ADVANCE PRAISE FOR *THE FREE WILL BAPTISTS*

"With the background and mind of a historian, Matthew Pinson has authored a new history of Free Will Baptists based on solid scholarly research and interpretation. His research has added much new material, which he has integrated into already known history. With his skill as a writer, Pinson has produced a well-written and very readable book for twenty-first-century students and interested readers and researchers of denominational history."
—GARY FENTON BAREFOOT, curator, Free Will Baptist Historical Collection, University of Mount Olive

"The subtitle of this book could easily read, "A New *and Definitive* History." Matthew Pinson is the foremost scholar of our day on Free Will Baptists, and he has provided a work that will shape this field of study for decades to come. He expertly offers a revision of Free Will Baptist beginnings, carefully weaves theological development within the historical narrative, and writes with a flair that makes the entire story informative and enjoyable."
— ANTHONY CHUTE, professor of Church History, California Baptist University

"The largest stream that shaped Baptist life in America was the Reformed-Calvinistic-Missionary Baptist tradition with significant influence from the evangelical revivals of the eighteenth and nineteenth centuries. Scholarship has consequently overstudied this mainstream to the neglect of other movements, suggesting that their influences and contributions can be ignored without loss to the wider Baptist family. We are indebted to J. Matthew Pinson for this critical monograph on the General-Free Will-Arminian stream of Baptist life in America that helps us to see that the Baptist story is diverse and contested. His emphasis on the discontinuity of Free Will Baptist groups from their evangelical Calvinistic counterparts shows that smaller does not mean less interesting or important. And if the genealogy of the Baptist movement is more like a river that ebbs and flows with rivulets that burst forth and return to main current than it is like branches of a tree that never return to the trunk, perhaps we may look to the Free Will Baptists to refresh the waters that vitalize our shared life."
—CURTIS W. FREEMAN, research professor of Theology and Baptist Studies and Ruth D. Duncan director of the Baptist House of Studies, Duke University Divinity School

"Readers looking to understand where Free Will Baptists came from and what they are doing today need look no further than Matthew Pinson's *The Free Will Baptists: A New History*. No one knows more about the Free Will Baptists than Pinson. In a long-overdue and gap-filling denominational history, he carefully examines the personal, ecclesial, organizational, and institutional foundations underlying a fascinatingly unique expression of the Baptist genius. Pinson brings into the light Free Will Baptist treasures old and new. With the appearance of this book, students and scholars of Baptist and American history now have a definitive resource for teaching and researching a diverse and evolving Baptist tradition."

—JOHN INSCORE ESSICK, associate professor of Church History, Baptist Seminary of Kentucky

"I welcome the opportunity to add my enthusiasm for Pinson's new book on Free Will Baptist history. For too long our historians have devoted most of their attention to the two well-known streams of our history: namely, the Palmer movement in the South and the Randall movement in the North. Dr. Pinson deals with those in a fresh way, of course, but he also gives much needed attention to the way the Free Will Baptist movement coalesced and spread—especially in the important South—in various areas. From this book you will learn things you didn't already know, and you'll gain a fresh perspective on the history of the denomination as a whole. Pinson has ably explored Free Will Baptist history, including new sources of information, not just for things we're already familiar with but also throughout the entire Free Will Baptist movement as we know it today. Kudos to him and to the University of Tennessee Press for this innovative book."

—ROBERT E. PICIRILLI, professor emeritus of New Testament and former academic dean, Welch College

THE FREE WILL BAPTISTS

The Free Will Baptists

A NEW HISTORY

J. Matthew Pinson

AMERICA'S BAPTISTS
Keith Harper, *Series Editor*

THE UNIVERSITY OF TENNESSEE PRESS
Knoxville

Copyright © 2025 by The University of Tennessee Press / Knoxville.
All Rights Reserved.
FIRST EDITION.

Library of Congress Cataloging-in-Publication Data
Names: Pinson, J. Matthew, 1967- author
Title: The Free Will Baptists : a new history / J. Matthew Pinson.
Description: First. | Knoxville : The University of Tennessee Press, [2025] | Series: America's Baptists | Includes bibliographical references and index. | Summary: "In this scholarly treatment of a lesser-known denomination, J. Matthew Pinson offers a comprehensive history of the Free Will Baptist movement—a distinct theological tradition within the larger Baptist family. He traces the beginnings of the Free Will Baptists in the Carolinas from the late 1600s; the denomination's early expansion across the Southeast; the rise and decline of the Northern Freewill Baptists; and the identity and development of the Free Will Baptist movement into the twentieth and twenty-first centuries"—Provided by publisher.
Identifiers: LCCN 2025025163 (print) | LCCN 2025025164 (ebook) | ISBN 9798895270424 hardcover | ISBN 9798895270431 epub | ISBN 9798895270448 adobe pdf
Subjects: LCSH: Free Will Baptists (1727–1935)—History | National Association of Free Will Baptists (U.S.)—History | Baptists—History
Classification: LCC BX6373 .P56 2025 (print) | LCC BX6373 (ebook) | DDC 286/.209—dc23/eng/20250925
LC record available at https://lccn.loc.gov/2025025163
LC ebook record available at https://lccn.loc.gov/2025025164

To William F. Davidson,
Michael R. Pelt,
and
Robert E. Picirilli,
on whose shoulders I stand.

CONTENTS

FOREWORD		
	by Timothy George	ix
SERIES EDITOR'S FOREWORD		
	by Andrew Smith	xiii
INTRODUCTION		1

PART I: BEGINNINGS IN THE CAROLINAS

One	English General Baptists in North Carolina to 1750	17
Two	The Calvinist Proselytization and Recovery, 1750–1794	41
Three	Free Will Baptists in the Carolinas, 1794–1865	61

PART II: EARLY EXPANSION ACROSS THE SOUTHEAST

Four	Origins in Southeast Alabama, Florida, and Georgia	89
Five	Origins in Alabama and Tennessee	111

PART III: THE RISE AND DECLINE OF THE NORTHERN FREEWILL BAPTISTS, 1780–1911

Six	The Rise of the Randall Movement	131
Seven	Doctrine and Decline in the North	159

PART IV: GROWTH AND IDENTITY IN THE SOUTH, 1866–1910

Eight	Southern Free Will Baptists: New Beginnings and Westward Expansion	191

| Nine | The Development of Southern Free Will Baptist Institutions Through 1910 | 219 |
| Ten | Doctrine and Practice in the South | 237 |

PART V: DEVELOPMENT IN THE TWENTIETH AND TWENTY-FIRST CENTURIES

Eleven	The Precursors and Founding of the National Association	275
Twelve	The Early Development of the National Association	297
Thirteen	Growth and Controversy After 1950	323
Fourteen	Institutions and Identity Since 1950	347

EPILOGUE	371
NOTES	383
BIBLIOGRAPHY	473
INDEX	499

FOREWORD

This book is a detailed and finely textured study of the Free Will Baptist movement. It is an example of what historian Margaret Bendroth has called "the spiritual practice of remembering."[1] The Christian faith presupposes the necessity of the past. It is not primarily a philosophy of religion, a code of morality, an order of liturgy, nor even a system of theology—though it embraces each of these. But at its core, the Christian faith is a record of what God has once and for all done to redeem the world through Jesus Christ and to call unto himself a special people, which is referred to in the sacred Scriptures as the *church*, the body of Christ. Christians have always been concerned to tell the story of this called-out community of faith—its struggles, temptations, setbacks, and advance—believing all the while that "the church's one foundation is Jesus Christ her Lord."

Some Baptist believers have claimed to be the heirs of an unbroken line of true visible churches stemming from the time of Jesus and the earliest apostles right down to the present day. This view is called Baptist successionism. However, most historians today connect the beginnings of the modern Baptist movement with the Protestant Reformation, an ecclesial and spiritual renewal of the Christian faith in the sixteenth century. The early Baptists did not intend to start a brand-new church from scratch. Like the reformers Luther, Calvin, Zwingli, and Cranmer, their aim was to renew or re-form the one, holy, catholic, and apostolic church, which had sadly lost its way in the intervening centuries since the New Testament.

Baptists as a distinct group emerged in the late sixteenth and early seventeenth century as part of this general reforming milieu. Matthew Pinson identifies three reforming streams at the headwaters of the early Free Will Baptist movement: (1) continental Anabaptism, especially through John Smyth and Thomas Helwys, who in 1609 reconstituted their exiled congregation on the basis of believer's baptism; (2) English Puritanism, a revival movement within the Church of England based on the sole sufficiency of the Holy Scriptures and the supremacy of divine grace mediated through Christ alone; (3) evangelical Arminianism, a renewal movement within the

Dutch Reformed church identified with Jacobus Arminius, which resisted the strictest forms of Calvinist soteriology.

Eventually, two distinct currents of Baptist life emerged in early seventeenth century England: the General Baptists and the Particular Baptists. The Generals received their name from their doctrine of general redemption, the teaching that Christ had died indiscriminately for all persons. The Particulars were so-called because of their adherence to the Calvinist doctrine of particular redemption, the belief that Christ's atonement was efficient for only those persons whom God had elected to salvation. Both groups were advocates for religious liberty and both practiced baptism for believers only—from the 1640s onward by immersion only. While Generals and Particulars met in separate associations and held differing views on soteriology, they both published confessions of faith, wrote catechisms for their children, and stressed the importance of family worship. On occasion, they could work closely together. For example, John Bunyan, the great superstar of the age, was a Calvinistic Baptist who practiced open communion—a persistent trait of later Free Will Baptists. Bunyan defended Henry Denne, a General Baptist evangelist, whose preaching had been opposed by the Anglicans.

The Baptist view of religious freedom was born out of the experience of persecution and martyrdom. Thomas Helwys, who planted the first General Baptist church in England in 1612, argued for universal religious toleration: "Let them be heretics, Turks, Jews, or whatsoever, it appertains not to the earthly power to punish them in the least measure."

Beginning in the late seventeenth century, a number of English General Baptists began to migrate to the New World, largely settling in what was then known as *Terra Carolina*. These General Baptists insisted on the practice of feet washing as a gospel ordinance based on the command of Jesus in John 13:14–15. They also practiced the laying on of hands for all baptized believers in accordance with the six principles set forth in Hebrews 6:1–2. They also brought with them an already well-developed confessional tradition. They were loyal to the *Standard Confession* of 1660, which would later be condensed, revised, and used widely by Free Will Baptists in America. Thomas Grantham was the leading General Baptist theologian in the Old World. His writings would be revered and read by many Free Will Baptists in America. The first Free Will Baptists were associated with Paul Palmer and his predecessors in North Carolina in the late seventeenth and early eighteenth centuries. From that initial beginning, the movement spread throughout the southern United States.

FOREWORD

Matthew Pinson has given us here a thorough, comprehensive survey of Free Will Baptist history, theology, and church life. The story bristles with drama, including internal squabbles over Masonic affiliation and the doctrine of apostasy, as well as external struggles and conflicts, especially with the more Calvinistic Baptists of the Philadelphia Baptist Association, whose aggressive proselytizing against the Free Will Baptist Church issued in a bitter conflict. Attention is also given to Benjamin Randall and a different expression of the Freewill Baptist experience arising in New Hampshire in the context of the Second Great Awakening.

Randall himself played an important role in establishing a number of Baptist churches and must be considered an evangelical in terms of his own beliefs and experience. He was converted under the preaching of the famous George Whitefield. However, by the early twentieth century, the movement he began had grown weak in its commitments, tending toward ecumenism and theological liberalism. In 1911, the remnant of the original Randall movement merged with the Northern Baptists, a mainline denomination which became known as the America Baptist Churches USA. On the other hand, the movement associated with Paul Palmer has maintained its own distinct identity. In 1935, various streams of this movement joined remnants of the Randall movement to form the National Association of Free Will Baptists, which now numbers more than 2,500 churches. They continue to hold evangelical Arminian beliefs, practice feet washing as a gospel ordinance, and support expanding missionary and educational ventures.

Cotton Mather, the Puritan scholar and pastor of Boston's Old North Church, died in 1728 when Palmer's Free Will Baptist movement was just getting off the ground. Mather was dubbed "the Lord's remembrancer" for his expansive recounting of the history and growth of the Christian faith in New England. This, his magnum opus, he titled *Magnalia Christi Americana*, the Great Acts of Christ in America. On a different scale and focused on a different region and while pursuing a different narrative, Matthew Pinson has also served as "the Lord's remembrancer" for his own distinctive ecclesial community and thus has helped all of us to engage in "the spiritual practice of remembering."

Timothy George
Beeson Divinity School of Samford University

SERIES EDITOR'S FOREWORD

On April 23, 2025, Dr. Keith Harper, professor of Baptist Studies at Southeastern Baptist Theological Seminary, friend and mentor to countless students and scholars in his field, passed away after a brief battle with cancer. His editorship of the monograph series of which this volume is the latest installment was and remains both a professional and a personal triumph: professional, because of the rich scholarship it has generated, and personal, because of the network of colleagues and friends that Dr. Harper both drew on and built in the process of shepherding these volumes to print.

Dr. Harper loved scholarship that studied Baptists as people who were never untouched by their wider social, cultural, political, and economic environment. As he noted in one foreword to another entry in this series, institutional histories can devolve into a catalog of "pastors, building programs, and so forth." Dr. Harper was keen to make sure that the America's Baptists series at the University of Tennessee Press would publish works that were "not that kind of . . . history." He was proud of this volume, Matthew Pinson's *The Free Will Baptists: A New History*, exactly because it is not "that kind of history."

In this book, readers will meet a small but energetic group of Baptists whose very name indicates that they stood outside the mainstream of not only American religious life, but even mainstream American Baptist life. At the same time, the story of the Free Will Baptists reflects their constant interaction with their environment, as the subjects of Pinson's story react to sectional conflicts and identities, the reality of slavery, matters of gender, and, in the twentieth century, nascent evangelicalism. Scholars who are fascinated by the finer points of Baptist and American Protestant polity will find plenty here to ponder, as Dr. Pinson's subjects resist single-minded congregational autonomy while still framing a polity with more flexibility than their larger Arminian neighbors, the Methodists. Additionally, the Free Will Baptists offer a unique perspective on the nature of salvation, offering an alternative to Calvinism within the Baptist tradition without embracing a Wesleyan interpretation of Arminianism. It was this "betwixt and between" element of the Free Will Baptist story that Dr. Harper found so fascinating; this is a book that will make a contribution not only to Baptist studies, but also to our understanding of wider American religious history.

Dr. Harper was able to guide this fine volume through the editorial process at the University of Tennessee Press, but he did not live to write the foreword. He would want you to know that what you hold in your hands is scholarship of the highest quality, evidence of the continuing vitality of both the Free Will Baptist tradition and the practice of denominational history. Dr. Pinson tells an important story well.

Andrew Smith
Carson-Newman University
Jefferson City, Tennessee

INTRODUCTION

This book tells the story of a unique American religious tradition. Any account of the Free Will Baptist Church will necessarily begin with theology, with the doctrines and practices that distinguish Free Will Baptists from other Protestants. The most important of these differences centers on the Christian doctrine of salvation, or soteriology.

A Distinct Theology

Free Will Baptists are most obviously distinct from other Baptists because of their Arminian doctrine of salvation. The earliest Free Will Baptists were English General Baptists who had sailed across the Atlantic to the colony of Carolina in the late seventeenth century. Thus, as General Baptists, they were distinct from their Particular Baptist cousins. ("General" signified a belief in a general or universal atonement and provision of grace for humanity. "Particular" represented an affirmation of particular atonement and provision of grace only for the elect.) Even later, when most Baptists from a Particular Baptist heritage had moderated their Calvinism to the point that they held only two points—total depravity and the certain perseverance of the saints— Free Will Baptists still doggedly maintained a full Arminian posture. They affirmed the possibility that a genuine believer could apostatize. Preaching this doctrine, which was shocking to non-Arminian Baptists, always kept the Free Will Baptists at arm's length from other Baptists.

However, Free Will Baptist soteriology was also distinct from other Arminian-oriented bodies in the American context. These included the Methodists and later the Holiness movement as well as the Stone-Campbell tradition of restorationist Christianity. The Free Will Baptists, especially in the South, were more Reformed in their doctrines of human depravity and moral inability in salvation, the nature of atonement, and justification by the imputed righteousness of Christ. Thus they diverged from the Christian perfectionism of much Wesleyan and Holiness evangelicalism, rejecting a second work of grace and crisis-experience orientation. There was also more resistance in the South to some of the manifestations of Romanticism seen in much of the pietism and revivalism of the American evangelical experience. Still pietism and revivalism exerted widespread influence on the movement—and dominated it in the North.

In addition to the soteriological differences with other Baptists, Free Will Baptists also maintained distinctions in their doctrine of the church, or ecclesiology. Their polity, from their start as General Baptists in England, struck a delicate balance. It was something of a hybrid between the strict independency of many Congregationalists and Particular Baptists on one hand and Presbyterian church government on the other. Some early Calvinist Baptists gave as robust a role to the local conference or association as the General/Free Will Baptists did. However, most did not, especially after the forces of what Nathan Hatch calls "democratization" began to take hold this side of the Atlantic. In brief, Free Will Baptist polity gave more power to local gatherings of churches called conferences or associations. This included a rigorous confessionalism by which local presbyteries or ordination councils ordained ministers and deacons and held them accountable to the entire body of churches for orthodoxy, fidelity to the confession of faith, and morality. However, unlike Presbyterian polity, General/Free Will Baptists typically maintained the ultimate right of self-government and dissent of the local congregation.

Another key ecclesiological difference concerned liturgical observances such as confirmation (the laying on of hands of newly baptized converts), open communion, the washing of the saints' feet, and the anointing of the sick with oil. The Free Will Baptists continued observing these practices, especially in the South. Many Free Will Baptists in that region maintained the imposition of hands until well into the twentieth century, and some have revived the practice. Free Will Baptists have consistently practiced open communion, and most continue the ritual of anointing of the sick, to the present day. The vast majority persist in the ancient rite of the *pedilavium* (Latin for the washing of feet), ensconcing it in their confessions of faith as a divine ordinance. Many other Baptists early in the American experience, while always maintaining closed communion, had practiced these other rituals but gradually abandoned them, except in the most rural corners of Appalachia and among the ultra-Calvinist Primitive Baptists.[1]

Distinct Origins and Existence

Free Will Baptists' adherence to these distinct beliefs and practices caused them to maintain a separate existence, even as a very small religious body, since their late seventeenth-century founding in North Carolina. That is another unique thing about this movement: its four-century history. The Free Will Baptist Church, starting with English General Baptists who had migrated to the American colonies in the 1680s, dates to the first General Baptist church on English soil, established by Thomas Helwys in Spitalfields outside London in 1612. Yet the movement has a definite American stamp. Most Free Will Baptists originated from this General Baptist strand, tracing themselves back to English General Baptists like Paul Palmer in North Carolina. Some came from quasi-Calvinist Baptists in the South who gradually jettisoned the last vestiges of their Calvinism under the influence of Free Will Baptists, fully taking on the Free Will Baptist confessional identity.

A small portion of the modern Free Will Baptist movement, however, originated from a completely different tradition. Another Arminian Baptist group, the Randall movement of Freewill Baptists, sprung up in New England in the 1780s under the leadership of Benjamin Randall. That movement blossomed over the nineteenth century. However, it eventually moderated its distinctive Freewill Baptist beliefs, was influenced by ecumenism and theological liberalism, and merged with the Northern Baptist Convention in 1911. A small minority stayed out of the merger, eventually uniting with groups of southern Free Will Baptists. These unions would eventuate in 1935 in the formation of the National Association of Free Will Baptists, by far the largest existing Free Will Baptist body.

Free Will Baptists also exist in numerous iterations outside the National Association, such as the predominantly African American denomination, the United American Free Will Baptists. They belong to several disparate conferences in the United States and gather fraternally in the National Convention of Free Will Baptists, USA. Another substantial body of Free Will Baptists, the Convention of Original Free Will Baptists, separated from the National Association of Free Will Baptists in the early 1960s. This schism largely centered on the Convention of Original Free Will Baptists' affirmation of a more strongly connectional form of church polity. Furthermore, there are hundreds of Free Will Baptist congregations that are either independent or affiliated with independent associations and conferences that are not members of the National Association. This book will tell the story of this American religious expression, which is heterogeneous in some ways but whose constituent streams are very much alike in others. Most of the book, admittedly, will concern the history of the largest body to which the vast majority of Free Will Baptists belong, the National Association of Free Will Baptists.

Excursus: The Reformed and General Baptist Context

A word needs to be said about the background of the Free Will Baptists in the English General Baptist movement and the Reformed wing of the Protestant Reformation out of which it emerged. The earliest Free Will Baptists in America were English General Baptists who lived in the English colony of Carolina in the region known after 1712 as North Carolina. Thus they were heirs to the General Baptist faith and practice associated with leading figures such as Thomas Helwys and Thomas Grantham.

Helwys founded the first Baptist church just outside London in 1612, having separated from his mentor John Smyth. A former Church of England priest, Smyth had made the transition from conformity (Anglicanism) to Puritanism to radical Puritanism (separation from the Church of England). After their self-exile in Amsterdam because of the persecution radical Puritans were experiencing in England, Smyth and Helwys came into contact with the Dutch Waterlander Mennonites.

The Waterlanders exerted some influence on Smyth and Helwys's doctrine of the church. In Amsterdam, like the Waterlanders, Smyth and Helwys came to believe that the Bible taught a believers' church ecclesiology. They affirmed that only believers ought to be baptized and admitted as church members. Thus they reconceived the church as a gathered community of voluntary believers. With this, they jettisoned the amalgamation of the institutional church with the state. In that traditional system, infants baptized into the church became members of the state church—for example, the Church of England or the Church of Scotland. Smyth and Helwys boldly rejected this view. Their rite of the washing of the saints' feet, which was a common General Baptist practice, was likely derived from the Waterlander Mennonites. The General Baptists' strong intercongregational polity may also have been influenced by the Waterlanders. That practice emphasized the power of associations of churches in ensuring accountability of churches and their leaders, while maintaining congregations' self-governance.

Helwys broke with Smyth after the latter embraced Mennonite doctrine, which affirmed more separation from the state and the larger culture than Helwys believed was taught in Holy Scripture. This included a rejection of the Mennonite teaching that Christians cannot serve as civil magistrates, bear arms, or fight in a just war. Helwys's view, like the sixteenth-century Anabaptist theologian and martyr Balthasar Hubmaier, steered a middle course. On one side it avoided the radical dichotomy between church and culture that characterized most of the Anabaptists, or Radical Reformers. On the other, it demurred from the symbiosis between church and state that characterized Magisterial Reformers such as Martin Luther, Huldrych Zwingli, and John Calvin. Other reasons Helwys cited for his departure from Smyth were the latter's embrace of the Waterlander belief in the necessity of a succession of believer's baptism from the apostles and their rejection of original sin and the imputation of the righteousness of Christ alone in justification. Helwys also vehemently disagreed with their view that Christ's flesh did not derive from Mary but was "celestial."

Thus the Anabaptist movement serves as one Reformation tributary into the General Baptist river. However, there were two other tributaries: the Puritan movement and the Arminian movement. The radical Puritan Helwys longed for a more thorough reformation than he thought most mainstream Puritans were willing to engage in. However, he was less radical in his move away from his Puritan moorings than his mentor Smyth. Because they were Puritans, the English General Baptists valued the Reformed interpretation of the five *solae* of the Magisterial Reformation: *sola Scriptura* (Scripture alone) *sola gratia* (grace alone), *sola fide* (faith alone), *solus Christus* (Christ alone), and *soli Deo gloria* (the glory of God alone).

The Puritan movement emphasized reforming the church according to Scripture and thus purifying it of unbiblical elements they believed had accrued during church history. They exemplified on the British Isles the thrust of the Reformed movement on the European continent associated with Reformers such as Zwingli and Calvin. Thus they interpreted *sola Scriptura* the way Zwingli and Calvin did, teaching that the doctrine and practice of the church should be based solely on apostolic precept and example in the New Testament. To devise new doctrines or practices in the worship and service of God, they thought, would be to add to God's revelation of how he wished to be worshipped and served. Further, it would bind the consciences of the people of God to priests, bishops, or popes who demanded the people's submission to doctrines and practices not taught in Scripture. This approach to the sufficiency of Scripture, shared with the Anabaptists, who had emerged from the Zwinglian wing of the Reformed movement, is precisely what led the General Baptists, along with their spiritual brothers and sisters the Particular Baptists, to insist that the baptism of believers was the only practice of baptism warranted by precept and example in Holy Scripture.

In addition to this Reformed interpretation of the *sola Scriptura* principle, the English General Baptists also inherited from the Puritans the Reformed interpretation of the other *solae*. Believers are saved by grace alone through faith alone in the merit of Christ alone. No works or merit can contribute to one's salvation, and neither priests nor Mary nor the saints can intercede for believers to the Father. All believers are priests and need the intercession of only one high priest, Jesus Christ. The theology of glory given to human beings in the pomp and ceremony and ritual and festival of the medieval church must give way to a theology of the cross whereby God's people approach him in order, simplicity, and humility.

The third Reformation tributary that flowed into the General Baptist river was Arminianism, a theological movement that arose from the Dutch Reformed theologian Jacobus Arminius. Their Arminianism is why the General Baptists were later known as *General* Baptists. They affirmed general redemption and general atonement, that God provided redemption for everyone and Christ died for everyone. Thus they differed from the Particular Baptists, who believed in particular redemption, that God provided redemption only for the elect. The General Baptists were, in fact, closer to the theology of Arminius than his own successors in the Netherlands, the Remonstrants. Reformed theology was defined differently in the sixteenth and early seventeenth centuries, and the Reformed tent was big enough to accommodate people who affirmed the five *solae* but still were not Calvinist in their soteriology. This broad Reformed faith and practice was encapsulated in the sixteenth-century Reformed confessions of faith and catechisms. These included the Belgic Confession and Heidelberg Catechism, to which Arminius himself eagerly subscribed. The "five points" of Calvinism were not added until 1619, when the Synod of Dort interpreted Reformed doctrine to require it.

Arminius's own "Arminianism" was a Reformed Arminianism that held tenaciously to total depravity, believing that divine grace drawing an individual was necessary for conversion. He was like Calvin on what it means to be a sinner, strongly resisting semi-Pelagianism, the idea that God gives grace to those who "do what is in them." He also agreed with Calvin in his robust opposition to views on justification characteristic of late medieval Roman Catholicism and some Anabaptists. Instead, he affirmed that only Christ's righteousness, wrought on the cross to satisfy the demands of divine justice and imputed to the believer, provides justification before God. Arminius's view of the nature of atonement and justification was soon rejected by his Remonstrant successors as well as Anglican and Puritan anti-Calvinists. Yet Helwys articulated an approach like that of Arminius.

Helwys's views on original sin and justification caused him to break with John Smyth. The latter had come to espouse the more semi-Pelagian views of the Dutch Waterlander Mennonites, arguing against the doctrines of original sin and justification by the righteousness of Christ alone. Helwys's approach would be articulated by Thomas Grantham and other General Baptists a generation later.

However, while Arminius agreed with Calvinists on what it means to be in a state of grace, he differed with them, like many other Reformed Christians of his day, on how one comes to be in a state of grace. Thus, unlike Calvin, who affirmed that divine grace was particular—only for the elect—and irresistible, Arminius believed it was universal and resistible. In his own mysterious manner and timing, Arminius thought, God comes to every individual with grace. Because God desires everyone's salvation, the Holy Spirit draws everyone and Christ atones for everyone's sins. Yet this desire, drawing, and atonement for sin can be freely resisted by the individual.

The General Baptist movement, and the Free Will Baptist movement that originated from it, cannot be understood apart from the Anabaptist, Puritan, and Arminian tributaries that flow into it. All three of these movements originated in the Reformed wing of the Reformation. This background provided the movement its distinct soteriology and ecclesiology, which caused a theological clash with Calvinistic Baptists on the one hand and Methodists on the other. This distinction allowed this small, unique religious tradition to persist for centuries alongside its two giant sisters in the American Protestant landscape.

The Impetus for This Book

This book originated with a course I teach on the history of Free Will Baptists at Welch College and Welch Divinity School. In that course we have read two main surveys: William F. Davidson's *The Free Will Baptists in History* and Michael R. Pelt's *History of Original Free Will Baptists*. Those two books are excellent histories that plowed new ground, providing an evidentiary basis for most of what the tradition maintained. However, students clamored for a new, updated volume. Robert Picirilli has done just as much groundbreaking work as Davidson and Pelt, but his books consist more of detailed studies scholars call "micro-history" and thus are not as useful as a main textbook for a survey course. Thus I decided to write a new book that surveys the entire history of the movement. The work, I hoped, would be a scholarly volume that presents fresh research and original insights. Yet it would be accessible for a general audience and could serve as a textbook for college and seminary courses in Free Will Baptist history.

The Free Will Baptist tradition provides a fascinating study in American religious history. The General and Free Will Baptist traditions have been under-studied. Thus there is a need for far more scholarly research and writing on this transatlantic movement. A renaissance of interest in Free Will Baptist history has occurred among younger scholars. There has been a need, not only with this trend among emerging scholars, but also in the Baptist and evangelical scholarly communities, as well as the discipline of American religious history, for a new history of this unique Baptist movement, which is too Reformed to be Wesleyan and too Arminian to be Calvinist.

This book, like the Free Will Baptist experience it explores, touches on the transatlantic/colonial religious experience in America, the polemics between Calvinism and Arminianism, the influence of pietism and revivalism on American Protestantism in the context of Romanticism, the crosscurrents of religious social reform and the move toward the social gospel and Protestant liberalism in the late nineteenth century, the fundamentalist-modernist controversy, relationships between majority-Black and majority-White Baptist expressions, the sect-to-denomination process, and more. This makes it a stimulating study for scholars of religious history in the American context.

The Free Will Baptist story—to allude to the title of the book from the pioneer mid-twentieth-century historian Damon Dodd—enriches several communities of discourse in the evangelical and Baptist worlds. It is the story of a Baptist and Arminian communion that has managed to maintain its distinctive confessional character throughout its three and a half centuries in North America. It defies the "Calvinist confessional orthodoxy vs. Arminian pietism/revivalism" dichotomy so often discussed in American religious historiography. The movement had a mixed reaction to revivalism, especially in the South. Yet it remained very fully Arminian. Its Arminianism is, however, of a different sort. It is characterized not by a Finneyesque, Holiness, semi-Pelagian tone but has more in common with Calvinism on key theological emphases. Thus it manages a nuanced, "betwixt and between" role. It stands between Calvinism and various varieties of Arminianism (whether Wesleyan or Stone-Campbell). It is also characterized by a type of church government that is not fully connectional in either the presbyterian or episcopal sense but does maintain presbyteries that maintain authority over ministers (though the smaller Convention of Original Free Will Baptists and some African American Free Will Baptists have polities that are more connectional in a presbyterian sense). These unique characteristics have led to the survival of this small but vibrant movement, and these sorts of distinctive traits make it a fascinating study for students and scholars of American religious history.

INTRODUCTION

The Difficulty of Writing the Book

This book has been exceedingly difficult to write. The primary reason for that difficulty is the sparseness of records in the movement for much of its history. This problem does not exist for the wealthy Randall movement in the North, whose story has been told repeatedly by American Baptist and Southern Baptist scholars. Yet the paucity of archival evidence for the history of Free Will Baptists in the American South makes the recounting of their history an exercise in historical reconstruction. Owing to the relative poverty of these congregations led by ministers who during the week were southern yeoman farmers with little in the way of formal education, most of the printed material they produced was ephemeral. For instance, for most Free Will Baptist conferences and associations there are very few early extant minutes. The influential Mount Moriah Association in west-central Alabama is a perfect example. The association was formed in 1850 after Elder Ellis Gore had left the Regular Baptists in 1846 and ridden to North Carolina on horseback to be ordained by the Free Will Baptists there. Yet the association's first extant set of minutes is from 1874. The only other available information about this tradition's first forty-two years is one brief handwritten history from 1888 by the clerk of the Mount Moriah Church and some notes from Gore's grandson based on oral interviews he had conducted. The lack of information can make some of the recounting of the early years and origins of Free Will Baptist submovements read rather sparsely. This is simply because there is almost no personal data—only names, dates, and places.

Tracing the history of the much smaller African American Free Will Baptist denomination has been particularly challenging, as the reader will note. Because of slavery, poverty, and illiteracy, together with the decentralized nature of the movement, its extant records are exceedingly meager. I only wish more could be discovered and written about this important expression of American Christianity.

Thus the historian of Free Will Baptists must piece together a picture of the movement's history from scraps of evidence here and there. Readers will get a glimpse of this painstaking process as they read these pages. A unique feature of this book is its use of the burgeoning discipline of genealogical history. I must gratefully acknowledge here the hosts of the online repository Ancestry.com. Without that resource, much of the piecemeal historiography I have conducted would have been far more difficult. Because that site is a storehouse of archival material related to genealogy, it has enabled me to find bits and pieces of biographical data about various southern Free Will Baptists. All of this is especially informative in tracing the migration patterns of the movement—a major motif of the book. This information provides a clearer picture of one of the greatest mysteries of the movement's history: who influenced scattered movements of "Arminianizing" groups of United and Separate Baptists across the South to make the gradual transition to a full Free Will Baptist confessional identity? In some cases, this genealogical research has moved us forward greatly in our understanding of this problem. In other cases, more research is still needed.

Unique Features of the Book

Two other unique features distinguish this book from earlier surveys of the tradition. First is its engagement with interpretation. This is a luxury earlier historians did not enjoy because they had to focus more on establishing the basic evidence for what had been previously held by tradition. Thus some of the earlier historiographical debates among lay historians have already been settled by my predecessors and do not need to be reestablished. These debates include issues like whether the Palmer movement was an English General Baptist movement, whether nineteenth-century Carolina Free Will Baptists descended from Paul Palmer, and whether Benjamin Randall was the founding father of the denomination. That these questions have been settled by William F. Davidson and other historians allows more time in this volume for interpretation of the Free Will Baptist tradition. Still, as noted above, the question about the influences from the Palmer movement on Arminianizing Baptist movements across the South is an area of research that has not been settled. It necessarily looms large in this account.

Another distinguishing characteristic of this book is its engagement with intellectual history. This book is more concerned with the history of ideas than previous studies, and those ideas are primarily theological ideas and the implications that flow from them. In-depth consideration of the theological framework is more important for understanding this tradition than for much recent Baptist historiography. Because the General/Free Will Baptist movement is under-studied, many of the unique features of its intellectual structure—the very ideas that kept it aloof from other Baptist movements—are unfamiliar to historians of the Baptist tradition and of transatlantic evangelicalism. Because of this, these ideas will receive greater attention than in previous studies.

One note about nomenclature: As Robert Picirilli has pointed out, the

INTRODUCTION

names Free Will Baptists used in their history, and use even today, are spelled in many different ways, and this can be confusing. The mainstream spelling of the name in the twentieth and twenty-first centuries has been "Free Will Baptist." In the South that usage was in the majority, being used of all the major Free Will Baptist bodies in the South, both predominantly Black and predominantly White. However, they also sometimes used "Free-will" and "Freewill." In the North, I am satisfied that "Freewill Baptist" was far and away in the majority among the northern Randall movement, until simply "Free Baptist" gradually overtook it after the 1860s. "Freewill Baptist" was the official name of the General Conference until 1892, when it officially became "Free Baptist." Even then, one would see "Free-will" occasionally in the North and even (though far less common) "Free Will." Decades ago, Gary F. Barefoot, head librarian of what is now the University of Mount Olive and still curator of the Free Will Baptist Historical Collection there, began using "Free Will" for the Palmer (southern) movement and "Freewill" for the Randall (northern) movement. Robert E. Picirilli followed suit at the Free Will Baptist Historical Collection at Welch College. We will do the same here, though, as Dr. Picirilli reminds us, the nomenclature across the movement, especially in the localities, is somewhat more variegated.

At first glance readers may be confused by the use of the title "General Conference" by so many bodies. It will become apparent that I refer at different places to five separate general conferences: (1) the General Conference in North Carolina; (2) the Randall General Conference in the North; (3) Thomas Peden's General Conference in the late nineteenth and early twentieth centuries, mostly in the South but with some churches in the Midwest; (4) the (African American) United American General Conference; and (5) the General Conference in the southeastern United States started in the 1920s, which became part of the National Association in 1935.

An Expression of Thanks

This brings me to an expression of thanks to Dr. Michael Pelt and Mr. Gary Barefoot for befriending me more than thirty years ago when I began my journey as a Free Will Baptist historian. They made available to me the riches of the Free Will Baptist Historical Collection at the University of Mount Olive in Mount Olive, North Carolina. I also want to thank retired curator Dr. Robert Picirilli and current curator Mr. Phillip Morgan for their work with the Free Will Baptist Historical Collection at Welch College in Gallatin, Tennessee, and their help to me. The collection at Welch is administered by the Historical Commission of the National Association of Free Will Baptists, which maintains a website at FWBHistory.com. That site and its host Eric Thomsen have made available digitized copies of many of the primary sources (especially minutes) I used in the preparation of this book. I could never have completed this work without the above-mentioned collections. I also thank the Special Collections department at Bates College Library in Lewiston, Maine; the American Baptist Historical Society archives currently housed at Mercer University's Cecil B. Day Campus in Atlanta and formerly at Colgate Rochester Crozer Divinity School in Rochester, New York, where I first conducted research in it; and the Southern Baptist Historical Library and Archives in Nashville.

I wish to thank my primary scholar-mentors in this work, on whose shoulders I stand: Dr. William F. Davidson, professor emeritus and former dean of the seminary at Columbia International University in Columbia, South Carolina; Dr. Michael R. Pelt, professor emeritus and former academic dean at the University of Mount Olive; and Dr. Robert E. Picirilli, professor emeritus and former academic dean at Welch College. I dedicate this book to the three of them.

I owe special thanks to Dr. Picirilli and Dr. E. Darrell Holley, my colleagues at Welch College, for reading the manuscript. Their help and advice have been invaluable. I also appreciate Dr. William Davidson, Mr. Gary Barefoot, and Dr. Michael Pelt, as well as my Welch colleagues Dr. Kevin Hester and Dr. Jesse Owens, for reading portions of the manuscript. I am also thankful to my daughter Anna Pinson and my former student Joshua Hunter, both of whose proofreading and research assistance proved very helpful in the preparation and completion of this work.

I wish to express my appreciation to Dr. Keith Harper, editor of the America's Baptists Series, to the director of the University of Tennessee Press, Scot Danforth, and to associate director of the press Thomas Wells for believing in the value of this work and for carefully helping me get it in shape for publication. My other editors at UT Press, Jonathan Boggs and Maliea Ruby, also offered invaluable assistance.

I would especially like to thank my family. My wife Melinda and my children Anna and Matthew have offered so much support, encouragement, and feedback in this endeavor that they know is dear to my heart. I am also grateful for my parents, John and Linda Pinson, and my late grandparents, L. V. and Curro Pinson, who instilled in me a love for the Free Will Baptist Church and its history.

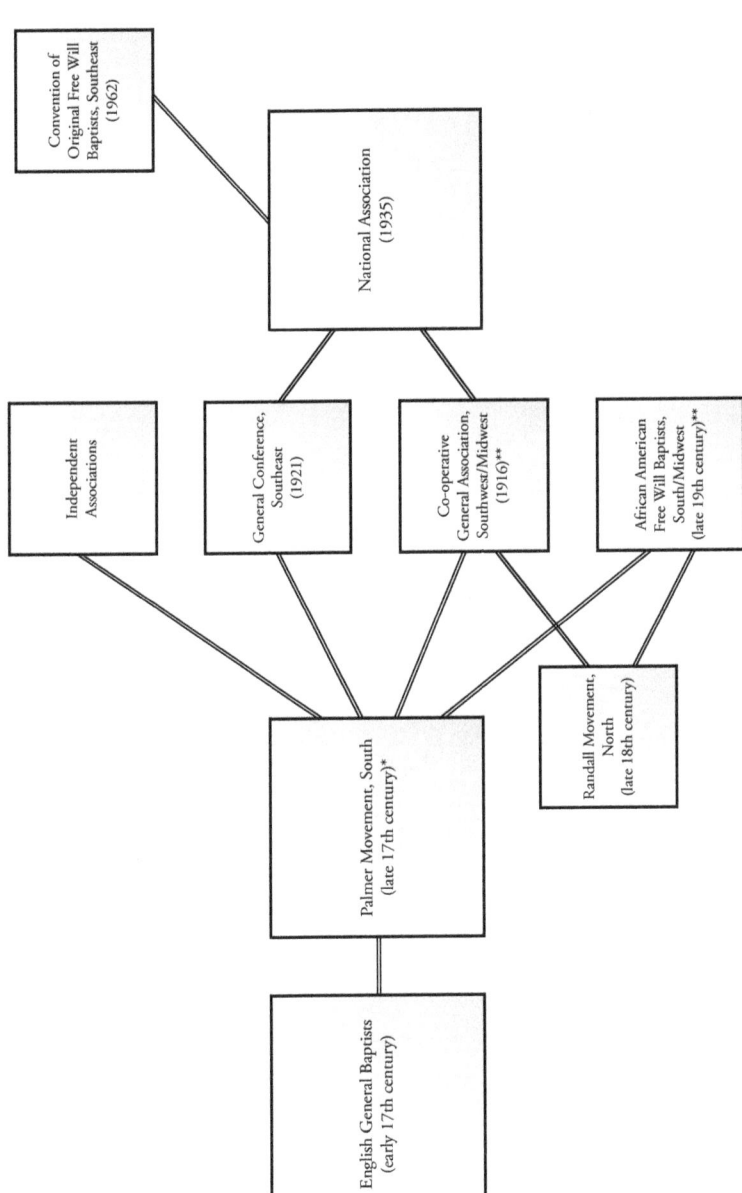

* See pp. 89–93 for a discussion of the origins of the Free Will Baptists of the South.
** Mixture of Palmer and Randall elements

Part I
BEGINNINGS IN THE CAROLINAS

One
ENGLISH GENERAL BAPTISTS IN NORTH CAROLINA TO 1750

THE FREE WILL BAPTISTS trace their origins in America to the English General Baptist minister Paul Palmer, who in 1727 organized a General Baptist church in Chowan Precinct, North Carolina, near his home in Perquimans Precinct.[1] For 250 years, historians had affirmed that Palmer was the founder of the General Baptist movement in North Carolina. However, in the mid-twentieth century, George Stevenson, an archivist for the state of North Carolina, discovered that Palmer had married into the family of the late Benjamin Laker. Stevenson's research, together with that of William Davidson and Michael Pelt, supported his conclusion that "although Palmer is generally given the sobriquet 'Father of North Carolina Baptists,' it seems probable from circumstances that the title properly belongs to Benjamin Laker." This author's research has discovered that Laker's neighbor, the Staffordshire General Baptist minister Thomas Hammersley, apparently predated Laker in his arrival in what would soon be known as Perquimans Precinct. Still, Laker looms much larger in the history of the period and is the primary link in the chain with Palmer.[2]

Benjamin Laker and His Influence

The first one hears about Benjamin Laker is that he signed the 1663 edition of the English General Baptist *Standard Confession* of 1660, the confession of faith of the General Assembly of General Baptists in England. This would have put him into contact with the eminent General Baptist leader and theologian Thomas Grantham. *Christianismus Primitivus*, Grantham's magnum opus, was one of Laker's prized possessions at a time when books were hard to come by on the American colonial frontier. This is known by the fact that he mentioned it by name in his last will and testament, bequeathing it to his daughter Sarah. Stevenson quipped that, given the fact that after her husband Thomas Harvey's death, Sarah would eventually marry an Anglican, Christopher Gale, "this was a regrettable bequest." It is a significant puzzle piece in Laker's story because of the volume's importance to him. Laker hailed from Betchworth in Surrey County, England. Surrey was home to a number of families whose surnames were the same as the best-known General/Free Will Baptist surnames in Eastern North Carolina in the eighteenth and early nineteenth centuries.[3]

Laker was one of the General Baptists whom Francis Smith, the foremost General Baptist publisher in the seventeenth century, was encouraging to move to Carolina in the 1680s. In 1682, Smith had published a new pamphlet by Samuel Wilson, *An Account of the Province of Carolina in America*. In it Wilson said, "I have here . . . described a pleasant and fertile country, abounding in health and pleasure, and with all things necessary for the sustenance of mankind, and wherein I think I have written nothing but truth, sure I am I have inserted no wilful falsehood. . . ." Wilson was secretary to the Lords Proprietors of England, eight political allies of King Charles II to whom he had given an enormous land grant in America in 1663. One of these territories was the "Province of Carolina," the land between Virginia and the Spanish territory of Florida. The Lords Proprietors promised religious freedom in this new land through a charter King Charles II had approved. That charter granted a surprising degree of religious liberty and local political control. However, early settlement of the region was slow. So the Lords Proprietors launched an advertising campaign in 1682 to encourage English people to emigrate to Carolina.[4]

Francis Smith himself considered emigrating to Carolina. Smith was heavily involved in promoting the move among Baptists and political radicals. Anthony Ashley Cooper, first Earl of Shaftesbury and a leading Whig in Smith's circle of influence, was one of the Lords Proprietors. Shaftesbury's influence held the promise of liberty of conscience, not just toleration, as well as a system of government based on John Locke's *Fundamental Constitutions*. This was in line with the sort of political publishing Smith had been doing alongside his Nonconformist religious publishing. Thus Smith was selected to be the publisher of Wilson's *An Account of the Province of Carolina in America*. The tract was in such demand that he had to print a second edition quickly. In 1682 the Lords Proprietors met the public for several weeks at the Carolina Coffee House on Birching Lane in London to promote the venture.[5]

It is likely that Thomas Hammersley was at one of those meetings and set out for America before his son John's birth in the Perquimans River region in 1683 or 1684. Another one of the ships bound for Carolina set sail in June 1684, with Benjamin Laker and his family on board. Laker was a man of means and was able to set up for his family a substantial estate in what would soon be northeastern North Carolina. A man named Richard Bentley, who owned 1,500 acres of land in Perquimans Precinct on the Albemarle Sound, sold Laker a 400-acre tract. Laker built a fine estate with his wife Elizabeth, their six children, a White laborer, and Black slaves named Francisco, Maria, and Mingo, and Mingo's family. By the next summer, Laker's son and oldest daughters had died of local fevers. Though the date of his wife's death or that of two of his other daughters is not known, he was widowed before his marriage to Juliana Taylor in May 1696. Taylor's daughter Joanna would marry Paul Palmer.[6]

In the late 1680s, Laker became a commissioner of the peace (justice of the peace) for Perquimans Precinct. In 1690, Philip Ludwell, the first governor of Carolina, selected Laker to represent one of the Lords Proprietors in Albemarle. Thus he became a member of the governor's council and sat on the highest courts in Carolina, including a post as General Court Justice. Laker's political influence expanded when his daughter Sarah married Thomas Harvey, deputy governor of Carolina, who had charge over the northern part of the large province. Laker continued in public service until 1698, when he stepped down and "lived as a private gentleman until his death."[7]

One interesting incident involved both Laker and Harvey in the court proceedings of the General Court of North Carolina on September 24–29, 1694. "Benjamin LaKar esqr" was summoned by the court on which he sat "to answer James ffewox in a plea of trespass." Fewox was alleging that Laker's plantation put "certain hogs" on his land, and "the plantifs corne thereon planted and growing hath been eaten up and destroyed." "Ye Honrbl Depty Governor esqur," being "nearly related" to Laker, recused himself. The court, finding "noe caus of action," ordered "that the sute be dismissed and that the said James ffewox pay costs."[8]

Laker died in 1701. On July 8 of that year, Juliana and Ruth Laker "Proved A Will of Beniamen Laker by ye Oathes of Richard ffrench And Elisabeth Steward Debro Thuston John More vars Daniel Snooks." In his will Laker stated: "I bequeath my Soul into the hands of Almighty God hoping for Salvation thro Christ my Redeemer & my body to a Christian buriall to be buried att the discretion of my Executrix hereafter Named...." In addition to leaving his cherished copy of Grantham's *Christianismus Primitivus* to his daughter Sarah, he willed his son-in-law George Blighton, the husband of his daughter Lydia, his copy of *Exposition of the First Five Books of Moses*.[9]

One of the witnesses to Laker's will was Richard French, who had settled in Perquimans Precinct in the late 1690s. French was likely attached to the Laker congregation. By 1701, he was going by the title "Minister of the Gospel" and performing marriages. He was still active in the ministry in the summer of 1711. That year John Urmston, an Anglican priest from the nearby Chowan Precinct who was also active in the other precincts of that region, complained about French's Dissenting activities. Urmston described French as "a rascal" who "pretends to the Ministry" and "prays extempore and does much mischief." In 1712 the governor's council summoned French to answer Urmston's charges that he was marrying people and administering baptism. However, later that year Governor Edward Hyde named French to the Court of Pleas and Quarter Sessions of Perquimans Precinct, and the record bears out nothing else about French until his death in 1716.[10]

The General Baptist believers Laker left behind in Perquimans Precinct were one of the four groups John Blair identified in his report to the Society for the Propagation of the Gospel in Foreign Parts in 1704. The society had sent Blair as an Anglican missionary to North Carolina in 1703. His narrative is contained in the North Carolina letter book of the society in London. In it, he explained that there were four sorts of people in North Carolina. The most numerous were Quakers, "the most powerful enemies to Church government, but a people very ignorant of what they profess." Another group consisted of those who "would be Quakers" if they were to become Christians at all. Yet he doubted they would because by being Quaker they would be "obliged to lead a more moral life than they are willing to comply to." Also present in North Carolina were Anglican parishioners who were "really zealous for the interest of the Church" and would "do very much" to see the Church of England advance in the region "if not opposed" by the sectarians. The only way Blair knew to describe the fourth group, the General Baptists, to his Anglican sponsors was as "something like Presbyterians, which sort is upheld by some idle fellows who have left their lawful employment, and preach and baptize throughout the country, without any manner of orders from any sect or pretended Church."[11]

The family of Laker's son-in-law George Blighton had General Baptist connections in southeastern Virginia. The General Baptist messenger Robert Norden began preaching in Prince George County, Virginia, in 1714.

This county was about a hundred miles away from Perquimans Precinct, and several General Baptist families migrated from there to northeastern North Carolina in the early eighteenth century. Blighton's next-door neighbor in Prince George County, Matthew Marks, registered his home as a meeting house for these Baptists, and Marks's will provided for Norden to have a home there as long as he remained a General Baptist minister in the region. Laker's daughter Lydia Blighton Clements and his grandson William Blighton were friends with John Hammersley, an ardent supporter of Norden's ministry who wrote about the Virginia Baptists to the Rhode Island General Baptist minister Nicholas Eyres in 1742. Incidentally, William was also brought up on charges for not attending Anglican services, which, as Stevenson surmises, probably meant that he was attending worship at a General Baptist meeting house.[12]

The Prince George County physician John Hammersley and his father Thomas's role among early North Carolina General Baptists has been overlooked by historians. Yet just as John's friend George Blighton had North Carolina connections, having married Lydia Laker in 1689 in what would soon become Perquimans Precinct, Hammersley also had North Carolina ties. He had been born and lived along the Perquimans River in North Carolina. His father had moved there from Staffordshire, England, gathering a General Baptist congregation there sometime before John's birth in 1683 or 1684. The Hammersley family had been influential among the General Baptists in England, with another John Hammersley of Staffordshire having signed the *Standard Confession* in 1660. These facts move the narrative back slightly before Laker's arrival and indicate that Thomas Hammersley had established a General Baptist congregation of which his neighbor, the layman Laker, must have been a member.[13]

The group of General Baptists Laker left behind in Perquimans Precinct, likely established by Hammersley, wrote to the General Association of General Baptists in England in 1702. That association was the group that had separated from the General Assembly of General Baptists in 1696 because it thought the latter body had not been diligent enough in addressing charges of christological heresy in its midst. In their letter, the struggling band of General Baptist believers asked the General Association to provide them with a minister or with books. As William Davidson shows, this was the General Baptist gathering in the Perquimans Precinct of North Carolina where Laker had exerted influence.[14]

At its meeting at White's Alley Church in London on June 3–5, 1702, the General Association adopted the following resolution:

> Whereas our Brethren of the Baptist perswation and of the Generall Faith who haue their aboad in Caralina haue desired us to Supply them wth a Ministry or with books, we being not able at present to doe the former haue collected ye Sum of Seuen pounds twelve Shillings whch wth wt can be farther obtain'd we haue put into the hands of our Bror S Keeling to Supply ym wth ye latter. & yt ye sd Bror Keeling doe wright a letter to them in the name of this Assembly.[15]

This episode is significant for historians in view of the sparse records from this early period because it ties the North Carolina General Baptists of the early eighteenth century to the more creedal General Association. Historians would love to know what volumes were in the crate of books the Perquimans General Baptists received from the General Association. Indeed, it was quite a shipment, since the amount of money the association allocated would likely be equivalent to more than $2,000 today.[16] Given the confessional polemical fervor of the General Association and the number of books that had been produced by its preachers in the previous few years, copies of the *Standard Confession* and Grantham's *Christianismus Primitivus* were no doubt included with more recent publications like Joseph Taylor's *Brief Enquiry* (1698), Joseph Hooke's *The Socinian Slain with the Sword of the Spirit* (1700) and *A Necessary Apology for the Baptized Believers* (1701), and Christopher Cooper's *The Vail Turn'd Aside* (1701).

Of course, it is more than mere coincidence that Paul Palmer, after marrying Laker's twice-widowed stepdaughter Joanna in 1722, left his Quaker meeting to join the General Baptist cause. In 1727 he would plant the first formally organized Free Will Baptist church historians know of, in that same locality.[17] Stevenson summarized the field that had been prepared for Palmer's labor:

> Besides the old group that had been led by Benjamin Laker in Perquimans Precinct, there was a pocket of General Baptists in Chowan, where two of them had sat on the vestry of St. Paul's parish in 1714. Northeastern Pasquotank, which never had been penetrated successfully by the Quakers, proved to be highly receptive to Baptist doctrine, while neighboring Currituck was home in 1718 to a lifelong Baptist physician whose six adult children had not been christened as infants. From his center on Lakers Creek in southwestern Perquimans Precinct, Palmer journeyed into the other three precincts preaching, baptizing, and laying his hands on the newly converted.[18]

Paul Palmer and His Fellow Laborers

The Life and Work of Paul Palmer

George Paschal, William Davidson, and George Stevenson did much in the twentieth century to reconstruct an accurate picture of the essentials of the life of Elder Paul Palmer. With the paucity of records, however, that was a difficult task. Thus very little is known about Palmer. For two centuries historians thought, based on Morgan Edwards's research in the late eighteenth century, that Palmer was a native of Maryland who was baptized in Delaware and ordained to ministry in Connecticut, later moving to North Carolina. Davidson and Stevenson moved away from this tradition, and in the late twentieth century, Stevenson discovered that Palmer was living in York County, Virginia, in 1717, where he married the widow Martha Hansford Hill, who had two small children and owned an "ordinary" (an inn or tavern). Martha died within a year of the wedding, and her brothers took the children and the inn, along with some of Paul's property—including his fiddle—leaving him in debt and hounded by creditors.[19]

Was Palmer born in England or Virginia or somewhere else? The extant records do not answer this question. The nineteenth-century Southern Baptist historian B. F. Riley asserted without citing his source that Palmer came directly from England. Citing Riley, the British Baptist historian W. T. Whitley thought Palmer might have migrated directly from England to North Carolina to take the place of the General Baptist messenger Robert Norden, whom the General Assembly had sent as a messenger to Virginia in 1714 but had retired back to England in 1725. Subsequent research has demonstrated that Riley and Whitley were mistaken.[20]

By 1719 Palmer had moved from Virginia about ninety-five miles southwest to Perquimans Precinct, North Carolina, where he married Benjamin Laker's stepdaughter Joanna Taylor Jeffreys Peterson. As Paschal said, Palmer married into one of the Precinct's "richest and most respectable families." Joanna enjoyed a high degree of wealth and prominence. Her late husband Thomas Peterson had been one of the most influential men in North Carolina. A political leader in Chowan Precinct, he owned an estate of five hundred acres, one hundred of which he had donated to help start the town of Edenton. Palmer himself soon became a significant landowner who had amassed 964 acres by 1729. He also participated in local politics, being named a permanent member of the precinct's grand jury.[21]

Palmer was a member of the Quaker meeting in Perquimans Precinct from at least 1719 but left and became General Baptist in 1722. Perhaps he had always been a Quaker and became General Baptist after marrying into the Laker family. Perhaps he was already General Baptist in southern Virginia before ever moving to North Carolina. Stevenson surmises that Palmer had the opportunity to discuss doctrine with General Baptists in southeastern Virginia and North Carolina. This could be true, since Palmer spoke fondly of the Virginia General Baptist Richard Jones in a 1729 letter to Elder John Comer of Rhode Island: "There is a comely little church in the isle of wight county, of about thirty or forty members, the Elder of which is one Richard Jones, a very sensible old gentleman, whom I have great love for. We see each other at every yearly meeting, and sometimes more often." He then went on to mention another southeastern Virginia General Baptist church in Surrey County, where Jones lived.[22]

The older Richard Jones, not to be confused with a younger minister by the same name whom the General Baptists in England sent to Virginia in 1727, had ministered alongside Robert Norden. The General Assembly sent Norden as a messenger to Virginia in 1714 "to propagate the Gospel of truth." In 1715 he was in Prince George County, Virginia, where he took the oath required of Dissenting Protestant ministers under the Toleration Act of 1689. In it he stated: "I, Robert Norden Profess faith in God the Father and in Jesus Christ his Eternall Sonn the true God and in the Holy Spiritt, One God Blessed for ever more, and I do acknowledge the Holy Scriptures of the Old and New Testament to be given by Divine Inspiration. Robert Norden." Norden ministered in southern Virginia until he returned to England in 1725, where he died that same year. No one knows whether Palmer was acquainted with Norden or any of the Virginia General Baptists before his move to North Carolina. So it is not known whether that relationship could have influenced him to accept General Baptist principles even before uniting with the Quaker meeting in Perquimans Precinct. Yet the records show that he married into a family of importance in the General Baptist cause in the region and went on to preach and teach General Baptist principles vigorously.[23]

A thirty-book library was noted in the inventory of Palmer's plantation house after his daughter's death. What if a list had survived with the titles of these volumes? Thirty books was a handsome collection at that time in rural colonial America, where only around half the population could read, or owned a single book. Had a list of Palmer's books survived, there would have no doubt appeared the titles of several General Baptist books. Perhaps there would even have been some of the books from the large shipment the General Association had sent from London twenty years before Palmer became a General Baptist. Had the several journals found in his daughter's possession after her death survived—historians have thought them to be Palmer's journals—they would likely have given us more information about his General Baptist roots.[24]

Certainly he must have had access to General Baptist books as he wrote his book manuscript *Christ the Predestinated and Elected*, which he sent to John Comer in March 1730, but which was never published and seems to be lost.[25] The fact that Palmer, an itinerant minister on the colonial frontier, probably with little formal education, would write an entire book on the Arminian doctrine of predestination indicates the importance he placed on theology and on the doctrine and practice of the General Baptist Church. Yet it also demonstrates a value placed on learning and books that would have been remarkable in his own day. Subsequent Free Will Baptist historians and theologians would have loved to have discovered this manuscript in a dusty archive in Rhode Island. Also, the fact that Palmer was interested enough in systematic theology to write such a manuscript and send it to a Calvinist minister six hundred miles away for his feedback perhaps provides some indication as to why the churches that remained Arminian after the Calvinist proselytization of the General Baptists in the 1750s were among those he most profoundly influenced. As Stevenson remarks,

> in view of the facts that the General Baptist churches founded independently of Palmer in the inner coastal plain were all destroyed by the particular form of Calvinism that swept into that area during the Great Awakening, and that most of Palmer's congregations in the outer coastal plain were perseveringly faithful to the doctrine of general provision taught by Palmer, it must be conceded that the Free Will Baptist churches (as the General Baptists came to be called) owe a debt both of doctrine and survivorship to the churches and clergy raised up under Palmer.[26]

Palmer enjoyed the life of a country gentleman and prosperous farmer with prominence in Perquimans Precinct. The information about his personal life is scarce. Yet his name appears in court records from time to time. One such time is in 1720 and 1721 when he and Joanna were brought up on charges from one of Thomas and Joanna Peterson's political adversaries, the Anglican Nicholas Crisp. Crisp alleged that Paul and Joanna's slave Cush, who also went by the name Quashey, "did feloniously seduce take carry & convey by force & Armes" a slave from a neighboring plantation. Crisp claimed that both the Palmers "did instigate order and comand" Cush's actions. Paul and Joanna both pled not guilty. The case was eventually dismissed when the attorney general "confesst" that "he would not Prosecute any further" because there was "no person appearing to prosecute or give Evidence to make good the charge" against them. As a Dissenter, Palmer was not without his enemies during his ministry. In early 1728, one John Dunnings accused Palmer of seducing his wife, which Palmer quickly and publicly denied. Eventually Dunnings dropped the allegation in open court.[27]

As mentioned above, very early, Elder Palmer preached, baptized, and confirmed converts in four precincts in which General Baptists were already active: Perquimans, Chowan, Pasquotank, and Currituck.[28] From his center on Laker's Creek in southwestern Perquimans Precinct, Palmer journeyed into the other three precincts. The community where Palmer "settled" the church in Chowan Precinct, close to the Chowan Indian Town—famous for being the first regularly organized Free Will Baptist congregation—had already been home to active General Baptists.[29] The congregation eventually built a meeting house on the road between Edenton and Nansemond and Isle of Wight Counties, Virginia. Many of the settlers in this community were from Nansemond County, Virginia, an area where Nonconformists and General Baptists were active. Earlier in 1714, two members of the vestry at St. Paul's had been known to be General Baptists. There was a small but fertile field of General Baptists in Chowan Precinct for Palmer to work with. This is why the records say that he "settled" the church at Chowan rather than that he gathered it, as historians traditionally assumed. It had to be Palmer's preaching that caused Thomas Roundtree, a vestryman in St. Paul's Parish Church to be "turned Anabaptist" toward the end of 1726. In 1728 the same thing happened to John Jordan, another vestryman at St. Paul's.[30]

The first extant record of Palmer's original Chowan congregation is in the diary of John Comer, to whom Palmer began writing in October 1729. Comer wrote:

> This day I received a letter from ye Baptist church in North Carolina, settled about two years (in ye year 1727) since, by Mr. Paul Palmer, signed by
>
> | | |
> |---|---|
> | John Parker, | Thomas Darker, |
> | John Jordan, | James Copland, |
> | Benjamin Evans, | John Welch, |
> | John Parker, | Joseph Parke, |

John Brinkley,	William Copland,
Michael Brinkley,	Joseph Parker.

This church consists of 32 members, it meets at Chowan.[31]

Paschal later demonstrated, through research on the above-named men, that this was the congregation in Chowan Precinct that was the first church settled by Palmer, not on the Chowan River in Perquimans Precinct, as Comer and Benedict had surmised. This is the congregation to which southern Free Will Baptists would trace their lineage.[32]

At the same time that Palmer was settling the church in Chowan Precinct, he was at work in Pasquotank. There he was supported by a young minister he had ordained, William Burges, who in September 1729 made his home a General Baptist meeting house. About this time Palmer and Burges petitioned the authorities to worship in Pasquotank (see petition below) and were publicly recognized as Dissenting ministers under the Toleration Act of 1689, which required Nonconformist ministers to take an oath of allegiance to the Crown and to orthodox doctrine.

North Carolina

To the Worshipfull Court of Pascotank Precinct Now Setting

The Humble Petition of us the Subscribers Humbly Sheweth That Whereas There is a Congregation of the People Calld Baptis Gathered In this Precinct meeting for Religious Worship In ye Dewelling House of William Burges on the North Side of Pascotank on the head of Ramonds Creek, he ye said Burges having granted ye Same for use of ye said meeting we Pray ye Same may be recorded and we ye humble Petitioners in duty bound Should Pray

W Burges

Paul Palmer

Frances Brockit

Thomas Heonrton

William Jones

Philip Torksey

Robert Wasson

Charles Leutrough[33]

The reason Burges's name was listed first on this document, as Pelt says, is probably that the church was meeting at his house, even though Palmer settled the church. Morgan Edwards was probably right that Burges became pastor of the congregation after Palmer moved on.[34]

Palmer's activities raised the concern of Governor Richard Everard. A letter Everard wrote to Edmund Gibson, the bishop of London, in October 1729 illustrates the concerns the Anglicans had regarding the activities of Dissenters. It also shows the success Palmer was having in gaining converts:

> My Lord, when I came first here, there was no Dissenters but Quakers in the Govt & now by the means of one Paul Palmer the Baptist Teacher, he has gained hundreds & to prevent it, tis impossible, when I have a Secretary, one John Lovick, that makes a jest of all religion & values not noe God, man, nor Devil a true enthusiast: when I promoted building the Church, he was the only man that hindered it, laid so many stumbling the way. . . .[35]

Also in 1729, Palmer opened his aforementioned correspondence with John Comer, a Calvinist Baptist minister who was friendly to the General Baptists, even serving as pastor of a General Baptist congregation. Palmer's acquaintance with Comer coincided with Palmer's frequent travels up and down the Eastern Seaboard. On those tours, Palmer visited other General Baptists, evangelized, and planted churches in places like Maryland and South Carolina. Because the records from this era are so sparse, no one knows for certain whether Palmer was ordained as a messenger, but his activities in Maryland and elsewhere indicate the probability that he was. Some modern historians have not read Palmer's itineracy through the lens of the General Baptist office of messenger, but this is the best explanation for the reason he established so many congregations and then moved on.[36]

Palmer's acquaintance with Comer, together with his tours, established Palmer as a knowledgeable and influential participant in the General Baptist community in the American colonies. To put the Laker-Palmer movement in perspective, one must note that by 1700, the year before Benjamin Laker's death, there were only thirty-one Baptist churches in the American colonies. By the early 1750s, that number had grown to around 112 congregations, around fifty of them Calvinistic, forty-three General Baptist, fifteen Seventh-Day Baptist, and three anti-paedobaptist congregations of unknown origin. Out of the roughly forty-three General Baptist churches stretching from what is now South Carolina to Massachusetts, twenty of them originated solely from the Laker-Palmer movement (with some in Maryland having Palmer's strong imprint). Thus by the early 1750s, about 47 percent of the General Baptist churches on the continent were Laker-Palmer churches, and about 18 percent of all the Baptist churches as a whole were in that group. Within Palmer's lifetime, there were General Baptist congregations in Massachusetts, Rhode Island, Connecticut, New York, New Jersey, Pennsylvania, Maryland, Virginia, North Carolina, and South Carolina. Owing to proselytization efforts by the Calvinist Baptists, as will be shown, the General Baptists lost a large number of their churches. Outside North Carolina, only a small contingent in the Northeast survived in General Six-Principle Baptist associations.[37]

One of the northern General Baptists that John Comer was acquainted with was the hatter Constant Devotion, who by 1734 was in North Carolina with Palmer. Comer's first diary entry regarding Palmer, on September 27, 1729, refers to the first of the letters Palmer exchanged with him, which tells of the original church Palmer settled in Chowan Precinct. Comer also referred in the same entry to a letter he had received from the Calvinist Baptist church in Charleston that contained a few General Baptist congregants. He noted that there had been "a difficulty in that church with ye minister, Mr. Palmer," which appeared in a letter they sent to the General Baptist church in Boston. Yet Comer remarked that the difficulty had been resolved. This is informative, given a second altercation Palmer would have with the Calvinist leadership of the church in Charleston six years later.[38]

Palmer's correspondence with Comer resulted in a friendship between them, and Palmer sent his book manuscript *Christ the Predestinated and Elected* to Comer for review in 1730. In the autumn of that year, Palmer sailed to New England and visited the General Baptists there. He traveled first to Massachusetts and Connecticut, then to Rhode Island, and later to New Jersey. Comer mentioned in his diary on October 6, "This day I went over to North Kingstown, to see Mr. Paul Palmer, the minister of North Carolina, who was come into ye country to visit ye churches and was returning home by land without coming over to ye Island by reason of an Act of Assembly prohibiting all from Boston except they lay four days currenteen [quarantine] by reason of the small pox being there. He is a man of parts and worthy."[39] On this journey Palmer aided John Drake, pastor of the General Baptist church in Piscataway, New Jersey, in the ordination of Henry Loveall. This action was later criticized by the Philadelphia Baptist Association because of Loveall's alleged checkered past and sexual indiscretions. Rather than sailing back to North Carolina, Palmer traveled overland. In Baltimore County, Maryland, he preached to a gathering in the home of the General Baptist layman Henry Sater, which he would later help constitute into an organized church.[40]

One can infer from court records that Paul and Joanna had two children. In 1734, Paul and Joanna deeded some real estate to Martha Ann (about fourteen years old) and Samuel (about twelve). That same year Palmer entered into the last phase of his evangelistic and church planting ministry. In these years he moved beyond Perquimans Precinct and Albemarle into the region below Albemarle Sound. This involved him in church plants in the North Carolina precincts of New Hanover, Beaufort, Craven, Onslow, Hyde, and Bladen, and his labors or those of his ordinands resulted in congregations in Pamlico and Pitt Counties as well. He also ventured into Maryland and South Carolina during these last years of his life. Stevenson surmised that there was probably a "division of labor," perhaps agreed to at the 1734 yearly meeting of the North Carolina and Virginia General Baptists, because Palmer ministered on the outer coastal plain, leaving the inner coastal plain to others.[41]

In February 1735 the General Baptists in Charleston invited Palmer to preach at the South Carolina yearly meeting. The Baptist church in Charleston comprised both General and Particular Baptists. Though the General Baptists had financially endowed the meeting house, they constituted a minority of the membership, and the pastor was Calvinistic. They furtively issued Palmer the invitation, and Palmer walked into a hornet's nest of angry Calvinists who never let him preach. This incident exacerbated poor relations among the General and Particular Baptists of Charleston. The General Baptist party talked with Palmer about their future. He tried to get them a minister from Rhode Island, but to no avail. However, in 1736 Robert Ingram moved from England to be their pastor, allying them to the General Baptists in England, who in 1739 sent Henry Heywood as a messenger to South Carolina. This tiny band of General Baptists would not survive.[42]

Palmer spent some time in Maryland in 1735. The first thing he did there was to take the oaths for Dissenting ministers and register six church meeting sites. The Somerset County Court records say:

> The Reverend Paul Palmer a dissenting Baptist minister Came here into Court in his proper person & prays that he may be admitted to preach and teach the Severall Congregations that shall Come to hear him in the County of Somerset . . . which is granted him he Complying with the act of parliament in such Case made and provided &. whereupon the said Paul Palmer took & subscribed the oath of fidelity as by the Said act of Parliament is directed and Subscribed to the articles of religion Except what part of the Said Articles is Excepted against in favour of Such dis-

senting Ministers by said act and Likewise took the severall oaths to the Government as by act of assembly is directed with the test and Subscribed the Same Oath of abjuration and declaration as is afd by the afd act of assembly required &.[43]

While Palmer was preaching in Somerset County on the Eastern Shore, he purchased a half-acre tract of land on "Luke Watson's place" for the purpose of building a meeting house. However, his primary ministry in the state was about 160 miles northwest, with a group of General Baptists at Chestnut Ridge in Baltimore County. That body had been gathered by a General Baptist layman named Henry Sater who had moved from England in 1709. Sater first hosted the meeting in his home and later built a meeting house for them. The congregation, which still exists, was the first Baptist church in Maryland.[44]

Sater had asked the General Baptist minister George Eaglesfield to preach for the congregation before 1725, when the latter took up the pastorate of a General Baptist church in New Jersey. Soon Sater invited Palmer to come up from North Carolina to serve as preacher for the church and to help them, along with the other churches Palmer was working to settle. Palmer was to have a long relationship with Sater and the General Baptists at Chestnut Ridge, helping settle the group into an established congregation in 1742. Edwards would later describe the congregation as "holding the doctrine of general redemption &c in opposition to those who limit the extend [sic] of Christ's death to the elect" and said, "Laying on of hands and washing feet were practiced in this church."[45]

Palmer was back in Perquimans Precinct by October 1735. Over the next four years, he would continue his messenger-like work throughout the region. His ministry was often associated with rivers and creeks because that is where he held his baptismal services. Later in the eighteenth century, one of his baptism places on the Trent River was known as "Paul Palmer's Landing" and "Paul Palmer's Dipping Hole." Palmer utilized his financial means to aid the ministry of the General Baptists. In April 1738, for example, he had a carpenter and millwright named John Pratt build two small frame houses for meeting houses. One of these was in Perquimans Precinct at his plantation and another was in Edenton.[46]

Palmer also used his influence in public life to expand the religious liberties of Nonconformists in North Carolina. Under heavy opposition from the Anglican authorities, he worked to obtain a more comprehensive solution with the government that would keep Dissenting ministers from having to take oaths at the courthouses of every community in which they preached.

Thus in October 1738, Palmer was granted a license allowing him to preach in any precinct in North Carolina.

LICENCE OF REV. PAUL PALMER TO PREACH.

(Original in Court House at Edenton, NC)

North Carolina.

Permission is hereby granted to Paul Palmer of Edenton a Protestant Minister to Teach or preach the word of God in any part of the said Province (he having qualified himself as such) pursuant to the directions of an Act of Parliament made in the first year of King William and Queen Mary Intituled an "Act for Tolerating Protestant dissenters."

Given under my hand at Edenton the 4th day of October Anno Dom. 1738.[47]

This move was important, given the increasing antipathy Anglican magistrates were exhibiting toward the General Baptists. Palmer experienced this himself in 1739 in Craven Precinct, where magistrates reacted against the "misbehaving speeches" of William Fulsher and Francis Ayres, two ministers Palmer had ordained. These men led the General Baptists in Craven Precinct to go to the chief justice of the province, John Montgomery, to obtain the same broad preaching rights Palmer had received. Their petition involved not only Fulsher and Ayres but also Josiah Hart. Fulsher and Hart would be important leaders in the ongoing movement.[48]

The next thing known about Palmer is the death of his son Samuel in November 1739 at just shy of eighteen years of age. In the title page of the family Bible, Palmer wrote these words: "Samuel Palmer, my Dear Son Departed this Life on the 24th of the M. of Novr., 1739, being in the 18th year of his life. The Text preached at his burial are these: 'I love them that Love me and those that seek me Early shall find me.' Prov. ye 8:17. PAUL PALMER." These are the last words of Palmer's of which there is a record.[49]

In the years after Samuel's death, Palmer spent time helping settle the church at Chestnut Ridge and other General Baptist congregations in Maryland. There he preached and evangelized, conducted baptisms and confirmations, aided congregations, and led congregations to build meeting houses, all the while arousing the suspicions of the authorities. One justice of the peace, William Young, summoned Palmer to appear before the Baltimore County Court in March 1742, but the complaints were subsequently dropped.[50]

The Constitution of the Chestnut Ridge Church in 1742, recorded by

Edwards, gives greater insight into the faith and practice of Palmer and his General Baptist associates than any other extant record. It says the members were "baptized upon a declaration of faith and repentance" and that they believed the doctrine of "general redemption for the free grace of God extended to all mankind." They committed themselves to "contend for the faith once delivered to the saints, owned by the best reformed churches in England, Scotland, and else where, especially as published and maintained in the forms or confessions of the Baptists in England." Furthermore, in a manner similar to that of the English General Baptist *Orthodox Creed*, the document stated, "We do also bind ourselves hereby to defend and live up to the protestant religion," and it stated that the congregation "differed in nothing" from the Churches of England and Scotland except the doctrines of salvation, baptism, church government, and liturgical ceremony. Also similar to earlier Baptist confessions of faith in England—and interesting in this era three-and-a-half decades before the American War for Independence—was a statement of loyalty to the Crown: "We do also engage with our lives and fortunes to defend the crown and dignity of our gracious sovereign king George."[51]

The document also distinguished the General Baptists from Anabaptism in its statement that the church was "not against taking oaths, nor using arms in defence of our king and country when legally called thereto; and that we do approve and will obey the laws of this province." The similarity to the General Baptists in England is spelled out in detail. The congregation bound itself "to follow the patterns of our brethren in England to maintain order, government and discipline in our church." The document made specific reference to how that order, government, and discipline was "especially" laid out in the English General Baptist Francis Stanley's book *The Gospel's Honor and the Churches' Ornament* (also known as *Christianity Indeed*), "dedicated to the churches in the counties of Lincoln, Nottingham, and Cambridge." Last, the document stated that every member who joined the church would be required to consent to and sign "this our solemn league and covenant."[52]

Nothing more is known of Palmer after his time in Maryland in 1742. Edwards mentioned that he planted a church in the southeastern part of North Carolina near the South Carolina line "about the year 1743." Thus one can surmise that Palmer was active in this area at some point in 1743. The fact that Joanna purchased land in her own name in the summer of 1743 suggests that he was probably dead by then. Joanna died four years later at sixty-one years of age, and two years after that Martha Ann gave birth to a son whom she named after her beloved brother Samuel, who had sought the Lord early.[53]

Palmer's subsequent reputation among Arminian Baptists has been that of a faithful minister of the gospel who was as concerned for evangelism, church planting, and lovingly shepherding the Lord's flock as he was doctrine, theology, preaching, and the nuts and bolts of organizational leadership. Calvinist Baptists, on the contrary, have tended to paint him as a disturber of the brethren, fomenting theological error and inculcating a cold formalism that opposed the sweet wind blowing in from the northern awakenings. Yet this is a caricature born of late eighteenth-century Calvinist Baptist polemics. Morgan Edwards is, perhaps unintentionally, guilty of painting this unfair picture since the only people in the region whom he interviewed were the General Baptists' bitterest critics. While Edwards could easily have interviewed General Baptist ministers such as Elder Joseph Parker who had a personal relationship with Palmer, he never did. Edwards must have at some point intended to interview the pastors of the continuing General Baptist congregations. Toward the end of his discussion of North Carolina Baptists, under the heading "Treats of the general Baptists in the province of Northcarolina," he reserved a place in his handwritten notes for the churches at "Contantony," "Matchipungo," "Meherin," and "Bear-River." However, he never got around to it. Those pages are left blank.[54]

It would take Southern Baptist historians William Whitsitt (president of Southern Baptist Theological Seminary), J. D. Hufham, and George Washington Paschal in the late nineteenth and early twentieth centuries to resurrect Palmer's reputation as a sound folk theologian, warm-hearted gospel preacher, and effective organizer. Hufham, for example, in the 1890s, called Palmer "that hero of the faith," remarking, "Paul Palmer was the greatest North Carolinian of his time. Not one of the men with whom he came into contact or collision can be compared with him" in "loftiness and firmness of purpose; in quickness and keenness of insight; in breadth of vision which enabled him to plan large enterprises and mastery of details which gave him success in the execution of them; in the courage and patience with which he awaited his opportunity...." Free Will Baptist historians Davidson, Stevenson, and Pelt would round out that picture more precisely in the late twentieth century.[55]

William Surginer, Josiah Hart, and Their Associates

Earlier historians thought that an epidemic had driven William Surginer (spelled variously as Sojourner, Surgeoner, and Surgenor) from Isle of Wight County, Virginia, to Kehukee, Edgecombe County, North Carolina, in 1742. However, recent research has shown that he moved in the 1720s. He probably came as a teenager, but evidently by 1729, at the age of twenty-two, he had purchased fifty acres of his own on Kehukee Swamp. In those early years, the General Baptists of Kehukee likely stayed in contact with their brothers and sisters at the General Baptist church at Burley in Virginia. They probably attended the Virginia yearly meeting with which Paul Palmer later united his North Carolina churches. Surginer would have been baptized by either the younger Richard Jones or Palmer. Surginer married Mary West Boykin, with whom he had at least three children, Jacob, Ann, and Tamar, and probably another son, Brown.[56]

By the late 1730s, Surginer was serving as a General Baptist elder along the Roanoke and Tar Rivers. Around 1742 he gathered a church on Kehukee Creek near the present-day town of Scotland Neck. There the church built a twenty-by-forty-foot meeting house that was still in existence by 1772 when Morgan Edwards conducted his research tour. Edwards spoke of Surginer in better terms than he did the other Arminian Baptists, referring to him as "a most excellent man." Paschal averred that he was obviously a "man of much wisdom and influence as well as an active and energetic minister." Even though Surginer pastored only one congregation, in a short time he mentored several young ministers from influential Anglican families. Over the next six years, he also started the Falls of Tar River (1744), Fishing Creek (1745), and Lower Fishing Creek (1748) churches. Surginer died at forty-three years of age in February 1749, according to a cedar grave marker made by his dear friend Josiah Hart.[57]

One of Elder Surginer's earliest associates in ministry seems to have been the mutual friend of Paul Palmer and John Comer, the hatter with the remarkable name of Constant Devotion. Devotion, born in 1706 to John and Elisabeth Devotion, had grown up in the First Baptist Church in Swansea, Massachusetts, which Palmer's friend John Comer had served for a time. Devotion's father was a deacon and later pastor of the church. No one knows whether Devotion was an ordained minister or a lay preacher, but he did a great deal to assist the work of Surginer in the late 1730s and early 1740s. Comer had recorded in his diary that he had received a visit from Devotion in November 1729. This was just after the church Palmer had settled in Chowan Precinct had appealed to Comer for help finding ministers to come south and aid in the work. Whether or not Devotion came as a result of that appeal, there is evidence that, by 1734, he met with Palmer, and in 1735 and 1736 he appeared in Edenton with another Baptist from Rhode Island, Joseph Witter. By 1739 Devotion had set up shop in Kehukee, where he served that year on a coroner's jury. The next year he bought a tract of land next to John Surginer's farm. In 1742 Devotion fell from his horse while visiting Lower Fishing Creek that summer and soon died.[58]

Surginer also associated with Peleg Rogers, a native of Washington County, Rhode Island, who in 1728 had lived in Perquiman's Precinct, Palmer's home precinct. Rogers was a minister who took the oaths for Dissenting ministers in Edgecombe County in 1744. The General Baptist church near Town Creek and Toisnot Swamp likely resulted from Rogers's ministry by 1748. Rogers had already moved to Duplin County before 1758, when the church was reorganized as a Particular Baptist church.[59]

Josiah Hart was the most remarkable of Surginer's associates. "Among all the General Baptists who labored in the gospel ministry in the Province of North Carolina," Paschal averred, "none was more active and able than Dr. Josiah Hart." Apparently a bachelor and a physician, Hart had the freedom to move from place to place preaching, baptizing, laying hands on newly baptized converts, and planting churches. He was very active in Craven and Beaufort Counties. Since Hart was active in Palmer's most entrenched early fields of ministry, he was probably one of Palmer's converts. He continued to cultivate these areas after Palmer's death in 1742. Later Hart was active in Edgecombe and Halifax Counties, where he worked closely with Surginer in the latter's closing years. As Paschal said, no one knows why Hart "left Beaufort for Edgecombe, the Edgecombe of that day, whether on the invitation of Parker or Sojourner [Surginer], or independently. But whatever the occasion it is certain that his purpose in going was to give the Gospel to the settlers along the frontier who were then utterly destitute of gospel privileges." While Surginer seems to have worked more as a pastor of one church and discipled young elders to go out and plant other churches, Elder Hart's labors were, like Palmer's, more like that of a General Baptist messenger.[60]

Edwards referred to him as "Dr. Josiah Hart of Scotland Neck" because of his work near Surginer on Kehukee Creek. According to Lemuel Burkitt and Jesse Read, historians of the Calvinistic Kehukee Baptist Association formed after the proselytization of the General Baptists, "Doctor Josiah Hart" was the founder of the Reedy Creek Church in Warren County. "He came about the year 1750, and preached and baptized. He was the first preacher of the Baptist persuasion who preached here.... Soon after him, Wm. Washington, James Smart, Samuel Davis, William Walker, and others joined in the work of preaching and baptizing, upon what is called the *Free-will* plan, and numbers came and were baptized. But nothing like a church constitution."[61]

After some of the young ministers who had been recently ordained became Calvinists following Surginer's death, Hart remained committed to

Arminianism until his death in 1758. However, he was unable to affect those ministers because he was no longer there. In his later years, he had to move back to the outer coastal plain in Tyrrell and Beaufort Counties to deal with business disputes that had arisen while he had worked further west with Surginer. Thus in some of the most crucial years of the transformation of General Baptist churches into Calvinist churches, Hart was gone. One can only wonder how many of the young ministers Hart had mentored would have been kept from proselytization by Calvinists had he not been occupied elsewhere.[62]

Joseph Parker's Early Years

Joseph Parker is the most important link in the chain between Paul Palmer and the later Free Will Baptist movement. Thus it is unfortunate that Morgan Edwards failed to interview him for his important historical research that has shaped the opinion of so many about the Calvinist proselytization of the General Baptist movement in the mid-eighteenth century. The victors write the history, and the one-sided account of Edwards, who for many years had been close friends with the best-known proselytizer John Gano, has shaped the way most Calvinist historians have interpreted the early General/Free Will Baptist movement in North Carolina. At the time Edwards conducted his extensive research tour through the region in 1772, he could have easily interviewed Parker, since the latter had lived in Dobbs County since 1758. Edwards knew about Parker, because he stated in his notes that the Lower Fishing Creek Church had "been a society belonging to Mr. Parker for about eight years and on the Arminian plan but in 1756 it was formed into a church on the Calvinistic order."[63]

Burkitt and Read made reference to Parker, noting, "The churches of this [the General Baptist] order were first gathered here by Elders *Paul Palmer* and *Joseph Parker*...." Speaking of the proselytization of the General Baptist churches by the Calvinists, they said, "Elder *Palmer*, we believe, died before the reformation took place; and Elder *Joseph Parker*, we cannot learn, was ever convinced of his errors, or receded from them; but continued in his way as before."[64]

S. J. Wheeler, who in 1847 wrote the history of the Meherrin Church, said that this Joseph Parker was the same one who had with his father-in-law John Welch signed the letter that Palmer's church in Chowan Precinct had sent John Comer in 1729.[65] Paschal and most subsequent historians have agreed with him. However, Stevenson has recently argued that Parker was the son of the prosperous planter Francis Parker who with his wife Elizabeth and their family moved with other families from Surrey, Nansemond, and Isle of Wight Counties, Virginia. Francis Parker settled with his family on Deep Creek below Kehukee Swamp, the area where William Surginer was active. Stevenson said that before 1735 they relocated to Lower Fishing Creek and that Joseph was constable of the district. Constant Devotion witnessed two deeds that Francis Parker made in 1742, placing this Joseph Parker in contact with Devotion.[66]

Whether our Joseph Parker is the one from the original Chowan congregation or the son of Francis Parker who moved from Virginia to Kehukee, he was tied to Palmer. The Joseph Parker in Comer's diary would have been intimately associated with Palmer. Either way, Parker was mentored by Josiah Hart, and thus at least indirectly by Palmer. Still, this Parker would have interacted with Palmer, who did not pass from the scene until 1743. Regardless, Joseph Parker would prove to be the steward of Palmer's Arminian legacy, enabling a small General Baptist remnant to survive the Calvinist onslaught from Philadelphia.[67]

Paschal lauded Parker for "preaching the gospel of the Savior," "calling men to repentance," and "walking in all the commands and ordinances of the Lord blamelessly." Several decades earlier Wheeler had said, "Elder Parker was a consistent Christian, a zealous and successful minister" who "was highly esteemed." Wheeler quoted one aged Baptist minister, Lewis Whitfield of Carteret County, who said that "Elder Joseph Parker 'was a square-built man,' with a broad face, about five feet eight inches high, and in his later years wore on his head a cap continually. His manner of preaching was full of animation." Whitfield could not tell Wheeler whether Parker and his wife Lucia had any children.[68]

From what little information can be scraped together, one notes that Parker was witness to a deed that William Surginer made in November 1745, and Surginer presided, with Josiah Hart, at the constitution of the Lower Fishing Creek Church in Edgecombe County and at Parker's ordination. Yet there is even more evidence of Parker's acquaintance with Hart. It is known that Hart preached, evangelized, baptized, and confirmed converts in the Lower Fishing Creek area in 1747. The next year the General Baptist church there was constituted, and it called Parker as pastor. Records show that Hart was in Lower Fishing Creek again in 1749. On that visit, he baptized Charles Daniel, whom he, with Henry Ledbetter, ordained as an elder in August 1753 to assist Parker.[69]

Soon Parker traveled to Dobbs County, near where there were already General Baptist churches at Stoney Creek and Swift Creek pastored by George

Graham and Joseph Willis, respectively. Graham was one of Palmer's colleagues; Graham and William Fulsher, another of Palmer's followers, had ordained Willis. Parker bought a hundred-acre farm in 1756 on Little Contentnea Creek in what is now Greene County. The congregation he planted there would survive the proselytization efforts of the Particular Baptists, plant new churches, and play a role in the continuing Free Will Baptist saga. Parker's story will be picked back up in the next chapter in the discussion of the General Baptist remnant that survived the Calvinist offensive.[70]

Two

THE CALVINIST PROSELYTIZATION AND RECOVERY, 1750-1794

The Calvinist Proselytization

The General Baptist movement that would become the Free Will Baptist Church in the American South was nearly snuffed out of existence by Calvinists abetted by the Philadelphia Baptist Association. Or, as Robert Gardner said, they "were invaded by missionaries from the Philadelphia Baptist Association."[1] During most of the colonial period, the General Baptists up and down the Eastern Seaboard were growing rapidly. In the first half of the eighteenth century, they were planting churches and having such evangelistic success that the Southern Baptist historian William Whitsitt later said they "dominated in America" from 1639 to 1740 and that Palmer's movement in particular was "the most prosperous body of Baptist people at that time in the world."[2]

Thomas Kidd, who lauds the Philadelphia Association's proselytization of the General Baptists of North Carolina, is partly right that the General Baptists in the 1750s "mostly opposed the new revivalism."[3] Yet they were no different in their misgivings than many Congregationalists, Presbyterians, and Calvinist Baptists. Most Calvinist Baptist historians have repeated the mistaken views of John Gano and the Philadelphia Association Calvinists of the 1750s. They have painted the General Baptists as cold, rationalistic, uninterested in spiritual fervor, and even unregenerate. This caricature, however, is belied by the General Baptists' evangelistic zeal and church planting success in difficult fields.[4]

As early as 1750, some of the young, recently ordained converts of William Surginer and Josiah Hart had surreptitiously accepted Calvinism, and they were slowly and quietly attempting to lead their congregations down that path. Morgan Edwards said that one of Hart's young converts, James Smart, whom he ordained in June 1750, embraced the New Light Calvinism sweeping in from the North within six months of his ordination. Though there were no Particular Baptist churches in North Carolina at that time, there were a few in South Carolina. News of the Calvinist wing of the Great Awakening, centered on the preaching of Gilbert Tennent, Jonathan Edwards, and especially George Whitefield, had reached North Carolina.[5] Smart's change to Calvinism was followed quickly by that of another of Hart's ordinands, Henry Ledbetter. Morgan Edwards said that Ledbetter's Calvinist preaching was so distasteful to his congregation that he felt compelled to leave and went to Charleston for tutoring in his newfound doctrine. Just after Surginer's death in 1750, two of his young converts at the Upper Fishing Creek Church, whom he had recently ordained, became Particular Baptists.[6]

Over a period of five years, Robert Williams, a North Carolina native who had moved to be a part of the Particular Baptists in Charleston in 1745, had influenced Smart and Ledbetter. Williams also convinced a layman in the Kehukee Church known as William Wallis the sleigh-maker, and the church's pastor Thomas Pope, to become New Light Calvinists. There was also some influence from Stephen Hollingsworth. He had always been a Particular Baptist and later started a church in Bladen County in 1756. Edwards later remarked that Ledbetter was "taught to be a Calvinist by Mr. Hollingsworth." Williams also convinced others to embrace Calvinism. These included William Walker of the Fishing Creek Church; John Moore of the Falls of Tar River Church, who had come out of the Kehukee Church; Edward Brown of the Great Cohara Church; and Charles Daniel (Surginer and Hart had both laid hands on Daniel at his ordination). Daniel said his reading of a collection of Whitefield's sermons in 1755 had convinced him of Calvinism. Influenced by William Wallis, Moore eventually read John Bunyan's *Law and Grace* and Edward Fisher's *The Marrow of Modern Divinity* and subsequently embraced Calvinism. He succeeded in convincing William Surginer's brother Robert, a member of the Falls of Tar River congregation, to accept Calvinism as well.[7]

These men, however, were unable to transform those General Baptist churches into Particular Baptist congregations. So they asked the Philadelphia Association, the stronghold of Baptist Calvinism in the North, for help. In 1754 that association sent their brightest young minister, the twenty-seven-year-old John Gano, to aid these Calvinist converts. Their objective was to convert the General Baptists to Calvinism. Stevenson was right in characterizing the representatives of the Philadelphia Association as having embraced a form of Calvinism that had been "greatly heightened by the Great Awakening." He explained that, like Whitefield, "they believed themselves justified in going uninvited into other ministers' churches, and they followed Whitefield's example of denouncing as unregenerated, hypocrites, or wolves in sheep's clothing those clergy who were opposed to their practices and theology."[8]

Within the next few years, Gano and other "missionaries" the Philadelphia Association sent down helped proselytize and assume control of as many General Baptist churches as possible. They alleged that these congregations were filled with false converts because they did not require their members to "relate" an "experience of grace." "Experience of grace" and "relation" were technical terms for a long, drawn-out litany of how individuals came to know they were one of the elect.[9]

The General Baptist Understanding of Conversion and Church Membership

Instead, the General Baptists simply ensured that their new members had been converted and admitted to church membership according to the Six Principles of the Christian Religion in Hebrews 6:1–2. The Six Principles were deeply embedded in General Baptist piety, constituting the General Baptists' own scripturally rooted "morphology of conversion." New believers must have—to use the language of the Geneva and King James Bibles—repented from dead works, placed their faith in Christ, and been baptized. Converts must have had the elders' hands laid on them, symbolizing the reception of the Holy Spirit (which, incidentally, the Philadelphia Association also required as a Christian ordinance), and acknowledged that as believers they would one day be resurrected by Christ and stand at the judgment.

This was standard English General Baptist practice on both sides of the Atlantic. Paul Palmer's friend John Comer referred in his diary to what the General Baptists in eighteenth-century America believed about the lives and profession of those who are baptized. Comer spoke positively of the Rhode Island General Baptist church pastored by James Clarke and Daniel Wightman, a Six-Principle Baptist congregation "owning ye Doctrine of Genl Redemption." The Calvinist Comer quoted their church covenant approvingly:

> By faith and practice with us, we mean and intend those that are dipped into water with a verbal demonstration of their faith and repentance, yielding obedience to all the rest of the ordinances of our Lord Jesus

Christ, as laying on of hands with a real faith in the Resurrection of the dead, and the Eternal Judgment; as also keeping their holy union and fellowship in Breaking of Bread and Prayer; as will be better seen and is set forth more at large in a printed sheet or declaration of faith and practice of ye Baptized churches, falsely called Anabaptists, in London and in other places in England; which sheet is signed by certain Elders and Brethren of said churches to the number of 73, printed in the year 1691.[10]

The declaration of faith to which they referred is the 1691 edition of the *Standard Confession*. It is informative to notice the almost direct quotation of the Six Principles of the Christian Religion from Hebrews 6:1–2. This was an integral part of the fabric of the General Baptists of that time—what it meant to be a General Six-Principle Baptist. As Burkitt and Read, the historians of the Calvinized Kehukee Association, later pointed out, the General Baptists of North Carolina also subscribed to the *Standard Confession*.[11]

That confession outlined how General Baptists received members. "The right and only way, of gathering Churches, (according to Christs appointment, Mat. 28. 19, 20.)," the confession read, "is first to teach, or preach the Gospel, Mark 16. 16. to the Sons and Daughters of men; and then to Baptise (that is in English to Dip) in the name of the Father, Son, and holy Spirit, or in the name of the Lord Jesus Christ; such only of them, as profess repentance towards God, and faith towards our Lord Jesus Christ, Acts. 2. 38. Acts 8. 12. Acts 18. 8." Thus one must receive with suspicion the rhetoric of the New Light Baptists, whose strict Calvinism and zeal for the northern awakenings caused them to question the Christianity of the General Baptists, just as their New Light Congregationalist and New Side Presbyterian counterparts had done with their Old Light and Old Side opponents in the North.[12]

The most important evidence that the Palmer churches were not "lax" in church membership and discipline is the "league and covenant" of the Chestnut Ridge Church Palmer helped form in Baltimore County, Maryland, in the early 1740s. The precise detail into which the document goes about the congregation's view of the "order, government and discipline" of the church and its members indicates the opposite about Palmer's and his protégés' views than what their Calvinist adversaries alleged. That document not only states that the congregation's members are only those who have been "baptized upon a declaration of faith and repentance." It also goes on to state explicitly, "We do bind ourselves to follow the patterns of our brethren in England to maintain order, government and discipline in our church," especially as laid out in Francis Stanley's book *Christianity Indeed*. That book outlined strict parameters for the membership and discipline of English General Baptist congregants. Last, the league and covenant was required to be consented to and signed by everyone who joined the Chestnut Ridge Church.[13]

The sticking point, then, was that the New Light Calvinist Baptists required an often lengthy and emotional "relation" of how applicants for church membership came to be converted and see themselves as elect. This had become popular during the Great Awakening in non-Baptist circles. "New Light" Congregationalist and "New Side" Presbyterian churches began to require these experiential exercises for admission to church membership. The "Old Lights" vehemently objected, arguing that this practice was adding things to the ordinary means of grace and to the sufficiency of Scripture.[14]

This dynamic is similar to what the General/Free Will Baptists said. One sees this posture exemplified by the nineteenth-century Free Will Baptist Elder Rufus K. Hearn. He stated in his *Origin of the Free Will Baptist Church of North Carolina*:

> These early churches took the Bible for their guide, they practiced its sacred teachings, and as the Apostles never required an experience, and as it was nowhere authorized in Holy Writ, they practiced what they found the gospel required, that is, faith in the Lord Jesus Christ, repentance towards God, and baptism by immersion; and baptized their members on a profession of their faith in the Lord Jesus Christ, and not by experience. Every Free Will Baptist will see that this is his doctrine, and the true doctrine of the New Testament, and it is our practice to the present day to baptize members on their profession of faith in the Lord Jesus Christ. They may call it lax in discipline, if they choose; we cannot, for we find no warrant in the New Testament for an experience of grace, as they term it.[15]

Philadelphia, Gano, and the Process of Proselytization

One of the most famous episodes in the annals of Free Will Baptist history is when Philadelphia Association minister John Gano intruded uninvited into a meeting of General Baptist ministers gathered in a meeting house. This incident took place about two years after the Philadelphia Association began working to take over these congregations. As Philip Mulder puts it, "Gano crashed the meeting, claimed the pulpit, and preached from the text 'Jesus I know, and Paul I know, but who are ye?'" Eventually, Gano "coerced" many of the ministers into "accepting his teaching" by "frightening, challenging, and shaming" them.[16]

After Gano returned from his tour, the Philadelphia Association sent two more ministers, Peter Vanhorn and Benjamin Miller, to continue the work of proselytization. Within a year, Miller and Vanhorn reorganized Fishing Creek Church, Kehukee Church, Bear Creek Church, and Swift Creek Church. After this, from October 1757 to April 1761, eight more churches were reconstituted as Particular Baptist congregations: Lower Fishing Creek, Falls of Tar River, Pasquotank, Toisnot, Red Banks, Great Cohara, Tar River, and Sandy Run.[17]

The most astonishing fact about these reconstituted congregations is that they were so much smaller than the General Baptist churches they succeeded. One assumes that these Calvinist converts worked slowly and astutely to avoid the fate of Henry Ledbetter, whose strong preaching of his newfound Calvinist doctrine to his congregants backfired. As Pelt explains, there is evidence in some instances of "open hostility on the part of the lay members to the fact that their church was being 'dissolved' and replaced by a new organization of which they did not approve." However, he explains, "without pastors to lead them, what remained of these General Baptist congregations would in time wither away. Even those who contested the ownership of their meeting houses, as at Toisnot in Edgecombe County, were not able to survive without pastoral leadership."[18]

However, the pressing questions for the modern reader are, how did these General Baptist laypeople allow their churches to be taken over, why did the reorganized Calvinist churches retain a minority of the members, and how could a minority take over a church? The most likely answer points to the not-uncommon occurrence today of aggressive and persuasive pastors making radical changes in modern-day congregations, with the majority of their members, a little at a time, becoming discouraged and simply ceasing to attend rather than "fighting the pastor." Then the pastor reconstitutes the church with the remaining members. Another possible answer, which Pelt proposes, is that the pastors in these early congregations sometimes held title to the meeting houses, which they had built at their own expense.

Either way, the majority of the individuals who had been members of these General Baptist congregations were no longer members after the churches' reconstitutions. The church covenant to which these members were now required to assent contained not only the relation of an "experience of grace," but also an affirmation of a statement of faith that contained what Paschal called a Calvinism that "was indeed of the most rigid kind." Both these standards were employed to ascertain the elect status of these congregants. Historians do not know what happened to most of the General Baptists who did not assent to the new terms of membership. Yet they were sheep without a shepherd, having no pastor to shepherd them in these rural frontier communities when congregations were a distant wagon-ride away from each other. Most probably went back to the earlier practice of meeting in homes with lay preachers. Some might have found it easier to attend a local Anglican church or Quaker meeting than to remain in a setting with a pastor who judged them unregenerate because of their honestly held doctrine and practice.[19]

This of course brings up the whole question of the allegation that the majority of these congregants were unregenerate because they could not "relate" an "experience of grace." This requires an in-depth consideration of the context of mid-eighteenth-century American evangelicalism. Calvinist historians have for 250 years repeated the Philadelphia Association's claim that the eighteenth-century General Baptists of North Carolina were cold, devoid of spiritual life, and filled with unregenerate church members. As Pelt observes, "It is amazing how later Baptist historians could be so forthright in passing judgment on these early General Baptists, even though they lack the kind of evidence to support their conclusions that would satisfy an impartial observer."[20]

It does not take a reader long to see how despised the General Baptists were in the eyes of their Regular Baptist counterparts. The origins of the traditional interpretation of Calvinist historians lie in the interviews Morgan Edwards conducted in 1772 and 1773. The problem with Morgan's research, as intimated above, is that it was one-sided. Morgan, a close friend of Gano's for many years, based his research solely on interviews with the General Baptists' enemies. They were bitter opponents who had been trying to root out what they saw as the dangerous false teaching of Arminianism.

This oppositional dynamic is seen in the 1803 statement made by Particular Baptist preachers Lemuel Burkitt and Jesse Read. They authored the history of the Kehukee Baptist Association, which was formed from the General Baptist churches that had been proselytized. At one point in their narrative, they spoke of the church at Flat Swamp, a General Baptist church that had become Calvinist. The church, they said, "began to experience severe difficulties; as the love of some of her members began to wax cold, it gave an opportunity to the enemy of souls to sow seeds of discord amongst them, which caused the Arminians and Universalists to look out of their dens, where they had been driven by the refulgent beams of Gospel truths." In another passage, Burkitt and Read recounted the account of a General Baptist preacher who had slumped to his death in the pulpit while preaching. They declared that this was an example of God's "avenging" his church, "for the fox was spoiling the tender grapes." Modern historians such as Bryan

LeBeau and Philip Mulder label this attitude among New Lights as "an acrimonious, controversial spirit."[21]

In the 1830s the New Englander Elias Hutchins visited the North Carolina Free Will Baptists and gave them copies of a northern Freewill Baptist hymnal. They reacted "with grief and almost indignant astonishment" at the words of a hymn that commended the New Lights:

> Come all who are New Lights indeed,
> Who are from sin and bondage freed;
> From Egypt's land we've taken flight,
> For God has given us a New Light.[22]

Had Morgan Edwards interviewed even one General Baptist, he would have encountered a different story that would have offered balance to his other sources. Later Arminian historians would point out that Edwards himself was a partisan in a time when New Light Calvinist revivalism was still very much affecting his analysis of his subject matter and when aggressive Calvinist proselytization of General Baptists was still occurring.[23] Paschal, whose 1930 analysis generally assumes the veracity of Edwards's account, said, "Probably the statement of Burkitt and Read that Palmer and his successors admitted the unconverted to baptism is not quite fair" and added that the General Baptists congregants "should not be judged too harshly."[24]

The "Relation" of an "Experience of Grace" in the Culture of the Great Awakening

Even more basic for the modern reader is the fact that what played out in North Carolina had occurred throughout the North in the paedobaptist denominations. There, New Lights consistently criticized Old Lights for being too devoid of spiritual fervor to be considered regenerate. Old Lights who relied on what the Westminster Shorter Catechism termed the "outward and ordinary means of grace" pushed back on such criticism, insisting they were regenerate. When one adds this novel thrust produced by the Great Awakening context in the North to the rigorous Calvinism of the Philadelphia Association and those sympathetic to it, a different light is cast on the situation with the General Baptists.[25]

More than anyone else, Douglas Winiarski has conducted painstaking research into the practice of what was often called the "relation" of an "experience of grace." His primary focus is the transformation that practice underwent in the fervor of the Great Awakening. His research sheds much light on the clash between the New Light Calvinist Baptists and the General Baptists. The conflict had played itself out hundreds of times in the North. New Lights had raised the bar on church membership requirements in unprecedented ways. Winiarski explains how they began stipulating that candidates for church membership publicly "relate" their emotional experience of how they came to discover they were one of the elect. Many of the New Lights caricatured Old Lights as cold and dead and even unregenerate. Old Lights resisted the new practices, wishing to adhere to what they called the "ordinary means of grace."[26]

In the seventeenth century, Calvinist Puritans in New England had required candidates for church membership to provide a "relation" of their conversion to be admitted to membership. Winiarski says this was "part of a unique genre of devotional literature with deep roots in the history of New England Congregationalism." However, even before the Great Awakening, critics "balked" at the "anxiety-inducing standards for church membership" that had come to characterize New England Puritanism. These critics believed that these "relations" did not rest on a "scriptural foundation." They accused the New England Puritans of "excessively narrowing the gates of the church." Yet with the onset of the Whitefield revivals, the standards for relating an "experience of grace" became inordinately high.[27]

Thus the 1740s, with the onset of the revivals, witnessed a sharp shift in the requirement of "relations" as well as in their tone. For example, as Winiarski explains, "Only a handful of lay men and women referenced the dangers of hell in relations composed before 1740, but, for those galvanized by Whitefield, Tennent, and their itinerating New England colleagues, the danger was imminent, inevitable, and desperately real. Threats of eternal damnation increasingly supplanted tales of providential affliction in the narratives of young converts." Increasingly in these "relations," "lay men and women zealously embraced Whitefield's powerful new oratorical style as well as his sustained assault on the sandy foundations of faith."[28]

By "sandy foundations" was meant those things the New Lights criticized about the traditional Puritan "relations." These emphasized theological beliefs, repentance, faith, and reliance on ordinary spiritual disciplines such as "secret prayer," Bible study, family worship, and "closet meditation." Whitefield and the New Lights denounced these as "crafty stratagems that led only to spiritual dullness." These were things that Satan had used to lull people into spiritual complacency. Instead, the New Lights "lavished attention" on "dramatic conversion experiences." Many individuals, in relating their "experience of grace," detailed "frightening images of Satan more often than prospective church members earlier in the century, and they described being driven 'allmost to dispare' by the prospect of 'hell opened wide.'" Some individuals related experiences of dreams and visions and "scanned their experiences for evidence of the precise moment when Christ began 'Courting my Backward Soul,' as one woman explained."[29]

John Crowley describes the reaction of one Carolina Anglican minister to some New Light Baptists' relation of their experience of grace through "dreams and visions": "But another vile Matter that does and must give Offence to all Sober Minds Is, what they call their *Experiences*.... To see a sett of Mongrels under Pretext of Religion, Sit, and hear for Hours together a string of Vile, cook'd up, Silly and Senseless Lyes, What they know to be such, ... must grieve and give great Offence to ev'ry one that has the Honour of Christianity at Heart."[30]

The Puritans before the Awakening had accepted written testimonies for membership. Yet the Awakening spurred the restoration of oral testimonies. As one Separate document stated, those who would not recite the emotional experiences that led to their conversion would be "Looked upon as an open Contemner of the Gospel-Commands." Some New Lights even required this of transfer members:

> Each time the Separates organized a new church, the founding members—both men and women—"stood confidently and zealously declared" their "Experences how the Lord brought them out of darkness into his marvelus light."... Some relations functioned like awakening sermons. Minister Paul Parke noted that many candidates were "filled with the holy Ghost"—some to "Greate Rapture"—when they recited their conversions and were admitted into "Visable fellowship" with the Separate church in Preston, Connecticut.... When delivered with power, oral conversion narratives provided certain evidence of election, ensured the purity of Separate church membership, edified the assembled congregation, and, on rare occasions, propelled onlookers into raptures of their own."[31]

The even more rigorous application of the relation of an "experience of grace" by the Separates is seen among the Separate Baptists (largely Congregationalist Separates who later adopted believer's baptism by immersion). Ironically, when they came to North Carolina in the late eighteenth century, they did the same thing to the Regular Baptists that the latter had done to the General Baptists a generation earlier: they claimed that the Regular Baptist churches were filled with members whose relation of their "experience of grace" was not convincing enough, accusing them of coldness and the lack of evidence of true conversion.[32]

Yet it was not just the more enthusiastic Separates who instituted rigorous requirements for the relation of an "experience of grace." Jonathan Edwards exemplified the heightened requirements for church membership characteristic of the Awakening. When he started requiring such "relations" of candidates for membership at his church in Northampton in 1749, several of his congregants resisted him and called for his resignation, which they eventually got. Even some of Edwards's allies in strengthening requirements for observing the Lord's Supper believed that he had gone too far in requiring elaborate "relations" for church membership. Thomas Foxcroft, for example, led his congregation "to allow candidates who 'have a Scruple upon their Minds about making a Relation as usual' to exhibit a written statement of their theological knowledge instead." Members of the Old South Church in Boston completely eliminated "relations." Instead, they had membership candidates affirm a "standardized profession of doctrine."[33]

The increasingly narrow requirements for membership candidates to testify publicly of their religious experiences led to hundreds of church splits in the North. Still, "across New England, in towns that had suffered through divisive revival seasons and those that had not, many lay men and women continued to submit relations that remained closely tied to the older ideal of the godly walk," Winiarski explains. "Even in revival hotbeds such as Malden and Norton, Massachusetts, and Suffield, Connecticut, people still envisioned church membership in the contractual terms of sacramental obligations." Winiarski argues that historians writing on the "Puritan conversion narrative" have "often moved briskly from the earlier practices," which emphasized the ordinary means of grace, to the practices of the Great Awakening. This has tended "to flatten the meaning of church membership, leaving scholars struggling to account for the unexpected conflicts and schisms that developed in the wake of the Whitefieldian revivals." Yet, he cogently argues, "relations" of an "experience of grace" during the Great Awakening were drastically different from "oral church admission narratives" in the seventeenth century. Winiarski's groundbreaking research reorients the way one reads what took place in the clash between the Calvinist New Lights and the General Baptists in North Carolina in the mid- to late eighteenth century.[34]

The General Baptist Reaction

Modern readers must place themselves into the shoes of these rural General Baptists who were the only Baptists in North Carolina up to this point.

They were surrounded on one side by the Quakers, whom Paul Palmer had left to join the General Baptists and whom they considered fanatics. On the other side were the Anglicans, whom they considered formalists. First, the Puritan conversion narrative itself, which arose in a Calvinistic context and emphasized peculiarly Calvinist piety surrounding particular and irresistible grace—doctrines strange to them and every other Christian outside the Calvinist fold—was completely foreign to the General Baptists. Second, the transformation that the "relation" of this narrative underwent in the fervor of the Great Awakening was shocking to them. They were accustomed simply to following the Six Principles of the Christian Religion and the *Standard Confession*'s prescription that "the right and only way, of gathering Churches," following Christ's direction, was "first to teach, or preach the Gospel . . . to the Sons and Daughters of men," then to "Baptise . . . such only of them, as profess repentance towards God, and faith towards our Lord Jesus Christ."[35]

Later Free Will Baptist historians saw the proselytization efforts of the Calvinists and their abettors from the Philadelphia Association as a playing out of the same divisive and unprecedented actions that led to the schisms and takeovers of hundreds of American churches in the 1740s and 1750s. They criticized the Calvinist Kehukee leaders Burkitt and Read for thinking it was reprehensible for an Arminian preacher named Frost to attempt to proselytize Calvinist churches yet for not applying the same standards to the very Calvinist proselytizers who founded the Calvinist Baptist movement in North Carolina. As southern Free Will Baptist historian Rufus K. Hearn would later argue, the acceptance of Calvinism was the basic reason for the proselytization. The secondary reason was the General Baptists' adherence to their traditional practices for accepting members, which flew in the face of the New Light innovations regarding the "relation" of an "experience of grace" that had recently caught on up north.[36]

Hearn said, "The enemies of the Arminian Baptists in North Carolina were greatly elated at the revolution, and regarded it as a great and beneficial change. . . . But considering the manner in which the revolution was brought about, and the unhappy results of it, there is much room to doubt the propriety of the measure." Had the New Lights, "as the Calvinistic Baptists were then called, been invited to visit and remodel these churches, no objection could probably be made to their course," he said. However, going in "uninvited to proselyte them, was obtrusive and provoking. There was surely work enough to be done in North Carolina by the Baptist ministers without interfering with a few churches who felt that they had a right to their organizations, and to labor unmolested in the fields they entered peaceably and had occupied some twenty-five years without molestation." Later Free Will Baptist historians asked why the Philadelphia Association did not evangelize those great numbers of people in the North Carolina wilderness who made no profession of faith, or attempt to proselytize the Anglicans or Quakers, who were further from the truth, according to the association's tenets, than the General Baptists.[37]

This episode nearly killed what is now known as the Free Will Baptist movement. However, the churches that survived would later develop into the Free Will Baptist Church of the South. As the historian William Whitsitt, president of Southern Baptist Theological Seminary, later said, "I am a Particular Baptist throughout, but I have sometimes been moved to tears by the sad fate of Paul Palmer, when his flourishing field—the most prosperous body of Baptist people at that time in the world—was overrun and trampled down by his enemies. Paul Palmer excites my imagination and evokes my sympathy. He was a great and worthy man, and ought to have a monument somewhere...."[38]

This chapter in Free Will Baptist history marks the beginning of a tension in Free Will Baptist life and thought between what scholars such as D. G. Hart and James Tunstead Burtchaell have referred to as confessionalism vs. pietism. As they explain, pietism became more than merely a renewal movement in Protestantism. Rather, it began to exhibit traits characteristic of Romanticism's extreme reaction against Enlightenment rationalism. Hart contrasts pietism and revivalism with "confessional Protestantism" in America. The latter was characterized by the sustaining of an old tradition of doctrine and piety rooted in the creeds of ancient Christianity and the confessions of faith of the Protestant Reformation. While sometimes the distinctions between these two poles are too neat and clearcut in Hart's analysis, his categories are exceptionally helpful. As he explains, "Like its European antecedents American pietism dismissed church creeds, structures, and ceremonies as merely formal or external manifestations of religion that went only skin deep." The transatlantic revivals in the First and Second Great Awakenings exhibited a fast-increasing tension between pietism and confessionalism, with the Second Great Awakening and the revivals of the nineteenth century becoming even more entrenched in a pietistic posture.[39]

Scholars such as Hart and Burtchaell have emphasized that one sees the impact of pietism on American religion not so much in its emphasis on the importance of a reformist mentality or an attempt to balance it with a proper Christian emphasis on the affections of the heart. Rather, their concern is how often pietism overemphasized individual religious experience. After all, Burtchaell argues, reformist movements such as the "early Renaissance outburst of mendicant, pacifist, and devotional lay reforms," and the Protestant Reformation itself were renewal movements that brought revitalization to the church by retrieving biblical and patristic streams of true piety. The same can be said, he noted, about much of the European Pietist movement of the late seventeenth and early eighteenth centuries, despite some of its extreme features.[40]

What began increasingly to characterize what Burtchaell calls "American pietisms," however, was their placing of "the religion of the heart"—subjective spiritual experience—at the center of Christianity, downplaying or even displacing theology and ecclesiology. Thus the corporate and communal dimensions of Christian spirituality were supplanted by a tendency toward individualism. The intellectual and theological dimensions of Christianity became underemphasized, and the emotional, experiential dimension was overemphasized. As Burtchaell says, pietism "propounded the primacy of spirit over letter, commitment over institution, affect over intellect, laity over clergy, invisible church over visible." Pietism, he notes, "was driven by fervor, and even in the hands of scholars it was naïve about history: it underestimated the need of Christianity to grow through time and circumstance, and its ability to modify or molt older forms without renouncing their purposes. The emphasis on spirit, enthusiasm, and unmediated grace repressed any strong sense of the visible church as an incarnate undertaking, as the body of Christ."[41]

Eventually, Burtchaell explains, pietism "persuaded itself that the individual, and perhaps the local congregation, is the only authentic bearer of the adjective 'Christian.' By the time pietism had devolved this far, it could not possibly be the sponsor of a stable sense of church." In pietism, doctrine became more "transient," bowing to individual experience. Under the influence of pietism, doctrines became "free-floating concepts" of subjective experience instead of the "manifold convictions" of a tradition or "continuous community."[42]

Revivalism mediated pietism to American Christianity. Thus, as Hart explains, revivalists "taught American believers to expect" that the institutional church plays "a small role" in authentic spiritual life. "Clergy, creeds, rituals, and church order did not matter since they did not affect the heart noticeably." The extremes of pietism and revivalism were aided and abetted by what Nathan Hatch has termed the "democratization of American Christianity." This force dovetailed with extreme pietism and revivalism's de-emphasis on creeds, confessions, and clergy, which often emphasized populism, cultural relevance, and individual emotional expression at the expense of church and tradition, theology and the intellect.[43]

One sees evidence throughout Free Will Baptist history of this tension between confessionalism on one hand and pietism and revivalism on the other, which is characteristic of the larger evangelical movement in America. The Randall movement of Freewill Baptists in the North, born out of the New Light revivalism of the Great Awakening, would fully embrace the Finneyesque revivalistic ethos of the Second Great Awakening. While the North Carolina General Baptists resisted the extremes of that New Light revivalism, their heirs in the nineteenth-century South would experience tension over the innovations of the Second Great Awakening. Some would experiment with the increasing pietism of the nineteenth-century Romantic milieu, while others would resist it, hearkening back to instincts rooted in their pre-revivalistic and confessional General Baptist past.[44]

The Continuing General Baptist Witness

Were it not for four stalwart pastors, the General Baptist witness would have been scrubbed from the scene in eighteenth-century North Carolina. The southern Free Will Baptist movement would not have survived. Those four ministers were Joseph Parker, William Parker, William Fulsher, and John Winfield. Out of the twenty General Baptist churches planted in North Carolina between 1727 and 1755, only four remained in existence. Joseph Parker pastored Little Contentnea Creek. Meherrin was led by William Parker. William Fulsher led the church at Pungo. John Winfield pastored Bear River.[45]

Joseph Parker's Later Years

Joseph Parker was the most important figure in carrying on the Palmer legacy. By either account of his origin, he was an associate of Palmer who was profoundly influenced by the latter's theological vision. Parker's Arminian theological commitments enabled him to keep the New Light Calvinist wave from overtaking his area of influence near the Neuse River. Historians know as little about Parker after the Calvinist proselytization as before it. "It was precisely because he was a General Baptist and so continued until his death that we know so little of him," Paschal wrote, "for the Particular Baptists who wrote our early histories say little of the work of any General Baptist, and nothing at all except as it throws light on Particular Baptist history." Paschal went on to describe Parker as "a true and faithful servant of Jesus Christ." With a "soul burning with missionary zeal," Paschal said,

Parker "carried the gospel from frontier settlement to frontier settlement even to extreme old age."[46]

Soon after the death of his father in 1757 and his brother in 1758, Parker moved to the area south of the Tar River and north of the Neuse River, in what was then Dobbs County (now Lenoir County). He had already begun to evangelize in this area, having bought one hundred acres of land there on December 25, 1756. The Calvinist intrusion that was taking place in the counties to the north never worked its way into Parker's new territory. The base of his field of activity was Little Contentnea Creek (later known as "Little Creek"). Like many Baptist churches of this era, Parker started branches of that church that later became fully constituted, self-governing congregations. Sometime between 1758 and his death in 1791 or 1792—one cannot be sure when—he established branches at Wheat Swamp and Louson Swamp near Kinston. Then he went on to gather congregations at Grimsley's meeting house in Greene County near Snow Hill and Gum Swamp in Pitt County near Greenville. Parker probably pastored all of these congregations, holding preaching services once monthly, as was not uncommon in Baptist circles in the late eighteenth and nineteenth centuries.[47]

This activity of Joseph Parker in the Neuse River area of modern-day Pitt and Green Counties would form the nucleus of the nineteenth-century Free Will Baptist movement. Wheat Swamp would survive as Wheat Swamp Free Will Baptist Church. Gum Swamp Original Free Will Baptist Church exists to this day. The Minutes of the North Carolina Free Will Baptist General Conference show that it was "Held at Grimsley's meeting house, Greene county, N.C. *On the 6th, 7th, 8th, and 9th days of November, A. D. 1845*."[48]

Elder Parker also preached elsewhere among the General Baptists. He established the Flat Swamp Church, which never got off the ground and was swallowed up by the Calvinist Baptists in the early 1790s, after Parker's 1785 move to Lenoir County. His successor, James Roach, worked in the Conetoe community that Parker had cultivated, planting a church there in 1798. The seeds Parker sowed in Little Swift Creek, Clayroot, and Kitts Swamp resulted in congregations established by Free Will Baptists in the early nineteenth century. He also occasionally preached at Pungo and at Meherrin to William Parker's congregation.[49]

According to Wheeler, Joseph Parker died in 1791 or 1792 and was buried in Robert Wyrington's burial ground on Wheat Swamp. Parker left behind his protégé James Roach, who had come from Craven County and had assumed the pastorates of Wheat Swamp and Louson Swamp Churches. He would help inch the movement forward into the nineteenth century, witnessing growth in the congregations Joseph Parker had planted. Wheeler could say in the 1840s that the three thousand members he estimated in the Free Will Baptist churches in North Carolina were "probably the descendants of the handful on Wheat Swamp, Pungo, and Conetoe." Thus the Free Will Baptists of the South, as Stevenson has said, "very nearly owe their continued life to Parker" who, as Davidson remarks, provided the seedbed for the later movement: "In every community south of the Tar River that had boasted a Parker church or preaching point, a Free Will Baptist church soon appeared."[50]

William Parker

William Parker's primary role was as the pastor of the Meherrin Church in Hertford County near present-day Murfreesboro. With Joseph Parker and John Winfield, he was one of the links between the earlier General Baptist movement and the developing Free Will Baptist movement of the nineteenth century. Almost every scrap of the paltry information that is extant on William Parker comes from Wheeler's *History of the Meherrin Church*, which later historians have corrected at a few points.

Parker was pastor of the Meherrin Church as early as 1773. Yet he probably came there much earlier. Paschal believed he could have been pastor there as early as 1748. Wheeler wrote his history in 1847, having interviewed several older people who had memories of Parker. They described him as "a remarkably pungent and practical preacher—seeking every opportunity to do good, and deeply devoted to the spiritual interests of his flock." Wheeler commented that, after the "reformation" of the churches into Calvinist Baptist congregations, "some ministers persisted in their [General Baptist] opinions and practices, and among them, as above remarked, was Elder William Parker." R. K. Hearn also wrote of an eyewitness account of a Free Will Baptist woman who was more than one hundred years of age and was a member of a Free Will Baptist church at her death. She recalled William Parker's preaching his first sermon at Gum Swamp Church.[51]

John Asplund, in his *Annual Register of the Baptist Denomination in North-America*, which he started publishing in 1791, listed the Meherrin Church as the only Baptist congregation in Hertford County in 1790. He said it had about one hundred members at that time. Wheeler believed that Meherrin was the only church of any sort meeting in Hertford County in 1790. Parker's preaching was the only preaching, "with the exception of an occasional service by an Episcopal clergyman, in whom the people lost confidence as a leader of the flock of Christ." Many people also regularly came from Gates, Bertie, and Northampton Counties to hear Parker preach.[52]

During Parker's ministry, it is notable that the Meherrin Church held worship services with Parker preaching every Sunday. This was remarkable in a day when many churches held worship services with preaching by an ordained minister only once or twice a month. Wheeler lamented that, even in 1847, this was not the case with the congregation: "In all the improvements of modern days, we have yet to reach this point, where our fathers stood," he said. "Before these peaceful plains were trodden by the heavy feet of hosts in battle in our revolutionary struggle, our forefathers were wont to repair to this consecrated spot, on *every Sabbath day* to listen to the sweet invitations of the gospel from the lips of their venerated pastor. Let us not tarry in the march of improvement until we reach that desirable point."[53]

In 1775, the Parker family, along with Peter Deberry and others, built a new meeting house "with their own hands, which was afterwards enlarged by the addition of sheds on the western and northern sides." That meeting house remained in use until 1802. Parker continued pastoring the church at Meherrin until January 1794. His funeral was attended by a large congregation from miles around. That he was respected by those across denominational lines is indicated by the fact that his funeral sermon was preached by the Regular Baptist minister David Barrow from Isle of Wight County, Virginia.[54]

Wheeler mentioned the same sorts of things the Calvinist Baptists customarily said about the General Baptists by Calvinists: that Elder Parker did not require the relation of an "experience of grace" and therefore that the church was in decline because it had unregenerate members. After Parker's death, Lemuel Burkitt came as pastor and soon reorganized the church along Calvinist lines. However, as Paschal said several decades later,

> It is probable that, in his severe censure of Mr. Parker, Wheeler, *Meherrin Church*, was only repeating things said by Calvinists against all General Baptists, and that most of the disturbance in his church was due rather to the natural desire of the members to conform to the standards of the neighboring Baptist churches and possibly the proselyting zeal of Burkitt than to any disorders engendered by Mr. Parker's looseness in receiving members. One would suppose from Wheeler's statement that the church had dwindled to nothingness in 1794: but according to Asplund it contained about 100 members.[55]

William Fulsher and John Winfield

Precious little is known about Elders William Fulsher and John Winfield, the other two of the General Baptist pastors who withstood the Philadelphia blitzkrieg. As mentioned earlier in the chapter, Elder William Fulsher had been mentored and ordained by Paul Palmer and remained active in the primary field of Palmer's ministry in northeastern North Carolina. Fulsher also worked closely with Dr. Josiah Hart, having joined with him and others in a petition of Dissenters from the Bay and Neuse Rivers appealing for expanded preaching rights. He is known to have been active in New Bern, Craven County, and Flea Point, Beaufort County, in the 1740s. By the time Morgan Edwards came through in the 1770s, Fulsher was the pastor of the Matchipungo (Pungo) Church.[56]

The pastor who succeeded Fulsher at Pungo, and remained true to his Arminian General Baptist faith and practice, was Elder John Winfield. Even less is known about Winfield. He took Fulsher's place sometime between 1773 and 1790. The year 1773 is the last recorded mention of Fulsher. In 1790 Winfield appeared as pastor of Pungo in Asplund's *Register*, which reports that the congregation numbered about one hundred that year. Wheeler mentioned Winfield as one of the pastors who, with the two Parkers, "refused to unite" in "the great reformation which took place among the Baptists of North Carolina." Burkitt and Read referred to Winfield, along with Joseph Parker, as one who "frequently preached" for William Parker at Meherrin. Historians do not know precisely when Winfield died, but the nineteenth-century Free Will Baptist minister Henry Smith, who was born in 1789, said that Winfield was influential in his youth. The Pungo Church would continue as a Free Will Baptist church, being on the roll of Bethel Conference until it was taken over by the Disciples of Christ in 1845.[57]

A Bridge to the Future

Joseph Parker, William Parker, William Fulsher, and John Winfield were bridges between the English General Baptist tradition of Palmer and the later Free Will Baptist movement. These four elders steadfastly resisted the New Light Calvinism that swept away the other sixteen original North Carolina General Baptist congregations and passed down the legacy of General Baptist faith and practice to the generation that followed them. The younger Richard Jones, along with Caspar Mintz—both of whom had come to Virginia from England in 1727 to replace Robert Norden two years after his death—had likewise sought the help of the Philadelphia Association in 1756 in reorganizing their churches into Calvinist congregations. Joseph Parker, William Parker, Fulsher, and Winfield now constituted the sole General Baptist ministerial presence in the South.[58]

In addition to ministering in their own localities, these four ministers traveled to preach for each other, as is seen, for example, in Burkitt and Read's comment that both Joseph Parker and John Winfield preached "frequently" at Meherrin. Joseph Parker, despite his distance from William Parker, Fulsher, and Winfield in the northeastern part of the state—a seven-or-eight-hour ride by horse and carriage—visited and preached frequently in that area. These remaining churches continued to use the *Standard Confession* of 1660, which their successors would condense a couple of decades after William Parker's death into the *1812 Abstract*, which will be considered in the next chapter. Writing in 1803, Burkitt and Read described the North Carolina General Baptists as holding "the Arminian tenets," and as "descendants of the *English General Baptists*," because they had found in "some original papers, that their Confession of Faith was subscribed by certain elders and deacons, and brethren, in behalf of themselves and others, to whom they belonged, both in London, and several counties in England, and was presented to King Charles the Second." This is a close paraphrase of the title page of the *Standard Confession*. Thus, as Paschal averred, the Free Will Baptists of the nineteenth century were simply the older General Baptists associated with Joseph and William Parker "under a different name."[59]

Three

FREE WILL BAPTISTS IN THE CAROLINAS, 1794–1865

The Remaining General Baptist Movement

Elder Jesse Heath, the most prominent of the early nineteenth-century pastors, said that when he was ordained in 1807, there were only five General Baptist churches and three ministers. Almost no information survives about the period between William Parker's death in 1794 and 1812 when the struggling movement entered a new chapter with the publication of a new confession of faith that condensed their earlier confession, the *Standard Confession* of 1660. This body had been "trampled down by their enemies," as Southern Baptist Seminary president William Whitsitt later said. Thus relations were profoundly tense between them and the Regular Baptists in North Carolina, whose entire origin owed itself to the latter's hard-hitting proselytization of General Baptist congregations.[1]

The first minister of whom there is record after Joseph Parker, William Parker, William Fulsher, and John Winfield was Elder James Roach, who succeeded Joseph Parker after the latter's death in 1791 or 1792. Asplund listed Roach in his *Annual Register of the Baptist Denomination in North-America* as a licensed minister in 1790. Even though Asplund identified Roach with the Goose Creek Church, which was Regular Baptist, Roach presumably identified with a General Baptist faction in the congregation. In any event, he was soon living in Greene County, where he was serving as pastor of churches that Parker had started, including Wheat Swamp, Louson Swamp, and Gum Swamp. Roach was likely ordained by Joseph Parker, the only General Baptist minister in the area in which Roach served along the Neuse River. Roach was still in Greene County in 1820, according to the census that year.[2]

As William Davidson observes, Elder John Winfield might have been one of the two ministers other than James Roach whom Jesse Heath said were active when he was ordained in 1807.[3] The Free Will Baptist minister Henry Smith said that Winfield was influential in his youth.[4] Smith was born in 1789; thus it is very possible that Winfield was still active in 1807, when Smith was around eighteen years old. R. K. Hearn's father, Elder Howell Hearn, could well have been one of the three ministers to whom Heath was referring. Or it could have been Henry Smith's father, the General Baptist preacher Josiah Smith, who with James Roach founded the Concord Church in Pamlico County in 1802.[5]

The 1812 Abstract

No minutes survive of a conference of the five or so North Carolina General Baptist churches that existed at the end of the eighteenth century and the beginning of the nineteenth. Because of the scarcity of records at this time, no one knows when the General Conference of North Carolina was established. However, it was meeting by 1812, because that year the General Conference authorized the revision of the English General Baptist *Standard Confession* of 1660. The preface stated that "OUR last general conference met at a meeting house called A Jones, on little Contentney, Green County, on the 5th of November 1812." The use of "our last general conference" indicates that the conference had probably been meeting for a while before 1812.[6]

At the 1812 session of the General Conference, considering "the general interest of the Gospel and especially the interest of the Churches they were related unto and did then represent," the delegates elected to "reprint the former confession of faith, put forth by the former Elders and Deacons" as well as to "annex a proper code of our discipline." The body appointed Roach and Heath, who "had recourse to all the former articles of faith and rules of Discipline now extant," to do the work. They were charged to let some elements of those documents "stand without variation and some things with variation." The document was entitled

AN ABSTRACT

of the

FORMER ARTICLES OF FAITH

confessed by the original

BAPTIST CHURCH
Holding the
Doctrine of General Provision.
With a Proper
CODE OF DISCIPLINE
For the Future Government of the Church

One infers several things from the *1812 Abstract*'s title and preface. First, its articles of faith were a revision of the *Standard Confession* of 1660. They were intended as an "abstract" or summary of that confession, those articles of faith "put forth by the former elders and deacons." This language in the preface is a paraphrase of the title of the *Standard Confession*, which said it was "Subscribed to by certain Elders, Deacons, and Brethren, met at London, in the first month (called March, 1660.)" This is the confession of faith these General/Free Will Baptists had been using up until that time.[7]

Further, these articles of faith were those of "the original Baptist church holding the doctrine of general provision." This refers to the General Baptists who held the doctrine of the general, or universal, provision of grace to all humanity, together with general, or universal, atonement. This was opposed to the Calvinistic doctrines of particular grace and particular atonement, for only the elect, as held by the Particular Baptists. One is tempted to presume that the use of "original" in "the original Baptist church holding the doctrine of general provision" is a reference to the fact that the first Baptists in England were General Baptists. However, it is more likely a reference that the original Baptists in North Carolina, before the onslaught of the Calvinist Baptists aided by the Philadelphia Association, were General Baptists, and the Baptists drawing up these 1812 articles were a continuation of that movement.

As noted in the previous chapter, in 1803, the Calvinist Baptist preachers Lemuel Burkitt and Jesse Read wrote a history of the Kehukee Association, the Particular or Regular Baptist association that comprised the formerly General Baptist congregations in the region. Their history, which was hostile to the General/Free Will Baptists, had said that the churches they took over had held "the Arminian tenets" and were "descendants of the *English General Baptists*." Burkitt and Read explained that they knew this because they had seen some "original papers" that said their confession of faith was "subscribed by certain elders and deacons, and brethren, in behalf of themselves and others, to whom they belonged, both in London, and several counties in England, and was presented to King Charles the Second." This is a near-verbatim quotation from the title page of the *Standard Confession*.[8]

Some parts of the *1812 Abstract* were identical to the *Standard Confession*, while other things were different. This was in keeping with the directions of the General Conference to have some things "without variation" and some "with variation." This confession will be referred to as the *1812 Abstract*. In the late twentieth century, following Elizabeth Smith, historians (including this author) often referred to this confession as the "1812 Former Articles." That is, however, technically a misnomer, since "the former articles" are those in the *Standard Confession* of 1660. This 1812 document is an *abstract* of those earlier articles first drafted in 1660. In this book, *1812 Abstract* will refer to the statement of doctrine, while *Discipline* will refer to the entire document, which includes the "code of discipline" of which the preface spoke.[9]

That brings us to the second charge the Conference gave Elders Roach and Heath. In addition to revising the *Standard Confession*, the conference tasked them with gathering the "rules of Discipline now extant" so that they could compose "a proper code of our discipline" for church government and order. That code of discipline is why Free Will Baptists soon began to refer to it in shorthand as "the *Discipline*," a phrase that was used well into the twentieth century. The fact that there were extant rules of discipline implies a level of organization that would mean that a conference had existed for quite some while.

Thus the *1812 Abstract* is essentially a revised and condensed version of the *Standard Confession* of 1660. Several of the lengthier ecclesiological articles were shortened or eliminated, probably because their subject matter was dealt with under the code of discipline later in the document. Other articles that were relevant only in the seventeenth-century English context were not brought over into the new document. Statements referring to issues such as obedience to magistrates and matters of conscience, penned during the Restoration era in England when Dissenters were denied basic religious liberty, were not seen as applicable to the nineteenth-century American context and were thus deleted.

The lengthier articles on the resurrection of Christ and general eschatology in the *Standard Confession* were replaced by a brief statement appended to the article on the person of Christ and two other brief articles. Article 2 states that Jesus "was buried and rose again the third day and ascended into Heaven, from whence we look for him, the second time in the clouds of Heaven, at the last day to judge both quick and dead." Article 19 asserts "a general resurrection of the dead and final judgment at the last day," while article 20 confesses that "the happiness of the righteous is eternal and the torment of the wicked is endless."[10]

Article 15 on justification by faith was newly written: "We believe that no man has any warrant in the holy scriptures for justification before God through his own works[,] power[,] or ability which he has in and of himself, only as he by Grace is made able to come to God, through Jesus Christ, believing the righteousness of Jesus Christ to be imputed to all believers for their eternal acceptance with God." Yet Article 14 stated "that good works are the fruits of a saving faith, and that in the use of the means of grace, and not out of the use of those means, eternal life is promised to men." A new article defining ordinances in an open-ended and inclusive way was also added: "We believe as touching Gospel ordinances in believer's baptism, laying on of hands, receiving the sacrament in bread and wine, washing the saints' feet, anointing the sick with oil in the name of the Lord, fasting, singing praises to God and the public ministry of the Word, with every institution of the Lord we shall find in the New Testament."[11]

The most surprising of the "things with variation" when compared with the *Standard Confession* of 1660 was the article on perseverance, which affirmed that "the Saints shall persevere in grace, and never finally fall away." This is shocking to later Free Will Baptist readers because it militates against the Arminianism that was the hallmark of the movement. Historians have wondered if this was something that a majority approved, which the minority believed would later be overturned. If any records had survived, there might be answers, but there are no records until 1827. That year Elder Jesse Heath, in a letter to the northern Freewill Baptists, assured his northern readers that the North Carolina Free Will Baptists were essentially like them doctrinally. When, in the next few years, the northern Freewill Baptist Elias Hutchins traveled among the Free Will Baptists of the Carolinas, he sensed no deviation from the basics of Freewill Baptist doctrine. The original article on perseverance is an enigma, but in any event it was permanently deleted in 1831, bringing the document back in line with historic General/Free Will Baptist belief.[12]

Jesse Heath and the Growing Movement

Fourteen years passed between the printing of the *1812 Abstract* in 1813 and the next extant record of the Free Will Baptists of North Carolina. In 1827, Elder Jesse Heath, who had been ordained as a Free Will Baptist minister twenty years earlier and had helped produce the *1812 Abstract*, wrote to the editor of the northern Freewill Baptist newspaper *The Morning Star*, which he had found out about and to which he had subscribed. The June 28, 1827, issue carried a letter Heath had written the previous month. One learns several things from this letter and the editor's comments on it. Heath was living at Cox's Bridge, North Carolina, and this was the second letter he had written. The editor's comments also indicate that this was the first the New England Freewill Baptists had heard about their North Carolina counterparts.[13]

In editor John Buzzell's first reply to Heath, he had written a brief summary of the basics of the northern Freewill Baptists' doctrine. Heath, using the exact wording he had used in the preface of the *1812 Abstract*, said the North Carolina Free Will Baptists agreed with Buzzell's summary of doctrine in "Principle"—"there is not the least difference." He hoped the same would be true regarding their "Practice." Thus Buzzell describes them as being "in sentiment similar to us." Concerning open communion, Heath remarked that "no application has been made for liberty to eat and drink with us; but if any in good standing were to ask that liberty, they would not be denied." His use of the phrase "good standing" in this context indicates their acceptance of the older notion of open communion as not barring from the Lord's Supper people who had been baptized as infants or by sprinkling or pouring. This contrasted with later notions of open communion that emphasized that anyone, whether in good standing with an orthodox church or not, would be invited to the Lord's Supper. Heath also noted that the North Carolina Free Will Baptists practiced "the imposition of hands on all newly baptized members, according to the examples of St. Peter, John, and Paul," as well as the "washing of feet, believing it to be a gospel ordinance."[14]

At this point the northern Freewill Baptists did not yet know how long the North Carolina Free Will Baptists had existed. It was in this letter that Heath said that twenty years earlier, when he had been ordained, there were only three ministers and five churches. Thus the editor inferred "that their connexion is several years younger than ours," not understanding that the North Carolina Free Will Baptists' origins in America dated back roughly a century and a half, almost a hundred years before Benjamin Randall started the Freewill Baptist movement in New England.[15]

Heath had not yet mentioned anything about the long history of the movement and the takeover of most of it by the Regular Baptists in the latter half of the eighteenth century. Yet he did say that, despite the few congregations that existed in 1807, recently they had been "highly favored, and the work at this moment is gloriously reviving among us." Heath mentioned that "the most useful ministers" among them were Frederick Fonville, Isaac

Pipkin, Henry Smith, Levi Braxton, Jesse Alfin, Jeremiah Heath, Jeremiah Rowe, James Moore, and Robert Bond. He also reported membership statistics from the 1825 session of the North Carolina General Conference, which met once a year but had not met in 1826 "[o]n account of its being very sickly in this section of our country last fall." He reported the 1825 membership as being around eight hundred.[16]

On December 13, 1827, *The Morning Star* referred to another letter Heath had written to Buzzell reporting on the conference's annual session in the fall of 1827. Nineteen ministers had attended the session, and "about as many churches were represented." In the May 28, 1828, issue, the newspaper printed a copy of a letter Heath had sent "Br. Buzzell" on April 25. In that letter, Heath mentioned a tour he had taken of Free Will Baptist congregations "in the lower part of this state." He mentioned "Eld. Smith," presumably Elder Henry Smith. He also noted several other churches and their pastors he had visited, two of whose names he had not mentioned in previous letters: "Poly Bridge, Duplin co. under the care of Eld. Alfin; Gum Swamp, Pitt co. under the care of Eld. Lockham; Newbern, Craven co. under the care of Eld. Pipkin, and in Poiny Nick, Newbern co. under the care of Eld. Hollace." He spoke of the growth of these congregations, exclaiming, "Blessed be the Lord. I am also happy to state that a gradual work appears to be progressing generally among us." He also spoke of his expectation of a visit from Elias Hutchins, a New England Freewill Baptist minister with whom he had been corresponding.[17]

Heath spent a considerable portion of his letter discussing correspondence from a minister named Elijah H. Callaway "in West Florida, Jackson co. who wishes to be taken into connexion with us." Callaway would be examined at the conference's next session "in order that he may receive ordination and form some acquaintance with the people of his choice." The letter of April 25 is notable because it mentions two men with connections in the West Florida and southeast Alabama region, both of whom will be discussed in the next chapter: Elijah Callaway and Brinson Hollace (Hollis). Ten years later Hollace would move southward and in the 1840s would end up in southeast Alabama, eventually living out his life in Jackson County, Florida, while pastoring churches across the state line in Southeast Alabama and preaching and evangelizing in southwest Georgia. This information is especially interesting given that the next notice in *The Morning Star* of a letter from Heath says that he was talking about how Free Will Baptists were doing well in the South, including "in the Floridas, in Georgia, and in Tennessee."[18]

Things were going so well in the Carolinas that, by the time Heath wrote Buzzell in November 1830, membership had more than doubled in five years—up from 800 members to 1,892. "The work of reformation in almost every part of the Connexion is going on," Heath declared. "The old and the young, the rich and the poor, the black and the white are the happy subjects of the revival; and we rejoice most of all that, while other denominations are divided, and party spirit and prejudice prevails, with us brotherly love continues."[19]

However, the North Carolina brethren quickly found something with which to disagree in *The Morning Star*. About this same time, Thomas J. Latham of Pantego, North Carolina, had been corresponding with some of the New England Freewill Baptists. Latham was aware that there was a move in the latter denomination to make the washing of the saints' feet an optional liturgical practice, not an ordinance of divine appointment. That development had been discussed in *The Morning Star*. He was obviously concerned that if the newspaper gained subscribers among the Free Will Baptists of North Carolina the rite would diminish among the latter, and he wished to register his opinions:

> As the question concerning *"washing the saints' feet,"* is one in which the Free-Will Baptists in this section of North Carolina feel deeply interested; and as your paper circulates amongst us, I hope you will pardon my entering into the discussion of it. It is the practice of the Free-Will Baptists here to wash each others' feet, whenever they partake of the Eucharist. If it is not a gospel ordinance, we ought to discontinue it—but we wish to be fully satisfied before we do so. In proof of its being a gospel ordinance, I shall endeavor to sustain the two following propositions.

The two propositions for which Latham proceeded to argue were, first, that the rite "is expressly and unequivocally enjoined by our Saviour himself" and, second, that it "was the practice of the primitive Christians in the Apostolic days." Latham appealed to John 13 to support the first proposition and to 1 Timothy 5:9–10 to support the second. He answered an objection raised by one of the writers for *The Morning Star* who had suggested that if Jesus had intended the washing of the saints' feet as "an ordinance of the Gospel," he would have mentioned it in "his commission to his disciples" in Mark 16:15–16. To this, Latham replied:

> The omission of the command to wash feet, in this place, does not invalidate the propriety of practicing it as a Gospel ordinance, any more than the omission of the Eucharist in the same place, invalidates it. Besides,

in the parallel text in Matthew, the commission is in these words, "Go ye therefore and teach all nations, baptizing them in the name of the Father and of the Son and of the Holy Ghost, teaching them to *observe all things whatsoever I have commanded you. . . .*"[20]

Jesse Heath, in one of his letters in 1827, said, "But I must tell you something of our situation in the ministry; we are all men of families, of little property and not a single scholar amongst us, so that the work is of God and not of us." In comparison to the wealth of the New England Freewill Baptists, which provided greater opportunities for education, Heath's comment provides a glimpse into the socioeconomic situation of the southern Free Will Baptists, most of whom were yeoman farmers and had fewer educational opportunities than the New England Freewill Baptists. Illiteracy rates were anywhere from ten to 20 percent of the White population in the antebellum South, and this is when censuses reflected a bare minimum of functional literacy, which usually required only two years of primary schooling. Especially given this context, the literary acumen and reasoning of Heath and Latham strike the modern reader as superior to many professionals in our modern, highly literate society.[21]

People like Heath and Latham's readership of publications such as *The Morning Star* and their obviously high level of literacy as seen in their letters, combined with the reality that they left such few records and writings behind, raise a number of questions. Beth Barton Schweiger investigates these themes in her book *A Literate South*. She argues that rural, literate Southerners in the nineteenth century are too often ignored by historians, mostly unintentionally, because their literacy did not leave the same sort of evidence behind that the industrialized North did in the nineteenth century. "Aside from cheap steady-sellers like schoolbooks, Bibles, and hymnbooks, books were expensive. Rural readers read mainly ephemera—broadsides, magazines, newspapers, tracts, pamphlets, and almanacs—which for the most part were never intended to survive, and predictably did not."[22]

The wealthy New England Freewill Baptists lived closer to urban centers and to each other and had the economic resources to sponsor schools and print hardcover books early on. However, the relative poverty of many rural southern Free Will Baptists produced ephemeral (paperback) literature that did not survive. This problem was exacerbated by the frequency of fires in the days before electricity. These considerations explain why copies of hymnals published in hardcover by southern Free Will Baptists in the nineteenth century survived, while the majority of minutes, *Disciplines*, pamphlets, newspapers, and magazines, published in small print runs of cheaper paperback editions with cheaper paper and less sturdy binding, did not.

Furthermore, most Free Will Baptist ministers in the South throughout the nineteenth and well into the twentieth century had to work six days a week as farmers or merchants or tradesmen while serving two or three congregations at the same time, with many congregations having preaching only once or twice a month. This way of life contrasted with that of the full-time pastor in New England who had the economic wherewithal to have attended a college sponsored by his wealthier denomination, to hold a full-time pastorate, and to enjoy the luxury of having time to study and write. The introductory words of Rufus K. Hearn's "Origin of the Free Will Baptist Church of North Carolina" illustrate these dynamics:

> I now make the feeble attempt, as I promised a few weeks ago, to show by whom the Free Will Baptists of North Carolina were organized. The account will be very imperfect, owing to our forefathers having kept no record of the proceedings, and as all the facts concerning the Free Will Baptists that we can get are derived from our enemies and tradition. The limited circumstances and education of the writer—I say limited circumstances, because I have to work hard and have no time to read or write only of a night, after my day's labor is finished—precludes a thorough examination.[23]

The reality is not that records from the eighteenth and early nineteenth centuries were not kept but rather that small numbers of ephemeral minutes were printed but did not survive to the 1870s when Hearn was writing.

The Visits of Elias Hutchins

The letters from Heath, Latham, and others burst onto the scene in the late 1820s and early 1830s, offering a sudden, fuller glimpse of Free Will Baptist development and life in the Carolinas. In addition to this, the visits of the New England Freewill Baptist minister Elias Hutchins among the Free Will Baptists of the Carolinas provide a clearer understanding of this period. The October 30, 1829, issue of *The Morning Star* gave notice that "Eld. Elias Hutchins sailed from Boston . . . for North Carolina—where, by Divine permission, he intends to spend the winter in preaching the gospel." Hutchins, ordained as a Freewill Baptist evangelist in Wilton, Maine, was one of a very few northern Freewill Baptists who ever traveled South before the late nineteenth century to visit their spiritual cousins in the Carolinas. He itinerated and preached extensively among the New England Freewill Baptists, but later went west to states such as Ohio and Indiana, before he made his trips to North and South Carolina.[24]

Hutchins sailed into Newbern (now New Bern) on October 23, 1829, and soon connected with Jesse Heath, with whom he traveled extensively in the region over the coming weeks. Hutchins also connected with two ministers from the Christian Connection. This group was sometimes mistaken by later Free Will Baptists for the Christian Church–Disciples of Christ movement associated with Thomas and Alexander Campbell. This is likely because it was similar to the latter in its aversion to written confessions of faith and to denominational nomenclature. Still, recent historians have been correct in surmising that this relationship probably paved the way for later links with the Campbell movement, which would eventuate in their "conversion" of several of Free Will Baptist ministers and their congregations to the Disciples of Christ later in the century.[25]

Heath took Hutchins deep into the North Carolina backcountry, where they preached at services during the week that had more than two hundred attendees, with one Sunday morning crowd numbering around a thousand. Hutchins wrote that at one of those church meetings to which Heath took him to preach, around five hundred Black people were in the congregation. As Davidson remarks, "Hutchins especially was impressed with the reverence that was evident in the worship service of the Free Will Baptists. He spoke often of the well-behaved, solemn, and attentive audiences." One of Hutchins's letters described a baptismal service in which twenty converts were baptized. Hutchins said, "The scene was solemn and impressive, well calculated to animate the Christian, and fill the minds of sinners with sensations of a favorable character; and the large congregation that witnessed the performance by a commendable decorum evinced great respect to the ordinance...."[26]

In late November Hutchins stayed at the home of Thomas and Clarissa Hood of Lenoir County, preaching in churches such as Louson Swamp and Wheat Swamp there. Early the next month, Hood took him on a trip on horseback to South Carolina, where he met the well-known preacher and founder of South Carolina Free Will Baptists, Redding Moore. Moore had lived and ministered in the Marion District of South Carolina since 1816 but was still a member of the North Carolina Conference during Hutchins's first visit. The day after their arrival back in North Carolina, they attended a quarterly meeting at Louson Swamp Church, which, Hutchins wrote, was "attended with much solemnity and with obvious manifestations of the Divine presence."²⁷

Hutchins also spoke of the transformation of some of the communities he visited after religion had taken hold on them. He spoke of one community that he described as having been "filled with dissipation of almost every description" yet had experienced a revival of religion that brought about palpable moral transformation: "The obscene songs of the drunken and lascivious had given place to the sweet music of Zion; prayer had taken the place of swearing and lying; the Sabbath, formerly a day of drinking and gambling, of fighting and horseracing, was religiously observed; and the salutary influences of pure religion were too obvious to be denied by its most inveterate enemies."²⁸

The Bethel and Shiloh Conferences

The 1830 General Conference was held at Grimsley's meeting house in Greene County, North Carolina, on November 11–14. At that conference, at which Elder Howell Hearn was elected moderator and Thomas Hood clerk, Jesse Heath made a motion calling for an amicable division of the conference into two conferences, one eastern and the other western, for greater ease of travel. The body appointed a committee consisting of Henry Smith, Jesse Heath, Jesse Alfin, Brinson Hollace, Nathaniel Lockhart, William Latham, and William Isler to recommend a plan for how to divide the conference. The eastern division was to be called the Shiloh Conference, while the western division was to be called the Bethel Conference. The Shiloh Conference would comprise thirteen congregations in Craven, Beaufort, Martin, and Pitt Counties. Thomas J. Latham was appointed treasurer of the Shiloh Conference, and that conference's first session was to be held at Pungo River Church the following October. "On motion, Elders Braxton, Moore, Johnson, Heath, and Thomas Moore were appointed messengers to the Shiloh Conference." Though it is known that the Shiloh Conference continued because the two conferences sent representatives back and forth, none of its early minutes have survived.²⁹

The next available minutes of the Bethel Conference in 1831 feature an example of the circular letters that were often printed in the minutes of southern Free Will Baptist conferences and associations. Howell Hearn was asked to write the circular letter that year. In it he said, "I would, brethren, admonish all to remember the covenant made in Baptism, and study to understand the word of God; as it is profitable for doctrine, for reproof, for correction, for instruction in righteousness, rather than to be influenced by the traditions of men; for there is one Lord, one faith[,] one Baptism, one God and Father of all." Hearn then directed some admonition toward the conference's ministers: "I fervently desire that our preaching brethren may always remember the counsel of our Divine Teacher, and not aspire to greatness in the world, only, but to righteousness; and be willing to be servants of all." Alluding to several Pauline scripture texts, Hearn exhorted the elders to commend "themselves to every man's conscience, being gentle, apt to teach, patient in spirit, instructing those that oppose themselves and especially when they feel constrained to declare the whole counsel of God, against all ungodliness, and unrighteousness of men, who hold the truth in unrighteousness, and that they exercise that charity, so highly recommended by the Apostle to the Corinthian church."[30]

In 1832 one sees an example of another practice that would become common: that of sending out itinerant ministers. These were ministers the conference would select to travel, preach, and perform the duties that among the English General Baptists had been associated with the office of the messenger. However, in this case, the conference usually appointed them for a limited period of time, often only a year, after which they would go back and serve one or more local congregations as pastor. In 1832, the Bethel Conference adopted the following resolution:

> Resolved that we employ two itinerant preachers; also that the Clerks open subscriptions in their respective churches for the purpose of obtaining money to support them; the sums thus voluntarily subscribed, to be paid quarterly, that is one fourth part every three months, to the clerk of the church, and that he pay those subscriptions quarterly to those itinerant preachers, and forward in the church's letter to the next Annual Conference, an account of the sums thus paid.[31]

This system was adopted by Free Will Baptists across the South in the nineteenth century. No doubt most of these itinerant preachers still had farms or other occupations to supply the majority of their income, but "subscriptions" by local churches provided supplemental income that enabled them to travel more frequently among the churches. That year, Elders Robert McNab and Lewis Hartsfield were elected as itinerant preachers. The extra time they had to commit to this sort of ministry probably explains why *The Morning Star* printed several letters from McNab and Hartsfield during this time.[32]

Hartsfield and McNab were responsible for extending the movement further westward into the region beyond Greene County. This area had before this time largely been undeveloped by Free Will Baptists.[33] Elder Frederick Fonville had been one of the few to venture further west. Hutchins had referred to this area in his letters about the North Carolina "back country."[34] In his second visit to North Carolina, he talked about a trip he took to the west of Fonville's home in Orange County, near present-day Chapel Hill. The church Fonville pastored, Strong Creek, was the westernmost Free Will Baptist church before one came to the mountains of western North Carolina. Despite the slowness of the development of the movement in this area, by 1833 Hartsfield and McNab had planted churches in Duplin and Sampson Counties, respectively.[35]

The North Carolina Free Will Baptists continued to show interest in other Arminian Baptists outside their fellowship. At the 1832 session of the Bethel Conference, a letter was read from Elder Jesse Lane, a General Baptist from Indiana. The conference approved a motion to invite Lane to represent the General Baptist Association of Indiana and Kentucky at the next annual conference. This General Baptist association was from a group of Arminian Baptists that had arisen in the American Midwest in the 1820s when its founder Benoni Stinson embraced Arminian tenets. Stinson's break with Calvinism led to his and his wife's schism with New Hope Baptist Church and the Calvinistic Wabash District Association of Baptists in Indiana in 1823. This denomination identified with the English General Baptists and took on the name for themselves, noting in their literature their similarities to the Free Will Baptists of North Carolina, whom they noted had descended directly from the English General Baptists who had migrated to the American colonies. While the two groups often shared fraternal delegates, they never entered into organic union.[36]

At that same session, the conference appointed Jesse Heath and Elias Hutchins to write and publish "a history of our connection in this and the adjoining states." Heath and Hutchins apparently never published this history, but subsequent historians would have loved to have had access to it. The language of "this and the adjoining states" illuminates Heath's statement a few years earlier stating that the movement was gaining ground "in the Floridas, in Georgia, and in Tennessee." That two of the states Heath mentioned, Tennessee and Georgia, were also two of the states adjoining North Carolina, in addition to South Carolina and Virginia, suggests that there was a history of Free Will Baptists in "adjoining states" to be written.

Redding Moore and South Carolina Free Will Baptists

This is a fitting place to discuss the origins of the movement in South Carolina, which emerged from the North Carolina body. North Carolina Free Will Baptists had been active across the state line in South Carolina as early as 1816. That year Elder Redding (Reading) Moore moved to the Marion District after his ordination as a Free Will Baptist minister, thus founding the movement in South Carolina. At the 1831 annual session of the Bethel Conference, Moore made a motion asking the conference to release its congregations in South Carolina to form a new Free Will Baptist "Annual Conference" there. The conference approved his motion and also appointed Jesse Heath and Robert Bond as messengers to the new conference. At the next session of the Bethel Conference in 1832, a letter from the South Carolina Conference was "read and accepted." The delegates then appointed Elder Jesse Vause to write a letter informing the South Carolina Conference of the proceedings of the Bethel Conference. This was a common practice among Baptist associations of this era.[37]

Much of the scant information that exists about Moore comes from some historical notes his grandson Elder J. B. (John Beaty) Moore recorded in 1901 in the preface to the record book of the Bethel (later "Old Bethel") Free Will Baptist Church. According to Moore, his grandfather first came to South Carolina in 1816 from Greene County, North Carolina, where he was a member of the congregation that met at Grimsley's meeting house and a licentiate among the North Carolina Free Will Baptists. J. B. Moore confirms that in the fall of 1816, Moore went back to North Carolina for ordination but then returned to the Marion District of South Carolina. In 1818 he started the South Carolina Conference out of three churches he had organized. That conference is still known today by the same name and is a member of the South Carolina State Association of Free Will Baptists.[38]

Almost nothing is known about Moore before 1816. He appears to have been born sometime between 1774 and 1781 to Reading Moore and Annie Norcott. Moore was still living in Greene County in 1812, serving on the grand jury for the county that year. As J. B. Moore indicated, Redding Moore had been a member of the church in Greene County associated with Elder Jesse Heath, which met at Grimsley's meeting house. He married his first wife, Ann, while he was still in North Carolina. They had four children. After Ann's death he married Nancy Ann Jones around 1823. They had at least three children. J. B. Moore's date for his grandfather's move to South Carolina is supported by Elias Hutchins, who visited Redding Moore in his home in

December 1829. In a letter to *The Morning Star*, Hutchins said that Moore had been serving in South Carolina for thirteen years. The censuses of 1820, 1830, and 1840 show that Moore was living in Marion District during that period with his family and one or two slaves (though by 1840 no slaves are listed as members of Moore's household). He died in 1849, probably in his seventies.[39]

The first three churches Moore organized, which formed the nucleus of the South Carolina Conference, appear to be Mother Church in Clarendon District; Little Sister Church in Williamsburg District about ten miles from Mother Church; and Piney (Pine) Grove Church, also in Williamsburg District. Little is known about the origins of these congregations other than that Moore gathered them. Records show, however, that Samuel McKenzie was the "first regular minister" of the Piney Grove Church. J. B. Moore also said that Moore organized the "Old Bethel" Church, located in the Marion District between the Pee Dee River and Jeffries Creek, sometime in the 1820s. Owing to the sparseness of records in this early period, we do not know what other churches Moore planted.[40]

An 1830 record in the minutes of the Hookerton Free Will Baptist Church in Hookerton, North Carolina, discusses Moore's visit there:

> On the evening the brethren met to commemorate the Lord's death. Elder Readding Moore administered the sacrament—the meeting solemn and interesting. A door again being opened for the reception of members, one came forward for fellowship and confessed her faith in the Redeemer and accordingly received the right hand of fellowship in order to baptism.
> On Sunday morning the brethren retired to water; there five candidates followed the dear Redeemer into the watery grave. The ordinance was administered by elder Readding Moore.[41]

The 1897 Minutes of the South Carolina Conference list the annual session that year as its seventy-ninth, indicating that they dated the beginning of the conference to 1819. Thus they imply that the South Carolina churches had a union meeting prior to their formal amicable dismissal from the Bethel Conference in 1831. Elias Hutchins mentioned two ministers who were assisting Moore in 1829. He was probably referring to Samuel McKenzie and Moab Hewitt. McKenzie owned the land on which the Piney Grove Church was built. He was born around 1790 to Daniel and Rebekah Sarah Dotson McKenzie (MacKenzie) and was married to Margaret Peggy McElveen in 1814, with whom he had eleven children. He remained active as an elder in the South Carolina Conference until his death in 1864. Moab Hewitt was born about 1795 and married Sarah (apparently Glenn), with whom he had at least four children. The 1860 census lists him as a Free Will Baptist clergyman. His name is in the Minutes of the South Carolina Conference as a minister until 1861, and his son William Hewitt was also a minister in the Conference.[42]

T. F. Harrison and J. M. Barfield listed Hewitt and four other ministers who were influential assistants to Moore: John Wilson, Samuel Moore, Wright Wilson, and Nathan Hall. While Hall's name does not appear in the minutes of the South Carolina Conference until 1864, the other three ministers Harrison and Barfield mentioned had important early ministries alongside Redding Moore.[43]

John T. Wilson (1789–1869), who married Ruth Ellis in 1812, is said by local tradition to have crossed Lynches River on horseback each month when he traveled to his pastorate at Piney Grove Church. He was active in the South Carolina Conference into old age and was even known to have preached after he had become infirm and his son Thomas had had him declared a "lunatic." That same son also was an active minister in the conference. Samuel Moore, Redding's oldest son, was born in North Carolina in 1807 and married Judith Hicks in 1826. Samuel Moore was extremely influential, alongside McKenzie, Hewitt, John Wilson, and Wright Wilson, in the early development of the South Carolina Conference. At one time he pastored the Old Bethel Church, and he remained a Free Will Baptist minister until his death in 1880, having served twice as moderator of the conference. Wright Wilson appears to have been related to John T. Wilson, since he named one of his sons by the same name. Very little is known about Wilson except that he was born in 1804, died in 1881, and served as moderator of the South Carolina Conference four times and one year as itinerant minister for the conference.[44]

The first extant records of the South Carolina Conference are the minutes of the 1858 annual session held with Ebenezer Church in Williamsburg District. Letters were read from churches in the Clarendon, Williamsburg, Darlington, Marion, and Sumter districts. By 1859, membership in the conference stood at 4,538. In 1860 several names of the earlier associates of Moore are listed: Elders John Wilson, Samuel Moore, Moab Hewitt, Samuel McKenzie, and Wright Wilson, along with Elders J. R. Lloyd and Benjamin Joiner, with J. N. Ridgeway as a licentiate. The Civil War decimated the churches, which after the War comprised only 671 members. Growth would occur in the 1870s, however, requiring that the conference be divided into two sections, one on either side of Black River.[45]

The South Carolina Conference, with origins as early as 1816, was the oldest Free Will Baptist presence in the South outside North Carolina. Its character was shaped by its direct identity with North Carolina Free Will Baptists, with whom it exchanged delegates throughout the nineteenth century, shared the same *Discipline*, and was alike in most ways. As the South Carolina Conference grew, it gave birth to the Eastern and Western Conferences in the early twentieth century. A state convention was begun in South Carolina in 1912, but the modern-day South Carolina State Association was formed in 1943 by the union of the South Carolina and Eastern Conferences with the Beaver Creek Association, Rock Fish Association, and Pee Dee Association.[46]

The Campbell Movement Schism

In 1834 Thomas J. Latham, whose letter to *The Morning Star* was considered earlier, invited a minister named Thomas Campbell, who had been touring and preaching across Eastern North Carolina, for a visit in his home. Campbell and his son Alexander became the chief leaders, along with Barton Stone, of the new Disciples of Christ movement sweeping the country. Thomas Campbell had already influenced David Hartsfield of the Hookerton Church with the views of the Disciples. This very aggressive movement proselytized churches from across denominations, urging them to leave behind the divisiveness of denominations and seek to be only "Christians" or "Disciples of Christ," not in denominational congregations but in "Churches of Christ."[47]

The Campbells and Stone adopted a posture that scholars such as Timothy George have called *nuda Scriptura*. This mentality is to be distinguished from *sola Scriptura*. The latter, while holding that Holy Scripture is the *norma normans*, the norming norm, which is the sole infallible authority for the church's doctrine and practice, placed great value on the creeds and councils of ancient Christian orthodoxy and on the wisdom and consensual exegesis of the saints and martyrs of the church's past. The *nuda Scriptura* mindset of the Stone-Campbell movement took firm hold on the consciousness of many nineteenth-century evangelicals. Its mantra was "no creed but the Bible," and it called for the elimination of any and all humanly composed creedal or confessional documents. Soon Latham began promoting Thomas Campbell's views among his congregants at the Concord Church and other churches nearby.[48]

The anti-confessional posture of the Disciples of Christ movement collided with the confessionalism of the Free Will Baptists during the 1830s and 1840s. The Free Will Baptists of North Carolina are a notable example of the loss of members in many denominations to the Disciples of Christ, who set about actively proselytizing Free Will Baptists, and a number of churches were lost. Free Will Baptists who came under the influence of the Disciples were required to renounce their traditional commitment to written confessions of faith—to "discard as utterly useless all human creeds, traditions, or commandments of uninspired men." Thus leaders such as Latham, David Hartsfield, and Henry Smith began to preach against the use of written confessions of faith.[49]

Reuben Barrow, a layman who himself had served on the 1836 revision committee for the *Discipline*, stated in 1842 that all rules of discipline "written by uninspired men, are altogether useless and unprofitable; and that they are one great cause of the divisions and contentions which pervade the Christian world at the present day." Over and over again, churches were asked to vote to choose whether to "take the written discipline or the word of God, upon which [some] voted to take the word of God." Yet those Free Will Baptists who remained committed to their received faith and practice saw this as a false dichotomy and continued to confess the *Discipline*. This controversy would actually strengthen the confessional posture of the continuing Free Will Baptist movement.[50]

At the 1839 annual session of the Bethel Conference held with Fellow's Chapel Church in Pitt County, Jeremiah Heath made a motion that "all the ministers confess that they will preach the doctrine, and support the principles and practices of the Free-Will Baptists, and that this confession and pledge be inserted in the minutes." Heath was simply reiterating what was already in print in the *Discipline*. That document stated that its precepts were binding on the conference's ministers. To receive ordination, the *Discipline* said, ministers were required to abide by the "ordinances and decrees" of the conference, to be "found orthodox" and "believe the Faith and Order of this Church to be altogether consonant with the Holy Scriptures." So even though what Heath called for came directly from the *Discipline*, the conference voted Heath's motion down, and then he demanded that his name be "erased" from the minutes.[51]

There are no surviving records of the 1840 Bethel Conference, but in 1841, an invitation was issued for the churches of the Shiloh Conference to attend. However, owing no doubt to the controversy surrounding the Disciples of Christ, most of the Shiloh congregations did not send delegates. This session was the turning point for the impact of the Disciples on the Bethel Conference, and it voted to drop "Free Will Baptist" from its name. Disciples of Christ historians mark this conference as the beginning of the Disciples of Christ movement in North Carolina.[52]

In addition to their concern over the anti-confessionalism of the Campbell movement, the Free Will Baptists were concerned about the accountability for orthodox faith and practice ensured by the conference and its presbytery, which ordained its ministers and held them accountable. They believed that the Disciples' view of the radical autonomy of local congregations threatened these standards and the unity of the church. The churches taken over by the Disciples encapsulated this sentiment in a resolution later passed by the Bethel Conference after it had gone over to the Campbell movement. This statement illustrates the way radical independency and anti-confessionalism went hand in hand:

> Resolved that this Conference consider each Church of Christ, composed of its Elders, Deacons, and other members, as the highest ecclesiastical tribunal recognized in the New Testament, and therefore disclaims any ecclesiastical or controlling power over the churches of Christ as are willing to unite with us, on the Holy Scriptures, as the Rule of Faith and Discipline, reserving to themselves, respectively, the right to interpret the same, for their own regulations, and that they be affectionately invited to represent themselves by Delegates in this Conference.[53]

The Free Will Baptists of the Carolinas, as well as other southern Free Will Baptists, as chapter 10 will show, maintained the ultimate right of the local congregation to govern itself and decide which conference or association to unite with. They were resolutely averse, however, to the independency of the Disciples of Christ, who believed that no conference or association should impose any parameters of doctrine or practice on its member congregations or their ministers.[54]

In 1842, despite the listing of forty-three churches in the minutes of the Bethel Conference, only fourteen churches sent delegates, the same number represented at the 1843 session, and only ten represented in 1844. Several Free Will Baptist leaders called a special conference in 1842 at the Louson Swamp Church in Lenoir County. The meeting was intended to rally the support of as many congregations as possible in the Shiloh and Bethel conferences for Free Will Baptist doctrine and practice. This resulted in the founding of a wholly new conference. The first extant minutes of this conference, which was held at "Grimsley's meeting house in Greene County, N.C." in 1845 called it "the North Carolina Free Will Baptist General Conference."[55]

The statistical tables for that meeting show the havoc the Disciples of Christ had wreaked on the Free Will Baptists. Thirty-eight churches and thirty-two ordained ministers were left. Uncoincidentally, Elder Thomas Moore "preached from the 4th chapter and 14th verse of St. Paul's letter to the Ephesians, viz. 'That we henceforth be no more children, tossed to and fro, and carried about with every wind of doctrine, by the sleight of men, and cunning craftiness whereby they lie in wait to deceive.'" The clerk of the conference, Elder Calvin Ruff, concluded the minutes with these words:

> Dear brethren, while in the discharge of the duty devolving upon me by order of the General Conference, I feel happy to say in conclusion, that during the sitting of our Conference peace and harmony seemed to prevail; for which I feel abundantly to thank our adorable Creator, hoping that God will abundantly bless our endeavors, and crown our meeting with the best of consequences. O that God may help us to love each other more fervently, and conform us more to his holy and righteous will, and strengthen us in his love, is the prayer of your brother.[56]

Harrison and Barfield would later say, "The Campbellites, during all this time [1833–1847], had been vigorously proselyting the Free Will Baptists." The churches remaining in the Bethel Conference after the founding of the new General Conference united with the union meeting of Disciples of Christ, which consisted of six small churches that were formerly Regular Baptist. Twelve congregations sent delegates to this meeting, though it listed several Free Will Baptist churches that had not represented to the Bethel Conference since the early 1840s.[57]

More than twenty-five ministers were lost, but unlike the Regular Baptist proselytization in the previous century, the Free Will Baptists held their own. This is indicated by the fact that thirty-eight congregations were on the membership roster of the new General Conference in 1845, as compared with six former Free Will Baptist churches that sent delegates to the new Disciples of Christ union meeting. The Free Will Baptists became more entrenched in their confessional solidarity, bounced back stronger, and continued to grow again. This was a marked contrast to their situation after the Calvinist incursion in the eighteenth century. Some of the Disciples of Christ ministers came back to the Free Will Baptist Church a few years later, such as Thomas Reaves, Wilson Daniels, Henry W. Mears, and Jeremiah Rowe in 1844 and Thomas C. Baker and Fred B. Silverthorne in 1847.[58]

In many ways, the Disciples of Christ represented a trend in nineteenth-century evangelicalism brought about by the increasing American emphasis on democracy, as it combined with the pietistic and revivalistic emphases of the Romantic era. Nathan Hatch has termed this trend "the democratization of American Christianity." Denominations such as the Episcopalians and Presbyterians decried this democratization and newfound radical independency as a denial of ecclesiastical authority, creed, and accountability. In some ways the reaction of the traditional Free Will Baptists against the Stone-Campbell movement was similar to the General Baptist reaction against the New Light revivalist trend in the eighteenth century. The General Baptists bore resemblance to the Old Side Presbyterians and Old Light Congregationalists. They were concerned that much New Light revivalism in the Great Awakening was watering down doctrinal clarity and accountability and ecclesiastical authority in protection of sound biblical doctrine and practice, substituting individualized subjective experience instead. Similarly, the democratized Stone-Campbell movement, a product of the Second Great Awakening, was emphasizing individual experience and downplaying the use of creeds and confessions of faith and the authority of conferences or associations in ordaining ministers and ensuring their doctrinal orthodoxy. In the face of the eighteenth-century trend, the General Baptists did not fare so well. In the face of the nineteenth-century trend, they fared better. Subsequent historians would note that when the Free Will Baptists were most confident in their own convictions, they were least apt to be laid waste by trends in the ever-evolving American evangelical landscape.[59]

The Anti-Masonry Controversy

The 1850s brought another controversy that hampered the growth of the movement, this time over anti-Masonry. This controversy, like the Stone-Campbell controversy, was tied to trends arising from the influence of Pietism and Second Great Awakening revivalism on nineteenth-century American Protestantism. Elder James Moore, one of the early ministers Jesse Heath had mentioned in the early 1830s, seems to have been the most outspoken opponent of membership in secret societies such as the Freemasons. Moore gained a following, and in 1847 the General Conference passed a resolution against membership in the Freemasons. At the 1850 session, however, a motion by Calvin Ruff passed, that the 1847 resolution be "expunged" from the record. Then Jesse Vause introduced a motion that gave each local church the right to make its own decision regarding membership in secret societies. Yet the right of an individual in a congregation to make an appeal to the conference was maintained. As the controversy raged, confusion ensued, and at the next conference in 1851, Ruff made a motion to rescind the Vause resolution and replace it with one that said, "That no member shall be excluded or any person debarred from becoming a member of any church belonging to this connection, for being or becoming a member of any of the following orders: Free Masons, Independent Order of Odd Fellows, or Sons of Temperance." The motion passed.[60]

The controversy soon reached a new level of intensity. At the 1853 meeting of the General Conference, Elder Alfred Moore presented a new resolution that no church in the conference could reject or excommunicate members of the Freemasons or Oddfellows. Someone proposed the addition of the words "unless a majority of the members shall so decide," but Alfred Moore rejected it. Before a vote was taken, James Moore, the vigorous opponent of secret societies, proposed another motion "giving to each church its own key—the privilege of transacting its own business." That motion was approved by a margin of nearly two-to-one. Still, the conference split, with both bodies claiming to be the original conference.[61]

The Masonic controversy depleted the numbers of the General Conference, which had thirty-six ministers and forty-five churches in 1851 but only seventeen ministers and twenty-one churches in 1853. The James Moore faction survived the schism. Some of the Alfred Moore faction, later in 1858, affiliated with James W. Hunnicut's Union Baptist movement, which sought to unite all "Liberal" (open-communion and Arminian) Baptists. However, in 1855 seven ministers who had been affiliated with the pro-Masonry group organized a new conference of eight churches comprising 370 members, the Cape Fear Free Will Baptist Conference, at Stoney Run Church. This conference would later enter into reunion with the North Carolina General Conference. Some years later, some of the Union Baptists moved to Oklahoma and, ironically, a century later they united with the Oklahoma State Association of Free Will Baptists and continue that affiliation to this day.[62]

Regrouping and Growth

A ray of light shone through the mist of the controversy in 1853, the first year that conference minutes make reference to Elder Rufus K. Hearn, who that year was added to the roster of ministers. Thirty-four-year-old Hearn, whose story will be told in chapter 9, would go on to become the most influential Free Will Baptist of the South in the latter half of the nineteenth century, leading in the development and promotion of organizations that would form the center of the southern movement in the late nineteenth and early twentieth centuries.[63]

Over the next few years, both the General Conference and Cape Fear Conference showed gradual growth, with several ministers and numerous members added to both groups. Hearn quickly became the most prominent name in the General Conference. In 1856 the body "took steps to rescue the history of the Conference" by appointing him as recording secretary to keep accurate records of the conference "and such other facts as may seem proper and right; also a sketch of the lives of the several ministers composing the same." He and Elder William May were appointed as correspondents with the United Baptists of Georgia, who, as will be seen, were interested in uniting all Free Will Baptists in the South. Yet, having been riddled with controversy, the General Conference was leery of uniting with this group. The Cape Fear Conference, on the contrary, was a leader in "union movements" among "Liberal Baptists" in the South, which will be explored in chapter 9.[64]

The 1856 General Conference at Grimsley's meeting house also shored up the movement's confessionalism in outlining a process of practicing "what the Discipline require[s]" regarding the examination of the conference's ministers. That year all the ministers were conferred with, and they all "passed examination," except for one minister who "was arraigned for keeping a grog shop." The process of annual examination of ministers continued thereafter. At the 1857 annual session of the conference, held with Gum Swamp Church in Pitt County, the minister who had been disciplined sought the conference's forgiveness and was reinstated. The body then approved a motion from Hearn that the conference would "not recognize any minister that engages in the traffic of spiritous liquors." This was at the height of the temperance movement in the North. The South was slow in implementing temperance reform. Yet the northern Freewill Baptists had decades earlier moved from the "O.P.," the Old Pledge, which involved drinking only beer and wine and not "ardent spirits" or liquors, to the "T." pledge—T for "Total." This pledge led to the use of the term "Teetotaler" as someone who practiced total abstinence from all intoxicants. The Free Will Baptists in the South would become more involved in the temperance movement as the century progressed.[65]

An important development took place in the 1859 meeting of the North Carolina General Conference at Reedy Branch Church in Pitt County. "On motion of Eld. B. B. Albritton," it was "agreed that we hold Union Meetings in our connection on the fifth Sunday in every month that has five Sundays." A committee was appointed, which the next day brought back a method for holding union meetings. The minutes refer to the groupings of churches that were to hold these union meetings as "districts." Despite a rocky start in the first few years, these districts would eventually evolve into regional conferences that held their meetings quarterly, meeting annually with the larger conference. This was a method that became common among southern Free Will Baptists.[66]

With the exception of the first three years of the Civil War, the 1860s witnessed the steady growth of both the General Conference and the Cape Fear Conference. Both these conferences continued to increase in church membership and the addition of newly ordained ministers. Having learned valuable lessons from the past through schism and controversy, they also focused increasingly carefully on the dictates of the *Discipline* and the continued care of the conferences' ministers and their doctrine and conduct. The 1860 General Conference exemplifies this increasing precision:

> We, a part of the committee appointed at last Conference to examine the Discipline and Minutes, beg leave to report that the 3d clause of resolutions introduced by Bro. Jesse Smith, in the Minutes of 1853, may be construed in a way to conflict with section 5th, in rules of Church Discipline, where the Discipline provides for the trying of a minister. We beg leave further to report that all business shall be decided by the Discipline, independent to all other laws; as any law coming in contact with our Discipline is unconstitutional according to our Discipline, and according to Bro. Smith's resolution, Art. 2.
>
> R. K. Hearn.
B. B. Albritton.
J. S. Bell.
Wm. May.[67]

This move was accompanied by more emphasis on the financial support of the General Conference, which requested that each church contribute to the conference's treasury.[68]

On the eve of the Civil War, at the 1861 General Conference held with Gum Swamp Church, a resolution was approved requesting "the President," Abraham Lincoln, to "set apart a day for fasting and prayer, for peace in our land." The Free Will Baptists of the Carolinas would overwhelmingly support the Confederacy in the Civil War. Those few who had left the General Conference during the Masonry controversy and united with James Hunnicut, an ardent Unionist, opposed the Confederacy. As a result, the Hunnicut group left the state. Most Free Will Baptists across the South were like their counterparts in the Carolinas in support of the Confederacy. Some of the Free Will Baptists in Western North Carolina and East Tennessee were a strong exception to this rule, however. As Robert Picirilli explains, the Toe River Association wanted to stay out of the War, as there was strong Union sentiment in western North Carolina and East Tennessee both inside and outside the Free Will Baptist Church.[69]

In 1861 the North Carolina General Conference also approved a motion to maintain formal correspondence with the Cape Fear Conference. Soon the two conferences began exchanging visiting ministers. In 1864, for example, Elder B. B. Holder, an illustrious minister in the Cape Fear Conference who would a few years later be sent by that conference as a home missionary to southeast Alabama, was seated as a visiting brother by the General Conference. During the first three years of the Civil War, the numerical growth of the churches in North and South Carolina paused, and there were fewer baptisms. The South Carolina churches suffered the greatest. However, the North Carolina Free Will Baptists held their own and witnessed surprising growth in the last two years of the War. The stage was set for an unprecedented period of growth and expansion among the Free Will Baptists of the Carolinas following the conclusion of the Civil War.[70]

Part II
EARLY EXPANSION ACROSS THE SOUTHEAST

Four
ORIGINS IN SOUTH ALABAMA, FLORIDA, AND GEORGIA

Migration and Identification

Historians have typically referred to the Free Will Baptists of the South as the Palmer movement and the northern Freewill Baptists as the Randall movement. While there has been popular interest that emphasizes the Randall movement, most recent published scholarship has tended to emphasize southern Free Will Baptists, probably because of their outsized role in the formation of the National Association.[1]

One of the enduring problems of Free Will Baptist history has arisen from the fact that Free Will Baptists in many areas of the South were originally United or Separate Baptists who became Free Will Baptist. Many United and Separate Baptists—dubbed "free willers" by their Calvinist interlocutors—had already diverged from Calvinist views of absolute predestination, limited atonement, and irresistible grace but still balked at the possibility of apostasy. Historians have wondered how and why they came to adopt Free Will Baptist faith and practice and how the Palmer tradition of the Carolinas influenced their transition. Early twentieth-century historians G. W. Million and G. A. Barrett said that after the decimation of the North Carolina General Baptist movement by the Calvinists in the mid-eighteenth century, it was "likely that the greater part of the membership of the remaining four churches migrated into Tennessee and Kentucky." Yet they did not give their reasons for thinking this.[2]

Modern historians hypothesize that Million and Barrett were right and that Carolina Free Will Baptists' westward migration influenced United and Separate Baptists to adopt a Free Will Baptist confessional identity, or there were other sorts of influence by the Palmer movement on "proto-Free Will Baptists" or "developing Free Will Baptists" throughout the South. However, more archival research needs to be done to unearth data that has not yet come to the surface to shed light on how United Baptists and Separate Baptists became Free Will Baptist. Genealogical research will make a major contribution to future research in this area. One of the contributions of this book is that it begins exploring this question, establishing more connections between different groups of Free Will Baptists, utilizing genealogical research. However, this volume is only a beginning; far more research needs to be done on this question.[3]

Frontier Migration Patterns

One important piece of this puzzle is an understanding of frontier migration patterns, especially the out-migration from North and South Carolina during the antebellum period. Out-migration from the Carolinas was much higher than from other southern coastal states. By 1860 North Carolina had dropped from third (in 1790) to twelfth in population among the states. Thirty percent of those born in North Carolina—more than four hundred thousand—had left the state before the Civil War. The vast majority of these moved to Georgia, Tennessee, Alabama, and Mississippi. Any theory of southern Free Will Baptist origins must account for the few thousand Free Will Baptists who migrated from the Carolinas during the antebellum period. One ascertains from frontier migration patterns in general that North and South Carolinians migrated to just the areas where various Free Will Baptist groups originated in the nineteenth century. The driving question for research on southern Free Will Baptist origins is, what happened to them?[4]

Historians have hypothesized that most new Free Will Baptist groups must have been influenced by Free Will Baptists from the Carolinas, or those who had been influenced by them. It is too much of a stretch to think that men and women, churches, and associations that emerged from a United Baptist or Separate Baptist background that jettisoned the doctrine of eternal security and closed communion, adopted the rite of the washing of the saints' feet, began writing confessions of faith, and took on the Free Will Baptist name simply did this spontaneously. This book emphasizes the *discontinuities* between the identity, faith, and practice of Free Will Baptist groups and the past identity, faith, and practice of their Separate, United, or Regular Baptist backgrounds. Of course, people can espouse Arminian principles simply based on their reading of Scripture alone. However, it is unlikely that most southern Free Will Baptist traditions would ever have existed—in the full confessional, ecclesiastical, and sociological sense of what it meant to be Free Will Baptist in the evangelical Protestant ethos of the nineteenth-century South—were it not for either direct lineage or strong influence from the Palmer movement. That would simply be too great a coincidence.

Examples of the Influence of the Palmer Tradition

This question cannot be completely answered before more research is done. Yet the influence of the Palmer movement on United and Separate Baptists who adopted full Free Will Baptist confessional identity is a more tenable explanation for this transition than the positing of a spontaneous origin. Several examples illustrate this dynamic, giving evidence of the influence of the Free Will Baptists from the Carolinas on the origins of those in other parts of the South. These examples indicate the kind of impact Elder Jesse Heath referred to in his aforementioned 1829 letter to John Buzzell about the flourishing of the Free Will Baptist work in the South. Heath had been writing with news of the growth they were experiencing in North Carolina. This letter, summarized in *The Morning Star*, mentioned the impact being made in "the Floridas, in Georgia and in Tennessee." It is also seen in the fact that in 1832 the North Carolina General Conference called for the writing of a history of Free Will Baptists "in this and the adjoining states."[5]

MINISTERS FROM THE CAROLINAS OR THOSE INFLUENCED BY THEM

Origin stories will be told in this and the coming chapter of "Arminianizing" Baptists in regions to the west and south of the Carolinas who sought ordination from North Carolina Free Will Baptists.[6] These include ministers like Ellis Gore in west-central Alabama and Elijah Callaway in West Florida. There is also evidence of North Carolina ministers who moved to other places and took up pastorates there. These include, for example, Brinson Hollis, Levi Griffin, B. B. Holder, and J. W. Lucas in southeast Alabama and southwest Georgia;[7] David Poyner, whose ministry touched North Carolina, Tennessee, Illinois, Missouri, Arkansas, and Oklahoma; Reddin R. Hayles in Central Florida;[8] and J. T. Eason in Texas. There are ministers in other states who were influenced by North Carolina ministers, such as James Hartsfield, Henry Boyett, Benjamin Tipton, and A. M. Stewart in the tri-state area of southeast Alabama, West Florida, and southwest Georgia; and Charles Stetson in Texas.[9] There were also ministers in other states who became Free Will Baptists who were originally from the Carolinas. However, historians do not know at this point whether there was any influence from Carolina Free Will Baptists on them. These include C. C. Vandiver in south-central Tennessee, J. A. Blanton in southeast Georgia, Kimbrell Massey in southwest Georgia, as well as the aforementioned Ellis Gore, Henry Boyett, and James Hartsfield. Finally, there were ministers from the Carolinas such as Lewis Hartsfield who migrated to other states (in his case, Alabama and later Texas), but no one knows whether they were Free Will Baptists after they left the Carolinas.

THE 1812 ABSTRACT

That the *1812 Abstract* was utilized by so many conferences and associations across the South is also evidence of the widespread influence of Carolina and the Palmer movement. This is especially true given the democratized nineteenth-century American context when so many local Baptist associations drafted their own articles of faith. One notes the *1812 Abstract* touching not only North and South Carolina but also Georgia, Florida, Alabama, Mississippi, Tennessee, Virginia, Kentucky, West Virginia, Ohio, and Indiana among predominantly White Free Will Baptists. These states would in turn influence other states where they would plant new churches in the nineteenth and twentieth centuries. Most Black Free Will Baptist churches across the United States have always employed this venerable confession of faith. Its use among them further illustrates the influence of Carolina and the Palmer tradition as it radiated out across the southern United States.[10]

LAITY WHO MIGRATED TO REGIONS THAT SOON HAD A FREE WILL BAPTIST PRESENCE

Finally, among the Free Will Baptists who were part of the nearly half-million individuals who migrated from the Carolinas during the antebellum period, some migrated to areas where, soon, Baptists would become Free Will Baptist. One example of this is Matthew Spivey, the son of Elder Caleb Spivey in the Bethel Conference in North Carolina in the 1820s. Spivey migrated to southeast Georgia. His story will be told later in this chapter.

A similar story is that of a father and son named Thomas Hood mentioned in chapter 3.[11] Thomas Hood Sr. was an active layman in Lenoir County, North Carolina, who served as clerk of the Bethel Conference there from 1829 through 1831 and on one of the conference's committees in 1832. He and his wife Clarissa entertained Elias Hutchins in their home when he visited North Carolina, and Thomas Sr. took Hutchins on a horseback ride into the backcountry to visit Free Will Baptist churches. One assumes it was Thomas

Sr. who did this; both father and son lived in the same household when the 1830 census was recorded. Thomas Sr. would have been around fifty-four years of age, and Thomas Jr. around twenty at this time. Nothing more is heard in North Carolina from either Thomas after 1832. They appear in no more conference minutes and on no more North Carolina censuses. Sometime between then and 1840, Thomas Sr. and Clarissa moved to Dallas County, Alabama. By 1843, Thomas Jr. was in Washington County, Texas, where he married Catherine Edney. They raised seven children there and lived a long life until 1871, when Thomas Jr. died. Catherine and some of her children moved to nearby Comanche County, Texas, where some of the earliest Free Will Baptist churches in Texas would originate. While there is no record of the church affiliation in Texas of these two families who were so deeply tied to the work of the Free Will Baptist Church, future research will no doubt turn up more. Future archival research will likely yield more information about other individuals like the Spiveys and Hoods who were among the half million or so people who migrated from the Carolinas during the antebellum period, a percentage of whom were Free Will Baptists.[12]

Beginnings in South Alabama, Florida, and Georgia

Free Will Baptist beginnings in south Alabama, Florida, and Georgia are tied to North Carolinians who migrated to those areas in the early and mid-nineteenth century. The center of activity there was the tri-state area of southeast Alabama, West Florida, and southwest Georgia. It radiated out from Jackson County, West Florida, and Henry (now Houston) County, Alabama, into the perimeter of southwest Georgia. This movement, along the way, entered into fellowship with Arminian-leaning Baptists from the Chattahoochee United Baptist Association who, accepting open communion and the possibility of apostasy, became Free Will Baptists. Eventually these people named their newly established associations "United Free Will Baptist."

Elijah Callaway

It appears that the first time the Free Will Baptist General Conference of North Carolina learned of a Free Will Baptist presence in southeast Alabama and West Florida was in 1828. In a letter to John Buzzell, editor of the northern Freewill Baptist paper *The Morning Star*, dated April 25, 1828, Jesse Heath recounted a special session of the conference called to consider a letter from a minister named Elijah H. Callaway from "West Florida, Jackson co."

Callaway had written the North Carolina Free Will Baptists seeking ordination from them. The conference voted "to receive him as a member and preacher in connexion with us until our next Annual Conference," at which they would examine him. Callaway was born in Sussex County, Delaware, in 1790 to Thomas and Nancy Callaway. It appears that as a child he moved to South Georgia with his family. He married Elizabeth Banks in Bulloch County, Georgia, in 1812, with whom he had ten children, some of whom were born while the family was living in Laurens County, Georgia. By 1825 they were living in Jackson County, West Florida, within a few miles of the state lines of Georgia and Alabama. Owing to the paucity of records, nothing else is known about Callaway. However, he might have been reporting back with news of success, since Heath mentioned in another letter to Buzzell a year and a half later how well things were going for the movement down south, including in Florida.[13]

Brinson Hollis and Henry Boyett

One of the North Carolina ministers who would have known about Callaway's work was Brinson Hollis (Hollace). Hollis was born in 1795 in Craven County, North Carolina, to Isaac Newton and Martha Prescott Hollis. He was married to Jennet Anderson in Craven County in January 1815, and they had nine children. In 1838 they decided to move to Georgia. That year the Bethel Conference voted that Hollis's name "be discontinued" from the record of ministers because of his "removal from the State." Hollis was one of the early Free Will Baptist ministers Heath had mentioned in his 1828 letter to Buzzell. Heath had said Hollis was serving as pastor of the Poiny Nick Church in Newbern (now New Bern), North Carolina. Census records show that Hollis was living in Georgia by 1840, then in Dale County, Alabama, in 1850, about fifteen or twenty miles northwest of present-day Dothan. Before 1860 he had settled in Jackson County, West Florida, where he died in 1880.[14]

The next mention of Elder Hollis in Free Will Baptist sources is by his younger colleague in ministry, Henry Boyett, of Jackson County, West Florida. One first learns of Elder Boyett when he writes Jeremiah Heath (who had served with Hollis in the North Carolina General and Bethel Conferences) in 1852 asking for assistance from North Carolina for a Free Will Baptist conference in the tri-state area of West Florida, southeast Alabama, and southwest Georgia. Boyett was born in 1816 in Duplin County, North Carolina, to James David and Mary Boyett. He had been exchanging letters with Heath and referred to the "refreshing" correspondence that had "left so sweet a savor in my mind that I feel as if I wanted a few minutes to converse with you, and it gives me great consolation my dear Brother to see your heart is fixed on your Masters work. I received your affectionate epistle with that Christian love, known only to the followers of a crucified redeemer."[15]

Boyett had presumably moved with his parents to Crenshaw County, Alabama, where they were living in 1837 when he was seventeen or eighteen years old. He married Allie Guy (who was also from Duplin County, North Carolina) in Pike County, Alabama, in 1848, and they had eight children. Boyett had ministered in different places in that area of southeast Alabama and West Florida. When he wrote Heath in 1852, he was pastoring two churches in the region, Post Oak, in Henry County, about halfway between present-day Blakely, Georgia, and Dothan, Alabama, and Kind Providence, whose location he did not mention. He wrote the letter from Henry County but gave his address as the Millwood Post Office, Jackson County, Florida. Were it not for this letter, almost nothing would be known about Brinson Hollis's ministry after he left Craven County, North Carolina, in 1838. Boyett spoke in his letter as though he and Heath (also from Craven County) had mentioned Hollis in previous correspondence. Boyett explained that "our beloved Brother Hollis is still progressing on, and many souls is added to his crown, and the Lord is still blessing his labors, in this part of his moral vineyard." He went on to identify Hollis as maintaining membership in the Post Oak Church that Boyett was serving as pastor, stating that Hollis was serving as the itinerant minister that year for the Free Will Baptist conference of which they were members.[16]

That conference, the name of which he did not mention, had thirteen member congregations and twelve ministers, "besides a great many licentiates." Obviously, the existence of such a well-established conference means that many years of church planting had been going on prior to his letter in 1852, presumably by Free Will Baptist ministers such as Callaway and Hollis. Boyett, who was in his mid-thirties, said, "I am young my dear Brother in the cause." He had been in the ministry at that time for only three years, and he asked for Heath's "prayers and Brotherly advice."[17]

After referring to the growth being experienced by Free Will Baptists both in the Carolinas and in his own area, Boyett mentioned that the movement he was part of was "fast gaining ground," having received "a great many" Missionary Baptists and Methodists who had "come over and joined the Free Will Baptists as the denomination of their choice." He had referred to these Missionary Baptists in a previous letter to Heath as some "United Baptists" with whom he had made contact. They had now become Free Will Baptists and wanted Boyett to pass along their greetings to the Free Will Baptists in North Carolina. Boyett made a formal request that Heath attend the next annual session of their conference, which would be held the following October, and "assist us in our deliberations." ("Conference" was the word Free Will Baptists in the Carolinas at that time used to refer to their intercongregational gatherings.) Boyett also said he would love to hear from any of the Free Will Baptists in North or South Carolina and asked Heath to pass along "our Brotherly love to all our Brothers and Sisters" there. Boyett asked Elder Heath to sell him a copy of the *Discipline* and a hymn book. "They would meet with great sale here," he assured Heath. He closed his letter by saying:

> We want help, my dear Brother. "Come over and help us" (Acts 16:9). "The harvest is plenteous, but the laborers are few" (Matthew 9:37).
>
> > Too many do not know
> > That Scripture is the only cure of woe
> > That the field of promise flings abroad,
> > Its odor o'er the Christian's thorny road.
> >
> > The soul, reposing on assured relief,
> > Feels herself happy amidst all her grief,
> > Forgets her labor as she toils along,
> > Weeps tears of joy and bursts into song.
>
> H.B.[18]

Historians do not know what happened to this conference, since the associations in this area trace themselves back no further than the First Free Will Baptist Church in Dothan in 1867. Yet Hollis and Boyett continued their ministry (Hollis lived until 1880, Boyett until 1909) and contributed to the ongoing Free Will Baptist movement in the region. Hollis's legacy lived on through his son B. B. (Benjamin Brinson) Hollis, who served as a Free Will Baptist minister in southeast Alabama and West Florida. B. B. Hollis, born in Craven County, North Carolina, in 1818, thus links the early North Carolina Free Will Baptist movement directly to the continuing work of Free Will Baptist associations in West Florida and southeast Alabama that are still in existence in the twenty-first century.[19]

Boyett's children and grandchildren were active in the work of Free Will Baptist churches and associations in southeast Alabama and West Florida after Boyett's death in 1909 in Geneva County, Alabama. His son D. J. (David James) Boyett was active in the Hinson Free Will Baptist Church in Geneva County in the 1910s and the Love-Wood Free Will Baptist Church in Jackson County in the 1920s. D. J.'s son Henry S. Boyett served as clerk of the Hinson Church. Both were active in the Liberty Association.[20]

Impact in Georgia

LEVI GRIFFIN

The Hollis-Boyett movement reached into southwest Georgia as well. Another relationship Elder Boyett mentioned in his letter to Heath was Heath's own brother-in-law, Levi Griffin. Griffin was born in Craven County, North Carolina, in 1788. After fighting in the North Carolina second regiment in the War of 1812, he married Jeremiah Heath's sister Winifred in Craven County in 1814. By 1850, the Baker County, Georgia, census shows the couple living there. Together they had five children, four of whom were born in Georgia. In his letter, Boyett told Heath about his sister and brother-in-law: "Your Brother-in-law, Levy Griffin, and your sister are well. They live in Baker County, Georgia. O! How can I relate the good news to you that our beloved Brother Griffin is standing on the walls of Zion pleading the merits of a crucified Redeemer, and calling on sinners to repent, as a Free Will Baptist preacher." Boyett said that Hollis and another Free Will Baptist minister, Benjamin Tipton, had ordained Griffin in March 1852.[21]

These connections illustrate frontier migration patterns among Free Will Baptists, and how groups of Free Will Baptists that arose outside of North Carolina were influenced by their brothers and sisters in North Carolina. Here was a Free Will Baptist minister, Levi Griffin, living forty miles away from the church pastored by Henry Boyett of Duplin County, North Carolina, and this minister's brother-in-law was one of the best-known Free Will Baptist ministers in North Carolina. Boyett also mentioned Heath's mother and nephew, who then lived in Randolph County, Georgia, about fifty miles from Boyett's church, as well as another relative, Heser Heath, who Boyett said lived only sixteen miles from him. "I am sorry to tell you he is a man of the world," Boyett lamented. "But of late, he has told me he intends to quit his wild ways and try to seek the Lord. I have conversed with him on a future state, and he has appeared much affected. I am in hopes he will repent and accept of that heavenly invitation that is intended to all that will receive it on the terms of the Gospel." So here was a relative of a Free Will Baptist minister in North Carolina who lived within sixteen miles of Jackson County, Florida, talking about his spiritual life with another Free Will Baptist minister who was originally from North Carolina.[22]

It is likely that the sizable, well-organized conference of which Hollis and Boyett were members formed the basis of the later Free Will Baptist movement in southeast Alabama and West Florida. The Southeastern United Free Will Baptist Association was not formed until 1879, when the Chattahoochee United Free Will Baptist Association (formerly Chattahoochee United Baptist Association) dismissed a number of churches in southeast Alabama to constitute it. Yet it is likely that churches from the Hollis-Boyett movement were part of this association. Boyett had mentioned union with the United Baptists. Thus there is merit to Chester Pelt's theory that the Hollis-Boyett group of Free Will Baptists influenced the Chattahoochee United Baptist Association to become Free Will Baptist and joined with them, taking on the name United Free Will Baptist.[23]

BENJAMIN TIPTON

Another interesting set of connections raised in Boyett's letter concerns Elder Benjamin Tipton, who assisted Hollis in Griffin's ordination. Records show that Tipton had been a United Baptist minister but was, after some point in the late 1860s, a minister in the Chattahoochee United Free Will Baptist Association in southwest Georgia. That association, which will be considered shortly, was a United Baptist Association up until some point in the 1860s or 1870s. Tipton was one of the "Missionary Baptists" Boyett had mentioned who had "come over and joined the Free Will Baptists as the denomination of their choice." He was likely one of the links that was instrumental in moving his fellow Chattahoochee ministers to do as he had done and become Free Will Baptist. A native Georgian born in Burke County in 1804, he lived until October 1878, when he was laid to rest in the Cedar Springs United Free Will Baptist Church cemetery in Early County, Georgia. Before moving to Early County, he had lived in nearby Decatur County, where he had married his wife Elizabeth Bostwick in 1829.[24]

Tipton's obituary in the 1879 Minutes of the Chattahoochee Association (the first set of extant minutes since 1854)—which by then was using the name "United Free Will Baptist"—says he had formerly been a pastor in the United Baptist Church in Metter, in southeast Georgia. He was in southwest Georgia as early as 1829, the year he was married, and by 1852 he was an associate of Henry Boyett and Brinson Hollis, having participated with the latter in Levi Griffin's ordination. Tipton served as the first pastor of the

Open Pond Church near Blakely, which appears to have originated before 1850. However, the church did not begin meeting at Open Pond until it built a log meeting house there in 1867. The church was listed as a member of the Chattahoochee Association in 1879. Thus Tipton, whom Boyett had said in 1852 was associated with Free Will Baptists and who was not a member of the Chattahoochee Association in the 1850s even though he was in the same area, shows up in the Chattahoochee Association in the late 1860s.[25]

The Tipton connection is fascinating because it ties three Free Will Baptist ministers who were from North Carolina—Hollis, Boyett, and Griffin—with a Free Will Baptist minister in southwest Georgia. Yet at the time Boyett wrote his letter in 1852, the Chattahoochee Association had not yet become fully Free Will Baptist. They had not yet, as a body, accepted open communion, the washing of the saints' feet, or the possibility of apostasy. Yet here was a former United Baptist minister who had become Free Will Baptist by 1852 and who, by at least as early as 1867, was in the Chattahoochee Association.[26]

It is impossible, with the extant records, to know precisely what to make of all this. Had some of the ministers in the Chattahoochee United Baptist Association already been allowed to hold distinctive Free Will Baptist doctrines as early as 1852? Probably not. It is more likely that Tipton, who had already embraced Free Will Baptist views by 1852 as a result of the influence of Hollis, Boyett, and Griffin, slowly helped convince more of the Chattahoochee brethren to become Free Will Baptists. Was Tipton part of the Hollis-Boyett conference in 1852, since he was not listed in the Chattahoochee statistical table in any of the extant minutes of the association in the 1840s and 1850s?

The two churches that Boyett's letter names as being in his and Hollis's conference were not listed in the Chattahoochee United Baptist Association minutes in 1854, even though Chattahoochee contained a few Alabama churches that year. The next extant minutes are from 1879, the year after Tipton's death. Cedar Springs United Free Will Baptist Church, the church with which he was affiliated at his death, was a member of the Chattahoochee United Free-Will Baptist Association, which it was called by 1879. That year the association released its Alabama churches to start the Southeastern Association, but no one knows the names of those congregations. Thus no one knows what happened to the conference and churches associated with the Hollis-Boyett group. Still, First Church, Dothan, Alabama, was founded in 1867, fifteen years after Boyett's letter. Therefore one is left to infer that the Southeastern Association was a successor association to the conference of which Hollis and Boyett were members. Or perhaps their conference united with Chattahoochee at some point between 1854 and 1879. Further research will likely provide the answer.

Benjamin Tipton had yet another intriguing connection tying A. M. Stewart, one of the founders of Texas Free Will Baptists, to these North Carolina Free Will Baptists in the tri-state area. Elder Tipton, whose ministry was intimately intertwined with that of Hollis, Boyett, and Griffin, would have had to be acquainted with Stewart. Seventy-two-year-old Tipton was living in Cedar Springs, Georgia, when Stewart left there for Texas at age twenty-three. Given Tipton's friendship with Hollis and Boyett, and the fact that the latter lived so close to Cedar Springs, the young Elder Stewart would have been acquainted with these men.[27]

Cape Fear Home Missionaries in Alabama

By 1868 there was another North Carolina presence in southeast Alabama. B. B. Holder and J. W. Lucas served as home missionaries from the Cape Fear Free-Will Baptist Conference in North Carolina to the area near Lawrenceville, Alabama. This was about twenty miles north of the Post Oak Church where Hollis and Boyett were serving in 1852. Holder was in southeast Alabama in 1868, and two churches he planted there, Judson in Lawrenceville and Bethsaida, apparently a little further north in Barbour County, became members of Cape Fear in 1870. The churches planted by Holder were later part of the Southeastern Association in Alabama, which was founded in 1879. There is a record of the Judson Church in Lawrenceville on the roster of the Southeastern Association as late as 1946. In 1870 the Cape Fear Conference formally sent Holder and Lucas back as missionaries of the conference. Lucas still had an address in Lawrenceville, Alabama, in 1873. Later Lucas answered a call to East Tennessee to serve with William Bonaparte Woolsey at Woolsey College in Greene County. Lucas remained in East Tennessee the rest of his life, starting a classical and theological academy at Unicoi.[28]

Later Development in Southeast Alabama and West Florida

Chester Pelt's theory that the Hollis-Boyett movement influenced the Chattahoochee United Baptists to adopt Free Will Baptist faith and practice is most plausible. Furthermore, the research for this book has shown that the tradition associated with Hollis and Boyett continued its witness, after their deaths, in the Southeastern Association and the State Line Association that emerged from it. As Wayne Love said, congregations such as Dothan and Howard Grove in Alabama (founded in 1867 and 1879 respectively) and Love-

Wood and Hickory Grove in West Florida (both founded around 1879) were part of the Southeastern Association.[29]

Southeastern became involved with a union movement associated with B. W. Nash and followed him in wanting to make the washing of the saints' feet an optional practice.[30] This action resulted in a schism that led to the founding of the State Line Association in 1886 and the Liberty Association in 1888. Both these associations wished to continue to view feet washing as a divine ordinance. In 1889 the Liberty Association was amicably formed out of the State Line Association. The Florida churches in the State Line Association later formed Salem Association in 1896.[31]

Elder John Thomas Knight was chiefly responsible for the growth of Free Will Baptists in North and West Florida in the 1880s. He and his wife Ella moved to Jackson County, West Florida, in the mid-1880s, from Randolph County, Georgia, where Elder C. C. Martin was involved in Knight's ordination by the Chattahoochee Association. Knight helped establish both Liberty and Salem Associations. He planted fifty-four Free Will Baptist churches in Jackson, Calhoun, and Washington Counties. Knight died in 1930 and was buried with his wife in the Nettle Ridge Cemetery, the cemetery of Nettle Ridge Church, later known as Christian Home Free Will Baptist Church in Blountstown. Knight's protégé, the blind preacher E. L. St. Claire from southeast Georgia, also planted several churches in northeast Florida, such as Harmony Church in Lake Butler. St. Claire, who will be discussed further in chapter 10, went on to become prominent among Free Will Baptists in the South.[32]

Little research has been conducted on Florida Free Will Baptists from the turn of the century until the establishment of the Florida State Association in 1944. Floridians would loom large in the early documents of the National Association of Free Will Baptists in 1935. Chipley deacon Ernest Owen and his wife Etha Mae would be instrumental in the founding of the Florida State Association in 1944. Four associations were represented: Liberty, Salem, State Line, and Union Hill (the latter two had more Alabama than Florida churches). Interestingly, the association took on the name the Sectional Association of South Alabama and West Florida. However, the association changed its name at its second annual session—held at a church in Alabama—to the Florida State Association of Free Will Baptists. This association would grow during the twentieth century, especially being a strong supporter of missions. This support was seen in its ministry to Cuban immigrants after the Castro regime assumed power in Cuba. Several Spanish-speaking and bilingual churches became members of associations in Florida in the mid- to late twentieth century, including the Hispanic Association in South Florida, which was founded in 1984.[33]

Chattahoochee and Similar Movements in Georgia

Around half the Free Will Baptist movement in Georgia originated from the Chattahoochee United Baptist Association. Its foremost leader, Elder Cyrus White, was an illustrious Baptist minister and movement builder who began to question the strict Calvinism of his Georgia Baptist culture.[34] In 1829, White was pastoring Bethlehem Baptist Church in the Ocmulgee Baptist Association, which maintained membership in the Georgia Baptist Convention. One of the Ocmulgee churches raised the question in the association whether Christ died for all or only for the elect, and the association replied by asserting that Christ died only for those God had unconditionally elected. White published *A Scriptural View of the Atonement*, a pamphlet that argued that Christ died for everyone. The Calvinist Baptist Jesse Mercer took issue with it, responding to it in ten letters published in his newspaper, *The Christian Index*.[35]

The United Baptist Association

In 1830 the Ocmulgee Association withdrew fellowship from White and Bethlehem Church. That congregation joined with other like-minded congregations to form the United Baptist Association in 1831. The name United Baptist harked back to the earlier United Baptist movement that brought together Regular and Separate Baptists in Virginia. That group had agreed to disagree on whether election was conditional or unconditional, whether the atonement was unlimited or limited, and whether divine drawing grace was resistible or irresistible. Seeing themselves as in agreement with the Separate Baptists, these Georgia United Baptists departed from the strict Calvinism of most Georgia Baptists toward a milder *via media* between Calvinism and Arminianism that would come to characterize most Southern Baptists later in the century. Thus what one sees in White is an "Arminianizing," not a full-blown embrace of Arminianism with affirmation of the possibility of apostasy. As Robert Picirilli states, "It is clear that the early United Baptist churches *were not Free Will Baptists*. They held free will views of the atonement, conditional election, and human responsibility for the gospel. They did not hold to the possibility of apostasy, open communion as a definite commitment, or feet-washing as an ordinance of the church."[36]

The Formation of the Chattahoochee Association

The Chattahoochee United Baptist Association was formed out of the United Baptist Association in 1835 because the latter was growing too large. The two associations maintained close relations at least up to 1854, the last Chattahoochee minutes extant before 1879. In 1842, The *Christian Index* said the strongly Calvinistic Regular Baptists should not make United Baptists be rebaptized or reordained to be integrated back into the mainstream of Regular Baptist life. In 1843, both the United Baptist Association and the Chattahoochee Associations were included in the statistical list of Georgia Baptists.[37]

According to Picirilli, in 1843 both those associations published a confession of faith that affirmed neither Calvinism nor universal atonement nor any other Arminian doctrine. In fact, the *Christian Index* mentioned it favorably, stating that some Regular Baptist associations had adopted it. Later, however, in 1846, 1848, and 1850, they printed as their "Abstract of Principles" the Sharon Confession of Faith, a confession issued by a group of United Baptist congregations meeting with the Sharon Baptist Church in 1830. However, even though the Sharon confession was closer to Arminianism, it did not affirm the possibility of apostasy. By 1879, as seen in the next extant minutes, the Chattahoochee Association would move away from the Sharon confession, printing a slightly altered version of the New Hampshire Confession of Faith that made room for the possibility of apostasy. However, even at that juncture, the association made clear that it had not come to the point where it fully required ministers and churches to assent to the confession in every point. This seems to have allowed freedom on the doctrines that divided the United Baptists from Free Will Baptists.[38]

As the Calvinist Baptist historian David Benedict stated, the United Baptists were a dying breed precisely because they were neither fully Calvinist nor fully Arminian. Benedict said that they were "gradually becoming assimilated in all respects to the old body [mainstream Regular Baptists] and will soon again be wholly absorbed in their ranks." If people were United Baptist who were gradually becoming more Arminian and even open communionist, they had a choice to make: between being a "Baptist" and a "Free Will Baptist." The Chattahoochee Association eventually chose the Free Will Baptist side sometime between its 1854 minutes and the next available minutes in 1879. Yet even for a while after that point, the association seemed to allow freedom for ministers who had not fully made the transition.[39]

The Difficulty of Making the Transition to Free Will Baptist Identity

One must remember how difficult it was to make this transition. In the small towns and rural areas of the American South in the nineteenth century, Baptist culture was dominated by various mild and strong versions of Calvinism. The "Missionary Baptists" dominated Baptist life and, in many cases, the culture of rural southern communities. These Baptists were deeply committed to closed communion, and many of them, especially after the spread of the Stone-Campbell movement in the 1830s and 1840s, even began to reject what they referred to as "alien immersion." That is, they would require re-immersion of new members from fully Arminian denominations that affirmed the possibility of apostasy.[40] Thus full adoption of Free Will Baptist faith and practice was a seismic shift for these people. It marked them as people "without a country." They were neither Methodist paedobaptists nor Stone-Campbell Restorationists nor (strong or mild, modified) Calvinist Baptists. Furthermore, the embrace of open communion was as scandalous as the acceptance of full-blown Arminianism, not to mention the acceptance of the rite of the washing of the saints' feet.

Later in the century, the thrust of Chattahoochee turned into a full-blown Arminianism. It seems that for a time among the Chattahoochee United Baptists there was a détente that allowed freedom on the doctrine of the possibility of apostasy, either to accept or reject it. Eventually, however, the doctrine of the possibility of apostasy was universally acknowledged.[41]

When one considers the origins of Middle Tennessee Free Will Baptists below, it becomes evident that the demarcation lines between Separate and Free Will Baptists involved more than simply being a "free willer," that is, disagreeing with Calvinism on particular and irresistible grace before conversion. Becoming Free Will Baptist also involved an embrace of the possibility of apostasy, written confessions of faith, and open communion. The vast majority of United Baptists, including those in the Chattahoochee movement, did not oppose humanly composed confessions of faith. Yet, unlike the Separate Baptists, most of them did not practice the washing of the saints' feet. Thus the demarcation line between the United Baptists and Free Will Baptists consisted of disagreement over the possibility of apostasy, open communion, and the *pedilavium*.

What one sees occurring among the Chattahoochee ministers in the mid-nineteenth century is a growing comfort level with Free Will Baptist faith and practice. Then, eventually, they fully embraced the distinctive Free Will Baptist doctrines of the possibility of apostasy, open communion, and the rite of the washing of the saints' feet. By 1879 the association had begun advocating the washing of feet, which the Church Decorum mentioned but left up to the local church. As mentioned earlier, these are the first extant minutes since 1854, when nothing at all was said about feet washing. In 1883 the association published a strong circular letter by Elder T. H. Griffin affirming the rite, in connection with the Lord's Supper, as a binding ordinance of Christ. In 1891, the association made it an ordinance that all churches were obliged to practice.[42]

Correspondence with North Carolina

Of special note regarding the question of when the Chattahoochee United Baptists became Free Will Baptists is their correspondence with the Bethel and General Conferences of Free Will Baptists in North Carolina. In 1839 one finds the following in the minutes of the Bethel Conference: "On motion, a letter was presented (directed to this Conference) from the Union Baptist connection in Georgia, requesting a correspondence, which was read and laid on the table for a more deliberate consideration of the Conference." Later in that same session, "the letters from the United Baptist connection in Georgia" were "taken up and received, and Elds. Bond, Parrot and Vause were appointed a committee to correspond with said denomination."[43]

It is important to understand that no one knows which group of United Baptists in Georgia made this request. It could have come from United Baptists farther east out of which the South Georgia Free Will Baptist (formerly Ogeechee) Association emerged. One must bear in mind that direct influence from North Carolina is evident in the South Georgia Association: it and its sister associations in southeast Georgia used the *1812 Abstract* as their articles of faith. Or the group that corresponded with the Bethel Conference in 1839 could have been the Chattahoochee Association. After all, James Moore later said that he knew a Greene County, North Carolina, Free Will Baptist minister who started a church in Georgia "at a place called Chatahoochee." Perhaps that minister's move to Georgia resulted from the 1839 contact.[44]

Who was this North Carolina Free Will Baptist minister to whom Moore referred, who moved to Georgia and started a church associated with Chattahoochee? It is not yet known. It could have been Chattahoochee Association minister Kimbrel Massey, a North Carolina native who was active in the association in the 1840s and 1850s. He was in Muscogee County, Georgia, by the time he was about twenty-six years old in 1836. Massey was later associated with the Chattahoochee-affiliated Shiloh Church in Macon County, Georgia. To date, nothing is known of any Free Will Baptist connections Massey had in North Carolina.[45]

However, Massey's younger colleague in ministry at Shiloh Church, Elder James R. Hartsfield of Grangersville in Macon County, Georgia, did have Free Will Baptist connections. A native of North Carolina, Hartsfield was the son of Andrew and Gashie Hartsfield. He was born in North Carolina in 1820. No one knows when he moved to Georgia or when he married his wife Elizabeth Ann Childs, with whom he had nine children. He died at forty-four years of age in 1864. Yet records show that he was a minister in the Chattahoochee Association and a member of Shiloh Church as early as 1847. Nothing is known of Hartsfield before this, but records show that he had Free Will Baptist connections. His cousins Lewis and David Hartsfield had been active ministers in the Bethel Free Will Baptist Conference in North Carolina in the 1830s. It will be left to future researchers to uncover which North Carolina Free Will Baptist James Moore was referring to who became affiliated with the Chattahoochee group. However, James Hartsfield does provide evidence of a Free Will Baptist connection in the Chattahoochee Association as early as the 1840s.[46]

While the answers to all these questions are unknown, there was to be no union between the Bethel Conference and whichever Georgia United Baptist group reached out to them in 1839. One sees no mention of Georgia in the North Carolina minutes for another sixteen years. The 1855 minutes of the North Carolina General Conference stated: "This Conference opened a correspondence with the Free Will Baptists of Georgia, by appointing Eld. R. K. Hearn corresponding Secretary." The following year, the conference appointed Hearn, along with William May, as correspondents with "the Georgia brethren." It is not known if this was the same group as the United Baptists that contacted the Bethel Conference sixteen years earlier. It certainly was the Chattahoochee Association, though, because the next year the minutes referred to them as "the Chattahoochee, United, or Free Will Baptist Association of Georgia." They read aloud a letter from Chattahoochee with a proposal "to hold a convention for the purpose of a union of the Free Will Baptists South." The conference agreed to keep up talks with Georgia. However, for unknown reasons the body voted in 1858 to reject the proposal to hold the proposed convention. No one knows why, because no minutes survive from the Chattahoochee Association between 1854 and 1879.[47]

In 1854 the Chattachoochee United Baptists were still closed communionists and eternal securitists, though they considered themselves "free willers" in comparison to their strict Calvinist counterparts in the Georgia Baptist Convention. There seems to be no evidence that they became fully Free Will

Baptist until the 1860s or 1870s. This is probably the reason the North Carolina General Conference did not pursue a union in 1858.[48]

The Transition to Free Will Baptist Identity

The fact that Chattahoochee wanted to get "Free Will Baptists" together in 1857 and that one of its congregations, Providence Church in Muskogee County, held such a convention in 1859 with representatives from Virginia, North Carolina, Georgia, and Alabama indicates that they considered themselves "free willers" of a sort in the 1850s, though by 1859 they still had not added "Free Will" to their name (one must remember that there are no extant associational minutes for the years between 1854 and 1879). It is known, however, that by 1876 they considered themselves Free Will Baptists, because that year their participation in B. W. Nash's Southern Baptist Association listed their name as "United Free Will Baptist." Furthermore, their participation in Nash's organization—which, while maintaining an open posture of whether people accepted feet washing as an ordinance, unambiguously affirmed the possibility of apostasy—indicates that Chattahoochee had by that time accepted the possibility of apostasy.[49]

One must remember that in this area there were at least two North Carolina ministers who remained active after the 1853 death of Levi Griffin, brother-in-law of the prominent North Carolina minister Jeremiah Heath: Brinson Hollis and Henry Boyett. It is very likely that Heath continued his correspondence with his friend Henry Boyett. No doubt Boyett continued to inform Heath of the ministry of Elder Benjamin Tipton, who seems to have been serving the Open Pond church in the Chattahoochee Association by the time that congregation began meeting at Open Pond in 1867. Hollis (Heath's former colleague in the Bethel Conference) and Boyett had since the early 1850s been co-laborers in ministry with Benjamin Tipton of Early County, Georgia, who was clearly in step with them doctrinally. This is not to mention the North Carolina pastor who James Moore said established a congregation in Georgia at "a place called Chatahoochee," nor Chattahoochee minister James Hartsfield, who was from North Carolina and whose cousins were North Carolina Free Will Baptist preachers. There were likely other convinced Free Will Baptists in this area. It seems likely that they slowly helped nudge their brothers and sisters in the Chattahoochee Association over to a full-fledged Free Will Baptist position sometime in the 1860s.

Other Movements in Georgia with United Baptist Backgrounds

Other United Baptists on the other side of the state also became Free Will Baptists. The largest such movement, which began with the Ogeechee United Free Will Baptist Association, which was founded in 1877 and changed its name to the South Georgia Free Will Baptist Association in 1903, was different from the Chattahoochee Association in that it used the *1812 Abstract* as its confession of faith. This is a clear indication of North Carolina Free Will Baptist influence. It coincides with the fact that Free Will Baptists had migrated to that region of southeast Georgia in the 1850s and probably influenced the United Baptists in this area.

One example of this is Matthew Spivey, the son of Elder Caleb Spivey in the Bethel Conference in North Carolina in the 1820s. By 1850 Matthew had moved with his wife Delilah to Coffee County in southeast Georgia. They later moved to nearby Ware County. United Baptists in this area would become Free Will Baptists at some point in the 1860s or 1870s. It is especially interesting that, among the Free Will Baptists of Southeast Georgia, the *1812 Abstract* was used rather than the "Doctrinal Views" of the Chattahoochee Association. This story provides another piece of the puzzle in this area. It prompts one to think that influence by people like Spivey was why the South Georgia and allied associations in southeast Georgia used the *1812 Abstract* when they became Free Will Baptist and, beyond that, why such influence led them to begin questioning their theology and eventually to adopt Free Will Baptist views. This is the sort of evidence that future research will no doubt produce, and the more pieces of the puzzle surface, the more definitive the picture of Free Will Baptist origins will become.[50]

One of the older ministers in the South Georgia Association, John Abraham Blanton, was born in 1857 in Pender County, North Carolina, into a family with deep roots in Sampson and Duplin Counties. Yet nothing is known of his religious background there. The South Georgia Association had several sister associations in the same region of the state that also used the *1812 Abstract* as their articles of faith. Georgia Union was established in 1895. Union was founded in 1926 by merging two earlier associations, Liberty and Ochlocknee. Little River was formed in 1907, Ogeechee in 1909, and the Marietta Union Conference in 1912. This group of associations had numbers similar to those of the Chattahoochee and its sister associations Martin and Midway and would have larger numbers in the twentieth century.[51]

A third Free Will Baptist movement with Georgia United Baptist origins is first seen in the Middle Georgia United Baptist Association. Though their extant minutes from 1897 did not use the word "Free Will" in their title, their articles of faith were entitled "Doctrinal Statement of General Principles Taught by United Free Will and other Liberal Baptists." They also favorably mentioned the Chattahoochee Association, which by that time had been referring to itself as "United Free Will Baptist" for at least twenty-one years. The Middle Georgia minutes also spoke positively of the Georgia State Convention of Liberal Baptists.[52]

Middle Georgia had common ancestry with the "United Free Will Baptist Church of Christ" movement in southwest Alabama, West Florida, and south Mississippi. This is indicated by the same unique associational decorum and articles of faith that comprised quotations from Scripture. These associations included Liberty No. 1 (founded 1892), Liberty No. 2 (founded 1910), and Southern Union (founded 1927) in southwest Alabama and West Florida, and Zion Rest (founded 1908) in south Mississippi. All these associations were later members of the Alabama and Mississippi State Free Will Baptist associations.[53]

Conclusion

Research for the present study has demonstrated the validity of Chester Pelt's theory that the Hollis-Boyett movement probably influenced the Chattahoochee United Baptists to adopt a full Free Will Baptist confessional identity. The Hollis and Boyett tradition continued its witness, after their deaths, in the Southeastern, State Line, and other associations in southeast Alabama and West Florida.

Though records are paltry from the Chattahoochee Association of this era, it seems there was a period of time in which it allowed freedom on the questions of open versus closed communion and the possibility of apostasy versus eternal security. The question of exactly when and how the association made the full transition in faith and practice from "United Baptist" to "United Free Will Baptist" is mired in mystery, owing to the paucity of records from the period. The research for this volume has borne out the cogency of Chester Pelt's view that the Free Will Baptist movement in that region, and on the edges of southwest Georgia, likely influenced the Chattahoochee United Baptists to embrace full Arminianism, open communion, and the washing of the saints' feet, becoming full-orbed Free Will Baptists. Elder Benjamin Tipton is the main link in this chain.

The equally significant Free Will Baptists on the other side of the state who also had United Baptist origins were influenced by North Carolina Free Will Baptists who brought with them the *1812 Abstract*. This is further substantiated by the fact that there were Free Will Baptists who migrated from North Carolina to this area in the 1850s. Furthermore, the majority of the United Free Will Baptist associations in South Georgia, southeast Alabama, and West Florida used the articles of faith of the *1812 Abstract* from the *Discipline* of North and South Carolina Free Will Baptists. However, until minutes, letters, or other documents are discovered, the precise reason and timing of the shift of United Baptists in this region to the new United Free Will Baptist identity, doctrine, and practice will be shrouded in mystery.

Five

ORIGINS IN ALABAMA AND TENNESSEE

Ellis Gore in Central and West Alabama

The first church in Alabama that would become Free Will Baptist met at Kingcade meeting house in Pickens County. It originated as a Regular Baptist church in November 1838. The congregation, which had in its membership both Whites and Black slaves, changed its name to Mount Moriah at the suggestion of a young member named Ellis C. Gore. The son of Thomas T. and Nancy S. Gore, he was born in Chester County, South Carolina, on October 3, 1800. His family had moved to Pickens County, near present-day McShan, by 1816. By 1841, Gore was pastor of the Mount Moriah Church, which he pastored for forty-two years until September 1883. He was married to Dorcas B. Thomas in 1823, with whom he had twelve children. Dorcas died in 1866, and in the next year Gore married Anna Mae Burdine Smith, with whom he had nine children. He died in 1883.[1]

Charges were brought against Gore in his Regular Baptist association in 1845 for "preaching spurious doctrine." F. L. Smith, the church clerk of Mount Moriah Free Will Baptist Church, wrote in 1888 that Gore continued preaching "the doctrine of Free Salvation, of open Communion." His congregation, which concurred with his teaching, seceded from the Regular Baptists, declaring themselves Free Will Baptist. Despite attempts of the Tuscaloosa Association to maintain control of the church and its property, they eventually voted to dismiss the congregation.[2]

It is not known how long Gore had been preaching Arminianism and open communion, but he had been for several years. However, he did not know of any Free Will Baptists in his region to ordain him. The Bethlehem Association, organized in 1844, had churches in south-central and West Tennessee and North Alabama. Bethlehem was using "Free Will Baptist" in its official name by 1846. Yet the Bethlehem Association seems to have been unknown to Gore. Thus he journeyed six hundred miles on horseback to Fayetteville, North Carolina. There he "joined the Free Will Baptists," receiving ordination from them and bringing back with him copies of the *Discipline* that included the *1812 Abstract*. Upon his return, Mount Moriah Church formally became a Free Will Baptist congregation. While it is not certain exactly when this transition to Free Will Baptist identity took place, the traditional account is that it occurred in 1846. It occurred sometime between 1845 and 1849. Mount Moriah Association was started in November 1850, and the body elected Gore as moderator and William Easterwood as clerk. This association comprised two churches in addition to Mount Moriah: Macedonia and New Salem. Mount Moriah and Macedonia exist to this day.[3]

Gore organized all three of these early churches.[4] In the original associational covenant, the member churches united around three resolutions:

> 1st Resolved That having been as we trust, brought by divine Grace to embrace the Lord Jesus Christ, & to give ourselves wholy up to him, we do Solemnly and Joyfully covenant with Each other, to walk together, in him with brotherly Love, as our common Lord. We do therefore, in His Strength, engage to exercise a mutual care as members one of another, to promote the growth of the whole body in Christian knowledge, holiness & comfort in all the will of God.
>
> 2nd Resolved That we will Cheerfully contribute of our property for the Maintenance of the Poor, and support of the Gospel.
>
> 3rd Resolved That we will neither omit Family and Closet religion at home, nor the too common neglect of religiously training of our Children with others under our care, & that we will Frequently exhort one another in the Spirit of meekness, according to St Matthew 18 ch.[5]

In a circular letter to the new association, Gore emphasized the free offer of the gospel that he believed was consistent with his Arminian theology: "I exhort you by a Godly walk and a pious conversation to invite sinners to Christ," he counseled. He also urged his brothers and sisters to invite Christians who "believe as we do, to Associate with us in the Great work of Salvation." He cautioned them, however: "Be not too anxious for numbers and seek not for refuse material of other Churches. The faithful, however humble their station in life, are the proper materials, "lively Stones" of God's Spiritual building. Such we invite to receive our articles and judge for themselves." Gore reminded them that sound theology must be wed to piety and morality: "If it be not our object to raise the Standard of experimental and practical religion, we will fail to accomplish much in the cause of Christ."[6]

However, sound theology was the main reason for their break with the Regular Baptists. "We assume our ground which forbids any compromise with the Calvinistic doctrines, or with those that believe them," Gore declared. "They could have no confidence in our veracity were we to accede to any compromise upon Calvinistic principals [sic] [.] [W]e have freed ourselves from their fetters, never again to be entangled by them, and we will suffer no vestige of fatalism to be introduced into the articles of faith by which we are to be governed." The circular letter illustrates the tension between Free Will Baptists and other Baptists amid the Calvinist culture of Baptist life in the American South in the mid-nineteenth century:

> I have suffered too much from this already. The divisions of the Baptist Church show, conversely, that all is not right in her doctrines. The Tree is known by its fruits. There is nothing wanting to effect a revolution, and to expunge the doctrine of unconditional eternal election, with its concomitant reprobation, eternal passing by or non-election, but a firm and persevering stand against the Changes [,] refinements an[d] concealments of Calvinism prove its final overthrowe. May the Grace of God keep us my beloved Brethren faithful until death. Amen.
>
> Ellis Gore[7]

The Mount Moriah tradition is unique in that it broke from full-fledged Calvinism. By contrast, almost all Baptist movements that became Free Will Baptist were already Arminianizing. They had already softened their Calvinism and accepted everything about Arminianism except for the possibility of apostasy. Gore and his movement, however, broke from strong Regular Baptist predestinarianism.

One of the three original churches, New Salem, burned and disbanded soon after the association's founding. There was no growth beyond the Mount Moriah and Macedonia churches until the 1860s, when ministers such as Thomas Molloy and Woods Springfield joined Gore in the work. They started churches in Pickens, Lamar, Marion, and other counties. Though records are sparse, it is certain that by 1874 there were nineteen congregations in Pickens and Sanford in Alabama and Monroe and Lafayette Counties in Mississippi. One distinguishing mark of this association is the striking fact that none of the congregations in 1874 shared its pastor with another church, in this era in which quarter-time and half-time (preaching once or twice a month) churches were common in many denominations.[8]

Another notable characteristic of Gore and the Mount Moriah tradition in Alabama was their larger vision for union with other Free Will Baptists and even other baptistic non-Calvinists. This was prefigured by the fact that Gore rode a horse all the way to North Carolina to receive ordination from the Free Will Baptists there. This would be the beginning of many miles Gore and his colleagues would travel in the interest of inter-regional unity among Arminian Baptists. Gore also served as an official representative to other Free Will Baptist associations outside his Alabama-North Mississippi region, such as the Chattahoochee United Free-Will Baptist Association in southwest Georgia. For a while he participated in B. W. Nash's union movement that sought to bring together all Liberal Baptists (open-communion and baptistic non-Calvinists) into fraternal relations. Gore even served as moderator of one of Nash's gatherings.[9]

Several associations emerged from the original Mount Moriah Association in the nineteenth and early twentieth centuries, such as Vernon (primarily in Alabama) in 1880, Tupelo (Mississippi) in 1884, and Jasper (primarily in Alabama) in 1887. Eventually these associations came together with churches in north Alabama associated with the Bethlehem Association and south and east Alabama to form the Alabama Free Will Baptist Conference in 1911. Many of the churches in the northern part of the state had emerged from the Bethlehem Association associated with C. C. Vandiver, discussed below. Those in south and east Alabama had emerged from the movement associated with Brinson Hollis, Henry Boyett, and the United Free Will Baptist movement that resulted from their union with former United Baptists of the Chattahoochee Association across the state line in southwest Georgia. Of the current churches in the Alabama State Association, around half owe their origins to the Gore/Mount Moriah movement, close to a third owe their origins to the Hollis/Boyett movement, and the rest owe their origins to the Bethlehem/Vandiver movement.[10]

The Origins of Tennessee Free Will Baptists

Four nineteenth-century movements gave rise to the Free Will Baptist movement in Tennessee. The earliest was the Bethlehem Association in West and south-central Tennessee, North Alabama, and North Mississippi, which formed in 1844. Cumberland Association in Middle Tennessee was founded as a Separate Baptist association in 1843 and became Free Will Baptist probably in the early 1850s. The Toe River Association in East Tennessee and Western North Carolina originated in 1850. The movement that would eventually be the Stone Association in the Cumberland Plateau began in the 1850s and fully became Free Will Baptist in 1887 or 1888. While the Bethlehem Association and some of the associations formed out of it, as well as the Stone Association, never formally united with the broader Free Will Baptist movement, many churches and individuals that emerged from those movements would go on to play influential roles in the wider Free Will Baptist Church.

Bethlehem Association

The Bethlehem Association in south-central and West Tennessee, which also included churches in North Alabama and North Mississippi, was founded in 1844 by Elder Carlisle Coleman (C. C.) Vandiver.[11] Almost nothing is known about Vandiver. He was born to George H. and Ascenith Vandiver in Anderson County, South Carolina, in 1811. Yet no one knows if his family had contact with Free Will Baptists in that state. His sister Elizabeth was born in Lawrence County, Tennessee, which indicates that he was there by the time he was about ten years old. Vandiver was married to Mary Ann Melton by 1833, and they had at least eight children. The barely legible occupation listing in the 1850 census for Lawrence County appears to say "Sep B Preacher." However, Vandiver was a Free Will Baptist at least by 1846, because a periodical published near Florence, Alabama, entitled *The Baptist* reprinted the minutes of the third annual session of the "Bethlehem Association of Free Will Baptists" with "Carlile Vandivere" as moderator. Furthermore, the 1850 census for Lawrence County lists Vandiver's brother Elisha's occupation as a "Freewill B. Preach," which is corroborated by an article on Elisha's son Carlisle G. Vandivere, which describes Elisha as "a Free-Will Baptist preacher." It is not certain how the Vandivers or these churches came by their Free Will Baptist identity. The North Carolina Free Will Baptist minister David Poyner sojourned in this vicinity for a time, but that was after 1850.[12]

The first extant copy of the minutes of Bethlehem Association show that they were in fellowship with the Cumberland Association in 1871, as well as a "Forked Deer Association of Free Will Baptists," somewhere in West Tennessee near the Forked Deer River. Like other nineteenth-century Free Will Baptist associations in the South, Bethlehem, which protected local congregations' self-government while seeing membership in an association as a "duty," maintained close care of their ordained ministers. They did not believe that the association should "lord it over God's heritage." Yet they viewed the association as a body that had a duty to "give the Churches the best advice she can, in all matters of difficulty."[13]

In the early 1870s, Vandiver had at least five relatives who served as ministers in churches in the Bethlehem Association. By 1874 the association had seventeen member congregations in Hardin, Wayne, Perry, and Lewis Counties, Tennessee; Lauderdale County, Alabama; and Prentiss County, Mississippi. Total membership was 610. In his circular letter that year, announcing his retirement, Vandiver thanked God that the "connexion" had been united for thirty-four years around the teaching that "Christ delivered ... to his Apostles," despite "winds of false doctrines" of the "Campbellites," Methodists, and "papalism" that would threaten to bring about "scism in the body." Stressing the difference between Free Will Baptist and "Campbellite" doctrine on one hand and Methodist doctrine on the other, Vandiver disavowed baptismal regeneration. He explained that, in baptism, the believer is "all over burried [sic] with Christ in baptism as a seal of the inward pardon or washing of the soul. Now brethren, any of our preachers teaching baptism as any part of regeneration, is not of us; but is taking sides with the enemies of Christ."[14]

The first extant copies of the minutes of the Tennessee River Association are from 1891, indicating that it was established in 1878, three years after the last extant minutes from Bethlehem. Tennessee River had formed out of the Bethlehem Association, and, according to the *Free Baptist Cyclopaedia*, two others had been founded: the Flat Creek and Flint River Associations. By 1889 there were 2,700 members in all these associations, with 1,062 in the Tennessee River Association. These associations covered West and south-central Tennessee, North Alabama, and North Mississippi. The Little Brown's Creek Association in North Mississippi, which later joined the Mississippi State Association, was started out of the Tennessee River Association in 1892 when the latter amicably divided into two associations.[15] By 1891, before their division, there were thirty-two congregations and forty ministers in the Tennessee River Association alone. Among them was C. C. Vandiver's brother, George Washington Vandiver, of Hardin County, Tennessee. The first extant minutes for Tennessee River (1891) had no printed articles of faith. In 1910, the minutes, printed by Free Will Baptist Press in Ayden, North Carolina, contained articles of faith that consisted of the *1812 Abstract*. Sometime in 1936 or 1937, after the formation of the National Association, Tennessee River started using the brief articles of faith printed with the *Treatise* of the National Association in 1935.¹⁶

The Flint River Association was started in 1882 in North Alabama. Another association constituted out of the Tennessee River Association was the Muscle Shoals State Line Association, in 1921. About half its churches were in south-central Tennessee, and about half were in North Alabama, with the southernmost church being in Cordova, Alabama, and the northernmost in Manchester, Tennessee. This association, like Tennessee River, used the *1812 Abstract* and had a strong presbytery. Bethlehem, Tennessee River, Flat Creek, and Flint River were united in a quadrennial meeting that gathered in 1888 for its third session. Like Tennessee River (until it finally united with the Tennessee State Association in 2021), Muscle Shoals State Line was historically an independent association, though it was a member of the "Alabama State Conference" for a time in the 1920s and 1930s and as of 2024 was in talks with the Tennessee State Association about membership. Still, leaders in the latter body in the twentieth century were products of congregations that emerged from the Bethlehem tradition. Current associations in the National Association from this tradition include the Tennessee River Association in Tennessee (with some churches in North Alabama), the Little Brown Creek Association in North Mississippi, and the Flint River Association in North Alabama. The Muscle Shoals State Line Association remains independent.¹⁷

Cumberland Association

The Cumberland Association owes its origins to a wealthy landowner by the name of Robert Heaton. He was born in 1756, entered the ministry in 1812, and in 1813 organized Zion Church at White's Creek in Davidson County. Soon he had established other churches such as Sycamore in 1823 and Charity in 1826. In these early years, Heaton was a Separate Baptist, the tradition from which most Southern Baptists in the mid-South descended. Separate Baptists had originated from New Light "Separates" who had come out of the Congregationalist churches and later accepted believer's baptism. They got their start in the South under the ministry of Shubal Stearns in the Sandy Creek Baptist Church in Guilford County, North Carolina. Separate Baptist churches were less formal, less cerebral, and more emotional than their Regular Baptist counterparts. While some Separate Baptists were more Calvinistic, they allowed for greater diversity in views on salvation, though they all agreed on the doctrine of final perseverance. Separate Baptists were closed communionist and averse to written confessions of faith. They practiced nine ordinances, including the washing of feet, the laying on of hands, and the dedication of children.[18]

Heaton was affiliated with the South Kentucky Association of Separate Baptists, and later with the Nolynn Association. No one knows what influences came to bear on Elder Heaton or his fellow ministers to persuade him to move toward Free Will Baptist doctrine and practice. Indeed, it is difficult to prove whether Heaton himself was ever a Free Will Baptist in the full, confessional sense of the term. While historians believe that he may have become fully Arminian—including affirmation of the possibility of apostasy—before his death in 1843, it seems that he did not affirm open communion by that point. That same year, or perhaps the year before, Heaton and his protégé Wilson Gower were the prime movers in forming the Cumberland Association. Some of the congregations that formed that initial association, such as Heads Church in Cedar Hill and Good Springs Church in Pleasant View, are still in existence and are members of the Northern Quarterly of the Cumberland Free Will Baptist Association to this day.[19]

Most of the information about the Cumberland Association in the nineteenth century has come from Robert Picirilli, who has conducted most of the research on Heaton and the founding of the Cumberland Association. As Picirilli shows, originally Heaton and Gower served churches in the Nolynn Association of Separate Baptists, which had member congregations in Kentucky and Tennessee. Many Separate Baptists were referred to by their strict Calvinist counterparts as "free willers" and even "Arminian" because they had modified their Calvinism to the point where the only Calvinist doctrines they held were total depravity and the final perseverance of all true believers. Separate Baptists were sharply opposed to the use of humanly composed confessions of faith, holding a "no creed but the Bible" stance that became common among many Baptists in the South. Separate Baptists were closed communionists but practiced the laying on of hands and the washing of the saints' feet. So the demarcating points between Separate Baptists and Free Will Baptists were open communion, the possibility of apostasy, and the use of written confessions of faith. When these three were accepted, the transition to a full Free Will Baptist confessional identity was formally complete.[20]

As Picirilli notes, while some have said that Heaton might have accepted open communion sometime before the Cumberland Association's founding, one cannot know for certain. The group within the Nolynn Association of Separate Baptists with which he and Gower were affiliated was being referred to as "free willers" as early as 1823. By 1825, the publishers of the testimony of Lucretia Patterson referred to them as "the Society of Free Will or Separate Baptists." However, they were still Separate Baptists who did not affirm the possibility of apostasy, a doctrine that horrified Separate Baptists. The problem with the use of the word "free willer" (or "freewiller") is its ubiquitous use by strict Calvinist Baptists to refer to anyone who had abandoned unconditional election, limited atonement, and irresistible grace, including those who did not accept the possibility of apostasy.[21]

When approached by a group of Calvinist Baptists about uniting with them, the Heaton group wanted to unite only on the basis of Scripture, not confessions of faith. For example, Thomas Chilton, a "free willer" Separate Baptist in the Nolynn Association, was said to be "an enemy of creeds and decorems." As late as 1839, Heaton did not believe in subscribing to humanly composed articles of faith. His churches, Charity and Zion, were "constituted upon the broad bases of the Scriptures of the old and new testament protesting against all human rules and articles of faith or decorems...."[22]

In 1826, Heaton had had some sort of controversy (it is not certain what) with Elder John M. Chaudoin of the same group of Arminianizing Separate Baptists. That was the year Heaton started the Charity church near Marrowbone Creek and was followed by sixty-five members from two of Chaudoin's congregations, Zion and Sweet Spring. Wilson Gower, who would help found Cumberland Association in the early 1840s, was on the list of members of the Zion Church. Heaton himself had baptized Gower and his wife Lucindy. Soon Gower started preaching. Heaton's and Gower's names appeared on the list of the Nolynn Association for the last time in 1833. Records do not indicate much more from them until 1837, when the minutes of the Concord Separate Baptist Association, composed entirely of Tennessee churches, show Gower representing the Blue Spring Church to the association. The Concord Association of Separate Baptists had separated from the Concord Baptist Association (United Baptists). The United Baptists were a group of Regular Baptists (strong Calvinists) and Separate Baptists who joined together despite their differences. However, this approach did not work in Middle Tennessee, and the United Baptist Association split back into Regular and Separate camps around 1826–1827.[23]

By 1838 the minutes of the Concord Separate Baptist Association listed Gower and Heaton as elders in good standing, with both of them preaching at the annual session. In 1838 there is a record of "the old Good Spring Baptist Church," represented in the Concord Association by its pastor Thomas W. Felts. The congregation is apparently the precursor to the present Good Springs Free Will Baptist Church. Heaton became pastor of this church sometime in 1839 or 1840. By 1841, there was a small band of churches associated with the ministry of Heaton and Gower: Heads, Good Spring, Charity, Blue Spring, and Liberty. Liberty Church was planted in 1841 several miles northwest in Stewart County at "Hays Fork Meeting House." It was the precursor to Brandons Chapel and Pleasant Hill Free Will Baptist churches, which exist to this day.[24]

The Cumberland Association of Separate Baptists was formed in 1843. This happened when the Concord Association of Separate Baptists decided to rejoin the United Baptists. In 1842 the Heaton and Gower churches petitioned for letters of dismissal, and the next year the Cumberland Association held its first session. The first set of Cumberland Association minutes extant is from the session "held at Head's Meeting House, Robertson County, Tenn. On the Saturday before the first Lord's day in October, 1843, and the two succeeding days." It shows that seven churches were represented: Liberty, Blue Spring, Good Spring, Charity, Mount Zion, Head's, and Sycamore. Heaton and Gower were joined by other elders such as William Barton and James Cherry, both of whom were selected, along with Gower, to "occupy the stand on Sabbath," preaching "to a large and attentive congregation." These churches would later become the Cumberland Free Will Baptist Association.[25]

The pressing question, however, is when did the new association make its final transition to a full Free Will Baptist confessional identity? Owing to the scarcity of records, no one knows. No minutes are extant between 1843 and 1876. It is certain that the Bethlehem Church in Ashland City, which Gower organized in 1847 as "The Separate Baptist church of Christ at Bethlehem," had by 1854 changed its name to the "Free Will Baptist Church at Bethlehem." G. V. Frey, in a brief history of the Cumberland Association written in 1911 and included in the associational minutes, said that the association adopted the Free Will Baptist name in 1851. One assumes that a copy of those minutes was available to him, but they are no longer extant.[26]

Nothing else is certain about when or why the Cumberland Separate Baptists became Free Will Baptist. Yet by 1876, the next year of extant minutes, the entire association had embraced the Free Will Baptist practice of publishing written articles of faith and affirming in those articles the possibility of apostasy of genuine believers: "We believe that the faithful Christian will never fall from grace; not withstanding: we believe in the free moral agency of man, after justification, and that there is a possible danger of falling into sin, and being finally lost." The next article read: "We believe, according to the Scriptures, Paul's letter to the Hebrews, 6th chapter, 1st to 7th verses, that after a man has been made partaker of the Holy Ghost, if he shall fall from grace, it is impossible ever to renew him again unto repentance, or restore him again into the favor of God."²⁷

The Cumberland Association would develop into one of the most influential associations in the Free Will Baptist Church. Many of the efforts toward the union of all Free Will Baptists emerged from this association. Occasionally in the late nineteenth century, there was even talk about union with the Randall movement of the North, and one year they petitioned the General Conference of the North. Yet nothing ever came of it. In 1898 H. M. Ford, the field secretary for the Free Baptists, gave a report to the northern General Conference of a visit he had made among Free Will Baptists in the South. This report demonstrates that, despite feeble attempts in the 1880s and 1890s, there was almost no relationship between Free Will Baptists in Middle Tennessee and the Randall movement:

> I have visited the General Association of the South twice, and the Cumberland Association twice, and the Western Division of the Stone Association once. These white Freewill Baptists of the South spring from different denominational ancestry than the Free Baptists of the north. There are between forty and fifty thousand of them. They are true to Free Baptist instincts, but uneducated, unsystematic, and not well organized.... These people believe intensely what they believe, and are tenacious especially of footwashing.²⁸

The Cumberland Association would grow significantly. From the original seven churches it comprised in 1843, it grew to nineteen churches by 1876. Today it has sixty member churches and stretches more than 150 miles north-to-south from Bowling Green, Kentucky, to Leoma, Tennessee, and one hundred miles east-to-west from Gallatin to Dover.²⁹

The Toe River Association

The first Free Will Baptist Association in East Tennessee was the Toe River Association. Its founding ministers were Moses Peterson, John Wheeler, and William Bonaparte Woolsey. Very little is known about the origins of these men or how or why they became Free Will Baptists. Peterson and Wheeler came out of the French Broad Baptist Association in western North Carolina. According to David Benedict, that association had split into strong Calvinist and Arminianizing factions around 1828, and by 1829 an association was formed that was later called the Big Ivy Association.³⁰

Woolsey became the most influential of these early ministers. He was born in Greene County, Tennessee, in 1821, into a Calvinist Baptist family. He married Alice Bird in 1842, the same year he was converted. He was licensed to preach in 1843 and ordained in 1847. Elder Woolsey began to question strict Calvinism as a result of his acquaintance with Peterson and Wheeler. The original group that broke with the French Broad Association appears to have still practiced closed communion. Soon, however, Peterson and Wheeler, along with Woolsey, somehow became convinced of open communion. This resulted in a new association that was both Arminian and open communionist: the Toe River Association, which was organized in November 1850 at Jack's Creek Church in Yancy County, North Carolina. Peterson was elected moderator and Woolsey clerk.[31]

Woolsey was intensely interested in education, not only for ministers but also for the poor children of his area of East Tennessee. With little formal education, he taught himself to read New Testament Greek. This high esteem for education is seen in attempts by the Toe River Association to establish a school. As early as 1858, Toe River had a committee on education, which noted in its report "the great importance of it in advancing a literary, moral, and esthetical training, and acquiring a sound evangelical literature." Thus they recommended that the association "select some suitable place in the bounds of this Association for the purpose of erecting a School-house and building up a School of high character." That dream eventually came to fruition in the establishment of Woolsey College, which was primarily a high school but also offered theological training. Woolsey donated land and timber, and a brick structure was completed in 1872, with eight classrooms and two larger auditoriums. It is not certain who influenced the early leaders of the Toe River Association or how they came by their Free Will Baptist identity. Later in the nineteenth century, they identified themselves with other Free Will Baptists in Tennessee and other parts of the South, but it is not known how early. Woolsey also read *The Morning Star*, the newspaper published by the Northern Freewill Baptists.[32]

The Toe River Association published articles of faith, a mark of the Free Will Baptists in contradistinction to the Separate Baptists. Their confession was very clear on Arminian principles, as well as open communion and the washing of the saints' feet. In 1852 a query came before the association whether "to have no articles of Faith but the Bible." However, subsequent associational minutes show that they continued to make reference to the association's confession of faith. In fact, they often directly quoted from it in the minutes to deal with questions—what they (and other associations and conferences) called queries—of faith and practice that local congregations would bring before the association. Free Will Baptists in the South universally withstood the anti-creedal trend popular in American revivalism and common among Separate Baptists as well as Disciples of Christ and Churches of Christ. By contrast, they subscribed to written confessions of faith, which they often called "creeds." The southern Free Will Baptists believed it was improper to recite creeds in public worship and affirmed that creeds and confessions were always subservient to the Bible and thus could be revised. Yet they did publish creeds and hold their ministers accountable to them, and Toe River provides an example of this.[33]

Like other Free Will Baptists in the South, the Toe River Association had a much stronger associational polity than other Baptists in this age of what Nathan Hatch calls "the democratization of American Christianity." Calvinist Baptists had never had as strong an associational polity as General and Free Will Baptists. However, some earlier Calvinist Baptists, such as those in the Philadelphia Association, were much stronger in their polity than most Baptists. This entailed careful emphasis on the ordination and care of ministers and their subscription to a confession of faith. However, as Gregory Wills discusses, the nineteenth century witnessed the decline in the authority of associations and their confessions in Baptist life. This would not characterize the Free Will Baptists of the nineteenth century. The Toe River Association, like other Free Will Baptist associations, enacted resolutions to bind the local churches and their ministers to the faith and practice of "the Free Will Baptist Church of Christ." This is how they referred to themselves—not as scattered, isolated congregations that happened to gather for fellowship from time to time. Instead, they viewed their association together in the larger "Free Will Baptist Church of Christ."[34]

One tidbit that appears in the early handwritten minutes of the Toe River Association is the following resolution from 1866: "We recommend to the Churches, to build good meeting houses." One sees two things here: First, early Free Will Baptists referred to their places of meeting not as a "church" but rather as a "meeting house." They saw the church not as the building but as the body of believers who met in the building. Second, they believed that churches should take special care to build meeting houses that were pleasing and well-constructed.[35]

The Toe River Association is also indicative of the sympathy for the Union in the Civil War that characterized many southerners in East Tennessee. Although the Toe River Association was not willing to say that holding slaves was sinful, its members did want to stay out of the Civil War, as there was strong Union sentiment in their region. Another interesting fact is that the

Toe River Association passed some anti-war resolutions after the War, in 1867 and 1868, threatening to exclude members for going to war, and petitioning the US Congress "to relieve us from military duty."[36]

By 1868 Toe River comprised thirty-two congregations. These churches would provide the nucleus of the East Tennessee movement that would expand throughout the latter nineteenth century. Some smaller associations formed out of Toe River are now extinct, such as the American and New American Associations. The American Association—aptly named at this time by a group of Unionists in the South—was established in 1868 but reunited with Toe River in 1878. They amicably separated again in 1882, however, with the daughter association taking on the name "New American Association."[37]

SOUTHWEST VIRGINIA

The existing movement of Free Will Baptists in southwest Virginia originated from the Toe River tradition. While the Randall movement had fostered several Black Freewill Baptist congregations among freed slaves in Northern Virginia after the Civil War, these were absorbed by the Northern Baptist Convention when it merged with the Free Baptist General Conference in the north in 1911. The Clinch Valley Association, earlier known as the Clinch River Association, started out of Toe River in 1876. This association, which is now part of the Virginia State Association of Free Will Baptists, exchanged corresponding delegates with Toe River. This brings up a common practice: the exchanging of visiting brethren between sister associations, in which associations would welcome and formally recognize visiting members of other associations. It is telling that these people, who had to drive horse-drawn wagons across winding, mountain dirt-roads, were eager to exchange visiting delegates between sister associations.[38]

The John Wheeler Association, which was founded in 1881, had some Tennessee churches, but most of them were in southwest Virginia with a few in western North Carolina. These churches lay to the east of those in the Clinch River Association. This association seems to have split from Toe River on account of more sympathy with the northern Free Baptists. *The Free Baptist Cyclopaedia*, a northern Free Baptist publication, described a "spirited contest" between advocates of the *Treatise* of the northern Freewill Baptists and of what they called the "John Wheeler Platform." It seems that the John Wheeler Association, ironically, sided against the "John Wheeler Platform" and adopted the northern *Treatise*. Elder Wheeler had died in 1870 and thus was unable to give his opinions on the matter. The association is a member of the present-day Virginia State Association of Free Will Baptists. That body would be founded in 1939. In addition to southwest Virginia, the Virginia State Association would consist of churches started by North Carolinians who moved to the Tidewater area and southwest Virginians who moved to Northern Virginia, both in the mid-twentieth century.[39]

UNION ASSOCIATION

The major East Tennessee association formed out of the Toe River Association in the nineteenth century was the Union Association. It was to become the largest association of East Tennessee Free Will Baptists in the twentieth century. It was founded out of Toe River and American Associations in 1872, with thirteen congregations as members. At one point, the Toe River, American, and Union Associations had sent letters of admission to the Freewill Baptist General Conference of the North. This unusual action among southern Free Will Baptists might have resulted from Unionist sentiment in East Tennessee at that time. Yet even among these associations, it was controversial, as seen in the debate over whether to adopt the Randall *Treatise* or continue on the "John Wheeler platform."

However, of the three associations, it was only the Union Association that would pursue this original plan of fellowship with the Randall movement. When the northern General Conference folded and became a part of the Northern Baptist Convention, Union stayed out. They adopted the following resolution in 1912: "Whereas the Union Association is not within the territory of the Northern Baptist Convention, but surrounded by Southern Baptists our relation to whom can in no way be effected by the proposed union between Free Baptists and Baptists of the Northern Convention, therefore Resolved, that Union Association take no action for or against the proposed union." For a while, the association changed its name to "Free Baptist," like that of the northern movement, but eventually changed it back.[40]

WESTERN NORTH CAROLINA

Historians know very little about the early history of the churches in western North Carolina, except that they were a product of the Toe River Association, which held its founding session at Jack's Creek Church in North Carolina. The records from the early history of this area of North Carolina are paltry, and very little research has been done. However, an autobiographical sketch by one of the early ministers, John H. Ballard (1844–1934), offers insight into the Free Will Baptists of this region from the mid-nineteenth through the early twentieth centuries. Ballard was converted in 1862 and had influence from Methodists, Missionary Baptists, and Free Will Baptists. Because he believed Scripture teaches baptism of believers only, by immersion, and because he was Arminian and open communionist, he felt drawn to the Free Will Baptists. He united with the Free Will Baptist church at Union Valley in Buncombe County, North Carolina, in December 1862. Despite the adherence of most southern Free Will Baptists to the Confederate cause, Ballard's loyalties in the Civil War exemplify many others of this region. Though he was drafted into the Confederate army, he and a fellow soldier deserted and "made our way through the mountains into East Tennessee, and joined the Federal army." Ballard decided that "if the South should succeed in establishing a Confederacy, I would never return to the old home again."[41]

After the war, Ballard returned to western North Carolina where he married "a young school Miss, by the name of Mattie J. Honneycutt." She was the daughter of a Free Will Baptist minister, Stephen Honneycutt, who would later lay hands on Ballard when he was ordained to the ministry in 1872. Ballard's early service at the Pensacola Church in Yancey County, North Carolina, would lay the groundwork for a long ministry of pastoring and church planting. He helped organize eight congregations. Ballard's ecumenical spirit is seen in his comment that he conducted revival meetings not only among Free Will Baptists but in "various Methodist, Baptist, and Presbyterian churches." His tutor and mentor in ministry was Presbyterian, and one of his closest friends was a Methodist who eventually asked Ballard to baptize him, after which he was ordained a Free Will Baptist minister. Ballard had been "personally acquainted with the fathers of our church," Wheeler, Peterson, and Woolsey.[42]

Stone Association

The fourth major tributary into Tennessee Free Will Baptists was the Stone Association in the Cumberland Plateau region of Tennessee. This movement had its roots in the 1850s but did not establish an association until 1865. Little is known about the religious background of Elder Corder Stone, the founder of the movement, except that he was a Baptist. The Stone Association, which now exists in Eastern and Western Divisions in Tennessee and also has sister churches in Indiana, dates to the withdrawal of Corder Stone, his son Thomas, and several other ministers from the Caney Fork Baptist Association around 1850. The Stones and their colleagues were leaning away from the strict Calvinism of Caney Fork. By 1865 they founded a new association named the "Stone Association of Christian Baptists, Church of Christ." Some observers have surmised that this was because of the movement of the Christian churches and Disciples of Christ associated with Barton Stone and Alexander and Thomas Campbell. However, as Picirilli notes, there is no evidence of this connection. It was common for Baptists and non-Baptists of all stripes to utilize formally the language of "Church of Christ" in its traditional, generic sense.[43]

The Stone Association formally became Free Will Baptist in 1886. The association already had written articles of faith that stated that "man is unable to recover himself from the fallen state that he is in by reason of sin, only by the grace of God through the exercise of faith" and that "the washing of the saints' feet" is an "ordinance of Jesus Christ." Their practice of open communion is indicated by the confession that "all members of the church of Christ have a right to the sacramental table upon the principles of their acceptance with him. . . ." In 1886 they added the following statement: "We believe according to the scriptures—Paul's letter to the Hebrews 6:1-7 and other scriptures—that after a man has been partaker of the Holy Ghost, it is possible to fall away and forever be lost."[44]

The Stone Association's full transition to a Free Will Baptist identity resulted from the efforts of John L. Welch Sr. Welch had come of age in the Stone Association and had preached in its churches in DeKalb County as a young man. About 1885, Welch moved with his family to Dickson County, Tennessee, where he united with the Cumberland Association. This led to a correspondence between the two associations, both of which took on the name "Free Will Christian Baptist" in 1886 (which Cumberland stopped using in 1920, and the Eastern Division of the Stone dropped in 1968). Some of the congregations of the Stone Association became Southern Baptist in 1918.[45]

Aside from one year when the Western Division of the Stone Association held membership in the Tennessee State Association, the Stone Association has maintained a separate existence from the Tennessee State and National Associations. Still, the Stone Association has enjoyed warm relations with other Free Will Baptists in the Middle Tennessee region. Furthermore, the Stone tradition has produced ministers who would later have an outsized influence on the larger movement. The most notable of these is John L. Welch Sr., whose son would go on to become the most important figure in the founding of the National Association in 1935. In the late twentieth century, a few Stone congregations united with the Liberty Association, which was founded in 1976 and united with the Tennessee State Association. This, in part, has caused the Liberty Association to triple its charter membership of three churches. At present there appear to be fifty-six congregations in the Eastern and Western Divisions of the Stone Association.[46]

Conclusion

It is not certain what led the founders of the five movements in the west-central and northern region of Alabama and the state of Tennessee to embrace Free Will Baptist confessional identity. If the founders of these movements knew about the existence of the others at the time of their founding, no evidence of that knowledge exists. The Mount Moriah tradition of west-central and North Alabama appears to be the only movement in the South to have originated directly from the Regular Baptists. Ellis Gore left his Regular Baptist association and traveled to North Carolina where he was ordained by Free Will Baptists, thus indicating influence from that movement. C. C. Vandiver and Robert Heaton, the founders, respectively, of the Bethlehem tradition of south-central and West Tennessee (as well as North Alabama and North Mississippi) and the Cumberland tradition of Middle Tennessee, both came from Separate Baptist backgrounds. The founders of the Toe River tradition of East Tennessee (as well as western North Carolina and southwest Virginia) had been United Baptist, while the background of the Stone tradition of the Upper Cumberland Plateau has not yet come to light. Future research will likely unearth more information about who or what influenced these traditions to embrace the full Free Will Baptist confessional identity.

Part III
THE RISE AND DECLINE OF THE NORTHERN FREEWILL BAPTISTS, 1780-1911

Six

THE RISE OF THE RANDALL MOVEMENT

The Context of the Second Great Awakening

The Second Great Awakening was the period of religious revival that swept the United States from the 1790s through the 1830s. The term "second" has been used to distinguish this time of religious revival from the Great Awakening of the mid-eighteenth century. Mark Noll's definition of the Second Great Awakening exemplifies the difficulty in pinning it down. He says that it is an "imprecise term that is usually taken to refer to a series of revivals managed by Presbyterians and Congregationalists (from the 1790s? from the early 1800s? into the 1830s?) that brought great numbers into the American churches." Noll wonders if the term should even be used, but if so, he says, it "should feature the less publicized efforts of Methodists and Baptists who did most of the work in churching and civilizing the American populace between the War for Independence and the Civil War." Paul E. Johnson makes a convincing case that the Second Great Awakening per se lasted until the late 1830s. Yet its mood continued later in the century.[1]

The revivalists of the First and Second Great Awakenings had many of the same goals, foremost of which was the salvation of souls. However, several differences distinguished the Second Great Awakening from the First. One difference was theological. Whereas the First Great Awakening had been largely conducted in a Calvinistic theological context, with the workings of the Spirit of a Sovereign God the primary focal point, the Second Great Awakening was more anti-Calvinist. Many of the leaders of the Second

Great Awakening believed that revival of religion was based on individual people responding with their free will to the gospel and its demands. With this often came a leaning toward moralism and perfectionism, an outlook that revivalists like Charles G. Finney shared with the Wesleyan and Holiness movements.[2]

Second Great Awakening revivalism also had its own set of methods called "new measures." These included emotionally intense, high-pressure altar calls and other techniques that critics believed psychologically manipulated individuals, pressing them for immediate conversion, getting them to repeat a sinner's prayer, and other techniques that featured a heightened experientialism and what critics decried as theatrics. Many of these measures coincided with the New School theology of evangelists like Finney, which downplayed human depravity, emphasizing the natural ability of men and women to respond to gospel appeals without divine grace. These new measures scandalized "old light" and "old school" Protestants, who were skeptical of what they saw as the excessive emotionalism and new evangelistic methods that characterized the revivalism of the Second Great Awakening. This involved not simply things like shouting "Amen" but practices like those described by the popular evangelist Peter Cartwright: wailing, laughing, jerking, convulsing, running, and dancing. As Cartwright reminisced: "To see those proud young gentlemen and young ladies, dressed in their silks, jewelry, and prunella, from top to toe, take the jerks, would often excite my risibilities. The first jerk or so, you would see their fine bonnets, caps, and combs fly; and so sudden would be the jerking of the head that their long loose hair would crack almost as loud as a wagoner's whip."[3]

The Second Great Awakening took place on three major fronts. The first was in New England, where men like Lyman Beecher and Nathaniel Taylor followed Timothy Dwight, president of Yale, in his non-Calvinistic "New Divinity" revivalism with its emphasis on the moral reform of individuals and society. The second was the revivalism of Charles G. Finney, which was much like that of Beecher and Taylor, and took hold in New York State, Ohio, and other parts of the Old Northwest. The third part of the movement took place on the American frontier, in both the North and South. The revival on the frontier took much of its lead from the Beecher-Taylor and Finney branches of the Second Great Awakening, making the "camp meeting" a popular "new measure."[4]

By the 1830s, the revivalistic ethos of the Second Great Awakening was well-entrenched in American culture. Its adherents desired to transform their culture into a Christian society by employing moral reform. They worked toward this transformation through a strong network of benevolent societies that were committed to such causes as ridding America of beverage alcohol, providing homes for rehabilitating prostitutes, caring for widows and orphans, alleviating poverty, and most of all, ending the institution of slavery.[5]

These evangelicals were confident that their society would indeed be transformed. This optimism was based, in large part, on the three primary theological tenets of the Second Great Awakening: anti-Calvinism, perfectionism, and millennialism. Second Great Awakening revivalism and anti-Calvinism, as Timothy L. Smith has said, "went hand in hand." The theology of the Second Great Awakening was strongly anti-Calvinistic, placing less emphasis on humanity's depravity and more emphasis on the innate ability of the individual to do good works. Thus one characteristic of the theology of the Second Great Awakening was perfectionism. Charles Finney was the chief spokesman for this view, preaching that not only should perfection for individual Christians be sought, but also perfection for all of society.[6]

Along with anti-Calvinism and perfectionism, postmillennialism had an inestimable impact on the Protestantism of this era. Postmillennial doctrine held that Christ's millennial rule on the earth would be ushered in by the perfection and Christianizing of the world by God's people. The world, it was held, would grow increasingly more righteous until Christ would return to establish his kingdom on earth. An example of the prominence of postmillennialism in evangelical social thought is found in the *Freewill Baptist Quarterly* of January 1865, in which a northern Freewill Baptist minister wrote that Christians are "duty bound to testify against prejudices which deprive [freed slaves] of their rights and equality before human law. When they are emancipated the struggle is not over. It is yet a long march to millennium." This postmillennial vision dovetailed with the stress on perfectionism. Since individual Christians could attain sinless perfection in this life, it was reasoned, and since the human will is the primary factor in bringing about moral and spiritual change, then societal perfection could be attainable through the efforts of Christians to bring about social righteousness.[7]

Northern Freewill Baptists, both in their theology and their concerns for public morality and social reform, fit very well with the revivalistic ethos of the Second Great Awakening. Indeed, in many ways, they were ahead of their time. Emerging out of the Calvinist Baptist tradition in the 1780s, Freewill Baptists had broken with the Calvinism exemplified in the Great Awakening at the beginning of the less-Calvinist Second Great Awakening. They fit the Second Great Awakening milieu, both with its anti-Calvinist, perfectionist, and millennial theology and its emphasis on public morality and social reform. Indeed, northern Freewill Baptist theology prefigured the theological emphases of the Second Great Awakening, especially anti-Calvinism and perfectionism.[8]

These doctrines, as with most evangelical revivalists of the day, provided the motivation for social reform. From the very earliest times, Freewill Baptists were active in such ventures as missions, Sabbath schools, temperance, abolition, the anti-Masonry movement, sabbatarianism, and a host of other concerns. They were also ahead of their time in the areas of women's rights and equal rights for African Americans. They were, for example, among the first in the United States to admit Black and female students into their schools. They pioneered in their efforts to establish racial equality, as is demonstrated by a resolution that passed at the first meeting of the General Conference in 1827: "Resolved, that the color of a candidate for the ministry should have no influence on his ordination, provided he be other wise qualified."[9]

This spirit is seen in the way the movement promoted the ministry of Elder Charles Bowles, a well-known Black Freewill Baptist minister. His biography, *The Life, Labors, and Travels of Elder Charles Bowles, of the Free Will Baptist Denomination, Together With an Essay on the Character and Condition of the African Race*, was widely promoted by the denomination and used in the abolition cause, especially the fight against the Fugitive Slave Act of 1850. The son of an African slave, Bowles took up residence in New Hampshire after fighting in the War for Independence. He started preaching for the Freewill Baptists in 1816 and preached throughout New England until his death in 1843 at eighty-two years of age. His biography denounced "negro-hate" and its effort "to drive the colored man from within the pale of human society."[10]

Though the Freewill Baptists of the North followed the New England "New Light" tradition as exemplified by men like Timothy Dwight of Yale, they were much more closely identified with the western revival tradition led by Charles Finney. *The Morning Star*, the official periodical of the Freewill Baptist denomination, was among the first to reprint Finney's *Revival Lectures* and was instrumental in establishing his prominence in New England. Theodore Dwight Weld, Finney's disciple and the foremost leader of the evangelical offensive against slavery, hailed the Freewill Baptists as perhaps contributing more than any other single denomination to the antislavery cause. David Marks, the foremost evangelist of the Freewill Baptist denomination and a leading antislavery activist, died at Oberlin College, the leading bastion of evangelical social reform. Finney himself, then president of Oberlin, preached Marks's funeral, hailing him as one of the greatest evangelists and reformers of the day. Northern Freewill Baptists in the middle part of the nineteenth century were indeed identified with and involved in the "Finn-eyesque" revivalistic ethos of the day.[11]

Benjamin Randall and the Origins of the Movement

The Freewill Baptist movement in the North had its beginning in the religious experience of Benjamin Randall. Born in New Castle, New Hampshire, in 1749, Randall made his home in New Hampshire his entire life, aside from his off-and-on stints as a sailor on his father's ship and a short term in the army during the Revolutionary War.[12]

Randall's Ecclesiastical Pilgrimage

During childhood and early adulthood, Randall moved through a series of stages in his religious development. William Davidson refers to these as the period of unconverted piety, the period of converted Congregationalism, the period in the Calvinistic Baptist tradition, and the period of Freewill Baptist sentiment. The turning point in Randall's religious development was the death of the famous Great Awakening evangelist George Whitefield. Earlier, Randall had heard Whitefield preach but had ignored him. On hearing of Whitefield's death, Randall recalled Whitfield's sermon and was converted. Randall joined the Congregational Church in 1773 only to leave two years later because of his disagreement with infant baptism. He and some close friends withdrew from the Congregational Church in May 1775 and joined the Baptist church at Berwick, Maine, in October 1776.[13]

The church at Berwick, like the vast majority of Baptist churches in New England at that time, was strongly Calvinistic. Randall soon publicly questioned the predestinarianism he encountered there, speaking out not only about the freedom to resist divine grace but also about his belief in the universality of Christ's atonement and provision of grace. He came under harsh criticism and was soon excommunicated by the Berwick Church for his adherence to Arminian principles. From there he was invited by a group of Baptists to New Durham, New Hampshire, where he went in March 1778 and eventually established the first Freewill Baptist church in the North in 1780. Randall began preaching his free will doctrine throughout New Hampshire and Maine, and soon other Freewill Baptist congregations formed. Several quarterly meetings were started, and churches were established in Vermont, Massachusetts, and other areas of New England.[14]

In his excellent scholarly biography of Randall, Scott Bryant argues that the early northern Freewill Baptists, as exemplified by Randall, served as a bridge movement between the First and Second Great Awakenings. Of course, the primary difference between Randall and his New England religious counterparts was his brand of Arminianism. Bryant argues correctly, yet in contradistinction to previous historians, that Randall was never a predestinarian Calvinist, citing Randall's statement that he never knew anything about Calvin's doctrine of election. Thus Randall did not go through a predestinarian phase, as historians had concluded. According to Bryant, Randall was theologically naive when he first began preaching: "Randall wrongly assumed that he was theologically in line with his Baptist peers. He recounted, 'As the doctrine of Calvin had not been in dispute among us, I had not considered whether I believed it or not.'" When asked on one occasion early in his ministry why he did not preach predestinarian Calvinist doctrine, Randall responded plainly, "Because I do not believe it." Previous historians have concluded that, because Randall left the Congregational Church and became a Regular Baptist, he had, during that period, accepted the Calvinist theology of those two denominations. Yet Bryant succeeds in showing that Randall never saw himself as a predestinarian Calvinist.[15]

Bryant's portrayal of the Arminianism of Randall and his colleagues, while accurate on the whole, does not delve into the nuances of Arminian thought in the seventeenth and eighteenth centuries. Bryant discusses only the doctrines all Arminians have in common: universal atonement, predestination conditioned on God's foreknowledge, the resistibility of divine calling and grace, and the possibility of apostatizing from the faith. However, his treatment does not explore important features of Randall's Arminianism that are closer to Wesleyan thought than to the views of his southern counterparts and their General Baptist ancestors.

Randall's Experientialism

Another difference between Randall and his southern counterparts was his heightened experientialism. Before his conversion, Bryant explains, Randall was an Old Light critic of Whitefield, seeing much of New Light revivalism as "delusion" and "enthusiasm." Randall recounted that he had viewed the Great Awakening preachers as "breaking up churches—frightening the people—And that their earnest and loud preaching, was only designed to make the people cry out, and make a noise." Yet Randall's conversion brought about an acceptance of the experientialism he had once criticized. Bryant highlights this, showing that, early on, Randall rooted his Arminian theological views in a supernatural vision he said he experienced when he was converted.

Bryant notes that Randall's original church covenant that he wrote for his first church in New Durham, New Hampshire, emphasized "the power of the Holy Spirit to teach and lead the congregation." Bryant argues that this view was different from that of the Calvinist Baptists, who did not allow "for the possibility of the Holy Spirit leading outside of what is already established in Scripture." Thus Bryant infers that Randall made his own experience a source of revelation or theological truth alongside Scripture.[16]

However, there is no reason to infer this from Randall's writings. His views are evidenced by his statement in his church covenant: "We promise to practice all the commands of and the ordinances of the New Testament of our Lord and Savior Jesus Christ, so far as they are or shall be made known unto us by the light of the Holy Spirit of truth, without which, we are sensible, we cannot attain to the true knowledge thereof." Bryant attempts to contrast Randall's view with the Calvinistic Second London Confession (1689), which said, "The whole Councel of God concerning all things necessary for his own Glory, Mans Salvation, Faith and Life, is either expressly set down or necessarily contained in the Holy Scripture; unto which nothing at any time is to be added, whether by new Revelation of the Spirit, or traditions of men." However, there is nothing in Randall's covenant that suggests that he believed in new revelation. The "light of the Spirit" of which he spoke, which makes known the "commands" and "ordinances of the New Testament," is, as all the early Freewill Baptists of the North taught, the Spirit speaking in Scripture.[17]

Doubtless, Randall and some of his pietistic early followers in the north did place more emphasis on mystical experience, such as Randall's own cornfield experience, a second work of grace, and other supernatural phenomena that would embarrass later more rationalistic Freewill Baptists in the mid- to-late nineteenth century. However, they stopped short of asserting that private experience is on par with Scripture.

Still, the differences between Randall and the southern Free Will Baptists concerning experientialism are very striking. As noted in chapter 2, one of the chief criticisms of the eighteenth-century New Light Calvinist Regular Baptists regarding the General Baptists (later dubbed "Free Will Baptists") in Carolina was that the latter were not experiential enough. As John Crowley explains, it was likewise commonplace for the Calvinistic Separate Baptists to require, before baptism, an experience of grace consisting of dramatic visions and dreams. This is precisely what Bryant describes of Randall, which would have been expected, given Randall's context as being a part of the Separate Baptist milieu in New England. But the lack of an experiential approach to conversion and church membership is precisely what the Philadelphia

Association Baptists criticized the southern Free Will Baptists for, accusing many of them of being unconverted. However, later southern Free Will Baptist leaders such as R. K. Hearn defended their practice, arguing that such an approach to conversion was not warranted in the New Testament and was not apostolic in origin.[18]

This understanding of experientialism in Randall also dislodges Bryant's notion of Randall's experientialism as somehow being radically different in character from the Calvinistic Baptists of his day. On the contrary, Randall's vision was commonplace among the Calvinistic Separates, even though his southern General Baptist counterparts would not have countenanced it. Indeed, when Elias Hutchins, a Randall Freewill Baptist, traveled among some of the southern Free Will Baptists in the 1830s, he sold them some hymnals, and one of the hymns spoke positively of New Light revivalism. Hearn, the leading minister and historian of the North Carolina Free Will Baptists in the nineteenth century, stated, "The hymn, which commends all New Lights . . . was read by the purchasers with grief and almost indignant astonishment."[19]

Randall shared Arminian views with other Baptist ministers at the time, such as Edward Lock and Tosier Lord, who participated in his ordination service. Thus Randall had co-laborers in the founding of the Freewill Baptist movement in New England. Randall began to be persecuted for his Arminian theology because it was so rare in New England in his day. This caused him to doubt his theological convictions. Then, in June 1780 he had what later became known as his "cornfield experience." "Prior to this mystical experience, Randall had difficulty reconciling the passages of the opponents with his own theology," Bryant explains.

> Randall then experienced a revelation that enlightened him on how the passages of the opponents could in fact be consistent with his own personal theology. The spiritual authority of this trance-like experience did not supercede that of the scriptures, but it did enable him to reconcile his theology with the scripture. Even a spiritual revelation directly from God in the form of his vision could not keep Randall from recognizing the authority of the scriptures as the rule for faith and practice of the Christian tradition.[20]

Randall's doctrine and practice laid the foundation for a new Freewill Baptist movement that would radiate out from New Hampshire to every corner of New England, then from there to the frontier of the Old Northwest.

The Early Growth of the Randall Movement

The growth of the northern Freewill Baptist movement in the early nineteenth century was phenomenal. By 1827, the year in which the Freewill Baptist General Conference first gathered, Randall's initial group of churches had grown to nearly three hundred congregations with a total membership of more than sixteen thousand. These churches were members of twenty-five quarterly meetings that represented to the newly formed General Conference. The Freewill Baptists moved west, expanded rapidly, and continued to preach their gospel of free grace, free salvation, free will, and free communion. By the 1830s, the Freewill Baptist General Conference supported two schools, a printing establishment, and a periodical, *The Morning Star*. The 1830s was also a time of increasing involvement in mission endeavors, with the Freewill Baptist Foreign Mission Society established in 1833 and the Freewill Baptist Home Mission Society founded in 1834. The denomination grew rapidly during the 1830s, and by 1835 the number of congregations in the General Conference had grown to 434, with a total membership of 33,876.[21]

Institution Building

The Morning Star and the Freewill Baptist Printing Establishment

The first institutions the northern Freewill Baptists fostered centered on getting the word out about the faith and practice of the denomination as well as news of its developing ministry. The first major church-wide vehicle for communication was a weekly newspaper called *The Morning Star*, and often, for short, the *Star*. The Freewill Baptist Printing Establishment grew out of this periodical. It began publication in Limerick, Maine, in 1826, under the direction of Elder John Buzzell, who had formerly published the *Religious Magazine*. A few years after its first issue, Elder William Burr wrote an article about the need for the denomination to publish its own books. Eventually this idea gained the interest of the illustrious preacher David Marks, who promoted the idea and in 1831 was named the agent of a "Book Concern." Its first published books included copies of the English General Baptist J. G. Pike's *The Character of Christ*. A year later, the owners of *The Morning Star* agreed to sell the paper to the General Conference.[22]

After Marks's resignation in 1835, the Book Concern and the *Star* merged. It was agreed that Dover, New Hampshire, would be the location for the publishing house, but the New Hampshire Legislature, wary of the antislavery stance of the *Star*, balked at granting a charter. Eventually the charter was granted, and in 1846 the Book Concern changed its name to the Freewill Baptist Printing Establishment. It would operate exclusively in Dover until 1887, when it relocated to Boston. It continued operation until September 1911. That year, as part of the merger with the Northern Baptists, it transferred its assets to the American Baptist Publication Society, and *The Morning Star* merged with the Northern Baptist periodical *The Watchman*.[23]

The Freewill Baptist Foreign Mission Society

Foreign mission work among the northern Freewill Baptists began in 1832, when English General Baptist missionary Amos Sutton wrote a letter to *The Morning Star* asking for help from his like-minded brothers and sisters for his mission in Puri, Orissa, India. This led *Morning Star* publisher John Buzzell, Hosea Quinby, and others to host a discussion about establishing a foreign missionary society. They formed the society and incorporated it with the Maine Legislature the next January, and by March they had chosen a name for the new organization, the Freewill Baptist Foreign Mission Society. The society elected Buzzell as its first president, a post he held for thirteen years.[24]

The society was governed by a fifteen-member executive board elected by its membership, which consisted of churches that donated at least $100 annually and individuals who donated at least $20 annually. Churches were allowed one voting delegate, and individuals presumably had a vote. This was at a time when $100 would be equivalent to more than $3,000 today. After Sutton traveled to the United States in 1834 to preach, Elder David Marks said in *The Morning Star*, "How criminal has been our ignorance and neglect of this holy enterprise, and how wonderful that providence which has illumined our darkness!" Sutton took the job of corresponding secretary for the society, which he held for one year. These initiatives laid the foundation for an engaged foreign mission ministry among the Northern Freewill Baptists. In 1883, the name was changed to the Free Baptist Foreign Mission Society.[25]

The mission field of the Freewill Baptists was India, in the districts of Midnapore and Balasore. The first missionary the society selected was Jeremiah Phillips. He had walked 150 miles to hear Sutton speak in Guilford, New Hampshire. When the offering plate was passed, $100 was raised, but more significant was a piece of paper Phillips placed in the plate, which read, "I give myself." The first ship to sail for India in 1835 had Phillips and his new wife Mary on it.[26]

The other Freewill Baptist couple on board were Eli and Clementina Noyes. In addition to his reputation as a missionary and evangelist, Noyes was an accomplished scholar who would go on to publish a Hebrew language reader, a book on apologetics, and another book on Hindu mythology. These two families ministered against all odds in the first years of their mission. One of Eli and Clementina Noyes's children died, and Jeremiah Phillips lost Mary and their firstborn child. Yet Phillips and the Noyeses continued laboring diligently and had their first convert in 1839. They laid the groundwork for a strong Freewill Baptist mission work that would continue as long as the denomination existed. When the denomination merged with the Northern Baptist Convention, the society dissolved and transferred its assets to the American Baptist Foreign Mission Society.[27]

The Freewill Baptist Home Mission Society

The year after the formation of the Foreign Mission Society, David Marks called for the establishment of a Freewill Baptist Home Mission Society, which was founded in 1834 in Dover, New Hampshire. Like the Printing Establishment, at first the Home Mission Society encountered difficulty being granted a charter from the New Hampshire Legislature, owing to the Freewill Baptists' strong antislavery stance. Eventually, however, a formal charter was granted in 1838. Marks was on the first board. While several men served as president, the ones who gave the society its vision and character were William Burr and Silas Curtis. Burr served as treasurer from 1834 to 1866, and Curtis served as corresponding secretary from 1839 to 1869. Jonathan Woodman was another early influential leader in the society, serving as its first missionary. The work of the society's home missionaries consisted of both "organizing" and "strengthening" churches. Home missionaries would also start schools, and schoolteachers would go as missionaries to staff these academies. In addition to New England, in the early years, the society sent missionaries to the frontiers of Nova Scotia, Ohio, Michigan, Illinois, and Indiana.[28]

In the 1840s through the 1860s, the society opened mission fields in Iowa, Minnesota, and Wisconsin. In the later nineteenth century, fields were opened in Quebec, Pennsylvania, Nebraska, Virginia, West Virginia, Louisiana, Missouri, South Dakota, California, Washington, and Texas. In Virginia, West Virginia, Louisiana, and Texas, most of the missions revolved around planting churches among freed slaves. One such work resulted in the establishment of Storer College, an institution of higher learning for freed slaves in Harpers Ferry, West Virginia. The Freewill Baptist Home Mission Society, more than any other force, aided the expansion and westward migration of the northern Freewill Baptists into the frontier. Because of its efforts, Freewill Baptists would become a major force in the religious life of the Old Northwest, even establishing colleges in Michigan and Ohio that would be major centers of learning in those states. The society continued operation until the merger with the Northern Baptist Convention, when the society dissolved and transferred its assets to the American Baptist Home Mission Society.[29]

Northern Freewill Baptist Higher Education

PARSONFIELD ACADEMY

Many of the earliest northern Freewill Baptist preachers were characterized by an anti-intellectual spirit. The denomination, however, began to see the need for ministerial education as its members' socioeconomic level increased, its borders expanded south and west, its social reform engagement widened, and its institutions formed and grew. Elder John Buzzell, the publisher of *The Morning Star*, probably the most influential early leader of the movement after Randall, opposed formal education for the ministry, as did his "Buzzellite" followers. Thus it is ironic that he founded the first Freewill Baptist educational institution, Parsonfield Academy, in North Parsonfield, Maine, in 1832. Yet Parsonfield provided general education, not theological education. The school was endorsed by the General Conference beginning in 1832. Buzzell was president of the board, and distinguished northern Freewill Baptist leaders such as Hosea Quinby, John Fullonton, and Oren B. Cheney served as early principals. Parsonfield's success led to the founding of a number of other such academies among the New England Freewill Baptists. The Strafford (later Austin) Academy, was founded in New Hampshire in 1834, and the Smithville Seminary was started in 1839.[30]

Unsurprisingly, the upsurge in classical high school education among Freewill Baptist youth in New England led to young ministerial candidates' desiring theological education. Thus many of them began attending colleges, divinity schools, and seminaries of other denominations. This state of affairs led Elders John Chaney, Silas Curtis, Dexter Waterman, and John J. Butler, in an 1839 article in *The Morning Star*, to call for a convention to discuss ministerial education. Despite vociferous opposition from the "Buzzellites," a Freewill Baptist Education Society was formed in 1840.[31]

THE BIBLICAL SCHOOL

The society tried to get a theological department at Parsonfield off the ground, but Buzzell's opposition made it unsustainable. So they moved the fledgling operation to Dracut (present-day Lowell), Massachusetts, in 1842. Though the Biblical School, as it was named, was designed for college graduates, those who had not graduated from college would be admitted if they could prove that their preparation in mathematics, history, philosophy, and composition was sufficient to succeed in the three-year postgraduate program. The Biblical School moved again in 1844, this time to Whitesboro, New York, partnering with an existing school there.[32]

Soon the leadership began to think it was unfeasible to aim the school's education at college graduates. Thus the rigorous Greek and Hebrew requirements were placed in the third year, meaning that many of the early students, who left before completing the three-year course, received no instruction in the original biblical languages. Two of the most distinguished Freewill Baptist scholars would start their teaching careers at Parsonfield: John J. Butler and Joseph Fullonton. The school was relocated to New Hampton, New Hampshire, in 1854, and was affiliated with a Freewill Baptist academy there called the New Hampton Literary Institution. Finally it made its fifth and last move, in 1870, to Bates College, the Freewill Baptist institution in Lewiston, Maine, where it became that institution's theological school and was renamed Cobb Divinity School. Other academies with limited theological studies included Geauga Seminary, founded by Ransom Dunn and others in Ohio in 1844 but merged with Hillsdale College in Michigan in 1854. However, in the 1840s and 1850s, institutions of higher learning were started to meet the increasing demands of the northern Freewill Baptist churches.[33]

HILLSDALE COLLEGE

Hillsdale College was the first full-fledged baccalaureate-level institution established by the Freewill Baptists that today would be thought of as collegiate level. Hillsdale's beginnings can be traced to Michigan Central College, an academy started in 1844 by the Michigan Yearly Meeting in Spring Arbor, Michigan, which evolved into a full college. The school opened with eight students and had increased to three hundred by the early 1850s. In those years the administration and trustees began to sense the inadequacy of the facilities and the infeasibility of expanding the campus in Spring Arbor. Thus they began looking at alternate locations. The town of Hillsdale, Michigan, was chosen early in 1853, and the last classes were taught in Spring Arbor in the spring of 1854.[34]

The town of Hillsdale raised some of the funds to help the college relocate there, and college leaders set about raising most of the capital needed to build the campus and make the move. The Freewill Baptist people began to see that an excellent institution of higher learning was central to their future. From wealthy to poor, they sacrificed to see the campus built and the college relocated. As the *Free Baptist Cyclopaedia* said, "From log houses, from shanties, from homes destitute, not only of the luxuries but often of some of the necessities of life, came the first endowment of Hillsdale." The college opened in newly constructed buildings on a twenty-five-acre parcel of land donated by one of Hillsdale's citizens, and classes opened in the fall of 1855. Soon several endowed professorships were created. The Freewill Baptist Printing Establishment gave the lion's share of the funds for the Burr Professorship of Pastoral and Systematic Theology, named for longtime editor of *The Morning Star*, William Burr. The Central Association funded the Marks Professorship of Ecclesiastical History, named for Elder David Marks. There were also endowed professorships of mathematics, Latin, and Christian Metaphysics and Theology.[35]

Many credited trustee and theology professor Ransom Dunn for keeping the college alive during the devastating years of the Civil War, when it incurred great financial losses. (Dunn would go on to serve as Hillsdale's president from 1884 to 1886.) Tragedy struck in 1874 when two of the buildings were destroyed by fire. Later that year the college unveiled its fundraising plan for the campus reconstruction, relying on "the general patronage and the confidence of the people, and especially our Churches. . . . A burnt-out college must be restored, and we expect our ministry, our church membership, our old subscribers, our alumni, our former students, and all our friends wherever our necessities shall be made known, to bear some part in the work." The Hillsdale constituency rallied, and the college got back on a firm footing and continued its growth throughout the rest of the century.[36]

Unlike most colleges of the day, Hillsdale from the start accepted students regardless of race or sex. When Ransom Dunn gave a speech to a gathering of Hillsdale citizens, he said, "One thing must be distinctly understood, and that is that the school from the first is to be a denominational one, but not sectarian, furnishing no special advantages to any denomination, nor refusing favor to any. Neither does it propose to make distinctions on the ground of sex or color. While there is at this time no intention to teach a denominational theology, we do intend to make the college strongly religious." Despite the fact that the theology department claimed not to teach denominational theology, many Freewill Baptist ministers received their education at Hillsdale. The social reform aims of the northern Freewill Baptists, from antislavery to temperance to efforts to alleviate poverty, support the reform of prostitutes, and establish orphanages were at the center of Hillsdale's character. The institution continued to prosper until it was absorbed by the Northern Baptist Convention. After that it continued to grow in its offerings and influence. In the latter half of the twentieth century, it would become involved with the growing conservative movement within the Republican Party. By the beginning of the twenty-first century, it would earn the reputation of being one of the country's leading conservative higher education institutions, providing a nerve center for the intellectual right in the United States.[37]

BATES COLLEGE AND COBB DIVINITY SCHOOL

Bates College, another significant higher education institution of the northern Freewill Baptists, was chartered as Maine State Seminary in 1855. The primary figure behind the founding of the institution was President Oren B. Cheney, a Freewill Baptist minister who had graduated from Dartmouth and who molded Bates for its first four decades. When the trustees gathered in July 1863, they voted to make the academy a college. They also changed the institution's name to Bates College, after the Hon. Benjamin E. Bates, from whom Cheney had solicited a very large gift to see the college and the city of Lewiston, Maine, in which it was located, prosper. Bates obtained a new charter in 1864. From its beginning Bates was open to students of both sexes and all races. This was very unusual for the 1850s and 1860s, in both the North and South. Aside from Middlebury in Vermont, which graduated its first Black graduate in 1823, and Bowdoin in Maine, which had one Black graduate before 1864, almost no colleges enrolled students unless they were White. Bates College had the strong imprint of O. B. Cheney, who remained president until 1894, when George Colby Chase succeeded him.[38]

Bates was, like its sister college Hillsdale, deeply committed to religious social reform. This resulted in the college's admissions policies regarding sex and race. In addition to antislavery, the campus was a center for the temperance movement, for efforts to help women leave prostitution, to alleviate poverty, and to raise orphaned children. Foreign missions was also a major thrust at Bates. The northern Freewill Baptists' heightened emphasis on religious social reform also resulted in strict "rules and regulations which the Trustees have adopted." The first catalog after the name change and relocation in 1863 stipulated, for example, that students were to attend "public worship twice on the Sabbath." No student, "when in the city," was to use guns or gunpowder "without permission from some member of the faculty." Students were prohibited from the use of "any intoxicating liquors as a beverage," and no student was to "chew, smoke, or snuff tobacco." Furthermore, students were not allowed to engage in "violation of the Sabbath" and were to abstain "from cardplaying, from visiting bowling alleys and billiard saloons, from attending balls and dancing schools, and, in general, to observe all the laws of common social morality." Male and female students could not "walk or ride in company without special permission," and they could meet only "at such times and places as may be designated by the faculty."[39]

As noted above, the Biblical School merged with Bates in 1870, being renamed Cobb Divinity School. Bates grew into one of the most prestigious colleges in New England. It gradually grew more secularized and less conservative in its religious outlook, continuing that trajectory at an even swifter pace after the merger with the Northern Baptists in 1911. Ironically, the two most important northern Freewill Baptist educational institutions would go on in the twentieth century to earn the reputation of being one of the most progressive colleges in America (Bates) and one of its most conservative (Hillsdale). Later in the century, the northern Free Baptists would establish other colleges: Rio Grande College was founded in 1876 in southern Ohio, and in 1890 Keuka College was established in New York.[40]

Women's Endeavors among the Northern Freewill Baptists

The Freewill Baptists of the North were at the forefront of promoting women's leadership in ministry in the nineteenth century. The Female Mission Society was the first organization dedicated to the service of northern Freewill Baptist women. It formed at the General Conference's 1847 session in Sutton, Vermont. Its primary purpose was to galvanize Freewill Baptist women in the support of home and foreign missions and to aid in women's spiritual formation. In 1865 the society changed its name to the Free Baptist Female Systematic Beneficence Society and finally, in 1873, became the Free Baptist Woman's Missionary Society.[41]

After 1873, the society gained the right to send and support its own missionaries, which were approved by the Free Baptist Foreign Mission Society board. Miss Susan R. Libby was the society's first missionary in 1874. The society's missionaries established schools and an orphanage, spreading the gospel in the Balasore and Midnapore districts of India. By 1883, O. B. Cheney had worked to gain a charter for the organization, granted by the Maine Legislature. Woman's Missionary Society chapters were formed in most quarterly and yearly meetings, and by the late 1880s, 250 such chapters were members of the organization. Outside India, a major field of endeavor for the society was work among freed slaves, especially at Storer College in West Virginia, at which the society opened Myrtle Hall, a boarding house for young women, and Anthony Hall, a building with classrooms, a chapel, and a library.[42]

These societies were born out of an extremely active women's movement among northern Freewill Baptists, which distinguished it not only from its southern Free Will Baptist counterpart but also from most other denominations of this period.[43] Among the northern Freewill Baptists, female exhorters appeared surprisingly early. Mary Savage is perhaps the earliest example of a female exhorter among the northern Freewill Baptists. She is known to have been an active preacher, if unordained, in New Durham, New Hampshire, the birthplace of the northern Freewill Baptists, as early as 1791. In 1792, Sally Parsons, to her father's initial dismay (he was eventually converted and supported her Christian faith), professed faith and united with the Freewill Baptists. In 1797, there is a record of the collection of an offering at the New Durham Yearly Meeting to buy her a horse, saddle, and bridle so that she could travel as a Freewill Baptist exhorter. Four years later she married one of Benjamin Randall's sons, Benjamin Walton Randall. Nineteenth-century Freewill Baptist historian I. D. Stewart explained that in 1796, a committee chaired by the elder Benjamin Randall moderated a dispute in a congregation in the Farmington Quarterly Meeting in Maine about women preaching publicly. Stewart reported that the committee "soon satisfied all present of its Scriptural propriety, and this decision was placed on the Quarterly Meeting records."[44]

Perhaps the most notable of the early preachers among northern Freewill Baptist women was Clarissa H. Danforth. Converted in 1809 after hearing the famed Freewill Baptist evangelist John Colby preach, she began preaching in her native Rhode Island by 1819 and conducted evangelistic campaigns in Massachusetts, New Hampshire, and Vermont. "Her labors were not confined to the Freewill Baptists," Stewart remarked, "but 'almost all the houses of worship in that region were opened for her, and ministers and people in multitudes flocked to hear, and listened with deep emotion.'" After marrying Danford Richmond, she preached less, but still exhorted occasionally.[45]

Stewart explained that though a "few" Freewill Baptist women had "felt themselves called to this work in different periods of our early history," and "some in the denomination could give them no encouragement," others thought "that women were truly called of God to the work." However, he noted, writing in 1862, "This number has greatly diminished in later years, so that now it doubtless constitutes a small minority."[46]

Danforth does not appear to have been licensed to preach by the New England Freewill Baptists. However, the northern Freewill Baptists of Wisconsin and Iowa licensed at least one woman to preach, Ruby Bixby, whom the Freewill Baptist Home Mission Society in 1846 commissioned with her husband as a home missionary, but she was not ordained as an elder. However, a Freewill Baptist congregation in Clayton County, Iowa, listed her as its minister from 1849 to 1877. It appears that the first Baptist woman to be formally ordained was M. A. Brennan, whom a Freewill Baptist church in Pennsylvania recognized as its minister. She was ordained in the Belle Vernon Freewill Baptist Church in Fayette County, Pennsylvania, in 1876. The second was Lura Maines, whom the annual reports of two Freewill Baptist congregations in Michigan indicate was ordained in the late 1870s. The northern Freewill Baptists led the way in the ordination of women; the first Northern Baptist woman to be ordained, for example, was May Jones of Puget Sound, Washington, who was not ordained until 1882.[47]

The Freewill Baptists' Socioeconomic Background

An examination of the socioeconomic and political background of the Northern Freewill Baptists demonstrates that they fit the profile of evangelical reform groups in the antebellum North. Like other leaders of the religious social reform movements, most northern Freewill Baptists in the first five decades of the denomination's existence were from New England. The rank and file of New England Freewill Baptist churches were in a higher socioeconomic stratum than that of the average New Englander. Unlike the southern Free Will Baptists, the early northern Freewill Baptists, as Davidson notes, "drew from the more wealthy elements of society and most often their churches were to be found within the city limits of the hill towns of northern New Hampshire and Southern Maine."[48]

That Freewill Baptists were at the higher end of the socioeconomic spectrum in the small towns of New England is seen in the following chart from Stephen Marini's *Radical Sects of Revolutionary New England*. The chart, based on data from the town inventory for New Durham, New Hampshire, in 1784, compares the property holdings of the Freewill Baptists who lived in New Durham, New Hampshire, to those of the townspeople of New Durham, per capita (see Table 1 below). Men like Shadrack Allard, Ebenizer Bickford, Colonel Thomas Tash, and Joseph Boody—all wealthier citizens of New Durham—were members of the Freewill Baptist church. Tash had two years previously been elected to the New Hampshire state House of Representatives. "In a hill town like New Durham," Marini notes, "early settlers like Tash, Bickford, Allard, and Boody constituted the social and economic infrastructure. Through their carefully calibrated evangelism, Benjamin Randel and other Freewill itinerants were able to attract such leaders as well as average subsistence farmers, creating a sectarian community of respect-

Table 1

	Oxen	Cows	Horses	Tillage	Mowing	Pasture	Wild
Freewill Baptists	2	1.67	2.75	1.22	4.6	1.88	90.3
New Durham Per Capita	1.15	1.57	1.33	1.1	3.15	2.25	83.35

able rural citizens." Freewill Baptist life continued in much the same way for the first five decades of the denomination's existence, with the Freewill Baptists reaching out to the subsistence farmers as well as the upper crust of the small towns of New England and, eventually, the rest of the North.[49]

Antislavery as an Illustration of Their Social Reform Thrust

Northern Freewill Baptist political convictions were strongly tied to the moral and social reform causes they embraced. Though at first the Freewill Baptist General Conference tried to avoid mixing church and politics, the Freewill Baptists eventually became politically outspoken. Early in the nineteenth century, most Freewill Baptists were Democrats, but later they made the transition to the Free Soil Party and eventually to the new Republican Party. For the northern Freewill Baptists, their moral concerns transcended the question of party affiliation. Freewill Baptist politicians in fact abandoned the traditional party system when it did not suit their social reform-oriented needs and goals. For example, John P. Hale, who had tried to run for the Senate as a Democrat only to be suppressed by party leaders because of his strong antislavery sentiments, was elected in the 1846 race as an Independent Democrat. He was voted into office by Whigs, Democrats, and Liberty Party adherents alike. The antislavery question clearly transcended the problem of party affiliation in this instance.[50]

Northern Freewill Baptist political positions were consistent with the moral convictions they believed so strongly should be upheld in society. With this motivation, Freewill Baptists would be leaders in the evangelical-revivalist efforts at social reform in the antebellum period. The movement's commitment to the cause of antislavery provides the most accurate illustration of their dedication to social reform.

> It gives me great pleasure to mention one Christian denomination somewhat numerous in parts of New England, as well as in other states, that deserves to be excepted from the censures I have been compelled to bestow upon the rest. I allude to the Freewill Baptists, who, from the beginning, refused to receive slave-holders into communion, and most of whom were prompt to espouse the doctrine of immediate emancipation.[51]

Oliver Johnson, in his biography of the abolitionist William Lloyd Garrison, used these words to express the great debt the northern abolitionist movement owed to the small but influential Freewill Baptist denomination. The northern Freewill Baptists were, along with the Quakers, the first of the few strong antislavery denominations that paved the way for much of the abolitionist movement in and outside New England. With their New England base and their Arminian, evangelical, and revivalist theology, the Freewill Baptists armed themselves for mortal combat with the social and moral evils of the day, chief of which was the "peculiar institution," slavery.

This antislavery stance affected every aspect of church life. The satirical hymn below, which appeared in the 1851 edition of *Sacred Melodies*, a popular Freewill Baptist hymnal, illustrates the northern Freewill Baptists' deeply held sentiments about slavery.

> My country! 'tis of thee,
> Strong hold of slavery,
>   Of thee I sing:
> Land where my fathers died,
> Where men man's rights deride,
> From every mountain side
>   Thy deeds shall ring.
>
> My native country! thee,
> Where all men are born free,
>   If white their skin:
> I love thy hills and dales,
> Thy mounts and pleasant vales,
> But hate thy Negro sales,
>   As foulest sin.

> Let wailing swell the breeze,
> And ring from all the trees,
> > The black man's wrong;
> Let every tongue awake
> Let bond and free partake,
> Let rocks their silence break,
> > The sound prolong.
>
> Our fathers' God! to thee,
> Author of liberty,
> > To thee we sing;
> Soon may our land be bright,
> With holy freedom's right
> Protect us by thy might,
> > Great God, our King.[52]

Though Freewill Baptists were among the first denominations to take a strong stand for the immediate emancipation of slaves, it was not until the 1830s that the Freewill Baptist antislavery movement began gaining ground. The denomination's long-held belief in racial equality is evidenced in a resolution passed at the first meeting of the Freewill Baptist General Conference in 1827: "Resolved, that the color of a candidate for the ministry should have no influence on his ordination, provided he be otherwise qualified."[53] The northern Freewill Baptists were also among the first to admit African Americans and women to their schools. A graduate of Oneida Institute in New York, commenting on Whitestown Seminary, a Freewill Baptist school begun in 1841, stated:

> The school will be open to candidates for the ministry of all denominations and of ALL COLORS free of a slaveocratic cast. Here young men looking forward to the work of the ministry, can study theology without having the font out of which they drink polluted with a slaveholding spirit. Whitestown Seminary is the only school of a high order in this state, that is conducted upon the anti-slavery principle.[54]

Still, many northern Freewill Baptists were wary of mixing church and politics. *The Morning Star* remained silent on the issue during the first seven years of its existence because the editors were afraid of a church owned and operated paper's becoming too involved in politics. Many of *The Morning Star*'s readers had warned the paper against taking political stances. Soon, however, the Freewill Baptists began to distinguish between "regular" politics (i.e., party politics) and the political implications of Christian moral concerns. Antislavery, they reasoned, fell into the latter category. Thus the *Star* began to take an unequivocal abolitionist stance, speaking out for total, immediate emancipation of the slaves. "In June, 1834, the New Hampshire Yearly Meeting endorsed its [*The Morning Star*'s] position, and recommended it to the patronage of all 'brethren and friends.'" *The Morning Star*, therefore, became the most important agent in disseminating the antislavery platform to the Freewill Baptist public.[55]

At the 1835 General Conference, which met at Byron, New York, there was much discussion on abolition. The delegates resolved that slavery was "an unjust infringement on the dearest rights of the slave." They further resolved that "as Christians and philanthropists, we ought to exert our influence to induce all slaveholders to use their best exertions, in their respective states, to procure the abolition of slavery," and that Christians should pray fervently that slavery be abolished.[56] These resolutions stopped short of the forceful positions that various quarterly and yearly meetings had taken, as well as the strong stance of the *Star* and the even stronger position that would be taken by the General Conference in subsequent years.[57]

A year later, trouble arose. In June 1836, the trustees of the Freewill Baptist Printing Establishment applied for the second time to the New Hampshire Legislature for the incorporation of the printing establishment but were refused because of the abolitionist stance of *The Morning Star*. Many people within and outside the denomination became displeased with the *Star*'s position. Some thought it too political while others simply disagreed with the concept of immediate emancipation. Many people, both Freewill Baptists and non-Freewill Baptists, refused to renew their subscriptions unless a different position was taken with regard to the slavery question. The Printing Establishment, however, continued its unflagging support of abolition. A similar set of circumstances had prevailed for the Freewill Baptist Home Mission Society. "For several years the act of incorporation was refused the Home Mission Society lest, as was then said, it would send forth 'missionaries to preach abolition.'"[58]

Against this backdrop, the General Conference of 1837 issued strong statements that differed radically from the resolutions made just two years earlier at Byron, New York. The first resolution reiterated the long-held northern

Freewill Baptist tradition of not mixing religion and politics while at the same time reaffirming the strong antislavery stance. This resolution regarded the abolitionist position that had been taken by *The Morning Star*.

> (1.) Resolved, that the Morning Star should be strictly what it purports to be, a religious paper.
>
> (2.) Resolved, That we approve the course which the Star has taken on the subject of Slavery, inasmuch as we do not consider this a political subject, but a crying sin and a great moral evil, and we recommend that it continue the same mild but decided course.
>
> (3.) Resolved, That religion and religious subjects should be kept separate from the political party politics of the day; and we approve the course which the Star is taking in this respect, and recommend to the editor that, in his selections of summary news and the doings of Congress, he take that course which shall give no just cause of offence to any one, or to show that he favors any one political party more than another--also, that he in no case publish, as editorial, any thing that can be properly or justly construed to have political bearing.
>
> (4.) Resolved, That it is the duty of all religious men to withhold their suffrages from all immoral, intemperate and licentious men, without regard to the political parties of the day.[59]

Two main factions in the denomination kept up the heat against the *Star* in protest, one from Maine and the other from New Hampshire. In 1839, eleven men, primarily from New Hampshire, signed a "protest," which they submitted to the *New Hampshire Patriot*. It stated that, though the signers believed slavery to be "a moral and political evil, and to be very much regretted that it should ever have been countenanced on Columbia's free soil," they as religious people could not "lend influence to any Society that we think has for its ultimate object the dissolution of the Union...." According to the protest, they disapproved of the measures of the American Anti-Slavery Society, which were "propagated in the *Morning Star*," as well as a rejection of the resolution passed in the Rockingham Quarterly Meeting, which had lent support to the American Anti-Slavery Society. They also disapproved of "a religious paper descending so far below the object for which it was intended (agreeably to the Prospectus), as to meddle with the political contentions of the day."[60]

In the early 1840s, several new associations were formed among the northern Freewill Baptists that opposed the strong antislavery stance taken by the General Conference. Members of these associations held conventions in western Maine in 1845 and 1846. The purpose of the conventions was to denounce abolitionism and to call Freewill Baptists away from its "excesses." The leaders of these associations were reputed to have a strong loyalty to the Democratic Party, which accounted for their hesitance to accept the abolitionist platform.[61] In 1843 this group began the publication of a newspaper called *The Freewill Baptist Repository*, which was designed as an alternative to *The Morning Star* and its abolitionist stance. The *Repository* did not last long, however, and the opinions of the *Star* held the day.[62]

By this time the General Conference had already affirmed the practice of excommunicating slaveholders. At the 1839 meeting of the General Conference in Conneaut, Ohio, the Freewill Baptists were put to the test regarding the stringency of their rule of withholding fellowship from slaveholders. Dr. William M. Housley of the Free Communion Baptists in Kentucky came to the floor. He stated that he had left the Free Communion Baptists because of their Calvinist sentiments and that he wished to join a group that was not Calvinistic in theology. He added that many Baptists in Kentucky and other parts of the South agreed with him and would join the Freewill Baptists if they would accept him.[63]

The question came up about slaves Housley owned—a mother and her three children—who lived in his own house with his family. A committee questioned Housley about what he thought of "American slavery." He answered that he thought it was a "great moral evil, a scourge and a curse." When asked if he was willing to release his slaves, he said that he would not feel right about releasing them because they did not have the education or means to survive. The committee then asked if he would let them go if they were promised three years of education and a livelihood in New England, and if he were remunerated for their value. He replied that he would. Finally, Housley was asked what he would do if his slaves tried to escape to Canada and he caught them. His reply was, "I should arrest and claim them as my property." Thus the committee "decided that as Dr. H. claimed property in human beings, they could not ordain him as a minister, nor fellowship with him as a Christian; and he was so informed." An 1847 edition of *The Church Member's Book* mentioned the practice of disciplining slaveholders: "Again—slave-holding, or as the Bible terms it, man-stealing, I Tim. 1:10, is a flagrant transgression of the gospel of Jesus Christ, and is by no means to be tolerated in the church."[64]

This logic was applied to the northern Freewill Baptists' stance toward the Free Will Baptists of the South, particularly in the Carolinas. The Free Will Baptists of North Carolina, though a separate movement of entirely different origin, had a few times corresponded with the northern Freewill Baptists and had welcomed at least one visitor from their midst, Elder Elias Hutchins. That this contact took place is all that the documentary evidence will support. However, some of the leaders of the northern denomination asserted that the North Carolina Free Will Baptists were members of the northern General Conference. In 1881, for example, I. D. Stewart stated that the Free Will Baptists of North and South Carolina were "in fellowship with the Freewill Baptists of the North, slavery excepted." He went on to say that the same denomination that could not tolerate William Housley did not wish to "continue fellowship" with the Carolina Free Will Baptists because the latter did not prohibit slaveholders from being members.[65]

The question of relationships between the northern Freewill Baptists and their southern counterparts arises here. In his comments Stewart implied the Southerners were officially in fellowship and were disfellowshipped because there were some among them who owned slaves. Yet there is no documentary evidence that there was ever any official fellowship between the two groups. The General Conference, in its ecumenical zeal, was famous for including associations and conferences on its membership rolls that never actually formally joined or sent delegates. In the very late nineteenth century, delegates were sent on rare occasions from places like East Tennessee. Yet most often the names on the roll indicated a kindred spirit, not official membership. This difficulty was acknowledged by the committee that orchestrated the 1911 merger with the Northern Baptists. They reported how difficult it was to get a vote of the bodies making up the General Conference because so many of them that were listed as being in fellowship were not active or did not report:

> A much more serious difficulty arose when an attempt was made to count and tabulate the vote of the constituent bodies. There is a list of these bodies published in the Free Baptist Register and Year Book. But this is an unofficial publication, made up from returns from quarterly meetings, which are not constituent bodies, and put forth without a thought of establishing legal or formal rights. There is a list, accompanied by statistics, published in connection with the Minutes of the General Conference. But this is a compilation made by the clerk and the committee on publishing minutes in their editorial capacity, and is not a criterion by which to determine accurately membership in General Conference. A list, more formal in

appearance, is appended as a footnote to Article I of the Constitution of the General Conference. This, however, is a mere accretion of names, to which each new name has been added without reference to the old names which in some instances should have been removed."[66]

Nonetheless, the posture of the northern Freewill Baptists toward the Free Will Baptists of the South demonstrates the former's indefatigable commitment to the excommunication of slaveholders and to making that commitment known. The Free Will Baptists in the South, being primarily of the yeoman farmer class, did not have a large slaveholding constituency. Slavery for them was not a great issue. Davidson comments that, owing to the "vehement hostility" of abolitionists toward the South, "one would expect that the minutes of the Southern Free Will Baptists would speak often of the slavery issue. But, surprisingly enough, such was not the case. . . . The controversy simply did not touch the [southern] denomination."[67]

The most extensive literary treatment of benevolence and social reform in the Freewill Baptist denomination was that of J. J. Butler in his 1840 book *Thoughts on the Benevolent Enterprises, Embracing the Subjects of Missions, Sabbath Schools, Temperance, Abolition of Slavery, and Peace*. Butler was the foremost theologian in the General Conference, having taught theology at Parsonfield Seminary in Maine and later publishing the standard Freewill Baptist book on systematic theology. His book was the definitive work on Freewill Baptist benevolence, and it continued to have great influence into the 1850s and 1860s. Butler's major theses on the abolition of slavery in his chapter by the same name offer insight into the lines of argument employed by the Freewill Baptists in their polemics against slavery. Replying to the notion of many northern Freewill Baptists that the antislavery stance was too politicized, Butler wrote: "If so, which political party does it favor? Not the Whig surely, for Mr. Clay, the champion of that party, is its avowed opponent. True, many Whigs are abolitionists, and so are Mr. Morris, of Ohio, one of the most distinguished Democrats in the Union, Judge Morton, the Democratic governor of Massachusetts, and many others of the same party."[68]

Though some northern Freewill Baptists opposed the underground railroad, many prominent Freewill Baptists were involved in efforts to get slaves to freedom in Canada. They maintained, for example, an underground railroad outpost at Parsonfield Seminary in Maine, where fugitive slaves were hidden and nurtured on their way to the Canadian border.[69]

As leaders in the northern evangelical ethos of the day, the northern Freewill Baptists made their own unique contribution to perfect sinful humanity as best they could and usher in the Millennium. Indeed, their contribution far outweighed their size, and when the slaves were finally freed, the Freewill Baptists were assured that fundamental to this accomplishment was their radical call to the church and society around them:

> Waken from your sinful slumber,
>   Shake off now your lethargy,
> Burst oppression's chains asunder,
>   Set the willing captive free.
>
> To the contest—onward freemen,
>   Sound aloud the Jubilee;
> To the rescue, sons of freedom
>   Give the slave his liberty.[70]

Seven
DOCTRINE AND DECLINE IN THE NORTH

The Sufficiency of Scripture

The faith and practice of the Randall movement of northern Freewill Baptists grew out of its understanding of the sufficiency of Scripture. Benjamin Randall's church covenant stated: "We promise to practice all the commands of and the ordinances of the New Testament of our Lord and Savior Jesus Christ, so far as they are or shall be made known unto us by the light of the Holy Spirit of truth, without which, we are sensible, we cannot attain to the true knowledge thereof." This doctrine became stock and trade for the northern Freewill Baptists. For example, the 1854 *Treatise* stated that the Holy Scriptures "reveal the will of God sufficiently to direct us in all important duties, and should be held by every Christian as his only infallible rule of faith and practice."[1]

An unsigned article on baptism in the *Freewill Baptist Quarterly* echoed all the major points of the doctrine of the sufficiency of Scripture. It stated that the church's practice is "absolutely dependent upon *Divine precept* or *scriptural precedent*. . . . It is on this principle that Protestants . . . reason, when contending with Catholics, about their claims to prerogatives and their numerous rites, viz.; that nothing short of an explicit grant, a *positive* command, or a *plain* example in the New Testament can prove their Divine origin." Thus, the article continues, "Nonconformists demand of Episcopalians, saying '*Produce your warrant* for this, that, and the other, *from our only rule of faith and practice*, a Divine precept, an apostolic example relating to the point in dispute.' So Baptists ask of Pedobaptists, Where is your Divine command or apostolic example in support of Pedobaptism?"[2]

The northern Freewill Baptists, like their General Baptist and southern Free Will Baptist counterparts, often used the phrase "ordinary means of grace" to describe the sufficiency of Scripture. One sees this, for example, in *The Church Member's Book*, a handbook for laypeople that was widely distributed in the movement. In its post-Second Great Awakening context of "new measures" and emotionalism, the book urged a return to the "ordinary means of grace." Using the broader definition of ordinances discussed above, the writer described the ordinary means of grace as things like "the regular and prayerful reading of the Scriptures as a religious exercise; attendance on the ordinances of the gospel, and daily self-examination." If Christians "turn their backs on the ordinances which Christ has enjoined on believers, are contented to be 'novices' in the word of God, and neglect diligent and frequent self-examination, these are so many reasons why they do not grow in grace." Many Christians, the author said, "overlook or undervalue the ordinary means of grace." These Christians, "on the stretch for something great," emphasize "extraordinary means," while the "common church prayer meeting, the family altar, and closet devotions, are not duly appreciated. This indulgence for something great and out of the common course, has a bewitching influence for evil over the heart; and diminishing the relish for the ordinary means, is prejudicial to growth in grace."[3]

Another example of the sufficiency of Scripture in the Randall movement is seen in an 1868 article by S. E. Root in the *Freewill Baptist Quarterly*: "God has fixed the conditions of his own worship, and we can neither alter nor abridge them." Root goes on to say, in phrases reminiscent of the General Baptists' notion of despising the means of grace, that God has "given us our hand-book of instructions, and will not accept our worship unless we use it as our guide. To prefer the speculations of reason to the authoritative truths of revelation is an insult to God which He will not allow." Root also appealed to the concept of divine institution: "God has instituted various forms of worship, each of which enjoined in Scripture has its uses."[4]

John J. Butler summarized the Randall movement's approach in his 1861 work *Natural and Revealed Theology*, the most widely used theology text in northern Freewill Baptist schools:

> The gospel church was organized by Christ. He is its chief corner stone, its head, and its lawgiver. The constitution of the gospel church rests wholly upon the precepts and practice of Christ and his inspired apostles. They

not only organized and governed churches, but also transmitted a record of their doings to us, to be followed in the perpetuation of the church. Essentials in church building are not left as matters of indifference to be regulated by uninspired men. The acts of popes, councils, or any other mere human authority, have no right to change the Divinely established constitution of the Christian church.[5]

These principles from the Randall movement lived on in the confessional documents later adopted by the National Association of Free Will Baptists in 1935, whose church covenant and *Treatise* were adapted from the Randall movement. For example, the church covenant states that we have "adopted the Word of God as our rule of faith and practice." The "Articles of Faith" state that the Christian Scriptures "are our infallible rule of faith and practice." Chapter 1 of the *Treatise* states that the Scriptures "are a sufficient and infallible rule and guide to salvation and all Christian worship and service."[6]

Sin and Salvation

The Arminianism of the northern Freewill Baptists grew out of the affirmations of its founder, Benjamin Randall. Reflecting on the days before he went public with his Arminian views, Randall noted that Calvinism had not been a point of controversy, and thus he had never really considered it. When asked on one occasion early in his ministry why he did not preach Calvinist doctrine, Randall responded plainly, "Because I do not believe it."[7] The northern Freewill Baptists' Arminianism upset the equilibrium of New England Calvinism. Some New England Baptists who were inclined toward Calvinism became more rigorous in their Calvinism in reaction to the Freewill Baptists. Yet other New England Baptists felt the need to soften their Calvinism, as is seen in the New Hampshire Confession of Faith. That confession in turn set the stage for the softening of Calvinism among Baptists across the country during the nineteenth century.[8]

The soteriology of the northern Freewill Baptist *Treatise*, to which all Freewill Baptist ministers subscribed, is a mixture of Reformed elements with quasi-Wesleyan doctrine. This stands in contrast to the southern Free Will Baptists, who diverged from Wesleyanism in their soteriology. The Randall movement's doctrine of depravity, like that of their southern counterparts, leaned much more Calvinistic than many anti-Calvinists of their day, who tended toward semi-Pelagian understandings of free will. Moses M. Smart, principal of the Biblical Department at Parsonfield Seminary, exemplifies this approach: "What we mean by total depravity is, that man of himself has become by nature wholly unable to do any thing good." Were it not for divine grace, "the conscience would have been as dark and silent, as cloudy midnight." Because of human inability, the northern *Treatise* averred that "[t]he power to believe is the gift of God." Likewise, the northern Freewill Baptists, like their English General Baptist and southern counterparts, affirmed the imputation of Adam's sin to the race. Though they left open the question of whether that imputation was mediate or immediate, most of their theologians affirmed mediate imputation, which even many Calvinist theologians of their day, such as the Presbyterian Robert Dabney, advocated.[9]

Prevenient grace, they taught, was necessary to counteract total depravity and give sinners an opportunity of salvation. They cited John 1:9, "That was the true light, which lighteth every man that cometh into the world," and Titus 2:11, "The grace of God which bringeth salvation hath appeared to all men." Only by this special grace can sinners be "rendered capable" of responding to the gospel.[10] This grace has been provided for everyone, but it can be freely resisted. This *gratia universalis* and *gratia resistibilis* is the theme of the northern Freewill Baptists' Arminian doctrine, as seen in their first *Treatise* published in 1834:

> The grace of God, the influences of the Holy Spirit, and the invitations of the gospel are given to all men, and by these they receive power to repent and obey all the requirements of the gospel. Hence it appears a perfect inconsistency to suppose that God would provide salvation for a less number than he really loved.... The fact being admitted that God loves all men, that Christ died for all men, that the Holy Ghost reproves all men, that the gospel invites all men, and that by virtue of these all men have the ability to repent and believe, what other conclusion can be drawn than that the salvation of all is possible? We mean only to say that salvation is possible, for though in its provision it is free and absolute, yet in its application it is expressly conditional. Salvation then being freely provided and man being capable through grace of obtaining it, if he perish, whom can he blame but himself? The charge must fall upon him with aggravated weight: *"Thou hast destroyed thyself."*[11]

The *Treatise*'s chapter on Christ's atonement and mediation affirmed the Arminian understanding of the *gratia universalis* that "Christ gave his life a sacrifice for the sins of the world and thus made salvation possible for all men." The confession also affirmed penal substitutionary atonement: "He died for us, suffering the penalty of the law in our stead to make known the righteousness of God that he might be just in justifying sinners who believe in his Son." The atonement provided "satisfaction for the violation of [God's] law."[12]

The northern Freewill Baptists affirmed a penal substitutionary doctrine of atonement, unlike most Wesleyans of their day. Yet they tended toward agreement with Wesleyans in denying the imputation of Christ's righteousness in justification. In this way they were unlike virtually all General Baptists and southern Free Will Baptists. An anti-imputational view was not universal and was not required by their *Treatise*. Still, the main theologians of the movement did not affirm the imputation of the righteousness of Christ in justification. Smart is fairly representative of these thinkers. He approvingly quoted seventeenth-century Puritans Richard Baxter, the four-point Calvinist anti-imputationist, and John Goodwin, the Arminian anti-imputationist. Smart averred that "there is no weight in the argument, that as our sins were accounted his, so his righteousness is accounted ours. Our sins were never so accounted Christ's as that he did them, and so justly suffered for them. Our transgressions are never said to have been imputed to him in the *fact* but only that they were laid upon him in the *penalty*."[13]

The confession's doctrine of sanctification was more like Wesleyanism's and differed strongly from that of the southern Free Will Baptists: "The attainment of entire sanctification in this life is both the privilege and duty of every Christian." However, by 1871, the Freewill Baptist General Conference had revised the *Treatise* to exclude the doctrine of entire sanctification completely.[14]

The Freewill Baptists affirmed that divine salvific grace continues to be resistible even after conversion. Thus perseverance is not "certain." Though believers are "kept by the power of God through faith unto salvation," this power is "only used to keep the saints *through their faith*," but Scripture teaches that "some have put away faith and a good conscience and concerning faith made shipwreck." The movement's primary systematic theologian John J. Butler explained these doctrines systematically in his book *Natural and Revealed Theology*. That book was revised later in the century by Ransom Dunn as Butler and Dunn's *Systematic Theology*.[15]

The Believers' Church and Believer's Baptism

The earliest Randall *Treatise* in 1834 defined the church more broadly than many nineteenth-century Baptists did. Like their counterparts in the South, the northern Freewill Baptists emphasized the local congregation but also the church outside the context of the local body. The *Treatise* defined the church as "an assembly of persons who believe in Christ and worship the true God, agreeably to his word" and in "a more general sense," as signifying "the whole body of real Christians throughout the world." They stressed a regenerate church membership received into the local church's fellowship by profession of faith and baptism by immersion.[16]

The northern Freewill Baptists taught that baptism is solely for believers. As the confession stated in a footnote, believers' being the only valid subjects of baptism is "evident" from three facts. First, the "commission of Christ" authorizes no baptism but that of believers. Second, there is no New Testament evidence of anyone other than believers being baptized. Third, the whole purpose of baptism is to be a "sign of regeneration," of an individual's death, burial, and resurrection with Christ, which can occur only in a believer. It is improper "to affix a sign where there is no evidence that the thing signified does really exist." They did not see sprinkling as true baptism. The 1834 *Treatise* stated that the reason immersion is the only valid mode of baptism is Paul's statement to the Colossians (2:12) and Romans (6:4–5) that believers are "buried with him in baptism." The only way baptism can be an accurate sign and symbol of burial is immersion. They pointed out that apostolic practice always indicated that large amounts of water were needed to baptize. In the footnotes, they also made arguments from church history similar to the ones of the southern Free Will Baptists discussed in chapter 10.[17]

The Lord's Supper and the Washing of the Saints' Feet

The northern Freewill Baptists, like their southern counterparts, saw the Lord's Supper as a sign and seal of Christ's body and blood that he gave as a sacrifice for sin. The *Treatise* stated that the Lord's Supper "is designed to commemorate the sufferings of Christ, and to represent, in the use of bread and wine, the communion which saints have with him, and with each other."[18]

While the Freewill Baptists were not sacramentalists in the typical sense of that word, they did not affirm a "bare memorialism." They saw the Lord's Supper as a deeply meaningful sign and seal of Christ's body and blood and their significace for the beleiver. Moses Smart distanced himself from transubstantiation, that "the bread and wine are literally changed into the body and blood of Christ; so that they are no longer bread and wine," as well as consubstantiation, which Smart identified with Luther's view that "the bread and wine remained the same; but, that *together with them*, the body and blood of Christ are *literally* received by the communicants." He described as the "correct view" that the bread and wine "represent" Christ's body and blood, and that "communicants who are in a right frame of mind, partake spiritually of the body and blood of Christ. So, then, it is more than a mere commemorative rite." This stands in contrast to the tendency of some later Baptists to make the Lord's Supper into a light and even trivial "passing of the plate."[19]

The Freewill Baptists were open communionists. The thrust of their practice was not to de-emphasize the necessity of baptism and church membership for partaking of the Lord's Supper. Instead, they wished to stress that people's error on the doctrine of baptism should not bar them from partaking in the Supper. Thus they welcomed to the Lord's table paedobaptists and non-immersionists who were members in good standing with other churches. In one place Smart addressed the concerns of closed communionists that, because the Lord's Supper is a church ordinance, it is inconsistent to welcome to the Table those who have not been truly baptized (by immersion). He responded:

> Well, admit that it is a church ordinance; if so, it extends to all church members. If, then, it does not extend to Congregationalists, Presbyterians, Methodists, &c., it must be because they are not churches of Christ, and if so, they have no christian ministry; and yet these same brethren who call us inconsistent, will associate with the ministers of these churches as ministers of Christ. They will exchange pulpits with them and in various ways manifest their fellowship; now do they not exhibit the greatest inconsistency for not communing with them at the Lord's Table? They know not how to affirm that these are not ministers of Christ, and their people not churches of Christ.[20]

While Randall and the earliest Freewill Baptists assiduously required the practicing of the washing of the saints' feet as a biblical ordinance, the denomination quickly moved away from this stricture. As early as 1831, the practice of the *pedilavium* was left an open question. At the fifth General Conference that year, the body passed a resolution acknowledging that the rite had "produced no small excitement" in the denomination. Some people believed they had "sufficient evidence from the New Testament to warrant the practice as an ordinance of the gospel," while others did not. Thus the body agreed that "all persons in connection with us have a free and lawful right to wash feet or not, as may best answer their consciences to God; neither the performance [n]or neglect of which should cause a breach of Christian fellowship." This statement was printed in the *Treatise* for thirty-seven years, after which all reference to the practice was dropped.[21]

Church Polity

The church polity of the Randall movement was almost identical to that of the English General Baptists and the Palmer movement. While placing great emphasis on the necessity of the interrelation of sister churches in quarterly meetings, the northern Freewill Baptists believed and practiced the self-government of the local church: "Every Free-will Baptist church is an independent body so far as it relates to its own government, the transaction of its own business, the choice of its officers, and the discipline of its members."[22]

The Randall movement affirmed that there were two offices in the New Testament church: "bishops or elders" and "deacons." In early northern Freewill Baptist usage (as in the Palmer movement), ministers of the gospel were referred to as "elder," as in "Elder Benjamin Randall" or "Elder John Buzzell." The Freewill Baptists equated elders and bishops, and also referred to these officers as "pastors." All those who were ordained preachers of the gospel filled this office. As the 1854 *Treatise* stated, "Bishops are overseers who have the charge of souls—to instruct and rule them by the word. They are called elders, and they perform the duties of pastors, teachers, and evangelists." John J. Butler argued, "The ministers mentioned in the New Testament were equal. Bishops, presbyters, and elders were all the same, and the terms denoting them are used synonymously in the Christian Scriptures."[23]

The northern Freewill Baptists also believed the same basic principles about deacons that the English General Baptists and southern Free Will Baptists did: they are ordained office-bearers specially marked by their spirituality and set apart by the congregation. The Randall *Treatise* stated that Scripture authorizes deacons as "assistants" to bishops (elders). This was especially true in the temporal affairs of the church, including helping the poor, but also in spiritual matters. Thus, they argued, there is warrant for this spiritual officer to exercise "helps" by serving at the Lord's table, "taking the lead of the meeting in the absence of the minister," and performing other spiritual services. Deacons were not to have limited terms of service, but were, like bishops, "regular or stated servant[s] of the church." Freewill Baptist views of the diaconate were different from the practice in high liturgical churches where deacons were clergy who wore vestments and were accorded more eminence and authority than Baptists believed Scripture warranted. Yet their practice also contrasted with later Baptist practice where sometimes congregations would treat deacons as "bosses" of the church and even of the pastor—or pendulum-swing, in reaction, by reducing deacons to a benevolence committee or to trustees who were in charge of church equipment or task management. The Randall movement, like all Baptists of the seventeenth through the nineteenth centuries, believed that, while certain people could exercise gifts of helps or administrations in the church (such as trustees, Sabbath school superintendents, clerks, and treasurers), these were not spiritual officers in the church.[24]

The northern Freewill Baptists thought significant decision-making should be done by the congregation. They believed that this principle disallowed the establishment of consistories or authoritative general boards in churches. Butler stated: "As a matter of expediency, it is doubtless true that in special cases the church may find it best to create a board; for instance, in case of a difficult and protracted labor. But this is quite another thing from having a standing board to govern in all cases. Neither Scripture nor experience warrants the creation of any such aristocracy in the church."[25]

The Randall movement believed that the New Testament warranted strong associations. They called these quarterly meetings, and these would usually unite together with other quarterly meetings into yearly meetings. While safeguarding the self-government of the local congregation, the Northern Freewill Baptists held that the quarterly meeting was responsible for the licensure, examination, and ordination of ministers. Its responsibility was also to offer wise counsel to local churches, especially in times of difficulty. However, churches did have the freedom to dissent from the quarterly meeting's decisions, after which the latter would often discipline such a congregation by removing it from fellowship. Butler, like the English General Baptists Thomas Grantham and William Jeffery, cited Acts 15 as apostolic warrant for associations: such bodies are not options for the churches, but apostolically approved means for their benefit.[26]

Worship

Some northern Freewill Baptists on the frontier were more emotionally expressive in their worship than their New England brothers and sisters. There was diversity in different regions, and Freewill Baptists emphasized the need to maintain simplicity in imitation of the apostolic pattern. As the movement entered the latter half of the nineteenth century, the movement's worship became more formal. Toward the end of the nineteenth century and the beginning of the twentieth, some northern Freewill Baptist worship was more liturgical. Thus, for example, one 1881 hymnal featured a section entitled "Chants and Occasional" with nine chant settings, three shorter entries entitled "Response to the Decalogue," and other liturgical elements.

Still, most northern Freewill Baptists, for most of the nineteenth century, engaged in worship that was non-liturgical or mildly liturgical. Like their southern counterparts, most of the differences within the Freewill Baptist denomination revolved around the questions of informality vs. formality, between churches that shouted "Amen!" and those whose worship was quiet and more cerebral.[27]

The Church Member's Book discussed public worship on "the Christian Sabbath" at some length. The author said, "It has pleased God to constitute the Christian church on such principles that it is free from those cumbrous ceremonies and complicated rituals with which the Jewish church was burdened." The book also urged Freewill Baptists to be faithful to their own congregations' worship services and other meetings. Some church members might say, "I can enjoy myself as well at other meetings as at our own," the author lamented. Every Christian should of course "possess so much of a catholic spirit as to be kind and free toward all saints" and to "enjoy the worship of God in other communions when circumstances put him in their way." However, every believer "should feel a *special* interest in the meetings of *his own church*."[28]

The book also emphasized reverence in worship. Believers should prepare themselves for worship and for hearing sermons even before they go to church: "On the Lord's day morning every Christian ought to make it a point to retire to his closet, and ... seek for the Holy Spirit's blessing on his own soul, and on the assembly about to convene for Divine service." Church members should be careful not to converse on non-spiritual matters before church when they reverently enter the sanctuary before divine service: "How much better to seat yourself immediately in the sanctuary, and have a few moments to raise the soul in silent yet fervent prayer to God for his blessing upon those services in which hundreds are about to engage." Free Will Baptists across the South also used the term "divine service" or "the divine service" to describe public worship services. Both denominations in the nineteenth century sharply distinguished the divine service from other church meetings such as singings, lessons, classes, prayer meetings, business meetings, conferences, and other less sacred gatherings.[29]

The Freewill Baptists in the North, no less than their southern counterparts, taught that worship on the Christian Sabbath was seen in the context of Sabbath-day observances outside the church sanctuary. Thus *The Church Member's Book* specified that it is a "parental duty" that "children be taught properly to observe the Christian Sabbath. God has consecrated the day as a *holy time.* ... Let parents particularly impress on the minds of their children, souls whom God has committed to their charge *to educate for eternity*, a high veneration for the Holy Sabbath, and the sanctuary of God on that Day. Should they not be guarded with sleepless vigilance against doing aught that shall desecrate the Lord's day?" This mentality would continue to characterize Black and White Free Will Baptists across the United States well into the late twentieth and even the early twenty-first century, though by that time mores about Sabbath-keeping were waning.[30]

Marriage, Sexuality, and the Family

Unlike the southern Free Will Baptists, whose sparse records make it difficult to reconstruct their views on women, there is ample information about northern Freewill Baptists' views, as discussed above. They were ahead of their time in advocating for women's rights to property, suffrage, and education. Thus the colleges of the Randall movement were among the first higher education institutions in the world to allow women as students. In other ways, however, the movement was similar to other nineteenth-century Protestants in its traditional understanding of sexuality, gender, and divorce.

Butler exemplifies the Freewill Baptists' views on marriage and sexuality. In his 1870 commentary on Jesus's words about maleness and femaleness in Matthew 19 and Mark 10, for example, Butler emphasized that "God made the distinction of sex [male and female] as a foundation of the marriage relation." Marriage, according to Butler, has a divinely given distinction between male and female at its essence. Butler went on to describe marriage as a "covenant," a "divine institution" in which "God joins the husband and wife together." Butler remarked that this is "not a mere agreement of their own, or civil contract; but when entered into in the appointed way, has the sanction and confirmation of Jehovah." He went on to say, "No man or body of men can dissolve this connection. None but God can do it, and that is by death. It is a relation sacredly and unconditionally entered upon for life, and cannot be violated without great sin. Adultery does indeed dissolve the connection, but this is a sin against God and man of fearful magnitude."[31]

One sees the northern Freewill Baptists' attitude toward sex outside marriage in *The Church Member's Book*, which emphasizes covenant marriage as a sign of the inviolable union between Christ and his church. The book quotes 1 Corinthians 6:10–12: "Be not deceived: neither fornicators, nor idolaters, nor adulterers, nor effeminate, nor abusers of themselves with mankind... shall inherit the kingdom of God." "Let the guilty fear," the author warned. "Do any think their guilt is atoned for by after-marriage? What will make amends for a sin which the gospel declares excludeth from the kingdom of heaven? . . . Let young brethren and sisters beware of temptation, and flee all youthful lusts." The author proceeded to say, "As fornication, so adultery, is evidence of a woful destitution of grace; and as expressly forbidden in the law of the Lord. 'He that goeth in unto his neighbor's wife; whoso toucheth her shall not be innocent. Whoso committeth adultery with a woman, lacketh understanding; he that doeth it destroyeth his own soul.'"[32]

Butler also exemplifies the northern Freewill Baptists' views on homosexuality, which were typical of the churches of their day. One sees this in his discussion in his commentary on Romans 1:27 ("likewise also the men, leaving the natural use of the woman, burned in their lust one toward another; men with men working that which is unseemly, and receiving in themselves that recompense of their error which was meet"). Butler stated that this verse described the male counterpart to the female sin mentioned in verse 26. That verse says, "Even their women did change the natural use into that which is against nature." Butler used the term "unnatural" to describe homosexual behavior. First Corinthians 6:9 listed the "effeminate" and "abusers of themselves with mankind" in a list of sinners who will not inherit the kingdom of God. In the commentary on that text, Butler simply said, "See notes on Rom. i." Butler's use of the word "unnatural" to refer to homosexuality had been common in Christian moral teaching and the traditional exegesis of Romans 1, which spoke of homosexual conduct as leaving behind the "natural use" or "natural function" of sexuality according to the law of nature and as seen in physical nature.[33]

The northern Freewill Baptists, like other Baptists of their day, tied together marriage and procreation. *The Church Member's Book* exemplifies this view when it says that Matthew 19 teaches that marriage is a divine institution and thus is "subject to his law alone. Hence the civil law is . . . binding upon the conscience only in so far as it agrees with the law of God. The contract of marriage is mutual; and those entering into it form a society, that is, they have something in common, which equally belongs to both. Hence they are mutually interested in the present and eternal well-being of their offspring."[34]

The northern Freewill Baptist view of divorce is likewise unremarkable when compared to other Protestant understandings of the day. *The Church Member's Book*, stated, for example: "The law of marriage is one for life, and not to be dissolved except for one cause only, the cause of whoredom." One also sees this later in the Freewill Baptist General Conference Minutes for 1907: "Whereas, the sanctity of the marriage relation is being undermined and family relations destroyed by loose and easy divorce laws; therefore, Resolved, . . . That we emphasize the one and only one scriptural ground for divorce, and advise our ministry not to perform the marriage ceremony of persons divorced for other than scriptural causes; and we would advise the enactment of uniform divorce laws."[35]

The *Church Member's Book* emphasizes the love and endearment of husbands and wives, parents and children, and brothers and sisters. This is especially true when it probes one of the author's favorite themes: family worship. "The relation of husband and wife, parent and child, brother and sister, are the most endearing and intimate on earth, these mutually bearing the sorrows or joys and dividing the ills of life among the other;—nothing can, therefore, be more rational and lovely than *religion in the family*. Religion in the domestic circle will always strengthen the various bonds of union and love, and cement the hearts of the various members of families."[36]

The Road to Dissolution

Theological Shifts

The Northern Freewill Baptists continued to grow and prosper into the late nineteenth century. Their publisher, mission boards, colleges and divinity school, and other institutions continued to develop. By the 1860s many of them would begin to use the appellation "Free Baptist," which would become the official name of the General Conference in 1892. The northern Freewill Baptists' intellectual output and theology was impressive. It included a theological journal, the *Freewill Baptist Quarterly*, published from 1853 to 1869. Each quarter, an association would "conduct" an issue of the *Quarterly*. Ministers of that association would write articles on Scripture and theology and their application to the church and the ministry of the gospel as well as to society and culture. Each *Quarterly* issue averaged around 120 pages. These quarterlies exemplified the Scottish Common Sense philosophy and Baconianism that was ascendant in nineteenth-century American Protestantism. This commitment combined an Arminian brand of Protestant orthodoxy with a staunchly postmillennial eschatology.[37]

Over the next four decades, that orthodoxy would begin to evidence fissures. What some scholars have called a Baconian thrust in nineteenth-century philosophy was part and parcel of the northern Freewill Baptist mind. Named for Francis Bacon, the Baconian impulse, allied with Scottish Common Sense realism, often overlapped with a strong confidence in the deliverances of reason and science. Free Baptist intellectuals in the late nineteenth and early twentieth centuries, like many of their northern

Protestant counterparts, began to feel that the older orthodoxy would not hold up under the scrutiny of modern science. This became more evident the more the consensus of the scientific community in the West affirmed modern science, especially the evolutionary views of leading thinkers such as Charles Darwin and Charles Lyell.[38]

Beginning in the 1880s, this trend combined with a growing interest in the currents of theological thought blowing across the Atlantic from Germany. Coincident with the upward social mobility of the northern Freewill Baptists and the increasing prestige of their academic institutions, some younger Freewill Baptist intellectuals studied theology at German universities. Many of them began to be concerned that the older Protestant orthodoxy they had been taught was incapable of withstanding the new historical criticism increasingly advocated in the mainstream of the academy in the West. Thus Freewill Baptist higher education in the north was on a trajectory similar to that of the colleges and universities of other mainline Protestant denominations, as explained by Jon Roberts and James Turner in *The Sacred and the Secular University*.[39]

In the introduction to that book, John F. Wilson accurately describes the process whereby the "old-time colleges" founded by Protestant denominations in the nineteenth century underwent a transformation as they began to reckon with the findings of modern science, the specialization that went along with that science and the Industrial Revolution, and the resultant fragmentation of knowledge in the emerging universities that contrasted with the unity fostered by the older religious vision. A "synergy between science and religion . . . had characterized the preceding era." In the traditional Protestant colleges of the antebellum period, there was an "interpenetration" between the older orthodoxy and natural science that "sustained a program of apologetics." In the older Protestant schools and colleges, the *raison d'être* of science was "finding in the world of nature evidence for the workings of divine order if not a divine mind." The required courses in Christian moral philosophy, often taught by college presidents, were "based on this evidence, namely, confidence that divine intention formed the framework of human endeavor." Wilson explains how the philosophical undergirding of this approach was Scottish Common Sense philosophy with its emphasis on natural theology rooted in empirical evidence available to anyone with common sense.[40]

Wilson is right when he argues that "the critical departure from this hegemonic construct took place in the 1870s. The central step was the impulse to endorse a more specialized pursuit in science" and the "adoption of 'methodological naturalism,'" which Wilson says "directly undercut" science's "usefulness to apologetics." The Free Baptists were slower to get on board with this trend, but leading intellectuals in the movement did so, and the colleges gradually followed suit. What was called the "theological modernism" of the secularizing higher education institutions in Europe and North America in the late nineteenth and early twentieth centuries went hand in hand with two other trends: first, a growing ecumenism—a desire to unite all Christian denominations. That trend was intricately intertwined with the second: the vision for comprehensive Christian social reform, which the regnant postmillennial eschatology held would help usher in the Millennium. Both ecumenism and what Northern Baptist thinker Walter Rauschenbusch called the "social gospel" became key components of the postmillennial impulse of the day, often uniting with a vision of scientific and technological progress. This vision usually dovetailed with the evolutionary understanding of the historical criticism of the Bible emerging from the European universities, which held that the Bible was a record of the evolution of the religious impulse in humanity.[41]

In the 1890s, what William Hutchinson called "the modernist impulse in American religion" began to manifest itself among the intellectual leaders of the Free Baptist General Conference. One sees this influence in the work of the northern Free Baptist scholar Alfred Williams Anthony, who would go on to become the chief architect of the merger with the Northern Baptist Convention in 1911. A graduate of Bates College and Cobb Divinity School, Anthony had done postgraduate study at the University of Berlin under Adolf von Harnack and Bernard Weiss. He became the Fullonton Professor of New Testament Criticism at Cobb in 1887 and was one of the most prominent voices in the denomination.[42]

By 1899 Anthony wrote *The Method of Jesus: An Interpretation of Personal Religion*. One of his primary goals in the book was to contrast personal religion with creedalism and doctrinal religion. "Certainly the Nicene creed gives a hundred-fold greater prominence to abstract theological conceptions than does the Sermon on the Mount," he wrote. "It was not faith of an abstract character that Jesus emphasized, certainly not a faith that embodied a definition of sin, and an explanation of salvation, and convictions concerning God's sovereignty and man's free agency." Anthony went on to drive a wedge between personal faith in Jesus and "orthodoxy," represented by "intellectual apprehension and syllogistic statement of Biblical history, chronology, and doctrine." Anthony downplayed orthodoxy as being at the center of the New Testament church's faith. His teachers at Bates, while evidencing a pietism characteristic of the Finneyesque milieu out of which they operated, had managed to maintain a commitment to the orthodoxy common to evangelical Protestants in nineteenth-century America. Anthony's pietism, however, moved in a direction that tended to dichotomize doctrinal orthodoxy and vital personal religion.[43]

In his chapter on "Progressive Revelation," Anthony reflected the ideas of the growing modernist movement in biblical and theological studies. He noted, for example, that the apostolic era does not provide "the most perfect examples of the Master's intent for his disciples and the application of his truth." The apostles were "so limited in their appreciation of the character of the Messiah and the Kingdom . . . that their examples and their utterances must be tested by the later and larger revelation that came as Christian experience enlarged the capacity to discern."[44]

Later in the chapter, he assured his readers they had "nothing to fear" from the latest currents in biblical criticism but "everything to gain." If biblical criticism can prove "that the book of Isaiah was written by two men at widely separated periods of time, that the book of Daniel was penned several hundreds of years after the date usually assigned to it, that the Pentateuch is a compilation from several earlier sources, then, though we adjust our present views of the Bible, we shall be in no sense losers, but shall better know what the Bible really is. . . ." Anthony proceeded to argue that Christians should not reject the science of Charles Darwin on the basis of his "ignoring supernatural force and law" but that Christian theology can and must be accommodated to the new science.[45]

Benjamin Francis Hayes, the leading theology professor at Bates from 1865 till his death in 1906, also exemplifies this trend. In his last public speech, Hayes, who had studied with the noted German philosopher Hermann Ulrici at the University of Halle, commented how positive the effects of the "transition from the traditional theology to acceptance of the views made necessary by recent progress of science" had been on Christianity. The "changed conceptions of the nature, mode of construction, purpose, and inspiration of the Scriptures which has resulted from the critical study of them" and the "world-view that has been gained by the progressive construction of philosophy," he explained, have resulted in "increased satisfaction and delight in the Holy Scriptures." He stated that his "re-examination of the grounds and substance of Christian faith during the past ten years" and "dropping" some of his "opinions which seem to have no rational foundation" had not weakened his faith but "greatly confirmed" it. In words like those used by Anthony, he noted, "It has resulted, also, in a confirmation of faith resting upon added evidence from many sources, especially upon the discovery that Christianity consists not in the decrees of councils of ancient ages, or necessarily in traditions handed down to us by the church, Catholic or Protestant—not in something from outside of us, but an experience within us."[46]

This embrace of the new liberal currents in theological study continued apace into the first decade of the twentieth century. This trend is demonstrated by the close relationship Bates College and Cobb Divinity School had with the University of Chicago. Shailer Mathews, Dean of the University of Chicago Divinity School, who would later pen the touchstone book for theological modernism, *The Faith of Modernism*, lectured at Cobb. Shirley Jackson Case, who later went on to become a distinguished New Testament scholar at the University of Chicago and a leading liberal critical scholar, was raised in a Freewill Baptist family in New Brunswick, Canada. He taught at Bates College and Cobb Divinity School from 1906 to 1908. Gary Dorrien has chronicled Mathews's and Case's signal role in the development of liberal theology in the mainline Protestant matrix of the early twentieth century. As Dorrien says, "Born into a liberal Christian home and grounded in German and American historicism, Case had a strong belief in the relevance of historical scholarship for modern Christianity, and an aversion to theology, philosophy, and displays of piety." As Jesse Owens shows, Case's 1907 inaugural address at his appointment at Cobb reflected his developing liberal understanding of theology.[47]

In his last report as corresponding secretary of the General Conference as the merger was fully finalized in 1917, Alfred Williams Anthony was frank about just how deeply connected these intellectual shifts were to the decline and ultimate demise of the denomination. He noted that these changes had been "spoken of privately at times among friends" but had "never been mentioned in public. I mention it now. Time enough has elapsed to permit at length perfecter frankness." Anthony reflected back to the time when "in all religious circles there was intellectual unrest" and "theological reconstruction was occurring." This process, he noted, had received vigorous opposition to the point that some opponents saw the appellation "higher critic" as being as bad as "'the Devil,' or 'Mephistopheles,' or 'Perdition.'" While no "heresy trials" were held, Anthony lamented that "we had what in many respects is worse," with "insinuations and innuendoes" and people advising students to stay away from educational institutions exploring new theological perspectives.

> We did not quarrel.... The men who cried at the gate, 'Wolf, wolf!', when there was no wolf, made men fear the gate. Experiences of pain came to

teachers who were seeking in all good conscience to discover and reveal the ways of God, when they found their scholarship an object of suspicion, their names whispered under bated breath, and the institutions with which they were connected made to suffer because of them.[48]

Anthony likened the denomination to a little boat in the middle of an ocean in the storm and stress of "Biblical Criticism" and "theological reconstruction." Bigger ships could come through the storm, but the Free Baptists could not. Thus many ministers jumped ship and continued their voyages in denominations in which they could "enjoy greater liberty of speech and action." They "discovered that ancient dogmas and a divisive propaganda, upon which denominations once thrived, were now destructive of denominational integrity and efficiency, and were not essential to the spirit of Christ."[49]

Ecumenism and the Social Gospel

The theology of modernism fit well with the ecumenism and social gospel that had come to characterize large swaths of the Free Baptist movement in the last decade of the nineteenth century. Norman Baxter identified the seeds of the Free Baptists' ecumenical aspirations in a comment Dexter Waterman made in 1859. Waterman had argued that the fact that "evangelical denominations are rapidly approximating each other" was proof that the Freewill Baptists had "successfully fulfilled their mission." The "views of people who expressed non-fellowship with Brother Randall have become so modified that in the opinion of many of their ministers, we might and ought to be one denomination." This ecumenical thrust mushroomed in the last three decades of the nineteenth century, as the Free Baptists talked increasingly of merger with other Protestant denominations. This vision manifested itself in the Free Baptists' involvement with the Federal Council of Churches (later National Council of Churches). As Dorrien explains, "The early Federal Council functioned, in effect, as a kind of laboratory for social gospel ideas that infiltrated the churches and seminaries. It placed divisive Christian doctrines off-limits and sought to advance social goals."[50]

The desire to unite with other denominations started out with discussions that—like those that their southern Free Will Baptist counterparts engaged in for a time—revolved around the union of non-Calvinist, baptistic, and open communion groups. This is seen in the report of an 1880 committee of the General Conference. As Jack Williams noted, 1886 was a "pivotal moment" in the move toward the dissolution of the General Conference. The resolution approved at that session would be quoted again and again over the next fifteen years. It affirmed the spiritual unity of all Christ's followers and the desire to form alliances with other denominations to advance Christ's kingdom, including a readiness to "join in organic union with such Christian bodies as may so far agree with us in doctrine and usage as to give assurance of continued harmony and peaceful relations in Christian work." Though official General Conference actions were not taken between 1886 and 1904, the drive to unite with another denomination grew in intensity in the last decade of the nineteenth century and continued into the twentieth.[51]

Some Free Baptists still seemed leery about a wider union with those outside the Arminian Baptist fold. In 1898, for example, in his report to the General Conference, field secretary H. M. Ford, using language reminiscent of the union movements circulating among southern Free Will Baptists, spoke of the need to unite "all liberal Baptists," referring to Free and Free Christian Baptists in Canada, Free Will Baptists in the South, and the General Baptists of the Midwest. He also mentioned the Church of God General Conference, an Arminian, baptistic body in the Midwest known as the "Winebrennarians" that practiced the washing of the saints' feet. Yet he was careful to say, "All these bodies substantially agreeing in polity and doctrine, no compromise and the surrender of no conviction being needed, there is no reason why the separation should longer continue to the detriment of the cause."[52]

In 1904 the General Conference named Alfred Williams Anthony the chair of the Committee on Conference with Other Christian People. He was just the right man for the job. He embodied a contagious zeal for what Baxter would fifty years later call the "reunion" of Free Baptists with the rest of the Baptist family. A 1904 initiative of George H. Ball, president of Keuka College, to unite with the Disciples of Christ gained some traction but had petered out by 1907. A merger with the Disciples of Christ would have made more sense for the Free Baptists. After all, the Disciples were thoroughly anti-Calvinist and baptistic but were moving away from their earlier views that tended toward baptismal regeneration. However, this was not to be.[53]

It is the height of irony that one of the greatest hindrances to union with the Disciples of Christ was that so many Free Baptists had given up on immersion as necessary for church membership. They thought the Disciples were too strict in requiring it of members transferring from paedobaptist or non-immersionist churches. It is just as ironic that the Free Baptists merged with the Northern Baptist Convention, which still contained large swaths of thoroughgoing Calvinism. Most Northern Baptists had moderated their Calvinism to the point that the only one of the five points of Calvinism they still affirmed was certain perseverance. This, however, speaks to the degree to which the Free Baptists' pietism and growing aversion to creedal and confessional formulas and sectarian doctrinal distinctions had led them to downplay even their Arminianism enough to be willing to call a truce on the doctrine of the possibility of apostasy.[54]

Other Factors in the Decline

Other considerations helped to hasten the decline of the Free Baptists. They did not move to growing areas fast enough to provide strong enough churches for Freewill Baptists who were moving to the cities from depressed rural areas and small towns. In addition to this, they were having difficulty getting their younger ministerial candidates to complete their education and keeping their younger ministers from going to other denominations. The Northern Baptists had softened their Calvinism and closed-communion stance, and Free Baptists had long before abandoned distinctive liturgical practices such as the washing of the saints' feet, the General Conference having decades earlier made it an open issue. There was only tepid disquiet about the one distinctive issue the denomination had left—the possibility of falling from grace—and the Free Baptists could not muster enough concern to vie for it. So younger ministers left for higher-paying pastorates that had similar baptistic practice but were willing to make things like open communion, the possibility of apostasy, and the requirement of immersion for church membership matters of indifference.[55]

Merger with the Northern Baptist Convention

After the 1904 General Conference, aggressive talks began to occur between the Free Baptists and Northern Baptists. However, the new Northern Baptist Convention had not yet formed. So the only union that could be achieved at that time was cooperation in mission and ministry. There was no formal body with which to merge. That problem was solved, however, when the Northern Baptist Convention was organized in May 1907. The 1907 Free Baptist General Conference voted to instruct the Committee on Conference to ask the Northern Baptists to agree on a "statement of common belief." They hoped such a statement would provide "a common principle under which our differences . . . so far as they still survive, may be tolerated." In March 1908 the committee met with their Northern Baptist counterparts and wrote a document entitled *The Basis of Union*. "Differences, if still existing, may be left, where the New Testament leaves them, to the teaching of the Scriptures, under the guidance of the Holy Spirit," the document specified.[56]

The Basis of Union read as follows:

After more than three years of conference, and careful study of the situation, a committee representing the American Baptist Missionary Union, the American Baptist Home Missionary Society, and the American Baptist Publication Society on the part of the Baptists, and the General Conference of Free Baptists on the part of the Free Baptists, under instruction of the Bodies appointing them, have formulated and do now recommend to their respective societies and constituencies the following plan for cooperation in missionary and denominational work.

First, the following brief historical statement shall be put into the records of each party to the co-operation: [This consisted of eighteen paragraphs of historical information about the Free Baptists.]

Second, it is recommended that the Constitutions of the American Baptist Missionary Union, the American Baptist Home Mission Society, and the American Baptist Publication Society be so changed as to admit to membership Free Baptists on the same terms as Baptists.

Third, that the general missionary work of the Free Baptists be adopted and carried on by the American Baptist Missionary Union, the American Baptist Home Mission Society, the American Baptist Publication Society, as the missionary agencies of the bodies thus united.

Fourth, that the churches of the united bodies will be expected to contribute to general missions through the above agencies, and the representatives of these agencies shall have equal standing in all the churches.

Fifth, that all the missionaries and pastors of the united bodies shall be recognized as on the same footing in all denominational activities.

Sixth, that this union shall go into effect January 1, 1909, provided that previous to that time the Free Baptists shall have approved it, and three-fourths of the Baptist State Conventions, where there are Yearly Meetings or Associations of Free Baptists, shall have approved it.

Seventh, it is suggested that in states where the Free Baptists equal twenty-five percent of the Baptists, or, more, the two organizations be consolidated into one new society to be called "The United Baptist Convention of the State of _____ and as a sub-title, "union of Baptist and Free Baptist Societies."[57]

The die was cast, and the merger was voted into being at the 1910 General Conference (because the conference met triennially, the decision could not be made until then). The report of the Committee on Conference noted that it was "impossible to obtain a full and adequate expression of conviction [of the yearly meetings and associations] within the time limit set in the basis itself, namely before January 1, 1909." The committee was also frank about the ambiguities of counting the vote of these constituent bodies. Their report stated that they were "satisfied" that two-thirds of the yearly meetings and associations, and "three-fourths of the resident church membership of the denomination" had voted to approve of the *Basis of Union*, "yet there was no definite record to which to turn and no court of appeal, excepting the General Conference itself." In other words, the General Conference would have to decide.[58]

Of the forty-eight constituent bodies with 53,799 members in the Free Baptist Register and Year Book of 1909, thirty-two constituent bodies representing 40,349 resident members would be needed to meet the terms of the *Basis of Union*. By that time, twenty-eight bodies representing 44,481 resident members had done so. Several bodies were undecided, but only five bodies, with a resident membership of 1,721, voted no. Fifteen bodies, with a resident membership of 2,558, either did not take action or did not report.[59]

The chart in the Minutes tallying the vote reveals that the negative votes came from "Ohio & Kentucky" (the Little Scioto and Kentucky Yearly Meeting), the Illinois Yearly Meeting, the Nebraska Yearly Meeting, the Northern Kansas Yearly Meeting, and the Southeast Missouri Yearly Meeting. These represented only about 15 percent of the yearly meetings and associations that voted, and only about 4 percent of the membership in the yearly meetings and associations that voted. In the discussion leading up to the vote, the three most outspoken opponents of the merger were T. C. Ferguson and S. L. Morris of Texas and John H. Wolfe of Nebraska. Ferguson was the most vigorous, wondering how the General Conference had the right to take funds that had been given by people for the purpose of supporting Free Baptist ministries and give them to another denomination. In response, Alfred Williams Anthony arose and said, "Away with the old dead hand of the past. We are looking for a new day." Some of the opponents of the union, such as T. J. Mawhorter of Indiana, ceased their opposition when Anthony explained that it was not to be an "organic union" but merely "fellowship." It took almost no time for this assertion to prove to be false. The vote was taken by ballot, and only 76 votes were cast, of which 61 were Yeas and 15 (about 20 percent) were Nays.[60]

It would take several years for the transition to be made, and in some areas where the merger encountered resistance, such as Nebraska, the fight was fierce. For example, the Nebraska Baptist Convention filed lawsuits against Freewill Baptists in the Nebraska Yearly Meeting for control of local congregations. Soon, however, the General Conference and its assets were dissolved. The colleges became Northern Baptist. The vast majority of yearly meetings, associations, and churches became Northern Baptist, though some retained Free Baptist or Freewill Baptist in their church names. Anthony tried to get the few holdouts in the Midwest and Southwest to make peace. With most he had success, but with others his efforts were to no avail.[61]

The Remnant of the Randall Movement

Most of the yearly meetings, associations, and congregations that stayed out of the merger were in Missouri; southern Illinois; southern Ohio, eastern Kentucky, and West Virginia; Nebraska and Kansas; and Texas. Many of these holdouts eventually became Northern Baptists. In Texas, for example, almost none of the current movement has roots in the Randall movement, and absolutely none in Nebraska and Kansas has. The present-day Free Will Baptist movements in Missouri, southern Illinois, southern Ohio, eastern Kentucky, and West Virginia have origins in both the Randall and Palmer movements. However, most of them had at one point united with the northern General Conference. Most present-day Free Will Baptist congregations whose origins are in the Randall movement are in the states of Missouri, Ohio, and West Virginia. The first Free Will Baptists in Kentucky originated out of the United Baptist movement and sought help from Ohio Freewill Baptists.[62] A discussion of the origins of Free Will Baptists in these states helps one understand the development of the movement in the Midwest and Southwest going forward. These groups would result in the formation of the Co-operative General Association in 1916, which would eventually help form the National Association of Free Will Baptists in 1935. While these states had origins in both the southern and northern movements, it will be convenient to consider them at this juncture. The objective of this section is to recount the origins of the present-day Free Will Baptist movement in these areas, not bodies that eventually united with the Northern Baptists or otherwise left the denomination.

Missouri

Because of the scarcity of records for the late nineteenth century, it is difficult to ascertain the origins of the Free Will Baptists of Missouri. While the majority of Missouri Free Will Baptists appear to have originated from Randall ministers who had moved westward, many of them started when ministers from the Palmer movement migrated westward. Chapter 8 will recount the origin story of the influential church planter David L. Poyner, a minister from North Carolina who moved to West Tennessee, then southern Illinois, then southeast Missouri, then northeast Arkansas, then finally northeast Oklahoma. Many of the Free Will Baptists of Missouri originated from the movement associated with Poyner, but no one knows how many. Poyner had been part of a "General Free Will Baptist" association in southern Illinois. That association had been established in the 1860s by a group of Free Will Baptists from the Cumberland Association in Middle Tennessee and a group of feet-washing General Baptists who had migrated from Kentucky. Poyner ministered in Ripley County, Missouri, where he lived from roughly 1870 to the end of the century.[63]

G. A. Barrett, one of Poyner's disciples, offered insight into the difficulty under which Poyner and other early Free Will Baptists in this area labored because of their Free Will Baptist confession of faith in an area with a large presence of "Missionary Baptists." Poyner stated that many of these early churches, like those in other areas, first held their meetings "under brush arbors. There were some few church buildings at this time belonging to the Missionary Baptists and Methodists. Very seldom was he allowed to preach in them, much less organize a church." Soon Poyner arranged to meet in two schoolhouses, out of which some of these early congregations were formed. Barrett remarked that these General Free Will Baptists encountered "persecution" from the "Close Communion Baptists, who styled the doctrine preached by Poyner as heresy." Yet Poyner preached "what he understood to be the doctrines taught by Christ and his apostles." Barrett said Poyner's opposition by the far more numerous Missionary Baptists was "like David against Goliath," and though sometimes Poyner felt weak, "yet he remembered his Lord had said, 'Out of weakness will I bring strength.'" Poyner's first two churches in Ripley County were Sugartree Grove and Brier Creek. Then, across the state line in Arkansas, his third church was Macedonia in Randolph County, of which Barrett was a charter member.[64]

According to Million and Barrett, the Western Mount Zion Association in Southwest Missouri originated from the Old Mount Zion Association in Northwest Arkansas. The origins of the Cave Springs Association, which continues to this day, are uncertain. Another likely indication of Palmer influence in Missouri is the fact that most of the churches in Missouri insisted on the washing of the saints' feet as an ordinance. This is instructive because many of the Missouri associations later joined the Co-operative General Association, and a few of its strong leaders, among them John H. Wolfe, militated against the rite. Wolfe affirmed the position of the northern Free Baptist General Conference, which had moved away from the washing of the saints' feet as a church ordinance as early as 1831. The first Randall *Treatise* said that, though Randall viewed the washing of feet as an ordinance, most Freewill Baptists of that time did not. That the Missouri churches held fast to it seems to indicate Palmer influence.[65]

While the majority of the movement in Missouri seems to have originated from the Randall movement, further research needs to be done to see how great a majority that was. The earliest known association in the state was the St. Francois Association, which continues to this day. Its origins were in the Randall movement in the mid-1860s. It was formed in 1869 as the St. Francois Quarterly Meeting from early congregations near Doe Run, De Lassus, and Loughboro. Elder Isaac Johnson was a minister from the northern movement who organized churches in Saline County as early as 1867. His work resulted in the founding of the Missouri Association, also called at various times the Missouri Central or Western Missouri Yearly Meeting. In 1869 these churches sent a letter to Elder D. G. Holmes of Chicago, which requested that he visit Missouri to help and instruct them. He came and helped form the yearly meeting, visiting annually for many years. Given Million's and Barrett's description of this association as "Central" or "Western," this may be connected with the "Central Western" quarterly meeting that joined the Missouri State Association at its initial meeting in 1914. It is evident that after the Free Baptist merger with the Northern Baptists, an association known as the Western Missouri Quarterly Meeting wrote a letter to the General Conference in 1917 asking to be dismissed from the General Conference. Further research may show that this is the same association.[66]

The Northwestern Yearly Meeting was started around 1870 from the efforts of O. S. Harding of Iowa. Was this the association that stayed out of the merger and would later help form the Missouri State Association? Or was it the Northwestern Missouri Association, to which Million and Barrett refer, that was formed in 1875 and changed its name to the Northwestern Missouri Yearly Meeting a year later?[67]

The present-day Missouri State Association of Free Will Baptists formed in the fall of 1914 at Philadelphia Freewill Baptist Church in Pattonsburg, Missouri. As Keith Garrison recounts,

> On the evening of November 25, 1914, a cool, damp evening permeated with light fog, the delegates arrived at the Philadelphia Church. Rural electricity had not yet made its mark on this tiny country hamlet, so oil lamps were used. A soft yellow glow shone forth from the windows as Rev. C. E. Mann, chairman of the Northeast Missouri Association, rose to the pulpit to deliver the introductory sermon and address of welcome.[68]

Many congregations in the northern part of the state had participated in the merger, but several yearly meetings and associations did not. The latter united to form the Missouri State Association. Its original members were the St. Francois Quarterly Meeting, the Northwest Association, the Northeast Association, and delegates from the Central Western Missouri and the Southeastern Kansas Associations. The next year, Western Mt. Zion, Laclede County, and Union Associations united with the State Association. The Missouri State Association would go on to be the leading influence in the new Co-operative General Association, founded in Pattonsburg in 1916.[69]

Illinois

Joshua Colson has recently shown that the present-day Free Will Baptist movement in southern Illinois had its origins outside the Randall movement. This movement eventually represented to the northern General Conference, but most of it did not participate in the merger with the Northern Baptist Convention. The earliest Free Will Baptist congregations in southern Illinois resulted from the work of Henry Smith Gordon. By 1837, Gordon had moved to Georgetown, Randolph County, Illinois, from across the river in Missouri. Soon he united with the Georgetown Missionary Baptist Church and was shortly thereafter ordained to the ministry. However, he came to reject closed communion and joined the Free Communion Baptists in 1851. It is uncertain precisely when Gordon became Arminian, but he came into contact with the General Baptist movement in Indiana, attending a meeting of the Liberty Association of General Baptists there in 1854 and meeting their founder, Benoni Stinson. Gordon's group changed its name to the southern Illinois Association of General Baptists in 1856 and kept that name for twenty years, when they changed their name to Freewill Baptist. In 1869, the association amicably divided into eastern and western branches, with the western association maintaining the old name. That association eventually united with the northern Freewill Baptist General Conference.[70]

The other main origin of southern Illinois Free Will Baptists, separate from the Gordon movement, had both southern Free Will Baptist and General Baptist connections in its origin. Colson has discovered through genealogical research that William Harvey Blankenship was born in 1824 in Davidson County, Tennessee, to John and Elizabeth Blankenship, noting that Robert Heaton, the founder of Middle Tennessee Free Will Baptists, said he baptized an "Elisabeth Blankenship" in Robertson County in 1826. This appears to be William Blankenship's mother, since her husband John died in Robertson County and a number of William's children were born there. Blankenship moved from Middle Tennessee to southern Illinois between 1860 and 1870. While there are no extant ordination records for Blankenship, it is certain that he was one of the Free Will Baptist ministers from the Cumberland Association who moved to Franklin County in southwestern Illinois and united with some General Baptists from Kentucky to form the Central Illinois General Free Will Baptist Conference. This is the conference David L. Poyner joined when he lived near Carbondale.[71]

Churches from both these groups apparently formed the Central Illinois Yearly Meeting, to which W. H. Blankenship belonged until his death in November 1879, recorded in the 1879 Minutes of the Freewill Baptist General Conference. There is little information about how, why, or which southern Illinois Free Will Baptists stayed out of the merger. However, one of the yearly meetings that is listed as a Nay vote in the vote of constituent bodies recorded in the Minutes of the 1910 General Conference is listed as simply "Illinois." Historians know that after the merger, the Central Illinois Yearly Meeting met in 1914 in West Frankfort. Henry S. Gordon's son George, a minister in the yearly meeting, helped persuade most of the members to join the merger. However, as Davidson shows, several congregations from the Franklin County and Wayne County Quarterly Meetings, which represented to central Illinois, refused to merge. Churches that stayed out of the merger tended to come from the Blankenship movement, including congregations such as Freedom, Union, and Harmony. This group named itself the Southern Illinois Yearly Conference and was composed of the Franklin County, Wayne County, and Freedom quarterly meetings. This conference would later dissolve, but the Illinois State Association of Original Free Will Baptists would form in 1960.[72]

Ohio, Kentucky, and West Virginia

The present-day movement in Ohio, Kentucky, and West Virginia also has mixed origins that are difficult to discern owing to the lack of extant records. Most of the early churches in these states seem to have been affiliated with the Randall movement at one time, and many of them directly originated from Randall origins. Others originated from southern Free Will Baptists who moved into the region either in the late nineteenth or twentieth century. This is especially true in Ohio, which had an influx of migration from the South after World War II. The Randall movement had planted a small number of Free Baptist churches in Northern Virginia and West Virginia that became Northern Baptist in the merger of 1911. They even sponsored two educational institutions in the region: a small college for freed slaves,

Storer College, in Harpers Ferry, West Virginia, and another school called West Virginia College in Taylor County, West Virginia. Ohio had been a very prosperous mission field for the Randall movement, which even started a college there, Rio Grande. However, almost all the Freewill Baptists of Ohio participated in the merger of 1911.[73]

One of the congregations that remained Freewill Baptist after the merger was the Old Kyger Church near Cheshire, which continues to this day. This was the first Freewill Baptist church in Ohio, founded in 1805 by Elder Eli Stedman, who moved to southern Ohio from Vermont that year. He organized and served Freewill Baptist churches in Ohio until his death in 1845. Another congregation that did not participate in the merger was the Porter Church, which continues to the present day. This congregation, which belonged to the Little Scioto Quarterly Meeting, was started in 1817 by Rufus Cheney of New York. Cheney also held credentials in the Meigs Quarterly Meeting, which would also remain Freewill Baptist. The Porter Church would host the meeting in 1939 at which the present-day Ohio State Association was formed. The Little Scioto and Meigs Quarterly Meetings together organized the Ohio River Yearly Meeting in 1833. A number of other quarterly meetings formed in the middle and later part of the century and joined Ohio River. One of these was the Jackson Quarterly Meeting, which was founded in 1873. The Pine Creek Quarterly Meeting began in 1879, joining that year with the Little Scioto Quarterly Meeting to form the Ohio and Kentucky Yearly Meeting. The Porter Quarterly Meeting was organized in 1901.[74]

The above quarterly meetings have been mentioned here because they did not participate in the merger of 1911. Their rejection of the merger can be traced to the influence of Ohio ministers with a strong sense of loyalty to the Freewill Baptist tradition and its faith and practice. The most influential of these was Thomas E. Peden. The vote of constituent bodies presented at the 1910 General Conference showed that the "Ohio & Kentucky" Yearly Meeting, which the minutes several pages later showed had changed its name to the Little Scioto and Kentucky Yearly Meeting, voted not to approve the merger. This yearly meeting was involved in the triennial General Conference that Peden helped start in protest after the 1892 northern General Conference officially changed its name to Free Baptist. The Ohio River Yearly Meeting, to which Peden originally belonged, also represented to this body.[75]

Alfred Williams Anthony referred to a group of southern Ohio Freewill Baptists in his report to the final session of the Free Baptist General Conference in 1917 as "the survivors of the followers of Rev. Thomas E. Peden, who severed their connection with General Conference in 1892, because of

DOCTRINE AND DECLINE IN THE NORTH 187

the incorporation of our body." The origins of the present-day movement in Ohio are found in churches and quarterly meetings that came out of these conferences. Three of the current conferences of the Ohio State Association (established 1939)—Jackson County, Pine Creek, and Porter—were Randall quarterly meetings that refused to participate in the merger. Another quarterly meeting that stayed out of the merger, Meigs, went defunct in the 1980s. Some of the churches that did not merge are members of the present-day Lawrence County Conference.[76]

Present-day Free Will Baptists in West Virginia originated from Randall influences, primarily in Ohio, as well as other influences from southwest Virginia and eastern Kentucky. The movement dates back to the establishment of the Kanawha Quarterly Meeting, which was founded by Randall Freewill Baptists from southern Ohio in 1883. Thomas Peden was active among West Virginia Freewill Baptists. In 1887 he moved across the state line from Ohio to become president of West Virginia College, which Freewill Baptists founded in 1868. Two of the conferences that formed out of the Kanawha Quarterly Meeting still exist: the Boone Conference, an independent conference that is not a member of the West Virginia State Association, and the Beckley Conference, which began as the Raleigh Quarterly Meeting. The West Virginia State Association would not be formed until 1946.[77]

The earliest churches in the present-day Free Will Baptist movement in Kentucky appear to have arisen from United Baptists who, for unknown reasons, accepted the possibility of apostasy, open communion, and the washing of the saints' feet and subsequently came under the influence of Ohio Freewill Baptists. These beginnings later combined with influences from southwest Virginia to form the modern-day Kentucky Free Will Baptist movement. There were Randall churches in Kentucky as early as the 1820s, but they had disappeared by 1879 when the first conference connected to the present-day movement started—the Johnson County Conference. The first congregation in this conference gathered when a group of members led by Thomas S. Williams and James, Nathan, and Eliphus VanHoose withdrew from the Mingo United Baptist Church in Johnson County in 1876 to form the Tom's Creek Freewill Baptist Church. No one knows how they came to be Free Will Baptists, but they formed the new congregation and later consulted with northern Freewill Baptists ministers in southern Ohio.[78]

Almost half of the more than eighty churches of the John-Thomas Association are in Kentucky. John-Thomas is the largest Free Will Baptist association that is not affiliated with the National Association. Through this association, Southwest Virginia Free Will Baptists had an impact on the

Kentucky movement. Little is known about the origins of either the John-Thomas Association or its member conferences. The association itself was not founded until 1923. The date of origin of its constituent conferences is not established. These churches appear to have a Palmer background, as evidenced in the association's use of the *1812 Abstract* as its articles of faith from its founding to the present. At its beginnings all its member churches were from Wise or Dickenson County, Virginia. Later in the century, it added two Kentucky conferences: Letcher County, which joined in 1936 or 1937, and Pike County, which joined in 1964. Outside Kentucky, most of the rest of its congregations are in southwest Virginia. Some of its member churches are in Indiana and Ohio. There has been pervasive cross-pollination between this association and the Free Will Baptists of Eastern Kentucky who are members of the Kentucky State Association. Earlier in the twentieth century, John-Thomas frequently exchanged delegates with the Kentucky State Association. The latter association was formed in 1939 in a meeting at Tom's Creek Church.[79]

One reason Ohio, West Virginia, and Kentucky did not form state associations until the 1930s and 1940s was that most of their churches and conferences were members of the Tri-State Association. That short-lived, regional association was formed in 1919 by conferences in Ohio, West Virginia, and Kentucky.[80]

Conclusion

The merger of the Free Baptist General Conference with the Northern Baptist Convention in 1911 signified the end of an era and, for all intents and purposes, the end of a movement. After the fallout from the merger of 1911, scattered Freewill Baptists who did not participate in the merger would regroup, some in existing quarterly and yearly meetings, others in new conferences and associations. Some of these Freewill Baptists united with congregations and associations in their regions that had origins in the Palmer movement. This was particularly evident in Missouri and Texas. These groups, primarily in the Midwest and Southwest, would soon unite with the Co-operative General Association. While the Free Will Baptists in Oklahoma had Palmer origins, Oklahoma would soon become a center of activity for this new Association, which in turn would later help form the National Association of Free Will Baptists.

Part IV
GROWTH AND IDENTITY IN THE SOUTH, 1866–1910

Eight
SOUTHERN FREE WILL BAPTISTS
New Beginnings and Westward Expansion

FREE WILL BAPTISTS had enjoyed a long history in the Carolinas. Their migration into areas such as Georgia, Florida, and Alabama had influenced some United Baptists there who later became Free Will Baptist. United and Separate Baptist groups in Tennessee had also become Free Will Baptist, but no one yet knows who or what influenced them to do so. Thus by the end of the Reconstruction period, there was a steadily growing movement of Free Will Baptists across the southern states. In the 1870s and 1880s, the same pattern repeated itself as Free Will Baptists moved west or Baptist groups became Free Will Baptist for reasons yet unknown. There are a few documented instances in the years after the Civil War of Free Will Baptists from the Eastern Seaboard eventually making their way to states west of the Mississippi. Most of the westward movement during this period, however, was from Alabama, Mississippi, and Tennessee.

Origins in Mississippi

Many of the Free Will Baptists in Mississippi find their origins in the Bethlehem Association associated with C. C. Vandiver and his brothers. That association had member churches in northeast Mississippi at least as early as the 1870s. Most of the rest of the Bethlehem congregations were in south-central and West Tennessee and North Alabama. Bethlehem churches appear to have been the earliest Free Will Baptist congregations in Mississippi.

The Bethlehem Association gave birth to the Tennessee River, Flat Creek, Flint River, and Muscle Shoals State Line Associations in the same tri-state region. Eventually the Little Brown's Creek Association in northeast Mississippi, which still exists, formed out of the Tennessee River Association in 1892. Before that, none of the Vandiver churches were in Mississippi-based associations but were in associations that comprised churches in all three states. Little Brown's Creek was the first association in Mississippi to emerge from this movement.[1]

The second-oldest group of churches in northeast Mississippi originated in the 1870s from the movement associated with Ellis Gore and the Mount Moriah Association in west-central and northwest Alabama. Some of Elder Gore's friends across the state line in northeast Mississippi started congregations that at first maintained membership in Mount Moriah and Alabama-based associations that had been allied with it, such as the Vernon and Jasper associations. Lowndes County, Mississippi, of which Columbus is the county seat, surfaces a great deal in records of Free Will Baptists across the South. Of course, the fact that Lowndes County was directly across the state line from Pickens County, Alabama, where Gore started the Mount Moriah movement of Free Will Baptists, means that there would have been much cross-pollination from Alabama Free Will Baptists in that area of Mississippi. For example, Gore's protégé Thomas J. Molloy maintained residence in Lowndes County for a time, where he married his wife Elmira in 1840. It appears that this area was alive with Free Will Baptist influence quite early. There also can be little doubt that Free Will Baptists from the Bethlehem Association further north developed relationships in this area as well. Another very early Mississippi minister was Z. D. Lawless, who was ordained in Alcorn County in 1877. There is no extant record of churches in Alcorn County in any of the Alabama associations. Lawless would later minister in Arkansas and Oklahoma.[2]

Eventually these churches were gathered into associations across the state line from Alabama. One early association, Union Grove, comprised churches in this region, most of which later became members of the Tupelo Association, which was organized in 1884.[3] Another association appears to have been started out of an amicable division of the Vernon Association. In 1883, the latter association resolved to divide itself into two "associational districts," the dividing line of which would be the Alabama-Mississippi state line. In 1883, Vernon had thirteen churches in Itawamba County, five in Monroe County, three in Lee County, and one in Prentiss County, all in Mississippi.

The Tupelo Association was established in 1884 from churches unaffiliated with the Vernon Association.[4]

A later movement with different origins was founded in south Mississippi at the turn of the twentieth century. The Zion Rest Association, which would in the mid-twentieth century change its name to the South Mississippi Association, was organized in 1908. Little is known about its origins, but its founders came out of the United Free Will Baptist movement associated with Georgia Free Will Baptists. Historians know this not only because of the use of "United Free Will Baptist" in the association's title, but also because its articles of faith are shared by United Free Will Baptist associations in south Alabama and West Florida that formed in the 1880s. This indicates that the founders of Free Will Baptists in south Mississippi were probably from the Liberty Association in south Alabama and West Florida. It is also clear that the articles of faith that Zion Rest had in common with Liberty were also shared by a small group called the Middle Georgia Association of United Baptists, entitled "Doctrinal Statements of General Principles Taught by United Free Will and Other Liberal Baptists."[5]

Leading Mississippi ministers such as M. L. Hollis would lead in the formation of a state association in 1942, which consisted of northeast Mississippi and Zion Rest Associations, with a visiting delegate from Little Brown Creek, which would soon join. This statewide association flagged but would be revived in the mid-1960s and exists to this day. Early leaders with Mississippi connections were influential in the organization of Free Will Baptist congregations and associations in Arkansas and Oklahoma.[6]

Origins in Arkansas

Little is known about the pluriform origins of Free Will Baptists in Arkansas. The movement in the eastern, central, and southwestern parts of the state originated from Free Will Baptists who had moved from other parts of the South, such as North Carolina, Alabama, Mississippi, and Tennessee. Less is certain, however, about the transition of the movement in northwest Arkansas from United Baptist to Free Will Baptist. Arminianizing United Baptist congregations and associations there began becoming Free Will Baptist, it appears, in the 1880s and 1890s. It is not certain if Free Will Baptist influences from southwest, northeast, and southeast Arkansas—movements started as Free Will Baptist—helped effect this shift or if it resulted from other influences. Yet the former seems most plausible.

Central Arkansas

By all accounts, the earliest Free Will Baptists in Arkansas were associated with Francis Marion Hudson, a deacon of the earliest known Free Will Baptist church in the state, organized in Pope County in 1850. That congregation was one of several congregations that formed the seedbed for the Antioch Association, which formed in 1892. Antioch comprised churches in Pope County, of which Russellville is the county seat. Hudson, a northwest Alabama native who had moved to Arkansas in 1846, was a charter member and deacon of that original church in Pope County in 1850.[7]

Little is known about this congregation and whether it was started as a Free Will Baptist church or later adopted Free Will Baptist faith and practice. It is certain, however, that in the 1890s the Antioch Association had ministers from northeast Arkansas such as W. C. Austin, who hailed from the Bethlehem tradition in West and south-central Tennessee. Hudson, who was not ordained as a minister until 1899, also helped organize a church in 1870 in Moreland, Pope County. Before it closed in the early twenty-first century, this was the oldest continuing Free Will Baptist congregation in Arkansas. Hudson was from Lauderdale County, Alabama, which means that his family might have been acquainted with the Free Will Baptist movement in that part of North Alabama and West and south-central Tennessee that was home to the Bethlehem Association identified with C. C. Vandiver.[8]

Southwest Arkansas

The Little Missouri River Association was founded in 1879. There was Free Will Baptist influence on this association from outside the state. Zedekiah D. Lawless was an ordained Free Will Baptist minister from northwest Alabama/northeast Mississippi who had been born in 1832 in Tuscaloosa County, Alabama, to Hiram and Mary Lawless. By the time he was four years old, he was living in Pickens County, Alabama. Z. D. married Mary Jane Howell in Itawamba County, Mississippi, in 1850, with whom he had thirteen children. He was ordained a Free Will Baptist minister in Alcorn County, Mississippi, in 1877. By 1878 when his son Charles was born, he was still in the northwest Alabama/northeast Mississippi region. By 1880, however, he was in Pike County, Arkansas, where his son John Henry, later also a minister in Little Missouri River, was married that year. It is reasonable to conjecture that Zedekiah was in Pike County by 1879 when the Little Missouri River Association was organized that fall. By 1891, the first year there are extant minutes for Little Missouri, Z. D. was a highly active minister in the association, serving as moderator. His son John Henry Lawless was also on the roll of ministers that year. The 1910 census shows Z. D. Lawless living in Pushmataha County, Oklahoma, a strong county in the early history of Free Will Baptists in Oklahoma. He died there five years later.⁹

Northwest Arkansas

Westin Goodspeed said that the first Free Will Baptist church west of the Mississippi was organized by Samuel Whitley in 1832 in Marion County, Arkansas. However, as Davidson shows, this congregation was not Free Will Baptist this early. The church Goodspeed referred to started as a United Baptist congregation and was joined by other United Baptist congregations such as Big Fork Church, also in Marion County. Charles Whitley and his brothers Isaac and Samuel came to Arkansas from Virginia. By 1838, Charles had started the Union United Baptist Church, having been active in the United Baptist movement in East Tennessee. Samuel came to Arkansas in 1842, having moved from Virginia and having lived in Tennessee for a time. Isaac arrived from Virginia in 1842.¹⁰

It is uncertain how these United Baptists became Free Will Baptists, thus adopting open communion, the possibility of apostasy, and the washing of the saints' feet. Yet their transition to Arminianism began when they broke from the Primitive Baptists over the issues of "foreordination" and "free salvation." They formed the Union Association of United Baptists in 1850, identifying themselves with the United Baptists formed in Kentucky in 1801 when Separate and Regular Baptists came together in the union of the Elkhorn and South Kentucky Associations. No one knows when they became Free Will Baptist, but by the 1880s, they were using the name and maintaining membership in the Old Mount Zion Free Will Baptist Association.¹¹

The origins of the Old Mount Zion Association in 1851 are hazy, but these Free Will Baptists also made the transition from United Baptist. That association originated from the Mt. Zion and Sugar Creek United Baptist churches, organized in 1847 and 1848 respectively. The *Free Baptist Cyclopaedia* states that W. J. Blackburn was ordained in 1865 in the Old Mount Zion Association. Blackburn's father, Sylvanus Walker Blackburn, was listed as a Free Will Baptist clergyman in the 1860 US census for Benton County. The elder Blackburn and his wife Catharine had moved from Hickman County, Tennessee, to Benton County by the mid-1830s. These factors raise several questions, the chief of which is, why did the census taker list Blackburn as a Free Will Baptist clergyman in 1860? This seems too early for this designation. The Old Mount Zion Association does not appear to have made the transition to confessional Free Will Baptist identity until the early 1890s, and there appear to have been no Free Will Baptists near Hickman County, Tennessee, in the 1830s when Sylvanus and Catharine Blackburn moved from there to Arkansas. Future research will no doubt tie up these loose ends.[12]

Little is known about the origins of the Arkansas Association, another very early association that formed in 1869. It appears that it also originated as United Baptist. Old Mt. Zion did not affirm the possibility of apostasy until the 1890s, and there is no knowledge when the Arkansas Association made the transition to full Arminianism, since the first extant minutes are from 1909. Did these associations become Free Will Baptist as a result of influence from Free Will Baptists from southwest Arkansas, which had Mississippi/Alabama Free Will Baptist roots? It seems likely. Further research will no doubt provide definitive answers to these questions.[13]

Northeast Arkansas

One of the most interesting migration stories in the history of the Free Will Baptist Church is that of Elder David L. Poyner. Davidson explains how Poyner organized the Social Band Association in northeast Arkansas in 1875, consisting of three congregations: Sugartree Grove, Brier Creek, and Macedonia. This association was started as a "General Free Will Baptist" association. The reason for this name was that Poyner had lived for a time in southern Illinois, where he had come into contact with a group that had started in 1862 or 1863 from a union of Free Will Baptists from the Cumberland Association in Middle Tennessee and some General Baptists from Kentucky. Both groups had migrated to southern Illinois. Poyner eventually moved to Ripley County, Missouri. There he established churches before moving across the state line into northeast Arkansas where he founded the Social Band Association.[14]

Harrison and Barfield, in their *History of the Free Will Baptists of North Carolina*, discussing "Free Will Baptists in Mo. and Ark." said that "Eld. David Leroy Poyner," who had moved to Ripley County, Missouri, "was born July 2nd, 1823, in Caswell County, N. C. He professed religion in the year 1845, and was ordained in 1867." Though Harrison and Barfield had some of the dates wrong, genealogical research shows that Poyner was born to Jesse and Nancy Poyner in Caswell County in 1820, where he lived in Yanceyville when his sister Louisa was born two years later. He was married and widowed three times and had seven sons and seven daughters.[15]

What makes Poyner's story even more interesting is that by 1849 he was in McNairy, Tennessee, where he married Nancy Kendall McAdoo. This is in the same area of south-central Tennessee where the C. C. Vandiver group was active. Eight of Poyner's children were born in this area of Tennessee from

1850 to 1863. By 1867 Poyner had moved to the Carbondale area of southern Illinois. If all this geographical confluence of Free Will Baptist influence were not fascinating enough, he moved to northeast Oklahoma sometime in the late nineteenth or early twentieth century and was laid to rest in Broken Arrow, Wagner County, in November 1903.[16]

South-central and West Tennessee had an impact on the Poyner movement in its second generation. According to G. W. Million and G. A. Barrett, Elder W. C. Austin, who helped found the Union Band Association in northeast Arkansas in 1893, and Elder C. S. Austin (it is not known if they were related) were both products of the Bethlehem tradition of south-central and West Tennessee, North Alabama, and northeast Mississippi. C. S. Austin was a member of the quadrennial meeting of the Bethlehem, Tennessee River, Flat Creek, and Flint River Associations.[17]

W. C. Austin was born in Hardin County, Tennessee, and was affiliated with the Bethlehem network of associations as early as 1882. He was well-known for his participation in highly attended debates he had on Free Will Baptist doctrine with ministers from other denominations at a time when such cross-denominational debates were popular. Million and Barrett cleverly (if partisanly) described the upper hand Austin had in one of the debates with the well-known Church of Christ minister J. G. Conner sometime before the latter's death in 1897: "Elder Conner being the experienced debater, and as this was Brother Austin's first, his opponent had considerable advantage in this respect. Brother Austin, however, being stationed on a solid rock and Elder Conner in the mud, rendered the battle more equal and the results were in our favor." In another debate, Austin's Methodist opponents "were getting worsted so badly that they stirred up a racket and stopped the debate. . . ." For a time Austin served Free Will Baptist churches in Oklahoma in an era when the Oklahoma movement was very young. In 1906 he moved back to Arkansas where he and G. W. Million participated in the publication of the *Free Will Baptist Banner*.[18]

The Tyronza Association in northeast Arkansas exemplifies another connection with the Bethlehem-Vandiver tradition. The two most influential ministers in this association were both Methodists named J. H. who became Free Will Baptists: J. H. Bullard and J. H. Johnston. Bullard organized most of the congregations in the Tyronza Association, which he helped gather in 1892 in Poinsett County. He was born in Tishomingo County, Mississippi, in 1848 but did not become a Free Will Baptist until 1890. He was ordained in West Tennessee by the Flat Creek Association, after which he planted three churches in Poinsett and Mississippi Counties in Arkansas. Johnston, who was born in Lawrence County, Tennessee, in 1854, left the Methodist ministry in his mid-twenties and joined the Mt. Cabo Free Will Baptist Church in Henderson County, Tennessee, which he served from 1889 to 1891. That congregation was a member of the Flat Creek Association, associated with the Bethlehem tradition. Johnston moved to Tyronza, Arkansas, in 1896, where he served Free Will Baptist churches for the next twelve years.[19]

Southeast Arkansas

The Hamburgh Association in southeast Arkansas was the product of Alabama Free Will Baptists associated with the Mount Moriah tradition given birth by Ellis Gore. One of Gore's protégés Thomas J. Molloy, a long-standing and influential minister in the Mount Moriah Association, moved to Ashley County, Arkansas, where he helped start the Hamburgh Association there. (Most of the early leaders in the association had the surname Molloy.) Hamburgh used the same unique articles of faith that Mount Moriah did, discussed in the next chapter. Molloy was born in Fayette County, Alabama, in 1820, to Daniel and Martha Molloy. He married Elmira Jane Wilcox in 1840 in Lowndes County, Mississippi. They had nine children, among them Daniel J. Molloy, also a minister in the Hamburgh Association, and another son, Ulysses C. Molloy, a layman and clerk of the association. This association eventually merged with the Saline Association, which still exists.[20]

Thus, to summarize, the origins of the Free Will Baptists in central Arkansas are unclear, though there was influence from the northeast Arkansas movement. The latter was started by a minister from Eastern North Carolina and involved a minister from West Tennessee. Origins in northwest Arkansas are uncertain, but it is likely that these Arminianizing United Baptists there were influenced by southwest Arkansas Free Will Baptists who were from northwest Alabama/northeast Mississippi. The movement in southeast Arkansas resulted from the labors of Alabama/Mississippi Free Will Baptists associated with the Mt. Moriah tradition. In 1898 the Arkansas State Association was organized at the Moreland Church in Pope County. That association's initial meeting included the Antioch, New Hope, Old Mount Zion, Arkansas, and Tyronza Associations. The body elected Jesse Jeffrey as moderator and George W. Burris as clerk.[21]

Origins in Texas

Some home missionaries from the Randall movement ministered among the White population in Texas in the late nineteenth century, and most of the congregations they planted seem to have been lost in the 1911 merger of that denomination with the Northern Baptists. The earliest ancestors of the modern-day movement in Texas, whose story will be told in recounting the history of the United American Free Will Baptists, were former Black slaves who had become Freewill Baptists through the ministry of home missionaries from the Randall movement. The vast majority of present-day, predominantly White Free Will Baptists in Texas derive from churches planted by ministers from the Chattahoochee Association in Georgia and from northwest Arkansas/southwest Missouri, with some influence from Eastern North Carolina.[22]

Historians traditionally held that Angus McAllister Stewart was the founder of Free Will Baptists in Texas. However, they did not know where he came from, and some conjectured that he was from the Randall movement. However, Robert L. Vaughn has shown that Stewart was a native of southwest Georgia. As noted in chapter 4, Stewart's connections with Benjamin Tipton, an older minister from Stewart's home county, Early County, Georgia, would have opened him up to association with Henry Boyett and Brinson Hollis. These were Free Will Baptist ministers from North Carolina who had migrated to the tri-state area of southeast Alabama, West Florida, and southwest Georgia. Thus Stewart is the link in a chain stretching from North Carolina in the early nineteenth century to Texas in the late nineteenth century.[23]

Stewart and fellow Chattahoochee pastor Joseph Apperson, son of David J. Apperson, one of the founders of Georgia Free Will Baptists, laid the groundwork for a vibrant movement of Free Will Baptists in Texas. Stewart started the first Free Will Baptist church in Texas at Clayton in Panola County in 1876 and founded the Texas Free Will Baptist Association two years later. Several of the congregations he had organized formed this association. Stewart, the son of John M. and Hulda Stewart, was born in Early County, Georgia, in 1853. He enrolled in Buford Academy in Gwinnett County, Georgia, at seventeen years of age, the same year he professed Christian faith, and was ordained the following year.[24]

One first learns of Stewart's work in Texas when he was a teacher in Marshall, Harrison County. He remained there for a few years, during which he organized a handful of churches that he formed into an association. Soon, however, he returned to Georgia, where he taught school, still single. He served as a pastor in the Chattahoochee Association in 1881 and 1882. However, he was back in Texas by November 1883, when he married Emma Ross in Panola County.[25]

According to the *Free Baptist Cyclopaedia*, Stewart planted five other churches in these early years in Panola, Rusk, and Cherokee Counties. One of these, Good Hope, exists to the present. He also assisted P. H. Adams in the organization of at least two congregations in Brazos County, more than 150 miles to the southwest of his main area of influence. One of these congregations, Bright Light, exists to this day. Stewart, mostly together with W. T. Woods, planted thirteen churches between Bright Light's founding in 1886 and the founding of the Grass Bur Church at Bowman's schoolhouse in 1899.[26]

While planting churches, Stewart continued his work as an educator, starting the Lone Star Institute in Cherokee County, the Hewitt Institute in Beckville, and the Academic and Collegiate Institute, informally known as the Free Will Baptist Academy, in Bryan. He also enjoyed an extensive itinerant ministry, preaching across the United States in Baptist and Free Will Baptist congregations. In this capacity he was involved in union movements to bring together all baptistic and open-communion non-Calvinists into one fraternal alliance. Stewart's wife Emma was also very active in the work of Texas Free Will Baptists, especially in youth ministry and the support of missions. She served a number of years as a member of the association's mission board and as president of its Young People's Society of Christian Endeavor.[27]

Joseph Lemuel Apperson was one of the other ministers who laid the foundation for Texas Free Will Baptists. Also from the Chattahoochee Association in Georgia, he was born in Macon County, Georgia, to Elder David J. and Sarah Apperson in 1842. The first extant minutes of the Texas Free Will Baptist Association in 1894 show that Apperson was the moderator of the association and pastor of the New Prospect Church in Cherokee County, and Stewart was pastor of the Union Springs Church in Rusk County and the Tatum Church in Panola County. Apperson, who was about nine years older than Stewart, served alongside him as a minister in the Chattahoochee Association in 1881 when Stewart was between his two stints in Texas. While Stewart was on the Chattahoochee roster of ministers in 1882, Apperson was not, meaning that he probably had moved to Texas by that time. Apperson's wife Eliza died while giving birth to their son Joseph Lemuel Apperson Jr. in Cherokee County in 1887. Joseph Sr. married Mary Davis two years later, who died in 1931. Apperson died in Jacksonville, Cherokee County, Texas, in 1935 at the age of 93, after a long and fruitful ministry among Free Will Baptists in Georgia and Texas.[28]

Not all the founders of Texas Free Will Baptists were from Georgia. Harrison and Barfield mentioned one North Carolina Free Will Baptist minister who had moved to Texas before the mid-1890s: J. T. Eason. They reported that Eason had moved from North Carolina to Texas, where he had planted a Free Will Baptist church. However, nothing else about him is known, except that he ordained another Free Will Baptist minister named Charles Stetson, known as the "Cowboy Preacher." Stetson later moved to Oklahoma, where he was active among Free Will Baptists there and helped publish the *Free Will Baptist Banner*. However, there is no other information about his ministry in Texas.[29]

Two brothers from northwest Arkansas/southwest Missouri, J. W. Ford and his brother J. A. Ford, were instrumental in establishing churches in central Texas in the late 1880s. They organized the West Fork District Association around 1890. Josephus Wesley Ford had a biographical entry in the *Free Baptist Cyclopaedia*, which was published in 1889, discussing his ministry among Arkansas Free Will Baptists. Ford was born in Washington, Arkansas, in 1848 to Richard and Martha Ford. He married Eliza Young in 1870, with whom he had thirteen children. Ordained to the ministry in 1880, Ford pastored several congregations in northwest Arkansas and southwest Missouri. Little is known about Ford's brother, James Alexander. However, by the late 1880s they were both in Decatur, Texas, about forty miles northwest of Fort Worth. J. A. Ford did write an article about the work in Texas for the Randall paper, *The Morning Star*, in 1901. J. W. died in 1898 in Decatur, Texas, at the age of fifty, and J. A. lived until 1912 when he died in Decatur.[30]

A small remnant of the Randall movement remained alive in Texas, but its origins are shrouded in mystery. Still, historians have noted the influence of this small contingent on the early history of the Texas State Association, which was founded in 1915. The vast majority of the continuing movement of predominantly White Free Will Baptists, however, originated from ministers who migrated to Texas from other parts of the South.[31]

Texas Free Will Baptists played a large role in the formation of a regional association of churches known as the Southwestern General Convention. This convention was made up of congregations that came from both Randall and Palmer backgrounds in Missouri, Oklahoma, Arkansas, Texas, and Louisiana. Million and Barrett said that about half the Free Will Baptist churches in those states were a part of the Southwestern General Convention. Two of that convention's most influential ministers were T. C. Ferguson and S. L. Morris, both of whom were serving in Texas at the time they both voted against the merger of the Randall Free Baptists of the North with the Northern Baptist Convention. Ferguson and his wife would travel many miles as half-time promotional agents for the convention. The Fergusons and Morrises would go on to play important roles in the Co-operative General Association alongside others, such as the Reverends Hiram and Lizzie McAdams and Dr. I. W. Yandell. The Texas State Association was constituted in 1915 at

Bradley Junction. At its first session it elected E. L. Hill as moderator and W. E. Dearmore as clerk.[32]

Origins in Oklahoma

Ministers such as David Poyner (originally from North Carolina but who had served in Tennessee, southern Illinois, Missouri, and Arkansas) and Zedekiah Lawless (originally from Mississippi but who had ministered in Arkansas) had moved to Oklahoma in the late nineteenth century. However, historians currently know nothing about their ministry or influence in northeast (Poyner) and southeast (Lawless) Oklahoma. Million and Barrett said that the founders of Oklahoma Free Will Baptists were "descendants of the Free Will Baptists of North Carolina." They did not discuss their reason for this assertion. Perhaps they were speaking of Poyner, who had been their primary mentor. They could also have been indicating that Mississippi and Alabama Free Will Baptists had ties to the original Free Will Baptist movement in North Carolina. Despite our lack of knowledge of Poyner's and Lawless's impact on the early history of Oklahoma Free Will Baptists, however, it is certain that other early pioneer Free Will Baptist ministers in the Oklahoma Territory hailed from Arkansas and Alabama.[33]

Fifty or sixty miles southeast of Broken Arrow, where Poyner was, and north of Pushmataha County, where Lawless was, Elders James M. Roberts and Thomas Jefferson Townsend had moved from Arkansas into Indian Territory in what became northeast Oklahoma. Very little is known about Townsend. He had lived in Howard and Pike Counties, Arkansas, the same counties in which Zedekiah Lawless and the Little Missouri River Association were active. Sometime between 1889 and 1891, Townsend moved to Oklahoma and established the earliest Free Will Baptist churches in Oklahoma. In 1891 Townsend sent letters inviting others to come and help him organize a Free Will Baptist association. He sent one of the letters to Elder William Coggins of Wise County, Texas. The organizational meeting of the Center Association was held in 1893 at Center, Indian Territory, just west of Ada. The body elected Elder Mark Harris as moderator and the deacon M. L. Hunt as clerk. Over the next ten years the Center Association would grow to six congregations, eight ordained ministers, and 175 members.[34]

Genealogical research, letters, and diary entries have revealed a little more about Roberts. He was born in Crawford County, Arkansas, in 1852, to Frans and Emily Roberts. He married Mary Elizabeth Witt in 1873, and they had nine children. In 1884, they moved from Sebastian County, Arkansas, to Webbers Falls in the Cherokee Nation in what is now Muskogee County, on the Arkansas River. There he rented land and started farming and, in his own words, "began preaching on Saturdays and Sundays in the little school houses here and there and under brush arbors and shade trees. I had a wife and seven children at that time, for which I made a living on the farm, so it took a lot of my time." Mary died in 1939, and Roberts was laid to rest in Stigler, Oklahoma, in 1940.[35]

According to Roberts, in 1892 a Free Will Baptist minister named "O. J. Tailor" moved from Texas to a place near McLain, also in present-day Muskogee County, and began preaching. This was Obediah Johnson Taylor, who was born in Anderson County, South Carolina, in 1851 to Talliaferro (Toliver) and Anna Taylor. He was still in South Carolina in 1870, when he married Elzira Findley. Sometime between 1870 and 1873, they moved to Paris, Logan County, Arkansas. Other than a brief stint in Texas, they lived in Arkansas until 1892. By 1894 Taylor was assistant moderator of a Free Will Baptist association in Indian Territory near Spiro, known as the Old Territorial Association. Having moved from South Carolina to Arkansas to Texas to Oklahoma, Taylor provides another example of patterns of migration and influence among Free Will Baptists across the South in the nineteenth century.[36]

Roberts said that he and Taylor "began preaching together" and, later in 1892, organized the Concord Free Will Baptist Church at the Buckhorn schoolhouse near McLain. This was "the first Free Will Baptist church organized in the Cherokee nation." For the next six years, Roberts and Taylor worked together planting many churches across eastern Oklahoma. The first two of these congregations were the Fields Chapel Church and the Star Villa Church. In 1895 they planted another congregation in Cullachaha near Cameron in the Choctaw Nation. The next year, Elder Roberts founded Mountain Home Church northwest of Webbers Falls, followed by Polks Chapel Church near Warner in 1897 and a congregation at Stigler in 1899. As Delbert Akin writes, "These were trying times. There was no money, no roads, and no bridges." Thus Roberts and his co-laborers often walked to their churches to preach, having to wade unbridged streams even in the coldest weather. "Sometimes," Akin narrates, Roberts "slept with his Bible for a pillow and his bed a pile of leaves or grass with the pale moon and the twinkling stars as a covering."[37]

Roberts's most influential early associate was Elder J. E. (Joshua Eiland) McGee, after whom, with Roberts, the Roberts-McGee Free Will Baptist Association was named. McGee represents still another migration story. He was not from Arkansas but from Vernon in Fayette County, Alabama, where he was born in 1857 to Peter and Annie Eiland McGee. Peter McGee was also a Free Will Baptist minister from Pickens County, Alabama, who was ordained by the Mount Moriah Association during the time when Ellis Gore was active there. Peter served until his death in 1887 in Vernon, Alabama.[38] J. E. McGee married Sarah E. Nabors in Lamar County, Alabama, in 1878, and the two had ten children. He died in Darwin, Pushmataha County, Oklahoma, in 1923. McGee was especially noted for his evangelistic work in the Choctaw Nation.[39]

McGee helped Roberts form the Territorial Association at Nubbin Ridge in 1894. This body grew to have churches from eighteen miles west of Tahlequah, east to Fort Smith, Arkansas, and south to Antlers, Oklahoma. The delegation elected Elder A. Barnhill as moderator, Elder O. J. Taylor as assistant moderator, and a layman, I. W. Graham, as clerk. Other than Barnhill and Taylor, several ministers were present: Roberts, McGee, L. D. Bearden, J. W. Burkhawlter, J. H. Brown, and W. G. Ramsey, representing the Cullachaha, Concord, Liberty, New Hope, Shiloh, Union Grove, and Kenida Churches. The next year twelve ministers attended, and eight congregations sent delegates. Over the next three years, the congregations of the Territorial Association experienced so much growth that an amicable division of the association was necessary. Thus the Territorial Association was split into two smaller associations on either side of the Canadian River. One was called Grand River Association, while the other was named the Roberts-McGee Association, for J. M. Roberts and J. E. McGee.[40]

In these early years, many young pastors were called into the ministry. The most outstanding of these was Dr. I. W. Yandell. He would go on to play roles of mammoth proportions in the development of Oklahoma Free Will Baptists. The first of those roles was that of moderator of the Oklahoma State Association. The work of early Oklahoma pioneers such as Townsend, Roberts, McGee, and Taylor led to the establishment of numerous churches that comprised seven associations. These bodies united in 1908 to form the Oklahoma State Association.[41]

The Beginnings of the African American Free Will Baptist Church

Early Developments in North Carolina

Records concerning the origins and history of Black Free Will Baptists are especially meager. Thus it is difficult to piece together the movement's history. Shortly after the Civil War, a separate movement of African American Free Will Baptists began to form, with origins primarily in the Carolinas and

Georgia. A series of resolutions in the 1866 annual session of the Cape Fear Conference dealing with "the colored members of our connection being allowed to preach the gospel" are illustrative of this development.[42]

The resolutions cited the change in "the political condition of the colored members of our connection, . . . they having formerly been slaves, and deprived of the privilege of preaching the gospel but now declared free by the authority of the United States." The resolutions stated that some of the Black members had petitioned the conference for authority to preach the gospel and that such members were "no longer to be deprived of such a privilege." The resolutions stipulated that "any colored member of our connection" who felt divinely called to the ministry could apply to his local congregation, be examined, and be granted a license to preach. However, they called for the racial segregation of the ministry and of the churches, stating that Black ministers would be licensed "to exhort among [their] own color." If the licentiate demonstrated he was "worthy, sound in faith and doctrine, and shall promise usefulness in the cause," then the congregation would recommend his ordination under the "jurisdiction of this conference, and governed by the same discipline." Such ministers were authorized to "raise up churches of their own color." The conference also appointed a committee to visit these newly formed congregations and provide annual statistical reports on them, enrolling them on the minutes as "the African Free Will Baptist Church." This would set the stage for a new conference of the African Free Will Baptist Church that would operate autonomously but in fraternal fellowship with the Cape Fear Conference. This new conference, eventually known as the Cape Fear United American Free Will Baptist Conference, would have its first official meeting in 1868 and would grow significantly over the next four decades. The first extant minutes in 1910 show that by that point the conference comprised forty-six congregations.[43]

A similar development occurred that same year in the North Carolina General Conference. The minutes of 1866 contain the first reference to Black members of Free Will Baptist congregations in the conference. The conference approved a motion that the "colored people who are, or wish to be, members of our churches remain as they have done heretofore." However, most of these members elected to move their membership to new Black congregations in which, as Pelt notes, "they could freely exercise their talents and interests without being dominated by their former masters." In these new congregations, they would enjoy the full rights and privileges of church membership and ministry, of which they had been largely deprived in most predominantly White congregations.[44]

This same scenario played out in this era in the South and North alike. Most White congregations had not granted the full privileges of church membership to African American members, whether enslaved or free. Whites had often kept Black members' names on separate rolls, seated them in separate seating, often in balconies or galleries, and limited leadership and teaching roles to Whites. This is evident in one of the few references to slavery or persons of color in the records of southern Free Will Baptists. In the 1855 *Discipline* of the North Carolina General Conference, a brief statement regarding church discipline stated: "No person of color within the pale of the Church shall give testimony against any person but those of color."[45]

That slavery and Black church members were mentioned so scarcely in extant records of Free Will Baptists in the South is unusual when compared with other southern denominations. There are a few other extant references to slavery among southern Free Will Baptists. Chapter 1 referred to Benjamin Laker's enslaved workers in the 1680s and the incident involving Paul and Joanna Palmer's slave in the 1720s. Another example is from Robert Heaton, the founder of Middle Tennessee Free Will Baptists, whom the 1840 census shows owned nine slaves. Another is from the Mount Moriah Association in Alabama, which refers to new churches being started by freed slaves. However, obviously, there were enough slaves among the North Carolina Free Will Baptists after the Civil War to justify the resolutions in the General and Cape Fear Conferences and form the nucleus of the new African Free Will Baptist Church. Together with the leanness of extant records for this period, the relative absence of reference to slavery probably owes itself to the fact that the majority of Free Will Baptists were primarily poor yeoman farmers who lacked the means to hold slaves.[46]

The North Carolina General Conference followed a similar course as Cape Fear. Realizing the desire of African American Free Will Baptists to have autonomous congregations, Elders Henry Dixon and R. K. Hearn introduced a motion at the 1867 annual session for "the colored members of this connection to unite and form churches to themselves; but if any of them wish to remain enrolled among the White members, they can do so as private members, and we also advise them to form a general conference to themselves." The conference appointed a committee to advise these new congregations, and the following year another committee was formed to aid in the organization of a "colored Free Will Baptist General Conference." The best known of these early congregations was Shady Grove Free Will Baptist Church in Snow Hill, Greene County, North Carolina, which was organized in 1867. Another of these early congregations was the "Colored Free Will

Baptist Church of Gum Swamp," organized by Black minister Arnold Spain and White ministers R. K. Hearn and Jessie Stancil in 1869. This congregation was first pastored by Elders Austin Atkinson and William Randolph, who constructed a meeting house with funds donated by the (majority-White) General Conference. This congregation later changed its name to Holly Hill Original Free Will Baptist Church. The more than 150-year history of this early congregation has been marked by long pastorates, with only four pastors having served the church between the founding pastors and the current pastor, Bishop James E. Tripp Jr. The success of these early churches led to the formation of numerous other congregations, which formed the first Annual Conference of Black Free Will Baptists in 1870.[47]

Understanding the Experience of Black Ministers after the Civil War

While no firsthand accounts of early Black Free Will Baptists survive, their experiences can be seen in autobiographical accounts of other African American ministers at this time in the South. The Colored Methodist Episcopal bishop Isaac Lane, for example, explored the difficulties he encountered with his call to preach the gospel during his enslavement: "I learned to read and write under the greatest difficulties. I was not only deprived of a teacher, but I was not allowed the use of a book or a pencil. I had to learn the best I could." A lengthy extract from Lane's autobiography gives insight into the probable conditions of Black Free Will Baptist ministers under slavery and shortly after emancipation:

> Shortly after my conversion I was overcome with a feeling that I ought to preach. I strove for months to get rid of it, but without success. I went to a man in whose piety and Christian virtue I had much confidence and made known to him my struggle and the feeling that was then strong upon me. He gave me his sympathy and directed me to a certain preacher for counsel and aid; but this man did not believe in Negroes preaching, and he gave me no encouragement. I next sought the advice of a colored man whom the Methodists had helped. He was a pure Christian man, and he told me that if God had really called me to preach he surely knew his own business better than man and advised me not to trouble myself, but trust God. I did trust him; and soon thereafter the inspiration came, and I firmly decided to enter upon the work of a minister.
>
> I sent in my petition to a Quarterly Conference of the Methodist Episcopal Church, South, for license to preach. The Conference did not grant my request, but gave me license to exhort instead. The committee

explained that the Church did not believe it proper to grant license to Negroes to preach. Rev. George Harris was the presiding elder, and Rev. A. R. Wilson was the preacher in charge of the local Church. Rev. Wilson was my personal friend up to the time of his death, and he took a lively interest in my career and my work. In the early days of my ministry I regarded him as a great and good man, and during all the years of our acquaintance thereafter the esteem in which I held him when I was a young man did not suffer in any way.

During the Civil War the attitude of the Southern Methodist Church toward granting license to Negroes to preach had undergone some changes, and so I appeared again for license to preach. This time I was sent before the Quarterly Conference presided over by Elder William H. Lee. After asking many questions bearing upon almost every phase of the doctrines of Christ and the Church, I was granted license to preach.

I have already spoken of the prayer meetings and the splendid opportunity they afforded in exercising the gifts that God had given me and the deepening of the work of grace in our hearts. These meetings proved to be a great preparation for the work that I was called upon to do after I had entered fully into the work of the Christian ministry. Being licensed to preach, I was frequently called upon to preach and exhort, especially on Sunday afternoons, not only to my people, but the white people also would come out in large numbers to hear me. At first I was very much embarrassed to preach before such large crowds, because I realized fully that I was without education and had but little opportunity of learning anything. But God helped me wonderfully and blessed my work.

From the time I was licensed to exhort up to 1865 I held meetings for our people. We had glorious times, and many converts would rise and "tell of Jesus and his love." These meetings made our country famous for Methodism during the war. . . . Many times my life was in great danger, and the white people were constantly being reviled and reprimanded because they had encouraged me in preaching. The persecutors went so far as to burn down the church houses in which I had preached to my people. But I had gone too far in the work to be stopped by such methods. Too many people, both white and colored, believed in me to be sidetracked by any such methods; for at this time not only Methodists, but Christian people of all denominations, upheld me and sought to give encouragement. One good old Presbyterian brother said to me after I had preached in his church: "Brother Lane, keep on preaching the gospel, and we will keep on building church houses until the trumpet blows. Let them burn down. We will build, and you shall preach."[48]

The Origins of the United American Free Will Baptist Church

The Annual Conference led to the formation of the United American Free Will Baptist Church (UAFWBC), which was incorporated in 1887. The growth of this body led to the planting of new churches and the organization of new conferences, and eventually in 1899 these conferences formed the General Conference, which was registered with the General Assembly of the State of North Carolina in 1901. Four years later, J. P. Parker (Governing Elder), T. T. Williams, and B. J. Mayes petitioned the General Assembly of the State of South Carolina to incorporate The African Free Will Baptist Church of South Carolina General Conference.[49]

In 1903 the UAFWBC adopted a Book of Discipline. The need for a new Discipline had been sensed at the 1899 formation of the General Conference. That body "saw that the advanced state of the connection, and the exigency of the times renders it necessary to revise our Book of Discipline, with such alterations and amendments as will make it expressive of the sentiments and usages of the denomination. Accordingly a committee of revision was appointed to accomplish the desired work." This was considered by the General Conference at its 1901 session at St. John's Free Will Baptist Church in Kinston, North Carolina, and its 1902 session at Dunn's Chapel Free Will Baptist Church in Dunn, North Carolina. The Discipline Revision Committee reported:

> The committee acknowledges its indebtedness to our former elders for the verification of the foundation of the principles upon which we stand. Yet we have labored most studiously to make a volume that would serve as an exponent of the practices of our beloved connection to those who are not personally acquainted with them. Also it will serve as a convenient textbook for the churchman.
>
> While we acknowledge the Scriptures as our only infallible rule of faith and practice, we need such a manual as this for convenient reference. It should be widely diffused and carefully studied by our ministry and membership, while we confess our inability to the arduous task set before us and the scrutinizing eye of the critical, we hope that this work will be the means of carrying the desired blessings to many.
>
> The committee have secured the copyright of this Book of Discipline, under the title of "The United American Free Will Baptist Faith" and

present it to you trusting that all the Brotherhood may find within this sacred volume that which they have long desired.

God speed the work, is the prayer of your humble servants.

Elder T. Draughton   Elder W. H. Randall   Elder G. B. McNeil

Elder J. H. Isler   Elder A. Blount[50]

The doctrinal portion of the *Discipline* reproduced the *1812 Abstract*. This remains the confessional statement of the present-day United American Free Will Baptist General Conference as well as several other Black Free Will Baptist bodies.[51] Similar groups of African American Free Will Baptists arose across the South. While extant records are extremely sparse, some information survives regarding the origins of movements in southern states such as Georgia, Alabama, Louisiana, Mississippi, Texas, Kentucky, Virginia, and West Virginia.

GEORGIA

Black Free Will Baptists in Georgia originated in a way very similar to those in the Carolinas. In 1872 the Chattahoochee Association appointed Elders C. C. Martin, D. J. Apperson, and L. Gibson to establish a new association called the Spring Creeks Association for the African American members who had been affiliated with Chattahoochee. Spring Creeks grew until it spun off another association, the Mount Hosea Association, in 1887. Three other associations followed: the Georgia Eastern Association in 1889, the Southern Union Annual Conference in 1898, and later the Star Bethel Association, apparently organized in 1936. According to Robert Gardner, based on oral testimony, these five associations existed into the early twenty-first century. The latest reliable membership statistics from these associations indicate that in the mid-twentieth century they comprised at least forty-one congregations with 1,600 members. Despite the segregation of Black and White associations and churches, the animus described below regarding the general population in Texas is not evident among the Free Will Baptists. There are several instances, for example, in which Chattahoochee sent visiting delegates to meetings of Black Free Will Baptist associations. Yet this was not a one-way street; Chattahoochee also received visiting Black ministers from Spring Creeks and Mount Hosea as delegates at its annual sessions.[52]

One of the most influential of the United American Free Will Baptist movements in Georgia was founded by Elder Samuel H. P. Edmonson. Edmonson was born in Lenoir County, North Carolina, in 1869 and was converted under the preaching of Elder J. H. Isler at Sutton Chapel Church in Kinston in 1889. Edmonson migrated to Berrien County, Georgia, where he served as a bi-vocational minister, eventually planting several United American Free Will Baptist congregations, creating a movement that multiplied in that area and further south into Florida.[53]

ALABAMA

Little is known about the origins of Black Free Will Baptists in Alabama, except for the fact that the Mount Moriah Association in 1869 underwent a process similar to those above, in setting up an association for freed slaves. However, Mount Moriah's policy on allowing African American members to remain in White congregations was more restrictive than those of North Carolina. Mount Moriah voted to "prevent amalgamation" of "negroes" and Whites in the same congregations. Yet they voted to help set up African American churches and ensure they were "properly taught by men of Ability."[54]

Precious little is known about the early Black Free Will Baptist presence in Alabama. However, there was a strong movement there as early as the 1880s. The 1891 Minutes of the Mallet's Creek Association provide a window into the faith and practice of the early Black Free Will Baptists of the South. Founded in 1890 in Lawrence County in North Alabama, with churches in Hillsboro and Athens, this association held its second annual session in late July and early August of 1891 over four days, Thursday morning through Sunday evening. The group had begun using "Rev." (for Reverend) as a title for ministers, as opposed to "Eld." (for Elder). This is early for the use of this title, which would become more common among Free Will Baptists and other Baptists in the early twentieth century. Still, the minutes referred to candidates examined by the "Committee on Ordination, for eldership."[55]

One of the ministers, J. M. Watkins, took his sermon text from "Paul's Letter to the Ephesians 2:20—'are built upon the foundation of the apostles and prophets,' etc." The body sang classic hymns such as "My Shepherd Will Supply My Need," a paraphrase of Psalm 23 by Isaac Watts. No doubt, for this hymn they used the tune "Sidney" from the *Sacred Harp*, which was very popular among Black Free Will Baptists in Alabama. Later a version of the *Sacred Harp* would be published by African Americans, *The Colored Sacred Harp*.[56] The proceedings of the association were marked with utmost seriousness and decorum:

> Recess having expired, the members of the Association reassembled. The moderator, being at his post of duty, called the meeting to order. He then

arose and charged the members of the Association how they should act, telling them not to forget their duty of respect and love for each other. He also charged them to enter into business with marked attention, and for each member to do his utmost to have the business carried on in a nice, quiet manner, and according to rules of order. After thus cautioning, he announced the house ready for business.

The moderator appointed committees: a Devotional Committee, committees on Finance, Preaching, Examining Credentials, and Annual Meetings—and a "Standing Committee on Printing, Education, Sabbath-school, Temperance, Ministry, Mission, Correspondence, and Morals." St. Mark Free Will Baptist Church, which had "come out from the Missionary Baptists," was received for membership at the meeting; "upon being examined," the congregation was "found orthodox and worthy of connection with us." The right hand of fellowship was extended to the new member congregation, after which a prayer of consecration was prayed. The minutes were detailed, containing comments on each sermon preached, using phrases such as "a well-argued discourse," "the text was wisely explained," and "the text was beautifully explained." The Saturday morning meeting was set aside for addresses on five queries, each presented by a different minister:

1. What is faith? and its importance, by Rev. I. Mays, which was nicely explained.
2. What is religion? and the requirements to obtain it, by Rev. J. M. Watkins, which was beautifully analyzed.
3. What is conversion? by Rev. G. McIntosh, which was beautifully discussed.
4. What should be the morals and character of a minister of the Gospel, by Rev. A. Watkins, which was very nicely elucidated.
5. Should a man educate himself to preach the Gospel? and why? By Rev. I. E. Holt, which was wisely explained.

The body passed a resolution that each church pay their delegates' travel expenses and resolved to encourage congregations to purchase books and periodicals from the Morning Star Publishing House in Boston, the publisher for the Randall movement.

Mallet's Creek had emerged from a Primitive Baptist background. The minutes stated in an "Ectype" that it was their "duty to come out from the

Primitive, or old school, Baptists, and rear up a Freewill Baptist church, as we do not believe that God made any one expressly for hell, as inculcated in the Primitive, or old school, Baptist churches." Their confession of faith consisted of the brief "Confession of Faith" found in the 1854 *Treatise* of the Randall movement before it was revised in 1871.[57]

TEXAS

The first Free Will Baptists in Texas were Black Freewill Baptists. Their churches originated from the efforts of home missionaries from the northern Freewill Baptists who moved to Texas to do mission work in African American communities. The first Free Will Baptist congregation in Texas, St. Paul Free Will Baptist Church in Lancaster, was a Black church. It was gathered in 1870, six years before Whites established Free Will Baptist congregations in the state. St. Paul Free Will Baptist Church exists to this day. Other congregations were planted in the Dallas area, resulting in the formation of the Northwest Texas Quarterly Meeting in 1883. Soon another quarterly meeting formed, the Dallas Quarterly Meeting. Northwest Texas and Dallas united in 1891 to establish the Northern Texas Yearly Meeting, which exists to the present.[58]

One of the White ministers from the North involved in the effort to plant churches in Black communities wrote to *The Morning Star* in 1873:

> I am in Texas and getting along as well as could be expected. The society is dull, and the people seem to have a form of religion, but they are so prejudiced against the colored people and Yankees, that they can have but a little of the love of Christ in their hearts. War and bitterness seem to fill their hearts. In some localities they have burned down the school houses built for the colored people, and do all they can to prevent their having any school. If a Yankee preaches he must look out for himself, or he will have trouble.... I think that I shall organize two Freewill Baptist churches soon. I find also many colored people that want to organize into a church. They like the Freewill doctrine because it is the teaching of the Bible. There are some of the Close Communionists that are coming over. There are some colored preachers that want to become Freewill Baptists, but they have been ordained in the close [communion] faith. We are very much in want of some copies of the Treatise and Register, which I will send for as soon as I get some money.[59]

Another association with an early existence in the state was the Northeast Texas Association, which was gathered as early as 1886, when it reported to the Randall General Conference. The association's letter to the General Conference stated: "We meet with great opposition here, because of our free doctrines, and our color. We are determined to live and enjoy our freedom. We ask admission to your body." That year they reported twenty-two churches and twenty-four ministers.[60]

LOUISIANA

Other Black Free Will Baptist movements in the South started as a result of efforts by the Randall movement. The earliest of these movements began in Louisiana during the Civil War, not by home missionaries but by a Union army chaplain, D. P. Cilley. Cilley was a northern Freewill Baptist minister who became acquainted with a Black Baptist minister named Charles Ready and his nephew J. Blackstone. He began sharing his Freewill Baptist doctrine with them, and they both became Freewill Baptists, were ordained, and began planting churches. Two of the earliest of these churches were in the towns of Angola and Algiers, Louisiana. At the time of Ready's death in 1877, these two congregations together had more than five hundred members. After Ready's death, Elder Isaac Williams took his place as the most influential leader among these churches. The work continued to prosper, adding congregations and ordaining numerous new ministers. Out of this nucleus three quarterly meetings were organized in 1873: New Orleans, Angola, and Baton Rouge.[61]

Later the Louisiana Yearly Meeting was formed and joined the Randall General Conference in 1883 with the following letter:

> It gives us great pleasure to be represented for the first time in your body. Although we are situated at a great distance from you, and belong to a race of people that has been ostracized and regarded in other days as goods and chattels, yet we have souls, and the Spirit of God has operated upon them, and we have been brought into the Christian fold. And the same spirit that made us Christians made us Freewill Baptists, and you may be assured, dear brethren, that we are loyal to the doctrines and polity of the denomination. We have three quarterly meetings and thirty churches. We have Sabbath schools in the most of our churches, and harmony prevails throughout all our borders.[62]

MISSISSIPPI

Also in the 1860s, a robust movement of Black Free Will Baptist churches emerged in Mississippi. No one knows whether these congregations were planted by heirs of the Palmer movement or Randall movement, though most were probably products of the latter. It is certain that one of the most influential early African American ministers in Mississippi and Louisiana was Elder Reuben Kendrick. The brief extant account of Kendrick discusses Black Free Will Baptist movements in both Kentucky and Louisiana. The well-traveled Kendrick was likely the leading church planter and organizer among the Black Free Will Baptists in the 1880s. Baptized by Elder Wesley Gule, pastor of a Kentucky congregation known as the Wamac Chapel Free Will Baptist Church, Kendrick was licensed to preach in 1868 in Baton Rouge, Louisiana. Elder Gule and another Kentucky minister, George Harris, ordained Kendrick in Baton Rouge two years later.[63]

Kendrick planted his first four congregations in Louisiana: Spring Hill, Zion Hill, Cockram Hill, and Pleasant Grove. Soon returning to Mississippi, Kendrick was elected as a representative to the Mississippi State Legislature in 1871, in which he served for four years. After he left office, he settled in Natchez, where he soon gathered a congregation. There he influenced the Missionary Baptist minister H. M. McIntyre to accept Free Will Baptist faith and practice, which led to a large group of Black Missionary Baptists becoming Free Will Baptist. Kendrick succeeded in forming the Mississippi Yearly Meeting in 1881, combining the Amite County and Natchez Quarterly Meetings. The Mississippi Yearly Meeting first represented to the Randall General Conference in 1886. Its letter to the General Conference stated: "Please receive us as a member of your body, and our delegate will tell you that we agree with you." In 1884, Kendrick moved to Louisiana, where he planted six more churches by 1888.[64]

VIRGINIA AND WEST VIRGINIA

Little is certain about the origins of the Black Free Will Baptists in Virginia. The first congregation in the state was organized in the Shenandoah Valley in 1867 as a result of missionary efforts of the Randall movement. Three years later there were enough churches to form two quarterly meetings with ten churches, which represented to a yearly meeting. This yearly meeting joined the General Conference in the North, which noted in its 1871 Minutes that these congregations were "composed almost entirely of those who were once slaves, and they are active and ambitious Christians." Most of these early congregations appear to have been absorbed by the Northern Baptists in the merger of 1911.[65]

Most of the West Virginia ministry among African American Free Will Baptists appears to have been swallowed up by the 1911 merger. However, early efforts in West Virginia are a vital part of the story of the early history of the Black Free Will Baptist movement. Nathan C. Brackett was one of the first home missionaries sent to work in communities of freed slaves in Virginia and West Virginia. His work, which started in 1865, was known as the Shenandoah Mission. It primarily consisted of establishing a network of schools for the education of freed slaves. Eventually, his work would result in the founding of Storer College in Harper's Ferry, West Virginia. In 1867, Brackett's activity shifted to the formation of Storer College, and A. H. Morrell assumed leadership of the Mission. Its first church was organized by two teachers, Miss Anne S. Dudley and Miss E. H. Oliver, at Martinsburg in June 1867. Eventually, enough congregations were gathered to be able to form the Harper's Ferry Quarterly Meeting. Soon Black ministers and teachers were trained and assumed leadership of the churches and schools of the Shenandoah Mission.[66]

In February 1867, Mr. John Storer of Sanford, Maine, pledged to Oren B. Cheney, president of Bates College, a matching gift of $10,000. The gift was designated for the establishment of a college for freed slaves, should another $10,000 be raised across the denomination by January 1868. The funds were raised, and, as Gideon Burgess and John Ward said, "notwithstanding the earnest opposition of those hostile to the education of the colored people," the West Virginia Legislature granted a charter in March 1868. Thus Storer College was founded. Storer became a favorite ministry of the Woman's Missionary Society, which in 1876 built Myrtle Hall, a girls' boarding house named after the northern Freewill Baptist youth magazine *The Myrtle*. Anthony Hall, the main building on campus, was renovated as a result of the generosity of the Freewill Baptist deacon L. W. Anthony, whose gift of $5,000 the Woman's Missionary Society matched in 1882.[67]

N. C. Brackett served as president for the first three decades of Storer's existence. His wife Louise Wood Brackett played a major role in the early years of Storer. An artist, Mrs. Brackett taught Latin, Greek, art, and literature. Burgess and Ward stated, "At first, bitter opposition from the white population was encountered. The teachers were ostracized and severe threats were made." Sharon D. Kennedy-Nolle, in her book *Writing Reconstruction: Race, Gender, and Citizenship in the Postwar South*, tells the story of furloughed cadets from the Virginia Military Institute harassing Storer students and female teachers, garnering an apology from Robert E. Lee, then president of Washington College. Storer was, Kennedy-Nolle says, "the only college for black West Virginians seeking teaching or academic degrees until 1892, when the state established the West Virginia Colored Institute."[68]

Burgess and Ward reported that by 1889, much of the hostility had been "overcome, and President Brackett, once of all men most hated and despised, has been for years a member of the city government. The school has won a place in the hearts of all." Storer College would be the center of a vibrant movement of African American Freewill Baptists in the region which, despite absorption by the Northern Baptist Convention in the 1911 merger, would form part of the history and character of the United American Free Will Baptist Church.[69]

Conclusion

During the forty-five years after the Civil War, mammoth changes occurred among Free Will Baptists in the South. The UAFWBC was started among African Americans after emancipation, developing and expanding quickly across the South, aided by efforts of the northern Freewill Baptists in providing education and church planting among freed slaves. The White churches in the South struggled as a result of the Civil War and Reconstruction. One sees a decline, for example, in the educational levels of southern Free Will Baptist ministers educated in this period as compared with those educated in the antebellum era. However, after the Reconstruction period, Black and White Free Will Baptists began to expand rapidly across the South and move west into the frontier in new areas such as Mississippi, Arkansas, Texas, and Oklahoma.

Nine
THE DEVELOPMENT OF SOUTHERN FREE WILL BAPTIST INSTITUTIONS THROUGH 1910

THE CIVIL WAR and Reconstruction period was a turbulent time for predominantly White Free Will Baptists in the South. From roughly 1861 to 1880, the momentum the Free Will Baptist movement experienced in the decades before the War was halted, and it experienced profound setbacks. After the 1870s, however, it grew and spread quickly. This numerical expansion was accompanied by a phenomenon similar to what Ruth Bordin, echoing Ernst Troeltsch, called the "sect-to-denomination process." This progression from what Troeltsch termed a "sect-type" religious organization to a "church-type" religious organization had occurred among the wealthier northern Freewill Baptists a generation earlier. In the latter decades of the nineteenth century and the first decade of the twentieth, the Southern Free Will Baptist development of institutions and organizations reflected this model. The three most obvious ways this process occurred in the South were in denominational education, publishing, and movements toward union.[1]

Education among the Southern Free Will Baptists

After decades of discussion and longing for the establishment of a Free Will Baptist institution of higher learning in the South, the Free Will Baptist Theological Seminary at Ayden, North Carolina, was founded in 1896. Owing to the poverty and geographical separation of Free Will Baptists, together with an anti-intellectual undercurrent in some segments of the movement, before the 1890s there had not been a long-standing Free Will Baptist educational movement. Had the movement not been racked by the Civil War and Reconstruction, no doubt sustainable schools would have been founded earlier. One can also detect a downturn in the quality of writing of Free Will Baptist ministers educated during and after the War when compared to older ministers whose schooling occurred before it.

Concern About Education in the South

In areas of the movement where education was emphasized, apprenticeship, mentoring, and self-education was the order of the day. The Chattahoochee Association's standards for its ministers in mid-nineteenth-century South Georgia exemplifies this approach:

> All ministers [must] agree to read the Scriptures daily, going through the Old Testament once and the New Testament twice per year, at least, consulting some commentator upon every obscure or difficult passage; to commit to memory the two epistles to Timothy, the epistle to Titus and the Lord's Sermon on the Mount; and to commit to memory the various passages relating to some or all of the following subjects: the existence and character of God, the original, present, and future state of man, the divinity of Christ, the office and operations of the Holy Ghost, faith, justification, regeneration, love or charity, works, etc. That these studies may be constantly and beneficially pursued, it is recommended that where two or more ministers reside in the same vicinity, that they have stated times of meeting for mutual examination, and select the subjects to be studied till the next meeting. The ministers of each association are to meet annually with the body, to report their progress and adopt a course of study for the ensuing year. . . .
>
> After this first meeting the plan of study will probably embrace ecclesiastical history, and some other important subjects. By this means it is hoped to raise up a body of well-informed and efficient ministers, trained to labor together in the vineyard of the Lord.[2]

This respect for learning, even if informal, is reflected in many of the circular letters printed in the minutes of the Chattahoochee Association throughout the nineteenth century. It obviously had an impact on A. M. Stewart, a minister in the Chattahoochee Association who was the first White Free Will Baptist to plant churches in Texas. Stewart was a schoolteacher who had studied at Buford Academy in Gwinnett County, Georgia. He held both the AB (Bachelor of Arts) and AM (Master of Arts) degrees. With

Col. Thomas Cocke, he started the Lone Star Institute in Cherokee County, Texas, which "emphasized cultural accomplishments in music and education," causing "many families" to relocate to Lone Star to enroll their children in the school. Stewart also established the Hewitt Institute in Beckville, Texas, and by 1903, he was principal of the Academic and Collegiate Institute, informally known as the Free Will Baptist Academy, in Bryan, Texas. Stewart's concern for education influenced the Texas Free Will Baptist Association. That Association's Committee on Education and Publication, of which Stewart was chair, called on the "board of examiners" for ministerial ordination to "prescribe" a "yearly course of reading" for all the association's ministers from a "circulating library" the association maintained. It advocated that "the churches should exert themselves for the education of the ministers that come from their ranks."[3]

One sees a similar emphasis in East Tennessee and Western North Carolina. These Free Will Baptists' high esteem for education appeared in early attempts by the Toe River Association to establish a school. As early as 1858, Toe River's committee on education said the following in its report:

> Dear Brethren—Having investigated the subject of Education, and viewing the great importance of it in advancing a literary, moral, and esthetical training, and acquiring a sound evangelical literature, it is therefore recommended that this Association recommend the Churches to send Delegates to Jack's Creek Church ... to select some suitable place in the bounds of this Association for the purpose of erecting a School-house and building up a School of high character.[4]

That vision eventually came to fruition in the establishment of Woolsey College in 1872. The Free Will Baptists of East Tennessee and Western North Carolina directed Elder William Bonaparte Woolsey and others to build a school, which Woolsey constructed on three-and-a-half picturesque acres he donated in the mountains of East Tennessee near Greeneville. A classical school that also offered a theological course of study, Woolsey College would provide education not only to ministers but also to students of all ages until it was absorbed by the public school system in Greene County in 1904.[5]

Another early call for a theological institution was made in an 1881 circular letter to the Mount Moriah Association in Alabama by Vernon pastor J. M. I. Guyton. He argued that ministers "should know more than any other class, for it is their business to teach." Even though young ministers are "taught and sent by the Spirit of God," they "need nevertheless to study the Bible; they need to know the rules, and power and right use of their own language" as well as "somewhat" of the biblical languages. This would better equip them "to repel the many forms of heresy that now assail the Christian faith." Guyton thanked God for older ministers like Ellis Gore and others, "men of the largest usefulness, who have never had the advantages of an education. They are self-taught men." Yet such men themselves advocated "an educated ministry." Guyton went on to press for formal theological education:

> Whence we conclude that we must have an educated ministry. . . . How are we to accomplish this end? Shall the young brethren be required to study in the scattered and brief remnants of time which they shall be able to save, or borrow from other pursuits? Shall they be required to buy, beg, or borrow the books they may need as best they can?
> No brethren, we must establish a Theological School and furnish it with a well stored library.[6]

That Guyton would lament Gore's limited formal education is ironic in light of the relative theological and rhetorical sophistication of some of the latter's circular letters in the Mount Moriah Association's minutes. It is noteworthy that notices of the deaths of ministers in nineteenth-century conference minutes across the South tended to praise ministers for their education or lament that they were unable to avail themselves of an education, owing to their poverty and difficult circumstances. Also one notices that the rhetorical and linguistic beauty of many of the extant writings of this period exceed that of our own day.

Ayden Seminary

It was not until 1896, however, that a long-standing institution for ministerial education would be established. This was the Free Will Baptist Theological Seminary in Ayden, North Carolina. This school, which would later change its name to Eureka College, served Free Will Baptists for thirty-four years. Its students were primarily from the Carolinas, but it also served students from across the southern states. Ayden Seminary, as it came to be called, laid the foundation for later institutions such as Zion Bible School, Free Will Baptist Bible College (later Welch College), and Mount Olive College (later the University of Mount Olive).[7]

In March 1896, a committee was appointed by a union meeting of the North Carolina General Conference to draw up bylaws, begin selling shares, and start construction of a building for an educational institution. A board was appointed, with J. M. Barfield as president of the board and T. F. Harrison as secretary. They located the school in Ayden. In an article in *The Free Will Baptist*, Harrison wrote that education

> should be of great and profound interest to all F.W.B., inasmuch as our future success and advancement depends on an education. Time after time have I had our old preachers to tell me what an awful struggle they have had in life trying to preach the Gospel of Christ, and especially when they were expecting to be assailed by some educated divine. The poor preacher would quake and tremble, not because he did not have the truth, but because he had no education. O may God bless us in our noble effort in building a F.W.B.T.S. to educate our preachers.
>
> Education is development. It aims to bring into harmonious action all the powers of the mind, not, as some supposed, a cultivation of a few, to the neglect of all the rest. Education should have reference to the whole man—the body, the mind, and the heart. To his body it will give vigor, activity, and beauty; to his heart virtue and praise; to his mind correctness and acuteness.

Harrison died the next year, at the age of twenty-four, thus cutting short the impact he would no doubt have had on the Free Will Baptist Seminary and on Free Will Baptists more broadly had he lived.[8]

Ayden Seminary was co-educational at a time when many colleges still did not enroll both men and women. Free Will Baptist men and women, primarily from the Carolinas but also from other parts of the South, came to Ayden to receive a classical education in the liberal arts and theology. The seminary changed its name to Eureka College in 1926. Students chose from four courses of study. The Classical Course covered Latin and Greek, classical literature, history, higher mathematics, natural science, and Bible and theology. The Scientific Course focused primarily on physics, chemistry, and biology but also required courses in theology and the liberal arts. The Commercial Course, in addition to a classical liberal arts core, required a concentration in commerce or business. The Biblical Course, primarily for ministers, concentrated on biblical and theological studies with several required courses in classical languages and literature, history, natural science, and higher mathematics. Students in the non-biblical courses of study were required to take a strong core of biblical and theological courses, yet the faculty attempted to teach all its subjects from the vantage point of Christian theology. Many of the graduates of the Biblical Course would serve as bi-vocational ministers, serving one or more smaller congregations while teaching in public schools.

In 1929, only four years after changing its name to Eureka College, the school ceased offering classes under the financial hardship of the recession that preceded the stock market crash in October 1929, which initiated the Great Depression. While there were still hopes of reviving it, the college officially closed early in 1930, and in 1931 it burned to the ground. However, the hopes for Free Will Baptist higher education did not burn with it. Ayden Seminary had been the fulfillment of years of hopes for a denominational college, and it would serve as a foundation for Free Will Baptist higher education in the twentieth century and as a catalyst for union and denominational growth in the South.[9]

Publishing among the Southern Free Will Baptists

As early as 1852, the Toe River Association in Tennessee had resolved "to recommend Sabbath Schools throughout our Association and that the members of the churches take a deep interest in keeping up the same." However, historians do not know when Free Will Baptists in other areas of the South began to hold Sunday schools, or when they began to publish a study curriculum for those schools. The Free Will Baptists of North Carolina had had "Sabbath school" committees in their conferences as early as 1872 and had printed some Sabbath school literature for Free Will Baptist congregations as early as the late 1880s and early 1890s. It is no surprise that these efforts began in North Carolina, the birthplace of the southern movement in which it had the most wealth and numerical strength in the South. The *Discipline* (the popular word for the 1812 *Abstract of the Former Articles of Faith Confessed by the Original Baptist Church Holding the Doctrine of General Provision With a Proper Code of Discipline*) had been published by the movement as early as 1813. Numerous printers were employed to print various editions of this confession, with one even being published in 1855 by a printing establishment in New York, New York.[10]

The southern movement had published its own hymnals as early as 1831, when William Lumpkin and Enoch Cobb published *The Free Will Baptist Hymn Book*. A year later Jesse Heath, the movement's most prominent leader in the early nineteenth century, published a hymnal with Elias Hutchins, *Psalms, Hymns, and Spiritual Songs, Selected for the United Churches of Christ, Commonly Called Free Will Baptists, in North Carolina; and for Saints in All Denominations*. The most widely used hymnal among southern Free Will

Baptists in the nineteenth and early twentieth centuries was *Zion's Hymns*, published by Rufus K. Hearn in 1854. This hymnal, edited by Hearn, with Joseph Bell and Jesse Randolph, was used until the early twentieth century.[11]

Toward the end of Reconstruction, in addition to confessions of faith and hymnals, the North Carolina Free Will Baptists began publishing a weekly newspaper as well as publications ranging from pamphlets to books to Sabbath school literature. These efforts resulted in a stock company known as the Free Will Baptist Publishing Company, later named the Free Will Baptist Press. It would provide Free Will Baptists in the Carolinas, and soon across the South, with reading material. The Press was founded in 1873 after R. K. Hearn made a motion at the 1873 North Carolina General Conference to "authorize Bro. E. R. Ellis to draw on the Treasurer for a sufficient amount to pay for printing a prospectus for a newspaper." Hearn is listed as a corresponding editor, and Ellis as managing editor, in the first extant issue of the newspaper on April 16, 1874.[12]

After a brief stint as *The Free Will Baptist Advocate*, Ellis changed the name of the paper to the *Toisnot Transcript* (after the town in which it was published). As a result of this re-titling, the publication languished, and soon R. K. Hearn was brought in as managing editor. Hearn changed the name to *The Free Will Baptist*. From its earliest years, it was often referred to in the denomination as "*The Baptist*." This publication, now known as *The Community* and published by the Convention of Original Free Will Baptists, has been published for more than 150 years and is the longest-running publication in the history of the movement.[13]

The Free Will Baptist provided readers with devotional and doctrinal articles and kept its readers informed about news regarding the denomination. In its earliest years, its subscription base was primarily in North and South Carolina, but even in the late nineteenth century, it had subscribers from numerous states. Until 1901 the words "The Organ of the Free Will Baptist Church of North Carolina" appeared on the masthead. That year it was changed to "The Organ of the Free Will Baptist Church North and South," indicating the publication's increasingly wider circulation and probably the influence of Thomas E. Peden. Dissatisfied with the drift of his own northern Free Baptist denomination, he had moved from Ohio to assume the principalship of the Free Will Baptist Seminary in Ayden, North Carolina. The paper was recommended as the official periodical of several associations across the South. According to one letter, Peden's new Ohio River Yearly Meeting, which had become disillusioned with the northern General Conference, had made *The Free Will Baptist* its official paper long before the turn of the century.[14]

The Free Will Baptist was the single most important unifying force among southern Free Will Baptists in the late nineteenth and early twentieth centuries. It aided greatly in moving the denomination from scattered churches, conferences, and associations to a more organized and cohesive movement.

The Role of Rufus K. Hearn

At the heart of much of this early development was Elder Rufus K. Hearn, the most notable early proprietor of the Free Will Baptist Press and publisher of *The Free Will Baptist*. Hearn was easily the most influential Free Will Baptist minister in the Carolinas in the nineteenth century. He was born in 1819 in Pitt County, North Carolina, to pioneer Free Will Baptist minister Howell Hearn and his wife Sarah. Howell and Sarah Hearn had both been born in the 1770s and had witnessed the devastation of the movement after the intrusion by the Calvinist Baptists. They had also lived through the recovery and growth during the early nineteenth century, with the adoption of a new name and a revised confession of faith (the *1812 Abstract*). Rufus married Lucetta Rives in 1846, and they had eight children. They were both baptized at Conetoe Mills and united with Gum Swamp Free Will Baptist Church in 1850, and in 1853 Hearn was ordained to gospel ministry. Gum Swamp Church called him as pastor three years later, a post he maintained for the next thirty-six years. He died in 1894, two years after retiring from the pastorate of Gum Swamp. Hearn was one of the few Free Will Baptist ministers who could remember the denomination's character in the early nineteenth century. His influence on the denomination was one of stabilization, conservation, and vision.[15]

Despite his own meager formal education, the illustrious farmer-preacher Hearn served as a voice for education, theology, and tradition among his people. Besides his directorship of the Press and editorship of *The Free Will Baptist*, as well as his leadership in the General Conference, one of his most enduring legacies was his short work "Origin of the Free Will Baptist Church of North Carolina," which self-consciously tied the denomination to its eighteenth-century General Baptist confessional identity. Even more influential was *Zion's Hymns*. This hymnal mediated the English hymn tradition to thousands of Free Will Baptists, who carried these small, leatherbound, pocket-size books to church with them each Sunday and took them back home for use in family worship during the week. For seventy years this volume, more than any other, shaped Free Will Baptists' theological sensibilities, not only with hundreds of rich hymns from the likes of Charles Wesley and Isaac Watts, but also songs that specifically addressed the distinctive confessional tenets of Free Will Baptists, including unique hymns teaching Arminian doctrine, open communion, and the rite of the washing of the saints' feet.[16]

Hearn served as editor and publisher of *The Free Will Baptist* and as director of the Free Will Baptist Press from 1880 to 1889. He persuaded the North Carolina General Conference to purchase a printing press and begin a regular publishing program supported by subscriptions from individuals and local congregations. For a few years, Hearn was the sole proprietor of the Press, publishing the paper at his own expense with help from subscribers. Hearn was the most significant figure in the late nineteenth century as the Free Will Baptist denomination in the South began the sect-to-denomination process. His vision of an educated ministry and biblical-doctrinal literacy for the laity set the stage for the development in these areas as the Free Will Baptist movement continued to grow across the South.[17]

The Expansion of the Free Will Baptist Press

In 1889, Hearn moved on from his editorial labors, and a stock company was formed to ensure the financial viability of the Press. The newly formed company took the name Free Will Baptist Publishing Company and was supported by stockholders, the majority of whom were Free Will Baptist individuals and churches. After a brief period when W. L. Bilbro served as editor for a year in Snow Hill, North Carolina, J. M. Barfield became the new editor. He operated the Press until 1892 when it was relocated to Ayden, North Carolina, where it operates to this day. Barfield employed Elder E. T. Phillips, who became assistant editor as well as secretary of the stock company. Phillips soon became editor, a post he held until 1916 and then again from 1921 to 1935. Though some Sabbath school literature had been published before his tenure, Phillips led the press to begin a full publishing program of age-graded Sabbath school curriculum in 1906. Several Free Will Baptist associations had promoted Sabbath schools since the 1880s, even hosting Sabbath school conventions. Many associations had previously recommended non-denominational curriculum, and a few encouraged the use of northern Free Baptist literature. However, these same associations began to recommend "Ayden literature" in the 1890s and especially after the expansion of the curriculum in 1906.[18]

In its early years, the Press published not only *The Free Will Baptist*, Sabbath school curriculum, and other denominational materials but also numerous pamphlets and books by leading ministers such as Barfield, T. F. Harrison, and E. L. St. Claire. Harrison and Barfield wrote the 430-page *History of the Free Will Baptists of North Carolina*, which the Press published in 1897. Harrison also co-wrote pamphlets with his twin brother T. H. Harrison on topics dealing with Free Will Baptist doctrine and practice. Soon the Press was publishing the minutes of various conferences and associations in states such as South Carolina, Georgia, Florida, Alabama, and Tennessee. With the foundation Hearn had built, and the superstructure laid by J. M. Barfield and E. T. Phillips, the Press served as a catalyst for bringing together Free Will Baptists across the southern United States.[19]

Efforts toward Union

Ecumenism and unity were the watchwords of late nineteenth-century American Protestantism. The ecumenical thrust was born of an optimism that went hand in hand with the Finneyesque optimistic anthropology and postmillennial eschatology of the era. That eschatological outlook saw divisions among Christians as an impediment to the ushering in of a millennial age of Christian righteousness, peace, and human flourishing, after which Jesus Christ would return. Among the northern Freewill Baptists, as noted in chapter 7, these elements often combined, at least in denominational institutions, with a more moderate and even liberal understanding of theology and church practice. This posture drove leading pastors and professors to be more au courant on the latest developments in the European universities. In the hinterlands it led to less interest in the unique marks that distinguished Freewill Baptists from other Protestants.[20]

Among the southern Free Will Baptists, the ecumenical thrust led to greater interest in union with other groups. However, the movement's leadership defined itself more in terms of the older orthodoxy that characterized the Protestantism of the South across denominations. Thus their interest in union was more about uniting with other broadly non-Calvinist, baptistic bodies that also held to open communion. Therefore, in the South, the question was not whether to forge more unions and come together with other Christians. Rather it was how wide to cast the net. This led to two different visions of Arminian Baptist unity among southern Free Will Baptists. One was motivated by broadly non-Calvinist and baptistic interests, combined with open communion. The other was motivated more by narrower concerns of confessional faith and practice. Indeed, this was a smaller-scale illustration of what was happening among many other Protestants in the South, who were slower to get on board with theological modernism than many of their northern counterparts.[21]

This was a time in the development of the Free Will Baptist movement in the South in which it could have developed in one of two ways. It could have progressed into a broader evangelical movement that was broadly non-Calvinistic and baptistic in nature yet maintained orthodoxy on what would come to be known as the "fundamentals of the faith." Or, in the face of modernity, as it was just beginning to come out of its cultural shell, it could retrench itself in Protestant orthodoxy and in a traditional account of its confessional identity.

This traditional identity would include open communion and a sort of Arminianism that distinguished itself not only from Wesleyanism and the Holiness movement but also from the anti-Calvinist thought forms of the burgeoning Stone-Campbell movement. Yet it would also include a distinctive polity that emphasized the interdependence of local congregations in strong conferences and associations with presbyteries that required their ministers to subscribe to a confession of faith. This militated against the radical independence of local congregations, which was becoming the trend in most low-church evangelicalism. Finally, most culturally distinctive of all, that traditional identity would involve holding fast to ancient liturgical practices that dated to patristic and medieval Christianity and flew in the face of an increasingly urbane, industrial, and modern evangelical Protestant world. This would include rites such as the *pedilavium*—the washing of the saints' feet—and the anointing of the sick. Another ancient rite that, while still a part of the written confessional distinctives of large swaths of the movement, the Free Will Baptists had largely begun to evolve away from by this point, was the ancient rite of confirmation—the imposition or laying on of hands after baptism. This would have made the movement seem even more retrograde.

Liberal Baptist Movements

B. W. Nash and his predecessor James W. Hunnicutt represented the first sort of union movement described above. Through his ironically named "Southern Baptist Association," Nash sought to unite all non-Calvinists who were baptistic and open communionist but carefully avoided other traditional General/Free Will Baptist distinctives historically characteristic of the southern movement. Robert L. Vaughn and Robert E. Picirilli have shed new light on this influential movement. Bushrod Washington Nash was the most influential leader of what Vaughn and Picirilli call "cross-denominational (and intra-denominational) unity movements" among many non-Calvinist baptistic groups at this time.[22]

In the early 1840s, James W. Hunnicutt had left the Methodist Church to start the Union Baptist movement, mainly in North Carolina and Virginia.

A few Free Will Baptists left their conferences to join Hunnicutt. The movement continued to gain adherents, and had it not been for Hunnicutt's "radical Republican" politics after the Civil War, the movement would have probably gained even more followers. Yet the most obvious difference between the Union Baptists and the Free Will Baptists was seen in the fact that the former rejected the washing of the saints' feet. This is illustrated in a large 1867 "Union Convention" that had delegations from the Union Baptists, the Disciples of Christ, and some Free Will Baptists. While the first two groups voted "aye" on a resolution that "we do not regard the washing of the saints' feet as an ordinance of the Christian church," the Free Will Baptists en masse voted "nay."[23]

This movement was often characterized by the term "Liberal Baptist." "Liberal" did not in this instance have any connection to debate between theological liberalism and conservatism but meant "free." The Liberal Baptist slogan, though it varied, usually went something like "free will, free salvation, free communion." Of course, the term "Liberal Baptist" meant different things to different people. Some Free Will Baptists who were strongly traditional in their faith and practice used the term. However, it tended to mean people who were broadly non-Calvinist, practiced open communion, and affirmed believer's baptism by immersion. However, it did not articulate anything further than that. Thus a Free Will Baptist could affirm each tenet, but so could an adherent of the Disciples of Christ/Churches of Christ. (This is illustrated by Nash's attempt to bring both Disciples of Christ and Free Will Baptists into the movement.) The devil was in the details of what was left unsaid.[24]

B. W. Nash took the foundation James Hunnicutt had laid and used his considerable organizational skill to build it into an even more influential network. His goal was to unite all Liberal Baptists into one movement. By 1860, Nash had taken what he called the "skeleton" of a dozen struggling churches and from them organized sixteen churches with "between twelve and fourteen hundred members." These were apparently congregations that had left the North Carolina Free Will Baptists after the Masonry controversy. As early as 1870, despite some interest of the North Carolina General Conference in talks with the Nash group, a motion by James Moore passed that "we dismiss from our conference the subject of uniting with other denominations." This was the first of several groups of Free Will Baptists across the South that would grow disillusioned with the Nash group.[25]

Nash, however, was just getting started. By 1876, he initiated his major organization, the Southern Baptist Association. It forged loose alliances with, for example, the Cape Fear Free Will Baptist Conference in North Carolina as well as with Free Will Baptists in Georgia and Alabama. Elder Ellis Gore of the Mount Moriah Association in Alabama for a time became a major influence in the movement. Several Free Will Baptist conferences and associations across the South began to recommend Nash's hymnals and his newspaper, *The Baptist Review*, and to have his printing press print their minutes. Also present at many of these gatherings of Liberal Baptists were representatives from the General Baptists of the Midwest.[26]

Nash's Southern Baptist Association eventually became influential enough that several Free Will Baptist conferences adopted its doctrinal articles as their own. Ironically, however, in many cases they continued to observe their distinctive Free Will Baptist doctrines and practices that distinguished them from Nash, most importantly the washing of the saints' feet. One example of this was the Little Missouri River Free Will Baptist Association, founded in Arkansas in 1877. In the first extant minutes of that fellowship (1891), the body passed a resolution to adopt the Southern Baptist Association's articles, but they specified "amending article 11," the article that advocated the practice of the Lord's Supper but not the washing of feet. The minutes refer to their observance, at the same meeting, of "communion and feet washing." In the next extant minutes, seventeen years later, Little Missouri River had stopped using the Southern Baptist Association articles and had begun using the articles of faith of the Arkansas Association.[27]

This first strategy of union would fail because the Free Will Baptist conferences and associations involved with the Nash group, one by one, took the route the North Carolina General Conference had taken in 1870. As Vaughn and Picirilli argue, the Union Baptist movement ultimately failed because Disciples of Christ and Free Will Baptists elected to remain in their respective communions. This is the perception of *The Morning Star* in a report it gave in 1889 that said that the "feeling between the Originals [Free Will Baptists of the Carolinas] and the Nash people is not generally very cordial." After the 1880s there was an increasing coolness between Free Will Baptists and the Nash movement. An 1889 convention in Columbus, Georgia, at which Nash was in attendance but apparently did not play a large role, self-consciously styled itself Free Will Baptist in contradistinction to Liberal Baptist.[28]

A competitor to the Southern Baptist Association, which did not meet with Nash's approval, was known as the Southern Unity Movement. A. D. Williams was the leader of this new movement. A well-known Randall Freewill Baptist, Williams was born in Pennsylvania but in 1889 moved from Nebraska, where he had been very active in the Freewill Baptist cause there, to Nashville, Tennessee. Nash referred to him as "the old renegade Yankee, A. D. Williams," excoriating Williams for his advocacy of "mixed schools and churches of white people and negroes." However, the Southern Unity Movement was short-lived, and after a couple of years Williams was in Oakland City, Indiana, helping the General Baptists start a college there. The Randall movement newspaper, *The Morning Star*, spoke of Williams's efforts as an attempt to unite the "scattered and separate Southern bodies" of Liberal Baptists into "one compact and potent organization." In August 1889, Williams started a newspaper, *The Christian Herald*, to work toward a fraternal organization to unite Free Will Baptists with other Liberal Baptists in the South.[29]

Williams generated quite a bit of interest in such an organization. This included that of John L. Welch Sr. whose son John L. Welch Jr. would later be at the forefront of establishing the National Association of Free Will Baptists in 1935 and Free Will Baptist Bible College in 1942. In the summer of 1889, Welch Sr. started publishing a paper out of Pleasant View, Tennessee, called the *Free Baptist Enterprise*, which promoted such fraternal union. As the editor of *The Morning Star* reported, for the movement to succeed, the largest organization of Free Will Baptists, the Original Free Will Baptists of North Carolina, would have to be involved, along with the sizable contingent of Tennessee Free Will Baptists. Yet, the editor conjectured, three conditions would need to be met for such a southern Liberal Baptist organization to get off the ground. They would have to be able to maintain their current associational structures and names, remain racially segregated, and be led by southern Free Will Baptists without uninvited interference from the northern Free Baptist denomination. Welch's paper eventually merged with *The Christian Herald*, and Williams and Welch brought in J. W. Lucas, the North Carolina educator who had moved to East Tennessee and started the Unicoi Institute, to be one of the paper's editors.[30]

Soon a call went out for the first meeting of this proposed organization that would unite all Liberal Baptists. It was set to gather at the North Nashville (later named Cofer's Chapel) Free Will Baptist Church in December 1889. Yet virtually all those calling for the meeting represented Free Will Baptist associations and conferences, from states as diverse as Tennessee, Alabama, Virginia, Georgia, Arkansas, and Texas. Only one non-Free Will Baptist group was represented in the call for meeting: the New Union Association of United Baptists in Tennessee. Despite Nash's attempts to dissuade his friends, such as the Cape Fear Conference in North Carolina and the Mount Moriah and allied associations in Alabama, from involvement, they pushed the new movement nonetheless. The meeting was held, and the group voted to name itself the "General Association of Baptists, believing in Free Will, Free Salvation, and Free Communion." However, unlike the more ecumenical Nash movement, almost all the participants were Free Will Baptists. Thus, though Williams intended it to be far more inclusive than just Free Will Baptists, the organization's end result was to bring together confessional Free Will Baptists across the South in a centralized location for the first time. This happened again the next year in Hartselle, Alabama, with a much smaller number present. The General Association had only a few more meetings after Williams moved to Indiana. Still, the short-lived effort proved to move southern Free Will Baptists more toward the goal of denominational union.[31]

The Move toward a Permanent Denominational Structure

Vaughn and Picirilli point out that "it may well be that the demise of the General Association was hastened by the birth of another unity movement," the (triennial) General Conference, behind which historians have seen Thomas E. Peden as the genius. This movement was also short-lived. Its first session was in 1895 in Ohio, Peden's primary field of endeavor before he moved to North Carolina to become principal of Ayden Seminary. This new General Conference held triennial sessions until 1910, when it met in Florence, Alabama. A subsequent meeting was planned for southwest Georgia in 1913, but no record of it is extant. Still, the (triennial) General Conference inched the Free Will Baptists of the South that much closer to union, but it was a different sort of union than that envisioned by previous union movements. Nash's movement had attempted to siphon off Free Will Baptists into a broader Liberal Baptist network, and Williams's movement had attempted a broader Liberal Baptist union, even though it unintentionally resulted in a more cohesively Free Will Baptist one. Peden's movement, however, started out with a self-consciously Free Will Baptist identity in mind.[32]

Ayden Seminary, *The Free Will Baptist*, and Free Will Baptist Press had already begun attracting a great deal of attention across the South, being recommended by many associations. Peden, who was ministering among the Freewill Baptists in Ohio in the 1880s, had become disenchanted with the northern Free Baptist movement because of its ecumenism. He found in the southern Free Will Baptists a new home when he became principal of Ayden Seminary in 1898. Peden was central in the growth of the (triennial) General Conference. Ayden, North Carolina, as the nerve center of the burgeoning Free Will Baptist movement on the East Coast, with its press, newspaper, and school, was already at the forefront of efforts to unite all southern Free Will Baptists. Peden increased its influence. Though the (triennial) General Conference would still not provide the permanent denominational structure that was hoped for, it moved that vision much closer to fruition.[33]

It cannot be overestimated how different the motivations and impetus of the (triennial) General Conference were from the union movements associated with Nash and Williams. After Peden's move to Ayden in 1898, the conference's driving force was the Carolinas. This was the region in which the most suspicion had grown over B. W. Nash and other more ecumenical unity movements that de-emphasized what they saw as key confessional commitments of Free Will Baptists that represented their historic identity. By the 1890s more and more Free Will Baptists of the South believed they were on the cusp of having a unified, coherent denominational movement. They longed for more fellowship and unity with others who shared their faith and practice. Yet they feared that uniting with other groups, even other Liberal Baptists, would do more to detract from the fulfillment of their vision than to benefit it.

Thomas Peden played directly into this dynamic. Many southern Free Will Baptists were becoming disillusioned with the sort of ecumenism embodied in the Southern Baptist Association and other union movements that downplayed Free Will Baptist confessional identity. At the same time, Peden was becoming disheartened with the ecumenical thrust in his own denomination, which he believed was in danger of destroying the northern Freewill Baptist movement. It is fascinating to see Peden leaving his denomination, which is at the epicenter of the strong movement in American mainline Protestantism toward ecumenism and ways of thinking that were not shackled to the older orthodoxy. Peden fled southward because he was militating against this mindset. At the same time, he encountered a group of Free Will Baptists in the South who were in the transition of the sect-to-denomination process. They were enthralled with the possibilities of their own vision of progress, unity, and more effective ways of fostering a coherent structure for the fulfillment of their mission as a unified church. However, because their confessional identity was at the heart of this vision, they, like Peden, were on a trajectory that did not comport with the typical ecumenical spirit of mainline Protestantism in America in the late nineteenth and early twentieth centuries. Yet in its unique way, theirs was an ecumenical and forward-looking spirit nonetheless.

This was a pivotal moment for the Free Will Baptists of the South. They had been decimated time and again in their two-hundred-year history in America by aggressive movements outside themselves with whom some of their number had developed relationships. They had never quite had the wealth and resources to fend off these attempts to peel off more of their members. Now, at the threshold of new vistas for education, publishing, and denominational organization, the movement's leaders made a key decision. In their weariness with ecumenically motivated efforts such as the one surrounding B. W. Nash, they chose instead to unite with each other around a common confessional framework. This decision would, more and more, bring denominational unity out of the diversity across the region, further aiding the movement's cohesion and development.

E. L. St. Claire as a Window into Denominational Development

The life and ministry of Dr. E. L. St. Claire serve as a window into the sect-to-denomination process the southern Free Will Baptists underwent in the quarter-century from approximately 1890 to 1915. His role was as influential in those years as Hearn's had been from 1860 to 1890. St. Claire was born in Alabama around 1866 and orphaned at the age of four. After graduating from the University of Alabama, he began a career in business, which likely contributed to his later skills in denominational leadership and development. St. Claire earned a master's degree and a doctorate, studying several ancient and modern languages, which aided him in becoming an accomplished preacher and teacher of the Bible and Christian doctrine. Early in his adulthood before his conversion and call to ministry, St. Claire contracted an illness that left him blind. He was ordained a Free Will Baptist minister in 1893. Like his mentor John T. Knight of the Chattahoochee Association, he specialized in planting churches, eventually establishing eleven churches and starting three associations in Georgia, Florida, and Alabama.[34]

St. Claire became well-known among Free Will Baptists in the Southeast, and in 1904 he was elected national evangelist of the General Conference. St. Claire was a sought-after preacher and engaging writer. His books and pamphlets on a host of topics, as well as his regular writing for *The Free Will Baptist*, made him the most prolific writer and communicator in the movement. He turned sermons into booklets such as *What Free Will Baptists Believe and Why*, which helped solidify his reputation as one of the leading teachers of and advocates for Free Will Baptist doctrine and practice of his day.[35]

St. Claire represented a continuation of the sort of southern Protestant orthodoxy of which E. Brooks Holifield wrote in his book *The Gentlemen Theologians*. St. Claire wrote about doctrinal topics from a confessional Arminian Baptist perspective that also contended for the distinctive Free Will Baptist practices of open communion and the washing of the saints' feet. He also galvanized his peers against the advances of what he saw as an encroaching liberalism in the mainline Protestant denominations, which he claimed was having a deleterious effect on modern culture. Not only did he warn of the problems of theological modernism, but he also wrote about the growth of cults that had moved away from traditional Christian orthodoxy. One sees this in a long poem he wrote that, while not the finest poetry, is very engaging and humorous: *The Great Debate at Fanatic's Hall, Prejudiceville: A Witty Book of Rhymes on Church Dissension.* The fascinating thing about this book, and about St. Claire, was the way it combined irenics and polemics. It contended for traditional orthodoxy and for distinctive confessional tenets. Yet at the same time it bemoaned infighting and disunity in the church and the lack of ecumenical relationships between different Christian denominations.[36]

St. Claire's other most notable contribution was to help inch the movement forward organizationally. He sensed the need to move the southern Free Will Baptist movement from a disorganized group of scattered congregations and associations that could never muster the resources to fund enduring institutions toward a more cohesive structure. That structure would, more and more, resemble the character of twentieth-century denominationalism. In addition to his role as a preacher and a sort of public intellectual among his brothers and sisters, St. Claire was a promoter par excellence. Marshaling the skills he had learned in establishing new congregations and associations early in his ministry, St. Claire flourished, first as national evangelist, then as an "agent" for Ayden Seminary and the Free Will Baptist Press. Like few others in the first two decades of the new century, he increased southern Free Will Baptists' interest in ministerial education, theology, full-time pastoral ministry, and missions. He accomplished this by promoting a more efficient, enduring denominational structure that he believed was necessary to bring the movement together so that it could foster more effective institutions.

Conclusion

When the desire arose among predominantly White Free Will Baptists to unite with others of similar faith and practice across the South, a sort of sect-to-denomination process ensued. This process eventuated in the establishment of institutions for education and publishing. These efforts toward union and institutional development would lay the groundwork for more formal Free Will Baptist alliances in the early twentieth century. Such alliances would more effectively promote theological education, publishing, and missions and eventually result in the formation of a national Free Will Baptist association.

Ten
DOCTRINE AND PRACTICE IN THE SOUTH

LIKE MOST OTHER Baptists in the South, the Free Will Baptists on the frontier often composed their own confessions of faith. Sometimes they wrote them originally, and other times they compiled them from older, commonly used articles of belief. Conferences and associations usually printed these statements in their annual booklet of minutes, referring to them with phrases such as "Articles of Faith," "Confession of Faith," or "Doctrinal Views."

In most ways, Free Will Baptists in the South were much like the majority of the Baptists in their region who emerged from the English Particular Baptist tradition, known at first as Regular and Separate Baptists and later by appellations such as Missionary Baptist, Primitive Baptist, Southern Baptist, or National Baptist. Thus, for instance, the southern Free Will Baptists of the nineteenth century affirmed basic Protestant orthodoxy. They were insistent on the cardinal doctrines of the Christian tradition regarding the inspiration and authority of Holy Scripture as divine speech and therefore true in its affirmations; Nicene orthodoxy in affirmation of the Holy Trinity; the incarnation; the person of Christ as fully God and fully human; Christ's virgin birth, bodily resurrection, and personal return; the personality and deity of the Holy Spirit; the immortality of the soul and the reality and everlasting character of heaven and hell; the necessity of knowing and being a disciple of Jesus Christ for salvation; and other traditional Christian teaching.

Like other Baptists, they affirmed the doctrines articulated in the five *solae* of the Reformation: *sola Scriptura* (Scripture alone), *sola gratia* (grace alone), *sola fide* (faith alone), *solus Christus* (Christ alone), and *soli Deo gloria* (the glory of God alone). These basic commitments continued to characterize

237

the Free Will Baptists of the nineteenth and early twentieth centuries, as they had their General Baptist forebears. Thus they resisted the tendency of much of the American church after the Second Great Awakening toward semi-Pelagianism, and they also adhered to the approach to the sufficiency of Scripture characteristic of the Baptist movement of their day on both sides of the Atlantic. Southern Free Will Baptists were always more in conversation with their fellow Baptists, who tended to lean toward various (weak or strong) forms of Calvinism, rather than their fellow Arminians, whose brand of Arminianism diverged from the Free Will Baptists' more Reformed approach to Arminianism. Therefore, the primary differences between southern Free Will Baptists and most other Baptists were that they affirmed the possibility of apostasy and practiced open communion and the washing of the saints' feet. Furthermore, in their polity, congregations were more interdependent and gave the conference or association more power than had come to characterize most Baptists in America. In other respects, Free Will Baptists were of a piece with the larger Baptist tradition. Thus this sketch of their doctrine and practice will spend more time emphasizing the Free Will Baptists' distinctions from their Baptist counterparts and less time discussing their similarities.[1]

The Sufficiency of Scripture

Like their English General Baptist forebears, Southern Free Will Baptists believed in the principle of the sufficiency of Scripture. They emphasized that God had ordained not only the church's doctrine but also its practice, having revealed both through apostolic precept and example in Holy Scripture. They used varied wording to describe this doctrine. The "*rule* of faith and practice" language is seen throughout their documents, as it is in the wider Baptist and Protestant traditions. The concept of "means of grace" is also employed. The *1812 Abstract*, for example, states that "in the use of the means of grace and not out of the use of those means, eternal life is promised to men." The Chattahoochee confession of faith speaks of "the means of grace connected with the establishment of the visible church." The Chattahoochee tradition, utilizing "rule" language, emphasized the necessity of continued faithfulness to the apostolic pattern of practice. Churches are to be "governed according to the rules laid down in the New Testament" and "these rules require churches to preserve the form of government and ordinances of the first Christian churches."[2]

Using the language of "ordinance," "precept," and "example," the church covenant from the Liberty tradition in south Alabama and West Florida, which spread to Mississippi and Texas, exemplifies the Southern view in this trinitarian statement: "We do hereby agree and covenant, by the help of God, our Father, and aided by the Holy Spirit, to keep the ordinances, precepts, and examples, as laid down in the New Testament of our Lord and Savior Jesus Christ." Likewise, the articles of faith of the Southern Baptist Association allied with B. W. Nash stated that the Bible's "teaching constitutes the only infallible doctrine for the government of the church."[3]

The *1812 Abstract* used "ordinance" the same way the General Baptists, like other Baptists and Puritans, used it in the seventeenth and eighteenth centuries: those practices God ordained for perpetuation in the church. It also used the well-worn General Baptist word "institution": "We believe as touching Gospel ordinances, in believer's baptism, laying on of hands, receiving of the sacrament in bread and wine, washing the saints' feet, anointing the sick with oil in the name of the Lord, fasting, prayer, singing praise to God, and the public ministry of the Word, with every institution of the Lord we shall find in the New Testament." The wording of the last phrase is common among southern Free Will Baptists. It was reproduced almost verbatim, for example, in a resolution offered by the eminent minister Neal Parrish at the 1923 session of the new General Conference of the South to "urge all our state conventions and conferences to remain steadfast, always abounding in the faith of the Free Will Baptist church, with every institution of the Lord that may be found in the New Testament."[4]

Of course, southern Free Will Baptists also engaged in certain practices that were based on circumstances of time and place yet which they believed proper and in accord with Scripture. This is intimated in the code of discipline that was attached to the *1812 Abstract*:

> The rules for the government of the Church of God are contained in the Holy Scriptures—But as many of them appear to be comprehended in general directions, it is necessary, for the better regulation of the Church, that certain fixed rules and principles of practice should be adopted,— provided those rules are in accordance with the Scriptures of Truth. For it is manifest that every religious society or community should make such local and temporary regulations as may secure obedience to the perfect law by which they are governed.[5]

Like their Calvinist Baptist counterparts, Free Will Baptists distinguished between "elements" and "circumstances." While various words were used in the Baptist tradition, what the Westminster Confession of Faith had referred to as "parts" or "elements" were invariable religious means and methods that must be observed. "Circumstances" were non-religious variables of time, place, and culture. For example, in church government, the Free Will Baptists tended to see their churches' uniting in conferences or associations as an essential element of the church. However, *how* this was done (regionally, statewide, nationally) varied depending on time, place, and other circumstances. In public worship, the Word was to be preached, but whether a megaphone or microphone was used, and whether the listeners were standing or seated in pews or chairs, or whether they were worshipping in a storefront building or an ornate sanctuary were non-religious circumstances of time, place, and culture. As with other Baptists, there were differences throughout Free Will Baptist history over whether certain practices were elements or circumstances. One example is whether instrumental musical accompaniment fell under the category of element or circumstance. Free Will Baptists came to believe that the use of instrumental accompaniment fell under the category of circumstance.

The views of southern Free Will Baptists are encapsulated by the influential nineteenth-century minister Rufus K. Hearn of North Carolina. In his "Origin of the Free Will Baptist Church of North Carolina," he discussed the takeover in the mid-eighteenth century of the majority of the North Carolina General Baptist congregations by the New Light Calvinists of the Philadelphia Baptist Association. One of the difficulties the New Lights had with the General Baptists, he narrated, was that the latter did not require their candidates for baptism to rehearse an "experience of grace." Common among the Great Awakening-era New Light Calvinists, this often involved a long rendition of the mystical experiences one underwent to ascertain one's status as one of the elect.[6]

Hearn's response is one of the best explanations of the southern Free Will Baptists' desire to have scriptural warrant for church practice. He believed that the Calvinists had added the recounting of an "experience of grace" to the simple New Testament precept and example of profession of faith and baptism as a prerequisite for church membership:

> These early churches took the Bible for their guide, they practiced its sacred teachings, and as the Apostles never required an experience, and as it was nowhere authorized in Holy Writ, they practiced what they found the gospel required, that is, faith in the Lord Jesus Christ, repentance towards God, and baptism by immersion; and baptized their members on a profession of their faith in the Lord Jesus Christ, and not by experience.

Every Free Will Baptist will see that this is his doctrine, and the true doctrine of the New Testament, and it is our practice to the present day to baptize members on their profession of faith in the Lord Jesus Christ. They may call it lax in discipline, if they choose; we cannot, for we find no warrant in the New Testament for an experience of grace, as they term it.[7]

E. L. St. Claire, one of the best-known preachers among southern Free Will Baptists in the first quarter of the twentieth century, epitomized the southern Free Will Baptist doctrine of the sufficiency of Scripture. In ways reminiscent of the English General Baptist *Orthodox Creed*, he painted Roman Catholic baptismal practice as an innovation and departure from apostolic tradition: "It was the Catholic Church that changed the rite of baptism to effusion or sprinkling. . . . The Free Will Baptists have not adopted the change—and will not! . . . We do not go to the Catholics for any of our doctrine, but to Christ and his apostles."[8]

In defending the practice of the washing of the saints' feet, St. Claire argued, "The Free Will Baptists, being a simple folk, have always accepted the New Testament as the only source of doctrine, adding nothing to it, taking nothing from it. Being a simple people, and finding in the New Testament that Christ washed his disciples' feet, . . . they have continued the holy example." Here one sees St. Claire's repeating of the concept of precept (or institution) and example. He concluded his comments on feet washing by stating that the Free Will Baptists "knew no better" than to follow "their Saviour, Priest, King, and Lawgiver. . . . The world must excuse them for their blind stubbornness in persisting in following and practicing this holy example of Christ. Having accepted Christ, the Free Will Baptists know of no other authority for doctrine. . . . Speak where the Bible speaks, silent when it is silent."[9]

Sin and Salvation

Unlike their other Baptist brothers and sisters in the South, the Free Will Baptists continued the confessional Arminianism of their General Baptist forebears. Other Baptists in the South preached various forms of Calvinism—from the hyper-Calvinism of some Primitive Baptists, to the strong five-point Calvinism of stalwarts such as Jesse Mercer, John Leadley Dagg, and James Pettigru Boyce, to the mild "post-Calvinism" that was fast becoming the majority position among "Missionary" Baptists.[10]

Like other Baptists of their day, Free Will Baptists preached the total depravity of humanity, owing to alienation from God because of the sin of

Adam and Eve, whose depravity was inherited by the human family. They also agreed with their Calvinist counterparts that a radical intervention of divine prevenient grace was necessary for sinners to respond to the gospel. Yet on the nature of this grace, their preaching differed from the Calvinist Baptists, who taught the historic Calvinist doctrine of *gratia particularis* and *gratia irresistibilis* (particular, irresistible grace). According to that account, God's sovereignty demands that he foreordain all things, including who receives grace enabling them to be saved. Thus divine prevenient grace is particular, designed only for the elect, those God chooses for salvation. Furthermore, this grace is irresistible. The elect cannot resist or reject it, either before or after conversion.

The Free Will Baptists, in contrast, preached the more typical view in the church catholic that divine prevenient grace is universal (*gratia universalis*) yet resisitible (*gratia resistibilis*). The universal call of the Spirit to everyone to be saved, they preached, is consistent with God's desire expressed in Holy Scripture for everyone to repent. That is why God provided atonement for everyone's sins in Christ's death. Thus God desires everyone's salvation, the Spirit calls and draws everyone to salvation, and Christ's death is for everyone, they maintained. The reason people are not converted is not God's design for them but their own will. God's gift of prevenient grace, which is necessary for sinners to respond to the gospel, they taught, is resistible, before and after conversion. Human resistance, not God's withholding of his grace, is the reason individuals are not converted.

Thus the Free Will Baptists of the South agreed with other Arminians on *how one comes to be* in a state of grace, but they were more like their Calvinist brothers and sisters on *what it means to be* in a state of grace. Unlike most Arminians of their day, they affirmed the notion that Jesus's death paid the penalty for sin and his righteousness was imputed to believers in justification. On the contrary, most Arminians in nineteenth-century America affirmed doctrines like the governmental view of atonement and the "impartation" of Christ's righteousness, rejecting penal substitutionary atonement and the imputation of righteousness, which they termed a "legal fiction." The southern Free Will Baptists also rejected the doctrine of Christian perfection and entire sanctification that was popular in the Wesleyan-Arminian and Holiness movements.[11]

Total Depravity

The Free Will Baptists of the American South went to much greater lengths to emphasize depravity than most Arminians of their day. In this way their theology was unlike much nineteenth-century Arminianism in America, let alone the semi-Pelagianism of many in the Holiness movement in the vein of preachers such as Charles Finney. Southern Free Will Baptists consistently affirmed the traditional Reformation doctrine of the total depravity of humanity. They preached that humanity had inherited total depravity from their first parents. Thus, they affirmed, human beings are completely sinful—dead in trespasses and sins. Nothing in their own nature or free will can muster up the desire for God. The only thing that can result from human reason or effort without divine grace, they believed, was idolatry.

This perspective was ubiquitous throughout the Free Will Baptist Church in the South. The Articles of Faith of the Alabama Free Will Baptists who were spiritual descendants of Ellis Gore and the Mount Moriah Association illustrate a great deal about the theology of formerly Calvinistic Baptists in the South who became Free Will Baptists. One must remember that Gore was a Regular Baptist who came to reject Calvinism and rode on horseback to North Carolina, where he was ordained by the Free Will Baptists there.

The Articles of Faith of Mount Moriah Association and its sister associations in Alabama, Mississippi, and Arkansas are especially interesting. They adapted material from five sources: the New Hampshire Confession of Faith, some Arminian articles common in popular nineteenth-century reference books, the Five Articles of the Remonstrance, the Regular Baptist Abstract of Principles, and other articles that appear to be original with Gore and Mount Moriah. It was a common practice in those days to utilize various common sources for statements of faith without attribution and to edit them to suit the purposes of the group. This is seen, for example, in the numerous Southern Baptist associational confessions throughout the South, which utilize articles from previous confessional documents and make changes as they see fit.[12]

One thing that is especially interesting is that some of the articles in the Mount Moriah confession that reflect Arminian doctrine are taken from a commonly repeated set of five articles that claimed to reflect Arminian belief and were repeated again and again in best-selling nineteenth-century reference books. These articles appear to have originated with Hannah Adams's 1784 work, *An Alphabetical Compendium of the Various Sects*, in which she put forward five articles that purportedly summarized Arminian views. Most notable, however, is that, while the Mount Moriah articles on conditional election and universal atonement quote the Adams articles verbatim, the article on depravity is opposite of Adams's inaccurate characterization of Arminian doctrine. Adams's third article is as follows: "That mankind are *not* totally depraved, and that depravity does *not* come upon them by virtue of Adam's being their public head, but that mortality and actual evil only, are the direct consequences of his sin to his posterity." This is of course a common misconception of Arminian theology.[13]

However, what is most fascinating is that the Mount Moriah articles, while quoting other articles from Adams's commonly repeated Arminian formula, affirm the opposite of her statement on depravity. Mount Moriah's Article 6 states: "We believe that true faith cannot proceed from the exercise of our natural faculties and powers, or from the force and operation of free will, since man, in consequence of his natural corruption, is incapable either of thinking or doing anything spiritually good." The significant thing is that this article is a direct quotation from the Five Articles of the Remonstrance. Gore probably got this from Mosheim's *Ecclesiastical History*, one of the best-selling church histories of the early nineteenth century, since the Archibald Maclaine translation of Mosheim uses the exact English wording that the Mount Moriah articles quote.[14]

Another interesting fact about Mount Moriah's Articles of Faith is that some of their language on depravity combines wording from the New Hampshire Confession and an early American Regular Baptist Abstract of Principles. The first part of article 3 is taken from the New Hampshire Confession: "We believe that man was created holy, under the law of his Maker, but from voluntary transgression, fell from that holy and happy state, in consequence of which all mankind are now sinners." The New Hampshire Confession follows that statement with the phrase "not by constraint but choice; being by nature utterly void of that holiness required by the law of God, positively inclined to evil; and therefore under just condemnation to eternal ruin, without defense or excuse." However, Mount Moriah substitutes the following phrase almost verbatim from a widely used Regular Baptist Abstract of Principles: "wholly unable of their own free will and ability to recover themselves from the fallen state in which they are by nature."[15]

That Regular Baptist Abstract of Principles was common among many early Calvinist Baptists in America, which vast numbers of Primitive Baptists kept using, and some still utilize. In its preface, the abstract stated that it was "agreeable to the Confession of faith adopted by upwards of one hundred congregations in England, and published in Philadelphia, 1742." That reference is to the 1689 London Baptist Confession, or Philadelphia Confession. It is ironic that this Free Will Baptist confessional statement is likely the only document that uses two phrases amalgamating wording derived from the staunchly Calvinistic Philadelphia Confession with language from the New

Hampshire Confession, which was specifically designed to tone down the Calvinism of the Philadelphia Confession.[16]

Arkansas's Hamburgh Association, founded in 1888 by Gore's colleague from Mount Moriah, Thomas Molloy, utilized the Mount Moriah Articles of Faith. Hamburgh's article on the Fall of Man is slightly more precise in its wording than the Mount Moriah article, or the New Hampshire Confession from which that article comes. Whereas the Mount Moriah Articles and New Hampshire Confession stated that "all mankind are now sinners," the Hamburgh article changed a word, saying that "all mankind are now depraved."[17]

This same approach to depravity is reflected in the first question asked in the "Rules of Ordination" of the Arkansas Association to the west of Hamburgh: "Do you believe in the Total Depravity of the Human Heart? Answer—I do." That tradition all over Arkansas and Oklahoma, integrating language from the New Hampshire Confession of Faith, confessed that "man voluntarily disobeyed" God and "fell under the just condemnation of the same." Thus the whole of humanity are "partakers of the sinful nature attained by the fall," and "man is unable to save himself with his own power." Another influential Arkansas tradition, which originated with the Old Mount Zion Association, employed the same basic wording Mount Moriah utilized from the Regular Baptist Abstract of Principles in the following statement: "We believe in the fall of Adam, and that by his transgression, all his posterity fell and were made sinners. . . . We believe in the corruption of human nature and the inability of man to recover himself by his own free will and ability."[18]

B. W. Nash's union movement, the "Southern Baptist Association," which sought to unite all "Liberal Baptists" (open-communion and non-Calvinist Baptists) across the South, was picked up by several churches and associations in western North Carolina, Georgia, Alabama, Mississippi, and Arkansas. That confession affirmed that "Adam was created holy, but by voluntary transgression fell into depravity, and consequently involved his posterity in sin."[19]

While affirming total depravity inherited from Adam, Free Will Baptists were quick to distance themselves from the doctrine of infant damnation that some Calvinists affirmed. The *1812 Abstract*, sticking closely to the language of the *Standard Confession* of 1660, stated regarding children who die in infancy that not "one of them dying in that state, shall suffer punishment in hell by the guilt of Adam's sin, for of such is the kingdom of God." Yet the *Abstract* did not go into the details of how infants are saved. The Cumberland Association did do so, however, confessing bluntly, "We believe in the justification of infants by the imputed righteousness of Jesus Christ." Likewise, The

Arkansas Association affirmed that "infants and idiots are saved by the merits of the Son of God." Immediately after the first question asked of ordinands in the Arkansas Association about total depravity was the question, "Do you believe that Infants are *Saved* while in a State of Innocence?" Answer—I do." These notions bear similarity to Thomas Helwys's and Thomas Grantham's views that infants are "saved" and not merely "safe."[20]

God's Purpose of Grace

The *1812 Abstract* communicated the same general-redemption Arminianism that had been taught by its General Baptist tradition. Because of "the great love wherewith he loved the world," God sent his Son, who "freely gave himself a ransom for all, tasting death for every man." God wants everyone to be saved through the knowledge of the truth, which means the gospel should be preached to everyone. The theme of the *gratia universalis* and *gratia resistibilis*, the "doctrine of General Provision made of God in Christ, for the benefit of all mankind," is encapsulated in article 6 of the *Abstract*, which repeats the *Standard Confession* of 1660 almost verbatim:

> We believe that no man shall suffer in hell for want of a Christ that died for him, but as the scripture has said for denying the Lord that bought them; because they believe not in the name of the only begotten Son of God. Unbelief therefore being the cause why the just and righteous God of Heaven, will condemn the children of men, it follows against all contradiction, that all men at one time or another are found in such a capacity as that through the grace of God, they may be eternally saved.[21]

This same teaching characterized all southern Free Will Baptists. Alluding to the Five Articles of the Remonstrance, the Mt. Moriah tradition stated, "We believe that God has not fixed the future state of mankind by an absolute and unconditional decree, but salvation is offered in the Gospel, free to all, and if sinners are lost forever, it will be their own fault." To them it made sense that if God desires everyone's repentance, the Spirit is calling everyone, and Christ died for everyone, then prevenient grace is universal.[22]

Like Arminius and other Arminians, the Free Will Baptists wondered why God would call everyone to salvation if his careful, intentional design for most of them was that they be deprived of his grace. Instead, God's public, revealed call in the gospel, they taught, is identical to his inward call. This flew in the face of the Calvinist doctrine of "two callings" and "two wills," in which God's revealed will and his public gospel calling are in contradiction to his secret will and secret call only to the elect. A circular letter written by D. J. Apperson, the moderator of the Chattahoochee Association in Georgia, said:

> Is it possible that God may have any secret counsel opposed to [his] public declaration? He has no decree that operates against his promise. He has no purpose that contradicts his oath. . . . Hear what the author of the Atonement says: 'This is the condemnation'—not that there is a settled decree of reprobation gone out, against any man or number of men, but that 'light is come into the world, and men loved darkness rather than light.' Hence, it is charged against the Pharisees as a heinous crime, that they 'rejected the counsel of God against themselves,' to their own ruin. This charge alleges that every thing in the counsel itself is for the benefit of the sinner, and nothing against him; that all the benefits of the counsel are freely and sincerely offered to the acceptance of the sinner; that the sinner voluntarily, but most perversely, rejects these benefits of the counsel; and that such rejection is a crime, and makes the sinner, and the sinner alone, the author of his own ruin.[23]

One sees in Apperson's words a common theme repeated by Free Will Baptists: the reason people receive condemnation is not that God designed them to be outside the scope of his grace with no chance of redemption, but that they resist him in the freedom of their will. Article 6 of the *1812 Abstract* quoted above suggested that the reason people suffer in hell is their denial of the Christ who provided atonement for them, not that God provided no atonement for their sin and no grace enabling their conversion.[24]

Free will is meant in the sense of freedom from necessity, not freedom from depravity. No one's will is free from the effects of depravity such that he or she can naturally desire God without grace, they declared. Everyone's will, however, is free from necessity in the sense that God gives the people he created in his image freedom to choose from more than one course of action. Their choices and actions are not divinely necessitated. Thus the Mount Moriah tradition affirmed "the moral free-agency of man, by the grace of God, before and after conversion, and that he is laid under no invincible necessity by his Creator, to act in any given way." D. J. Apperson averred that the atonement "effects no change whatever in the laws of liberty. It does not constrain the sinner to accept pardon. It does not constrain God to exercise mercy. As, therefore, this counsel of God can be administered without infringing on free agency, it is a sample and a proof that *all* the purposes of God may be so too."²⁵

The universal divine purpose and calling seemed natural to the Free Will Baptists because of what they saw as the clear teaching of Holy Scripture on the universality of the atonement of Christ. General provision of grace made sense in the context of general atonement. The strong affirmation of universal atonement cited above from the *1812 Abstract* is mirrored in the Articles of Faith in the Mount Moriah tradition, quoting the five articles of the Remonstrants verbatim: "We believe that Christ, by his death and sufferings, made an atonement for the sins of all mankind in general, and of every individual in particular; however, that none but those who believe in Him can be partakers of the divine benefits." Likewise, the Arkansas tradition affirmed: "We believe that Christ, by His death, burial, and resurrection purchased our pardon and offered it freely to all mankind upon the principles of repentance toward God and faith in the Lord Jesus Christ."²⁶

Article 9 of the *1812 Abstract* bears witness to the Free Will Baptist belief in universal prevenient grace in a new article written in 1812 that was not held over from the *Standard Confession* of 1660:

> We believe that sinners are drawn to God the Father, by the Holy Ghost, through Christ His Son, and that the Holy Ghost offers His divine aid to all the human family, so as they might all be happy, would they give place to His divine teaching; whereas such who do not receive the Divine impressions of the Holy Spirit, shall at a future day, own their condemnation just, and charge themselves with their own damnation, for willfully rejecting the offers of sovereign grace."²⁷

Mount Moriah spoke of the "general application of the grace of God to fallen man, sufficient to enable him" to have faith. Speaking of prevenient grace, Apperson alluded to Acts 16:14, which says God opened Lydia's heart, enabling her to receive the gospel. "When the Holy Spirit opens the heart to attend to the claims and influence of the Atonement," Apperson averred, "there is no more violence offered to the freedom of the will, than there was in Christ showing his wounds to doubting Thomas, to make him 'not faithless but believing.'"²⁸

These and other statements of southern Free Will Baptists of this era evince another difference between them and most Arminians of their day: they saw prevenient grace as a convicting, enabling, drawing power that is individually directed, not a general mitigating of the effects of depravity.

Many Arminians believed that every human being was born with depravity universally mitigated to the point that he or she was simply free to believe. While Free Will Baptists everywhere articulated universal prevenient grace, their emphasis was more individualized. This is indicated by language that someone was "under conviction" by the Holy Spirit at a given point in time, that the Spirit was "striving" with that individual, but that the individual should not resist this wooing while the "door of the ark" was open, because the Spirit "would not always strive" with him or her.[29]

The Nature of Atonement and Justification

Though they staunchly confessed Arminian tenets regarding *how one comes to be* in a state of grace, Free Will Baptists in the South differed from most other Arminians regarding *what it means to be* in a state of grace. They were much more Reformed in many ways than most of their other Arminian counterparts and somewhat more Reformed than many of their northern Freewill Baptist counterparts. Unlike other Arminians of their day, they believed, as the nineteenth-century western North Carolina pastor John Ballard stated, that Christ "paid the penalty" for sin.[30] They strongly affirmed the penal substitutionary view of atonement that other Baptists, as members of the broader Reformed family, believed. Thus they could heartily sing the words from the hymn "'Tis Finished! The Messiah Dies," which appeared as hymn 5 in *Zion's Hymns*:

> 'Tis finished! The Messiah dies,
> Cut off for sins, but not His own!
> Accomplish'd is the sacrifice,
> The great redeeming work is done.
>
> 'Tis finished! All the debt is paid;
> Justice divine is satisfied;
> The grand and full atonement made;
> God for a guilty world hath died.
>
> The veil is rent in Christ alone;
> The living way to heaven is seen;
> The middle wall is broken down,
> And all mankind may enter in.

> The types and figures are fulfill'd;
> Exacted is the legal pain;
> The precious promises are seal'd;
> The spotless Lamb of God is slain.
>
> Saved from the legal curse I am,
> My Savior hangs on yonder tree;
> See there the meek, expiring Lamb!
> 'Tis finished! He expires for me.
>
> Death, hell, and sin are now subdued;
> All grace is now to sinners given;
> And lo, I plead the atoning blood,
> And in Thy right I claim Thy Heaven![31]

Most formulations of penal substitutionary, or penal satisfaction, atonement were construed as entailing the imputation of the righteousness of Christ in justification. This understanding of justification as the crediting of Christ's obedience to those who are in union with him through faith was anathema to many Arminians of this era. The same can be said regarding adherents of Charles Finney's thought. They saw justification as consisting in the simple pardon or forgiveness of sin, emphasizing the impartation of Christ's righteousness, painting imputation as a "legal fiction." Even many northern Freewill Baptists in the Randall movement fit this profile.[32]

The Free Will Baptists of the South, however, preached a doctrine that was similar to that of Jacobus Arminius and their own English General Baptist forebears. The *1812 Abstract* is illustrative of this teaching. An original article that was added to the rest of the material, most of which was abstracted from the *Standard Confession* of 1660, states: "We believe that no man has any warrant in the holy scriptures for justification before God through his own works, power, or ability which he has in and of himself, only as he by Grace is made able to come to God, through Jesus Christ; believing the righteousness of Jesus Christ to be imputed to all believers for their eternal acceptance with God."[33]

Likewise, the Old Mt. Zion tradition in Arkansas said in its Articles of Faith: "We believe that sinners are justified in the sight of God, only by the righteousness of Christ imputed to them, and that good works are the fruits of faith, and follow after justification." The Cumberland tradition that originated in Middle Tennessee followed suit, even to the point of saying that Christ's righteousness is imputed to those who die in infancy. The Chattachoochee tradition maintained the New Hampshire Confession's language that justification is "bestowed, not in consideration of anything which we have done, but solely through his own righteousness and atonement."[34]

Typically these confessional documents followed up the statement on justification with a consideration of the role of good works, maintaining that genuine faith always results in good works, even though faith, not good works, is what secures justification. Thus the *1812 Abstract* states, "We believe that good works are the fruits of a saving faith, and that in the use of the means of grace, and not out of the use of those means, eternal life is promised to men." The Articles of Faith of the Little Brown's Creek Association in Mississippi, which is mostly taken from those of B. W. Nash's ironically named Southern Baptist Association, added the affirmation that while good works necessarily result from true faith and are therefore "necessary to an ultimate salvation," believers are not saved by works, because the works of the law "being dead could not save us; grace saved us from the law, creating us unto good works which God hath ordained that we might walk in them."[35]

Perseverance and Apostasy

The major difference on the doctrine of salvation between southern Free Will Baptists and their Calvinist-background Baptist counterparts is their affirmation of the possibility of apostasy of the converted. Even the "Arminianizing" United Baptists and Separate Baptists that dotted the southern landscape and rejected orthodox Calvinism's doctrine of particular and irresistible grace still held to the absolute perseverance of everyone who was initially converted. When some of these eventually became Free Will Baptists, acceptance of the doctrine of the possibility of apostasy was usually the point at which they formally declared themselves Free Will Baptist. This held true even though they sometimes had accepted the appellation "free willer" decades earlier because they had rejected unconditional election, limited atonement, and irresistible grace before conversion. For Separate Baptists, who already practiced the washing of the saints' feet, acceptance of open communion and written confessions of faith signaled, along with affirmation of the possibility of apostasy, the transition to Free Will Baptist faith, practice, and identity. For United Baptists, who already used written confessions of faith, acceptance of the washing of feet and open communion came together with the affirmation of the confessional Arminian position on apostasy as the mark of full Free Will Baptist faith, practice, and identity.[36]

It was natural for Free Will Baptists to affirm the possibility of apostasy because they believed it was a logical outworking of the doctrine of the resistibility of grace. To them, it was theologically and logically untenable to affirm that the Spirit, with his grace, strives with and influences individuals whom he created as personal beings, maintaining their freedom to resist that grace before conversion, while closing off the freedom of those same personal beings to resist his grace after conversion. This is why the Mount Moriah tradition was careful in its wording of its aforementioned article on free will when it spoke of "the moral free-agency of man, by the grace of God, *before and after conversion*, and that he is laid under no invincible necessity by his Creator, to act in any given way." It seemed to them confused to assert that human freedom from necessity would be graciously maintained before conversion but that after conversion, believers would be "laid under" an "invincible necessity." This seemed to them to mitigate their belief in how God deals with his free creatures whom he created as personal beings in his own image who think, feel, and make meaningful choices.[37]

The Chattahoochee tradition, after its adherents accepted the possibility of apostasy, used a slightly edited version of the New Hampshire Confession of Faith as their articles of faith. Yet they altered the statement on perseverance and eventually added a statement on the *pedilavium*. The New Hampshire Confession states: "We believe that such only are real believers as endure unto the end: that their persevering attachment to Christ is the grand mark which distinguishes them from superficial professors; that a special providence watches over their welfare, and that they are kept by the power of God through faith unto salvation." The change the Chattahoochee tradition made to the confession signifies their shift to full Arminianism. It deleted the clause "We believe that such only are real believers as endure unto the end." However, it kept the rest of the statement. Thus, they confessed that those who persist in genuine faith, as distinguished from mere professing Christians, are preserved, or, quoting 1 Peter 1:5, kept by God's power through that continued faith.[38]

Chattahoochee saw no contradiction between the latter part of the New Hampshire article—with its strong assurance of salvation for those who believe—and their affirmation of the possibility of apostasy. This is seen in a "Circular Letter on Apostasy" by Macon County, Georgia, pastor J. M. King in 1902. In that letter, King affirmed that believers must continue in justifying faith lest they commit apostasy, from which they can never recover. This letter was printed a few pages before the articles of faith that contain the above language. King maintained the consistency of his belief with the confession by insisting that only those who persist in belief will be kept by God. He argued that the keeping is through faith, but that faith can be rejected, rendering the apostate like the "trees twice dead, plucked up by the roots" in Jude 12.[39]

The Cumberland Association Articles of Faith articulated the same doctrine:

> Art. 5. We believe that the faithful Christian will never fall from grace; notwithstanding: we believe in the free moral agency of man, after justification, and that there is a possible danger of falling into sin, and being finally lost.
>
> Art. 6. We believe, according to the Scriptures, Paul's letter to the Hebrews, 6th chapter, 1st to 7th verses, that after a man has been made partaker of the Holy Ghost, if he shall fall from grace, it is impossible ever to renew him again unto repentance, or restore him again into the favor of God.[40]

This Arminian emphasis is maintained throughout the Free Will Baptist movement in the South, as exemplified by Arkansas Free Will Baptists. The Articles of Faith of the Arkansas tradition, for instance, says, "We believe that all Christians should persevere in grace and be faithful to the end if they inherit eternal life." Both the Social Band and Big Spring Associations in Arkansas appealed to the biblical formula "he that endureth to the end, the same shall be saved." Arkansas's influential Old Mount Zion Association, founded as a United Baptist Association in 1842, already affirmed both open communion and the washing of the saints' feet as an ordinance in its second extant minutes in 1889. However, despite the fact they were already calling themselves Free Will Baptist in 1889, they affirmed that "saints persevere in grace and not one of them will be finally lost." It appears that 1896 is when they finally made their transition to full Arminianism, because by that year, they dealt with the apostasy issue by inserting the word "may": "saints may persevere in grace and not one be lost." One of Old Mount Zion's sister associations in the region immediately to the South of Old Mount Zion, named simply "Mt. Zion Association," changed those same articles of faith to teach the possibility of apostasy in the following way: "We believe that saints *who* will persevere in grace unto the end will be saved and not one of them will be finally lost."[41]

In the mid-twentieth century, a debate would develop over whether (1) unrepentant sin could cause apostasy that is remediable through repentance or (2) believers are kept by faith and imputed righteousness alone and can apostatize only through renouncing faith, which is irremediable. However, this issue does not surface in the records until the 1890s and twentieth century. The emphasis in the extant sources from the nineteenth century is on being "kept by the power of God through faith" (1 Peter 1:5) and on irremediable apostasy in texts such as Hebrews 6:4-6 and 10:26-31, John 15:1-6, and 2 Peter 2:20-22.[42]

The Church

Nature, Membership, and Discipline

In their doctrine of the church, the Free Will Baptists of the South differed from most other Baptists in America in only three particulars: open communion, the washing of the saints' feet, and a stronger associational polity. Their doctrine of the nature and marks of a local church, the nature of the Lord's Supper, church membership, and discipline were much like that of other Baptists in the South in the nineteenth century. Thus they affirmed the baptism of only believers and taught that the sole mode of baptism prescribed in Scripture was immersion in water. They believed that only those who have undergone baptism as prescribed in this manner can be admitted to church membership. Like other Baptists in the South in the nineteenth century, the Free Will Baptists were strict on church membership and discipline. Applicants for church membership, they taught, must be repentant from sin and have faith in Jesus Christ. They must have been baptized by immersion and agree to live a holy life and "submit to all the rules of the church under whose care they are." Free Will Baptists required that members assent to orthodox Christian doctrine. Though leaders were required to subscribe to the confession of faith's distinctive denominational doctrines, every member was not.[43]

Alabama Free Will Baptist founder Ellis Gore's 1874 essay "Church Discipline" is representative of southern Free Will Baptists' understanding of the nature of the church, its membership, and its discipline. Like other Free Will Baptists but unlike many other Baptists, especially the Landmark Baptists popular in the South of that day, Gore did not define the church exclusively in terms of the local congregation. That is why he and many others referred to the denomination outside the local congregation as "the Free Will Baptist Church." This usage would be ubiquitous among Free Will Baptists until the mid-twentieth century, when independency movements from outside the denomination eroded this historic emphasis. Gore also emphasized the universal church, which had historically been referred to as "the church catholic"—what many Protestants would refer to as "small-c catholic" to distance themselves from Roman Catholicism.[44]

Gore began his definition of the church with the "general sense" of the word as "the whole body of believers in Christ, in every age of the world." Then he went on to discuss the term's "particular sense," which he said was an "assembly of Christians, united together by covenant in the faith and fellowship of the Gospel, observing the ordinances of Christ, governed by his laws, and exercising the rights, gifts and privileges invested in them by his word." A biblical church, Gore stipulated, requires at least five Christians who are "well-informed" in "the doctrine of the Bible" (though ideally, he averred, there will be more): a church must have at least two spiritual officers: "Bishops or Pastors, and Deacons." These officers have the responsibility of ensuring that the local church's members who have covenanted together "carry out the entire discipline, government and ordinances of the church." Pastors should not be authoritarian—should not "lord it over" the congregation—because the governance and discipline of the church "belongs to the body, as equals in government," to be "subject to one another, in humility." In this "community" of the faithful, the "authority" or "power" to "carry out the laws and regulations" of Scripture, while administered by the church's officers, is ultimately "invested" in "the body," and "a majority should rule" in the body's decisions.[45]

Gore's essay mostly concerned church membership and discipline. Because the members of Christ's local body have covenanted together "to walk according to the scripture," they are accountable to one another. They have the responsibility to "watch and care" for each other. This responsibility entails a "course of labor to be pursued toward transgressors" to "save the transgressor" and to protect as much as possible the spiritual and moral purity of the church and its witness before the watching world. Thus members' failure to walk according to Scripture in a publicly observable way, and their refusal to repent, "renders them subject to the discipline of the church." Church discipline, Gore stressed, was designed to be redemptive and restorative, not "selfish and oppressive, but tender, kind and affectionate," in the "spirit of forbearance and prayer," because "a soft answer turneth away wrath." Yet admonition must occur. Effective discipline requires a delicate combination of "plain, tender, pungent treatment."[46]

Gore distinguished between two sorts of offenses: "personal and private" and "public or general." He outlined Matthew 18. If the offense is personal and private, and the confronted individual repents, that is the end of church discipline and "you gain your brother." If he "gives you satisfaction, it should be a secret with you and him forever." If not, one should take "one or two confidential and judicious brethren" along and confront the erring brother or sister again. Only after the individual refuses to repent a second time should the offense be taken before the congregation. Yet Gore emphasized that "forbearing and forgiving one another in love, is a great christian virtue; hence we should not expect to agree in everything, and we should not make every little infirmity a matter of discipline, where the purity and piety of the individual, and the honor of the church, is not endangered." Regarding "public or outrageous offences," or refusal to repent of private ones, such cases should be taken before the church. The church officers will then hold a public trial, "that he may prove his innocence." The church should "labor" for the erring member's repentance, but the "honor and purity of the church must be sustained in their exclusion. At a proper time, by proving the sincerity of their repentance and reformation, such may be received back into the church."[47]

These principles are seen in numerous associational Articles of Faith across the South. The most common, the *1812 Abstract*, said, for example, that if one's sin was of a public nature, the church would deal with the individual according to the principles of Matthew 18. If the sin was private, "their private admonition and satisfaction shall be sufficient in that case." Should repentance not follow admonition, disorderly members "lay themselves liable to excommunication."[48]

Polity

The consensus of southern Free Will Baptist church government in the nineteenth century was that the local congregation is a self-governing body that has a duty to maintain fellowship and accountability with other local congregations in a formal conference or association. That the church is ultimately self-governing and has control over its own affairs was borne out in the controversy that occurred in North Carolina in 1853 about whether churches should let Freemasons be members. The North Carolina General Conference agreed that the "Rules of Discipline gives to each individual Church its own key—the privileges of transacting its own business independent of the General Conference."[49] The earliest extant copy of the *1812 Abstract* contained a statement that places jurisdiction over meeting houses squarely in the local congregation: "All the Meeting Houses belonging to our connection shall be under the jurisdiction of the Elders and Churches."[50]

This approach to the self-government of the local congregation was repeated throughout the South. Southern Free Will Baptists believed that the local church "shall control all her internal affairs."[51] They believed that decision-making authority in the local congregation was with the "majority" or "suffrage" of the congregation. The Carolina tradition is representative of this. In 1853, after the Masonry controversy, the General Conference agreed that "all matters shall be decided by a majority." Similarly, the Bethlehem tradition in Tennessee, Alabama, and Mississippi held that "a majority of members [of a church] shall rule in all cases."[52]

THE OFFICERS OF THE CHURCH

The southern Free Will Baptists saw pastors (elders) and deacons as the spiritual officers of the church. A church could have other positions as circumstances required, such as trustees, clerks, and so forth. Yet these were seen as administrative or "helps" roles and not as spiritual offices in which people were set apart or ordained for the work of ministry. Like their English General Baptist forebears, southern Free Will Baptists saw their pastors as holding the same New Testament office as "bishop" or "elder." The terms "elder," "bishop," and "pastor" were seen as referring to the same office. The Chattahoochee Association exemplified this approach in its statement "that elders are also called bishops or pastors; that all elders are equal in rank; though they may perform different functions since some may be bishops or pastors of a particular church, while others may be simply elders, having no pastoral charge."[53]

In many cases, both ministers and deacons were authorized to administer baptism. Furthermore, ministers, and usually deacons, were examined and ordained by the presbytery of the association or conference, as exemplified in article 13 from the Chattahoochee tradition: "The elders and deacons must be set apart to their office by ordination, by the imposition of the hands of the presbytery and prayer."[54]

FELLOWSHIP AMONG CHURCHES

Southern Free Will Baptists were consistent with the approach of their General Baptist forebears in their views of the relation of churches in conferences or associations. While they affirmed the self-government of the local congregation, they also believed it was a "duty" (e.g., the Bethlehem tradition) or "necessity" (e.g., the Arkansas tradition) to be "united" in association with other churches. This intercongregational relationship included counsel from the association in settling internal disputes. This practice was referred to as "calling aid" or "calling help" from "sister churches." It was a common practice for churches that were experiencing internal difficulties to ask for the help of the conference or association in settling such disputes. The Toe River Association in East Tennessee, for example, affirmed that local congregations were wise to allow local church disputes to be settled outside the local congregation, or as the minutes put it, to "remove a trial" from the local congregation "in litigated points." It was always acknowledged that the congregation had the right to make its own final decision. Yet the association's counsel was given great weight, and dissenting from it could result in the withdrawal of fellowship.[55]

One of the primary roles of the conference or association was the ordination and discipline of ministers. The usual name for the ordaining body of a conference or association was "presbytery." This usage was almost universal.[56] However, this body was sometimes referred to as an "ordaining council," and many times associations used both names. These presbyteries usually comprised only ministers. Some associations, however, sometimes elected deacons to their ordaining councils. The conference or association in some cases gave churches the right to deal with ministerial discipline cases. Yet it was understood that the association or conference had final jurisdiction over its ministers, in their ordination, care, and discipline. The Cumberland Association's requirements exemplify this commitment: "No minister shall be ordained until he can preach and defend the Free Will Baptist doctrine and not until he can fill the requirements in Paul's first letter to Timothy, 3d chapter, from 1st to 8th verse, and this shall be tested before a Presbytery."[57]

The Carolina tradition, for example, required churches to try ministerial discipline cases by calling in two or more pastors from other churches in the conference, "and if satisfaction is not made, the conference will appoint a committee to deal with him." More common was the practice of the Cumberland Association, which stated, "Presbytery shall have full power to try all ministers of the order for unchristian conduct, and, on proper testimony, the decision shall be final."[58]

While conferences and associations had the right and responsibility of giving counsel and aid to congregations, they were not to "lord it over God's heritage, nor infringe upon the inherent rights of the churches."[59] Conferences and associations also reserved the right to exclude the delegates of disorderly churches. The Arkansas Association, for example, gave itself the "power, for good cause, . . . to exclude the delegates from its session when they or their church are disorderly or fail to keep a good report."[60]

Ordinances

Southern Free Will Baptists in the nineteenth and early twentieth centuries tended to have a much broader understanding of ordinances than other Baptists in America. Early Baptists viewed ordinances closer to the way the Westminster Shorter Catechism used the word in its question on the "outward and ordinary means of grace." The Catechism defined those means of grace as "his ordinances, especially the Word, sacraments, and prayer." Most Baptists in America increasingly became uncomfortable with the word "sacrament" because of the sacramentalist overtones that often went with it. However, many Baptists, including Free Will Baptists in both the South and the North, continued to employ the term. Most Baptists in the nineteenth century simply began to use "ordinance" as a synonym for "sacrament," and eventually most Baptists "knew" there were only two of those: baptism and the Lord's Supper. However, most Baptists in the South originally defined ordinances in the older, multi-faceted way. It took Southern Baptists with Separate Baptist backgrounds longer to adopt the new and evolving Baptist definition of ordinance. After all, the Separate Baptists had required no less than nine ordinances: "baptism, the Lord's Supper, love-feasts, laying-on-of-hands, washing feet, anointing the sick, right hand of fellowship, kiss of charity, and devoting children."[61]

A broader approach to ordinances and sacraments characterized most Free Will Baptists in the nineteenth-century South. It is reflected in article 17 of the *1812 Abstract*: "We believe as touching Gospel ordinances in believer's baptism, laying on of hands, receiving the sacrament in bread and wine, washing the saints' feet, anointing the sick with oil in the name of the Lord, fasting, prayer, singing praises to God and the public ministry of the Word, with every institution of the Lord we shall find in the New Testament." The phrase "with every institution of the Lord we shall find in the New Testament" explained the Free Will Baptists' view of ordinances as practices the Spirit had instituted or appointed in the New Testament. These were what the Free Will Baptists, like their counterparts in the North, referred to as the "means of grace." These appointed means revealed in the New Testament, they taught, are God's cherished methods for gathering a people for his name and fitting them for his eternal kingdom. The language of "means of grace" is used in the *1812 Abstract*. It is also used in other documents, such as the Chattahoochee Association Minutes. It was carried over into the practices section of the *Treatise* of the National Association, which said that pastors and deacons were responsible for "promoting ... attendance on the means of grace."[62]

Though many southern Free Will Baptists still practiced the laying on of hands and the anointing of the sick in the early twentieth century, those practices had declined in some areas. By the time the National Association was formed in 1935, three ordinances were agreed on: baptism, the Lord's Supper, and the washing of the saints' feet. This formula is seen, for example, in the Arkansas Association's Articles of Faith: "We believe Baptism and the Lord's Supper and the Washing of the Saints' Feet, to be Gospel ordinances...."[63]

BAPTISM

Like the General Baptists before them, and like all Baptists, the Free Will Baptists of the South affirmed the baptism of believers only by immersion. Furthermore, they believed that Holy Scripture made this rite a prerequisite for church membership. Thus, while the Free Will Baptists affirmed open communion, they did not practice open membership. Only a tiny minority of Baptists, following John Bunyan, had made church membership open regardless of baptism in the seventeenth century, a practice that would be revived by some Baptists in the late twentieth century. The *1812 Abstract* summarized the Free Will Baptist doctrine of baptism: "We believe the Gospel mode of baptism is by immersion, and that believers are the only subjects for baptism."[64]

T. F. Harrison and J. M. Barfield defended this confessional statement at length in their book *A History of the Free Will Baptists of North Carolina*. Their summary of the basic Baptist teaching on the "subjects" and "mode" of baptism is typical of nineteenth-century Free Will Baptists in the South. They argued that the New Testament referred only to believers, never infants, when it described baptism, discussing texts such as Matthew 28:19; Mark 16:16; and Acts 2:38, 41; 8:12, 37; and 10:46. The description of baptism as a sign of the believer's death, burial, and resurrection with Christ indicated immersion as the mode, since the sign must accord with the thing signified. It also proved, they argued, that baptism was of believers only. Only believers have been buried and raised with Christ. "Infants cannot walk in newness of life, have the 'old man crucified with him.' ... Infants cannot 'put on Christ,' ... Infants cannot be 'risen with him,' ... 'through faith;' ... baptism is 'the answer of a good conscience'—another thing impossible for infants."[65]

Harrison and Barfield dealt with the paedobaptist argument that household baptisms in the New Testament proved that infants were baptized in the early church. Based on the teaching on baptism elsewhere in the New Testament, they urged, "Baptists are not required to prove there were no infants. It is necessary for Pedobaptists to prove there were, before the case can do them any good." They noted that the members of Lydia's household, who were baptized, were referred to as "brethren," indicating they were believers. Referring to the Philippian jailer's household being baptized, they pointed out that the members of his household were "all old enough to be intelligently preached to." Crispus "believed on the Lord with all his house": "No infants there, either." Similarly, Paul baptized the household of Stephanus, but the Bible refers to them as converts. Likewise, Harrison and Barfield maintained, the household baptism in Acts 19 was of "disciples" who had "heard" the gospel.⁶⁶

Regarding the mode of baptism, Harrison and Barfield explained that "there are various other Greek words to express various other applications of water," such as "sprinkle," "wash," and "pour." Yet "the Bible, while using them in other connections, never once uses any of them in connection with the ordinance of baptism—using always and only *baptizo*," the Greek word they explained meant to dip or plunge. Again, they argued, the sign must line up with the thing signified, and baptism is a sign of the believer's death, burial, and resurrection with Christ. Furthermore, citing numerous historical authorities, they argued that there was no aspersion (sprinking) until well into the medieval period and that the Greek Orthodox still baptized only by immersion.⁶⁷

While Free Will Baptists in the South disavowed baptismal regeneration, they affirmed that baptism is essential to normative Christian faith and obedience. Justification is by faith alone. Yet baptism, like all other works, necessarily accompanies Christian faith. Free Will Baptists were like other Baptists in this view, and it came to the surface primarily in conversations with representatives of the Stone-Campbell movement—Disciples of Christ, Churches of Christ, and Christian Churches—many of whom taught baptismal regeneration. Elder J. M. Bray of the Chattahoochee Association in Georgia emphasized this doctrine in a circular letter on "reasons why we are Free Will Baptists." While baptism is not "essential to salvation," he argued, it is "essential unto obedience." One cannot obey "the law of Christ" without undergoing baptism. To follow the New Testament "as our guide and as our rule of faith and practice . . . in all things will bring us into the water to be buried with Him in baptism."⁶⁸

The Lord's Supper

The extant sources in the South reveal little discussion by southern Free Will Baptists about the nature of the Lord's Supper. Most of the discussion is about open communion: inviting all members of churches to the table regardless of their denomination or their views on the subjects and mode of baptism. The *1812 Abstract* speaks of the Lord's Supper, which some nineteenth-century Free Will Baptists termed the Eucharist, as the "sacrament in bread and wine." One sees the word "sacrament" throughout the extant records in the South as well as the North. One thing is certain: the Free Will Baptists of the South took the Lord's Supper with the utmost seriousness. They were not, like many later Baptists, "bare memorialists." Rather, they believed that the Lord's Supper was a vivid and profound sign and seal of the atonement of Christ and of believer's feeding on Christ and communing with him as the only Bread of Life. Yet they also obviously eschewed transubstantiation and even theories about whether Christ's body and blood were spiritually present in the Supper any more than Christ was spiritually present in other ordinances God had instituted for perpetuation in the church.[69]

Open communion was what was discussed most in printed minutes and other extant documents of the southern Free Will Baptists. This is likely because it was one of the most controversial elements of their faith and practice. That open communion would be so controversial is foreign to many modern Baptists. Yet the fact that Free Will Baptists practiced open communion would have been just as horrifying to the average Baptist in the nineteenth-century South as the belief in the possibility of apostasy. The Toe River Association in East Tennessee exemplifies the southern Free Will Baptist position in its 1857 affirmation that it is "agreeable to Gospel order" to open "the sacramental table" to those in denominations that did not practice baptism by immersion. Article 13 of Mount Moriah's Articles of Faith exemplifies the strong affirmation of open communion: "We believe in open, or mixed communion, and the churches of our body are authorized, through their pastors, to invite christians of all orthodox churches who are in good standing in their respective churches, to commune with us at the Lord's table."[70]

An 1885 circular letter by Elder Wood Springfield, one of the early Mount Moriah ministers, encapsulated the Free Will Baptist concern about closed communion:

> Among evangelical denominations in this country the chief controversy on this subject is with the close communion Baptist. They will not admit members of the pedobaptist churches to the ordinance, on the ground that baptism is prerequisite to communion and pedobaptist have not been baptized; they also reject the Freewill Baptist, although they have been baptized, because they commune with pedobaptists. It will be seen, therefore,

that in their view that christian character, church fellowship, and baptism will not entitle one to communion: he must be of their faith and order. . . . Ought pedobaptist Christians be barred to admission to this ordinance? . . . Was not Dodridge, Brainard, and Whitfield Christians? but they were not baptized according to the Baptist faith. . . . [I]f we regard our pedobaptist brethren as christians we should not exclude them from the communion for the table is the Lord's, not ours. . . . [W]hat we mean by free communion is, that we believe that all Christians have an equal right to participate at any time and place that circumstances will admit. Oh! that the sectarian coat could be thrown off, and controversies would cease, and christians would seize hold of the word that is able to stand.[71]

B. W. Nash's Southern Baptist Association articles of faith, adopted by several Free Will Baptist associations across the South in the late nineteenth century, was emblematic of this "liberal communion" posture when it specified that "all Christians should unite in observing that sacred service, regardless of names or denominational distinctions." The southern Free Will Baptists felt they were making an impact in pressing their open-communion views, as more evangelicals, in the increasingly ecumenical mood of the late nineteenth century, became comfortable with open communion. As Elder J. H. Jenkins exclaimed in a circular letter to the Chattahoochee Association in 1899, "Already we have seen roseate gleams of the morning light heralding the brighter day, when the man-made doctrine and practice of closed communion will, like Calvinism, have vanished away before the resplendent rays of righteousness and eternal truth. Let us hold fast our terms of gospel communion, the communion of saints and not of sects."[72]

THE WASHING OF THE SAINTS' FEET

Most early Baptists in the American South practiced the washing of the saints' feet as an ordinance of the gospel. The very fact that the Calvinist Southern Baptist John Leadley Dagg got the practice in his crosshairs and felt the need to oppose it shows how widespread it was. Over the nineteenth century, as Baptists' socioeconomic prospects increased, the practice began to wane among mainstream Southern Baptists or "Missionary Baptists" in the South. By the beginning of the twentieth century, various Baptists in or from Appalachia, as well as Primitive Baptists, were the only Calvinist-background Baptists in the South still practicing the rite.[73]

The patristic liturgical observance of the *pedilavium* (Latin for feet washing) was continued as a "sacramental" in the Roman Catholic and Eastern

Orthodox communions throughout the medieval period and into the present day. It was recovered by mainline Protestants during the liturgical renewal movement and began to be practiced on Maundy Thursday in many mainline denominations. However, the washing of the saints' feet was generally uncommon among American Protestants in the nineteenth century. Other than Baptists and groups such as the Arminian-baptistic Church of God General Conference founded by John Winebrenner, most North American denominations that practiced the rite were from Anabaptist backgrounds, such as Mennonites and Amish, Brethren, and Hutterites. Some Wesleyan-Holiness groups practiced it, and it continues in the (non-Pentecostal) Church of God, Anderson, Indiana, and the (Pentecostal) Church of God, Cleveland, Tennessee. Adventist groups also embraced the practice in the nineteenth century.

Even many Free Will Baptist associations that were friendly with B. W. Nash's Southern Baptist Association in the late nineteenth century observed the rite. As seen in chapter 11, Nash's move to unite all Liberal Baptists militated against the washing of the saints' feet. The Little Missouri River Association, founded in Arkansas in 1877, exemplifies several Nash-oriented Free Will Baptist associations that still insisted on the rite. That association resolved, in 1891, to adopt the articles of the Southern Baptist Association but to add feet washing and amend article 11, which mentions the Lord's Supper but not the washing of the saints' feet. The same minutes refer to the observance of "communion and feet washing" at the association meeting itself. Mississippi's Little Brown's Creek Association is an example of a body that adapted the Nash articles of faith, adding their own articles on the person of Christ and of the Holy Spirit, editing some other articles, and inserting an article after the Lord's Supper article that said, "We believe the Saints ought to wash each others [sic] feet in commemoration of the love that was shown to us by our Savior and out of love toward each other; John 13:14—'If I then, your Lord and Master, have washed your feet, ye also ought to wash one another's feet.'"[74]

The same can be said of the "General Free Will Baptists" in southern Illinois, southeast Missouri, and northeast Arkansas. This group originated through a union of feet-washing General Baptists from Kentucky and Free Will Baptists from the Cumberland Association in Middle Tennessee, with influence from David Poyner, who was originally from North Carolina. The Articles of Faith of one of these General Free Will Baptist associations, Social Band in northeast Arkansas, were almost identical to those of the General Association of General Baptists. Yet while the General Association of General Baptists left the washing of feet an open question, Social Band's articles said, "We believe that baptism, the Lord's Supper, and the washing of the saint's [sic] feet are ordinances of Jesus Christ appointed in the church...."[75]

The "twin preachers" T. F. and T. H. Harrison of North Carolina, in their little book *Feet-Washing*, written in 1894, outlined the Free Will Baptists' reasons for continuing the liturgical practice of the washing of the saints' feet in the life of the church. They argued that the words of institution for the ritual in John 13 are even stronger than those for baptism and the Lord's Supper. They noted that the term "church ordinance" cannot be found in the Bible. The Harrison brothers argued that interpreters cannot be consistent in perpetuating the physical, ritual practice of baptism and the Lord's Supper unless they also do so with feet washing. In this way, such critics of the washing of feet were like many Quakers, who disavowed baptism and the Lord's Supper as "fleshly," treating them as object lessons on spiritual truths. Harrison and Harrison maintained that what Christ instituted in John 13 was an obvious ritual, which he elaborately enacted and explained.[76]

They countered the objection that only small sectarian groups practice the rite by pointing to the Roman Catholic and Eastern Orthodox churches' perpetuation of the liturgical practice. They quoted at length a Roman Catholic liturgical scholar defending the *pedilavium*, which he said was practiced by the church fathers and was still in practice as a sacramental in the modern Roman Catholic Church. Others made the same historical argument. For example, Elder T. H. Griffin, in an 1883 circular letter to the Chattahoochee Association, argued that many of the church fathers practiced the washing of the saints' feet. The Harrisons, Griffin, and other writers pointed to early Christianity's reflection on the widows who were to be cared for by the church in 1 Timothy 5:9–10 as being commended for "washing the saints' feet." If this were simply discussing the cultural practice of washing guests' dirty feet, they asked, why would these widows be singled out for commendation on a practice that believers and unbelievers alike routinely observed, and why would it only be for saints rather than unbelieving guests?[77]

Worship

Not much is recorded in the extant sources of the southern Free Will Baptists about their mode of worship. However, there is no reason to think it differed from that of other Baptists of their day. Nineteenth-century Free Will Baptists, in their emphasis on the sufficiency of Scripture and the ordinary means of grace, worshipped the Lord simply and saw themselves as patterning their worship after the precept and example of Christ and the apostles. When the northern Freewill Baptist Elias Hutchins visited the Free Will Baptists of

North and South Carolina, he "especially was impressed with the reverence that was evident in the worship service of the Free Will Baptists," William Davidson notes. "He spoke often of the well-behaved, solemn, and attentive audiences." One of Hutchins's letters described a baptismal service in which twenty converts were baptized. Hutchins said, "The scene was solemn and impressive, well calculated to animate the Christian, and fill the minds of sinners with sensations of a favorable character; and the large congregation that witnessed the performance by a commendable decorum evinced great respect to the ordinance...."[78]

There were differences among Free Will Baptists of various locations and subcultures. Some tended more toward formality and less emotional expressiveness, while others tended more toward informality and more emotional expressiveness. Yet until the late twentieth century, there was broad agreement on the simplicity of worship based on the sufficiency of Holy Scripture. A comparison with the wider Baptist tradition in the South will shed light on southern Free Will Baptist worship. It embodied a dynamic similar to what Walter Shurden described among Calvinist-background Baptists in the South. What he called the "Charleston" or Regular Baptist tradition was more ordered, formal, and intellectual. The "Sandy Creek" or Separate Baptist tradition was more informal and emotional. Yet, as Shurden explains, most Southern Baptists in the late nineteenth and twentieth centuries achieved a *via media* between these two approaches. Strong pockets of Charleston and Sandy Creek worship persisted, however, into the present day. The same can essentially be said of the Free Will Baptist Church in the South.[79]

Extant sources show that observers, like Hutchins, often used the word "solemn" to describe the worship services of the Free Will Baptists along the Eastern Seaboard. Yet observers were using the word in its traditional sense of "formal and dignified," from the Latin *sollemnis*, for customs or religious rites, rather than the modern connotation of "not cheerful or smiling."[80] Thus the southern Free Will Baptists sang:

> How great, how solemn is the work
> Which we attend today!
> Now for a holy, solemn frame,
> O God, to thee we pray.
>
> Awake our love, our fear, our hope;
> Wake, fortitude and joy;

> Vain world, begone; let things above
> Our happy thoughts employ.
>
> Whilst thee, our Saviour and our God,
> To all around we own,
> Drive each rebellious, rival lust,
> Each traitor from thy throne.
>
> Instruct our minds; our wills subdue;
> To heaven our passions raise;
> That hence our lives, our all may be
> Devoted to thy praise.[81]

This solemnity is also seen in a description of services of worship led by Redding Moore, the founder of South Carolina Free Will Baptists, in Hookerton, North Carolina, in 1830: "On the evening the brethren met to commemorate the Lord's death. Elder Readding Moore administered the sacrament—the meeting solemn and interesting."[82]

The worship was "solemn" yet also "interesting." Noah Webster defined the latter term, in the older sense of the word, as "engaging the affections." This sort of worship was like Shurden's Southern Baptist "Charleston tradition." However, some Free Will Baptists engaged in shouting "Amen" and "Hallelujah" and other practices of the more emotional worship characterized by what Shurden called the "Sandy Creek Tradition."[83]

However, all nineteenth-century Free Will Baptists in the South quoted St. Paul about the need to conduct church affairs "decently and in order." Even those who were more emotionally expressive treated worship with the utmost seriousness. They all wished to maintain the simplicity of worship as they believed they were encountering it in the New Testament. Both more formal and more informal congregations, like their radical Puritan ancestors, placed emphasis on Word-centered worship. Thus, not simply singing, but everything they did in worship, they claimed, was to "let the word of Christ dwell in [them] richly with all wisdom," as they sought to "teach and admonish each other" (Colossians 3:16). Thus they made preaching the central focus of worship. Yet other aspects of their worship were skewed toward this Word-centered objective. One sees this, for example, in the heavily theological hymns they sang. The hymns printed in *Zion's Hymns*, for example, show that the nineteenth-century Free Will Baptists were in agreement with the hymn tradition of English Nonconformity represented by figures such as Charles Wesley, Isaac Watts, and Calvinist Baptists of their day who appropriated that tradition.

The consensus of the English Nonconformist hymn tradition held that the purpose for the church's song was teaching, admonition, and giving glory to God alone with grace in one's heart. As the title page of North Carolinian Enoch Cobb's 1846 hymnal *The Free Will Baptist Hymn Book* quoted, worshippers were to "sing with the spirit" and "sing with the understanding also." Worship was thus Word-centered in its content as well as its form. As part of this tradition, Free Will Baptists believed that Scripture was calling them to worship God with "joy and trembling" (Psalm 2:11), in "reverence and godly fear: For our God is a consuming fire" (Hebrews 12:28–29). They believed that they could do this only by internalizing the divine revelation of Holy Scripture. Cobb also emphasized in his preface the purpose of the church's song to stimulate the fear of the Lord and to produce in the worshipper "an eye single to the glory of God" and of "the Lamb."[84]

As seen in *Zion's Hymns*, the southern Free Will Baptists agreed with the English hymn tradition that one of the primary purposes of the church's song is the teaching of doctrine. Hearn, Bell, and Randolph said in their Preface to *Zion's Hymns* that they had carefully selected the hymns they believed were most suitable to "public, private, and social worship," and they sent them forth as a "means of promoting the Redeemer's kingdom." One of those hymns, number 70, got to the heart of their view of the meaning, purpose, and activity of public worship. Like the other hymns, it had in bold print at the top the subject matter of the song: "Prayer for a Blessing on Public Worship." The hymn was an edition of James Montgomery's "To Thy Temple We Repair":

> To thy temple we repair;
> Lord, we love to worship there;
> There, within the veil, we meet
> Christ upon the mercy-seat.
>
> While thy glorious name is sung,
> Tune our lips, inspire our tongue;
> Then our joyful souls shall bless
> Christ the Lord our righteousness.

While to thee our prayers ascend,
Let thine ear in love attend;
Hear us when thy Spirit pleads;
Hear, for Jesus intercedes.

While thy word is heard with awe,
While we tremble at thy law,
Let thy gospel's wondrous love
Every doubt and fear remove.

From thy house when we return,
Let our hearts within us burn;
Then at ev'ning may we say,
"We have walked with God to-day."[85]

Southern Free Will Baptists, both Black and White, became serious about music education in their congregations in the nineteenth century. This took the form of the "singing school" or "fa-so-la" movement enshrined in three song books: *The Sacred Harp*, its African American counterpart *The Colored Sacred Harp*, and *Southern Harmony*. This a capella singing tradition, which had analogues across the Atlantic in the "west gallery music" in rural English parish churches, originated in America with the work of singing masters such as William Billings, using musical notes in four shapes, known by the terms "fa, sol, la, fa, sol, la, mi, fa" (similar to the later seven-shape concept of do-re-mi-fa-sol-la-ti-do). This was intended to help common people learn how to read musical notation so that any group of people could sing any new song in harmony.[86]

Sacred Harp and *Southern Harmony* "all-day singings with dinner on the grounds" not only served as an intergenerational socio-cultural outlet for Free Will Baptists but also taught them to sing in parts, thus enriching their worship services. Their hymnals were text-only without notation. Each psalm, hymn, and spiritual song had a metrical note at the top indicating what meter the hymn was in. For example, "Amazing Grace" was in the common meter—C.M. So it could easily be sung to any number of common meter tunes the singers had memorized at singing school. ("Joy to the World," "O, for a Thousand Tongues to Sing," and "Must Jesus Bear the Cross Alone" are examples of C.M. tunes.) The leader would announce the hymn number, then the tune, and the congregation would then sing the hymn to that tune.[87]

Other Areas of Practice

Owing to the scarcity of records, historians have precious little information about southern Free Will Baptist views on a variety of topics such as the role of women, sexuality, race, poverty, and social issues. Most of the information about nineteenth-century Free Will Baptists comes from minutes and is mostly doctrinal in nature. Very little is said about women directly, except occasional references to "sisters," mentioning female attendees by the title "Sister," or obituaries of active women in the conference, such as the following from the Chattahoochee Association in Georgia:

> Emeline, daughter of B. S. and Jane Johnson, was born the 10th of May, 1849, joined the church, and was baptized by Elder C. C. Martin, in 1864. Married to W. F. Simpson in 1866; departed this life February 20th, 1881. Her life was one of devotion. She lived to do good to all as she had opportunity. Lingering for a long time with consumption she neither murmured nor complained, but with christian meekness glorified God through all trials and sufferings, thus leaving an example to family and friends that those who trust in Christ are not left comfortless in tribulation.[88]

Sexuality and divorce are rarely mentioned in conference and association records, except in passing remarks about cases of ministerial discipline.

Regarding the alleviation of poverty and other benevolent enterprises, scattered comments occur throughout the records similar to this in the Mount Moriah tradition: "That we will Cheerfully contribute of our property for the Maintenance of the Poor." Other conferences and associations required their member churches to disclose the amount of funds they raised for "benevolent purposes" the preceding year or to maintain a benevolence committee. Also, numerous commendations appeared in obituaries about ministers, laymen, and laywomen who were strong supporters of benevolent organizations. For example, the 1893 obituary of North Carolina minister Elder R. A. Johnson, who died at forty-seven years of age, praised him for being "a very liberal giver to all benevolent organizations." Beyond this sort of acclaim in minutes, little has survived in the historical record, except the practice of local congregations being required to report to the annual session of an association or conference how much money they raised for "benevolent purposes." As will be seen in later chapters, as the denomination began to grow and coalesce, orphanages became one of its favorite benevolent enterprises.[89]

Paltry evidence survives about southern Free Will Baptist views on race, though it certainly must have run the gamut of opinions among Baptists in the nineteenth-century South. The handful of passing references to African Americans from White Free Will Baptists are to enslaved members of local churches during the antebellum period and to helping freed slaves start new churches, conferences, and associations following the Civil War, sometimes with funds provided by White Free Will Baptists. Phillip Morgan discusses a few references to the Middle Tennessee minister Robert Heaton, who died in 1843, which show that he evangelized African Americans and received them into membership as transfers from other congregations. The owners of some of the Black members listed as "servants" on the church's membership roster were members of other churches. Morgan infers that some of the African American members in Heaton's congregation may have been free Blacks, though most were clearly slaves. One of the few other antebellum references to slavery in the records of southern Free Will Baptists is that of the Toe River Association in East Tennessee and western North Carolina. At its 1851 session a query was brought forward asking "whether it be right to buy and sell men, women and children agreeable to the Holy Scriptures or not, though they be black." After being tabled for a year, the association answered the question in the affirmative. The Free Will Baptists in this association would be strongly anti-Confederate in their support of the Union in the Civil War.[90]

As noted in chapter 8, there are a few extant examples of letters written from African American associations that refer to hostility from Whites. The Northeast Texas Association, for example, wrote the northern General Conference in the 1880s, saying, "We meet with great opposition here, because of our free doctrines, and our color. We are determined to live and enjoy our freedom." One White Randall missionary to Texas wrote about racism there after the Civil War, even describing accounts of Black Free Will Baptists having their schoolhouses burned by hostile Whites. However, he mentioned nothing about the attitudes of White Free Will Baptists toward race relations. There was obvious racial segregation among the Free Will Baptists in the late nineteenth and early twentieth centuries. Still, the animus described in Texas does not appear to have characterized relations between Black and White Free Will Baptists. Black and White associations were known, for example, to have exchanged delegates, with White ministers visiting Black associations and Black ministers being received as "visiting brethren" at White associations.[91]

This is not to say that there was no racial animus among the Free Will Baptists of the late nineteenth-century South. It is simply to say that the sparse records provide no evidence of it. One interesting comment does arise from

H. M. Ford, the Field Secretary of the Free Baptist General Conference who made two tours among southern Free Will Baptists in the late 1890s. In his 1898 report to the General Conference, Ford remarked,

> When I said before an audience of five hundred or more that in matters of religion we in the north cared no more for the color of a man's skin than we did for the color of his eyes, and if a converted colored man or woman wanted to join any of our churches we would be glad to have them come, I could not see that it affected the audience in the least, but when they asked me point blank if we practised footwashing, and I replied 'No,' you should have seen the look of disappointment.[92]

More research needs to be undertaken, which will no doubt provide more specific information about attitudes toward race among Black and White Free Will Baptists in the nineteenth century.

While most Free Will Baptists in the South were supporters of the Confederacy during the Civil War, it is interesting to note, as aforementioned, the Toe River Association's sympathy for the Union in the Civil War despite their lack of opposition to slavery. Support for the Union was not uncommon in their region of East Tennessee and western North Carolina, as was seen with Elder John H. Ballard of western North Carolina, who deserted the Confederate army to fight with the Union army. Another interesting fact is that the Toe River Association passed some anti-war resolutions after the War, in 1867 and 1868, threatening to exclude members for going to war and petitioning the US Congress "to relieve us from military duty."[93]

Part V

DEVELOPMENT IN THE TWENTIETH AND TWENTY-FIRST CENTURIES

Eleven
THE PRECURSORS AND FOUNDING
OF THE NATIONAL ASSOCIATION

The Co-operative General Association

Reeling from the merger of the Free Baptist General Conference with the Northern Baptist Convention in 1911, a remnant of the Randall movement in the Midwest and Southwest were eager to unite for a more effective ecclesiastical organization and the ministry it could provide. At the forefront of this effort were T. C. Ferguson and John H. Wolfe, the two most outspoken opponents of the merger at the northern General Conference in Oceana, New York, in 1910. By 1916 Ferguson had moved from Texas back to Missouri, and he and Wolfe, a minister in the Nebraska-Kansas Yearly Meeting, had already been involved in rebuilding after the merger. Their efforts included helping to establish new institutions such as the periodical *The New Morning Star*. They rallied other Randall remnants, including those who had been involved with Ferguson and S. L. Morris of Texas in the work of the Southwestern General Convention. Yet they also joined forces with Free Will Baptists in the region who had originated from Palmer origins farther east. All this energy coalesced in the formation of the Co-operative General Association of Freewill Baptists at Philadelphia Church in Pattonsburg, Missouri, on the twenty-seventh day of December, 1916. The meeting, which adjourned on New Year's Day, was a joyous and hopeful celebration of the association's confessional identity and union around a common cause.[1]

The delegates to this first session were primarily from associations in Missouri and Texas, which T. C. Ferguson and S. L. Morris knew well. Also represented was the Nebraska-Kansas Yearly Meeting which had, just barely, survived the 1911 merger with the help of John H. and Delia Wolfe. The association elected John H. Wolfe as moderator, J. F. Duckworth of Greentop, Missouri, as assistant moderator, Ira Waterman of Eldridge, Missouri, as clerk, W. E. Dearmore of Elk Creek, Nebraska, as assistant clerk, and a layman, James Hardin of Novinger, Missouri, as treasurer.[2]

North Carolina pastor R. F. Pittman, though not representing a conference, was present as a visiting delegate. Pittman was fully included in the proceedings, serving on committees and even being named an associate editor of Morris's paper, *The New Morning Star*. Likely as a result of the report Pittman gave about the work in North Carolina, the association endorsed the Free Will Baptist Press, its weekly paper *The Free Will Baptist*, the Free Will Baptist Seminary in Ayden, North Carolina, and the Free Will Baptist Orphanage in Middlesex, North Carolina.[3]

Institutions and Early Development

In addition to adopting an existing mission work in Barbados conducted by a minister named Miss S. A. Esterbrook, the association also endorsed the Freewill Baptist Biblical Correspondent School, which Wolfe had recently started. A graduate of the "full theological" program at Hillsdale College in Michigan, Wolfe put his classical education in biblical studies, systematic theology, Greek, Hebrew, and Latin to good use as dean and instructor of systematic theology. G. S. Lattimer, a pastor from Haddam, Kansas, taught Church History and Evidences of Christianity. Another teacher was Ira Waterman, an influential minister from Eldridge, Missouri, who would later be mentioned by John L. Welch when he reminisced about the early merger talks between the General Conference of the South and the Co-operative General Association.

Very soon after its formation, the Co-operative General Association involved Free Will Baptists from the state of Oklahoma, from which a number of delegates represented to the association's 1917 session. That session was held at a new college that John H. Wolfe had started that year in Tecumseh, Oklahoma. Wolfe had been busy the entire year piecing together a Freewill Baptist organization with Oklahoma as its geographical base. Shortly after the organizational meeting of the Co-operative General Association in January 1917, Wolfe visited the town of Tecumseh and discussed a proposition with the president of Tecumseh National Bank and a group of town leaders for opening a college there. They agreed to buy the old Indianola Business College building and provide some funds for its renovation if Wolfe would open his college there. Wolfe took them up on their offer and made the transition from Nebraska to Tecumseh, convincing S. L. Morris and his wife to move the operations of *The New Morning Star* there from Weatherford, Texas. Tecumseh College opened for classes that August.[4]

In less than a year, Wolfe had assembled a faculty and staff of six. He served as president, head of the Department of Theology and Philosophy, and Fuller Professor of Systematic Theology. That chair in theology was named for Mr. and Mrs. William Fuller, Nebraska Freewill Baptists who had contributed the first $500 endowment to the college. At Wolfe's side were his wife, Rev. Delia Wolfe, who taught history and languages; Rev. S. L. Morris, who taught sacred history and apologetics; Morris's wife Grace, who taught mathematics and physics; and Rev. Samra Smith, a North Carolinian who had served at the Free Will Baptist school at Unicoi, Tennessee, who taught chemistry, biology, and "Expression." The curriculum was divided into eight "courses": Classical, Philosophical, Scientific, Literary, and Classical Theological, which, together with three years of preparatory (high school) work, took seven years to complete; "English Theological" and "Expression," which required four years; and "Normal," a teacher preparation program that lasted three years. The Biblical Correspondent School was still operating for those who could not make the move to Tecumseh.[5]

After S. L. Morris moved *The New Morning Star* to Tecumseh, Samra Smith approached him about merging the paper he edited, the *Biblical Beacon*, with *The New Morning Star* and donating all the *Beacon's* equipment and assets. Morris agreed, and this consolidation gave the paper even more subscribers than the five hundred it had before moving to Oklahoma. Smith became an associate editor of *The New Morning Star* with John Wolfe, who was already acting in that capacity. In his report to the Co-operative General Association, Morris said, "It is hard for those who are not acquainted with Bro. and Sister Smith to rightly appreciate their real worth to the work here. In fact we feel that we cannot do without them in the Star Office." If that were not enough, W. C. Austin, the Tennessean who had moved to Oklahoma by way of northeast Arkansas, merged his paper, the *Pruning Hook*, with the *Star*.[6]

The year 1917 also saw the appointment of several "field superintendents" to promote the work of the association. These included T. C. Ferguson and Ira Waterman as well as Texas minister Hiram M. McAdams. These men were instrumental in reaching out to other Arminian Baptist groups. Waterman had made contacts as far east as North Carolina (R. F. Pittman was back again as a visitor at the 1917 session), and Ferguson had been in touch with General Baptists in his Midwest region. The association also announced the recent election of the Revs. Hiram and Lizzie McAdams as its missionaries to the British West Indies, where the McAdamses would serve a short term in Barbados.[7]

The next year the Co-operative General Association extended its borders eastward, holding its 1918 session in Paintsville, Kentucky. Kentucky was the eastern state that would have the most involvement with the association, which was very grateful for its brothers and sisters from the Commonwealth. That relationship would last until the association's last meeting in 1937 held in Purdy, Missouri. The association's affection for the Kentucky brethren is illustrated in a break from business at the Thursday afternoon business meeting that year, when G. Peyton Gulick "played 'My Old Kentucky Home' on his violin, dedicating the number to the Vanhoose Brothers of Paintsville, Kentucky." Several other delegates from back east attended that 1918 session, hailing from the states of Ohio, West Virginia, North Carolina, and Tennessee. The Resolutions Committee mentioned associations from Michigan and Illinois, but no delegates from those states were present at the meeting. It was significant that John L. Welch of the Cumberland Association in Tennessee was a delegate, since he would later be the major catalyst in bringing together this body with the General Conference, which would be established east of the Mississippi in 1921.[8]

The field superintendents had done a great deal of work building interest for a union of all Free Will Baptists. R. F. Pittman of North Carolina was not able to attend the 1918 session but sent in a field superintendent's report by letter. Samra Smith, general secretary of the association, gave a report on his promotional work. In addition to discussing his visits in Missouri, he informed the body of his recent trip home to the North Carolina State Convention. He described the convention as "one of the strongest bodies" of Free Will Baptists. While he was there, he conducted a series of meetings at the church in Lucama, one of the congregations Pittman served as pastor. Smith mentioned contact with some Freewill Baptists in Michigan who had continued after the merger. He had also been corresponding with Free Will Baptists in Georgia, Alabama, Mississippi, and Tennessee. The association continued to promote the institutions in both Oklahoma and North Carolina.[9]

The institutions and ministries of the Co-operative General Association experienced gradual growth. Tecumseh College added a music department in 1918. The enrollment for that year was twenty-two. *The New Morning Star* added equipment and continued printing the paper, the Free Baptist *Treatise*, and limited books and pamphlets, and there continued to be a demand for northern Free Baptist books such as George Ball's *Christian Baptism* and John J. Butler and Ransom Dunn's *Systematic Theology*. Wolfe spoke hopefully about the future of the movement: "The outlook throughout the Denomination is exceedingly encouraging as we get the word from all quarters. Surely the Lord led in the great work that is in our hands and before us, and with confidence we are moving along the right road."[10]

The Failure of Union

At this early stage, Free Will Baptists on both sides of the Mississippi hoped that the Co-operative General Association would become the new national body for all Free Will Baptists. This is illustrated by the sizable delegation from the east at the 1918 session. That, however, was not to be. At the 1919 session held with Cofer's Chapel Church in Nashville, the issue of the washing of the saints' feet became a bone of contention. Some of the leaders of the Co-operative General Association, especially Nebraskans John H. Wolfe and the layman M. L. Morse, were strongly opposed to viewing the rite as an ordinance and did not want to make it an article of faith. Robert Picirilli recounts an unsuccessful attempt by Morse to try to get the churches of southern Illinois to give up the rite. "Now we are out with the Illinois brethren," Morse wrote to Wolfe. "Is there any show to get in with any of the Ohio or Indiana brethren? Feet-washing is all the talk in the south and is working up north." Despite the fact that most of the churches in the Co-operative General Association practiced the ordinance, Wolfe at that time was the glue that held the association together. His insistence that the washing of the saints' feet be made an open issue dissuaded Welch and the other major players that were east of the Mississippi from continued involvement.[11]

Morse's comments about the southern Illinois movement's attitude toward the washing of the saints' feet are unsurprising. Most of their origins were in Free Will Baptists from the Cumberland Association in Middle Tennessee and General Baptists from Kentucky. That was an area where feet washing was common among General Baptists. As mentioned before, those in Missouri also practiced the rite. Wolfe and Morse were receiving great opposition on this subject from within the Co-operative General Association itself. While the association's 1916 Articles of Faith did not mention the practice, as early as 1917 and 1918, it was included, with Wolfe allowing it because of the "give and take" he said would be necessary to achieve a larger Freewill Baptist movement. Picirilli rightly conjectures that the growing contingent in Oklahoma that was so resolute on the practice—thinking it was a necessary practice for "GENUINE" Free Will Baptists—likely played strongly into the tension. In a letter to Morse concerning North Carolina native Samra Smith's presidency of Tecumseh College, Wolfe worried that those "who do not practice footwashing" would be "crowded out" of the Co-operative General Association. This is likely the reason Wolfe and Morse exited the association in 1922.[12]

John L. Welch later indicated that there never would have been a National Association in 1935 had the leadership of the Co-operative General Association not agreed to make the washing of the saints' feet an article of faith. In an interview with Picirilli in the 1970s, Welch explained that the 1919 session of the association was decisive in the decision not to pursue a relationship with the Co-operative General Association. He explained that leaders such as Wolfe "wouldn't take a stand on it, they wanted to leave it an open question. The North Carolina and Tennessee people wanted it as an ordinance, you see. Well, the result of the argument was that the North Carolina group and our [Tennessee] group pulled out from the Co-operative . . . over this question of feet washing." With the hopes of the Co-operative General Association's becoming the national Free Will Baptist association dashed, the Free Will Baptists in the east formed the General Conference of the Original Free Will Baptists of the United States in 1921. Fourteen years later, this body would unite with the Co-operative General Association with a *Treatise* that confessed the washing of the saints' feet as a church ordinance.[13]

The Co-operative General Association continued to serve as a unifying organization for Freewill Baptists mostly west of the Mississippi. The movement in Oklahoma was growing, and delegates from that state began to comprise the majority of the delegates at the association's meetings. By 1922, John H. Wolfe and M. L. Morse had lost interest in the work at Tecumseh and the Co-operative General Association. They were absent from the 1922 and 1923 sessions, and by 1927 they were attempting to start another organization that they intended to name the "Inter-State Conference of Free Will Baptists," which sputtered before it could ever launch.[14]

Unlike at previous meetings, there was almost nothing said about Tecumseh College at the 1922 session of the Co-operative General Association, except for a simple recommendation of the institution from Committee on Education chair R. A. Roberts. Oklahoma pastor B. F. Brown reluctantly accepted the presidency of Tecumseh in November 1922 because he said Wolfe had "refused" the position. The small school was still proceeding at about the same pace, with twenty-one students enrolled, but all those students were from the town of Tecumseh. *The New Morning Star* had also fallen on hard times as well and had gone for a few months in the fall of 1922 without being printed. Brown said, "I feel that the college ought to be sustained, and that

God will hear our prayers, that necessary funds will be sent in. This is our testing time. I am sure that when our people do the will of God, to go and do and speak as He leads, we will have plenty and to spare and our school and paper will then work to an accomplished end."[15]

The next year, in November 1924, Brown resigned as president, and Grace I. Morris, S. L. Morris's wife, took the position. There was at least one other president, T. A. Searcy, in the 1926–1927 academic year. In a letter to M. L. Morse, Wolfe lamented Searcy's appointment because the latter, who was originally from Texas, had in the intervening years served as a Northern Baptist minister in Iowa. Interestingly, T. B. Mellette was on the faculty list that year. Mellette was a South Carolina minister who was always a staunch advocate of higher education and would later operate Zion Bible School in Blakely, Georgia, when there was no other Free Will Baptist school. Mellette was either teaching by correspondence or his move did not work out, because he was still in South Carolina in November 1926 and by June and November 1927 was in Southwest Georgia. Tecumseh College was struggling and by then offered only three programs, the High School Course, the Theological Course, and the Commercial Course. In February 1927, tragedy struck, and the building was destroyed by fire. Tecumseh would never recover. *The New Morning Star* followed suit and does not seem to have been published past 1927.[16]

Exploring the Possibility of Merger

Though discouraged, the Co-operative General Association did not give up hope. They continued to try developing ways to advance the movement. For example, a small publication known as the *Freewill Baptist Quarterly* was in publication in the 1920s, and in the early 1930s a printing press operated for a while, the Western Freewill Baptist Publishing Company. The association continued moving forward in its goal to achieve union among Free Will Baptists. Over the next seven years, its leaders would repair the breach with those of the General Conference. By the 1934 session of the Co-operative General Association in Denison, Texas, merger plans were underway, and a committee from the General Conference consisting of John L. Welch, E. C. Morris, I. J. Blackwelder, and K. V. Shutes came to work out the terms of a merger between the two groups.[17]

Also present at the 1934 session of the Co-operative General Association were representatives from the Tri-State Association. That body had been founded in 1919 and comprised Ohio, West Virginia, and Kentucky Free Will Baptists. A delegation from Texas was at the 1934 session that appears to have been new to the Co-operative General Association. Though there are no extant Co-operative General minutes between 1923 and 1934, it appears that the Tri-State Association was already a part of the Co-operative General Association before 1934. It sent an "Associational Letter," and one of its delegates, F. S. Van Hoose, was on the association's committee to discuss merger with the General Conference. Also at the 1934 session, a motion was carried to send delegates from the association to the 1935 annual session of the General Conference at Black Jack Church in Greenville, North Carolina. At the 1934 meeting, the committee from the General Conference met with a committee from the Co-operative General Association consisting of J. L. Waltman, Noel Turner, Bert F. Rogers, F. S. Van Hoose, and Selph Jones. This joint committee continued the merger talks that had occurred the previous June at the thirteenth annual session of the General Conference when it convened with East Nashville Church in Nashville, Tennessee. These talks would eventuate in the formation of the National Association of Free Will Baptists the following year.[18]

For more than two decades, the Co-operative General Association worked to consolidate the Free Will Baptist presence in the Midwest and Southwest. Though John H. Wolfe, the early genius behind the association and its institutions, would become disaffected with it, he was the primary figure to give it shape in its early years. His decision to locate Tecumseh College in Oklahoma coincided with, and likely contributed to, the growth of the movement in that state. The association drew from an amalgamation of Randall and Palmer elements—Missouri and Texas being a mixture of both and Oklahoma having originated from the southern movement. Yet it kept the Randall legacy from disappearing. Even after Wolfe's departure and the tragic fire that was the final stroke in the demise of Tecumseh College and *The New Morning Star*, the Co-operative General Association rallied and stayed the course, ever working toward a union of all Free Will Baptists into one body.

The General Conference

The failure of the 1919 attempt to unite the movement east of the Mississippi with the Co-operative General Association resulted from a vocal minority in the latter that wanted the washing of the saints' feet to be an open question. However, the majority of that body practiced the rite as an ordinance, as continued to be evidenced by repeated statements in its publications in the 1920s. Thus, after the departure of John H. Wolfe and M. L. Morse, the main voices raised in opposition to feet washing, relations began to warm again between the two groups. By that time, however, the General Conference had already been formed in 1921, since the eastern Free Will Baptists felt certain that union with the Co-operative General Association would not occur. This conference, much stronger in numbers and organization than the Co-operative General Association, would set the organizational stage for the National Association of Free Will Baptists, which would be founded in 1935.[19]

On Thursday, May 26, 1921, representatives from Free Will Baptist conferences and associations in Alabama, Georgia, North Carolina, and Tennessee assembled at Cofer's Chapel Church in Nashville "for the purpose of entering into a national organization." A telegram had come from a delegation from Ohio that were still on their way, so those already gathered agreed to wait until their arrival to call the meeting to order. Neal H. Parrish of Georgia offered the opening sermon. That afternoon, the group entered into a discussion about their desires for a multi-state organization, and on Friday morning the attendees agreed to form a "temporary organization," electing John L. Welch of Nashville, Tennessee, as president and E. C. Morris of Kinston, North Carolina, as recording secretary. Welch's name would loom large in the effort to bring all Free Will Baptists into a national body fourteen years later, and he can be credited with having been the chief architect of the new movement.[20]

Welch appointed Elders J. W. Alford and J. C. Moye of North Carolina, Neal H. Parrish of Georgia, and J. E. Hodgins of Alabama as a committee to draft a constitution and bylaws. The Committee on Constitution worked all Friday afternoon. On Saturday morning their report was adopted, and the body approved a motion to make the temporary organization into a permanent one. The organization was to be known as the General Conference of the Original Free Will Baptists of the United States and was to be "composed of the various Associations, Conferences and Conventions of the above-named states, together with other like bodies of the same faith and practice, which may hereafter be admitted." The delegates added to Welch and Morris Elder D. W. Alexander of North Carolina as vice president, Hodgins as treasurer, and Parrish as field secretary. They also elected an Executive Committee comprising Parrish, Hodgins, and Elders D. T. Armstrong of Tennessee and M. B. Hutchinson of Ohio.[21]

The second annual session convened in 1922 with Marshall Free Will Baptist Church in the small town of Marshall in western North Carolina near the Tennessee state line. Representatives from the French Broad Association in that region of North Carolina were present, as was the South Carolina delegation led by T. B. Mellette, of whom the Committee on Credentials felt "satisfied from our conference with Bro. Mellette that he is representing a loyal people and thoroughly orthodox in every respect." The next item of business was a report by E. T. Phillips, editor of *The Free Will Baptist*. Evident as early as the General Conference's second annual session in 1922 was its commitment to the confessional norms of the Free Will Baptist Church, including a repudiation of the then-growing Holiness and Pentecostal movements. The body approved the following resolution:

> Resolved, That Conference go on record and pledge itself to stand by and support in case of division that part of any church conference or association that contends for the original faith and practice of the Free Will Baptist church, even though it be in the minority, when such division is caused by the advent of new doctrines, which might disturb and destroy the harmony and life of the church.
>
> We further declare it to be our judgment that we will not recognize the doctrines of a second definite work of grace, nor the doctrines allied with it under the guise of sanctification or holiness. But it is our purpose to recognize and we do hereby recognize the doctrine of the Original Free Will Baptist church with all its ordinances unmodified.[22]

The Ladies Aid Society

At that second annual session, Mrs. Alice E. Lupton of New Bern, North Carolina, addressed the body on "The Value of Church Auxiliaries." She primarily discussed the key role that Sunday schools, youth ministry, and "Ladies Aid and Woman's Home Mission" societies could play in the church's ministry. Lupton's address would lay the groundwork for a strong women's movement in the General Conference, which would be adopted by the National Association in 1935. Local ladies aid societies had been in operation for several decades among the Free Will Baptists in the Southeast, especially in the states of Georgia, Tennessee, and North Carolina, where there are records from the last few years of the nineteenth and first few years of the twentieth centuries. In the 1890s a women's organization formed at the Free Will Baptist Church in Glennville, Georgia. In 1907, at the urging of Dell Upton, pastor of Cofer's Chapel Church in Nashville, a ladies aid society was established there. Two of the founding members of that society, Fannie Mae Polston and Mary Ann Weaver (later Mrs. John L. Welch) would go on to become leaders in the General Conference's Ladies Aid Society. Also in 1907, a ladies aid society with a strong interest in missions was started by Miss Lucy Linton at St. Mary's Church in New Bern, North Carolina.[23]

The General Conference thus led the way in the organization of such societies. Shortly after the beginning of the General Conference, that body began to sense the need to begin a formal women's ministry to further the work of women's groups throughout the denomination, such as the Woman's Home Mission Convention of North Carolina. At the third annual session of the General Conference in Damascus, Georgia, in 1923, Lupton spoke again on "the importance of the Ladies' and Young People's work in the church." At that same annual session, she proposed the following resolution:

> Realizing that the women of our denomination can render valuable service through what is known as Ladies' Aid Societies and Home Mission Societies, we are recommending that the ministers of this Conference make an effort to get the ladies of their various churches to organize one or more of these societies and that they blend their efforts to promote our denominational institutions along with other lines of service.

The body elected an "Auxiliary" committee. Presumably this committee was to consider women's, laymen's, and youth ministries, because the committee consisted of "Sister Alice E. Lupton, laymen D. H. Melvin and Jas. Cheshire" and presented a report on "Young People's Work."[24]

Because one of the primary ministries of local ladies aid societies was the support of missions, the missions committee of the General Conference in 1925 recommended that a "Board of Five on Woman's activities" be elected to pursue endeavors such as "Ladies Aid, Home and Foreign Missions Societies in churches, [and] Woman's Home Missions Conventions, in local Conferences." The body responded by electing a Ladies Aid Committee consisting of Fannie Mae Polston of Tennessee, Alice E. Lupton, Mrs. G. A. Connor of North Carolina, A. R. Carter of Georgia, and G. L. Shutes of Florida. In 1926, the Committee on Missions recommended the constitution and bylaws of the Woman's Home Mission Convention of North Carolina, suggesting that more of the constituent bodies of the General Conference start similar women's organizations, which would further the cause of world missions. That same year Fannie Polston was made general secretary of the General Conference's new ladies aid society. Thus the groundwork was laid for a thriving Ladies Aid Society for the General Conference that would continue to grow through the founding and first few years of the National Association.[25]

Under Polston's leadership, the Ladies Aid Society grew exponentially. John L. Welch, Polston's pastor and organizer par excellence, offered aid in planning and vision. The two centers of ladies aid work were Tennessee, which by 1928 had twenty-two societies, and North Carolina, which by that same year had thirty-five. Progress, however, was made in the late 1920s in states such as Mississippi, Alabama, Florida, Georgia, South Carolina, and Ohio. Pastors saw these societies as promising, not only as an avenue for interest and growth in their congregations, but also for fanning the flame of world missions among their congregants and in the wider denomination. The women in these societies were at the forefront of promotion of League work and Eureka College. These societies also strongly emphasized benevolence and the alleviation of poverty. In the Ladies Aid Society as a whole, that took its primary form in the support of Free Will Baptist orphanages.[26]

Welch and his wife Mary took a great interest in the progress of the ladies aid movement, helping start several "district auxiliary conventions" in the mid-South. Polston began reaching out more to foster a women's movement west of the Mississippi in states such as Missouri, Oklahoma, and Texas. The work continued to prosper, and by the time of the founding of the National Association in 1935, more than 135 societies were reporting in the states of North and South Carolina, Tennessee, Alabama, Georgia, and Texas alone.[27]

Educational Emphasis and Organizational Development

At the General Conference's third annual session in Damascus, Georgia, in 1923, a new delegation from Florida was added, represented by G. L. Shutes and D. H. Melvin. Conference President Welch appointed committees on Missions, Education, Auxiliary, Sunday School, and Publication. The General Conference continued its support of the work of the institutions in Ayden, North Carolina: the Seminary, the Free Will Baptist Press, and *The Free Will Baptist* paper.[28]

Increasingly, conference leadership stressed the importance of education. In 1923, the Education Committee, consisting of J. W. Alford, Neal H. Parrish, and the layman E. D. Parker of Tennessee, recommended that the conference "ask every conference and association of this General Conference to raise the educational standard for ministers, and we further request that no applicant for ordination be ordained who does not have at least a high school education." The report also said, "We urge all our young men aspiring to the ministry to go to college if possible." This was significant at a time when high school graduation rates in the US were less than 20 percent. The Publication Committee "urgently" recommended that all churches use the Free Will Baptist Press's Sunday school literature and recommended immediate planning for the writing and publication of "a Church History and Systematic Theology."[29]

An emphasis on education would continue throughout the 1920s, with strong support of the Seminary in Ayden, continued recommendations that a high school education be a prerequisite for ordination, and general encouragement of higher education. At the annual session in 1926, the Education Committee went as far as to "commend the Cumberland Association of Tennessee for the educational example that she has set for our people in the education of Rev. Wm. H. Oliver, who is completing his degrees from the Vanderbilt University." Oliver himself would continue this emphasis, later being named to the faculty of Eureka College, the new name for Ayden Seminary, being elected as superintendent of the public school system in Nashville, and later serving as a professor at Free Will Baptist Bible College there.[30]

Together with an emphasis on education, the complexity and effectiveness of the General Conference continued to increase throughout the 1920s. Boards were increasingly more efficiently administered, though volunteers led them. One sees this trend in the detail of the reports made by the "General Secretaries" of the various boards.[31]

It was the responsibility of Neal Parrish, field secretary for the General Conference, to reach out to unaffiliated groups who affirmed Free Will Baptist faith and practice to attempt to bring them into the conference fold. He reported to the 1924 annual session that he had communicated "with leaders among our people in a number of Southern States with the hope that they will be finally drawn into this great organization, having received assurances from some that they will finally bring their people to join us. I feel, brethren, that we have every reason to feel encouraged and to go on with this work, however, exercising due patience and working tenaciously." By 1924, the conference was also sponsoring a Committee on Evangelism and sponsoring three part-time "National Evangelists"—Parrish of Georgia, R. N. Hinnant of Eastern North Carolina, and R. V. Self of Western North Carolina. These ministers would hold evangelistic preaching services throughout the denomination, encourage evangelism, and promote the work of the General Conference and its endorsed institutions.[32]

Also at the 1924 annual session, the delegates approved a resolution urging Free Will Baptist ministers to write their US representatives opposing repeal of the Eighteenth Amendment. In 1919 that amendment had prohibited the manufacture and sale of alcoholic beverages in the US. It had been supported nearly universally by Protestants across denominational lines, by liberals and conservatives alike. The stance of the General Conference shows that Free Will Baptists of the South had by this time caught up with their northern brothers and sisters in their concerns regarding temperance. These concerns were reiterated in subsequent years. The 1924 annual session closed as the assembly rose and sang the hymn "Blest Be the Tie That Binds."³³

Confessional Solidarity and Concerns About Ecumenism

A recurrent theme in the early years of the General Conference was the confessional solidarity of the Free Will Baptist Church and the need to avoid formal alliances with other bodies. This generation of leaders had suffered firsthand from what they sensed as the depleting effects of ecumenical efforts among their movement. This feeling had been exacerbated by the failure of the union with the Co-operative General Association because of some of its outspoken leaders' opposition to the washing of the saints' feet, to which the General Conference determinedly clung.

This leeriness is palpable, coming to the surface again and again, for example, during the 1923 annual session. Elder Silas Moore of the Ohio Yearly Meeting, in words reminiscent of Ohioan Thomas Peden, commented that in these "days of apostasy in many Protestant churches, we believe that there should be no entangling alliances with other churches, but that we, as a denomination, should stand by the faith of our fathers who have left us so rich a heritage in faith and works." J. W. Alford, offering a formal "Resolution of Warning," referred to Moore's comments later in the meeting, lamenting the Free Baptist-Northern Baptist merger that had occurred only a little over a decade earlier. Alford mentioned that "in the past our denomination in many places has suffered much at hands of false and treacherous brethren, and that even yet, there are movements on foot for their further betrayal of our church, which would lead to the loss of our identity and independence, with the loss of our institutions in which are invested many thousands of dollars." He lamented that "history is in the habit of repeating itself."³⁴

T. B. Mellette, in another resolution that referred to a move by some in North Carolina to enter into fraternal fellowship with the "Southern Christian church," called on the General Conference to "urge" the North Carolina State Convention to "defeat all movements having tendency to destroy our independence, faith and practice." In another resolution, Mellette called on the General Conference to "remain steadfast . . . in the faith of the Free Will Baptist church with every institution of the Lord that may be found in the New Testament." That last phrase was a common phrase from the *1812 Abstract*'s article on the ordinances of the church. All these resolutions were approved.³⁵

The fundamentalist-modernist controversy was in full swing during the years of the General Conference, and southern Free Will Baptists in the

1920s tended strongly toward one side. The theological liberalism described in chapter 7, known as modernism, had characterized many of the leaders of the Free Baptist General Conference in the North. It was being countered in the northern mainline Protestant denominations by conservatives who had come to be known as "fundamentalists." That label had been used at first to describe a type of orthodoxy outlined in *The Fundamentals*, a series of books defending Protestant orthodoxy that were published between 1910 and 1915. However, the term later became associated with a brand of ecclesiastical and cultural separatism that did not characterize most of the writers of *The Fundamentals*. Those volumes contained essays from the classic evangelical orthodoxy regnant in the nineteenth century, represented by theologians such as the Presbyterian B. B. Warfield and the Southern Baptist E. Y. Mullins, whose writings appeared in the collection.[36]

The famous Scopes Trial of 1925, which concerned the town of Dayton, Tennessee's opposition to the teaching of evolution in public schools, was a flash point in the fundamentalist-modernist controversy. That event was no doubt fresh on M. H. Mellette's mind when the South Carolina pastor introduced a sharply worded anti-evolution resolution at the annual session in May 1926. Lumping Darwin's teachings with "dangerous doctrines and ideas that have crept into our ranks through the teachings of sciences of men, and especially as taught relative to the creation of all things material," the resolution advised "our teachers and publishers" to "refuse any teaching" not in keeping with Scripture.[37]

Foreign Missions

Foreign missions also became a major thrust of the General Conference, whose mission program would eventually become that of the National Association. In 1925 J. L. Welch, who was still the conference's moderator, appointed a Committee on Missions. In the early years, the raising of awareness and funds for foreign and home missions was primarily delegated to the Ladies Aid Society. In 1925 the Committee on Missions that Welch appointed recommended a five-member mission board with a part-time field secretary who would work with Ladies Aid and Woman's Home Mission societies to promote missions. At the 1926 annual session, the Committee on Missions recommended that all the churches financially support the existing Foreign Mission Board of the North Carolina State Convention. It also recommended that associations establish women's organizations modeled after North Carolina's Woman's Home Mission Convention.[38]

Increasing appeals were made for foreign missions. The Free Will Baptists of the South believed in foreign missions, as is indicated in their hymns. One of them described "The Missionary's Farewell":

> Yes, my native land, I love thee;
> All thy scenes I love them well:
> Friends, connections, happy country,
> Can I bid you all farewell?
> Can I leave you,
> Far in heathen lands to dwell?
>
> In the deserts let me labor;
> On the mountains let me tell
> How he died—the blessed Saviour—
> To Redeem a world from hell.
> Let me hasten,
> Far in heathen lands to dwell.[39]

However, organized overseas missions had been slow to catch on, probably because of the poverty and lack of development in the movement and the resultant lack of cohesion and infrastructure needed to fund and administer overseas ministries. The 1929 annual session was held in Glennville, Georgia, the hometown of Laura Belle Barnard, who would a few years later be the first foreign missionary supported by the General Conference. Remarks by the Committee on Foreign Missions at that Annual Session, chaired by Georgia pastor J. R. Hunt, illustrate the growing zeal for world mission during these years:

> We your committee on Foreign Missions, respectfully submit that we recommend a fuller mission activity of our Denomination. We believe that our home mission activities are miniature in action and deplore our utter lack of Foreign activity. We recommend that this Conference provide for the proper education of some acceptable men and women who give evidence of a divine call to foreign fields and that we provide for continual support of these missionaries. We further recommend that this body establish a Foreign Mission Board for the proper conduct of a Foreign program.[40]

Difficulty for Eureka College

The 1928 annual session was held on the campus of Eureka College, the school in Ayden, North Carolina, which had been renamed in 1925. The Education Committee, chaired by William Henry Oliver, continued to sound the trumpet about the need for greater support for Eureka. After the "Eureka Quartet Band" sang before the congregation, Oliver gave his committee's report. It implored every Free Will Baptist to send a gift to the college in the next year and to support Eureka's capital campaign, thanking those who had given in the past. The report also urged "every conscientious Free Will Baptist" to "solicit students for the college, especially prospective ministerial students."[41]

Things were not going well financially for Eureka, and one senses urgency in the financial appeals Oliver made. The North Carolina State Convention had divided Eureka's $35,000 debt into quotas each church would be responsible for raising. In January 1929 President L. R. Ennis, writing in *The Free Will Baptist*, urged congregations and individuals to send in their quotas, and several did. However, it was not enough, and the administration was forced to cut programs. The situation was exacerbated by the recession that set in that summer, which mushroomed into the Great Depression when the stock market crashed a few months later. Eureka was not able to open in the fall of 1929. Two weeks before the stock market crash, at a ministers' meeting in Goldsboro, North Carolina, a strategy was devised that the State Convention's Executive Committee would direct the remainder of the capital campaign, enlisting the aid of the four conferences that comprised the convention. Ladies Aid societies would be responsible for raising a third of the funds. Free Will Baptists in other states would continue to be solicited through the channels of the General Conference, which was still attempting to raise funds in the summer of 1930. However, swift recovery did not occur, and all hopes of reviving the college were lost when its Administration Building was destroyed by fire in the fall of 1931.[42]

The Move toward Union

In 1926, the General Conference had voted to send Welch back to the Cooperative General Association, indicating a desire to resume talks and an openness to do so on the General Conference's clear terms. It was at that time that momentum again began to build for a union of the two groups. The next year, Welch became Field Secretary for the General Conference, which allowed him to concentrate his efforts on the formation of a national association. Every year he would report more conferences and associations being added to the ranks of the General Conference.[43]

In 1930, in his report to the conference when it convened in Vernon, Alabama, Welch welcomed a new corresponding delegate from the Texas State Convention, saying he hoped to "have other states also to join in with us in a united effort for our cause." The body voted to send Welch and Mississippi pastor M. L. Hollis to visit the next session of the Texas State Convention. In 1931, Rev. C. B. Thompson visited from that convention, and it was announced that the 1932 annual session of the General Conference would be held with the Bryan Free Will Baptist Church in Bryan, Texas. This was the first time the General Conference would convene west of the Mississippi. The pastor of the Bryan Church was E. C. Morris, who had moved to Texas from North Carolina. Other items on the agenda related to a more comprehensive national organization, The delegates approved a committee consisting of R. F. Pittman and R. E. Tripp to prepare a draft of a "Treatise and Book of Discipline," and Welch was made chair of a new committee to consider the publication of "a complete Church Hymnal."[44]

Also at the General Conference's 1931 annual session, the body went on record endorsing Zion Bible School in Blakely, Georgia, which was being overseen by former conference moderator T. B. Mellette. The conference had recognized Zion in its 1930 annual session but now fully endorsed it. The Minutes indicate, however, that there were still hopes that Eureka College would be revived. For the first time, the Committee on Education recommended that a more formal Board of Education be established in the committee's place, "with one member from each state represented in the General Conference." It would be the responsibility of this board to "make an educational survey" of the denomination to ascertain its educational "needs and possibilities." At the 1932 annual session in Bryan, Texas, Welch would be made secretary of education, in addition to his current role as field secretary.[45]

That 1932 annual session was intended as a way to get the General Conference to meet in the territory of the Co-operative General Association so that representatives of the latter would participate, and that is what occurred: W. E. Dearmore, moderator of the Co-operative General Association, was present and was asked to give remarks. Oklahoma pastor B. F. Rogers presented a devotion. Also, there was a song sung at one of the worship services by "the Oklahoma-Missouri Quartet," and M. L. Morse of Nebraska—ironically one of the early leaders of the Co-operative General Association who had scared off the brethren from the East with his anti-feet washing rhetoric—was present and was called on to pray.[46]

When the Credentials Committee, chaired by Welch, gave its report, it informed the body that it had conferred with the "fraternal delegates" from the Co-operative General Association regarding the union of the two bodies. The committee indicated that representatives of both organizations wanted to pursue merger. It recommended that the Moderator appoint a five-member committee to confer with the Executive Committee of the Co-operative General Association and formulate "a satisfactory basis on which the two bodies may be merged," to be presented at the 1933 General Conference.[47]

The 1933 annual session of the General Conference held with East Nashville Church in Nashville, Tennessee, was a momentous occasion for that conference and the Co-operative General Association. There, delegates formulated the basis of the union of the two bodies into a new national movement. At the Friday morning session, the joint committee from the two conferences made its report. It called for the merger of the two groups according to the Articles of Faith of the 1901 *Treatise* of the Randall movement and its church covenant, forms, and usages. Yet it included the phrase "with such amendments as may be made and approved by the body when perfected into one organization." The body adopted the report, voting to allow the Executive Committees of both bodies to work out the details of the merger according to the agreed-on terms. The congregation then joined together in the singing of "Blest Be the Tie That Binds," "and a handshake was engaged in as a token of the reality of this tie."[48]

The issue that had formerly prohibited union, that of the washing of the saints' feet, was not mentioned here. It is not certain how the agreement was reached to insert the rite into the *Treatise* before it was voted on two years later at the founding meeting of the National Association of Free Will Baptists, but it happened. Still, at the 1934 annual session convened with Open Pond Church in Jakin, Georgia, the joint merger committee stated that "the merger could not be perfected at this time." The Executive Board, for unstated reasons, had asked for another year but still remained hopeful "to be able to settle the matter definitely." The negotiations would have to wait until the next Co-operative General Association meeting in November in Denison, Texas. At that session, the joint committee agreed that the name of the new organization would be the National Association of Free Will Baptists. The General Conference and Co-operative General Association would continue to operate as they had been. John L. Welch would act as moderator temporarily, with Winford Davis of Missouri as assistant moderator, at the first meeting of the new association scheduled for November 1935.[49]

The Founding of the National Association

When the First Session of the National Association of the Original Free Will Baptists of the United States convened November 5–7, 1935, at Cofer's Chapel Free Will Baptist Church in Nashville, it was a union of two bodies into one. The much larger General Conference, consisting mostly of churches east of the Mississippi, and the Co-operative General Association, consisting mostly of churches west of the Mississippi, became the Eastern General Association and Western General Association. At first, it was envisioned that these two bodies would continue to meet. However, by the time of the second session of the National Association in 1938, the two associations were considered superfluous, and each disbanded. Delegates at the founding session in 1935 approved a constitution and bylaws that outlined the structure of the new association. At this early stage, the National Association followed a model of organization very much like local conferences or associations; it would go on to develop greater complexity in the years to follow.[50]

The association elected the following officers: John L. Welch of Nashville, Tennessee, moderator; Winford Davis of Monette, Missouri, assistant moderator; I. J. Blackwelder of Nashville, Tennessee, secretary-treasurer; and B. F. Rogers of Oklahoma, assistant secretary-treasurer. Other officers at this early juncture included part-time, volunteer "General Secretaries" who would chair committees and oversee particular areas of ministry: I. J. Blackwelder, Secretary-Treasurer of Foreign Missions; Winford Davis, Secretary of Sunday School Work; Henry Melvin of Durham, North Carolina, Secretary of Free Will Baptist League Work; and Fannie Polston of Nashville, Tennessee, Secretary of Women's Work. To these were added a five-member executive board consisting of J. W. Alford of Kenly, North Carolina; B. F. Brown of Purdy, Missouri; Daniel F. Pelt of Abbeville, Alabama; E. B. Joyner of Lake Butler, Florida; and the lay leader C. F. Goen of Bryan, Texas.[51]

Local conferences sent delegates to the meeting, and if there was a state conference or association, it also sent delegates. Representation at this initial meeting took a variety of forms. For example, the North Carolina State Convention sent delegates, and three local conferences from North Carolina—the Western Conference, the Eastern Conference, and the Cape Fear Conference—also did. The same pattern was seen in the delegates from Alabama, Oklahoma, and Texas. At this early stage, most Free Will Baptists had not organized themselves into conferences based on the state their churches were in. Thus, for example, only one association in Tennessee, which had no state association, sent delegates: the Cumberland Association in Middle

Tennessee. Likewise, the delegates from Georgia and Mississippi were all from local associations. Missouri was the only state whose delegates were all from a state association with no local associational representation. The Tri-State Association, which consisted of Ohio, West Virginia, and Kentucky conferences, was a regional body that sent delegates, one of them being M. F. Vanhoose of Kentucky, who was elected to the *Treatise* Revision Committee at that session, the other being from West Virginia. The old Nebraska-Kansas Yearly Meeting, the shell of which had survived the 1911 merger, also sent delegates. The "State Conference" in Arkansas did not send delegates but sent visitors to observe the meeting.[52]

Four procedural committees were appointed: the Committee on Constitution and By-Laws, the *Treatise* Revision Committee, the Program Committee (which consisted of the moderator and general secretaries), and the Publicity Committee. Five other committees were also formed. A Joint Educational Committee came together, comprising members from both the General Conference and the Co-operative General Association. The Women's Auxiliary Work of the General Conference was "accepted by the Association," as was the Foreign Mission Work, with I. J. Blackwelder being made National Secretary of Foreign Missions. The Sunday School Work of the General Conference was also accepted, and Winford Davis of the Co-operative General Association was made its general secretary. The Free Will Baptist League, the General Conference's youth movement, continued as it had in the General Conference under the leadership of Henry Melvin and was adopted by the association.[53]

The *Treatise* Revision Committee made its report on that document, with which both sides were familiar and revisions to which had obviously been discussed. The revised *Treatise* was approved without the body hearing a public reading of it. Still, later in the session, there was a public reading of the document. The Constitution and By-Laws Committee made its report, and the document was read and adopted. That document called for a simple structure that would serve the new denomination in its infancy. Yet most of the document's policies and procedures continued into later years. According to the document, the General Conference, now the Eastern Association, and the Co-operative General Association, now the Western Association, would both be composed of state associations, which would comprise local or "annual" associations. Some of these local associations had smaller quarterly meetings that represented to them. The officers of the National Association—moderator, assistant moderator, recording clerk, assistant recording clerk, and treasurer—and an executive board would be elected at each session. The moderator would have the right to appoint ad hoc committees as needed. The Executive Board had the right and responsibility of acting "in behalf of and for the National Association" between sessions. The association was originally planned as a triennial association to meet every three years, but at its second session, it would shift to meeting annually.[54]

Conclusion

The year 1935 was a momentous year for Free Will Baptists east and west, as the General Conference primarily in the east and the Co-operative General Association primarily in the west united to form the National Association of Free Will Baptists. That historic gathering in Nashville would mark the beginning of the modern denominational organization of the Free Will Baptist movement that continues as the primary Free Will Baptist association to which the vast majority of Free Will Baptists are united to the present day.

Twelve
THE EARLY DEVELOPMENT OF THE NATIONAL ASSOCIATION

THE SECOND SESSION of the National Association convened with East Nashville Free Will Baptist Church in Nashville, Tennessee, in November 1938. This was a crucial meeting at which the organization of the new association took shape, and several decisions made at this session would set the pace for the development of the National Association. In addition to delegates from bodies that were represented at the first session, delegates registered from Florida, Ohio, Illinois, and Virginia. The major item of business was the consideration of the reorganization plan that had been submitted to the Eastern Association by the lay leader W. E. Coville of Nashville, Tennessee. Coville's proposal provided three key ideas that would structure the National Association. The association would (1) meet not triennially but annually, (2) would alternate between regions, meeting east of the Mississippi one year and west of the Mississippi the next, and (3) would be represented by state, not regional, associations. Coville's proposal was adopted unanimously by the delegates, after which the body sang "Blest Be the Tie That Binds."[1]

At the 1938 session, National Secretary of Education John L. Welch delivered remarks about the need for a centrally located higher education institution. His comments were followed by a speech from T. B. Mellette on behalf of Zion Bible School in Georgia, the only existing Free Will Baptist school for ministerial education. The body received reports from its other general secretaries on Foreign Missions, Home Missions, Women's Work, Sunday School, and Free Will Baptist League and accepted the Virginia State Convention for membership. The Statistical Report presented by Elder J. C.

Griffin listed a total of 1,142 churches representing to the association with a membership of 82,752.[2]

Developing Organizational Structure

Much of the basic organizational structure of the National Association of Free Will Baptists was set by the end of its fifth session in 1941. W. E. Coville, chair of the *Treatise* Revision Committee, reported at that 1938 session on several issues related to the changes in "usages" (organization). These included the changes that Coville had proposed at the General Conference as well as matters such as the listing of new standing boards, the deletion of "recording" in front of "clerk," and other routine matters. The report was signed "Layman W. E. Coville, Chairman," followed by all the other members of the committee, who were pastors, with the abbreviation "Eld." in front of their names (in other places in the Minutes, "Elder" was spelled out). This indicated that, though the use of "Reverend" as a title for ministers was becoming more common, the title "Elder" at this time, and at the National level, was still in use. It would continue in some areas as late as the 1970s. At the 1938 session, it was also determined that each board should consist of five elected members, including the General, Mission, and Superannuation (retirement) Boards. The general secretaries of these boards were elected and added to the list of standing boards that had been approved at the first session. The Superannuation Board got a slow start. Mrs. J. E. Simpson, its general secretary, reported a total in its treasury of only $190.24 when she made her first report in 1939.[3]

The organization of the National Association took a leap forward at the 1940 annual session held with Paintsville Church in Paintsville, Kentucky. The body approved an amendment to the constitution that called for a General Board. This new board was to consist of the general officers, the chairs of the standing boards, and "one member from each affiliated State Association and one member from each affiliated association comprising one or more states." Though recommendations of constituent bodies were taken with great seriousness, their representatives to the General Board were required to be elected by the National Association in annual session. In the early years after the formation of the General Board, it elected the Executive Committee from its own membership. Various associations continued to unite with the National Association, with South Carolina delegates registering for the first time in 1940, the Wolverine Association in Michigan joining in 1942, and Arkansas and West Virginia uniting with the association in 1946.[4]

At the annual session in 1941, the delegates approved a recommendation from the General Board to employ a full-time executive secretary with a salary of $50 per week. This annual salary of $2,600 was generous at a time when a new car cost less than $1,000 and gasoline was nineteen cents per gallon. The General Board informed the body at the Annual Session of its decision to hire North Carolina minister L. R. Ennis, former president of Eureka College, as the association's first executive secretary. However, the body approved a change to the constitution that required the executive secretary, as general promotional secretary of the association, to be elected by the body at its annual session. This development would move the promotion of the program of the National Association forward immensely over the course of the 1940s and in the coming decades.[5]

The bylaws of the General Board specified that the executive secretary would serve as the executive officer of the Executive Committee and General Board (but not as a member of the General Board). The primary duties of the office would include "charge of the home office" and provision for the accounting of all financial transactions of the association. The executive secretary's particular task was to "promote the interests, plans, and undertakings of the General Board and the National Association by personal contacts, public addresses, direction of organizations and special workers, newspaper and personal correspondence," especially the National Association's missions, educational, and benevolent work. Ennis would leave the office in 1944 to become president of Free Will Baptist Bible College. In the formative years of the National Association, its executive secretaries included the influential ministers Robert Crawford of Alabama (1944–1948) and Damon C. Dodd of Missouri (1949–1953). This office would exercise an incalculable influence on the development and growth of the National Association during this period.[6]

The Beginning of a Foreign Missions Effort

Both the General Conference and the Co-operative General Association had supported foreign mission works, and the General Conference was supporting Laura Belle Barnard of Glennville, Georgia, when the National Association was formed in 1935. Thus it was not as difficult for the new National Association to launch into foreign mission work as it would be to start a new educational institution. Among the first orders of business at the first session of the new National Association in 1935 was to appoint a National Secretary of Foreign Missions. The delegates elected Nashville pastor I. J. Blackwelder for the role, in addition to his election as secretary-treasurer of the association at the same meeting. Blackwelder had already been acting in the capacity of General Secretary of Foreign Missions for the General Conference. The night before, the assembly had heard a "lecture" on missions in South America by Thomas Willey. At the second session in 1938, Blackwelder gave the first report of the Foreign Mission Board, made up of "the Eastern and Western foreign mission boards, together with the National Secretary-Treasurer." He announced that the board had assumed the support of Miss Laura Belle Barnard in India, Thomas and Mabel Willey "among the native Indians in the interior of Panama," and Miss Bessie Yeley of Sciotoville, Ohio, in Venezuela, who had been supported by Ohio Freewill Baptists.[7]

Barnard had spoken at the General Conference in June 1935 about her calling to share the gospel with the people of India. She spoke about her most treasured text of Scripture, Psalm 16:11, "Preserve me, O God: For in thee do I put my trust. O my soul, thou hast said unto the Lord, Thou art my Lord: My goodness extendeth not to thee; But to the saints that are in the earth, And to the excellent, in whom is all my delight." Barnard set sail for India, arriving there in August 1935. After completing her training, she began her mission to the "untouchables" of the lower social orders of the caste system in the Kotagiri township in Tamil Nadu. Barnard would return to the United States from 1942 to 1945. During these years she helped start Free Will Baptist Bible College, teaching missions and English there. She also taught in various "institutes" held in local areas. In them she used a manuscript she had written about the history and theology of missions, *His Name Among All Nations*, which would be published by the Foreign Mission Board in 1946. After a brief stint in her home state of Georgia, she returned to India. Barnard served in India until 1957, when she returned to the college, completing her career teaching missions and Bible and writing her autobiography, *Touching the Untouchables*. India would become one of the great enduring mission fields of the National Association.[8]

The foreign missions effort of the National Association was essentially an adoption of the mission works of the General Conference. The Foreign Mission Board report to the General Conference in 1935 had mentioned Barnard and Yeley, though it was noted that Yeley had "sailed independent of the General Conference." The next year, the General Conference Foreign Mission Board reported that it had "helped in getting Miss Laura Belle Barnard to India where she has been working and studying the language of that section of India since August 15, 1935." It also reported that Thomas H. Willey was eager "to return to South America for the purpose of beginning independent mission work for the Free Will Baptist Church." The report urged that "this great door is open to us and we must accept the opportunity or reject it," indicating that Willey was ready to embark on his mission "as quickly as our people are willing to send him."[9]

The report also stressed how engaged "quite a few of our young people" were in their burden for "lost souls in the heathen lands." They were ready to go but needed financial support to get the necessary training to commence their overseas missions. These young people also had the support of the Free Will Baptist Leagues, youth organizations all over the country that wished to support missions with prayers and with funds. In addition to their endorsement by the General Conference, Thomas and Mabel Willey had received some support from the Co-operative General Association. Missouri pastor Winford Davis, chair of the Co-operative General Association's Foreign Mission Board, had mentioned Willey in his 1937 report to the Western General Association, and "Sister [Mabel] Willey brought a message on 'Attempting Great Things for God'" at the meeting, alluding to William Carey's famous dictum, "Attempt great things for God. Expect great things from God."[10]

After the 1938 session of the National Association, the Eastern and Western General Association mission boards disbanded, and delegates elected a new mission board with representation from both bodies. It consisted of three pastors, Blackwelder and Davis, as well as B. F. Rogers of Oklahoma, and two laypeople, C. F. Goen of Texas and Mrs. J. R. Bennett of North Carolina. In 1939, that board recommended the continued support of Barnard, Yeley, and the Willeys and recommended shifting the Willeys from Panama to Nicaragua, owing to the "intolerant government" of the former. The mission in Nicaragua did not materialize. In 1941, the board even considered sending the Willeys to India, but it also authorized dispatching a delegation to Cuba in consideration of sending them there. After their initial trip to Cuba in 1941, Thomas and Mabel Willey sensed a divine calling to establish a mission there, and with the Foreign Mission Board's blessing, they did so. At its July 1942 meeting, the board voted to begin raising support to build a mission station in Cuba, including a schoolhouse, and to send another missionary. It also agreed to purchase five horses for the work of Cuban itinerant evangelists. In 1943, the Willeys opened their first mission station in Pinar del Rio in western Cuba. There they built a schoolhouse to hold the Cedars of Lebanon Bible Institute, which would provide education for Cuban pastors and evangelists. Starting with seventy-six believers, within a year a Cuban association of five congregations was established.[11]

That same year they were joined by Bessie Yeley, who moved there from Venezuela to assist in the work. Yeley, a native of Portsmouth, Ohio, served in Cuba for several years and later ministered to immigrants along the Mexican border in Nogales, Arizona, and in Miami. In 1944, the board sent Miss Olive van Syok, who had to return home to Iowa in 1946 to care for her ailing mother. In 1946, the board sent Damon and Sylvia Dodd of Missouri to Cuba. The Dodds were two of the first students at the recently established Free Will Baptist Bible College. They had met with the Foreign Mission Board in 1943, indicating their desire "to go anywhere and any time the Lord and our people might see fit." Three years later, the board reported to the National Association that "Rev. and Mrs. Damon Dodd have gone to the field in Cuba and with them has gone a new jeep which is now proving to be a great blessing on the Cuban field."[12]

The Willeys' warm spirit endeared them to the people of Pinar del Rio, who affectionately called them "Pop" and "Mom" Willey. They ministered there until 1960 when, pressured to leave by the policies of the Castro regime, they began ministering to Cuban refugees in Miami until Thomas's life was brought to an end by cancer in 1968. Mabel continued her ministry among her beloved Cuban people in Miami.[13]

Other early missionaries appointed by the board, now named the "Board of Foreign Missions," included Paul and Nelle Woolsey, whom the board sent to India in 1947. Paul Woolsey was the grandson of the Free Will Baptist pioneer from the East Tennessee mountains, Elder William Bonaparte Woolsey, founder of Woolsey College. Paul Woolsey was a writer, producing booklets such as *The Quack Doctor*, which described the medical dispensary he and Nelle maintained (even though neither had medical training), and *A Modern Jonah*, in which Woolsey told the story of his call to missionary service in India. He also wrote a history concerning East Tennessee Free Will Baptists, *God, A Hundred Years, and a Free Will Baptist Family*. Ill health forced the Woolseys back home to East Tennessee in 1952.[14]

Dan and Trula Cronk took up the slack when the Woolseys left their North India mission in 1952. The Cronks were also two of the first students to enroll at Free Will Baptist Bible College. Dan was from Detroit, Michigan, and Trula had grown up in the Free Will Baptist Orphanage in East Tennessee. They had joined the Woolseys in North India in 1948 and began a mission among the Aboriginal Santal tribe there. They also served in the unevangelized region of Kishanganj in North India, as well as in South India. The board also sent Miss Zalene Lloyd to India in 1948, who served in South India for two years before resigning from the board and moving to North India, where she worked in an orphanage for three years. After twenty-seven years of missionary service in India, Dan and Trula Cronk returned to the

United States, where Dan would teach missions at Free Will Baptist Bible College and serve as a member of the Board of Foreign Missions.[15]

In 1950 there was a move to merge the Foreign and Home Mission Boards, but it was voted down by the General Board and never gained traction. The work of the Foreign Mission Board in its first fifteen years would provide a strong foundation for missionary outreach in the denomination in the late twentieth and early twenty-first centuries. The missions in India and Cuba would become two of the most fruitful areas of international presence for the Free Will Baptist Church.

The Establishment of Free Will Baptist Bible College

At its first session, the National Association elected a Joint Educational Committee and elected John L. Welch as National Secretary of Education. The memory was still fresh of the burning of Eureka College in North Carolina and Tecumseh College in Oklahoma. Zion Bible School in Southwest Georgia had been led by T. B. Mellette since 1930, providing education to small classes of ministerial students from different parts of the South. Yet there was a strong sense that the denomination needed a centrally located institution that could fill its need for Christian higher education from a confessionally Free Will Baptist perspective.[16]

This sense of need coalesced most around Welch, who desired to see a college built for the new National Association. Welch had been serving as field secretary as well as educational secretary for the General Conference. In his 1933 report to that body, he said he had "found a strong and growing sentiment among our people for a centralized educational institution which might serve all of our students who desire to take the proper training to prepare them for Free Will Baptist work." He spoke of the desire in the denomination for a school of high quality and reputation "that will not only meet our needs but reflect credit on our denomination." Welch recommended that the founding of "a centralized educational institution" be made a condition of the widely discussed merger of the General Conference and Co-operative General Association into one body.[17]

Furthermore, Welch recommended Nashville, Tennessee, as the ideal place for such a college because of its central location. However, he warned, such a school could not succeed if all Free Will Baptists did not come together and get behind it: "It is my candid conviction that it will be futile for us to undertake a school work at any place unless our people throughout the whole country become of one mind and one heart in this undertaking. So long as we are divided in sentiment and purpose we cannot have a successful school." His work as field secretary and educational secretary for the General Conference and the chief architect of the union of the General Conference and the Co-operative General Association made him the ideal choice for moderator and educational secretary of the new National Association. From this post, he would continue to lobby for a denominational college located in Middle Tennessee.[18]

Several other individuals joined Welch in his concern for founding an institution of higher learning for the fledgling denomination. These included some of the most important early leaders in the movement. Among them were L. R. Ennis and R. B. Spencer of North Carolina, both of whom had previously served as presidents of Eureka College, and T. B. Mellette of Georgia, who was leading Zion Bible School. Also influential in this effort were J. C. Griffin of North Carolina, J. R. Davidson of Georgia, Henry Melvin of North Carolina, and Melvin Bingham of Oklahoma. Several Tennessee women were also at the forefront of the movement for a denominational college: Fannie Polston, Agnes Frazier, Eva Ray, and Mrs. Ed Parker of the Cumberland Association of Middle Tennessee.[19]

The growing sense of the need for higher education for Free Will Baptists is captured by the words of Frazier in the January 24, 1940, issue of *The Free Will Baptist*:

> We who would meet the needs of this distraught age must look at our conditions and see that we as a church must recognize the interlacing of religious interest with every other interest in our national life.... If the Free Will Baptist message is worth preserving, it is worthy of intelligent interpretation to our young people ... who are to be the leaders of thought and life for their generation in our church.... These young people know that if they are to get a thorough grounding in truth and ethics ... they can only get it in an institution that is avowedly Christian.... These noble young people are begging that we furnish a Christian Institution, supported by Free Will Baptists, where they may become better equipped for God's service.[20]

At its first session, after electing Welch as National Secretary of Education, the delegates elected "five School Trustees," who would assist him in working toward the establishment of a national educational institution. Tasked with "sponsoring the Educational Program" of the denomination and called the "Joint Educational Committee," they consisted of Welch, Selph Jones of

Missouri, Henry Melvin of North Carolina, J. C. Griffin of North Carolina, M. F. Vanhoose of Kentucky, and E. A. O'Donnell of Oklahoma. At the 1938 session, Welch gave an education report, and a new board was elected, with J. R. Davidson as chair. Originally from North Carolina, he had recently moved from Georgia to Texas, where he pastored in Bryan. He was joined on the board by George Dunbar of Tennessee, J. R. Bennett of North Carolina, Melvin Bingham of Oklahoma, and D. S. (Selph) Jones of Missouri.[21]

The following year Miss Jean Welch, the daughter of John L. and Mary Welch, delivered a "heart touching challenge in behalf of the youth of the church" for the denomination to start a college. The Board of Education (the same as it was the year before, except that Selph Jones was replaced by Winford Davis of Missouri) proposed that it be authorized to obtain property for a school to be paid for out of funds it had already collected and be "authorized to establish and maintain a Bible College for the training of Ministers, and other Christian workers—this to include equipping the buildings, selecting a faculty, and necessary field workers."[22]

In 1941 L. R. Ennis was elected executive secretary of the National Association. As Picirilli notes, the "original motivation and funding" for this new office came from the Board of Education. Ennis was tasked with promoting the work of the Board of Education. This directly involved starting a system of Christian Workers' Institutes across the Free Will Baptist Church that would serve as a precursor to the foundation of the new school. These institutes, under the leadership of Ennis, then Robert Crawford and later Damon Dodd, would serve as feeders to the new institution. They continued until 1952, when at the annual session that year it was decided that the institutes "should be turned over to the Bible College."[23]

At the 1941 annual session, the body approved a resolution directing the Board of Education to "purchase, hold, and control suitable real property for a Bible School in the city of Nashville of the State of Tennessee, the title to which property shall be vested in said Board of Education as a Board of Trustees." Those trustees were to have "full authority to negotiate the complete transaction, including the encumbrance of said property as collateral to any unpaid balance which at the discretion of the Board of Education may be deemed wise and necessary." That next September, the Board of Education purchased one building, later known as Davidson Hall, at 3609 Richland Avenue in the historic Richland-West End neighborhood of Nashville. This twelve-room, two-story greystone residence was sold to the board for $15,000. The seller was a Presbyterian layman, W. O. Tirrill, who also donated $1,000 to the cause and wept for joy when he spoke at the building's dedication.[24]

The board, by this time chaired by J. R. Davidson, with the advice and counsel of John L. Welch, selected Free Will Baptist pastor Linton C. Johnson as the college's first president. Welch would later say that there was no question that Johnson should be the president of the new institution. In September of 1942, Johnson moved to Nashville from South Georgia with his wife Ruth, a native of Pennsylvania. This twenty-eight-year-old southern gentleman would come to exert more influence on the Free Will Baptist denomination than anyone else in the twentieth century, retiring in 1979 after thirty-four years as the college's president. Under his leadership, the college would move from a fledgling Bible school to an accredited Christian college with numerous new buildings and programs of study. Johnson envisioned more than a Bible school, placing great value on the Western tradition of the liberal arts and sciences and the canons of classical learning. He and his wife Ruth emphasized extending the kingdom of Christ as the aim of the new institution, as seen in the motto Ruth Johnson chose, from Psalm 43: "O send out thy light and thy truth."[25]

Nine or ten students—there are differences in the records on the number—gathered at that one building on Richland Avenue in September 1942. In accord with the hopes of the founders, they represented the geographical diversity of the young denomination, coming from North Carolina, Tennessee, Georgia, Illinois, Michigan, and Missouri. Several more students joined them in the spring of 1943. This original student body included such later Free Will Baptist leaders as Damon Dodd and his wife Sylvia (Dodd later served as executive secretary of the National Assocaition and general director of Home Missions for the National Association), Paul Ketteman (later director of development at the college), Marie Hyatt, and Daniel Cronk (who with his wife Trula served as a missionary to India and later taught missions at Free Will Baptist Bible College).[26]

The original faculty and staff numbered five. In addition to Johnson, who taught Bible, theology, and history, it included Laura Belle Barnard, who taught English and missions; Henry Melvin, who taught music; Gladys Lewis, the school's dietitian; and J. R. Davidson, who served as business manager. In keeping with the National Association's 1935 plan to "begin our school work on a small scale, confining the work to a Bible course and add other courses to the same as the Lord prospers us," the institution began a two-year program. The academic program initially consisted of history, English composition and rhetoric, grammar, literature, music, biblical studies, and theology, after which languages, philosophy, natural science, and mathematics were added. Ruth Johnson, a musician and amateur visual artist, oversaw a program of social and cultural education, performing classical piano concerts, holding formal dinners and parties, and teaching etiquette.[27]

From the beginning there were differences in philosophy of education among the trustees, with some desiring a Bible institute model and others favoring a program with strong cores in both biblical studies and the liberal arts. As Phillip Morgan has argued, Johnson favored a hybrid between the two typical approaches to evangelical higher education at the time. One approach, favored by most in the Bible college movement at that time, saw training for full-time Christian service as the only legitimate program. This was reminiscent of D. L. Moody's call for the training of "gap-men" who would "stand in the gap" and get as many people converted as possible because the world was coming to an end. Moody originally conceived of "gap-men" as standing between the laity and the ministry, but this concept would set the stage for the Bible institute and Bible college movement. The other approach, favored more among the evangelical liberal arts colleges, was broader, emphasizing a mix of classical education and career preparation and requiring little theological education unless students were studying for the ministry.[28]

Johnson's approach fell between these two. His vision would be mediated through the writings of the two most influential intellectuals he mentored in the late 1940s and early 1950s, F. Leroy Forlines and Robert E. Picirilli. They would flesh out this unique hybrid between standard Bible college and liberal arts approaches. More pietistic elements on the board opposed Johnson on the weight he gave to the liberal arts. Tradition holds that this was one of the reasons he resigned from the presidency in 1944 to assume the pastorate of First Free Will Baptist Church in Tupelo, Mississippi. What precipitated this move is uncertain. However, the board hired L. R. Ennis to replace Johnson, and the curriculum during Ennis's tenure was much more reflective of the Bible institute model than it had been under Johnson's. Ennis resigned in 1947, and the board asked Johnson to come back. Johnson would later say that during that three-year pastorate, "I found myself unable to free myself from the conviction that this work must have been in God's plan for my life." He went on to explain that when he returned, the college solidified its desire to move away from a Bible institute model. "This meant finding balance between biblical and liberal arts studies to give students a proper world view as well as training in biblical studies that would prepare them to proclaim God's Word."[29]

Morgan discusses several approaches to higher education in the denomination, but Johnson subscribed to the one advocated by those like Agnes Frazier, who chaired the Tennessee State Free Will Baptist Board of

Education. In a January 1940 article in *The Free Will Baptist*, she lamented what she implied was a widespread sentiment in Free Will Baptist churches: "There are colleges enough. Let them go to them." Frazier was not making this up. A few years earlier in the same publication, one minister had written, "Let the state have the responsibility of training the general public in its secular arts. Our responsibility is to train servants of the church in the art of holy living and rightly dividing the Word of God for ourselves and others."[30]

In words representative of the pro-education movement in the National Association in the early 1940s, Frazier wrote, "There are state and private owned institutions galore in which the teachings of the Bible and the truths of Christianity are debarred, though some teachers feel no restraint in teaching atheism and cutting the ground from under real ethics and morals, by the type of philosophy and psychology which is being taught." She said she prayed that

> in July we will say, unitedly, "Here, National Association, is this building (or the price of one) centrally located, which we are giving our denomination. It is to be used in the purposeful instruction, the training and direction of our boys and girls, ministers and laymen; so as to develop in body and mind, soul and spirit, all the beauty, perfection and power of which the individual is capable; and to direct this developed individual in the field of noble Christian service."
>
> But what is beauty? what is perfection? what is power? These are soul qualities. They belong to the great Christian postulants. No soul approaches perfection without the Spirit of Christ. No soul is powerful without a grip on God—without courage, manliness, honesty, and integrity. These are all spiritual qualities and are only procured by spiritual development.... Free Will Baptists must establish a school, equip it, endow it, and run it. Without this, Christianity, as accepted and interpreted by the Free Will Baptist Church, will not be free to create the atmosphere necessary to Christian education, nor will it be free to give the kind of instruction which has to be given if Free Will Baptist thought is to function in educational minded peoples.[31]

Frazier's article, which met with much positive response, emphasized the importance of the college's producing an educated ministry. Yet it also mentioned the need to "turn out men and women fitted to do the work of construction and order in our civilizations, whether they serve in the field of religion, medicine; or whether their chosen field be in some other sphere."

John L. Welch and L. C. Johnson were both broadly committed to this goal but believed that the way to accomplish it involved a thoroughgoing foundation in the teaching of the Bible and the Christian tradition.[32]

The two most important people who helped L. C. and Ruth Johnson put their educational philosophy into practice in these early days were Charles and Laura Thigpen. In 1948 Johnson learned of this promising young Southern Methodist couple who were serving in Tuscaloosa, Alabama. Thigpen was pastor of a Southern Methodist Church there. Johnson telegraphed the couple, gauging their interest in serving at the college and subsequently took the train to Tuscaloosa to meet with them to offer them positions. They took Johnson up on his offer and both began teaching at the college in 1948, Charles in Bible and English, Laura in English, speech, and drama. Thigpen also served in administrative roles as dean of men and registrar in those early years and would go on to become dean of the college, and after Johnson's retirement, president. Thigpen helped move the institution from a two-year to a four-year college, adding a third year of study in 1949 and a fourth year in 1950, culminating in the awarding of its first bachelor's degrees to five graduates—T. O. Terry, Adam Scott, Walter Reynolds, Marie Hanna, and Wesley Calvery—in 1951. Thigpen also convinced other colleges and universities to accept the college's credits.[33]

The Beginnings of Home Missions

The Women's Auxiliary of the General Conference had begun supporting home mission works before the formation of the National Association, and the Co-operative General Association had a home missions committee. The newly formed National Association would build on these earlier movements to make "church extension" a major thrust of the new, united movement. At the first session in 1935, the body approved in its constitution and bylaws the appointment of a part-time National Secretary of Home Missions. In 1938, the Eastern General Association elected a Home Mission Board consisting of "Eld. K. V. Shutes, Chairman, Glennville, Ga.; Eld. M. L. Hollis, Tupelo, Miss.; and Eld. J. K. Warkentin, Treas., Fort Worth, Texas." At the same meeting, the evangelist Lizzie McAdams of Texas reported on her tour visiting churches in Alabama, Florida, and Georgia, to raise awareness for home missions. In its report, the board stated its desire to raise funds so that they could get an "Evangelist" on the field to begin church planting as soon as possible.[34]

The 1938 Minutes of the National Association show that the new association implemented the home missions efforts of both the General Conference in the east and the Co-operative General Association in the west. Both these ministries would be amalgamated into the new Home Mission Board. M. L. Hollis, the well-known pastor from Mississippi who had planted numerous churches in northeast Mississippi and northwest Alabama, was made board chair. Lizzie McAdams of Texas, long attached to the Co-operative General Association but with many contacts in the General Conference, was elected to the board and named "Home Mission Worker." Agnes Frazier of Middle Tennessee was also elected to the board, as was East Tennessee pastor George Dunbar. McAdams and Frazier resigned from the board for unknown reasons in 1939, though McAdams continued as Home Mission Worker. She and Frazier were replaced by B. F. Brown of Missouri and J. W. Addington of Virginia. J. K. Warkentin of Texas, who had served on the Home Mission Board of the Eastern General Association, was also elected that year, along with M. E. Tyson of North Carolina.[35]

The Home Mission Board report to the 1941 annual session emphasized the work of M. L. Hollis and Hiram and Lizzie McAdams in raising awareness and financial support for the future of home mission work in the denomination. At that annual session, the General Board directed the Home Mission Board "to intensify its activities with a view to building up its treasury sufficiently to meet the expenses of a General Home Missionary." Fundraising and promotional work for home missions continued, and by 1944 the board had changed hands: J. F. Miller was elected chair, and J. B. Bloss, W. K. Jordan, and C. B. Dees were elected to the board. There was concern in the National Association that home missions was not being given adequate attention. This is reflected in Executive Secretary Robert Crawford's report to the 1944 annual session, in which he said, "We need to be more missionary minded, especially home missionary minded." While Crawford believed that "most of our people" were "wide awake on foreign missions," he urged Free Will Baptists to "pray very earnestly to our Heavenly Father to help us work out a Home Mission system, that will reach the masses at home." In 1946, the board began supporting church planting efforts by R. C. Wiggs in Norfolk, Virginia, and H. Ray Berry in Huntsville, Texas. That same year it presented a new constitution and plan for its future.[36]

In 1947 the Board appointed Oklahoma pastor Harry Staires as part-time Promotional Secretary for Home Missions, and activities started picking up. Soon the board began meeting with prospective home missionary candidates at the annual Bible Conference on the campus of Free Will Baptist Bible College and partnering with existing church planting efforts at the local and state levels. In 1948 the board reported its partnership with sixteen such church plants. That same year the board began a new thrust to start churches in cities, a bold step for a largely small-town and rural denomination. In its report to the 1948 annual session, the board appealed to the denomination, noting that "many of our people, especially young people, have left the rural communities and gone into the cities and find there no Free Will Baptist church, and are not willing to go to any other church." Free Will Baptists, he urged, need to "pray for Free Will Baptist churches to be planted in the cities" and "support Home Missions that this might be done."[37]

By the summer of 1949, the board reported four church plants in cities and growing towns: Raymond Riggs in Breckenridge, Michigan; Homer Parker in Pine Bluff, Arkansas; Weaver Welch in Kansas City, Missouri; and A. B. Chandler in Portsmouth, Virginia. Again that same year, the Resolutions Committee recommended that the Foreign Mission Board and Home Mission Board be merged, but again the attempt failed. In 1950, the Home Mission Board continued to gather steam, when Staires reported a new mission in Hobbs, New Mexico, as well as interest in work among the Choctaw Indians in Oklahoma and the Cherokee Indians in western North Carolina. These fledgling but persistent efforts would lay the groundwork for a burgeoning of church planting through the Home Mission Board in the 1950s.[38]

The Woman's National Auxiliary Convention

The beginnings of the Woman's National Auxiliary Convention were in the General Conference. Its vibrant women's movement was essentially taken over by the National Association in its early years. After the formation of the National Association, the Western General Association hosted Fannie Mae Polston at its 1937 session. The Minutes read that "a very convincing lecture on 'Auxiliaries of the Church' was given by Mrs. Fannie Polston of Nashville, Tenn., National Secretary of Women's Work of the Free Will Baptist Church." The women's Missionary Committee reported: "At this time, it seems impossible to organize a Women's Work of the Western General Association." It recommended that the Western Association's constituent bodies report annually to "our National Secretary of Women's Work," Fannie Polston, and that she be invited back to speak to the association's session the following year.[39]

The General Conference's Ladies Aid Society had set the stage for a strong women's movement when the conference united with the Co-operative General Association in 1935. During this first session, Polston, Agnes Frazier, and Mary Ann Welch presented a report on the work of the Ladies Aid Society of the General Conference. The work continued in the Eastern General

Association, and, as noted above, in 1937 the Western General Association exhibited a desire to become involved with that effort. At the second session of the National Association in 1938, Fannie Polston was elected to head what was variously called the "Women's Auxiliary" and "Women's Missionary Society" of the new association. Along with her, the body elected Mary Ann Welch, Mrs. L. J. Lawliss of Texas, Mrs. Eugene Miller of Missouri, and Mrs. J. C. Griffin of North Carolina to join Polston on the board. Momentum began to build as the women's movement of the east began to spark greater interest in the west. In 1938 the organization was called the Women's National Convention, and by 1939 it had settled on the name it would have for more than five decades: the Women's National Auxiliary Convention (WNAC).[40]

In the early years of the new, united body, WNAC continued its emphasis on home and foreign missions, youth work, orphanages, and other benevolent work. Its emphasis on higher education shifted from Eureka College, which had ceased operation in 1931, to Zion Bible School. Then it moved to the promotion of a new, centrally located national college that was on everyone's mind. The establishment of such an institution became one of the central interests of WNAC in its early years, as seen in a resolution approved at the 1940 convention, which stated: "Since our women feel very keenly the need of a Christian Educational Institution, we recommend that the 2nd. Vice President in every Organization put on a special campaign during the month of June to raise finance for this school and same to be turned over to the National Convention Treasurer."[41]

Prayer and "stewardship study classes" continued to dominate the movement's emphasis on spiritual formation. When Agnes Frazier revised the *Women's Auxiliary Manual* in 1940, she said, "There was a time in the history of our women's work when women had to resort to box-suppers, quilt sales, bazaars, etc. in order to get money to give to missions, Christian education, and orphanages; but a new day has dawned. As a result of our stewardship study courses, women are learning to give as good stewards." The stress on stewardship in the denomination's women's movement in the 1940s would lead to a flowering of denominational interest in stewardship in the 1950s. This emphasis would result in the sending of large numbers of missionaries and the growth and new buildings at Free Will Baptist Bible College. As Mary Ruth Wisehart, who would become executive secretary of WNAC in the late twentieth century, wrote,

> Among Mrs. Mary Welch's papers is a well-worn copy of *The Call to Christian Stewardship* by Julius Earl Crawford, published in 1926. The book is

marked and notated and filled with notes written on sheets of paper and cards. Under the scripture "He which soweth sparingly shall reap also sparingly," Mrs. Welch has written, "No wonder many have lean souls, unblessed lives, no testimony, stale experiences." The women aimed to have every woman a tither and the Lord's work supported by tithes and offerings from God's people.[42]

The convention continued the strong emphasis of the Ladies Aid Society on prayer. WNAC began sponsoring weeks of prayer that had a notable effect not only on women but on men and youth in local congregations. In 1935, Polston said, "Since prayer must precede and undergird all our service, let us begin there. . . . [B]y observing the Week of Prayer we seek to focus the power of prayer upon a world task, believing that prayer can do anything that God can do, and remembering the prayer of Jesus 'that the world may know.'" The convention hosted annual stewardship declamation contests, which, after the National Association started, were held at the annual sessions. These popular contests—prefiguring the annual Church Training Service (CTS) competitions of the later twentieth century—encouraged children to write speeches on the subject of stewardship, memorize them, and present them publicly. In the early years, the WNAC was dominated by Tennessee, North Carolina, and to some extent Georgia. Soon, however, greater delegation registered from states like South Carolina, Oklahoma, Missouri, and Ohio.[43]

In her 1941 report to the WNAC, first vice president Agnes Frazier described the difficulty getting materials printed for the organization. Her remarks are interesting because they evidence the possibility of a slight early tension concerning the Free Will Baptist Press in Ayden, North Carolina, which would in some ways foreshadow the controversy between the North Carolina State Convention and the National Association in the late 1950s. Yet her report also shows the tremendous growth of the WNAC and the need for more resources. She stated that "there is an urgent cry for literature," noting the need for a full-time worker in the Auxiliary Literature Department. That the denomination's women's movement would need a full-time literature worker—at a time when it had no college, both its missions agencies operated with part-time general secretaries, and a full-time executive secretary had just been elected at the 1941 annual session—explains how quickly the women's movement was growing and how influential it was at this early juncture of the National Association.[44]

Frazier explained that the convention had contracted with the *Free Will Baptist Gem*, the state paper in Missouri which was read widely across the denomination. The *Gem* would print wall charts "to be used in the auxiliaries, the requirements considered necessary for efficient and accurate work in crediting and marking their standings on the Standard of Achievement." The *Gem* had also printed the *Manual of Methods* and had agreed to give back to the convention a small percentage of the profit from sales. Those funds would in turn be used to print other materials. She then explained that the Free Will Baptist Press in Ayden, North Carolina, had been the printer for the *Year Book of Programs* back to the Ladies Aid Society nine years earlier. However, the convention had thus far been unable to reach an agreement with the Free Will Baptist Press whereby the WNAC could receive a share in the profits needed for other printing.⁴⁵

This instance, however slight, would prefigure a number of tensions between the fledgling National Association and the older, more established denominational entities in North Carolina. One detects in this situation a hint of internal tension within the leadership of the group. The Minutes of the 1942 Convention state that Mrs. J. C. Griffin, the WNAC president, had "instructed" Frazier to "give the work for that year to the Free Will Baptist Press, at Ayden, N. C." After all, Griffin said, the *Gem* had published the *Manual of Methods*, and she "thought it only fair that our printing be divided between them." Yet Frazier "did not comply." In the end, the membership voted to allow Frazier to make the final decision since "she is an unpaid worker."⁴⁶

WNAC appealed to the National Association's Board of Publications and Literature for help. That board was chaired by J. C. Griffin, the towering figure from North Carolina whose wife was WNAC president. He sought to smooth out the relationship between the WNAC and the Press. However, the issue lingered on, as is evidenced by the 1945 recommendation of the General Board that the Board of Publications and Literature "confer with" the first vice president of the WNAC to find a "solution to the publication of literature for the W. N. A. C." The next year, the Board of Publications and Literature itself published the Auxiliary's *Year Book of Programs*.⁴⁷

The organizational complexity of the WNAC at this early stage, and its coordination of its societies at the local church, district, and state levels, is also impressive. The convention elected five vice presidents, each in charge of different aspects of the organization's purpose. This division of labor illustrates the basic objectives of the WNAC. The first vice president, Frazier, was in charge of literature. The second vice president oversaw the promotion of denominational education. The third vice president was in charge of missions and general promotion. The fourth vice president was in charge of stewardship, and the fifth vice president directed "benevolences," especially the support of orphanages. This system of vice presidents operated at every level, state, district, and local church.[48]

As the time grew closer for the establishment of Free Will Baptist Bible College, the WNAC worked hand in hand with the National Board of Education and the Executive Office's Christian Workers Institutes to press for the start of a collegiate institution. Agnes Frazier, as seen above, was at the center of this effort. At the 1942 meeting of the WNAC, Frazier called on her Free Will Baptist sisters to "launch out into the deep" to accomplish this objective and the other objectives of the convention: "How we also need to beckon . . . our partners, the women in our churches, who are doing nothing," she declared. "If an automobile had as many useless parts as a church, it would not even run down hill." Frazier encouraged each woman in her audience not to be one of those useless parts: "So many Free Will Baptist women with incandescent light powers are doing tallow candle shining, or none at all. So many Free Will Baptist women with diamond and ruby abilities doing pewter work. . . . So many with Winchester powers doing popgun work. . . . The love of Christ should certainly constrain us to enlist these women."[49]

The 1940s witnessed enormous gains for the convention, primarily under the leadership of volunteers such as Fannie Polston, Agnes Frazier, and Lizzie McAdams. The women's movement continued to spur the denomination on in the support of missions and the newly established Free Will Baptist Bible College, featuring missionary speakers as well as speakers and singers from the college. They saw missions and education as twin tasks in the fulfillment of the Great Commission. Opal Bingham, second vice president for 1943, encouraged support of the new college in Nashville, which she believed would provide "an education that discovers the individual, duly emphasizes both rights and duties, and champions the doctrine of equality in opportunity. With a spirit of obedience to the Great Commission Free Will Baptists are making a close relation between its forces of evangelism and education."[50]

In his 1945 report, Robert Crawford, executive secretary of the National Association, noted the "marked increase" in the WNAC. He recognized a notable upsurge in their giving over the previous year, a time when the country was involved in a world war. "Praise is due unto our noble women for following the leadership of the Lord," Crawford exulted. In 1944, Frazier had proposed four important resolutions that would set the stage for the organization's development: that a monthly magazine be published, that a full-time editor be employed, that a central office be established in Nashville, and that the publications be printed by the lowest bidder. In 1947, Mrs. Huey Gower was employed and paid as the first executive secretary of the WNAC. The rest of Frazier's goals would have to wait until the next decade to be met. Still, by 1950, the Women's National Auxiliary Convention had made amazing strides, having grown to more than 184 local auxiliaries and spurring the Free Will Baptist Church on to greater heights in missions, education, prayer, stewardship, and benevolence.[51]

Publications and Literature, Sunday School, and League

The General Conference and Co-operative General Association had each supported its own publisher. The General Conference supported the larger and more established Free Will Baptist Press in Ayden, North Carolina, while the Co-operative General Association generally supported the printing press of the *Free Will Baptist Gem*, at Purdy, Missouri. At the formation of the National Association in 1935, it was decided that the new *Treatise*, the National Association's confession of faith, would be put out for bid to both presses and printed by the lower bidder. However, until 1951, the Press printed the Minutes every year except for three. In 1939, the assets of the Press were more than six times those of the *Gem*.[52]

From the start, the National Association provided in its constitution and bylaws for part-time National Secretaries for Sunday Schools and Young People's Work. Winford Davis of Missouri was elected Secretary of Sunday School Work. North Carolina pastor Henry Melvin was made secretary for the youth movement, which continued the work of the General Conference's "Free Will Baptist League" under the same name. One first sees the name "Free Will Baptist League" as the youth organization of the General Conference in 1924 in the report of Miss Ruth Stewart of Nashville, Tennessee. That year she chaired the Committee on Young People's Work. This name was first used in Nashville and was suggested by John L. Welch to the North Carolina State Convention. Melvin had been general secretary of this organization for nearly a decade.[53]

The Free Will Baptist League continued to have its literature printed by Free Will Baptist Press, its printer for many years. In the late 1930s and early 1940s, after the League was made the National Association's youth arm, Melvin moved the organization forward swiftly, announcing quarterly publications not only for children and adolescents but also for college-aged students. At its 1938 session, the National Association began electing five-member boards. It also began tallying the total number of Sunday schools in the association and their enrollment, but not those of Leagues, despite the fact that the League Board played a much larger role at the National Association level in its early years. By 1940, with 132,000 members across the denomination, Sunday school enrollment was listed at 78,000, while League enrollment was listed at 25,000. The realization that League membership was open only to young people through college age puts that number in perspective.[54]

At that first election of five-member boards in 1938, in addition to Melvin, the delegates elected to the League Board Texas pastor R. C. Wiggs and three laypeople, Esther Apple of Missouri, Everett Kieffer of Oklahoma, and Allene Reed of Tennessee. It elected to the Sunday School Board three laymen, G. W. Cloud of Florida, who succeeded Winford Davis as chair, L. E. Duncan of Mississippi, and Aston Pegues of Texas; and two ministers, R. P. Harris of North Carolina and Paul Purcell of Oklahoma. The desire to elect laymen and laywomen to the Boards of the National Association in its early years is notable. That trend would gradually decline in the 1970s as the association, its entities, and its annual sessions became more clergy-dominated. Though most of the denomination never supported women's ordination to ministry, the presence of women was ubiquitous in the elections, records, and annual session business meetings of the 1930s, 1940s, and 1950s but began to recede in the 1960s.[55]

In 1940, the Sunday School Board presented a first-ever "Standard of Efficiency." This document outlined the basic mission and principles of Sunday schools. It also monitored the use of Free Will Baptist curriculum, records and reporting of attendance, and benchmarks for enrollees' participation in the life of not only the Sunday school but also the wider church. The Standard specified that efficient Sunday schools would have 80 percent of their enrollees using their own Bibles and attending morning worship. Furthermore, the Standard stipulated monthly officers' and teachers' meetings and an Annual Teachers' and Officers' Training Institute in each Sunday school, with a 75 percent attendance rate of all elected officers and teachers at both. The document also included principles for age-grading and recommendations for the conduct of district Sunday school conventions. It further required that all the enterprises of the National Association would be promoted by Sunday schools. Along with this, the body ratified a "Constitution and By-Laws of the National Free Will Baptist Sunday School Convention." This document was designed to ensure the effectiveness of Sunday schools throughout the denomination. The Sunday School Convention was to be held concurrently with the annual session of the National Association each year. In 1941 W. E. Coville, the president of the Sunday School Convention, negotiated with Free Will Baptist Press, the *Free Will Baptist Gem*, and one other printer to have Sunday school "supplies" printed. The *Gem* came in with the lowest bid and was employed.⁵⁶

At the 1942 annual session, the General Board recommended a Board of Publications and Literature, which the delegates approved. J. C. Griffin was made secretary, and four other ministers were elected to serve with him: L. C. Johnson, Mark Lewis of Missouri, Charles R. Porter of Illinois, and K. V. Shutes of Alabama. That same year, for the first time, the Free Will Baptist Press and the *Free Will Baptist Gem* both gave official reports at the annual session, though neither were governed by the National Association. At its first report, to the annual session of 1943, the Board of Publications and Literature recommended the Free Will Baptist Press and its publication, *The Free Will Baptist*, as well as the *Free Will Baptist Gem*. That year, Coville consulted with the Board of Publications and Literature about publishing a "textbook" for the Sunday School Convention. The board declined the invitation because it was not in a position to act as a printer.⁵⁷

In the early 1940s, the number of Leagues, with their memberships, began to appear in the statistical tables. At the 1943 annual session, League General Secretary Henry Melvin reported that no department of the denomination had suffered during the past year like the Free Will Baptist League. "This has been due to the drafting of virtually all of the senior age boys into the armed forces of the Nation, and the shifting of much of the youthful population in defense work." Yet Melvin stressed that he was not being pessimistic and that the work was continuing strong. The Press in Ayden continued to publish the League's literature, also handling its sales and assuming "the risk of profit or loss."⁵⁸

The Board of Publications and Literature was not above occasionally making recommendations to the denomination that were broader than publishing concerns. For example, in its 1947 report at the annual session, J. C. Griffin, speaking for the other members of the Board—L. C. Johnson, L. E. Duncan of Mississippi, Ralph Staten of Arkansas, and K. V. Shutes of Alabama—made a recommendation concerning some in the denomination who desired a revision of the *Treatise*. These individuals had come to the Board wanting the *Treatise*, which was soon to be reprinted, to "further declare" a position on "certain doctrines" and "disciplinary matters." Many people, they reported, were claiming to be premillennialists, postmillennialists, or "non-millennialists" and wanted confessional clarity on these matters. Thus the Board recommended that a large, representative committee be appointed to revise the *Treatise*. The delegates elected a *Treatise* Revision Committee at that same annual session consisting of five ministers: J. C. Griffin of North

Carolina, J. F. Miller of Missouri, J. L. Welch of Tennessee, Raymond Riggs of Michigan, K. V. Shutes of Alabama, S. F. Vanhoose of Kentucky, and L. A. Holliday of South Carolina.[59]

The most substantial change in doctrinal wording in the 1948 revision occurred in the chapter on sanctification. Before 1948, that chapter had defined sanctification as "a work of God's grace by which the soul is cleansed from all sin and wholly consecrated to Christ. It commences at regeneration, and the Christian can and should abide in this state to the end of life, constantly growing in grace and in the knowledge of our Lord Jesus Christ." The new statement said simply, "Sanctification is the continuing of God's grace by which the Christian may constantly grow in grace and in the knowledge of our Lord Jesus Christ." It is not clear what precipitated this change. The other changes included changing the wording about the work of the minister from "a faithful pastor" to "a faithful minister," and the "general judgment" was changed simply to "judgment" in the chapter on judgment and retribution.[60]

Throughout the 1940s, the Board of Publications and Literature continued to endorse both the Press and the *Gem*, attempting to divide the publication of its books and booklets evenly between the two. For example, in 1948, the Board of Publications and Literature said in its report to the annual session:

> We find that our publishing houses are very co-operative with the Board of Publications and Literature, and are willing to work for the on going of the larger denomination, but they are what we Free Will Baptist[s] have made them, if we had given them better support we would have had a better set-up, but like our Educational Institutions we have been too prone to patronize and help other denominations to build up their work, thus our Literature and Institutions of learning have suffered.[61]

Almost all of the board's publications, however, were published by Free Will Baptist Press. This included J. C. Griffin's *Special Services Arranged for Ministers and Others Who Prefer to Use Them for Helpful Services* (better known by the much briefer title on the front cover, *Manual for Ministers*).[62]

Yet even at this early stage, one sees evidence of tension over the two publishers. While encouraging the use of both the Free Will Baptist Press and the Missouri *Gem*, Griffin commented: "We need more cooperation in all of our departmental work. We can never make progress by criticisms which are of a destructive nature. We are blessed with two denominational publishing houses which are anxious to seek and to give the best service possible. We can help them by patronizing and cooperating with them in their efforts."[63]

At the 1948 meeting of the National Sunday School Convention, still held in conjunction with the National Association's annual session, its president, Paul J. Ketteman, reported on the progress of the Sunday school movement in the denomination and for the first time indicated a developing partnership with the interdenominational Evangelical Teacher Training Association and its General Secretary Clarence H. Benson. Partnership with this organization, which emphasized teacher training for local churches, would thrive throughout the twentieth century and, with Free Will Baptist Bible College, into the twenty-first. The organization, later named the Evangelical Training Association, provided the model for teacher training for the National Association later in the twentieth century. The Free Will Baptist League continued to prosper, holding its first national conference in Nashville in June of 1948 with students from fourteen states and Cuba. This would be the first in a series of national youth conferences sponsored by the League.[64]

The Board of Publications and Literature continued to beat the drum about the need to promote Free Will Baptist literature, encouraging "the patronage of our people toward the use of safe, sound literature." In his 1949 report to the annual session, Griffin stressed to the body the need to "refuse to patronize book agents that go from door to door, with books that are contrary to the sound doctrines of the Bible," especially by groups such as Jehovah's Witnesses, Mormons, and Seventh-Day Adventists. "We say purchase no publication without careful examination and if you cannot satisfy yourself as to the soundness of the book, get your pastor or some one else who knows to give his opinion on the book."[65]

The Association's Makeup and Leadership

The statistics from the 1948 annual session provide a snapshot of the makeup and leadership of the National Association in its early years. It comprised 1,636 churches with 118,854 members. The average membership of its churches was seventy-three. More than 80 percent of its membership was east of the Mississippi River. Half its membership was found in states on the East Coast.[66]

North Carolina, Tennessee, and Missouri were the strongest states and most influential voices in the association in terms of delegation, participation, officers and board memberships, and financial support. North Carolina, the oldest and most established of any of the state organizations, dominated with a third of the association's membership, and its churches were wealthier and stronger. For example, while the average membership of churches in the denomination was seventy-three at this time, it was 107 in North Carolina, making that state the leader both in terms of overall membership and per-church membership. Tennessee's dominance at the National Association level was outsized compared to its percentage of membership in the association, even before denominational entities began to locate their operations in Nashville. While Tennessee provided only 7 percent of the association's members, its churches were much stronger than average, at ninety-two members per congregation, and more officers, board members, and general secretaries were from Tennessee than any other state. Missouri ran a close third to North Carolina and Tennessee, with Alabama and Georgia not far behind. While Missouri's churches were smaller, its participation and giving per capita were the highest in the Association. These five states—accounting for 60 percent of the National Association's membership and an even higher quotient of influence and funds—dominated the trajectory of the denomination in its first two decades.[67]

Thirteen
GROWTH AND CONTROVERSY AFTER 1950

"'WHEN THOU SHALT hear the sound of going . . . then shalt thou go out to battle.' I Chronicles 14:15. . . . God has given us the 'go' sign. . . . We have heard the sound of going and we are ready to go out to battle against the prevailing evils of the day." A palpable spirit of optimism characterized the report of Executive Secretary Damon Dodd to the 1951 annual session of the National Association, which opened with these words. Dodd exulted about a "spirit of denominational revival" which had "resulted in the best year which we have ever known as the National Association of Free Will Baptists." This is symbolic of the spirit with which the movement embarked on the second half of the twentieth century.[1]

Expansion in the Twentieth Century

The National Association continued both its organizational growth and geographical expansion. The latter resulted from two trends. The National Association increased its emphasis on home missions and church planting. Furthermore, many congregants migrated north in the years surrounding and after World War II, looking for work in urban industrial centers. Michigan is the ideal example of this phenomenon. There were Free Baptists in Michigan from the Randall movement left over after its merger with the Northern Baptist Convention in 1911. For a time, the Co-operative General Association was in contact with those congregations, trying to get them to unite with the association. Those churches, however, eventually became Northern

Baptist. Thus the entire Michigan Free Will Baptist movement in the present day originated from northward migration from southern states. In the early 1940s, several churches were planted in the Detroit area. By 1941, Hazel Park Church, Highland Park Church, Ecorse (later Woodhaven) Church, and First Church of Flint united to form the Wolverine Association. That body almost immediately joined the National Association. Seven ministers represented their congregations to the early Wolverine Association: N. P. Gates, C. E. Riggs, Maurice Roach, James Grisham, Raymond Riggs, Virgil Greenway, and George T. Warren.[2]

Later, illustrious preachers such as Lloyd Locklear, a Lumbee Indian who had migrated from North Carolina, came to the state, and growth continued to occur. Michigan became a hotbed of activity in the 1950s, as denominational personalities such as Charles and Laura Thigpen moved to the Detroit area to minister to growing suburban congregations. Soon the Metropolitan Association was formed and in 1956 joined with Wolverine to form the Michigan State Association. That initial state organization elected Charles Thigpen as moderator, N. P. Gates as assistant moderator, William T. Newsome as clerk, Paul Robinson as assistant clerk, and George Butler as treasurer. Michigan would become a microcosm of Free Will Baptists. Its pastors had migrated from east and west of the Mississippi—from North Carolina to Kentucky to Tennessee to Arkansas and beyond—from the mountains and the flatlands. They were both lively and quiet in worship, both amillennial and premillennial, from both "backsliding" and "apostasy" backgrounds.[3] Despite its small numbers, Michigan would go on to exercise an outsized influence on the National Association, especially Free Will Baptist Bible College and Foreign Missions.[4]

Indiana, like other areas of Free Will Baptist activity, would be birthed out of nearby states. Though the Randall movement had several churches in the state, they all became Northern Baptist as a result of the 1911 merger. Thus the present-day, majority-White Free Will Baptist movement in Indiana emerged from Kentucky, Virginia, and Tennessee Free Will Baptists. The first Free Will Baptist congregation in Indiana was planted by Melvin Staggs and Clarence Bailey, who were from Pikeville, Kentucky. That church united with the Floyd County Conference in Kentucky in 1952. The first conference in Indiana was the Kosciusko County Conference, which was organized in Claypool, Indiana, in 1954. The Floyd County Conference in Kentucky assisted with the organization of this conference, dispatching ministers such as Charles Rowe, William Amburgey, Douglas Burkett, and Carl Center to help.[5]

At first the Kosciusko County Conference represented to the Floyd

County Conference. However, in 1961, Indiana Free Will Baptists organized a new association known as the Wabash Valley Association of Free Will Baptist Churches. They elected Randall Goble as moderator, Charles Bailey as assistant moderator, Richard Cordell as clerk, and Bobby Whitaker as treasurer. The White River Conference, which was formed in 1962, had churches that had formerly been members of an Anabaptist denomination known as the New Dunkard Church of God. These and other associations united to form the Indiana State Association in 1971. Two other associations with Indiana congregations are unaffiliated with the Indiana State Association: the Stone Association of Indiana, which has ties to the Stone Association in Tennessee, and the John-Thomas Association.[6]

California Free Will Baptists are another example of migration in the mid-twentieth century. They grew as Free Will Baptists from several states, mostly west of the Mississippi, moved further west. As in other states, a small Randall presence in California was absorbed by the Northern Baptist Convention. According to Jack Williams, the earliest present-day Free Will Baptist churches in California in the late 1930s and early 1940s were the East Los Angeles Church, the Turlock Church, and the Porterville Church. The first annual session of the California State Association convened with the Turlock Church in 1944. The delegates elected Elder Ralph Geiger moderator and J. L. Waltman assistant moderator. The minutes of the second annual session were printed by the *Free Will Baptist Gem* in Missouri. In 1955, the State Association started California Bible Institute, which later became California Christian College. Ministry to the Hispanic community has also flourished among California Free Will Baptists, with a Hispanic Association founded in the late 1980s.[7]

Other movements associated with the National Association began to dot the American landscape in the twentieth and early twenty-first centuries as home missionaries moved north and west to plant new churches. These included local churches in Alaska, Hawaii, South Dakota, Wisconsin, and the US Virgin Islands; local and regional associations such as the Arizona Association, the First Colorado Association, the Idaho Association (with representation from Utah), the Eastern Iowa Association, the Mid-Atlantic Association (Delaware, Maryland, New Jersey, Pennsylvania), the Northeast Association (New Hampshire, Maine, and Rhode Island), the Northwest Association (Oregon and Washington), and the David Marks Heritage Association (Pennsylvania and New York); and state associations such as the Kansas State Association. The Atlantic Canada Association, which united with the National Association in 1981, comprises congregations that emerged from the Arminian "Primitive Baptist" movement in New Brunswick. Unlike other Canadian Arminian Baptists, this association did not participate in the merger with Calvinistic Baptists in Canada. The above movements, while small, began to represent to the General Board of the National Association, support the association's ministries, and affect denominational life.[8]

The North Carolina Schism and the Convention of Original Free Will Baptists

Four factors led to a schism with the North Carolina State Convention of Original Free Will Baptists in 1962: the centralization of the National Association, Sunday school publishing, philosophy of higher education, and church government. The first factor is somewhat sociological in nature and provides a matrix through which to understand the last three. The second factor was organizational, the third philosophical, and the fourth theological.

Centralization

After the formation of the National Association in 1935, tension gradually cropped up between the leadership of that association in Nashville, Tennessee, and the established institutions of North Carolina Free Will Baptists. The latter constituted the largest of all the member state organizations that constituted the National Association. As seen in the previous chapter, by 1950, about a third of the denomination's membership came from North Carolina. Its churches were older, larger, and stronger than those in other states, and its institutions were older and more established than those in other places.[9]

Tennessee had always been the other most prominent state in the National Association. However, its prominence was elevated exponentially more when decisions were gradually made that reflected the sentiment that Nashville was the most geographically central location and thus the institutions and ministries of the National Association were located there. In the first two decades of the association's existence, Nashville more and more became the center of gravity in the denomination. Thus it gained greater prominence than the older, more established institutions in North Carolina. This created tension, which coincided with, and likely contributed to, the founding of Mount Olive College in North Carolina in 1952. This institution was perceived by some as a competitor to Free Will Baptist Bible College, the college of the National Association. The establishment of *Contact* magazine by the National Association in 1953 also contributed to this friction. It was perceived by some as a competitor to *The Free Will Baptist*, the weekly periodical published in Ayden, North Carolina.[10]

Sunday School Publishing

This centralization aspect dovetailed with another component of the tension between North Carolina and the National Association: disagreements over the publication of the denomination's Sunday school curriculum. Free Will Baptist Press in Ayden, North Carolina, had been publishing Sunday school literature for around six decades. Yet as the National Association grew in the 1950s, its Sunday School Board began to clamor for changes in its curriculum. Those changes soon came into conflict with the established practice of the Free Will Baptist Press. As seen in the previous chapter, this was not the first time tension had arisen between one of the entities of the National Association and the Free Will Baptist Press. WNAC had expressed frustration with the Press in the 1940s, creating tension between WNAC's president, Mrs. J. C. Griffin of New Bern, North Carolina, and its first vice president Agnes Frazier of Nashville, Tennessee.[11]

By 1954, the Sunday School Board had arrived at a profit-sharing agreement with the Free Will Baptist Press. Seven and one-half percent of curriculum sales would come back to the board for its promotional work. Soon the board began to have greater aspirations. At the annual session of the National Association in 1957, the Sunday School Board asked the delegates to approve an expansion campaign. That initiative would entail the board's hiring a full-time executive secretary and publishing its own curriculum so that it could realize a 30 percent profit. These funds would then be plowed back into the expansion campaign, which had ambitious goals for teacher training and publishing. While this measure passed, it created a firestorm of controversy because Free Will Baptist Press would no longer be publishing the association's Sunday school curriculum.[12]

At the 1958 annual session held in St. Louis, Missouri, the Sunday School Department reported an increase in sales of Sunday school curriculum. It touted "astounding success" with its new curriculum. However, by January of 1959, the board had assumed liabilities three times that of its total assets, and before the 1959 annual session in July, the entire board resigned. The General Board of the National Association directed the Executive Committee to continue the publishing program until a course of action could be decided on. That same year the Executive Committee, chaired by Free Will Baptist Bible College dean Charles Thigpen, entered into a contract with Free Will Baptist Press for the publication of all Sunday school curriculum.

The General Board urged Free Will Baptists everywhere to buy shares in the Press, thus "giving them a voting voice in the control of literature." Purchasing shares did not involve profit, but it did get shareholders a vote. A new Sunday School Board was elected, consisting of former missionary Paul Woolsey of Tennessee, who was made chair; Roger Reeds of Missouri, who was made secretary-treasurer; Ralph Staten of North Carolina; Robert King of Arkansas; and L. H. Clayton of South Carolina. These actions dealt with the conflict temporarily. Yet the episode exacerbated the developing tension between North Carolina and the National Association.[13]

Higher Education

Another factor that reflected the tension between the establishment in North Carolina and the increasingly centralized denominational center in Nashville was higher education. There was growing dissatisfaction in North Carolina with Free Will Baptist Bible College's slow pace in moving beyond its focus on education for ministers and missionaries. Many in that state also believed that the college's requirement of such a large number of courses in biblical and theological studies for non-ministry students was onerous. Thus plans were made to open a liberal arts college that would require of its students only a few courses in religious studies. This new school, it was proposed, would emphasize career preparation for Free Will Baptist students as well as those of other denominations in North Carolina. There was also a sense by some supporters of the idea of a new North Carolina college that the college in Nashville was too narrow in the expression of orthodoxy it embraced. Thus Mount Allen Junior College was chartered in 1951 and began operations in 1952 at Cragmont Assembly near Black Mountain in western North Carolina. The college relocated to the town of Mount Olive in Eastern North Carolina in 1954. It called the young W. Burkette Raper as its president. Over his forty-year presidential tenure, with his remarkable organizational and fundraising skills, Raper would build Mount Olive College into one of the most respected and fastest-growing colleges in the state.[14]

In the late 1950s, tension developed between some of Free Will Baptist Bible College's supporters and Mount Olive College. Rumors began to circulate about tendencies among some on the campus toward secularization and an embrace of neoorthodox theology. These concerns were addressed by two different approaches in the Free Will Baptist Bible College orbit. The more irenic one was represented by Winterville, North Carolina, native F. Leroy Forlines, a theology professor at Free Will Baptist Bible College. The more rigorous critique coalesced around Durham, North Carolina, pastor

Ronald Creech. Forlines, in a dispassionate private correspondence with Raper, asked for assurances from him that Mount Olive was strong in ensuring that orthodoxy was being affirmed in its coursework. Raper, not wishing to countenance the controversy, simply replied that he was in good standing with his local presbytery and that the college affirmed the Faith and Discipline of North Carolina Free Will Baptists.[15]

Creech expressed privately to Raper his concern about whether the latter's distancing himself from indoctrination and sectarianism was not opening the door to theological liberalism. Creech was publicly critical of Mount Olive in his widely distributed newsletter *The Challenger*. He castigated the college's rules, which allowed students to attend movies and wear shorts, for being too loose and not encouraging the sort of piety that should characterize an institution training future ministers. Rumors swirled about the preference of Mount Olive faculty for Duke Divinity School and Raper's fondness for the mainline Protestant Bible commentary *The Interpreter's Bible*. Meanwhile, Mount Olive supporters criticized Creech and his comrades as being joined at the hip with John R. Rice's *Sword of the Lord* paper and its Independent Baptist brand of separatist fundamentalism. Exchanges between Creech and Mount Olive supporters exacerbated tensions that had up to this point remained under the surface. When a church polity dispute emerged in 1960 between Creech and the Western Conference of Free Will Baptists, of which his congregation, Edgemont Free Will Baptist Church in Durham, was a member, things quickly began to get out of hand.[16]

Despite the concerns about Mount Olive College, the Executive Committee of the National Association later said, "Let us state, first of all, that the educational philosophy of no institution—neither Free Will Baptist Bible College nor Mount Olive College—was the issue." The committee explained that these matters had not surfaced in any discussions of either itself, the General Board, or the National body in annual session. "For anyone to assert then that this was the basis for the action by the association is to either ignorantly or purposefully cloud the real issue on which the assembled delegates acted." That "real issue," the statement said, was church polity.[17]

Church Polity

A minority of the Edgemont Church had accused the pastor Ronald Creech and the congregation's majority, later known as the Miles faction, of doctrinal and administrative irregularities. That minority, later known as the Teasley faction, reported their concerns to the moderator of the Western Conference. The conference's Executive Committee held a regular meeting on August 12,

1960, at which some of the Teasley group were present. The committee decided to call a joint meeting of the Executive Committee and the Board of Ordination of the Conference to hear from any of Edgemont's members. Some of the congregation's minority had reported they feared recrimination for their actions. In response, the committee specified that "acts of reprisal against members giving information to this committee will not be tolerated." Subsequently, however, five of the Teasley group were disciplined by the church and warned of excommunication should interaction with conference officials continue. Creech did not attend the Western Conference meeting. Later, however, a witness stated in court that Creech had remained outside the building so he could see who attended the meeting. As a result of this hearing, the joint committee brought charges against Creech and the Miles faction. It required Creech to report to them at a subsequent meeting, which he declined to do. Thus the joint committee revoked his ministerial credentials for a week, pending another meeting to which he was summoned.[18]

Creech and the Miles faction brought their attorney to that meeting, whom Creech said would speak for him. The chairman ruled this out of order, saying the meeting was ecclesiastical, not civil. The attorney persisted, and the committee went into executive session. At that point, it voted to revoke Creech's credentials until he agreed to answer to the charges in person. Creech and his attorney sent the committee a letter ordering them to retract the charges, which they regarded as libelous. Yet the joint committee responded that they were following the Statement of Faith and Discipline for Original Free Will Baptists of North Carolina and other Western Conference standards. They insisted that Creech would have to "face the accusers and answer the charges." Creech insisted that, though he had requested a copy of the charges, he had never been given one. The joint committee subsequently requested Creech's and the Miles faction's presence at another meeting, which they declined to attend. Creech believed that the Western Conference's actions were a violation of the autonomy of the local church. The Western Conference believed that it was operating according to traditional Free Will Baptist polity and that ministers were subject for their credentials to the presbytery or board of ordination.[19]

Before that last meeting, Creech filed a $400,000 lawsuit and a temporary restraining order that would keep the Western Conference from reporting their findings. After a judge modified the restraining order in November 1960, the joint committee again called on Creech to answer the charges, which he declined to do. At its meeting the next January, the joint committee reiterated its stance before the full Western Conference. The conference upheld the joint committee's decision by a vote of ninety-eight to twenty-two. When Creech did not abide by the conference's actions, it filed a lawsuit to have the civil court of Durham County evict him from the pulpit. Furthermore, it insisted that the Miles faction not be allowed to present themselves as the true Edgemont congregation. In June 1961, a Superior Court judge issued a temporary restraining order against Creech. That order disallowed him from representing himself as a Free Will Baptist minister and awarded the Edgemont property to the minority (Teasley) faction. The judge clarified that the order would be reversed should Creech and the Miles faction submit to the conference's authority.[20]

Up to this point, many Free Will Baptists both inside and outside North Carolina had sympathized with the Western Conference, believing that historic Free Will Baptist polity required Creech to submit to the authority of the Western Conference Board of Ordination. The *Treatise* at that time stated: "When a minority of a church is aggrieved with the action of the majority, a council may be called by mutual agreement, or requested by the Quarterly Meeting. Such council may be called simply for advice, or as a board of arbitration whose decision shall be final." After the Western Conference filed its lawsuit, however, the tide of public sentiment in the wider denomination began to turn against the Conference. Most believed that, in attempting to declare a minority of a self-governing congregation to be the true church, the conference had overstepped its bounds and had violated the self-government of the local congregation. This is seen in an editorial by Billy Melvin, executive secretary of the National Association, entitled "Congregational or Connectional?" in the February 1962 issue of *Contact*. This essay recounted the history of Free Will Baptist statements defending the ultimate right of self-governance of local congregations. The article stated that even key leaders of the North Carolina State Convention in the years immediately preceding the controversy had affirmed this polity.[21]

As late as January 1962, an editorial in *The Free Will Baptist* stated: "One thing is certain, there are denominational leaders in other states who understand North Carolina's position. Many know what is practiced in other states. It is to these leaders that we believe many of our people will eventually turn for an honest and unbiased explanation." However, that was not to be. Many Free Will Baptist congregations in the Southeast continued to subscribe to the Sunday school and League literature of the Free Will Baptist Press. However, only a handful of ministers and churches outside North Carolina supported the State Convention's position.[22]

These sentiments were seen in a statement made by the Executive

Committee of the National Association, which was approved by the overwhelming majority of the delegation at its annual session in July 1961 at Norfolk, Virginia. That statement noted that Free Will Baptist tradition, both inside and outside North Carolina, had protected the self-government of the local congregation from ultimate intrusion from bodies outside itself. Though ministers were answerable to the presbyteries of their conferences or associations, they were free to unite with another conference if they dissented from a conference decision. Likewise, the committee argued, though congregations were obliged to receive with humility the counsel of the conference or association of which they were members, in the end they had the right of free dissent and self-governance, to break fellowship with that conference and unite with another. The committee statement pointed to official publications of North Carolina Free Will Baptists that had recently argued for this position. Noting that fifty-two North Carolina ministers had signed an affidavit stating that North Carolina Free Will Baptists had historically practiced "a connectional form of church government," the committee, followed by the General Board and the delegates of the National Association, called on the North Carolina State Convention "to repudiate any and all forms of connectional church government."[23]

The differences between the two positions are illustrated by statements from the Executive Committees of the North Carolina State Convention and the National Association. The State Convention's Executive Committee defended its commitment to connectional polity by citing its Statement of Faith and Discipline. That confessional document said that the conference or association was the "highest tribunal" and thus had "final disciplinary authority over the local church." It also said that each conference or association "assumes and exercises authority over Original Free Will Baptist ministers in its jurisdiction or bounds." The Executive Committee of the National Association said they supported the Western Conference's power over its ministers and disciplinary authority over its local congregations. Yet they argued that ultimately, in historic Free Will Baptist polity, after discipline had been administered, those congregations were self-governing. Thus the Western Conference, they maintained, should not have "placed itself in a position of determining the membership of a local church" and "take[n] the property away from the majority, thus interfering again in local, internal affairs."[24]

At the annual session in Norfolk that July, the General Board recommended that a special committee be appointed to study the matter and report back its findings to the next annual session in 1962. However, a subsequent motion carried, after intense floor debate, to declare vacant the seats of five members of National Association boards who had signed the affidavit affirming connectional church government. North Carolina ministers believed that this action constituted a violation of the due process of which they believed these board members had been deprived. The officers of the National Association insisted that the delegates to that body had always had the privilege of determining who held its offices. The National Association, after what it considered a breach of historic Free Will Baptist polity, issued an amicus curiae (friend of the court) brief in favor of Creech and the Miles faction. In this brief, the National Association indicated its belief that the rights of the Miles faction under historic Free Will Baptist polity had been abrogated. The brief stressed the National Association's position that "each local church is the highest authority over its own property and internal affairs and that no conference or association with which the church may voluntarily unite has authority to reverse any decision reached by the local church. . . ." In response, the North Carolina State Convention, as well as the Central, Eastern, and Cape Fear Conferences, filed an amicus brief in favor of the Western Conference and the minority group in the Edgemont Church, the Teasley faction. The North Carolina Supreme Court, however, would not consider either brief.[25]

After a series of articles and statements carried in *The Free Will Baptist* and *Contact*, followed by several Executive Committee meetings of the North Carolina State Convention, a special meeting of that committee and all the State Convention's standing boards was called in February 1962, as Michael Pelt says, to assess the State Convention's situation. The group agreed to call a special session of the State Convention, which would be held on March 29, 1962. At that meeting the State Convention formally severed its relationship with the National Association. In June, a minority of the North Carolina congregations withdrew from the State Convention and their respective conferences to form the North Carolina State Association. That new association united with the National Association. In the spring of 1963, the Supreme Court of North Carolina dismissed the cases before it relative to this controversy. It stated that these were ecclesiastical matters and the court could not rule on them. However, it did rule in favor of the Teasley faction in the case over the Edgemont property. In the end, by mutual agreement, the Teasley faction received the church building and the Miles faction received the parsonage.[26]

The Convention Retools

When the schism occurred, the North Carolina State Convention was already in a position of strength with regard to higher education, publishing,

Sunday school, and League. The convention also operated the orphanage in Middlesex as well as Cragmont Assembly in western North Carolina. Mount Olive Junior College had achieved regional accreditation with the Southern Association of Colleges and Schools in 1960. This positioned it for growth in the coming years. On a new ninety-acre parcel of land, the college began construction in 1964. Though many buildings were still utilized at the old downtown campus, the goal was to make a full transition to the new campus. Over the next decade, an academic building, men's and women's residence halls, Moye Library, named for Rev. and Mrs. J. C. Moye, and a new chapel were built. President Burkette Raper, a graduate of Duke Divinity School, received a master's degree in higher education administration from Florida State University and became adept at fundraising for the college. President Raper's influence would shape the institution more than anyone else's. Other key influences were Michael Pelt, who taught religion and for many years served as Academic Dean and Chairman of the Department of Religion, and Head Librarian Gary Fenton Barefoot, who with Pelt's assistance built a strong Free Will Baptist Historical Collection housed in Moye Library.[27]

Raper personally affirmed the classic evangelical theology of Protestant orthodoxy. Yet he self-consciously allowed for a broader approach to theology among the faculty. Thus Mount Olive came to identify more with views similar to those of the moderate wing of the Southern Baptist Convention, much of which is now part of the Cooperative Baptist Fellowship. This is seen in the joint MDiv program the university began sponsoring in 2010 with Campbell University Divinity School, a North Carolina school with ties to the Cooperative Baptist Fellowship.[28]

Mount Olive's accreditation by the Southern Association of Colleges and Schools laid the groundwork for its emergence as a well-known and respected private college in the region. In 1979 the North Carolina State Convention ratified a decision by the Board of Trustees to make Mount Olive a four-year college. A junior class was added in 1984, and a senior class in 1985. The institution's opening of a site at Seymour Johnson Air Force Base in nearby Goldsboro would provide the framework for a network of teaching sites. In the 1990s these sites exponentially expanded Mount Olive's reach in the region. In that decade it added campuses in New Bern, Wilmington, and the Research Triangle (Raleigh). It also expanded its online presence. In 2014, having grown substantially and having added several graduate programs, the board changed the college's name to the University of Mount Olive.[29]

Another educational institution among the Original Free Will Baptists of North Carolina was the Carolina Bible Institute. Rev. Floyd Cherry founded the school in 1975. This institution represented the outlook of American dispensationalism and fundamentalism. Some perceived the founding of this institute, which was independently owned and operated, as a reaction against the more open theological posture of the faculty at Mount Olive. Graduate studies were added in 1987, and after Cherry's retirement, the school was served by presidents such as Rev. Joseph Ingram and Rev. Rudy Owens. In 1996, Cherry edited a collection of essays on doctrine that included contributions by people from both schools, including Raper. The book was printed by the Free Will Baptist Press and officially endorsed by the convention. It espoused all the typical doctrines associated with traditional evangelicalism, including biblical inerrancy, the creation of Adam and Eve, the personality of the devil, and hell as eternal conscious punishment.[30]

After the 1962 schism, the Free Will Baptist Press continued publishing Sunday school, League, and women's auxiliary literature, as it had done for many decades. It also engaged in a publishing program of books and denominational resources, including books that it had published previously, such as J. C. Griffin's *Minister's Manual*. It reprinted classics such as T. F. Harrison's and J. M. Barfield's *History of the Free Will Baptists of North Carolina*. It also published denominational confessions of faith, including its confession that was substantially rewritten in 1976, *The Articles of Faith and Principles of Church Government for Original Free Will Baptists (of the English General Baptist Heritage)*, and *The Free Will Baptist Hymnal*. Most notably, it continued publishing *The Free Will Baptist* every week. Later this magazine changed its name to *Community* and began bi-monthly publication in 2022. The official name of the Press was changed to the Free Will Baptist Press Foundation. In 1990 Mount Olive College started its own publishing concern, Mount Olive College Press, now University of Mount Olive Press.[31]

The North Carolina Convention had to start from scratch in its missions ministry. Its existing Board of Missions ramped up its fundraising activities, setting a goal of $75,000 in gifts for 1963 and directing all contributions to be sent to its address in Ayden. That year the convention initiated its first mission field in Mexico, sending Rev. and Mrs. James Lanier there. The board employed Joseph Ingram as full-time Director-treasurer, under whose leadership the ministry witnessed growth. After a brief experiment in Rhodesia with missionaries Joe and Faye Barrow, it was agreed that the board would begin a mission in the Philippines in cooperation with the General Association of

General Baptists. The board sent Harold and Sandra Jones to the island of Mindanao in 1969, and they began a mission on the island of Palawan three years later. This would provide the structure for a growing Original Free Will Baptist mission work in the Philippines.[32]

Interestingly, an opportunity to initiate a mission in India arose when in the early 1970s Dr. E. M. Lall of Bareilly, Uttar Pradesh, India, wrote a letter to Eureka College in Ayden, North Carolina, which had been closed for more than four decades. The letter was given to the Director-treasurer of the Mission Board; it requested that a Free Will Baptist missionary be sent to India. This led to significant ministry in India on behalf of the convention and eventuated in an Original Free Will Baptist missionary presence in Nepal in the 1990s. The Foreign Mission Board, renamed OFWB International, continued opening new mission fields in the late twentieth and early twenty-first centuries. In 1991 the board opened a mission work in Bulgaria. In 2008, the board initiated a ministry in Guinea and also entered into an agreement with the Original Free Will Baptist Middle Eastern District Conference of America, a group of African American Free Will Baptists, to open a mission field in Liberia. The most recent field opened was Haiti, in 2011.[33]

Home missions had a slower start in the convention. Though administered by its Board of Missions until 1972, that year the convention invested home missions in a separate board known as the Board of Church Extension. At the same time, the Board of Missions was renamed the Board of Foreign Missions. In 1985, the name of the Board of Church Extension was changed to the Board of Home Missions and Evangelism. Most of the work of this board has been the promotion and support of church plants in North Carolina initiated by the conferences comprising the convention. In the 1980s the board began a joint project with the General Association of General Baptists to evangelize H'Mong refugees from Laos. Recently, assistance has been given to the planting of Hispanic Free Will Baptist congregations in North Carolina. Today the board is known as the Church Planting and Renewal Board.[34]

The convention, renamed the Convention of Original Free Will Baptists (COFWB) in 1990, continues to operate a variety of ministries. The COFWB headquarters moved from Ayden to Mount Olive in 2015. In addition to its Children's Home, Cragmont Assembly, the University of Mount Olive, OFWB International, Free Will Baptist Press Foundation, and the Church Planting and Renewal Board, it also operates a retirement program known as the Minister's Program, a Church Finance Association, and a group of homes for retired ministers. The convention also endorses two ancillary ministries: Camp Vandemere and the North Carolina Foundation for Christian Ministries. In 2022 the convention comprised more than 275 congregations, around 225 of them in North Carolina, South Carolina, and Georgia, and more than fifty in Bulgaria, Guinea, Haiti, India, Liberia, Mexico, and the Philippines.[35]

African American Free Will Baptists

The history of African American Free Will Baptists in the twentieth century is difficult to chronicle owing to the paucity of records. Numerous African American groups in the United States trace their origins to the 1899 founding of the United American Free Will Baptist (UAFWB) General Conference. This body was incorporated by the General Assembly of the State of North Carolina in 1901. Most of these groups point to Samuel H. P. Edmonson, discussed in chapter 8, as one of the earliest founders of the modern United American Free Will Baptist movement. A native of North Carolina, Edmondson migrated to Coffee County, Georgia, where he ministered until his death in the mid-1920s. He had an inestimable influence on the early UAFWB General Conference. His "Poem for the General Conference," written in 1920, encapsulates the values, vision, and aspiration of African American Free Will Baptists in the early twentieth century. Edmondson celebrated the church's past and its leaders, emphasized freedom and unity, and evidenced his vision for education, uplift, cultural impact, and forward movement:

> Behold the General Conference comes,
> To the Old Empire State,
> God is their Captain, they proclaim
> God's will they came to do.
> Ocilla Free Will Baptist Church,
> Saints, come, you are welcome here.
> The Delegates from North and South,
> From West and East may come.
> The General Conference "Watch Word" is,
> "United in their Lord,"
> Hodge and Suggs, and Davis too,
> Are all God fearing men.

> The General Conference now in parade,
> For God and all mankind,
> Thomas and Bryant and Ben McLean,
> Are all God fearing men.
> Behold the Free Will Baptists want
> More men like Smith and Brown,
> The Publishing House, and Colleges, too,
> Need more prepared men.
> Old Patrick Henry said of old,
> "Give me Liberty or give me death."
> That's what the Free Will Baptists cry,
> To God and all mankind.[36]

The Free Will Baptists of the original General Conference continued to plant new churches in the Carolinas. Many of these churches in the Carolinas bore the name "African Free Will Baptist." The movement experienced tremendous growth in the first quarter of the twentieth century. The United States Bureau of the Census publication *Religious Bodies: 1916* listed 170 congregations in Georgia, South Carolina, North Carolina, Virginia, Mississippi, Louisiana, Arkansas, Tennessee, and Illinois, which represented to seven conferences: Cape Fear, Columbus, Georgia Eastern, Northeast, Northwest, Southeastern United, and Union United. Except for Cape Fear (North Carolina), Columbus (Georgia), and Georgia Eastern, it is impossible to tell from this publication what regions of the country these conferences were in. It is evident from the 1936 issue of this same publication that the Northeast and Northwest conferences were both in North Carolina. In twenty years, the number of congregations had increased to 226, and Florida, Alabama, Kentucky, and Texas had been added to the list of states. The Mount Hosea, Southern, and Texas associations were now listed. Other data confirms that the Mount Hosea Association was in Georgia. As early as 1922, the General Conference, headquartered in Kinston, North Carolina, had a college known as Kinston College (now United American Free Will Baptist Bible College). It was administered by President L. E. Rasbury and by 1927 had announced a $300,000 building campaign. The conference also sponsored a publishing house which published a weekly paper, *The Free Will Baptist Advocate*, edited by Elder J. W. C. Smith.[37]

The United American Free Will Baptists soon began to radiate out from the Southeast. They moved, west, to states such as Texas and Louisiana, and north, to the Middle Atlantic and Northeastern states. In 1916 the movement, apparently amicably, divided into eastern and western divisions. Over the course of the twentieth century, various smaller conferences formed across the United States. Most of these conferences now send delegations to the National Convention of Free Will Baptists, USA. This is a loose-knit fraternal organization of Black Free Will Baptists that includes regional conferences such as the United American Free Will Baptist Denomination Inc. (Kinston, North Carolina), the United American Free Will Baptist Conference (Lakeland, Florida), the Western Division Free Will Baptist Conference (St. Louis, Missouri), the Northeast Original Free Will Baptist Conference (Greenville, North Carolina), and the Unified Free Will Baptist Church Inc. (New Haven, Connecticut).[38]

The United American Free Will Baptist Denomination

The United American Free Will Baptist Denomination Inc., is the oldest and largest of these fellowships. It is a continuation of the original General Conference that formed in North Carolina in 1899. Its churches are primarily in the Carolinas and other states on the Eastern Seaboard, and its offices are located in Kinston, North Carolina. Bishop J. E. Reddick has for more than fifty years been the presiding bishop of this fellowship of churches. During the mid-twentieth century, the term "bishop" began to replace "elder" as the preferred New Testament term for the ordained pastoral office in the UAFWBC. The United American Free Will Baptist Denomination Inc., owns and operates the longest-standing and most established college in the movement, United American Free Will Baptist Bible College in Kinston, North Carolina. Bishop Ronald Mayo serves as president of the college, which offers degrees in Bible, theology, ministry, counseling, and liberal studies.[39]

The Western Division of Freewill Baptists

The next-largest group of Black Free Will Baptists is the Western Division of Freewill Baptists. It started in 1917 as the Negro Free-Will Baptist Church, electing Elder Willie Jones as its first president. He and second vice president Henry Clay Maxwell had enormous influence on the conference in its formative years. Both these men had been educated at the J. S. Manning Institute, an African American Free Will Baptist school in Cairo, Illinois, founded in the late nineteenth century. Jones and Maxwell valued education and influenced young Edgar Warfield, who was present at the first session of the newly formed Negro Free-Will Baptist Church. Warfield would go on to become the most influential figure in what would eventually be known as the Western Division, serving as the conference's general bishop from 1938 to 1970. Serving nearly four decades of his ministry at First Free-Will Baptist Church, St. Louis, Missouri, Warfield also served churches in Illinois and Indiana. In the 1950s, the executive secretary of the National Association of Free Will Baptists, W. Stanley Mooneyham, invited Warfield to Nashville. On that trip, Mooneyham introduced him to the National Association and its ministries. Warfield toured the Free Will Baptist National Offices and Free Will Baptist Bible College. This led to the adoption of the Sunday school literature of the Free Will Baptist Press in Ayden, North Carolina, by many Western Division congregations. During this period, significant growth occurred in the Western Division. It purchased its first headquarters building in St. Louis and grew rapidly, with the addition of conferences from Mississippi, Texas, Louisiana, Arkansas, Illinois, and Kentucky.[40]

Bishop Raymond Captville of Baton Rouge, Louisiana, is currently general bishop of the Western Division, a post he has filled since 2003. In 2009, Captville started Trinity Online Bible College in Baton Rouge, which partners with Randall University in Moore, Oklahoma, for ministerial training. In 2016 he was elected president of the National Convention of Free Will Baptists mentioned above.[41]

The Western Division's church polity offers insight into the distinctive form of church government many African American Free Will Baptists affirm:

> The Western Division of Freewill Baptists is distinctive in that its organization and Church Government are a modified mixture between the Congregational and Episcopal forms of ecclesiastical government. Each Annual Conference, District Conference and Local Church has a right to govern itself as long as it abides by the constitution and by-laws, rules, regulations and guidelines as set forth by the General Conference Discipline.[42]

The General Conference of the Western Division is the "overseeing body for all the Western Division Churches and Conferences. The General Conference is the highest government and the final authority in the Western Division of Free Will Baptists Inc."[43]

The Western Division's website explains that the "worship styles within the Western Division churches range from that of quiet and contemplative to loud and very exuberant." Unlike the predominantly White National Association of Free Will Baptists, the Western Division, like some other African American Free Will Baptist conferences, comprises both charismatic and non-charismatic churches. The Quad State Annual Conference is an example of a charismatic conference within the Western Division. While most African American Free Will Baptists are not charismatic, some are, and those charismatic conferences maintain loose fellowship in larger Black Free Will Baptist organizations.[44]

The United American Free Will Baptist General Conference

The United American Free Will Baptist General Conference, headquartered in Lakeland, Florida, was founded in 1966 as an offshoot of the UAFWBC in North Carolina. It has around thirty member churches primarily in Florida but also in Georgia, South Carolina, Louisiana, and Arkansas. It comprises the East Florida, West Florida, South Florida "A," Louisiana-Arkansas, and South Carolina Conferences. Like most African American Free Will Baptist groups, its Articles of Faith are the same as those of the *1812 Abstract*.[45]

Rev. Elliott Titus Brown was probably the most influential minister in the twentieth-century history of this conference. Born in 1909 in Fernandina, Florida, he attended Jacksonville public schools. Embracing Christianity at an early age, he became a committed worker in his local United American Free Will Baptist congregation and went on to receive post-secondary Bible training. Brown's two long-term pastorates were Mt. Olive Free Will Baptist Church in Bartow, Florida, and Antioch Free Will Baptist Church in Deland, Florida. From his post as moderator of the South Florida Annual Conference, Brown exerted great influence on the movement in the Southeast until his death in 1972. He served in diverse roles in the old General Conference, such as president of the Education Department, editor of the Literary Department, and general secretary. His wife, the former Ozzie Fountain, whom he married in 1932, was also highly active in the UAFWBC, especially in the state of Florida.[46]

The Unified Free Will Baptist Church

Several Black Free Will Baptist churches in the Northeast are affiliated with the Unified Free Will Baptist Church. This body resulted from the migration of Black Free Will Baptists from the South to states such as Connecticut, New York, New Jersey, and Pennsylvania for greater employment opportunity. Exemplary of these congregations is the history of one of the oldest Unified congregations, St. Matthew's Unified Free Will Baptist Church in New Haven, Connecticut. Chartered in New Haven in 1918, the congregation had its origins in a group of African American Free Will Baptists who began meeting in a home in the Orchard Street area of New Haven. They formed a prayer meeting, covenanted as a church under the leadership of Rev. E. M. Hardy, and began meeting in a storefront on Henry Street in New Haven. Rev. Thomas O. Gorman was the first formal pastor, and Mother Matilda Gorman provided the funding for the initial charter of the congregation. The Unified Free Will Baptist Church Inc. maintains its headquarters in New Haven. The Unified Free Will Baptists have several annual conferences, one of the most active of which is the Middle Atlantic Annual Conference, which was organized in 1972 by Rev. Collie Edwards and consists primarily of congregations in New York and New Jersey.[47]

The Original Free Will Baptist Middle Eastern District

Another group of Black Free Will Baptists is the Original Free Will Baptist Middle Eastern District. Headquartered in Wilson, North Carolina, this fellowship comprises around thirty-five congregations primarily in North Carolina but with a few churches in Virginia, Maryland, New Jersey, and Georgia. Its presiding bishop is LaVaughn Hughes. There are also several Black Free Will Baptist churches in Washington, DC, and Maryland. It is difficult to ascertain what parts of the South these congregations originated from. However, it is certain that some of them in the District of Columbia originated from Black Free Will Baptists who migrated from North Carolina.[48]

Free Will Baptists and Race Relations

Majority-Black and majority-White groups of Free Will Baptists have enjoyed fraternal relationships over the twentieth and early-twenty-first centuries. Before the civil rights movement, this tended to involve White ministers being invited to preach in Black churches. While there were exceptions to this rule, the alternative did not typically occur. However, this has changed in recent decades, with predominantly White congregations becoming more racially integrated. Such efforts began in the mid-1960s. Little was said publicly about race during the mid-twentieth century. However, in its first issue in November 1953, *Contact*, the new periodical of the National Association of Free Will Baptists, carried a brief editorial on the first page on the "state of the Negro church." The editor, W. Stanley Mooneyham, executive secretary of the National Association, expressed concerns about the difficulties being experienced by the African American church, particularly concerning a shortage of ministers and ministerial education. "Justice and equal opportunity," he wrote, quoting African American minister H. L. Mitchell, "can come to the Negro race through tolerance and understanding."[49]

A 1967 article in *Contact* by Mark Vandivort, a home missionary in the National Association, however, reveals some of the attitudes prevalent in the National Association and signals a pattern in that body of commenting more frequently about race relations. The article, entitled "Black Power," with the tagline "In the past Free Will Baptists established schools for the American Negro," largely concerned the evangelization of African Americans.[50]

Vandivort insisted, "I believe we as Free Will Baptists have too long had a head-in-sand attitude toward our responsibility to the American Negro. We must not avoid the responsibility of evangelizing and training of the colored people because of prejudiced attitudes and traditions." While Whites who have "fellowship" with their "Negro brethren" will receive criticism from some Whites, he asserted, they must "launch forward into this ministry as God calls and leads with hearts filled with His love." Just as Free Will Baptist missionaries were sharing the gospel in Côte d'Ivoire, West Africa, Vandivort said, White Free Will Baptist ministers of the National Association should share the gospel with African Americans.[51]

Vandivort implored White Free Will Baptists to be "willing to come together at the foot of the cross" with African Americans and "recognize that they can be equal members of the body of Christ. The love of Christ is sufficient to melt racial and class barriers. The Spirit of Christ in our hearts can help us build bridges of fellowship between born-again believers of respective races and social-economic status." Yet Vandivort was hesitant to delve into questions of racial integration, stating that "integration of the local church would not be practical in some areas" yet in those areas where it is impracticable, Vandivort urged, White congregations should seek to forge partnerships with African American congregations, set up vacation Bible schools in Black neighborhoods, "help train the colored preacher both on the local institutional level and the college level," and cooperate with Black Free Will Baptists in missions endeavors. The "first solution to this overwhelming problem is to love the American Negro as a person for whom Christ died and to believe that the 'Gospel of Christ' is indeed 'the power of God unto salvation to everyone that believeth,' whether Jew or Gentile, red, yellow, black or white."[52]

The National Association in annual session has voiced opposition to racism in three separate resolutions, in 1965, 1995, and 2020. Most recently, in 2020, delegates unanimously passed the following resolution, which referred to two previous resolutions:

WHEREAS at the 1965 Annual Session of the National Association of Free Will Baptists, this body overwhelmingly affirmed that "the

National Association of Free Will Baptists believes that all persons should equally enjoy those freedoms and privileges intended by God from creation, taught in the Bible, and provided by the Constitution of the United States of America. The church of Jesus Christ must recognize the dignity of every person as a creation of God and must actively seek ways to bring that person into a right relationship with God, regardless of race or national origin.... We are convinced that the transformation of mankind through faith in Jesus Christ is the greatest instrument available to break down prejudices and cause justice to prevail. We are opposed to violence to secure human rights, and are equally opposed to force to prevent the achievement of such rights," and

WHEREAS at the 1995 Annual Session of the National Association of Free Will Baptists, this body overwhelmingly approved a "Resolution Concerning Racism," which stated, "Whereas all people are created in the image of God (Genesis 1:26) and, whereas all people have descended through 'one blood' from Adam (Acts 17:26), and whereas God desires for all people to be saved (2 Peter 3:9), be it resolved that the National Association of Free Will Baptists does hereby condemn racism in any form and does pledge to proclaim the Gospel freely to all men of every race,"

BE IT RESOLVED that we reaffirm and remain resolute in the established stance of this body.[53]

In the early twenty-first century, both predominantly Black and predominantly White groups regularly exchange associational delegates and preachers, and some United American Free Will Baptist congregations maintain membership in associations affiliated with the National Association. Welch College, along with Mount Olive, Randall, and Southeastern colleges, have led the way in forging relationships with Black Free Will Baptists. Randall University and the Convention of Original Free Will Baptists both have formal agreements with the United American Free Will Baptists.[54]

Conclusion

After 1950, the Free Will Baptist movement continued to expand, primarily through migration and church planting. Both Black and White Free Will Baptists moved north for job opportunities and started mission works and churches all over the Northeast, mid-Atlantic, and upper Midwest. The North Carolina schism of 1962 led to the establishment of a much smaller but still viable denominational organization in the Convention of Original Free Will

Baptists. Black and White denominational networks remained unofficially segregated but always had a small presence of the other race attending their congregations. While overtures of greater cooperation and integration were made during the early years of the civil rights movement, in the twenty-first century it would begin to occur at a more aggressive pace.

Fourteen
INSTITUTIONS AND IDENTITY SINCE 1950

AFTER THE FOUNDING era of the National Association of Free Will Baptists, its institutions began to expand and mature. These institutions were owned and operated by the National Association but governed by semi-autonomous boards elected by its delegates in annual session. They moved the work of the association forward in the areas of home and foreign missions; higher education; publishing; ministry to women, youth, and laymen; denominational promotion; and financing of ministerial retirement and denominational ministry.

Foreign Missions/IM

The 1950s and 1960s witnessed the flowering of the foreign missions effort of the National Association. Missionaries such as Carlisle and Marie Hanna and Volena Wilson in India, Wesley and Aileen Calvery and Herbert and Geraldine Waid in Japan, Lonnie and Anita Sparks and Dan and Margaret Merkh in Côte d'Ivoire, West Africa, and Dave and Pat Franks and Ken and Marvis Eagleton in Brazil opened up new missions in the 1950s under the leadership of the General Director of Free Will Baptist Foreign Missions, Raymond Riggs.[1]

Thomas and Mabel Willey were forced from Cuba by the Castro regime in 1960. Yet Cuba remained a thriving mission field. The sixties would continue the expansion of Free Will Baptist foreign missionary endeavor. Rev. Rolla Smith, who became general director in 1960, worked with Tom Willey

Jr. and his wife Alicia and John and Barbara Moehlman to reopen the field of Panama.[2] J. Reford Wilson, named general director in 1962, increased the number of missionaries from thirty-eight to ninety-four. The board sent Bill and Glenda Fulcher as well as Paul and Amy Robinson to open the field of Uruguay. They called the Merkh family from a successful work in Côte d'Ivoire to start a ministry in France in 1966. The mission in Côte d'Ivoire continued to thrive in the 1960s. Yet it underwent a paradigm shift to medical missions. Missouri physician LaVerne Miley and his wife Lorene started a medical clinic there in 1962 after he had taught at Free Will Baptist Bible College in the 1950s.[3]

The 1970s was a boom decade for the Foreign Missions Department. In 1972, the board introduced missionaries Dock and Norma Jean Caton into Spain. By this time most of the major fields of ministry open to Free Will Baptist missionaries today had been established. Thus the late 1970s and 1980s were a time of maturing and deepening existing mission fields, which Rolla Smith, who had reassumed the general directorship in 1975, successfully oversaw. The eighties and nineties witnessed a deepening of the foreign mission effort under the leadership of R. Eugene Waddell. He led in the formation of partnerships with parachurch ministries such as English Language Institute China and with existing Baptist groups in the former Soviet Union.[4]

James Forlines and Clint Morgan introduced innovations and more partnerships in the early twenty-first century, changing the department's name to Free Will Baptist International Missions (Forlines), then to IM Inc. (Morgan). The recruitment of a new generation of missionaries became a driving force of the ministry. It increasingly emphasized unengaged language groups and missions to countries that restricted missionary access. By 2022 IM had 114 missionaries in eight countries as well as partnerships with twenty-seven evangelical missions agencies in twenty-five countries.[5]

Free Will Baptist Bible College/Welch College

By 1950, Free Will Baptist Bible College had begun offering the four-year Bachelor of Arts (BA) degree. Under founding president L. C. Johnson's visionary leadership, not only the programs of study but also the physical plant increased. By the end of the decade, more than two hundred students were housed and educated in seven buildings, and the college had received accreditation from the Accrediting Association of Bible Colleges.[6]

Johnson steadily built the faculty, adding to Charles and Laura Thigpen and J. P. and Anna Barrow several key instructors who would profoundly shape the character of the college. These included F. Leroy Forlines (1953), Robert E. Picirilli (1955), Mary Ruth Wisehart (1956), and Ralph C. Hampton (1958). The 1960s and 1970s were a time of remarkable growth and expansion for Free Will Baptist Bible College. In 1965, Johnson and the Board of Trustees launched an aggressive campaign that would result in the construction of several new buildings on the campus on West End Avenue in Nashville. The college also continued acquiring historic residences, refurbishing them for academic use. Some of these buildings were notable historic Nashville structures, such as the stately Welch Library, named in honor of John L. and Mary Welch.[7]

In 1979, Johnson retired as president and was succeeded by Dr. Charles Thigpen, who had served as the college's dean for more than twenty years. Thigpen provided strong leadership during difficult days for the institution, when a group of alumni, including some trustees, started a new institution in 1982 because of their desire for a school that would embody a more rigorous sort of separatist fundamentalism than what they had perceived at Free Will Baptist Bible College. This development coincided with the entrance of the baby boomer generation into adulthood, leaving the enrollment of the college far lower than its peak of 648 in the 1981–1982 academic year. Thigpen retired in 1990.[8]

The 1990s and early twenty-first century saw growth under the tenures of presidents C. Thomas Malone (1990–2002) and J. Matthew Pinson (2002–). Malone achieved regional accreditation of the college by the Southern Association of Colleges and Schools and spearheaded several new academic programs. He also led an effort to sell the campus property in the Richland-West End neighborhood in Nashville and relocate the institution to a larger piece of land on which it could grow. Pinson continued adding new academic programs, including graduate degrees, as well as opening Welch Divinity School, which began offering the Master of Divinity degree. In 2012, the institution changed its name to Welch College, in memory of John and Mary Welch. The college fulfilled its vision of relocation when a new campus with Jeffersonian architecture opened in Gallatin in 2017, a small town that had grown into a significant suburb of Nashville.[9]

Home Missions/North American Ministries

The Home Missions Board brought on Damon Dodd, its first full-time secretary, in 1953. He brought visionary leadership to his role, sending out several unpaid bi-vocational ministers, such as Rev. and Mrs. Robert

Wilfong (Florida); Rev. and Mrs. George C. Lee (Nebraska); and Rev. and Mrs. Sylvester Crawford (California). The board sent longtime foreign missionary Bessie Yeley, who had been in Cuba since 1943, to work in Florida. Churches were also planted in Oregon, Washington, and, for the first time, in Mexico, which the National Association designated as a home mission field rather than a foreign one.[10]

General Director Homer Willis (1956–1968), sent full-time church planters to New Hampshire (Rev. and Mrs. Mack Owens), Alaska (Rev. and Mrs. Lee Whaley), and Hawaii (Rev. and Mrs. Luther Sanders). Rev. and Mrs. Ken Walker planted a church in the Washington, DC, suburb of Arlington, Virginia. Also in the 1960s, two later General Directors of Home Missions went out as church planters: Roy and Pat Thomas to Colorado, and Larry and Wanda Powell to the US Virgin Islands.[11]

The 1970s and 1980s witnessed continued expansion under Robert L. Shockey (1973–1978) and longtime church planter Roy Thomas (1978–1995). Thomas's more than twenty years with the department, first as associate director and then as director, had an inestimable influence on it, along with his book *Planting and Growing a Fundamental Church*. Trymon Messer, general director from 1995–2001, was the only layperson ever to be full-time general director of any department of the National Association, except for its Master's Men laymen's ministry and Woman's National Auxiliary Convention.[12]

In the early twenty-first century, Larry Powell (2001–2013) and David Crowe (2013–) led Home Missions. These years focused on the planting of new congregations in urban centers and ministering to the growing Hispanic population in the US (Powell) and diversifying Home Missions by transforming it into a broader organization that was renamed North American Ministries (Crowe). The denomination's laymen's ministry, Master's Men, came under the aegis of North American Ministries in 2015.[13]

North American Ministries placed missionaries in every state except Nevada, as well as the District of Columbia, Canada, Mexico, Puerto Rico, and the US Virgin Islands. The organization was also the endorsing agency for the placing of chaplains in the armed forces as well as other fields.[14]

WNAC

The Woman's National Auxiliary Convention went into the latter half of the twentieth century poised for growth. Agnes Frazier, named executive secretary in 1950, moved the organization forward in vital ways over her three-year tenure. In 1953, when the National Association purchased an old Greystone home on Richland Avenue, down the street from the college, WNAC moved its office there, along with the other national agencies. Gladys Sloan served there as executive secretary, followed by Eunice Edwards of Missouri, who filled the post until her retirement in 1963. Mrs. Cleo Pursell (1963–1985) was the longest-serving executive secretary in the history of the Convention. She oversaw relocation to the new National Association office building on Murfreesboro Road in Nashville.[15]

Under Pursell's leadership one of the memorable ministries of the Auxiliary, the "Missionary Provision Closet," was expanded in the warehouse space the national offices maintained. The Missionary Provision Closet had literally started as a closet under Edwards's leadership in 1962. In this "closet" were stored "provisions" of goods as varied as household electrical appliances, tableware, and other household items. These were shipped to Nashville by hundreds of Free Will Baptist women every year for missionary families. Medical supplies were also collected and provided for the clinic in Côte d'Ivoire.[16]

Dr. Mary Ruth Wisehart assumed the leadership of WNAC in 1985 and served for the next thirteen years. Under her tenure the agency changed its name to Women Nationally Active for Christ in 1993. As a result of her leadership, a number of changes occurred, including scholarships for female students at Free Will Baptist Bible College and the growth of the number of WNAC chapters.[17]

In the twenty-first century, the ministry has been overseen by Marjorie Workman (1985–2008), who came to the role from her post as Dean of Women at Free Will Baptist Bible College, Danita High (2008–2009), Elizabeth Hodges (2009–2022), who in 2014 led WNAC from being a self-standing auxiliary to an official agency of the National Association of Free Will Baptists, and former missionary to Japan Ruth McDonald (2022–).[18]

Sunday School, CTS, and Randall House/D6

The ministries that had to be completely re-created after the North Carolina schism were publishing, Sunday school, and church training (the latter had heretofore been known as Free Will Baptist League). During the controversy that surrounded the 1961 annual session of the National Association in Norfolk, Virginia, the Free Will Baptist Press asked to be released from its contract with the Sunday School Board. Despite subsequent negotiations by the Sunday School Board to attempt to maintain a relationship with the Press, the Press Board would not acquiesce. During that same meeting, the

Sunday School Board announced that it would be hiring a full-time Promotional Editor. Former executive secretary of the National Association. W. Stanley Mooneyham, whom the board had employed as interim editor, had been able to reduce the indebtedness of the Board drastically.[19]

The board hired St. Louis, Missouri, native Roger C. Reeds, who had been serving on the Sunday School Board since 1959. He outlined his plans for jump-starting the Sunday school ministry of the National Association, since the contract with Free Will Baptist Press had been severed in January of that year. The board had persuaded the Oklahoma State Association, which had begun printing Sunday school literature on its own in 1959, to "relinquish" its program, which it agreed to do. Reeds quickly got the department solvent and paid off all its debt. "The Sunday School Department is a service department," he announced. "It is no longer necessary for you to send your gifts to us. Send these to other needy areas of service within our ranks, but let us have the opportunity of serving you with your Sunday School needs."[20]

In 1963 Reeds brought on Florida pastor Harrold Harrison as promotional secretary. Together, these two men would craft a publishing program for the denomination that would set the stage for the next four decades. Harrison led the training for Sunday school officers and teachers—how to organize and administer Sunday schools, teaching methods, and training courses to teach Sunday school teachers the Bible, doctrine, and church history. Often Harrison utilized the materials of the Evangelical Teacher Training Association.[21]

The delegates to the 1971 annual session of the National Association voted in support of the Sunday School Board's desire to move its operations into a new 40,000-square-foot office building on Bush Road in Nashville, Tennessee, which it purchased just after the annual session for $178,000. The building was named "Randall House," after northern Freewill Baptist founder Benjamin Randall. Soon Reeds and Harrison were publishing training materials under the trade name Randall House Publications.[22]

The Free Will Baptist League Board had to regroup in a way similar to the Sunday School Board. After Free Will Baptist Press stopped giving the League Board a percentage of profits as a result of the controversy with the North Carolina State Convention in 1961, the board began publishing its own curriculum in October of that year. While the focus of the Sunday School Board was on Bible exposition, the focus of the League Board was on providing training for youth to lead and serve the church. Thus the curriculum covered subjects such as leadership, stewardship, character development, doctrine, ethics, and Christian living.[23]

In 1964, the National Association voted to change the name of Free Will Baptist League to Church Training Service, or "CTS," as it was usually called. By 1965 Henry Melvin was the chair of the CTS Board, and Samuel Johnson was its full-time general director.[24]

Johnson instituted a new "national competition" in 1964 in which students in various grade levels could compete in contests of Bible knowledge. One contest, known as "Bible Bowl" tested high school students' knowledge of Scripture, doctrine, and basic apologetics books such as Howard F. Vos's *Genesis and Archaeology* and W. Graham Scroggie's *Is the Bible the Word of God?* These competitions were held in conjunction with the annual sessions of the National Association each July. The CTS continued to have a larger representation of laypeople when other boards, other than WNAC and Master's Men, had become almost completely clergy-dominated. In 1963, three laypeople were members of the League Board: Sylvia Dodd of Tennessee, Harold Critcher of Tennessee, and Dorothy Phillips of North Carolina. By 1970 all the members of the CTS Board were clergymen.[25]

In his report, after a decade of service, Samuel Johnson announced that he was stepping down as general director of the CTS Department and that the board had chosen Malcolm C. Fry as his replacement. Fry immediately employed Jonathan Thigpen, son of Charles and Laura Thigpen and recent graduate of Free Will Baptist Bible College, as the Assistant Director of CTS. Fry also added a "Music and Arts Festival" to the slate of competition activities. He and his wife Mae continued the League and CTS tradition of training. They provided not only teacher training for youth ministry but also resources teaching children and adolescents about the Christian tradition, Christian theology, Christian personal and social ethics, Free Will Baptist distinctives of doctrine and practice, and Free Will Baptist history.[26]

At the 1978 annual session in Kansas City, Missouri, delegates to the National Association approved a merger of the Sunday School and Church Training Service departments. The Department, which came to be known officially as Randall House Publications, continued its growth. In the 1990s and early twenty-first century, under the leadership of Alton Loveless (1993–2002) and Ronald Hunter Jr. (2002–), the organization witnessed a number of innovations that moved it forward significantly. Under Loveless, it took leaps forward technologically and continued to develop new products utilizing digital technology. Integrating technological, design, and marketing savvy, Hunter created a new brand, D6, based on Deuteronomy 6, emphasizing family-based discipleship. D6 also began sponsoring an annual conference that featured influential speakers in the evangelical family ministry movement. The organization formally changed its name to D6 Family Ministry in 2023.[27]

The Executive Office

The Executive Department took a great stride forward in 1953 when Executive Secretary-Treasurer W. Stanley Mooneyham coordinated the purchase of a historic home at 3801 Richland Avenue, a block away from the campus of Free Will Baptist Bible College. Mooneyham served from 1953 to 1959 and would later go on to serve as president of World Vision International. The creation of a cooperative program of denominational giving as well as the initiation of a monthly denominational magazine, *Contact*, in 1953 exemplify Mooneyham's success in organizational development. Billy Melvin served as executive secretary from 1959 to 1967, after which he became Executive Director of the National Association of Evangelicals. Melvin helped guide the National Association through the North Carolina schism and also oversaw the relocation of the national offices to a new location on Murfreesboro Road in Nashville in 1965.[28] Later executive secretaries included Rufus Coffey (1967–1979); the longest-standing executive secretary, Melvin Worthington (1979–2002), who led in the move of the national offices in 1991 to a new 30,000-square-foot facility in the Nashville suburb of Antioch, Tennessee; Keith Burden (2002–2019), who replaced *Contact* with a new bi-monthly magazine, *ONE*; and Edward Moody (2019–), who emphasized congregational revitalization and denominational renewal.[29]

Financial Services Organizations

The Board of Retirement and Insurance grew out of the National Board of Superannuation, which was led by Mrs. J. E. Simpson. In 1955, the board hired its first full-time director, Rev. K. V. Shutes. After his resignation two years later, his wife Lora took over as executive secretary-treasurer.[30]

In 1969 the Board of Retirement and Insurance replaced the Superannuation Board, assuming the retirement plan of the North Carolina State Association of Free Will Baptists, which was formed after the schism with the North Carolina State Convention. Herman Hersey had been director of that program and continued as part-time director until 1973, when he and his wife Vernie moved to Nashville to administer the program full-time. William Evans succeeded Hersey (1993–2005). In the twenty-first century, the organization was led by Ray Lewis (2005–2015) and John Brummitt (2015–).

By 2021, the assets under management of the Board of Retirement and Insurance had topped 112 million dollars.[31]

The Board of Retirement created another financial institution, the Free Will Baptist Foundation, in 1980. It became a separate agency in 2005 with a unique board structure in which it had nine elected trustees as well as the directors of each of the agencies of the National Association: Free Will Baptist Bible College, International Missions, Home Missions, Randall House Publications, WNAC, Master's Men, the Board of Retirement, and the Executive Office. The foundation was established to help churches and church members in planned giving, allowing for the creation of trust funds, annuities, and other instruments for endowing Free Will Baptist ministries with future financial support. The foundation's first director after its separation from the Board of Retirement was William Evans, who remained director until 2007, when he was succeeded by David Brown, who had been chief financial officer of the Board of Retirement and Free Will Baptist Foundation. Under Brown's tenure, the foundation's assets increased to more than 113 million dollars, and the foundation began making charitable grants to Free Will Baptist ministries. The most notable of these grants was given to build a women's center in Côte d'Ivoire, West Africa.[32] Brown was succeeded by Brent Patrick, who was named CEO of the organization in 2025.

Origins of the Commissions of the National Association

A concern to ensure the continued orthodoxy of the National Association in the face of Protestant liberal theology resulted in the establishment of the association's first commission in 1959. The Resolutions Committee at the annual session that year recommended the formation of a committee to study and write about theological liberalism and secularism. In 1960, it was referred to as the Commission on the Study of Theological Liberalism, and its first five members were R. Eugene Waddell, Ronald Creech, Bobby Jackson, Paul J. Ketteman, and N. R. Smith. In its first report at the 1961 annual session, the commission said that, while "Modernism" was "not as bold as it once was, ... Neo-Orthodoxy hides behind the cloak of evangelical terms to disguise its infidelity. This could be our greatest threat in doctrine, because it is so difficult to uncover." The report also discussed the "dangers" of "secularism and materialism," noting that their goal was to "alert" the denomination to these trends by writing articles about them to be published in denominational periodicals.[33]

In 1962, F. Leroy Forlines, theology professor at Free Will Baptist Bible

College, was elected to what was by that time being called the Commission on Theological Liberalism. Forlines was immediately elected chair and would prove to be the longest-standing member of the commission, serving on it for fifty years and giving it much of its character. In the mid-1980s the commission's name was changed to the Commission for Theological Integrity.[34]

The second commission the National Association established was the Historical Commission, which was elected in July 1963. At the annual session that year in Detroit, Michigan, the body received a special report from the Executive Committee. That report recommended the founding of a commission for the archiving, researching, and writing of the history of the Free Will Baptist Church, recommending that the library of Free Will Baptist Bible College "serve as a repository for such historical materials as will be gathered." The original commission comprised Damon Dodd, Bill Hill, and George C. Lee Jr.[35]

In 1964, Bill (William F.) Davidson was added to the commission. He would go on to write a doctoral dissertation on the early history of the Palmer tradition and later would produce the first scholarly history of the denomination, *The Free Will Baptists in America*, in 1985. Robert E. Picirilli was elected in 1973. Picirilli would, in retirement, serve as curator of the Free Will Baptist Historical Collection at Free Will Baptist Bible College and would go on to write major books on the movement's history. Picirilli would serve five decades on the commission, four of them alongside *Contact* editor Jack Williams.[36]

The Media Commission of the National Association was founded as the Radio and Television Commission in 1983. That year, on the recommendation of the General Board, the body approved a motion to establish "a five-member commission to formulate and execute plans to bring into being television and radio programs commensurate to the needs and opportunities of our people." That original commission consisted of George C. Lee, Guy Owens, Sandy Goodfellow, Larry Hampton, and James Vallance.[37]

In 1997, the commission began emphasizing video media, producing the commission's first television commercial. Also that year it recommended a name change to "Free Will Baptist Media Commission." In 2001, it shifted attention to online media, beginning to offer advice and services to Free Will Baptist churches and associations and later livestreaming the annual session and leadership conference of the National Association.[38]

In 1987, the Executive Office of the National Association published *Rejoice: The Free Will Baptist Hymn Book*. The National Association had elected a Hymn Book Committee to produce the work. That committee consisted of Vernon Whaley (chair), R. Douglas Little (secretary), W. Blaine Hughes, Leroy Cutler, Bill Gardner, Ted Wilbanks, and Rodney D. Whaley, as well as an advisory group consisting of Robert Picirilli, Roger Reeds, and Melvin Worthington. At the annual session of the National Association in Kansas City, Missouri, in July 1988, the committee recommended that the association start a music commission.[39]

The commission's stated purposes were to "preserve" and "promote Free Will Baptist hymnody, publish the *Rejoice* hymnal for non-Free Will Baptist churches, publish choral music and recordings, and engage in a comprehensive, age-graded program of music education for the churches of the National Association of Free Will Baptists." The original commission consisted of Vernon Whaley, Douglas Little, Bill Gardner, Blaine Hughes, and Rodney Whaley.[40]

Other Educational Endeavors

Smaller educational institutions other than Free Will Baptist Bible College/Welch College were started in other regions, some because of perceived distance of the churches in a given region from the national college's location in Middle Tennessee, others for differences in theology and approaches to evangelical identity. For example, the California State Association started California Bible Institute in 1955, later known as California Christian College. The institution started as a stop-gap measure to provide ministerial training for California Free Will Baptist pastors because other educational options were a great distance away. The first Board of Christian Education of the California State Association of Free Will Baptists consisted of Dean Moore, Wade Jernigan, Jerry Dudley, Winston Lawless, and Ralph Hampton Sr. Hampton's commitment to education would become manifest in his sons Ralph and Charles, who would spend most of their careers on the faculty and administration of Free Will Baptist Bible College. California Christian College continued to serve the needs of those called into the service of the church among California Free Will Baptists until under financial strain it sold its assets to an evangelical nonprofit in 2022.[41]

Randall University was founded as Oklahoma Bible College in 1959. Oklahoma Free Will Baptists tended strongly toward amillennialism and the "backsliding" rather than "apostasy" view of perseverance (for the distinction, see chapter 10). Thus many were unhappy with the approach at Free Will Baptist Bible College, which taught the apostasy view and tended toward different varieties of premillennialism in the classroom. So when a series of Bible institutes began being taught across the churches of the Oklahoma State Association, there was momentum for a school owned and operated by that association. Oklahoma Bible College initially started in the basement of First Free Will Baptist Church in Tulsa and moved to Wagoner the next fall. Its founding board consisted of John West, Wade Jernigan, Melvin Bingham, Weldon Wood, and Marlin Bivins. The school's name was changed to Hillsdale Free Will Baptist College in 1971 and eventually to Randall University in 2016. Served by presidents such as Daniel Parker, J. D. O'Donnell, Bill Jones, Edwin Wade, Jim Shepherd, Carl Cheshier, Timothy Eaton, and Robert Thompson, the institution has largely been supported by the Oklahoma State Association but with some support and board representation from neighboring states. Randall is accredited by the Transnational Association of Christian Colleges and Schools (TRACS).[42]

Southeastern Free Will Baptist College started in 1983 as a result of a perceived drift toward neo-evangelicalism at Free Will Baptist Bible College by a group of separatist fundamentalist pastors, some of whom were on the latter institution's Board of Trustees. Southeastern's story will be told more fully below in connection with developments in fundamentalist-evangelical identity in the National Association. The TRACS-accredited school has been served by presidents such as Randy Cox, Joe Ange, Billy Bevan, Lorenza Stox, Jim Marcum, Nate Ange, and Jeff Jones.[43]

The Development of Orphanages and Children's Homes

Most of the southern Free Will Baptist energy toward social ministry and the alleviation of poverty in the twentieth century coalesced in the care of orphans and other children from disadvantaged backgrounds. Orphanages were seen as an ideal way to fulfill the sentiment in James 1:27 that the center of "pure and undefiled religion" was caring for widows and orphans in their distress. Often ladies aid societies and women's auxiliaries were leaders in raising awareness and financial support for orphanages. The state associations of North Carolina, South Carolina, Tennessee, and Alabama provided such institutions that were supported by Free Will Baptists throughout the United States and Canada.

The first modern Free Will Baptist children's home found its origins in discussions from 1910 to 1915 regarding the desire of many in the North Carolina State Convention to establish "a home for homeless boys and girls of our state." By 1916 the State Convention appointed an orphanage committee. Soon Rev. and Mrs. Ben Deans donated fifty acres outside Middlesex,

North Carolina. Over the next two years, the committee constructed a large, three-story building and planted numerous fruit trees on the land. The Free Will Baptist Orphanage was established at Middlesex, North Carolina, and admitted its first children in May 1920.[44]

The Tennessee State Association of Free Will Baptists established an orphanage in the mountains of East Tennessee in May 1939. The idea for an orphanage was a large part of the motivation for starting a state association in Tennessee. Mr. and Mrs. I. L. Stanley were employed as superintendents of the new Free Will Baptist Orphanage in Greeneville. The orphanage opened at the 160-acre Camp Creek School campus, which had formerly been owned by the United Presbyterian Church and then Greene County.[45]

In the 1940s, the Free Will Baptists of Alabama began to consider purchasing a dilapidated women's academy campus in Eldridge for use as an orphanage. Free Will Baptist men went to work to refurbish the campus, while ladies aid societies raised support. After the children's home was started, the children formed a choir and drove from church to church in a school bus singing in handmade choir robes and raising money for the orphanage, which began operations in 1948 and was eventually named Free Will Baptist Children's Home.[46]

The Free Will Baptist Children's Home, which began as a ministry of the South Carolina State Association, opened its doors in Turbeville, South Carolina, in October 1949. The South Carolina Children's Home provided nearly seven decades of foster care and other services for families in a Christian context until its closure under financial constraints in 2014.[47]

The most recent addition to children and family services ministries among Free Will Baptists was Harvest Free Will Baptist Child Care Ministries in Duffield, Virginia. In 1992, Harvest's founders began to sense the need for a children's home in southwestern Virginia. The home officially opened in 1993.[48]

Developments in Doctrine and Practice

Free Will Baptist faith and practice did not so much change from its basic commitments in the twentieth and twenty-first centuries as much as it was refined. The early twentieth century continued apace from trends in the nineteenth. While the National Association after its founding in 1935 funneled energy more toward organization than theology, it also proved to be a catalyst for the advance of Free Will Baptist theology. This occurred chiefly through the work of its educational institution, Free Will Baptist Bible

College/Welch College. Ironically, however, at just the point that Free Will Baptist theology began to attain maturity and influence in the late twentieth century, anti-intellectual influences from the wider culture and other segments of evangelicalism began to erode theological interest and concern. As market-oriented pragmatism became the watchword after the 1960s, a dynamic developed in some segments of the movement that was not so much anti-theological as it was atheological.[49]

The irony is that the desire for ministerial fitness and learning among Free Will Baptists in the nineteenth-century South had been enormous given the socioeconomic and educational disadvantages of most Free Will Baptist ministers. The extant circular letters of many Free Will Baptist ministers whose highest level of education was not even a high school diploma demonstrate an impressive concern for doctrine and theology. Yet they also evidence a level of rhetorical skill the modern reader would be surprised to find in a contemporary article written by a writer with a graduate degree. If one could bottle the seriousness regarding theology and ecclesial practice among nineteenth-century Free Will Baptists and pour it out into the contemporary context—with the ease of obtaining theological education and having thousands of free online books at one's fingertips—the result would be astounding. The general educational and theological level of the ministry continued to rise in the late twentieth and early twenty-first centuries. However, in the late twentieth century, a new form of technologically savvy anti-intellectualism replaced the older rural anti-education sentiment in some pockets of the denomination. A phenomenon that media ecologists call not illiteracy but aliteracy began to appear. Still the Free Will Baptist ministry, as a rule, became more theologically literate after World War II.[50]

Welch College produced two scholars who laid the superstructure for Free Will Baptist theology in the late twentieth and early-twenty-first centuries: F. Leroy Forlines (d. 2020) and Robert E. Picirilli. Forlines was a systematic theologian and cultural apologist, and Picirilli was a Greek exegete and biblical theologian. Forlines and Picirilli produced a body of work that built on what had been preserved from confessions of faith, sermons, and Sunday school and League literature but had not been written in systematic theologies and biblical commentaries. Starting with a course taught by L. C. Johnson, president of Free Will Baptist Bible College, they began to forge a Free Will Baptist theology built on a synthesis of their own doctrinal inheritance, the thought of Jacobus Arminius, and nineteenth-century transmitters of Reformed scholasticism such as William G. T. Shedd and Charles Hodge (especially Shedd). This product was very much like the thought of their

English General Baptist forebears Thomas Helwys and Thomas Grantham, though they had not read those thinkers until later in the twentieth century after they had already produced their systems.[51]

Two legacies of Forlines and Picirilli were the most enduring. First, they articulated what came to be known as Reformed Arminianism. Second, they articulated a broadly Reformed understanding of the Christian worldview and its posture toward modern culture that was characteristic of Evangelical Renaissance thinkers such as Carl F. H. Henry and Kenneth Kantzer. These two emphases would shape the subsequent trajectory of Welch College and through it the wider denomination. Forlines also served as chair for fifty years of the National Association's Commission for Theological Integrity. This commission provided a vehicle for Forlines's version of evangelical orthodoxy and his broadly Augustinian-Kuyperian approach to thought and culture—what he called "Christian worldview thinking." Picirilli mediated this approach not only through his own voluminous writings but also through the twelve-volume *Randall House Bible Commentary*, of which he served as general editor. This commentary series transmitted the exegetical rationale for Free Will Baptist theology to a wider audience.[52]

Reformed Arminianism was simply a refinement of the more Reformed themes of total depravity, penal substitutionary atonement, the imputation of the righteousness of Christ in justification, and the Reformed account of sanctification common in southern Free Will Baptist confessional documents (though not inconsistent with the northern Freewill Baptist *Treatise* after it was revised in 1871). The implications of this system for the doctrine of perseverance and apostasy caused ripples in the mid-twentieth century. In the twentieth century, the doctrine that the seventeenth-century Arminian Puritan divine John Goodwin had termed "repeated regeneration" began to become evident in the extant records. This doctrine held that believers could lose their salvation through sinful acts and be restored to salvation after repentance. This approach became the strongest in the areas that had been influenced by the Randall movement but was not limited to those areas.[53]

In 1959 Forlines wrote a booklet entitled *The Doctrine of Perseverance*. That work stated that, because believers are imputed with the obedience of Christ, they are as righteous as Christ in the divine estimation as long as they persist in faith. Only by making shipwreck of saving faith (an image from 1 Timothy 1:19) can individuals apostatize, after which they will be irremediably lost. The booklet was published and widely distributed by the Free Will Baptist Press in Ayden, North Carolina. Yet it created controversy in some quadrants of the denomination. The controversy bubbled to the surface in 1968, when the Oklahoma State Association recommended to the General Board the inclusion of a passage in the *Treatise* that affirmed that the backslider can be in a lost condition yet not be apostate. This statement was referred to the Executive Committee to study and return with a recommendation the following year. A motion was introduced, but failed, to prohibit Free Will Baptist Bible College faculty from teaching, for that year, that irremediable apostasy is the only kind of fall from grace. The delegates directed the Executive Committee to appoint "a representative group of persons from across the denomination" to consider the matter. That committee came back with an appendix to the *Treatise* in 1969 that was carefully written to satisfy both sides and was approved by the body. This controversy receded significantly over the next forty years as younger generations embraced the teaching of Forlines and Picirilli, and their former students, which would come to be called Reformed Arminianism. Many ministers, however, still hold to the other position and are in good standing with the denomination.[54]

Two other appendixes were added to the *Treatise* in the 1970s. The first arose from the controversy in the evangelical Protestant community regarding the inerrancy of Scripture and the resultant publication in 1978 of the Chicago Statement on Biblical Inerrancy. The National Association wished to clarify its position and thus in 1977 asked the Executive Committee to draft a statement on biblical inerrancy to be added to chapter 1 of the *Treatise*, as well as a more extended appendix to the *Treatise* on the subject. The delegates adopted those statements at the annual session in 1979.[55]

The charismatic movement became a second area of concern in the 1970s, as a small smattering of Free Will Baptist churches dotting the American landscape in the 1970s became charismatic and left the denomination. The memory had lingered of several churches in the Carolinas becoming Pentecostal in the early twentieth century, even forming a very small Pentecostal Free Will Baptist denomination. The charismatic movement associated with televangelists such as Oral Roberts had become popular in segments of American evangelicalism in the 1970s. Concern about the influence of this movement on the Free Will Baptist Church led the General Board to propose to the annual session in 1978 an appendix to the *Treatise* on "Glossolalia." The statement, which committed the denomination to a non-charismatic view of the gift of tongues and other modern interpretations of the charismatic gifts, was adopted in 1979.[56]

The 1970s and 1980s brought with them identity-forming episodes similar to those that occurred in the late 1950s and early 1960s with the North Carolina schism. After that division, the denomination moved slightly to the right on the spectrum of American evangelicalism. The separatist fundamentalism of figures such as the Independent Baptist John R. Rice and his widely distributed periodical *The Sword of the Lord* began to exert more profound influence in the National Association, especially in the states along the Atlantic coast.

Under Stanley Mooneyham's and Billy Melvin's tenures as executive secretary, the denomination had strengthened its relationship with the larger evangelical community. This is exemplified by the National Association's joining the National Association of Evangelicals (NAE) and the fact that speakers from that organization were prominently featured in the worship services of the annual sessions during the 1950s and 1960s. Furthermore, by 1971 Melvin, then NAE Executive Director, was still giving reports from the NAE at the annual session. This trend would be reversed when the delegates to the 1972 annual session voted to withdraw from the NAE. The resolution cited the fact that "there are individuals and churches in the denomination who object to our affiliation" with the NAE and that requiring membership in an "extra-denominational" body is "inconsistent with the autonomy of the local church." Ten years later at the 1982 annual session, a resolution was defeated that referred to the 1972 action, saying "that vote had been vindicated by the continued liberalism now so clearly evident in the NAE." The resolution called on the denomination to "re-affirm our position as a fundamentalist denomination." Urging the body to "go on record as opposing the liberal trends in the NAE," it directed denominational publications not to give "favorable coverage" to the NAE but rather seek to inform the denomination of the "dangers of the ecclesiastical and spiritual compromise of the National Association of Evangelicals." The resolution was defeated.[57]

This struggle for a separatist fundamentalist identity rather than a broader evangelical one manifested itself in a schism within Free Will Baptist Bible College (FWBBC) in the early 1980s. That division resulted in the formation of Southeastern Free Will Baptist College, which opened its doors to seventy-one students in the fall semester of 1983. The origins of the institution lay in the concerns of a number of separatist fundamentalist pastors, some of whom served on the Board of Trustees of Free Will Baptist Bible College. These pastors believed that the college was not robust enough on the distinctive tenets of separatist fundamentalism and had succumbed to neo-evangelicalism. They also believed that the college's support of Christian K-12 education was too tepid because it considered it appropriate to prepare students to teach in public schools as well as Christian schools. The college was also perceived as too focused on denominationalism and not enough on the local congregation. Further, these ministers believed that FWBBC, despite its strong core of biblical studies, had invested too many resources in the liberal arts and career preparation and was not committed enough to the training of students for full-time Christian ministry. The ministerial training program was perceived as producing ministers who lacked strong pastoral authority and were not aggressive enough in evangelism. Free Will Baptist Bible College issued a rebuttal to these assertions in a pamphlet entitled "The Record Speaks."[58]

Into this set of circumstances came the fact that FWBBC theology professor F. Leroy Forlines was asked in a class whether the wine Jesus made at the wedding at Cana, recorded in the Gospel of John, was fermented, to which he answered yes. There was a demand by some ministers for Forlines's resignation, which the administration of the college and a majority of its board refused to meet. After a series of ensuing events, in April 1982, a group of seventy-eight men met at Hilltop Free Will Baptist Church in Fuquay-Varina, North Carolina, and voted to start a new college. It was agreed that the board of directors would consist of nine permanent members in addition to seven rotating members and the college's president.[59]

The board of directors founded Southeastern Free Will Baptist College with a commitment to training ministers in the sort of thoroughgoing fundamentalism of which they believed the administration and faculty of Free Will Baptist Bible College had fallen short. Thus its founding principles consisted of an emphasis on the local church, strong pastoral authority, the "Fundamentalist-Separatist" approach to "personal sanctification" and "ecclesiastical affiliation," strong "personal soul-winning" and worldwide evangelism, and a mandate for Christian schools.[60]

The college opened in Virginia Beach, Virginia, at Gateway Free Will Baptist Church, the largest Free Will Baptist congregation at the time, which was being led by board member Dale Burden. The fledgling college utilized the facilities of the church and the large Christian school it maintained. Randy Cox, pastor of First Free Will Baptist Church in Raleigh, North Carolina, became the first president, on a part-time basis. In 1985, the board of directors elected Joe Ange as full-time president of Southeastern. In the previous decade, Ange had served at Free Will Baptist Bible College in the role of director of religious activities. The enrollment in the fall semester of 1985 was 170 students. In 1987, unable to acquire land in the area surrounding Virginia Beach, the college board purchased a new campus of sixty acres near Raleigh, North Carolina, in the community of Wendell, and began construction that year. Classes opened on the new campus in October.[61]

Difficulties arose as the college board adopted views that a minority of the board and some of the institution's faculty and supporters deemed problematic. These included the view that the King James Version was the only acceptable English translation of the Bible and that the blood of Jesus was divine. This state of affairs eventually led to the resignations of key faculty members who protested these affirmations, as well as to a splinter in the college constituency. A minority led by Dale Burden founded a new college in Virginia Beach on the campus of Gateway Christian School known as Gateway Christian College, with former Southeastern professor Bruce Barnes as president. This school would operate for ten years before closing under financial constraints in 2013.[62]

That no appendixes were added to the *Treatise* for the remainder of the twentieth century and the first eight years of the twenty-first points to the period after the schism between Free Will Baptist Bible College and Southeastern Free Will Baptist College as one less beset by controversy and development in doctrine and practice. The next appendix added to the *Treatise* originated in response to the increasing acceptance of same-sex marriage in American society. The delegates to the 2008 convention of Women Nationally Active for Christ passed a resolution opposing same-sex marriage and supporting a constitutional amendment against it. That same year the delegates to the annual session of the National Association approved an appendix on marriage and sexuality written by the Commission for Theological Integrity. That appendix affirmed the traditional Christian view limiting marriage to members of the opposite sex. In 2022 the National Association amended that appendix to include language affirming that one's sex at birth is determinative for one's gender.[63]

One shift in denominational practice in the twentieth century concerned the creeping clericalization of the denomination. While this was not unusual in the history of denominationalism in North America, it had its effects among Free Will Baptists at all organizational levels, local, state, and national. The early history of the National Association witnessed high levels of participation of the laity, with laymen and laywomen serving on local, state, and national boards and committees and holding offices. However, by the 1970s, such involvement had, for all intents and purposes, faded away. This would shift in the early twenty-first century, when greater efforts were made at the National Association level to involve laymen and laywomen in the business of the association.[64]

This issue dovetails with the role of women in the denomination. While there was a small number of female preachers when the National Association came together in 1935, mostly in areas that had had greater influence from the Randall movement, the denomination as a rule continued limiting ministerial ordination to men. Over the course of the twentieth century, as the denomination became more active in the wider evangelical community, the presence of women ordained to ministry became non-existent in the National Association, though it was accepted (but very limited) in the Convention of Original Free Will Baptists and among the African American Free Will Baptists. At the same time, the denomination's openness to women's leadership in non-ministerial roles also decreased markedly. It is difficult to discern whether this development resulted from the increasing clericalization of the denomination or its views on women's roles per se. In the twenty-first century, the denomination has, by and large, maintained solidarity with what has come to be known as the "complementarian" understanding of sex roles in the family and church. However, women have increasingly been accorded more and more influence and have been gradually invited into non-ordained-ministry leadership roles.[65]

Eschatology served as a minor source of conflict in the twentieth century. Some Free Will Baptists were amillennial, especially in Appalachia and west of the Mississippi River, while others were premillennial. Though in the nineteenth century postmillennialism was more common, and while there were always a handful of postmillennialists in the twentieth century, by mid-century that position had mostly dissipated. A few associations required their ordinands to affirm amillennialism, which was for many years the eschatological posture of Hillsdale Free Will Baptist College (later Randall University), the college of the Oklahoma State Association. Southeastern Free Will Baptist College in North Carolina was consistently dispensational premillennial. Welch College leaned toward different stripes of premillennialism but tolerated divergent views. However, by and large, the denomination, as it had always done since its origins in the English General Baptist movement in the seventeenth century, left the timing of the return of Christ and other related eschatological details as open questions.[66]

Other developments in doctrine and practice in the twentieth and twenty-first centuries included the trend that soteriology eclipsed ecclesiology as a focus of discussion and debate, as compared with the nineteenth century, when ecclesiology was at least as central to the Free Will Baptist consciousness. This coincided with the influence of the Independent Baptist and non-denominational megachurch movements on segments of the denomination. In the zeal to oppose the North Carolina State Convention's espousal of a connectionalism that resulted in a conference selecting which faction in a church schism was the true congregation, some Free Will Baptists pendulum-swung to a posture of hyper-autonomy of the local congregation. This approach de-emphasized the interdependence and accountability of local congregations to their associations and conferences. Along with this went a lessening of emphasis on the local conference's oversight of its ministers, and, in some cases, a decrease in emphasis of the subscription of ordinands and ministers to the confessional standards of the association or conference. Still, the vast majority of Free Will Baptists at the local level continued to require confessional subscription of their ministers, and most Free Will Baptist pastors continued faithful attendance at quarterly and annual meetings of their local conferences.[67]

In the twenty-first century, the National Association witnessed a renaissance of interest among many of its younger ministers in theology and its implications for the church, culture, and society. This is somewhat ironic, given the conventional wisdom of the day that younger people were uninterested in doctrine, theology, and the life of the mind; more interested in being segregated from older generations and entertained; and reticent to assume leadership roles. In general, the denomination's younger adults, especially those in ministerial, missionary, and diaconal roles, tended to exhibit a desire for renewal through retrieval of the Christian tradition in its Protestant and Free Will Baptist expressions.[68]

Growth Patterns in the National Association

In 1937, the first year for which a statistical report was made for the National Association, 1,142 churches and 80,344 members were recorded. The report acknowledged how difficult it was to get accurate records because some churches and associations were incomplete or inconsistent in their reporting. This difficulty would continue for the next eight and a half decades. Another difficulty with National Association membership records concerns the number of Free Will Baptist congregations or associations in any given year that are independent. At the present, it is estimated that, in associations that are not in fellowship with the National Association, apart from the African American Free Will Baptists and the Convention of Original Free Will Baptists, there are more than 325 churches with an estimated membership of more than 25,000. This does not include scores of independent Free Will Baptist congregations that are not members of associations for various reasons.[69]

After that initial statistical report in 1937, more associations began to affiliate with the National Association, and by 1948, 1,594 churches with 118,854 members were represented. In 1961, the year before the North Carolina schism, 2,150 churches reported with a membership of 193,664. The next year, after the North Carolina State Convention severed ties with the

National Association, that number was reduced to 1,974 churches with 168,706 members. Over the next two decades, the National Association would grow consistently. In 1972, 2,250 congregations reported with 198,274 members. In 1982, there were 2,505 churches reporting 243,658 members. That was the record year for the number of churches and their membership in the National Association. It represented a 44 percent increase in membership over 1962, the year after the schism.[70]

Over the next forty years, the denomination would decline in membership (see Table 2 below). This decline resulted from several factors, chief of which were four: first, the late twentieth and early twenty-first centuries witnessed the increasing secularization of society. Too many churches had an attractional model of ministry, based either on a mid-twentieth-century fundamentalist model or a late twentieth-century seeker-sensitive model. Neither of these equipped congregations with the depth needed to meet the challenges of secularization. Second, many congregations left their associations while remaining Free Will Baptist doctrinally, while others left for other denominations or non-denominationalism. This often occurred because of a lack of interest in theological concerns, which allowed them to call ministers who were unsupportive of the denomination's confessional vision. Third, and most importantly, seismic demographic shifts occurred around Free Will Baptist churches. These took place in hundreds of rural communities where factory farming and other economic shifts had drastically decreased the population in these areas during this period. Also, many urban churches found themselves languishing in neighborhoods that had undergone substantial demographic shifts in the late twentieth century. Often they lacked the ability to adapt to the socioeconomic changes in their churches' communities. These rural-urban demographic shifts came together with a decline in birth rates from a generation earlier to erode the denomination's membership base. The fourth factor loomed in the background of the others: independent movements outside the denomination had a deep impact on many churches, namely the Independent Baptist movement, which influenced the denomination's right flank, and the non-denominational megachurch movement, which influenced its left. These movements intentionally discouraged denominational identity, theology, and participation. This dynamic led many congregations to lose their Free Will Baptist identity and leave. It caused other churches to withdraw from the high level of denominational activity that had characterized them in previous decades. This phenomenon in turn weakened the support network for smaller, struggling churches at the local association and conference level.

In 2019, the last reporting year before the onset of the COVID-19 pandemic, the National Association comprised 2,035 churches with a membership of 132,631. Ironically, however, strong congregations of varied sizes and demographics had been carrying the weight of the financial support of the institutions of the National Association, and most of those organizations witnessed stability and growth over this same period. Despite the decline in North America, the international statistics reported by IM Inc., have increased. As of 2021, outside North America, 271 churches and 119 missions works and meeting points existed with a weekly attendance of 42,585. The National Association united with Free Will Baptist associations in other countries to form the International Fellowship of Free Will Baptist Churches in 1995. At the beginning of the third decade of the twenty-first century, denominational leaders were hopeful for stabilization. Those hopes were based on the numbers of the movement's youth who were willing to enter ordained ministry or missionary service and who, surprising to many, demonstrated increasingly greater interest in the theological and historical dimensions of their religious identity.[71]

Table 2
National Association Membership and Churches

Year	Reported Membership	Reported Churches
1938	82,752	1,143
1948	118,854	1,594
1958	184,287	2,166
1961	193,664	2,150
1962	168,706	1,974
1972	198,274	2,250
1982	243,658	2,505
1992	209,223	2,317
2002	194,583	2,331
2012	162,269	2,043
2019	132,631	2,035

1961 and 1962 are shown to indicate the drop in membership after the North Carolina Schism of 1962.

EPILOGUE

The Free Will Baptist story is one of resilience and survival in the face of incredible odds. The denomination has managed to persist for four centuries in its very nuanced doctrinal posture—Arminian but not Wesleyan, Reformed but not Calvinist, Baptist but not Anabaptist.[1] The survival of this minority Protestant group is, in itself, a compelling story, if for no other reason than that they consistently persevered in the face of repeated persecution and cultural pressures. In the seventeenth century, they were opposed by Anglicans, in the eighteenth by Calvinist Baptists, in the nineteenth by the Disciples of Christ, and in the twentieth by Pentecostalism and non-denominational fundamentalism and evangelicalism. Yet in each instance, they rebounded, giving more articulate voice to their theological tradition.

The Free Will Baptists were always betwixt and between. Their very origins reflected this liminal space. In the seventeenth century, their combination of Arminianism and Nonconformity put them at odds with the entire Protestant establishment. After all, Anglicans tended to be Arminian but suppressed Nonconformity. Nonconformists tended to be Calvinists. Both deplored believer's baptism. In the eighteenth century, the Free Will Baptists ran afoul of the strict Calvinist New Light Baptists of the Philadelphia Association, which all but destroyed them. In the nineteenth century, the movement was set upon by the Disciples of Christ, who heavily proselytized among its ranks.

Even after Baptists began moderating their Calvinism in the nineteenth century, the Southern Free Will Baptists maintained their historic faith and practice. It would have been easy (similar to the northern Free Baptists) for this small group of believers to accept the doctrine of eternal security, give up their historic practice of the washing of the saints' feet, and simply become Southern Baptist. This is especially true after the Civil War and Reconstruction left the largely southern denomination even poorer and weaker than before. Yet they persisted, time after time, in the face of opposition from larger movements with far greater resources. In the twentieth and twenty-first centuries, they have continued to maintain their tradition in the face of non-denominational fundamentalism and evangelicalism, which have, each in its own way, gnawed away at the edges of Free Will Baptist identity.

The history of the Free Will Baptist Church is a story of this survival as a denomination that remained aloof from the American Protestant mainstream, whether Baptist or Methodist. It is also interesting in its nuanced tension between poles in American religious history. These characterizations are accurate with regard to both the Palmer (southern) and Randall (northern) movements. The continued, separate existence of Free Will Baptists resulted from theological, not socio-cultural, differences with these larger movements in American evangelicalism. Tension between poles related to questions of confessionalism, pietism, orthodoxy, and ecumenism also make the Free Will Baptist story compelling. Theology looms so large in this narrative because it is what kept the Free Will Baptists as a distinct, smaller denomination, aloof from the larger, more dominant Baptist and Methodist expressions of American Protestantism.

The Palmer and Randall Movements

Before discussing these themes, it is important to draw together one of the overarching issues in this book: the Palmer and Randall movements and their influence on the continuing Free Will Baptist story. The modern popular history of the movement has tended to place too much emphasis on Benjamin Randall and the northern Free Baptist General Conference that originated from him. That movement largely disappeared in 1911 when it merged with the Northern Baptist Convention. Perhaps the reason for this imbalance is the fact that the northern denomination was a wealthy movement that led the way in American social reform and the abolition of slavery in the nineteenth century. Perhaps the reason is that, owing to its wealth, the Randall movement left behind an impressive record of intellectual output. The myriad hardcover books from the northern Freewill Baptists were far more accessible than the smaller, ephemeral output of their poorer cousins to the south.

However, the historian cannot help but notice how few of the churches that formed the National Association in 1935 hailed from the tiny percentage of the Randall movement that stayed out of the 1911 merger. In the late 1940s, for example, around 50 percent of the membership of the National Association was from the coastal states of the southeast. About 80 percent were from east of the Mississippi. While there was Randall influence in Ohio, West Virginia, and Kentucky, it was mixed with origins from the south. The same is true of Missouri, Oklahoma, and Texas.

This disparity is indicated in the statistical reports of the Western Association (formerly the Co-operative General Association) and the Eastern Association (formerly the General Conference) in the years immediately following the formation of the National Association. In 1937, the total membership of the Western Association (which included the Tri-State Association that consisted of Ohio, West Virginia, and Kentucky, in addition to Missouri and Oklahoma) was around 16,200. That same year, the Eastern Association (which included only one state from west of the Mississippi, Texas) comprised 80,344.

The Randall movement, as indicated by its inclusion in this volume, is clearly a part of the overall history of the modern Free Will Baptist movement. Yet its role in that history is much less significant than popular narratives often imply. This situation has resulted in far less research being done on the southern, or Palmer, movement. There is a great need for future historians to redress the imbalanced treatment of the Randall and Palmer movements by conducting more extensive research on the Free Will Baptists of the South and recognizing their dominance over the modern movement's character. Especially important is the need to continue the research that has been done for this volume on the influence of the Free Will Baptists in the Carolinas on United and Separate Baptist groups that would become Free Will Baptist in the nineteenth century.

Distinction from Other Baptists

The Free Will Baptists, whether southern or northern, did not fit in with the larger Baptist movement. Their distinctiveness is seen in the doctrines of salvation, the ordinances or sacraments of the church, and church polity or government.

One sees the Calvinist fear of Arminianism most clearly in the successful efforts of the Philadelphia Baptist Association to take over most of the North Carolina General Baptist movement in the mid- to late eighteenth century. The distinction between Calvinism and Arminianism is the most obvious reason for the separate existence of General/Free Will Baptists. Yet even after most Baptists in America moved away from the predestinarianism of traditional Calvinism, their aversion to the Arminian belief that genuine believers can fall from grace made them just as skeptical of the Free Will Baptists.[2]

However, the way most Free Will Baptists, especially in the South, viewed the liturgical practices of the Lord's Supper and the washing of the saints' feet distinguished them from other Baptists just as much as their Arminian soteriology. Many Calvinistic Baptists, such as the Primitive Baptists and Separate Baptists, continued practicing feet washing. Yet most Baptists in the nineteenth century moved away from the practice. This included the Freewill Baptists in the north. This liturgical rite increasingly made the Free Will Baptists of the South seem peculiar, adding to their uniqueness in comparison to other Baptists.

Even more than the *pedilavium*, the American Free Will Baptist practice of open communion was nothing short of shocking to other Baptists. Historians have failed to emphasize how this practice distinguished Free Will Baptists from other Baptists. It made them seem odd in the small communities that dotted the American landscape. This is especially true in the South, which was increasingly dominated by closed-communion Baptists. Thus when small groups of United and Separate Baptists throughout the South became Free Will Baptist, they were inviting the scrutiny and scorn of other Baptists. This opprobrium came as much because they differed from closed communion as it did because they disagreed with the doctrine of the eternal security of the regenerate.

Polity was another growing difference between Free Will Baptists and Baptists of other varieties. Unlike the Philadelphia Association in the eighteenth century, most Baptists became more and more democratized in the nineteenth century.[3] On the contrary, Free Will Baptists, whether southern or northern, had a stronger associational polity that reflected a hybrid between strict congregational and presbyterian models. Free Will Baptists in the nineteenth century always insisted that the local congregation governs itself. It chooses its own office-bearers, conducts its own business, holds title to its own property, and can decide which association or conference to unite with or ultimately become independent. Yet Free Will Baptists continued their traditional practice of a much stronger intercongregational polity and emphasis on "the church" being more than simply the local congregation. Southern Free Will Baptists had received this polity from their English General Baptist ancestors. The Freewill Baptists of the North were like their southern counterparts in this way. Tied to this polity was a stronger confessionalism than in most Baptist circles. With this approach, presbyteries in local conferences and associations examined and ordained ministers and deacons, requiring them to subscribe to a written confession of faith and holding them accountable if they veered from it.

This confessionalism is especially interesting when considering various Separate Baptist groups that became Free Will Baptist. Separate Baptists already practiced the washing of the saints' feet. Yet they conscientiously refused to have written confessions of faith and, thus obviously, ministerial subscription to those confessions. So the transition to Free Will Baptist identity for these Baptists involved not just an adoption of the doctrine of the possibility of apostasy and the practice of open communion. It also included a move to the requirement that ministers and deacons subscribe to written confessions of faith.

This stronger polity and approach to confessional subscription was challenged when the Disciples of Christ began forming from those discontented with denominationalism, including Free Will Baptists. The churches in North Carolina had a particularly damaging schism owing to proselytizing efforts from the Campbell movement. That group derided the strong polity, confessionalism, and "denominationalism" of the Free Will Baptists. Disciples of Christ leaders held the Free Will Baptist *Discipline* in one hand and the Bible in the other and challenged congregants to choose between the two.

Distinction from the Methodists

The uniqueness of Free Will Baptists from Methodists is even stronger than their demarcation from other Baptists. The most notable difference was over baptism. The Free Will Baptists baptized only believers, and their theology entailed their belief that Methodists baptized as infants were not truly baptized. Like other Baptists, they went as far as to say that even Methodists who had received aspersion (sprinkling) as believers must undergo immersion to unite with a Free Will Baptist congregation. They were willing to share Holy Communion with these paedobaptist Methodists, owing to their open-communion stance. Yet this practice did little to ameliorate the distance the baptismal differences created.

Another insurmountable difference between Free Will Baptists and their Methodist brothers and sisters was their polity. While most other Baptists thought Free Will Baptist polity was too connectional, Methodists thought it was not connectional enough. Thus, while Free Will Baptists' intercongregational polity was stronger than that of their Baptist brothers and sisters, they also differed from the highly connectional polity of the Methodists. The Methodist conferences and bishops had control over their congregations and the ministers in their care. This control extended even to the appointing of each congregation's pastor and controlling the ownership of its property. Thus, with regard to polity, the Free Will Baptists found themselves in a no-man's land between what they saw as the ultra-autonomy of the Baptists and the episcopal-connectionalism of the Methodists.

The differences between Free Will Baptists and Methodists were not only ecclesiological (the doctrine of the church). They were also soteriological (the doctrine of salvation). The Free Will Baptists' doctrine of salvation, especially in the South, was always colored with a Reformed hue on depravity, the nature of atonement, justification, sanctification, and assurance in Christ. Their most obvious difference with the Wesleyan Arminianism of the Methodists was on entire sanctification. Methodists believed that this state, initiated by a distinct second work of grace in believers' lives, could be obtained in this life. Instead, the southern Free Will Baptists insisted on a Reformed doctrine of progressive sanctification. Together with these differences went an understanding of atonement as penal substitutionary and of justification as consisting of the imputation of the righteousness of Christ. Believers, they argued, do not stand righteous by their sanctification or "imparted" righteousness, as the Methodists asserted. Instead, they are justified only by the righteousness of Christ imputed through faith alone. Salvation is by faith, from start to finish, not by good works. Renouncing that faith, they believed, results in an irremediable apostasy.

Many in the Randall movement diverged from their southern Free Will Baptist counterparts on certain soteriological points. The early Randall Freewill Baptists, for example, affirmed the doctrine of entire sanctification, though they later dropped it. Some even downplayed or denied the imputation of Christ's righteousness in justification. Yet they still upheld a penal substitutionary understanding of atonement. They placed more emphasis on good works and repentance to maintain salvation than the southern movement did. Yet, for most of its existence, the General Conference's *Treatise* was vague on these doctrines. Thus individuals could subscribe to it while affirming mediating approaches at various points on a spectrum between Wesleyan-leaning and Reformed-leaning versions of Arminianism.[4]

These theological differences with the two largest Protestant bodies in America, the Baptists and the Methodists, are the only reason the Free Will Baptists continued throughout the nineteenth and twentieth centuries as a separate denomination. The northern Freewill Baptists united with the Northern Baptist Convention, indicating their increasingly relaxed posture on the Arminian doctrine of apostasy. Yet a small remnant of the Randall movement was unrelenting and would eventually join their southern brethren in 1935 in the founding of the National Association.

Poles of Tension

The Free Will Baptist tradition is also fascinating in the nuanced tension it has maintained between two poles on issues such as confessionalism, pietism, orthodoxy, and ecumenism. The English General Baptist forebears of the southern movement had experienced their own controversy over orthodoxy in the late seventeenth century. This clash resulted in a schism in the General Assembly over issues related to the Trinity and the person of Christ. A new body, the General Association, formed in protest in 1696. Its members alleged that the General Assembly had not been vigilant enough in rooting out a tiny group that coalesced around Matthew Caffyn. He was rumored to have heterodox opinions on the doctrine of the Trinity and the two natures of Christ. Hindsight shows that the General Association's instincts were right. Yet at the time Caffyn would continually escape the accusations, insisting that he professed "the good old apostolical Trinity" and publicly signing orthodox confessional statements.[5]

Thomas Hammersley, Benjamin Laker, and Paul Palmer, the founders of the Palmer movement in North Carolina, were affiliated with the staunchly orthodox and more creedal General Association, which insisted on ministers and deacons subscribing to written confessions of faith. This confessionalism would go on to characterize the Free Will Baptist movement.

That confessional posture would be challenged and strengthened twice in the early movement. The first challenge was the incursion of the stoutly Calvinist Philadelphia Association in the mid- to late eighteenth century. The second involved the efforts of the Disciples of Christ/Campbell movement in the 1830s and 1840s to gain adherents from the Free Will Baptists. At both these junctures, these earliest southern Free Will Baptists lost ground numerically. Yet they held the more tenaciously to their confession of faith after debilitating proselytization.

For the first hundred years of its existence, the Randall movement was also strongly confessional, with associational ordination processes that undergirded that posture. Forces at work in that movement, however, competed with that confessionalism and eventually defeated it altogether when the General Conference merged with the Northern Baptist Convention.

Tension had always existed between pietism and ecumenism on one hand and confessionalism on the other. Successfully holding this tension usually rendered both the Free Will Baptists of the South and the Freewill Baptists of the North stronger in their denominational identity. Yet the history of the Free Will Baptist Church is a history of struggling with ecumenical relationships. Thus they struggled between isolation from other groups and fascination with them—whether Calvinists or Disciples of Christ in the early centuries or the Pentecostal-charismatic, independent fundamentalist Baptist, or non-denominational megachurch movements in the twentieth and twenty-first. The movement's confessionalist tendencies, contrasting with both pietism and ecumenism, tended always to bring it back to its roots.

By "confessionalism," scholars such as James Tunstead Burtchaell and Daryl G. Hart mean an emphasis on the institutional church, including the church beyond the local congregation. This includes the church's writing down its confession of faith or doctrine and having ecclesiastical structures to ensure fidelity to that confession on the part of church leaders. Scholars like Burtchaell and Hart define "pietism" not just as renewal movements in the Christian tradition that emphasize vital spirituality side-by-side with religious orthodoxy. Instead they characterize it as a moving of doctrinal orthodoxy and the centrality of the institutional church from the center of Christianity to its periphery, leaving only the religion of the individual's heart at the center.[6]

Burtchaell and Hart have persuasively argued that this tension between pietism and confessionalism was always at play in American Christianity. When a romanticized, democratized "religion of the heart" took center stage, moving a robustly doctrinal orientation from the center to the periphery, the received orthodoxy of a given religious group was usually marginalized. When that doctrinal orthodoxy was displaced at the center by mere piety, it was usually accompanied, eventually, by two characteristics: a desire to emphasize commonalities and downplay distinctions with other denominations and a desire to perfect society through religious social reform.[7]

A nuanced balance or successfully held tension was necessary to keep a given denomination committed to its unique confessional tradition and identity while at the same time finding ways to foster camaraderie across denominational lines and to employ Christian benevolence for the betterment of society. An over-emphasis on doctrinal conformity and a de-emphasis on vital spirituality could lead to a moribund orthodoxy. An over-emphasis on religious experience and a downplaying of doctrinal commitments could lead to an overpowering pietism that could squelch orthodoxy and true religion. Yet Burtchaell and Hart make a compelling argument that in most cases Protestant denominations did not successfully hold this nuanced tension. For those Protestants wishing to maintain doctrinal orthodoxy, letting go of the nuanced tension and having only the "religion of the heart" at the center and thus moving a theological orientation to the periphery was extremely debilitating.

The "pendulum-swinging" between a wholly pietistic orientation and a doctrinal-confessional one characterized both the southern and northern wings of the Free Will Baptist movements. This pendulum-swinging was exacerbated by the revivalism of the Great Awakening and the Second Great Awakening in the increasingly Romantic context of American culture. The General Baptists of the Carolinas had been on the receiving end of some of the excesses of the New Light revivalism of the First Great Awakening. The New Lights accused them of the lack of religion because they did not employ emotionalistic New Light practices to demonstrate their piety, sticking tenaciously to the "six principles of the Christian religion" in Hebrews 6:1–2. The Disciples of Christ were a quintessential example of the pietism of the Second Great Awakening. That movement reconfigured and unseated traditional Christian confessional categories, actively attacking the received confessionalism of the Free Will Baptists.

The northern Freewill Baptists had been birthed by the Great Awakening and became intimately intertwined with Charles Finney and the Second Great Awakening. They led the way in the Protestant world in ecumenism and social reform. The northern movement would succeed at completing the trajectory Burtchaell and Hart have outlined, moving doctrinal orthodoxy to the margins while maintaining their commitment to pietism, ecumenism, and social reform. Eventually, this path would result in the acceptance by some in the movement of liberal Protestant theological commitments that faculty in some of their educational institutions were gleaning from their study in German universities. Finally, their ecumenical thrust would result in the end of their existence as a separate denomination, with only a tiny remnant withdrawing from the merger with the Northern Baptists.

The movement in the South, as the Palmer movement migrated west, influencing other sorts of Baptists to become Free Will Baptist, resisted this temptation. Yet, as in evangelicalism at large, some in the movement would still pendulum-swing between pietism and confessionalism. One can see this in the loss of churches to the new Pentecostal movement in the twentieth century. In the 1920s, after the Pentecostal Free Will Baptist Church started out of a splinter in the Carolinas, the Free Will Baptists in the General Conference in the South again doubled down on their historic confessionalism.

Such retrenchment also occurred in response to the fundamentalist-modernist controversy. Some southern Free Will Baptists moved to so robust a separatist position that they would separate from orthodox co-religionists who did not separate sufficiently from liberal Protestant individuals and institutions. The schism with the North Carolina State Convention (later Convention of Original Free Will Baptists) was in some ways a playing out of this dynamic. Mount Olive College and some segments of the State Convention represented a stance vis-à-vis the fundamentalist-modernist controversy that leaned more toward mainline Protestantism. Thus it was in some ways similar to the Cooperative Baptist Fellowship, which left the Southern Baptist Convention in the late twentieth century after conservatives assumed control of the boards of that denomination. Still, in the Convention of Original Free Will Baptists, both fundamentalist and moderate factions persisted.

After the North Carolina schism of 1962, the separatist fundamentalist movement in the National Association gained even more ground, eventually resulting in the establishment of a new rigorously fundamentalist college twenty years later. Yet, ironically, the leadership of that college in its first few decades tended to identify more with the staunch fundamentalists in the Independent Baptist movement and thus was not a force for traditional confessional Free Will Baptist ideals.

The tension between confessionalism and pietism, and between denominationalism and ecumenism, continued to play out in the influence of the Independent Baptist and non-denominational megachurch movements among Free Will Baptists in the late twentieth and early twenty-first centuries. Those who emphasized confessionalism were critical of these influences. Some in this group became ultra-separatist in their aloofness from those outside the denomination. Others in this group maintained extra-denominational alliances with like-minded confessional groups in other denominations. Others in the movement became less confessional, stressing pietism and evangelism while de-emphasizing theological considerations and distinctive denominational commitments. Some congregations remained aloof from these larger movements and trends, simply maintaining the status quo.

Conclusion

The history of the Free Will Baptists in America has been the story of a minority religious tradition that has existed betwixt and between the mainstream American Protestant denominations, primarily the Baptists and the Methodists. Thus it has remained smaller and has always been beset with significant critique from these larger movements. This unique position predisposed the denomination in the South to proselytization efforts by other groups. These efforts were exacerbated by poverty. That poverty, until the late nineteenth and early twentieth centuries, hindered effective educational endeavors and institutions needed to maintain the theological commitments of the movement successfully.

The Randall movement in the North was a different story, with more wealth and a more educated ministry. Yet, losing its tension between pietism and confessionalism, it eventually marginalized the very reasons for having a separate Arminian Baptist denomination. It even went on to embrace the liberal emphases emerging in the early years of the fundamentalist-modernist controversy.

The founding in 1935 of the National Association, primarily a southern movement with which the remnant of the Randall movement that remained Freewill Baptist united, represented the tenacious spirit of the Free Will Baptists in the face of their minority status. The movement reached its peak in the four decades between 1950 and 1990. Since then, the denomination, like most Protestant denominations, has been in numerical decline. Yet it still remains a viable movement that is the object of study in cross-denominational research about American denominations. Its distinctive commitment to its unique expression of Arminianism, combined with a Baptist doctrine of the church, remains central to its identity. Its leaders cling to the hope that the Free Will Baptist people and churches will maintain their distinctive faith and practice, rally in the face of demographic shifts and the growing secularization of American life, and continue to fulfill their mission to "promote the success of the church and of the Gospel, . . . counting it our chief business in life to extend the influence of Christ in society, constantly praying and toiling that the kingdom of God may come, and His will be done on earth as it is in heaven."[8]

NOTES

FOREWORD

1. Margaret Bendroth, *The Spiritual Act of Remembering (Eerdmans, 2013)*.

INTRODUCTION

1. There is some debate over the language of "close" vs. "closed" communion. Many authors historically said "close" communion limited partaking of the Lord's supper to those who had been immersed, while "closed" communion limited it to a local church or to those from churches of like faith and order. One sees both these usages in the primary sources quoted in this book. For convenience and clarity, I will use "closed" communion to describe all non-open communion stances among Baptists.

CHAPTER ONE

1. Historians affirm that Paul Palmer, Joseph Parker, and their associates were English General Baptists. William F. Davidson painstakingly and cogently demonstrates not only the historical proof but also the universal historiographical support for this assertion (Davidson, *The Free Will Baptists in History* [Nashville: Randall House, 2001], 57–105). Proof that Palmer et al. were General Baptist first appears in three key primary sources: the Rhode Island Calvinist Baptist pastor John Comer's diary in the 1720s and 1730s, then the Calvinist Baptist historian Morgan Edwards's *Materials Towards a History of the Baptists* in 1772, then the Calvinist Baptist pastors Lemuel Burkitt and Jesse Read's *Concise History of the Kehukee Baptist Association* in 1803. These sources are cited by secondary sources from then on. Early nineteenth-century historians David Benedict (1813, Calvinist Baptist) and Richard Knight (1827, General Baptist) concurred, citing Edwards. Later nineteenth-century historians such as the northern Freewill Baptists I. D. Stewart (1862) and G. A. Burgess and J. T. Ward (1889), agreeing with an unsigned 1855 article, "The Early General Baptist Churches in the United States," *Freewill Baptist Quarterly* 3 (1855); the southern Free Will Baptists R. K. Hearn (1875) and T. F. Harrison and J. M. Barfield (1896); Northern Baptists George F. Adams (1885), Thomas Armitage (1890), Albert Henry Newman (1875), and Henry

Vedder (1907); Southern Baptists B. F. Riley (1898), William Whitsitt (1890s), and J. D. Hufham (1890s); and American General Baptist D. B. Montgomery (1882) join the chorus of all other historians in the nineteenth century affirming the General Baptist affiliation of Palmer and his associates. This argument was brought over into twentieth-century historiography by Southern Baptists John Christian (1926) and George Paschal (1930), as well as the British Baptist W. T. Whitley (1936). Subsequent historians affirmed and built on Paschal's magisterial research, e.g., Southern Baptists Joseph Watts (1953), M. A. Huggins (1967), Robert Gardner (1983), Leon McBeth (1987), and Douglas Weaver (2008); American Baptist Robert Torbet (1950); American General Baptist Ollie Latch (1954); and Free Will Baptists G. W. Million and G. A. Barrett (1911), Damon Dodd (1956), G. W. Million (1958), William Davidson (1974, 1985, 2001, 2006), George Stevenson (1991, 1994), Michael Pelt (1996), Matthew Pinson (1998), and Darrell Holley (2000); and North Carolina historian Lindley Butler (2022). See bibliography for detailed citations.

2. For more on the English General Baptists, see J. Matthew Pinson and Jesse F. Owens, *The English General Baptists of the Seventeenth Century* (Brentwood, TN: B&H Academic, forthcoming); George Stevenson, "Laker, Benjamin," in *Dictionary of North Carolina Biography*, vol. 4, ed. William S. Powell (Chapel Hill: University of North Carolina Press, 1991), 3–5. Joanna Taylor Jeffreys Peterson, Palmer's wife, was Benjamin Laker's stepdaughter. This section is indebted to Stevenson's research. His papers on Laker are held at the Free Will Baptist Historical Collection at the University of Mount Olive in Mount Olive, North Carolina. A recent book that makes use of Stevenson's research on Laker and Palmer is Lindley S. Butler, *A History of North Carolina in the Proprietary Era, 1629–1729* (Chapel Hill: University of North Carolina Press, 2022), 148, 212–16, 228, 389–90. On Hammersley, see p. 21 and notes 13–14 in this chapter.

3. His name is spelled "Laccar" in *A Brief Confession or Declaration of Faith, Set forth by many of us, who are (falsly) called Ana-Baptists, to inform all Men of our innocent Belief and Practice. Subscribed by certain Elders, Deacons, and Brethren, in the behalf of themselves, and many others unto whom they belong, in London, and in several Counties of this Nation, who are of the same Faith with us*, Early English books tract supplement interim guide / 816.m.24[59]; Wing (CD-ROM, 1996) / T2726. 1 sheet. London, 1691; W. T. Whitley, ed., *Minutes of the General Assembly of the General Baptists* (London: Kingsgate, 1909), 44; Stevenson, "Laker," 4:3–4.

4. Samuel Wilson, *An Account of the Province of Carolina in America* (London: Francis Smith, 1682), 17; Milton Ready, *The Tar Heel State: A New History of North Carolina* (Columbia, SC: University of South Carolina Press, 2020), 26.

5. Timothy Crist, "Francis Smith and the Opposition Press in England, 1660–

1688" (PhD thesis, Cambridge University, 1977), 267–68. Smith was the best-known Baptist publisher in the seventeenth century, publishing the *Standard Confession* of 1660, most of Thomas Grantham's and John Bunyan's books, and also—sometimes secretly—books from Whiggish or Republican political radicals. One can only imagine the impact on the early General Baptists of Carolina if the most distinguished Baptist publisher in England, himself a General Baptist, had migrated there. The Carolina Coffee House remained an important connection point between London and Carolina well into the eighteenth century; see James Raven, *London Booksellers and American Customers: Transatlantic Community and the Charleston Library Society, 1478–1811* (Columbia, SC: University of South Carolina Press, 2002), 126–28, 145–46.
6. Davidson, *Free Will Baptists in History*, 32–34; Michael R. Pelt, *A History of Original Free Will Baptists* (Mount Olive, NC: Mount Olive College Press, 1996), 23.
7. Stevenson, "Laker," 4:4. Stevenson mistakenly says 1697, but the Minutes of the Perquimans Precinct Court show that he was present as of January 1698. Minutes of the Perquimans Precinct Court, North Carolina. January 10, 1698, in Mattie Erma Edwards Parker, ed., *Colonial Records of North Carolina* (Second Series) (Raleigh: Department of Archives and History, 1963), 1:488–89; Davidson, *Free Will Baptists in History*, 32–34.
8. Minutes of the General Court of North Carolina, including Chancery Court minutes (September 24–29, 1694), in Parker, ed., *Colonial Records of North Carolina*, 1:414–15. With the fluidity of spellings in early modern English, Laker is alternately spelled "Laccar," "Lakar," "LaKar," and (in his will) "Lakaro."
9. Minutes of the Perquimans Precinct Court, North Carolina (July 7–9, 1701), in Parker, ed., *Colonial Records of North Carolina*, 1:549; will quoted in Davidson, *Free Will Baptists in History*, 34.
10. *Colonial Records*, 1:549, 771, 2:72; Stevenson, "Laker," 4:4. "Prays extempore" is a reference to the fact that Baptists, unlike Anglicans but like many other Nonconformists, did not use written prayers in worship.
11. "Reverend John Blair's Mission to North Carolina, 1704," in "Alexander S. Salley, ed., *Narratives of Early Carolina, 1650–1708*, Original Narratives of Early American History, J. Franklin Jameson, gen. ed. (New York: Charles Scribner's Sons, 1911), 216.
12. Clarence H. Urner, "Early Baptist Records in Prince George County, Virginia," *The Virginia Magazine of History and Biography* 41 (1933): 97–101; Davidson, *Free Will Baptists in History*, 20–21; Joyce D. Goodfriend, "The Baptist Church in Prerevolutionary New York City," *American Baptist Quarterly* 16 (1997): 220. Eyres had moved his church from New York City to Newport, Rhode Island, in 1731; Stevenson, "Laker," 4:4; Cf. Morgan Edwards, "Materials Towards a History of the Baptists in the Provinces of Maryland, Virginia, North Carolina, South Carolina, Georgia" (MS, 1772, held in Furman

University Library), 3:21–22. https://cdm16821.contentdm.oclc.org/digital/collection/jbt/id/220/rec/1.

13. More research needs to be done on the Hammersleys. See W. T. Whitley, "Thomas Hammersley," *Baptist Quarterly* 8 (1937): 316; Whitley, *Minutes*, 44; J. R. B. Hathaway, ed., "Births, Deaths and Marriages in Berkeley, Later Perquimans Precinct, N.C.," *The North Carolina Historical and Genealogical Register* 3 (1903): 204. Dr. Hammersley appears to have been born in what would later become Perquimans Precinct in 1683 or 1684. His father Thomas had migrated from Staffordshire and had apparently started a General Baptist church on the Albermarle Sound near the Perquimans River before the Lakers arrived. Thus Stevenson's picture of Laker as the first General Baptist in North Carolina should probably be revised, since the Hammersley family's arrival in what would become Perquimans Precinct seems to have predated that of the Lakers. See Alan Betteridge, "Early Staffordshire Baptists: A Further Note," *Baptist Quarterly* 38 (1999): 200–201, who says that the church Thomas Hammersley established in America carried on a correspondence with his original Staffordshire congregation "for some years." Genealogical research conducted on the Homersley/Hammersley family by Len Holmes corroborates this account (email correspondence with Len Holmes, June 25–26, 2024).

14. Pelt says (without citing his source) that the June 1702 request from Carolina for a minister or books, taken up by the General Association when it met at White's Alley, had originally been sent to General Baptists in Staffordshire. See Pelt, *History of Original Free Will Baptists*, 24. Whitley, cited above, noted that the Staffordshire General Baptists were sympathetic with the General Association and that Thomas Hammersley was influential among them. For Davidson's compelling argument regarding the origin of the 1702 letter being the Perquimans congregation, see Davidson, *Free Will Baptists in History*, 22–24, 34–35. For support for Davidson's view, see A. H. Newman, *A History of the Baptist Churches of the United States* (New York: Charles Scribner's Sons, 1902), 224–25, and Leah Townsend, *South Carolina Baptist History, 1670–1805* (Florence, SC: Florence Printing Company, 1935), 5–13. Pelt (*Original Free Will Baptists*, 24) concurs, as does Stevenson ("Laker," 4:4) and Butler (*North Carolina in the Proprietary Era*, 216). The only other scholar to discuss this is Whitley. Davidson shows that Whitley mistakenly assumed in a 1936 article that the plea could have come from either the Perquimans group or the Charleston, South Carolina, church. However, as Davidson persuasively argues, the Charleston church had a strong pastor, the Calvinist William Screven (since at least 1699, perhaps earlier). Yet by 1937 Whitley had concluded that John Hammersley's friends in Perquimans Precinct were the ones who wrote the letter. See W. T. Whitley, "General Baptists in Carolina and Virginia," *Crozer Quarterly* 13 (1936): 21–27; Whitley, "Thomas Hammersley," 316.

15. Whitley, *Minutes*, General Association (1702), 75.
16. Robert D. Hume, "The Value of Money in Eighteenth-Century England: Income, Prices, Buying Power—and Some Problems in Cultural Economics," *Huntington Library Quarterly* 77 (2015): 381.
17. I use "Free Will Baptist" here for convenience. That name would not be used until the late eighteenth or early nineteenth centuries.
18. George Stevenson, "Palmer, Paul," in *Dictionary of North Carolina Biography*, vol. 5, ed. William S. Powell (Chapel Hill: University of North Carolina Press, 1991), 12.
19. Davidson, *Free Will Baptists in History*, 25–26; Stevenson, "Palmer," 5:10. For a recent, engaging retelling of Palmer's story, see E. Darrell Holley, *Without a Monument: The Life of Elder Paul Palmer* (Nashville: Free Will Baptist Bible College, 2000), which can be found at https://fwbhistory.com/?p=603.
20. B. F. Riley, *A History of the Baptists in the Southern States East of the Mississippi* (Philadelphia: American Baptist Publication Society, 1898), 166; W. T. Whitley, "General Baptists in Carolina and Virginia," 26–27; Whitley, *Minutes of the General Assembly*, 125, 146.
21. *Colonial Records*, 596, 660; George Washington Paschal, *History of North Carolina Baptists*, 2 vols. (Raleigh: The General Board, North Carolina Baptist State Convention, 1930), 1:132–36; Davidson, *Free Will Baptists in History*, 25–26.
22. Stevenson, "Palmer," 10; Davidson, *Free Will Baptists in History*, 26–27. David Benedict reprinted this excerpt from Palmer's letter in his *General History of the Baptist Denomination in America, and Other Parts of the World*, 2 vols. (Boston: Manning and Loring, 1813), 2:24.
23. Urner, "Early Baptist Records in Prince George County, Virginia," 99; Davidson, *Free Will Baptists in History*, 19–20; Whitley, *Minutes of the General Assembly*, 125, 144.
24. Stevenson, "Palmer," 13.
25. C. Edwin Barrows, ed., *The Diary of John Comer*, in *Collections of the Rhode Island Historical Society* 8 (1893): 102.
26. Stevenson, "Palmer," 5:13.
27. Minutes of the General Court of North Carolina (1720–1722) in William Laurence Saunders, *Colonial Records of North Carolina*, 2:409–11, 415–16, 442, 444, 471, https://docsouth.unc.edu/csr/, For a discussion of the Palmers' innocence, see Paschal, *North Carolina Baptists*, 1:136–37, n. 29; Stevenson, "Palmer," 5:11.
28. The reader will remember that the General Baptists practiced the rite of confirmation: laying hands on all newly baptized believers.
29. The traditional notion that the Chowan church was "the first regularly organized Free Will Baptist congregation" is called into question by the fact that Thomas Hammersly appears to have been an ordained minister who gathered a congregation along the Perquimans River in the 1680s. Still,

the movement that would come to be known as "Free Will Baptist" in the American South arose from congregations Palmer had started. However, as noted above, there were other General Baptists in the American colonies before Palmer became a General Baptist. Thus, while Palmer's churches were the first "Free Will Baptist" churches in America, they were not the first "General Baptist" churches in America.

30. There were no Calvinist Baptists in Virginia before 1750. See Robert Gardner, *Baptists of Early America: A Statistical History, 1639–1790* (Atlanta: Georgia Baptist Historical Society, 1983), 99. See also Edwards, "Materials," 4:125. Edwards established that there were no Particular Baptists in North Carolina until the middle of the eighteenth century. See also Morgan Edwards, "Tour of Rev. Morgan Edwards of Pennsylvania, To the American Baptists in North Carolina in 1772–73," MS, University Library, University of North Carolina at Chapel Hill, 38, https://archive.org/details/tourofrevmorgane1893edwa/page/n5/mode/2up; Pelt, *Original Free Will Baptists*, 37; Stevenson, "Palmer," 5:11.

31. *Diary of John Comer*, 84–85; Davidson, *Free Will Baptists in History*, 29. "Thomas Darker" is a misprint for Thomas Parker, the father of one of the Joseph Parkers and one of the John Parkers in the church. Another John Parker, son of John Parker (Sr.) and another Joseph Parker, son of Joseph Parker (Sr.) were members of the extended Parker family. See Paschal, *North Carolina Baptists*, 1:140–41.

32. Paschal, *North Carolina Baptists*, 1:140–42; Davidson, *Free Will Baptists in History*, 29–30; Pelt, *Original Free Will Baptists*, 36.

33. *The North Carolina Historical and Genealogical Register* 1 (1900): 283. J. R. B. Hathaway was the editor of this serial published quarterly between 1900 and 1903; Davidson, *Free Will Baptists in History*, 30–31.

34. Edwards, "Materials," 4:130, 135; Pelt, *Original Free Will Baptists*, 38–39; Davidson, *Free Will Baptists in History*, 31.

35. Letter from Richard Everard to Edmund Gibson (October 12, 1729) in Saunders, *Colonial Records of North Carolina*, 3:48.

36. See, e.g., McBeth, who says that "settling down to one pastorate was not his style.... Parker apparently provided some of the stability which the volatile Palmer lacked." *The Baptist Heritage*, (Nashville: Broadman, 1987), 222–23. Recent historians (e.g., Pelt, *Original Free Will Baptists*, 35–36; Stevenson, "Palmer," 12) who have correctly viewed Palmer's activity in light of the General Baptist office of messenger have seen that as the most reasonable explanation of Palmer's itineracy.

37. As Davidson has shown, the number of General Baptist churches in North Carolina was higher than Gardner's number, which is reflected in the above numbers. Other than that, the numbers are from Gardner. Davidson, *Free Will Baptists in History*, 67; Gardner, *Baptists of Early America*, 30–57, 62–63;

"Baptists in the Colonies till 1750," *Transactions of the Baptist Historical Society* 7 (1920): 33–34; Ollie Latch, *History of the General Baptists* (Poplar Bluff, MO: The General Baptist Press, 1954), 115. By the mid-twentieth century the General Six-Principle Baptist denomination in the North comprised only around 325 members and by the late twentieth century had dwindled to nothing. A group of pastors has attempted to revive the General Six-Principle Baptist movement in the early twenty-first century and have a website under the name "General Association of Six-Principle Baptists." However, little can be ascertained about the small number of churches affiliated with that association.

38. *Diary of John Comer*, 85; Stevenson, "Surginer, William" in *Dictionary of North Carolina Biography*, 5:477; Pelt, *Original Free Will Baptists*, 48–49; Davidson, *Free Will Baptists in History*, 27–29.
39. *Diary of John Comer*, 111–12. "Man of parts" is an archaic term meaning a man of talents, gifts, and abilities in many different areas.
40. *Diary of John Comer*, 113–14, 117–18; Edwards, "Materials," 2–5. It is impossible to decipher from the evidence exactly what happened with Loveall. Yet the allegations gave the Philadelphia Association a club with which to beat the General Baptists. Comer reproduced a letter to Henry Drake from a Philadelphia Association minister criticizing Drake and Palmer for ordaining Loveall. Comer himself, however, preached at Loveall's church at his invitation, noting that his "evil actions" were committed before his conversion. Comer's parenthetical comment in his handwritten diary questioning whether the reports about Loveall were indeed true was left out of the printed edition by the editor, the Baptist pastor C. Edwin Barrows, in 1893 and replaced by the bracketed phrase "[*Certain particulars omitted.*]." However, allegations arose against Loveall later in his life. Paschal remarked that Loveall "had deceived Palmer as he had deceived Comer" (Paschal, *North Carolina Baptists*, 1:152; *Diary of John Comer*, 117–18; Manuscript copy of the diary of John Comer, 2 volumes in one, 1704–1731, original manuscripts at the Rhode Island Historical Society).
41. Stevenson, "Palmer," 11–12.
42. Stevenson, "Palmer," 12; Davidson, *Free Will Baptists in America*, 23; Pelt, *Original Free Will Baptists*, 42.
43. Somerset County Judicial Records, 1735–1737, vol. 851, 62–63; Davidson, *Free Will Baptists in History*, 27–29.
44. Edwards, "Materials," 2–5; Joseph T. Watts, *The Rise and Progress of Maryland Baptists* (Baltimore: Maryland Baptist Union, 1953), 10. Palmer is often credited with starting or settling the Chestnut Ridge Church, under Sater's sponsorship; see, e.g., McBeth, *Baptist Heritage*, 222; and William H. Brackney, *Historical Dictionary of the Baptists* (Lanham, MD: Scarecrow, 2009), 426; and Robert G. Torbet, *A History of the Baptists* (Valley Forge, PA:

Judson, 1963), 222. Davidson indirectly agrees when he indicates that Palmer was the primary ministerial influence on the Chestnut Ridge Church before Loveall was brought in to serve as a more permanent pastor of the congregation in 1742, when the church was formally constituted (*Free Will Baptists in History*, 28–29). The church now appears to be in the Southern Baptist Convention, having been swallowed up in the Philadelphia Association's proselytization activities in the region later in the eighteenth century. The church's website states that it subscribes to the Baptist Faith and Message 2000. The church's address is at "Sater's Lane" (https://crbclives.com/mission); Watts, *Rise and Progress of Maryland Baptists*, 10.

45. Edwards, "Materials," 2–5; Edwards's documentation of Palmer's association with the Chestnut Ridge Church is repeated by Benedict, *General History of the Baptist Denomination*, 2:213, then thereafter by numerous other historians, e.g., "The Early General Baptist Churches in the United States," 430; Adams, *History of the Baptists in Maryland*, 23; Isaac W. Maclay, *The Descendants of Henry Sater of Maryland* (New York: Barnes, 1895), 75. Twentieth-century historians that refer to it include G. W. Million and G. A. Barrett, *A Brief History of the Liberal Baptists in England and America from 1606 to 1911* (Pocahontas, AR: Liberal Baptist Book and Tract Company, 1911), 310; Paschal, *North Carolina Baptists*, 1:132, 152; Watts, *Rise and Progress*, 6, 10; Torbet, *History of the Baptists*, 222; Elmer F. Ruark, "Our Baptist Heritage," *The Quarterly Review* 27 (1967): 55; Davidson, *Free Will Baptists in History*, 28–29; McBeth, *Baptist Heritage*, 224; Stevenson, "Palmer,"5:12–13; and Pelt, *Original Free Will Baptists*, 40, 42, 46–47; Brackney, *Dictionary*, 426.

46. Stevenson, "Palmer," 5:12.

47. *The North Carolina Historical and Genealogical Register* 2 (1901): 195; Davidson, *Free Will Baptists in History*, 31–32.

48. "Petition from Protestant Dissenters of Bay and Neuse Rivers," in *The North Carolina Historical and Genealogical Register* 2 (1901): 198; Davidson, *Free Will Baptists in History*, 44; Stevenson, "Palmer," 5:12.

49. *The North Carolina Historical and Genealogical Register* 3 (1903): 475. Nothing can be ascertained about the existence of this page or of the Bible from which it was taken.

50. Stevenson, "Palmer," 5:13.

51. Edwards, "Materials," 12. Most General Baptists in the late eighteenth century appear to have sided with the thirteen American colonies in the War for Independence. For example, most of the Kehukee, North Carolina, pastor William Surginer's male relatives appear to have fought for the colonies, while others appear to have been loyalists.

52. Edwards, "Materials," 13. The reader will also remember that, according to Edwards, the church practiced the *pedilavium*. This document from the

Chestnut Ridge Church was reprinted widely in nineteenth-century books on Baptist history, especially regarding Maryland. Benedict is the first to reprint it in 1813 (*History of the Baptist Denomination*, 2:13–14). See also, e.g., "The Early General Baptist Churches in the United States," 430; D. B. Montgomery, *General Baptist History*, 131; Adams, *History of the Baptists in Maryland*, 24. The book to which it refers is the well-known General Baptist messenger Francis Stanley's widely read 1667 volume, *Christianity indeed, or, The well-disciplin'd Christian the Delight of Christ*, alternately known (as listed after the Epistle Dedicatory and Preface) as *A Treatise Setting forth the Gospel's Honour, and The Churches Ornament*. The volume was printed by Francis Smith. This information from the Chestnut Ridge Church is interesting in how clearly it ties Paul Palmer's General Baptist movement to the more-creedal General Baptists associated with figures such as Francis Stanley. It is also noteworthy that the congregation classed itself and other General Baptists among the "reformed" and that it practiced the washing of the saints' feet.

53. Edwards, "Materials," 126; Edwards, "Tour," 29; Stevenson, "Palmer," 5:13.
54. Edwards, "Materials," 4:164–67. That Edwards knew about Joseph Parker is indicated by his statement that the majority of North Carolina General Baptists had accepted the "sentiments of the Particular-baptists . . . except Mr. Parker and his church, and some others." Edwards, "Materials," 4:125; see also, e.g., 4:134, 136. "Contantony" is an alternate spelling for Contentnea. See also Edwards, "Tour," 28.
55. J. D. Hufham, "Notes, Queries and Criticisms," *North Carolina Baptist Historical Papers* 3 (1899): 225; J. D. Hufham, "The Baptists in North Carolina," *North Carolina Baptist Historical Papers* 1 (1896–1897): 243.
56. See Stevenson's argument for the earlier date for Surginer's move to North Carolina in "Surginer," 5:477; Edwards, "Materials," 4:125, 129; https://www.ancestry.com/family-tree/person/tree/46416227/person/6868346005/facts; *Abstract of North Carolina Wills Compiled from Original and Recorded Wills in the Office of the Secretary of State* (Raleigh: E. M. Uzzell, 1910), 398; Paschal, *North Carolina Baptists*, 1:172–73; Pelt, *Original Free Will Baptists*, 48; Davidson, *Free Will Baptists in History*, 21–22.
57. Edwards, "Materials," 4: 129; Paschal, *North Carolina Baptists*, 1:172–75; Pelt, *Original Free Will Baptists*, 48–50. Edwards said, "He died Feb. 18, 1749, aged 43 years and 7 months. This date I found on a cedar rail put over his grave by his surviving friend Rev. Josiah Hart" (4:129).
58. *Diary of John Comer*, 94; Stevenson, "Surginer," 5:477; https://www.ancestry.com/family-tree/person/tree/7749901/person/25352620016/facts; *American Genealogical-Biographical Index* (Middletown, CT: Godfrey Memorial Library, 1904), 43:147; Virginia Gunn Fick, "Hatting," *Encyclopedia of North Carolina*, ed. William S. Powell (Chapel Hill: University of North Carolina Press, 2006), https://www.ncpedia.org/hatting; "History of the First Baptist

Church, Swansea, Massachusetts," *The Baptist Memorial and Monthly Record* 4 (1845): 264. While the evidence for Devotion's association with Surginer is circumstantial, it is inconceivable that it did not occur.
59. Stevenson, "Surginer," 5:477; *American Genealogical-Biographical Index* (Middletown, CT: Godfrey Memorial Library, 1904), 149:100; https://wc.rootsweb.com/trees/158440/I14193/-/individual; Peleg Rogers, Find-A-Grave #34977631.
60. Pelt, *Original Free Will Baptists*, 49; Paschal, *North Carolina Baptists*, 1:173–74. When Paschal said "the Edgecombe of that day," he was referring to the fact that Edgecombe County, when it was first divided off from Bertie County in 1742, was much larger than it became after portions of it became parts of four other counties: Granville, Halifax, Nash, and Wilson.
61. Edwards said William Walker was "ordained in 1748 by Josiah Hart." Edwards, "Materials," 4:133; see also 138; Lemuel Burkitt and Jesse Read, *A Concise History of the Kehukee Baptist Association, from its Original Rise Down to 1803*, rev. by Henry L. Burkitt (Philadelphia: Lippincott, Grambo and Company, 1850), 234–35; B. P. Davis, "Notes from Records of Reedy Creek Church, Tar River Association," *North Carolina Baptist Historical Papers* 3 (1899–1900): 218, 221. "The *Free-will* plan" appears to be the first usage in print of the appellation "free will" for these General Baptists. Later historians such as R. K. Hearn inferred that this usage by the group's "enemies" eventually led to the formal use in the denomination's title. See Hearn, "Origin of the Free Will Baptist Church of North Carolina" in D. B. Montgomery, ed., *General Baptist History* (Evansville, IN: Courier, 1882), 167. Hearn's history was printed earlier in the *Toisnot Transcript* (May 20–June 17, 1875).
62. Stevenson, "Surginer," 5:477.
63. Edwards, "Materials," 4:134; Pelt, *Original Free Will Baptists*, 50–51.
64. Burkitt and Read, *Concise History of the Kehukee Baptist Association*, 32, 35–36.
65. *Diary of John Comer*, 85; *North Carolina Historical and Genealogical Register* 2 (1901): 299; S. J. Wheeler, "History of the Meherrin Church," *North Carolina Baptist Historical Papers* 1 (1896): 42. This issue of the serial was published in Henderson, North Carolina, in October 1896 by the North Carolina Baptist Historical Society. The original was entitled *History of the Baptist Church Meeting at Parker's Meeting House Called Meherrin* and was printed in 1847.
66. George Stevenson, "Parker, Joseph," *Dictionary of North Carolina Biography*, 5:19–20; Pelt, *Original Free Will Baptists*, 52–53.
67. Stevenson, "Parker," 20–22; Davidson, *Free Will Baptists in History*, 70–71.
68. Paschal, *North Carolina Baptists*, 1:170; Wheeler, "History of the Meherrin Church," 44; Stevenson, "Parker," 5:22.
69. Edwards, "Materials," 4:134; Pelt, *Original Free Will Baptists*, 54.
70. Pelt, *Original Free Will Baptists*, 50–51, 54–55.

CHAPTER TWO

1. Robert Gardner, *Baptists of Early America: A Statistical History, 1639-1790* (Atlanta: Georgia Baptist Historical Society, 1983), 108. H. Leon McBeth quotes Gardner, adding that it was a "rather blunt but accurate statement of the case." See his *The Baptist Heritage: Four Centuries of Baptist Witness* (Nashville: Broadman, 1987), 223.
2. Quoted in George Washington Paschal, *History of North Carolina Baptists*, 2 vols. (Raleigh: The General Board, North Carolina Baptist State Convention, 1930), 1:528, n. 88.
3. Thomas S. Kidd, "Calvinism Is Not New to Baptists: Grace Unleashed in the American Colonies," *Desiring God* (June 13, 2015), https://www.desiringgod.org/articles/calvinism-is-not-new-to-baptists.
4. See Jesse F. Owens's essay, "When General Baptists Became Particular Baptists," written for a doctoral seminar on American Religious History at Southern Baptist Theological Seminary. Other recent tellings of the story appear in Davidson, *The Free Will Baptists in History* (Nashville: Randall House, 2001), 57–71, and Michael R. Pelt, *A History of Original Free Will Baptists* (Mount Olive, NC: Mount Olive College Press, 1996), 56–67.
5. Thomas S. Kidd, *George Whitefield: America's Spiritual Founding Father* (New Haven, Yale University Press, 2014), 97.
6. Morgan Edwards, "Tour of Rev. Morgan Edwards of Pennsylvania, To the American Baptists in North Carolina in 1772–73," MS, University Library, University of North Carolina at Chapel Hill, 21, https://archive.org/details/tourofrevmorgane1893edwa/page/n5/mode/2up; Paschal, *North Carolina Baptists*, 1:205, 416.
7. Morgan Edwards, "Materials Towards a History of the Baptists in the Provinces of Maryland, Virginia, North Carolina, South Carolina, Georgia" (MS, 1772, held in Furman University Library), 4:125–26, 131–34, 141–42, https://cdm16821.contentdm.oclc.org/digital/collection/jbt/id/220/rec/1; Edwards, "Tour," 21; https://www.ancestry.com/family-tree/person/tree/46416227/person/6866335771/facts; Davidson, *Free Will Baptists in History*, 64; Pelt, *Original Free Will Baptists*, 60–61; Owens, "When General Baptists Became Particular Baptists," 5–7, 9–10.
8. Stevenson, "Parker," 5:20; Owens, "When General Baptists Became Particular Baptists, 7–8. See Owens for a discussion of Gano's modern biographer, Terry Wolever, *The Life of John Gano, 1727-1804* (Springfield, MO: Particular Baptist Press, 2012), who takes a very dim view of the General Baptists.
9. Davidson, *Free Will Baptists in History*, 36–38, 58–61; Gardner, *Baptists of Early America*, 108.
10. C. Edwin Barrows, ed., *The Diary of John Comer*, in *Collections of the Rhode Island Historical Society* 8 (1893): 104.

11. Lemuel Burkitt and Jesse Read, *A Concise History of the Kehukee Baptist Association, from its Original Rise Down to 1803*, rev. by Henry L. Burkitt (Philadelphia: Lippincott, Grambo and Company, 1850), 32; W. T. Whitley, ed., *Minutes of the General Assembly of the General Baptists* (London: Kingsgate, 1909), 10, 30–31.
12. *The Standard Confession*, 1660, art. 11, repr. in J. Matthew Pinson, *A Free Will Baptist Handbook: Heritage, Beliefs, and Ministries*, 2nd ed. (Nashville: Randall House, 2022), 137.
13. Edwards, "Materials," 13.
14. "Reunion of the Synods of New York and Philadelphia," [part two of a two-part article] *Presbyterian Quarterly Review* 28 (1859): 543.
15. Rufus K. Hearn, "Origin of the Free Will Baptist Church of North Carolina," 169–70. Historian of Appalachian Baptists John Sparks draws an analogy between this eighteenth-century phenomenon and twentieth-century interactions between some Free Will Baptist ministers from outside Appalachia and some natives of Appalachia. Rather than requiring intensely emotional experiences in conversion, he says, such ministers went "to an extreme of Arminianism actually very probably like that which Paul Palmer must have preached on the North Carolina coast in the days before the Great Awakening; more than a few 'progressive' Free Will Baptist ministers preach salvation as belief by nothing more than a conscious rational choice followed by an oral confession. . . ." John Sparks, *The Roots of Appalachian Christianity: The Life and Legacy of Elder Shubal Stearns* (Lexington, KY: The University Press of Kentucky, 2001), 274; Davidson, *Free Will Baptists in History*, 62–63.
16. Edwards, "Materials," 4:125–26; Philip N. Mulder, *A Controversial Spirit: Evangelical Awakenings in the South* (New York: Oxford University Press, 2002), 40. Mulder's account of the episode is much like Hearn, "Origin of the Free Will Baptist Church," 169–70.
17. Davidson, *Free Will Baptists in History*, 67–68; Owens, "When General Baptists Became Particular Baptists" (unpublished essay, 2014), 5–11.
18. Owens, "When General Baptists Became Particular Baptists," 9; Pelt, *Original Free Will Baptists*, 64; Davidson, *Free Will Baptists in History*, 66–68.
19. Paschal, *North Carolina Baptists*, 1:218. Paschal reproduces the covenant on pp. 220–22 from the "record book of Sandy Creek Church in Franklin County, which William Walker used at its organization of January 29, 1771, and from that it was copied for the church at Poplar Spring by the Church Clerk, Isaac Pippin" (Paschal, *North Carolina Baptists*, 1:216).
20. Pelt, *Original Free Will Baptists*, 66.
21. Burkitt and Read, *Concise History of the Kehukee Association*, 218, 263. See Bryan F. LeBeau, "'The Acrimonious, Controversial Spirit' Among Baptists and Presbyterians in the Middle Colonies During the Great Awakening," *American Baptist Quarterly* 9 (1990): 167–83. See also Mulder, *A Contro-*

versial Spirit, 37–42. Mulder refers to "a controversial spirit," citing LeBeau. Mulder has the best treatment of the New Light Calvinism of the Regular Baptists. He describes the way in which Gano and the Regular Baptists, though less emotional than the Separate Baptists, together with them "appropriated the immediacy of the New Light to bolster their insistent style, absolute choices, and sudden, complete transformations" (38).

22. Hearn, "Origin of the Free Will Baptist Church," 160; "The North Carolina Freewill Baptists," *Freewill Baptist Quarterly* 4 (1856): 335. See pp. 10–11 of the Introduction on the distinction between the use of the name "Free Will Baptist" for the southern movement and "Freewill Baptist" for the northern movement.
23. See, e.g., the American General Baptist historian Ollie Latch, *History of the General Baptists* (Poplar Bluff, MO: The General Baptist Press, 1954), 113–14.
24. Paschal, *North Carolina Baptists*, 1:157.
25. William Whitsitt was right when he noted that the "influence" of George Whitefield "upon the fortunes of the Baptists of North Carolina" was immense, and that "the Calvinistic Baptists" of North Carolina "do owe to Mr. Whitefield their present position, their power and their prestige." "Notes and Comments," *North Carolina Baptist Historical Papers* 1 (1896–1897): 133. Similarly, the British Baptist historian W. T. Whitley said, "For thirty years the General Baptists were being overtaken by the Particular Baptists, and this is to be traced directly to the untiring energy of Whitefield." W. T. Whitley, *A History of the British Baptists* (London: Charles Griffin and Company, Limited, 1923), 206.
26. Douglas L. Winiarski, *Darkness Falls on the Land of Light: Experiencing Religious Awakenings in Eighteenth-Century New England* (Chapel Hill: University of North Carolina Press, for the Omohundro Institute of Early American History and Culture, Williamsburg, Virginia, 2017).
27. Winiarski, *Darkness Falls on the Land of Light*, 31, 33–34.
28. Winiarski, *Darkness Falls on the Land of Light*, 34–36, 155–56.
29. Winiarski, *Darkness Falls on the Land of Light*, 470–71.
30. Richard J. Hooker, ed., *The Carolina Backcountry on the Eve of the Revolution: The Journal and Other Writings of Charles Woodmason, Anglican Itinerant* (Chapel Hill: University of North Carolina Press, 1953), 102–3, quoted in John G. Crowley, *Primitive Baptists of the Wiregrass South, 1815 to the Present* (Gainesville, FL: University Press of Florida, 1998), 8.
31. Winiarski, *Darkness Falls on the Land of Light*, 396–97. "Separates" were New Lights who had left the Old Light Congregationalists. Separates who embraced believer's baptism were known as "Separate Baptists."
32. Pelt, *Original Free Will Baptists*, 67.
33. Winiarski, *Darkness Falls on the Land of Light*, 457–58, 462.
34. Winiarski, *Darkness Falls on the Land of Light*, 466, 528–29.

35. *Standard Confession, 1660*, art. 11.
36. Hearn, "Origin of the Free Will Baptist Church," 155–56, 158–59.
37. Hearn, "Origin of the Free Will Baptist Church," 155–57, quoting "The North Carolina Freewill Baptists," *Freewill Baptist Quarterly*, (1856): 331–32.
38. Quoted in Paschal, *North Carolina Baptists*, 1:528.
39. D. G. Hart, *The Lost Soul of American Protestantism* (Lanham, MD: Rowman and Littlefield, 2002), xxiii.
40. James Tunstead Burtchaell, *The Dying of the Light: The Disengagement of Colleges and Universities from their Christian Churches* (Grand Rapids: Eerdmans, 1998), 839.
41. Burtchaell, *Dying of the Light*, 839–41.
42. Burtchaell, *Dying of the Light*, 841.
43. Hart, *The Lost Soul*, 21; Nathan Hatch, *The Democratization of American Christianity* (New Haven: Yale University Press, 1989), 211–13.
44. See Kevin L. Hester, "Free Will Baptists," in *Encyclopedia of Religious Revivals in America*, Michael J. McClymond and Lisa Smith, eds. (Westport, CT: Greenwood Press, 2007).
45. Edwards, "Materials," 4:169–70. Edwards spelled it "Wingfield." Historians affirm that the Free Will Baptists in the Carolinas in the nineteenth century are direct descendants of the General Baptists associated with Paul Palmer, Joseph Parker, et al. William F. Davidson painstakingly and cogently demonstrates not only the historical proof but also the universal historiographical support for this assertion (Davidson, *Free Will Baptists in History*, 57–105). Proof of this direct connection first appears in four key primary sources: John Asplund's *Annual Register of the Baptist Denomination in North-America; To the First of November, 1790* (Southampton County, VA, 1792), Burkitt and Read's *Concise History of the Kehukee Association* (1803), the *1812 Abstract*, and then the 1820s–30s correspondence between the North Carolina Free Will Baptists and the northern Freewill Baptists (see chapter 3). In the nineteenth century, historians speak with one voice in affirming that the Free Will Baptists in North Carolina were direct descendants of the Palmer/Parker General Baptists. This includes northern Freewill Baptists I. D. Stewart (1862) and G. A. Burgess and J. T. Ward (1889), agreeing with an unsigned 1855 article, "The Early General Baptist Churches in the United States," *Freewill Baptist Quarterly* 3 (1855); southern Free Will Baptists R. K. Hearn (1875) and T. F. Harrison and J. M. Barfield (1897); Southern Baptists S. J. Wheeler (1847) and B. F. Riley (1898); Northern Baptists Albert Henry Newman (1898) and Henry Vedder (1907); and all other nineteenth-century historians who comment on the origins of the southern Free Will Baptists. This argument is brought over into twentieth-century historiography, with affirmations by Southern Baptists J. H. Grime (1902), George Paschal (his 1930 book as well as his article "Morgan Edwards' Materials Toward a His-

tory of the Baptists in the Province of North Carolina," *North Carolina Historical Review* 7 [1930]), M. A. Huggins (1967), Robert Gardner (1983), Leon McBeth (1987), Bill Leonard (2005), Albert Wardin (2007), and James Leo Garrett (2009); American Baptist Robert Torbet (1950); Disciples of Christ historian C. C. Ware (1927); American General Baptist Ollie Latch (1954); and Free Will Baptists G. W. Million and G. A. Barrett (1911), Damon Dodd (1956), Million (1958), William Davidson (1974, 1985, 2001 2006), George Stevenson (1991, 1994), Michael Pelt (1996), Matthew Pinson (1998), and Darrell Holley (2001). See bibliography for full citations.

46. Paschal, *North Carolina Baptists*, 1:171.
47. Stevenson, "Parker,"5:21–22; Pelt, *Original Free Will Baptists*, 54. Stevenson mistakenly surmises that John Stancill, who failed his ordination examination in the newly established Calvinist association in the 1700s, may have linked up with Joseph Parker. However, this Stancill was actually a Universalist and would play a large role in the subsequent history of the Universalist denomination in this region. Burkitt and Read refer to him as "Stansill" in *Concise History*, 218. He was referred to as the "Hell Redemptionist" John Stansel in an article entitled "Progress of Universalism in North and South Carolina," *The Universalist Magazine* (August 11, 1827), https://universalist-christian.net/universalist-history/progress-of-universalism-in-north-and-south-carolina-1827/.
48. After 1845, when it was proselytized by the Disciples of Christ, Wheat Swamp became Wheat Swamp Christian Church. See Naomi Dail Holder, *History of Wheat Swamp Christian Church* (1977), 65; "Gum Swamp OFWB History," https://gumswampchurch.org/gum-swamp-ofwb-church-history/, accessed August 2, 2021. This history says the church was founded in the 1750s; Minutes of the North Carolina Free Will Baptist General Conference November 6–9, 1845.
49. Stevenson, "Parker," 5:21; Davidson, *Free Will Baptists in History*, 62, 68–69. There is disagreement as to whether William Parker was Joseph Parker's cousin. All historians prior to Stevenson thought he was. Davidson sticks with this tradition, and Pelt seems ambivalent.
50. Paschal, *North Carolina Baptists*, 1:167; Stevenson, "Parker," 22; Davidson, *Free Will Baptists in History*, 70.
51. Wheeler, "History of the Meherrin Church," 47, 49; Hearn, "Origin of the Free Will Baptist Church," 165; Paschal, *North Carolina Baptists*, 1:521n76.
52. John Asplund, *The Annual Register of the Baptist Denomination in North-America; To the First of November, 1790* (1791), 37; Wheeler, "History of the Meherrin Church," 45.
53. Wheeler, "History of the Meherrin Church," 45.
54. Wheeler, "History of the Meherrin Church," 48.
55. Paschal, *North Carolina Baptists*, 1:222.

56. Davidson, *Free Will Baptists in History*, 44–45.
57. Asplund, *Annual Register of the Baptist Denomination*, 37; see Davidson's explanation of Asplund's listing (*Free Will Baptists in History*, 69–70); Edwards, "Tour," 28; Wheeler, "History of the Meherrin Church," 43; Burkitt and Read, *Concise History of the Kehukee Association*, 213. Henry Smith was a Free Will Baptist pastor who joined the Disciples of Christ in the 1840s. Charles Crossfield Ware, *Pamlico Profile* (New Bern, NC: Owen G. Dunn, 1961), 11; Charles Crossfield Ware, *Albemarle Annals* (Wilson, NC, 1961), 22.
58. Edwards, "Materials," 3:21–22; Benedict, *General History of the Baptist Denomination in America, and Other Parts of the World*, 2 vols. (Boston: Manning and Loring, 1813), 2:24; Wheeler, "History of the Meherrin Church," 48. Edwards noted that the church in Baltimore County started by Henry Sater was also proselytized by the Particular Baptists in the 1750s.
59. Burkitt and Read, *Concise History of the Kehukee Association*, 32; Paschal, *North Carolina Baptists*, 223.

CHAPTER THREE

1. Letter of May 28, 1827, from Jesse Heath to *The Morning Star*, June 28, 1827; See William F. Davidson, *The Free Will Baptists in History* (Nashville: Randall House, 2001), 76–91, for the most in-depth treatment of the evidence that the Free Will Baptists of the Carolinas in the nineteenth century emerged from the four churches left behind by the Palmer General Baptists. See also note 45 in chapter 2. According to R. K. Hearn, B. W. Nash alleged that the movement had started with Elders James Moore and Hearn himself. Yet the General Baptist origin of the movement, for which Davidson marshals great evidence, is undeniable, having been universally acknowledged by church historians of all varieties, inside and outside the Free Will Baptist Church. See Hearn, "Origin of the Free Will Baptist Church," in D. B. Montgomery, ed., *General Baptist History* (Evansville, IN: Courier, 1882), 170. Hearn's history was printed earlier in the *Toisnot Transcript* (May 20–June 17, 1875).
2. John Asplund, *The Annual Register of the Baptist Denomination in North-America; To the First of November, 1790* (Southampton County, VA, 1791), 36; Michael R. Pelt, *A History of Original Free Will Baptists* (Mount Olive, NC: Mount Olive College Press, 1996), 107–8; https://www.ancestry.com/discoveryui-content/view/359429:7734?tid=&pid=&queryId=6f04b6bf6b7b123dbb9253db8c63f7e2&_phsrc=owG1780&_phstart=successSource; James Roach, 1820 U. S. Census, Greene County, North Carolina, p. 256, NARA roll: M33_82, image: 150.
3. Davidson, *Free Will Baptists in History*, 87–88.
4. C. C. Ware, *Pamlico Profile* (New Bern, NC: Owen G. Dunn, 1961), 11. Smith later joined the Disciples of Christ. The proselytization of North Carolina

Free Will Baptists by the Disciples of Christ will be discussed later in this chapter.
5. Ware, *Pamlico Profile*, 24–25. Both Davidson and Pelt appear to agree that Winfield must have been one of the three, in addition to Roach. For the third, Hearn is put forward by Davidson (*Free Will Baptists in History*, 88), while Pelt says Smith is a possibility (*Original Free Will Baptists*, 108).
6. *An Abstract of the Former Articles of Faith Confessed by the Original Baptist Church Holding the Doctrine of General Provision With a Proper Code of Discipline* (New Bern, NC: Salmon Hall, 1814), hereafter referred to as the *1812 Abstract* (capitalization and punctuation in original). See Davidson, *Free Will Baptists in History*, 91–92. When "General Conference" is used with regard to North Carolina, it speaks of the main body of Free Will Baptists in Eastern North Carolina before that conference's amicable division into the Bethel and Shiloh Conferences in 1830. During the period between 1830 and 1850, the titles "Bethel" and "Shiloh" are used. After 1842, "General Conference" became the official name, though "Annual Conference" was often used informally.
7. *1812 Abstract*; *Standard Confession* of 1660. These confessions are reprinted in J. Matthew Pinson, *A Free Will Baptist Handbook: Heritage, Beliefs, and Ministries*, 2nd ed. (Nashville: Randall House, 2022), 137–54. For a facsimile of the title page of the *Standard Confession* of 1660, see the cover of *The Free Will Baptist* (July 27, 1960). See Davidson, *Free Will Baptists in History*, 91–99, for a comprehensive discussion of the relationship of the *1812 Abstract* and the *Standard Confession* of 1660.
8. Burkitt and Read, *A Concise History of the Kehukee Baptist Association, from its Original Rise Down to 1803*, rev. by Henry L. Burkitt (Philadelphia: Lippincott, Grambo and Company, 1850), 32; Davidson, *Free Will Baptists in History*, 91–92.
9. Elizabeth Smith, "The Former Articles of Faith of the North Carolina Free Will Baptists," *The Free Will Baptist* (July 27, 1960), 10; Davidson, *Free Will Baptists in History*, 93; *1812 Abstract*, repr. in Pinson, *Free Will Baptist Handbook*, 149–54.
10. *1812 Abstract*, arts. 2, 19–20. The *Abstract* is consistent with the entire General/Free Will Baptist tradition in having an open posture on whether there is a Millennium and, if so, whether Christ returns before or after it.
11. *1812 Abstract*, arts. 14, 15, 27.
12. *1812 Abstract*, arts. 14, 15, 27; Letter from Jesse Heath, May 29, 1827, *The Morning Star*, June 28, 1827, with editor's remarks; T. F. Harrison and J. M. Barfield, *History of the Free Will Baptists of North Carolina* (Ayden, NC: Free Will Baptist Publishing House, [1896]), 213; Minutes of the Annual North Carolina Bethel Conference (1831), transcribed by Robert E. Picirilli, 4 (hereafter referred to as "Minutes of the Bethel Conference"; all these have been transcribed by Picirilli from the reprinted versions in Harrison and Barfield

above, supplemented by material from *The Morning Star*, and are available at https://fwbhistory.com/?page_id=2978); Davidson, *Free Will Baptists in History*, 172–74. See pp. 16–17 of the Introduction to this book on the distinction between the use of the name "Free Will Baptist" for the southern movement and "Freewill Baptist" for the northern movement.

13. *Morning Star*, June 28, 1827; Davidson, *Free Will Baptists in History*, 85–86. These early letters have been gathered into a file by William Davidson and Robert Picirilli in the Free Will Baptist Historical Collection at Welch College under the title "Elias Hutchins and His Visit to North Carolina Free Will Baptists."

14. *Morning Star*, June 28, 1827. Robert E. Picirilli reprints these letters by Heath in his book *Little Known Chapters in Free Will Baptist History* (Nashville: Randall House, 2015), chapter 3.

15. *Morning Star*, June 28, 1827.

16. *Morning Star*, June 28, 1827.

17. *Morning Star*, December 13, 1927; May 28, 1828. "Newbern co." appears to be a misprint, since New Bern, North Carolina (then spelled "Newbern") was the county seat of Craven County. "Poiny Nick" seems to be a phonetic spelling of the "high-tider" pronunciation of what would later be known as the "Piney Neck" Church. For more on this dialect, see Walt Wolfram and Natalie Schilling-Estes, *Hoi Toide on the Outer Banks: The Story of the Ocracoke Brogue* (Chapel Hill: University of North Carolina Press, 1997).

18. *Morning Star*, May 28, 1828; October 30, 1829. "The Floridas" refers to West Florida and East Florida, into which the area had been divided before the acquisition from Spain in 1821.

19. Letter from Jesse Heath, November 13, 1820, *Morning Star*, December 22, 1830.

20. Letter from Thomas J. Latham, December 23, 1830, *Morning Star*, January 19, 1831.

21. William J. Collins, "Education, Migration, and Regional Wage Convergence in the United States," in T. J. Hatton, Kevin H. O'Rourke, and Alan M. Taylor, eds., *The New Comparative Economic History: Essays in Honor of Jeffrey G. Williamson* (Cambridge: MIT Press, 2007), 165–91. Interestingly, Collins shows that illiteracy in the South during the Reconstruction years and the early 1880s doubled from its rate in 1860. Thus it is not coincidental that the careful reader can detect a decline in the quality of writing by southern White Free Will Baptist pastors reared in the years following the Civil War when compared to writing of older ministers earlier in the nineteenth century. Of course, Black Free Will Baptist pastors' literacy increased after their emancipation from slavery, since they were then permitted by law to learn to read and write.

22. Beth Barton Schweiger, *A Literate South: Reading before Emancipation* (New Haven: Yale University Press, 2019), xv–xvi.

23. Hearn, "Origin of the Free Will Baptist Church," 148.
24. *The Morning Star*, October 30, 1929; "Hutchins, Rev. Elias," *Free Baptist Cyclopaedia* (Chicago: Free Baptist Cyclopaedia Company, 1889), 283. For the best information on Hutchins's visits, see Picirilli, *Little Known Chapters*, chapter 3.
25. Pelt, *Original Free Will Baptists*, 121. The Christian Connection was a small Arminian group, originally known as Republican Methodists, started by former Methodist minister and North Carolinian James O'Kelly. Its members, who largely came out of Methodist, Baptist, Congregational, and Presbyterian churches, were baptized by immersion and practiced open communion. Though it remained distinct from the Stone-Campbell movement, it was similar to it in its dissociation from denominationalism, its "no creed but the Bible" views, and its revivalism.
26. Davidson, *Free Will Baptists in History*, 162; Letter from Elias Hutchins, June 20, 1830, *Morning Star*, July 28, 1830; letter from Elias Hutchins, November 25, 1829, *Morning Star* December, 23, 1820; D. M. Graham, "Biographical Sketch of Rev. Elias Hutchins," *Freewill Baptist Quarterly* 8 (1860), 96; Pelt, *Original Free Will Baptists*, 121.
27. "Elias Hutchins in North Carolina," *Freewill Baptist Quarterly* 10 (1862), 293, repr. as chapter 4 in Picirilli, *Little Known Chapters*. Thomas Hood is obviously the layman of the same name who was in the 1820 and 1830 censuses for Lenoir County, rather than his twenty-year-old son who lived in his household. Hood Sr. migrated to Alabama by 1840 and died there near Selma in 1857. https://www.ancestry.com/family-tree/person/tree/103330334/person/260027316331/facts; Thomas Hood, 1820 U. S. Census, Lenoir County, North Carolina, p. 293, NARA roll: M33_80, image: 265; Thomas Hood, 1830 U. S. Census, Lenoir County, North Carolina, series: M19, roll: 122, p. 295, Family History Library Film: 0018088; Thomas Hood, 1840 U. S. Census, Perry County, Alabama, roll: 10, p. 293, Family History Library Film: 0002334.
28. "Elias Hutchins in North Carolina," 293.
29. Minutes of the Annual North Carolina (Bethel) Conference (1830), 4, transcribed by Robert E. Picirilli; Harrison and Barfield, *History of the Free Will Baptists of North Carolina*, 203–4; Pelt, *Original Free Will Baptists*, 117.
30. Harrison and Barfield, *History of the Free Will Baptists*, 214–15; Minutes of the Bethel Conference (1831), 5.
31. Harrison and Barfield, *History of the Free Will Baptists*, 219–20; Minutes of the Bethel Conference (1832), 4.
32. Harrison and Barfield, *History of the Free Will Baptists*, 219–20; Minutes of the Bethel Conference (1832), 4. Picirilli reprints the letters from McNab in *Little Known Chapters*, 103–15. See also *Morning Star*, November 14, 1833; September 3, 1834.

33. This association in the mountains, which will be discussed briefly in the next chapter, was founded by former United Baptists who had abandoned mild Calvinism and closed communion, adopted the washing of the saints' feet, and became Free Will Baptists. Extant records do not provide the circumstances or influences that led to their becoming Free Will Baptists.
34. Fonville's son, John Averette Fonville, was a minister in the Free Will Baptist conference in North Carolina until 1836 when he was "discontinued from these minutes: he having united with the South Carolina Conference [of Free Will Baptists]." Later he moved to Lowndes County, Alabama, where he eventually became a "Missionary Baptist" minister, but we do not know when he made the transition. See Harrison and Barfield, *History of the Free Will Baptists*, 224, 226; Minutes of the Bethel Conference (1836), 4; "Sketch of Rev. John Averette Fonville" (Montgomery Alabama, Alabama Department of Archives and History), 2, https://www.ancestry.com/imageviewer/collections/9581/images/32569_1220706416_0044-00000?ssrc=&backlabel=Return; Davidson, *Free Will Baptists in History*, 153–54.
35. Davidson, *Free Will Baptists in History*, 149–50. Hartsfield and his brothers exemplify the migration patterns of many North Carolina Free Will Baptists. Born in Johnston County, North Carolina, in 1799 and brought up in Lenoir County, Hartsfield married Lillian "Lovie" Barfield around 1826 near Hookerton in Greene County. They had ten children. His father John died in 1838 in Wheat Swamp. The Hartsfields moved to Butler County, Alabama, in 1836 and by 1855 were in Nacogdoches County, Texas, where Lillian died in 1864 and Lewis followed her in 1866. Hartsfield's move to Alabama coincided with a controversy that arose with him about which nothing is known, resulting in a resolution by the Bethel Conference held at Wheat Swamp in November 1835 to discipline the churches he pastored, which indicates he was under discipline for a reason undisclosed in the minutes. One infers from C. C. Ware that Lewis Hartsfield had not, like his brother David Hartsfield, joined the Disciples of Christ. Ware mentions both brothers, specifying that David became Disciples of Christ but referring to Lewis only as a Free Will Baptist minister. By 1840 David Hartsfield had moved to Columbus, Mississippi, along with his and Lewis's other brother Benjamin Franklin Hartsfield. David died there four years later, and Benjamin died in nearby Clay County, Mississippi, in 1887. It will be left for future researchers to ascertain what Lewis Hartsfield's ministerial labors entailed after his move from North Carolina, although he was evidently still a minister in 1856, when he solemnized a marriage in Nacogdoches, Texas. Harrison and Barfield, *History of the Free Will Baptists*, 213, 220–21, 224, 227; Charles Crossfield Ware, *North Carolina Disciples of Christ: A History of Their Rise and Progress, and of Their Contribution to Their General Brotherhood* (St.

Louis: Christian Board of Publication, 1927), 240–41; https://www.ancestry.com/family-tree/person/tree/47079702/person/6688756400/facts; https://www.findagrave.com/memorial/194510670/lewis-hartsfield; Lewis Hartsfield, 1830 US Census, Lenoir County, North Carolina, series: M19, roll: 122, p. 295, Family History Library Film: 0018088; Lewis Hartsfield, 1840 US Census, Butler County, Alabama, roll: 1, p. 157, Family History Library Film: 0002332; David Hartsfield, and Ben Hartsfield, 1840 US Census, Lowndes County, Mississippi, roll: 215, p. 216, Family History Library Film: 0014841; Lewis Hartsfield, 1850 U. S. Census, Beat 4, Butler County, Alabama, roll: 2, p. 226a; Lewis Hartsfield, 1860 US Census, Beat 7, Nacogdoches County, Texas, roll: M653_1301, p. 175, Family History Library Film: 805301; "History of Butler County Alabama," 187 (cited on Ancestry.com page noted above); "Marriage Records of Nacogdoches County, Texas, 1824–1881," 40, 131 (cited on Ancesry.com page noted above); cf. also Pauline Shirley Murrie, ed., "Marriage Records of Nacogdoches County, Texas, 1824–1881" (Houston: n.p., 1968), found at https://www.seekingmyroots.com/members/files/H011199.pdf; John Hartsfield, Find-A-Grave #147898579; Lewis Hartsfield, Find-A-Grave #194510670.

36. Harrison and Barfield, *History of the Free Will Baptists*, 220. For a brief discussion of Stinson and his soteriology, see J. Matthew Pinson, "Dissent from Calvinism in the Baptist Tradition," in *Calvinism: A Biblical and Theological Critique*, ed. David L. Allen and Steve W. Lemke (Nashville: B&H Academic, 2022), 254–55.

37. Harrison and Barfield, *History of the Free Will Baptists*, 212, 218; Minutes of the Bethel Conference (1831), 3; (1832), 3. In the early nineteenth century, what are now known as counties in South Carolina were called districts.

38. W. J. McKnight and Robert E. Picirilli, "The Spread of the Free Will Baptists from North Carolina to South Carolina: Redding Moore and the First Churches and Preachers, 1816–1849," in Robert E. Picirilli, *Free Will Baptist History: Exploring Our Origins and Identity* (Nashville: Randall House, 2019), 36; this book contains almost all the information about early South Carolina Free Will Baptists. See also Davidson, *Free Will Baptists in History*, 193–95. (Interestingly, Picirilli is a descendant of Moore.)

39. McKnight and Picirilli, "The Spread of Free Will Baptists," 36–40; https://www.ancestry.com/family-tree/person/tree/118235569/person/352137881475/facts; Reddin More, 1820 US Census, Marion County, South Carolina, p. 63, NARA roll: M33_121, image: 122; Reddin Moore, 1830 US Census, Marion County, South Carolina, series: M19, roll: 172, p. 33, Family History Library Film: 0022506; Reden Moore, 1840 US Census, Marion County, South Carolina, roll: 513, p. 156, Family History Library Film: 0022510; Reddin Moore, South Carolina Department of Archives and History, Columbia, South Carolina, US Census Mortality Schedules, South Carolina, 1850-1880, roll:

3, year: 1849, Marion, South Carolina; Letter to *The Morning Star* printed February 17, 1830.
40. McKnight and Picirilli, "The Spread of the Free Will Baptists," 36, 40–43; William Willis Bodie, *History of Williamsburg: Something About the People of Williamsburg County, South Carolina, From the First Settlement by Europeans About 1705 Until 1923* (Columbia, SC: State Company, 1923), 194.
41. Minutes of the Hookerton Free Will Baptist Church (Later Hookerton Disciples Church), 1830–1869 (November 30, 1830), 5. At this time, "interesting" according to Noah Webster's 1828 American Dictionary of the English Language, meant "engaging the affections . . . exciting emotions or passions."
42. Bodie, *History of Williamsburg*, 194, 241, 312–13; McKnight and Picirilli, "The Spread of the Free Will Baptists," 46–48; https://www.ancestry.com/family-tree/person/tree/6002978/person/-1338123290/facts; Saml McKenzie, 1850 U. S. Census, Sumter County, South Carolina, roll: 859, p. 406b; https://www.ancestry.com/family-tree/person/tree/170555479/person/312211140411/facts; Moab Huiet, 1860 US Census, Clarendon County, South Carolina, roll: M653_1217, p. 220, Family History Library Film: 805217; Moab Hewitt, Find-A-Grave #53656070; https://www.findagrave.com/memorial/53656070/moab-hewitt; McKenzie's son William appears to have moved with his family to West Florida in the 1880s, but there is no knowledge of his church affiliation. https://www.ancestry.com/family-tree/person/tree/6002978/person/-1320726830/facts; Wm McKenzie, Schedules of the Florida State Census of 1885, (National Archives Microfilm Publication M845, 13 Rolls), Records of the Bureau of the Census, Record Group 29, National Archives, Washington DC, 54.
43. Harrison and Barfield, *History of the Free Will Baptists*, 402.
44. McKnight and Picirilli, "The Spread of the Free Will Baptists," 49–50.
45. Davidson, *Free Will Baptists in History*, 195.
46. Minutes of the South Carolina State Association (1943). Nothing is known about the origins of the Beaver Creek Association, but McKnight and Picirilli conjecture that it might have come from the movement in the mountains of western North Carolina. See McKnight and Picirilli, "The Spread of the Free Will Baptists," 53. See also Davidson, *Free Will Baptists in History*, 195; Paul Reid, "The South Carolina State Association," in Robert E. Picirilli, ed., *History of Free Will Baptist State Associations* (Nashville: Randall House, 1976), 89.
47. Ware, *North Carolina Disciples of Christ*, 66, 241.
48. Pelt, *Original Free Will Baptists*, 129–30. See Timothy George, "An Evangelical Reflection on Scripture and Tradition," *Pro Ecclesia* 9 (2000): 205–6. Keith Stanglin says that *nuda Scriptura* was Campbell's approach, yet Stanglin is an example of some modern scholars in the Stone-Campbell movement who do not affirm *nuda Scriptura*. See Stanglin, *The Letter and Spirit of*

Biblical Interpretation: From the Early Church to Modern Practice (Downers Grove, IL: Baker Academic, 2018), 168, 222.
49. Pelt, *Original Free Will Baptists*, 140; Charles C. Ware, *Tar Heel Disciples* (New Bern, NC: Owen G. Dunn, 1942), 36.
50. Pelt, *Original Free Will Baptists*, 135, 137; Ware, *Tar Heel Disciples*, 22–24. See Pelt, *Original Free Will Baptists*, 128–43, for the best documentation and analysis of this controversy. Portions of this and the previous paragraph are adapted from J. Matthew Pinson, "Confessional, Baptist, and Arminian: General-Free Will Baptists and the Nicene Faith," in Timothy George, ed., *Evangelicals and the Nicene Faith: Reclaiming the Apostolic Witness* (Grand Rapids: Baker, 2011), 100–15, 218–25, repr. as chapter 7 in J. Matthew Pinson, *Arminian and Baptist: Explorations in a Theological Tradition* (Nashville: Randall House, 2015).
51. Harrison and Barfield, *History of the Free Will Baptists*, 231–32; Minutes of the Bethel Conference (1839), 4.
52. Harrison and Barfield, *History of the Free Will Baptists*, 232; Minutes of the Bethel Conference (1841), 3; Pelt, *Original Free Will Baptists*, 134; Ware, *North Carolina Disciples of Christ*, 92–93.
53. Ware, *Tar Heel Disciples*, 27–28; Pelt, *Original Free Will Baptists*, 139.
54. See J. Matthew Pinson, *Free Will Baptists and Church Government* (Antioch, TN: Historical Commission, National Association of Free Will Baptists, 2008), 9–11, as well as the discussion of church polity in chapter 10 of this book.
55. Minutes of the North Carolina Free Will Baptist General Conference (November 6–9, 1845), 1–4.
56. Minutes of the North Carolina Free Will Baptist General Conference (November 6–9, 1845), 1, 4.
57. Harrison and Barfield, *History of the Free Will Baptists*, 234; Ware, *North Carolina Disciples of Christ*, 86; Pelt, *Original Free Will Baptists*, 140–41.
58. Pelt, *Original Free Will Baptists*, 142.
59. Nathan O. Hatch, *The Democratization of American Christianity* (New Haven: Yale University Press, 1989), passim; for the Stone-Campbell movement, see esp. 67–80. Sometimes Hatch overplays his hand. There were democratic elements in early Christianity as well as in the confessional Anabaptist, Baptist, and other Free Church movements long before the Great Awakening. Such elements need not necessarily produce a *nuda Scriptura* approach to confessional subscription or a radically autonomous approach to church polity. See J. Matthew Pinson, "Free Will Baptists," in *Encyclopedia of Religious Controversies in the United States*, vol. 1, ed. Bill J. Leonard and Jill Y. Crainshaw (Santa Barbara, CA: ABC-CLIO, 2013), 318–20.
60. Harrison and Barfield, *History of the Free Will Baptists*, 236–40. See also James M. Woods, "Anti-Masonry," in Leonard and Crainshaw, ed., *Encyclopedia of Religious Controversies*, 27–29.

61. Harrison and Barfield, *History of the Free Will Baptists*, 241–42; Pelt, *Original Free Will Baptists*, 146–47; Davidson, *Free Will Baptists in History*, 184–85.
62. Pelt, *Original Free Will Baptists*, 151; Gary F. Barefoot, Alan K. Lamm, Michael R. Pelt, Ricky J. Warren, *A History of the Cape Fear Conference of Original Free Will Baptists, 1855-2010* ([no city], NC: Cape Fear Conference Historical Committee, 2011) 2; Minutes of the Oklahoma State Free Will Baptist Association, 1954, 8, 12; Picirilli, *Free Will Baptist History*, 159–60.
63. Harrison and Barfield, *History of the Free Will Baptists*, 243.
64. Harrison and Barfield, *History of the Free Will Baptists*, 244–46.
65. Harrison and Barfield, *History of the Free Will Baptists*, 244, 246; Davidson, *Free Will Baptists in History*, 244–45.
66. Harrison and Barfield, *History of the Free Will Baptists*, 249–50. Many larger conferences and associations in the South came to hold quarterly meetings with a smaller group of churches called quarterlies or union meetings, which would gather with the entire larger conference or association annually.
67. Harrison and Barfield, *History of the Free Will Baptists*, 254.
68. Harrison and Barfield, *History of the Free Will Baptists*, 255.
69. Robert E. Picirilli, *History of Tennessee Free Will Baptists* (Nashville: Historical Commission, Tennessee State Association of Free Will Baptists, 2012), 20.
70. Pelt, *Original Free Will Baptists*, 165; Harrison and Barfield, *History of the Free Will Baptists*, 257, 260–61, 263; McKnight and Picirilli, "The Spread of Free Will Baptists," 49–50.

CHAPTER FOUR

1. This statement must not be interpreted to downplay the influence of Randall-origin individuals and congregations on the formation of the National Association, who were from states that had both Palmer and Randall origins, especially Ohio, West Virginia, Missouri, Texas, and the Nebraska-Kansas Yearly Meeting. However, most of the Randall-origin churches in Texas and all those in Nebraska-Kansas either became Northern Baptists or are now defunct. As will be discussed in chapter 12, more than 80 percent of the membership of the early National Association was in churches east of the Mississippi River, the vast majority of which had their origins in the southern movement. Even of those west of the Mississippi, the origins of the states that provided most of the congregations in that region—Arkansas and Oklahoma—were from the Palmer movement.
2. G. W. Million and G. A. Barrett, *A Brief History of the Liberal Baptist People in England and America from 1606 to 1911* (Pocahontas, AR: Liberal Baptist Book and Tract Company, 1911), 177. While most of the Baptists throughout the South who became Free Will Baptist were United or Separate Baptist, at least one, Ellis Gore of the Mount Moriah Association in west-central Ala-

bama, came directly out of a Regular Baptist association. His story will be told later.
3. "Proto-Free Will Baptist" is my term, and "developing Free Will Baptist" is Robert Picirilli's term (he uses it in email correspondence on May 4, 2022). These terms describe the journey of United and Separate Baptists toward full Free Will Baptist confessional identity. Often these groups would go through periods of ambiguity and tolerance of various views before finally settling on the typical Free Will Baptist confessional affirmations, including the possibility of apostasy, open communion, the washing of the saints' feet, and the use of written confessions of faith.
4. Michael R. Pelt, *History of Original Free Will Baptists* (Mount Olive, NC: Mount Olive College Press, 1996), 131; Charles C. Bolton, *Poor Whites of the Antebellum South: Tenants and Laborers in Central North Carolina and Northeast Mississippi* (Durham, NC: Duke University Press, 1994), chapter 4, "Poverty Moves West: The Migration of Poor Whites to the Old Southwest," 66–83; Donald R. Lennon and Fred D. Ragan "Searching for Greener Pastures: Out-Migration in the 1800s and 1900s," *Tar Heel Junior Historian* 34, no. 2 (Spring 1995), https://www.ncpedia.org/anchor/searching-greener-pastures.
5. *The Morning Star*, October 30, 1829; T. F. Harrison and J. M. Barfield, *History of the Free Will Baptists of North Carolina* (Ayden, NC: Free Will Baptist Publishing House, [1896]), 220; Minutes of the Annual (Bethel) Conference of North Carolina (1832), 4 (transcribed by Robert E. Picirilli), hereafter referred to as "Minutes of the Bethel Conference."
6. Most of the brief examples in this paragraph will be fully narrated and documented later in the book.
7. Harrison and Barfield reported Elder James Moore's comment that a Free Will Baptist pastor from Greene County, North Carolina, moved to Georgia and planted a Free Will Baptist church "at a place called Chatahoochee." Harrison and Barfield, *History of the Free Will Baptists*, 128.
8. Hayles was amicably dismissed from the North Carolina General Conference at some point in the nineteenth century and established a Free Will Baptist church in Marion County, Florida. He stayed in contact with the General Conference until his death in Florida in 1888 and was mentioned in the 1889 minutes as a Free Will Baptist minister. Harrison and Barfield, *History of the Free Will Baptists*, 390.
9. The aforementioned Stewart, from southwest Georgia, was the first southern Free Will Baptist to start a Free Will Baptist church in Texas.
10. In addition to the Carolinas, use of the *1812 Abstract* is seen in at least the following predominantly White bodies: the Tennessee River and Muscle Shoals State Line Associations (south-central and West Tennessee, North Mississippi, North Alabama); the South Georgia, Little River, Georgia Union, and Old Line Associations and the Marietta Union Conference

(South Georgia); the Union Association (South Georgia, Florida), the Salem Association (Florida), the West Florida and South East Alabama Liberty Association (Florida, southeast Alabama—it used a shortened version of the *Abstract*) the John-Thomas Association (with churches in Virginia, Kentucky, Ohio, West Virginia, Indiana), and the Mount Olive Association (Kentucky, Tennessee).

11. While the above examples are briefer and will be narrated and documented later, the story of Thomas Hood Sr. and Jr. will be detailed and documented here at greater length.

12. https://www.ancestry.com/family-tree/person/tree/103330334/person/260027316331/facts; Thomas Hood, 1830 US Census, Lenoir County, North Carolina, series: M19, roll: 122, p. 295, Family History Library Film: 0018088; Thomas Hood, 1840 US Census, Perry County, Alabama, roll: 10, p. 293, Family History Library Film: 0002334; Thomas Hood, 1850 US Census, Pences, Dallas County, Alabama, roll: 4, p. 282a; https://www.ancestry.com/family-tree/person/tree/103330334/person/260027316330/facts; Thomas Hood, 1860 US Census, Washington County, Texas, roll: M653_1307, p. 154, Family History Library Film: 805307; Thomas Hood, 1870 US Census, Beat 3, Washington County, Texas, roll: M593_1608, p. 219B; Texas, US, Marriage Index, 1824-2017, Texas Department of State Health Services; Austin, Texas; https://www.ancestry.com/family-tree/person/tree/103330334/person/260027317743/facts

13. *The Morning Star*, May 28, 1828; October 30, 1829; https://www.ancestry.com/family-tree/person/tree/2049754/person/1772550866/facts?_phsrc=owG1667&_phstart=successSource; Rev. Elijah Hosea Callaway, Find-A-Grave #76606619; https://www.ancestry.com/family-tree/person/tree/2049754/person/1772550920/facts; *Marriages, Vol. 1A, 1809-1816, Georgia, US, Marriage Records From Select Counties, 1828-1978, County Marriage Records, 1828–1978*, The Georgia Archives, Morrow, Georgia, 162.

14. Harrison and Barfield, *History of the Free Will Baptists*, 229; Minutes of the Bethel Conference (1838), 3; https://www.ancestry.com/family-tree/person/tree/82618410/person/30517747975/facts; https://www.ancestry.com/family-tree/person/tree/17480198/person/18018564157/facts; Brinson Hollis, 1850 US Census, Southern Division, Dale County, Alabama, roll: 4, p. 175b; Brinson Hollis, 1860 US Census, Jackson County, Florida, roll: M653_107, p. 744, Family History Library Film: 803107; *Index to Marriage Bonds—Abstracts (1780–1865)*, North Carolina County Registers of Deeds, Microfilm, Record Group 048, North Carolina State Archives, Raleigh, NC; *Loose Wills and Estate Papers, 1746-1890*, North Carolina, County Court of Pleas and Quarter Sessions (Craven County).

15. All these references are to a letter from the papers of Jeremiah Heath held in the Free Will Baptist Historical Collection at the University of Mount

Olive. A transcription and photocopy of the handwritten letter is reprinted in Chester H. Pelt, *A History of the Salem Association of Free Will Baptists of West Florida* (Marianna, FL: Salem Free Will Baptist Association, 1987), 8–10; Boyett is alternately spelled "Boyt" and "Boit"; https://www.ancestry.com/family-tree/person/tree/9548447/person/-782713363/facts, accessed July 27, 2022; James Boyet, 1810 US Census, Duplin County, North Carolina, roll: 40, p. 682, image: 00052, Family History Library Film: 0337913; James Boyett, 1820 US Census, Duplin County, North Carolina, p. 170, NARA roll: M33_80, image: 170; Henry Boyt, 1850 US Census, Pike County, Alabama, roll: 13, p. 204b; Henry Boyt, 1860 US Census, Division 2, Santa Rosa County, Florida, roll: M653_109, p. 713, Family History Library Film: 803109; Henry Boyett, 1900 U. S Census, Wrights Creek, Geneva County, Alabama, roll: 17, p. 2, enumeration district: 0072, FHL microfilm: 1240017; Allie Boyett, 1910 US Census, Fadette, Geneva County, Alabama, roll: T624_12, p. 10A, enumeration district: 0097, FHL microfilm: 1374025; Alabama Department of Archives and History, Montgomery, Alabama, *Confederate Pension Applications, 1880-1940*, collection #: Microfilm in the Research Room, roll description: Boyd, Jasper—Bradford, Wm. N.

16. https://www.ancestry.com/family-tree/person/tree/9548447/person/-782713363/facts?_phsrc=0wG1663&_phstart=successSource; https://www.ancestry.com/family-tree/person/tree/9548447/person/-782709822/facts; Bureau of Land Management, *US, General Land Office Records, 1776-2015*, Washington DC, USA, Federal Land Patents, State Volumes, 324; *1809 – 1885, Alabama, US, County Marriage Records, 1805-1967*, Marriage Records. Alabama Marriages, County courthouses, Alabama, 358. Allie Guy's family had moved from Duplin County, North Carolina, to Alabama by 1844, when her brother S. J. Guy was born (https://www.ancestry.com/family-tree/person/tree/9548447/person/-782701840/facts); County Court Records at Kenansville, NC and FHL # 0422156 item 2, North Carolina, US, Marriage Index, 1741-2004; S. J. Guy, 1860 US Census, Precinct 5, Butler County, Alabama, roll: M653_3, p. 117, Family History Library Film: 803003). Pelt mistakenly inferred that Hollis was Boyett's sibling, no doubt misinterpreting Boyett's use of "our dear Brother," "Brother Hollis," and "my Brother Hollis." However, this can only refer to the Free Will Baptist minister in the region Brinson Hollis. There was never any Hollis Boyett, Boyt, or Boit anywhere in these parts or any in federal census records. "Our dear brother" makes sense because Hollis had also ministered alongside Jeremiah Heath in the same conference, and the two were from the same county in North Carolina.

17. Pelt, *History of the Salem Association*, 8–10.
18. Pelt, *History of the Salem Association*, 8–10. "Missionary Baptists" refers to non-Free Will Baptists who split from what came to be known as Primitive Baptists over the latter's opposition to missions societies or missionary

endeavors outside the local church. Most Southern Baptists were known as Missionary Baptists.

19. Hollis is on the roster of ordained ministers in the 1893 Minutes of the Eighth Annual Session of the State Line Free Will Baptist Association with a Highfall, Henry County, Alabama, address. (He is also listed in the 1897 Minutes.) Born in 1818 in Craven County, North Carolina, he lived until 1906 and was laid to rest in nearby Holmes County, Florida, https://www.ancestry.com/family-tree/person/tree/29668469/person/112152170614/story; Benjamin B. Hollis, Find-A-Grave #31958321.

20. Henry Boyett, Find-A-Grave #193685028. Boyett was drawing a Confederate army pension when he died (https://www.ancestry.com/imageviewer/collections/1677/images/32719_237101-00340?pId=2432781); Alabama Department of Archives and History, Montgomery, Alabama, *Confederate Pension Applications, 1880–1940*, collection #: Microfilm in the Research Room, roll description: Boyd, Jasper - Bradford, Wm. N.); David James "D. J." Boyett, Find-A-Grave #42440922, accessed August 8, 2022. D. J. Boyett was an active layman in Free Will Baptist churches in this area. For example, he represented Hinson Free Will Baptist Church in Geneva County, Alabama, as a delegate to the 1911 annual session of the Liberty Association. See Minutes of the West-Florida and South-East Alabama Liberty Free Will Baptist Association (1911), 2. He and his son Henry S. Boyett were both delegates from Hinson Church in 1914, and Henry S., who lived in Slocomb, Alabama, was the church's clerk.

21. https://www.ancestry.com/family-tree/person/tree/153604746/person/3220 53420983/facts?_phsrc=owG125&_phstart=successSource; Levi Griffin, 1850 US Census, District 7, Baker County, Georgia, roll: 61, p. 51b; Levi Griffen, *County Court Records – FHL # 0296803-0296808, North Carolina, US, Marriage Index, 1741-2004*, North Carolina State Archives, Raleigh, North Carolina; John Griffin, North Carolina, US, Compiled Census and Census Substitutes Index, 1790-1890; Pelt, *History of the Salem Association*, 8–9.

22. Pelt, *History of the Salem Association*, 8–10.

23. Pelt, *History of the Salem Association*, 8–10. For more information on the Chattahoochee United Baptist Association and its process of becoming Free Will Baptist, see the next section.

24. The 1870 census shows that Benjamin Tipton was a "minister of the gospel" in Early County, Georgia. See https://www.ancestry.com/imageviewer/collections/7163/images/4263444_00113?usePUB=true&_phsrc=owG129 &_phstart=successSource&usePUBJs=true&pId=3106823; https://www.ancestry.com/family-tree/person/tree/4849389/person/25338154896/facts?_phsrc=owG132&_phstart=successSourcem; Benjamin Tipton, 1870 US Census, District 26, Early County, Georgia, roll: M593_148, p. 55A; *Marriages, Book AA, 1824-1841, Georgia, US, Marriage Records From Select Coun-*

ties, *1828-1978*, County Marriage Records, 1828-1978, The Georgia Archives, Morrow, Georgia, 23; Rev. Benjamin "Ben" Tipton, Find-A-Grave #30833596.

25. Minutes of the Chattahoochee Association (1850, 1851, 1854, 1879); there are no extant minutes for 1852 or 1853. See also Jo Smith Webb, *Linkage: The Study of a Family*, vol. 2 (self-published, 1984), 301; Minutes of the First Twenty Years of Quarterly Sessions of the Paul Palmer Fellowship Conference of the Original Free Will Baptist, "History of the Churches," 110. The United Baptist Church in Metter never appears to have been a member of the Chattahoochee Association.

26. Minutes of the Chattahoochee Association (1850, 1851, 1854); Pelt, *History of the Salem Association*, 8-10.

27. The information about Stewart comes from R. L. Vaughn, "The Founding of the Free Will Baptist Work in Texas: The Story of A. M. Stewart from Georgia," in Robert E. Picirilli, *Free Will Baptist History: Exploring Our Origins and Identity* (Nashville: Randall House, 2019), 110-12. Cedar Springs Church was in the Chattahoochee Association's minutes in 1879 and 1881-83, and 1885. See Minutes of the Chattahoochee Association (1879, 1881, 1882, 1885), "Statistical Table" (1883), 16. Cedar Springs left to help form Martin Association in 1887. See Minutes of the Chattahoochee Association for those years and the Minutes of the First Annual Session of the Martin Freewill Baptist Association (1887).

28. Million and Barrett, *Brief History of the Liberal Baptist People*, 199; Gary F. Barefoot, Alan K. Lamm, Michael R. Pelt, and Ricky J. Warren, *A History of the Cape Fear Conference of Original Free Will Baptists, 1855-2010* (Cape Fear Historical Committee, 2011), 5; Picirilli, *Free Will Baptist History*, 182-83; Minutes of the Southeastern Association (1946). There are no extant minutes for this association before 1927, and none between that year and 1946. See Picirilli, *Free Will Baptist History*, 179-231, for detailed information about Lucas.

29. Wayne Love, *History of the Howard Grove Free Will Baptist Church* (Cottonwood, AL: Howard Grove Free Will Baptist Church, 1960), 5; Pelt, *History of the Salem Association*, 13.

30. B. W. Nash was a non-Free Will Baptist who attempted to get all baptistic non-Calvinists together, including Free Will Baptists, General Baptists, and Disciples of Christ. For more on Nash, see chapter 9.

31. Love, *History of Howard Grove*, 5; Pelt, *History of the Salem Association*, 13-17. The Nash influence is much more probable than Randall influence, which Pelt posited. Pelt did not know about the Nash movement, the research on which has largely been done in the twenty-first century by Robert Vaughn and Robert Picirilli, *Free Will Baptist History*, 131-77. More information will be provided for other areas of Alabama later in the chapter.

32. Jerry Whitworth, *The History of Nettle Ridge Church, 1856-1994* (1994), 10-15;

Pelt, *History of the Salem Association*, 11, citing the organizational minutes of Salem Free Will Baptist Church (1889); J. Matthew Pinson, "E. L. St. Claire and the Free Will Baptist Experience, 1893–1916," *Viewpoints: The Journal of the Georgia Baptist Historical Society* 17 (2000): 21.

33. Ernest Owen and Darrell Holley, "A Brief History of the Florida State Association," *The Historical Review: A Journal of Church History Published by the Florida State Association of Free Will Baptists* 2 (1994): 51–52.

34. Picirilli, *Free Will Baptist History*, 55–108, has done more than any historian to shed light on this background. This information is from "Genealogy Report: Ancestors of Osiris Merlin Johnson," *Genealogy*, printed November 30, 2001, https://www.genealogy.com/ftm/j/o/h/Osiris-M-Johnson/GENE 1-0030.html; *The* (Milledgeville, GA) *Reflector* (Nov. 17, 1818), 3.

35. Picirilli, *Free Will Baptist History*, 62–63; Minutes of the Ocmulgee Baptist Association, 1829, 2–3, as cited by Daniel Williams, "Origins of the Free Will Baptists in Georgia," *The Journal of Baptist Studies* 6 (2014): 37. For more information about the exchange between White and Mercer, see Anthony L. Chute, *A Piety Above the Common Standard: Jesse Mercer and the Defense of Evangelistic Calvinism* (Macon, GA: Mercer University Press, 2004), 83–92.

36. Picirilli, *Free Will Baptist History*, 75; Williams, "Origins of Free Will Baptists in Georgia," 40–41. This is explicitly stated later in a circular letter in the Minutes of the Chattahoochee Association (1850), 4–6.

37. Picirilli, *Free Will Baptist History*, 70.

38. Picirilli, *Free Will Baptist History*, 70–72. No confession of faith is printed in the 1847, 1851, or 1854 Chattahoochee minutes, which are extant. See chapter 10 for a discussion of Chattahoochee's later emendation of the New Hampshire Confession to make it consistent with the doctrine of the possibility of apostasy. This is seen in the first extant minutes after 1854, which are from 1879. In 1842, the minutes stated that "we never did adopt the Sharon Confession of Faith, nor did we ever design to do so." Minutes of the Chattahoochee Association (1842), 5; (1879), 14–16. See Williams, "Origins of Free Will Baptists in Georgia," 50. That design apparently changed after 1842.

39. David Benedict, *A General History of the Baptist Denomination in America and Other Parts of the World* (New York: Lewis Colby and Co., 1848), 744, as cited by Williams, "Origins of Free Will Baptists in Georgia," 49; Picirilli, *Free Will Baptist History*, 69.

40. See Walter B. Shurden, *Not a Silent People: Controversies That Have Shaped Southern Baptists* (Macon, GA: Smyth and Helwys, 1995), 48–50. Even as late as the twenty-first century, this was the view of many Southern Baptists, as indicated by the fact that the SBC International Mission Board would require re-immersion of missionary candidates whose baptism had been in churches that affirmed the possibility of apostasy. See James A. Patterson, *James Robinson Graves: Staking the Boundaries of Baptist Identity*, Studies in

Baptist Life and Thought, ed. Michael A. G. Haykin (Nashville: B&H Academic, 2012), 199–201.
41. See chapter 10 for more on the Chattahoochee Association's views on perseverance.
42. Minutes of the Chattahoochee Association (1883), 7–12; (1891), 3, 11.
43. Harrison and Barfield, *History of the Free Will Baptists*, 230–31; Minutes of the Bethel Conference (1839), 3–4. This is an obvious reference to the United Baptists, despite the use of the term "Union Baptist" the first time they are mentioned in the Bethel Conference minutes.
44. Harrison and Barfield, *History of the Free Will Baptists*, 128.
45. https://www.ancestry.com/family-tree/person/tree/41932790/person/1970 7490310/facts?_phsrc=owG1806&_phstart=successSource; Kimbrel Massey, 1840 US Census, District 921, Muscogee County, Georgia, roll: 47, p. 330, Family History Library Film: 0007045; Kimbrill Massey, 1850 US Census, District 9, Muscogee County, Georgia, roll: 79, p. 389a; Kimbrel Massey, 1860 US Census, Georgia Militia District 814, Macon County, Georgia, roll: M653_130, p. 76, Family History Library Film: 803130; Rev. Kimbrell Massey, Find-A-Grave #76365053, accessed August 8, 2022.
46. https://www.ancestry.com/family-tree/person/tree/178491448/person/2623 24708880/facts; https://www.ancestry.com/family-tree/178491448 /family?cfpid=262323221140&fpid=262324708880&usePUBJs=true; James Hartsfield, 1860 US Census, Georgia Militia District 757, Macon County, Georgia, roll: M653_130, p. 101, Family History Library Film: 803130; James Hartsfield, Find-A-Grave #53705596, accessed August 8, 2022.; Minutes of the Chattahoochee Association (1847), 3; (1848), 2; (1851), 9; (1854), 7.
47. Harrison and Barfield, *History of the Free Will Baptists*, 243–46.
48. Minutes of the Chattahoochee Association (1854), 3–5.
49. Picirilli, *Free Will Baptist History*, 137. The Mount Moriah Association in Alabama referred to the "Chattahoochee United Free Will Baptist Association" in the minutes of its 1874 annual session. See Minutes of the Mount Moriah Association (1874), 1. What was meant by the statement in the Minutes of the North Carolina General Conference that the Chattahoochee Association wanted to unite all "Free Will Baptists"? Is this meant in the narrow denominational sense or in the broader "free willer" sense that militated against particular and irresistible grace?
50. Minutes of the Annual North Carolina (Bethel) Conference of North Carolina (November 5–8, 1829), transcribed by Robert E. Picirilli, 7; https://www.ancestry.com/family-tree/person/tree/21341855/person/29125305480 /facts?_phsrc=owG1352&_phstart=successSource; https://www.ancestry.com /family-tree/person/tree/21341855/person/29125263128/facts; Matthew Spivey, 1850 US Census, Columbus County, North Carolina, roll: 626, p. 258b; Matthew Spivey, 1860 US Census, Georgia Militia District 1170, Coffee County,

Georgia, roll: M653_117, p. 539, Family History Library Film: 803117; Matthew Spivey, 1870 US Census, Subdivision 130, Ware County, Georgia, roll: M593_181, p. 15A; Lila An Spivey, 1880 US Census, Millwood, Ware County, Georgia, roll: 170, p. 34C, enumeration district: 095.

51. Minutes of the South Georgia Association (1903); Picirilli says that Union was formed out of the former Liberty and Ochlochnee Associations; see *Free Will Baptist History*, 98; Minutes of the Georgia Union Association (1900); Minutes of the Union Association (1926); Minutes of the Little River Association (1936); Minutes of the Ogeechee Association (1940); Minutes of the Marietta Union Conference (1912); https://www.ancestry.com/family-tree/person/tree/11792679/person/-243225605/facts. John A. Blanton, 1900 US Census, Militia District 1364, Appling County, Georgia, roll: 178, p. 18, enumeration district: 0104, FHL microfilm: 1240178; John A. Blanton, 1920 US Census, Surrency, Appling County, Georgia, roll: T625_233, p. 3A, enumeration district: 6; John A. Blanton, 1930 US Census, Militia District 1239, Appling County, Georgia, pg. 4A, enumeration district: 0008, FHL microfilm: 2340071; Rev. John Abraham Blanton, Find-A-Grave #43863591, accessed August 8, 2022; David Blanton, 1850 US Census, South Division, Duplin County, North Carolina, roll: 629, p. 56a. The original name of the South Georgia Association, Ogeechee, is not to be confused with the later-established Ogeechee Association nearby. Both these associations exist to this day.

52. Minutes of the Middle Georgia Association of United Baptists (1897), 6 (cover page missing); Picirilli, *Free Will Baptist History*, 91–92.

53. The Birmingham District, Liberty, and East Alabama Associations also have their origins in the United Free Will Baptist movement, though it is uncertain whether they developed from Georgia Free Will Baptists who moved west or from the southeast Alabama Free Will Baptists who migrated north. See Minutes of the Liberty Association [southwest Alabama] (1906); Minutes of the Liberty Association No. 2 [southwest Alabama] (1925); Minutes of the Southern Union Association (1931); Minutes of the Birmingham District Association (1939); Minutes of the Liberty Association [East Alabama] (1936); Minutes of the East Alabama Association (1958). Most of these associations, in their early years, added "Church of Christ" to their name, using it in a generic sense unconnected to the usage of the phrase in the Stone-Campbell movement.

CHAPTER FIVE

1. F. L. Smith, "Rise and Progress of Mt. Moriah Church and Mt. Moriah Association with Some of Their Labors," handwritten MS, July 10, 1888 (held in the Free Will Baptist Historical Collection, Welch College); Notes of

M. P. Gore, grandson of Ellis Gore, McShan, Pickens County, Alabama, November 12, 1971 (held in the Free Will Baptist Historical Collection, Welch College); William F. Davidson, *The Free Will Baptists in History* (Nashville: Randall House, 2001), 202–4; https://www.ancestry.com/family-tree/person/tree/154088415/person/172242224010/facts; Notley Gore, Find-A-Grave #52961646; Alabama Surname Files (Montgomery: Alabama Department of Archives and History), Box or Film Number: M84-4690; Obituary, Ellis Gore, *Pickens County Herald & West Alabamian* (November 14, 1883), 3.
2. Smith, "Rise and Progress of Mt. Moriah Church."
3. M. P. Gore notes; Smith, "Rise and Progress," 4; Davidson, *Free Will Baptists in History*, 204; J. D. O'Donnell, "The Alabama State Association," in Robert E. Picirilli, ed., *History of Free Will Baptist State Associations* (Nashville: Randall House, 1976), 1; Historical Marker, Mount Moriah Free Will Baptist Church, Pickens, County, Alabama (https://www.findagrave.com/memorial/28783043/ellis-gore/photo); "A Discovery," *The Baptist* (November 21, 1846), 194–95; *The 2019 Free Will Baptist Yearbook* (Antioch, TN: Executive Office, National Association of Free Will Baptists, 2019), B-6.
4. M. P. Gore notes.
5. Smith, "Rise and Progress," 4.
6. Smith, "Rise and Progress," 9–10.
7. Smith, "Rise and Progress," 10.
8. Minutes of the Mount Moriah Association (1874), 8; Davidson, *Free Will Baptists in America*, 204–5; O'Donnell, "Alabama State Association," 1.
9. For more on the Liberal Baptist movement associated with B. W. Nash, see chapter 9. See Minutes of the Mount Moriah Association (1874), 1; Robert E. Picirilli and R. L. Vaughn, "Unity Movements," in Robert E. Picirilli, *Free Will Baptist History: Exploring Our Origins and Identity* (Nashville: Randall House, 2019), 154–55. Extant records seem to indicate that Gore did not practice the washing of the saints' feet, likely as a result of Nash's influence.
10. Minutes of the Vernon Association (1883); Minutes of the Tupelo Association (1916); Minutes of the Jasper Association (1887); *The 2019 Free Will Baptist Yearbook* (Antioch, TN: Executive Office, National Association of Free Will Baptists, 2019), B-3–9.
11. There is disagreement from the numbering of the minutes and from a circular letter from C. C. Vandiver in 1875, but the association seems to have been founded in 1844. See the Minutes of the Bethlehem Association (1871, 1875). The November 21, 1846, issue of *The Baptist* mentions undated minutes that indicated it was the association's "third session," thus indicating that the first session was in 1844. This lines up with the association's own dating in its Minutes. The confusion surrounding the founding date is exacerbated by the fact that the *Free Baptist Cyclopaedia* says Vandiver founded the Bethlehem Association in 1839. See G. A. Burgess and J. T.

Ward, "Tennessee," *Free Baptist Cyclopaedia* (Chicago: Free Baptist Cyclopaedia Company, 1889), 641.

12. https://www.ancestry.com/family-tree/person/tree/164264219/person/292223200343/facts; https://www.ancestry.com/family-tree/person/tree/60507190/person/182021525379/facts; Carlisle Vandiver, 1840 US Census, Wayne County, Tennessee, roll: 536, p. 89, Family History Library Film: 0024550; Carlile C. Vandiver, 1850 US Census, District 7, Lawrence County, Tennessee, roll: 886, p. 358b; C. C. Vandiver, 1860 US Census, District 7, Lawrence County, Tennessee, roll: M653_1260, p. 442, Family History Library Film: 805260; C. C. Vandiver, 1880 US Census, District 2, Perry County, Tennessee, roll: 1274, p. 387C, enumeration district: 146; "A Discovery," *The Baptist* (November 21, 1846), 194–95. This article in *The Baptist* also lists C. C. Vandiver's brother, Elisha (Elias) Vandiver, as a member of a select committee (which included C. C. and their father G. H.) elected to "arrange the unfinished business." For mentions of Elisha Vandever as a Free Will Baptist preacher, see Elisha Vandever, 1850 US Census, District 7, Lawrence County, Tennessee, roll: 886, p. 361b; "Carlisle G. Vandivere," *A Memorial and Biographical History of McLennan, Falls, Bell and Coryell Counties, Texas* (Chicago: Lewis Publishing Company, 1893), 984.

13. Minutes of the Bethlehem Association (1871, 1875). The Forked Deer Association, of which no records have survived, is now defunct.

14. Minutes of the Bethlehem Association (1875). The minutes of the Bethlehem Association from 1872 and 1873 indicate that they authorized the publication of a hymnal, of which no copies are extant. The only extant minutes for Bethlehem Association are from 1871, 1872, 1873, and 1875.

15. Minutes of the Tennessee River Association (1891); Minutes of the Little Brown's Creek Association (1899).

16. Minutes of the Tennessee River Association (1891, 1924, 1927); Minutes of the Little Brown's Creek Association (1899); G. A. Burgess and J. T. Ward, "Tennessee," *Free Baptist Cyclopaedia*, 641–42.

17. Minutes of the Flint River Association (1937); Minutes of the Muscle Shoals State Line Association (1927); G. W. Million and G. A. Barrett, *A Brief History of the Liberal Baptist People in England and America from 1606 to 1911* (Pocahontas, AR: Liberal Baptist Book and Tract Company, 1911), 196. Individuals such as J. B. Bloss, L. V. Pinson (this author's grandfather), and Fay Gilbert Forlines came from congregations that emerged from this movement.

18. See William L. Lumpkin, *Baptist Foundations in the South: Tracing through the Separates the Influence of the Great Awakening, 1754–1787* (Nashville: Broadman, 1961); Morgan Scott, *History of the Separate Baptist Church* (Indianapolis: Hollenbeck, 1901); John Sparks, *Roots of Appalachian Christianity: The Life and Legacy of Elder Shubal Stearns* (Lexington, KY: The University Press of Kentucky, 2001), 209, 235, 267–69; Keith Harper, *A Mere*

Kentucky of a Place: The Elkhorn Association and the Commonwealth's First Baptists, America's Baptists (Knoxville: University of Tennessee Press, 2021), 3–6, 65–76; Steve W. Lemke, "History or Revisionist History? How Calvinistic Were the Overwhelming Majority of Baptists and Their Confessions in the South until the Twentieth Century?" *Southwestern Journal of Theology* 57 (2015): 235–36; J. H. Spencer, *A History of Kentucky Baptists from 1769 to 1885*, rev. Mrs. Burilla B. Spencer. 2 vols. (Cincinnati: J. R. Baumes, 1885).

19. In 1820 the Nolynn Association, with Heaton as moderator, affirmed the typical Separate Baptist *via media* between Arminianism and Calvinism, which included universal atonement, the opportunity for anyone to repent and believe, and the certain perseverance of the saints. See Minutes of the Nolynn Association of Separate Baptists (1820), 6, http://www.separate-baptist.org/downloads/nolynn/NolynnMinutes1819-1884.pdf. It would be a great coincidence if the "Old Good Spring Baptist Church" was not the same church as the modern-day Good Springs Free Will Baptist Church. However, as Robert Picirilli points out, there is no documentary proof that this is the same congregation. Nothing would be known about the origins of Cumberland Association were it not for Picirilli's research, which is summarized in his chapter on the subject in *Little Known Chapters in Free Will Baptist History* (Nashville: Randall House, 2015), 27–72. Some of his earlier research is found in "A Study of Separate, Free Will Baptist Origins in Middle Tennessee," *The Quarterly Review* 37 (1977), 44–52. See also Phillip T. Morgan, "Founding of the Cumberland Association," in Roy W. Harris and Phillip T. Morgan, *The Cumberland Association: Celebrating 175 Years of Leadership, Ministry, and Service* (Lebanon, TN: RHM, 2018); Phillip T. Morgan, "Robert Heaton (1765–1843)," in *Arminian Baptists: A Biographical History of Free Will Baptists*, ed. David Lytle and Charles Cook (Nashville: Randall House, 2022).

20. The Nolynn Association's 1825 pronouncement that Separate Baptists, having been accused of open communion, "deny" it, and "Open communions are not expressions in the holy Scripture. Therefore, we have nothing to do with them" exemplifies the Separate Baptists' commitment to closed communion in the nineteenth century. See Minutes of the Nolynn Association of Separate Baptists (1825), 32. Peter Lumpkins makes it clear that Separate Baptists, even though the more Arminian-leaning of them were accused of Arminianism or of being "free willers" by their strict Calvinist counterparts, were always modified Calvinists or modified Arminians—depending on one's perspective— affirming the final perseverance of all true believers. See E. Peter Frank Lumpkins, "The Decline of Confessional Calvinism among Baptist Associations in the Southern States during the Nineteenth Century" (PhD diss., University of Pretoria, 2018), e.g., pp. 92–95, and passim. As John Sparks says, Kentucky

Separate Baptists washed feet and practiced closed communion at this time. See John Sparks, *The Roots of Appalachian Christianity*. Shubal Stearns and Daniel Marshall had constituted their church based on the six principles of the Christian religion plus the "perseverance of the saints." (Quoted in J. D. Hufham, "The Baptists of North Carolina. Part II—Third Paper," *North Carolina Baptist Historical Papers* 3.1 [1899], 38). Thus while some Separate Baptists were more Calvinistic, others leaned more Arminian but still held that true believers would of necessity persevere in grace to the end of life. This doctrine continued among the Separate Baptists in the nineteenth century.

21. Picirilli, *Little Known Chapters*, 50.
22. This was in an entry in his record book in September 1839, quoted in Picirilli, *Little Known Chapters*, 49, 59–60, 64.
23. Picirilli, *Little Known Chapters*, 52, 59.
24. Picirilli, *Little Known Chapters*, 65–66, 70n65.
25. Concord minutes cited in Davidson, *Free Will Baptists in History*, 120; Minutes of the Cumberland Association of Separate Baptists, (1843).
26. Picirilli, *Little Known Chapters*, 70.
27. Minutes of the Cumberland Association (1876), 11–12.
28. Picirilli, *History of Tennessee Free Will Baptists* (Nashville: Historical Commission, Tennessee State Association of Free Will Baptists, 2012), 14.
29. Concord minutes cited in Davidson, *Free Will Baptists in America*, 120; Minutes of the Cumberland Association of Separate Baptists, October 1843; *2019 Free Will Baptist Yearbook*, B-109–B-113; Picirilli, *Tennessee Free Will Baptists*, 12.
30. David Benedict, *A General History of the Baptist Denomination in America and Other Parts of the World* (New York: Lewis Colby and Company, 1850), 698.
31. Paul Woolsey, *God, A Hundred Years, and a Free Will Baptist Family* (Chuckey, TN: Union Free Will Baptist Association, 1949), 3–4.
32. Minutes of the Toe River Association (1958), handwritten minutes with unnumbered pages held in the Free Will Baptist Historical Collection, Welch College; Woolsey, *God, A Hundred Years, and a Free Will Baptist Family*, 12–13, 43–51,
33. Minutes of the Toe River Association (1852).
34. Minutes of the Toe River Association (1854). In addition to Hatch, *Democratization of American Christianity*, see Gregory A. Wills, *Democratic Religion: Freedom, Authority, and Church Discipline in the Baptist South, 1785–1900*, Religion in America, ed. Harry S. Stout (New York: Oxford University Press, 1997).
35. Minutes of the Toe River Association (1866).
36. Picirilli, *Tennessee Free Will Baptists*, 20.
37. Minutes of the Toe River Association (1868, 1878, 1882); "Tennessee," in *Free Baptist Cyclopaedia*, 640.

38. The Clinch Valley Association has one church in Tennessee, but most of its churches are in Virginia and it maintains membership in the Virginia State Association. The Holston Valley Association is defunct.
39. "Tennessee," in *Free Baptist Cyclopaedia*, 640; Million and Barrett, *Brief History of the Liberal Baptist People*, 197; James Myers Jr., "The Virginia State Association," in *History of Free Will Baptist State Associations*, 106–7; *2018 Free Will Baptist Yearbook* (Antioch, TN: Executive Office, National Association of Free Will Baptists, 2018), B-126–28.
40. Minutes of the Union Association (1912), 7–8. The name was "Free Baptist" from 1901 or 1902 to 1920 or 1921 (there are no extant minutes for 1901 or 1920).
41. "The Life of Rev. John H. Ballard," https://moc.libguides.com/c.php?g=779604&p=5590014#s-lg-box-17667065. William F. Davidson discovered two issues of early minutes from the aforementioned Arminianizing association of which David Benedict had spoken, which separated from the French Broad Association of United Baptists in 1827 in opposition to Calvinism. This association even took on the name "Free-Will Baptist," but it adopted the Big Ivy Baptist Association's articles of faith, which affirmed certain perseverance. The new association also practiced closed communion. That it practiced feet washing is unremarkable, since the Big Ivy Association, like many other Baptists of the day, did as well. While Paul Woolsey mentioned this association, he did not indicate that it had any direct connection with the Toe River Association. Though it came out of the French Broad Association, like Moses Peterson, John Wheeler, and William Bonaparte Wolsey did two decades later, there appears to be no organic connection between the two groups. See Minutes of the Free-Will Baptist Association (Salisbury, NC: Philo White, 1830); Davidson, *Free Will Baptists in History*, 148–49; Woolsey, *God, A Hundred Years, and a Free Will Baptist Family*, 14–15.
42. "The Life of Rev. John H. Ballard."
43. Picirilli, *Tennessee Free Will Baptists*, 27. See the article by Judge Ernest Hurston Boyd in the *Putnam County Herald*, November 19, 1953; http://osafreewillbaptist.org/blog1/history/.
44. "History of Dodson Branch Free Will Christian Baptist Church."
45. Fleetwood Ball, "Cleveland Calls Christly Clans—Tennessee Baptists Meet, Undaunted by Rain," *Baptist and Reflector* (November 20, 1919): 5–6; Picirilli, *Tennessee Free Will Baptists*, 27–29.
46. "Churches," Original Stone Association of the Free Will Christian Baptist Church of Christ, http://osafreewillbaptist.org/blog1/churches/; "Freewill Baptist Church Covenant," Allardt Freewill Baptist Church, https://allardtfwbc.wordpress.com/fwb-covenant/; Minutes of the Liberty Association (1976) 1; (2020), 2.

CHAPTER SIX

1. Mark A. Noll, *America's God: From Jonathan Edwards to Abraham Lincoln* (New York: Oxford University Press, 2005), 567; Paul E. Johnson, *A Shopkeeper's Millennium: Society and Revival in Rochester, New York, 1815–1837* (New York: Hill and Wang, 2004), 4–5.
2. Mark A. Noll, *A History of Christianity in the United States and Canada* (Grand Rapids: Eerdmans, 1992), 169–70; J. R. Fitzmier, "Second Great Awakening" in *Dictionary of Religion in America*, ed. Daniel G. Reid (Downers Grove, IL: InterVarsity, 1990), 1067–68; Charles G. Cole, *The Social Ideas of the Northern Evangelists, 1826–1850* (New York: Columbia University Press, 1954), 61. Select portions of this chapter are adapted from J. Matthew Pinson, "Religious Social Reform in the Antebellum North: Anti-Slavery and Temperance Reform among the Northern Freewill Baptists, 1800–1860" (MA thesis, University of West Florida, 1993).
3. Cole, *Social Ideas*, 61. The Cartwright quotation is from Douglas A. Sweeney, *The American Evangelical Story: A History of the Movement* (Grand Rapids, MI: Baker, 2005), 73. For a discussion of nineteenth-century critiques of Second Great Awakening revivalism, see Russ Patrick Reeves, "Countering Revivalism and Revitalizing Protestantism: High Church, Confessional, and Romantic Critiques of Second Great Awakening Revivalism, 1835 to 1852" (PhD diss., University of Iowa, 2005).
4. Fitzmier, "Second Great Awakening," 1067–68.
5. John L. Thomas, *The Liberator: A Biography of William Lloyd Garrison* (Boston: Little, Brown and Company, 1963), 163–67.
6. Timothy L. Smith, *Revivalism and Social Reform* (Nashville: Abingdon, 1957), 27; John R. McKivigan, *The War against Proslavery Religion: Abolitionism and the Northern Churches, 1830–1865* (Ithaca: Cornell University Press, 1984), 19–21.
7. Smith, *Revivalism and Social Reform*, 27; Cole, *The Social Ideas*, 233–34; "The Presidential Election in 1864," *Freewill Baptist Quarterly* 13 (1865): 87; McKivigan, *War against Proslavery Religion*, 198.
8. There is some debate over the eschatology of Benjamin Randall, but the early Freewill Baptist denomination was, like the rest of evangelical revivalism, generally characterized by a belief in postmillennialism. The first doctrinal statement of the Freewill Baptist General Conference, drafted in 1834, stated a belief in entire sanctification (perfectionism): "The attainment of Entire Sanctification in this life, is both the privilege and duty of every Christian." *A Treatise on the Faith and Practice of the Freewill Baptists* (1834) (this doctrine remained in the *Treatise* until it was expunged later in the century); William F. Davidson, *The Free Will Baptists in History* (Nashville: Randall House, 2001), 171.

9. Damon C. Dodd, *The Free Will Baptist Story* (Nashville: Executive Department of the National Association of Free Will Baptists, 1956), 94; Milton C. Sernett, *Abolition's Axe: Beriah Green, Oneida Institute, and the Black Freedom Struggle* (Syracuse, NY: Syracuse University Press, 1986), 105; *Minutes of the General Conference of the Freewill Baptist Connection* [1827-1859] (Dover, NH: Freewill Baptist Printing Establishment, 1859), 1827, 27. Hereafter referred to as Minutes of the General Conference.
10. "Bowles, Rev. Charles," in G. A. Burgess and J. T. Ward, *Free Baptist Cyclopaedia* (Chicago: Free Baptist Cyclopaedia Company, 1889), 63; John W. Lewis, *The Life, Labors, and Travels of Elder Charles Bowles, of the Free Will Baptist Denomination, Together With an Essay on the Character and Condition of the African Race* (Watertown, ME: Ingalls and Stowell's Steam Press, 1852); Eric Thomsen, "In the North," FWBHistory.com, https://fwbhistory.com/?page_id=88.
11. Marilla Marks, ed., *Memoirs of the Life of David Marks* (Dover, NH: The Free-will Baptist Printing Establishment, 1847), 451, 456–61, 494; "Anti-Slavery Society," in *Free Baptist Cyclopaedia*, 21.
12. I. D. Stewart, *The History of the Freewill Baptists for Half a Century*, vol. 1 (Dover, NH: Freewill Baptist Printing Establishment, 1862), 32 (Stewart never followed up with a second volume to this work); Dodd, *Free Will Baptist Story*, 69.
13. John Buzzell, *Life of Elder Benjamin Randall* (Limerick, Maine: Hobbs, Woodman, and Co., 1827), 11; Davidson, *Free Will Baptists in History*, 127–30.
14. Stewart, *History of the Freewill Baptists*, 44–45; "Randall, Rev. Benjamin," in *Free Baptist Cyclopaedia*, 558–59; G. W. Million, *A History of Free Will Baptists* (Nashville: Board of Publications and Literature, National Association of Free Will Baptists, 1958), 59–60.
15. Scott Bryant, *The Awakening of the Freewill Baptists: Benjamin Randall and the Founding of an American Religious Tradition* (Macon, GA: Mercer University Press, 2011), 83. I am one of the historians who has learned from Bryant on this point.
16. Bryant, *The Awakening of the Freewill Baptists*, 67, 91–92, quoting John Buzzell, *A Religious Magazine, containing a short history of the Church of Christ, gathered at New-Durham, N.H., in the year 1780 . . . also a particular account of the late Reformations and revivals of religion* (Portland, ME: J. M'Kown, 1822), 210.
17. Bryant, *The Awakening of the Freewill Baptists*, 91–92.
18. John G. Crowley, *Primitive Baptists of the Wiregrass South, 1815 to the Present* (Gainesville, FL: University Press of Florida, 1998), 8; R. K. Hearn, "Origin of the Free Will Baptist Church of North Carolina," in D. B. Montgomery, *General Baptist History* (Evansville, IN: Courier, 1889), 169–70. Hearn's history was printed earlier in the *Toisnot Transcript* (May 20–June 17, 1875).

19. Hearn, "Origin of the Free Will Baptist Church," 160; "The North Carolina Freewill Baptists," *Freewill Baptist Quarterly* 4 (1856): 335.
20. Bryant, *The Awakening of the Freewill Baptists*, 95–96. This statement seems to mitigate somewhat Bryant's earlier statements about non-scriptural data being a source of revelatory authority for Randall.
21. Davidson, *Free Will Baptists in History*, 156, 227; Minutes of the General Conference (1835), 121; Norman Allen Baxter, *History of the Freewill Baptists* (Rochester, NY: American Baptist Publication Society, 1957), 138–40.
22. Marks, ed., *Memoirs of the Life of David Marks*, 271–73; Minutes of the General Conference (1832), 78–79; "Printing Establishment, The Free Will Baptist," in *Free Baptist Cyclopaedia*, 543–44; Baxter, *History of the Freewill Baptists*, 41.
23. Minutes of the General Conference (1832), 74; "Printing Establishment," 544–45; Baxter, *History of the Freewill Baptists*, 178–79. In this book the year for the merger of the Free Baptist General Conference with the Northern Baptist Convention will be considered 1911. The merger was voted on and approved in 1910 but did not occur until 1911. The General Conference was technically still in existence until 1917, when all the details of the merger were finalized and the General Conference officially ceased to exist. Yet after 1911 all the institutions affiliated with the General Conference and the vast majority of the churches had united with the Northern Baptists.
24. "Foreign Mission Society," in *Free Baptist Cyclopaedia*, 198–99; Baxter, *History of the Freewill Baptists*, 66–67, citing *The Morning Star* (April 13, 1832).
25. "Foreign Mission Society," in *Free Baptist Cyclopaedia*, 198–200; Marks, ed. *Memoirs of the Life of David Marks*, 314–15. In the 1860s and 1870s, the denomination would begin gradually to use the term "Free Baptist" as an alternative title to "Freewill Baptist." This title was first used in the 1840s. The General Conference would formally change its name to "Free Baptist" in 1892. Alfred Williams Anthony explained in 1917 that the name was changed because it more accurately encapsulated the overall emphases of the denomination on free will, free grace, free salvation, and free communion. See Minutes of the General Conference (1917), 61–62. See also Robert E. Picirilli, *Little Known Chapters in Free Will Baptist History* (Nashville: Randall House, 2015), 11; and Baxter, *History of the Free Will Baptists*, 1 n. 1.
26. Baxter, *History of the Freewill Baptists*, 68.
27. Baxter, *History of the Freewill Baptists*, 69–70, 178; Marks, ed., *Memoirs of the Life of David Marks*, 347; Minutes of the General Conference (1835), 121.
28. "Home Mission Society," in *Free Baptist Cyclopaedia*, 271–72; Marks, ed., *Memoirs of the Life of David Marks*, 333.
29. "Home Mission Society," in *Free Baptist Cyclopaedia*, 273–75; Baxter, *History of the Freewill Baptists*, 178.
30. Minutes of the General Conference (1832), 76; "Parsonfield Seminary," in *Free Baptist Cyclopaedia*, 509; Baxter, *History of the Freewill Baptists*, 86–87.

31. Baxter, *History of the Freewill Baptists*, 86–87.
32. Minutes of the General Conference (1844), 243; Baxter, *History of the Freewill Baptists*, 87–89.
33. Baxter, *History of the Freewill Baptists*, 89–90; "Geauga Seminary," in *Free Baptist Cyclopaedia*, 223; Davidson, *Free Will Baptists in History*, 232.
34. "Michigan Central College," in *Free Baptist Cyclopaedia*, 408.
35. "Hillsdale College," in *Free Baptist Cyclopaedia*, 256–66.
36. *Hillsdale College. Sketch of Its History—Recent Loss of Its Buildings—Change of Plans and Description of the New*, booklet printed in September 1874, 1–3. (This booklet was bound with several historical documents from Hillsdale College and was obtained from Google Books under the title "Hillsdale College, 1862.") See also "Hillsdale College," *Free Baptist Cyclopaedia*, 266–67. Dunn would later go on to serve as the first president of Rio Grande College, a Freewill Baptist institution in Ohio.
37. *Hillsdale College. Sketch of Its History*, 1–3; "Hillsdale College," in *Free Baptist Cyclopaedia*, 264.
38. "Bates College" in the *Free Baptist Cyclopaedia*, 45–48; "A Brief History," https://www.bates.edu/150-years/history/; Timothy Larson, "Faith by Their Works: Our Progressive Tradition," BA thesis, Bates College, 2005, https://www.bates.edu/150-years/history/progressive-tradition/chapter-2/.
39. *Catalogue of the Officers and Students of Bates College* (Lewiston, ME: Daily Journal Office, 1863), 36–37.
40. Steven Hasty, "Did They Survive?" *Contact* (July 1988), 12–13.
41. Minutes of the General Conference (1849), 299; "Woman's Missionary Society," in *Free Baptist Cyclopaedia*, 713.
42. *The Free Baptist Woman's Missionary Society: Faith and Works Win, 1873–1921* (Providence, RI: The Free Baptist Woman's Missionary Society, 1922), 20, 25–27, 30–32, 83, 102; "Woman's Missionary Society," 713–14.
43. Free Will Baptists in the South did not ordain women to ministry (though a portion of the southern movement in the early twentieth century showed some openness to ordained female preachers from the Midwest and Southwest).
44. I. D. Stewart, *The History of the Freewill Baptists*, 191–92.
45. Stewart, *History of the Freewill Baptists*, 300, 306–10, 318, 338, 366, 377, 389–91. The quotation is found on p. 318; Stewart does not indicate whom he is quoting. See also the account of Salome Lincoln Mowry, another female preacher among the northern Freewill Baptists: Almond H. Davis, *The Female Preacher, Or, Memoir of Salome Lincoln, Afterwards the Wife of Elder Junia S. Mowry* (Providence, RI: Elder J. S. Mowry, 1843).
46. Stewart, *History of the Freewill Baptists*, 192.
47. Pamela R. Durso, "She-Preachers, Bossy Women, and Children of the Devil: Women Ministers in the Baptist Tradition, 1609-2012," *Review & Expositor*

110 (2013): 33–47; James R. Lynch, "Baptist Women in Ministry Through 1920," *American Baptist Quarterly* 13 (1994): 311.

48. Davidson, *Free Will Baptists in History*, 160–61. See Edward Magdol, *The Antislavery Rank and File: A Social Profile of the Abolitionists' Constituency* (Westport, CT: Greenwood, 1986), which establishes that the evangelical social reformers were primarily drawn from the middle classes rather than from the lower or upper classes. They came more from the ranks of merchants, artisans, gentleman farmers, and skilled laborers than from the ranks of the privileged classes.

49. Stephen A. Marini, *Radical Sects in Revolutionary New England* (Cambridge: Harvard University Press, 1982), 97 (Marini uses an alternate spelling of Benjamin Randall's surname); Davidson, *Free Will Baptists in History*, 160–61.

50. McKivigan, *War Against Proslavery Religion*, 148, 152; Emeline Burlingame-Cheney, *The Story of the Life and Work of Oren B. Cheney, Founder and First President of Bates College* (Boston: Morning Star Publishing House, 1907), 56–57.

51. Oliver Johnson, *W. L. Garrison and His Times* (Miami: Mnemosyne, 1969 [1881]), 75–76.

52. *Sacred Melodies* (Dover, NH: The Free-Will Baptist Printing Establishment, 1851), no. 257.

53. Sernett, *Abolition's Axe*, 105.

54. *Liberty Press* (October 10, 1843), cited in Sernett, *Abolition's Axe*, 105.

55. I. D. Stewart, "Anti-Slavery" in *The Centennial Record of Freewill Baptists, 1780–1880* (Dover, NH: Freewill Baptist Printing Establishment, 1881), 192.

56. Minutes of the General Conference (1835), 123.

57. "Anti-Slavery Society," *The Free Baptist Cyclopaedia*, 20.

58. *Fifth Annual Report of the Freewill Baptist Anti-Slavery Society* (Dover, New Hampshire: Wm. Burr, Printer, 1851), 11; J. M. Brewster, *Fidelity and Usefulness: Life of William Burr* (Dover, NH: Freewill Baptist Printing Establishment, 1871), 124–25; Stewart, "Anti-Slavery," 196; "Anti-Slavery Society," *Free Baptist Cyclopaedia*, 20. Later, Freewill Baptists in Ohio experienced similar difficulty. When they applied to the Ohio Legislature for the incorporation of Geauga Seminary, "proslavery men interested themselves for its defeat. They could not prevent the granting of a charter, but they succeeded in procuring the insertion of a clause that excluded colored persons from the privileges of the school." (*Fifth Annual Report*, 13.)

59. Minutes of the General Conference (1837), 140.

60. I. D. Stewart, "The Anti-Slavery Record of the Freewill Baptists," *Freewill Baptist Quarterly* 16 (1868), 55–56.

61. Stewart, "Anti-Slavery Record," 59–60.

62. Stewart, "Anti-Slavery Record," 60.

63. Minutes of the General Conference (1839), 178. One wonders which Baptists Housley had in mind.
64. Stewart, "Anti-Slavery Record," 177–79; *The Church Member's Book: Or Admonitions and Instructions for All Classes of Christians* (Dover, NH: The Free-will Baptist Printing Establishment, 1847), 130.
65. Stewart, "Anti-Slavery," 198. See the *Fifth Annual Report of the Freewill Baptist Anti-slavery Society*, 18, which reads: "The subject of our connection with the slaveholding churches of North and South Carolina, was brought before the Conference, and this connection entirely dissolved."
66. Minutes of the General Conference (1910), 100–104.
67. Davidson, *Free Will Baptists in History*, 242–43.
68. John J. Butler, *Thoughts on the Benevolent Enterprises, Embracing the Subjects of Missions, Sabbath Schools, Temperance, Abolition of Slavery, and Peace* (Dover, New Hampshire: Published by the Trustees of the Freewill Baptist Connection, 1840), 83, 131–32; "Professor John J. Butler, D.D." in *Free Baptist Cyclopaedia*, 91-92.
69. Burlingame-Cheney, *Life and Work of Oren B. Cheney*, 24.
70. *Sacred Melodies*, no. 251.

CHAPTER SEVEN

1. Quoted in Scott Bryant, *The Awakening of the Freewill Baptists: Benjamin Randall and the Founding of an American Religious Tradition* (Macon, GA: Mercer University Press, 2011). Some of this section is adapted from J. Matthew Pinson, *Free Will Baptists and the Sufficiency of Scripture* (Antioch, TN: Historical Commission, National Association of Free Will Baptists, 2014); "Introduction" to *A Treatise of the Faith of the Free-will Baptists* (Dover, NH: Free-will Baptist Printing Establishment, 1854).
2. "The Baptismal Question in the Light of the Scriptures and Church History," *The Freewill Baptist Quarterly* 7 (1859), 139. Italics in the original.
3. *The Church Member's Book: Or Admonitions and Instructions for All Classes of Christians* (Dover, NH: Free-will Baptist Printing Establishment, 1847), 29. See also pp. 70, 75, 82, 100, 140, 143, and 160. The author did not consider things like camp meetings and protracted meetings as ordinary means of grace. Most Free Will Baptists, however, came to see these events as mere gatherings where worship and preaching would occur and at which the ordinary means of grace would be administered. Thus their concern would not have been holding camp meetings or protracted meetings but with ensuring that those meetings were administering only the ordinary means of grace. The language of "means of grace" occurs in the *Treatise* that was revised in 1854 on pages 8 and 47. In the 1868 revision and thereafter, the Randall *Treatise* stated that the pastor and deacons are to "promote . . . attendance on

the means of grace." *Treatise on the Faith and Practice of the Freewill Baptists* (Dover, NH: Freewill Baptist Printing Establishment, 1871), "Usages" section 4. This same language was carried over verbatim into the *Treatise* of the National Association, where it remained until that document's 1969 revision. See *Treatise* (1969).

4. S. E. Root, "The Philosophy of Divine Worship," *Freewill Baptist Quarterly* 16 (1868): 223–24, 226.
5. John J. Butler, *Natural and Revealed Theology* (Dover, NH: Freewill Baptist Printing Establishment, 1861), 361. Ransom Dunn retained this statement in his 1892 revision of the book, which was widely read until the 1911 merger (and thereafter by Free Will Baptists in the South). J. J. Butler and Ransom Dunn, *Lectures on Systematic Theology* (Boston: Morning Star, 1892), 341.
6. *Treatise*, National Association (1936), 3, 65, 68; "Usages" section, 37.
7. Scott Bryant, *The Awakening of the Freewill Baptists: Benjamin Randall and the Founding of an American Religious Tradition* (Macon, GA: Mercer University Press, 2011), 83. Some of this section is adapted from J. Matthew Pinson, "Dissent from Calvinism in the Baptist Tradition," in David L. Allen and Steve W. Lemke, eds., *Calvinism: A Biblical and Theological Critique* (Nashville: B&H Academic, 2022).
8. J. Matthew Pinson, "Dissent from Calvinism in the Baptist Tradition," 260–63, 273; Mark A. Noll, *A History of Christianity in the United States and Canada* (Grand Rapids: Eerdmans, 1992), 178–79; James Leo Garrett, *Baptist Theology: A Four-Century Study* (Macon, GA: Mercer University Press, 2019), 151.
9. Moses M. Smart, *A Brief View of Christian Doctrine* (Lowell, MA: N. L. Daton, 1843), 121–22, 126–27. I have not been able to find anyone in the northern or southern group before the twentieth century who denied the imputation of Adam's sin to humanity, though it appears E. L. St. Claire did in the early twentieth century.
10. Smart, *Brief View of Christian Doctrine*, 121–22; see also J. A. Howe, "The Relation of the Doctrine of Total Depravity to Other Christian Doctrines," *Freewill Baptist Quarterly* 13 (1865): 311–21.
11. *A Treatise on the Faith of the Freewill Baptists. . . .* (Dover, NH: David Marks, for the Freewill Baptist Connexion, 1834), 64–69.
12. *Treatise* (1834), 55–57, 61, 73, 82; Minutes of the Freewill Baptist General Conference (1871), 236; *Treatise* (1871), 32.
13. Smart, *Brief View of Christian Doctrine*, 163.
14. *Treatise* (1834), 82; *Treatise* (1871), 24–25, 33.
15. Butler, *Natural and Revealed Theology*; Butler and Dunn, *Lectures*; *Treatise* (1834), 55–57, 61, 73, 82. Minutes of the Freewill Baptist General Conference (1871), 236; *Treatise* (1871).
16. *Treatise* (1834), 91–93.

17. *Treatise* (1834), 107-8.
18. *Treatise* (1834), 109.
19. Smart, *Brief View of Christian Doctrine*, 280-81.
20. Smart, *Brief View of Christian Doctrine*, 281-82.
21. *Treatise* (1854), 95; By the time of the 1871 *Treatise*, the washing of feet was no longer mentioned.
22. See Butler, *Natural and Revealed Theology*, 366-67; see also *Usages of the Free-Will Baptist Connexion*, Revised by Order of the Thirteenth Annual General Conference, Assembled in Oct., 1847, v-vi; *Usages of the Free-Will Baptist Connexion*, 11. Some of this section is adapted from J. Matthew Pinson, *Free Will Baptists and Church Government* (Antioch, TN: Historical Commission, National Association of Free Will Baptists, 2008).
23. *Treatise* (1854), 81, 87, 381. The Randall movement had itinerant ministers who would plant, settle, and advise churches, but they did not hold to a separate office of messenger.
24. Butler, *Natural and Revealed Theology*, 378; *Treatise* (1854), 87-90.
25. Butler, *Natural and Revealed Theology*, 365.
26. Section VI of the 1847 *Usages of the Free-will Baptist Connexion* discusses the reasons for the "connection of the church with the quarterly meeting." It says, "Every church in order to be connected with the Free-will Baptist denomination must become a member of some Q. M. in the denomination. The objects for which churches unite together in a Q. M. are union, strength and mutual aid, that they may thereby be better prepared to glorify God, advance truth, and benefit the world." See *Usages of the Free-Will Baptist Connexion*, 14, 16; Butler, *Natural and Revealed Theology*, 367.
27. *The Freewill Baptist Selection of Spiritual Songs with Music for the Church and the Choir* (Dover, NH: Freewill Baptist Printing Establishment, 1881). I am thankful to my colleague Jacob Lute for pointing me to this source.
28. *Church Member's Book*, 138, 142.
29. *Church Member's Book*, 139.
30. *Church Member's Book*, 189.
31. John J. Butler, *Commentary on the New Testament: Critical and Practical: The Gospels* (Dover, NH: G. T. Day and Company, 1870), 122.
32. *Church Member's Book*, 128-29.
33. John J. Butler, *Commentary on the New Testament: Critical and Practical: Acts, Romans, Corinthians* (Biddeford, ME: J. E. Butler, 1871), 295.
34. *Church Member's Book*, 180-81.
35. *Church Member's Book*, 180; Minutes of the General Conference (1907), 146, 180.
36. *Church Member's Book*, 72. For more on northern Freewill Baptists and social reform, see chapter 6, as well as J. Matthew Pinson, "Religious Social Reform in Antebellum New England: Abolition and Temperance Reform

among the Northern Freewill Baptists, 1800–1860" (MA thesis, University of West Florida, 1993).
37. See J. Matthew Pinson, "Baconianism and Scottish Common Sense Philosophy among the Northern Freewill Baptists" (unpublished essay presented at Yale University American Religious History doctoral study group, 1993). The reason for the shift from "Freewill" to "Free" Baptist was probably the union with the Free Communion Baptists as well as the common use of the slogan "free will, free grace, free salvation, free communion."
38. Pinson, "Baconianism and Scottish Common Sense"; Theodore Dwight Bozeman, *Protestants in an Age of Science: The Baconian Ideal and Antebellum American Religious Thought* (Chapel Hill: University of North Carolina Press, 1977). Baconianism is shorthand for the primacy of the scientific method of Francis Bacon for human knowledge. Its first cousin, Scottish common sense philosophy, or Scottish realism, is Thomas Reid and Dugald Stewart's view that opposed the skepticism of David Hume and the idealism of George Berkeley and held that everyday people can gain valid knowledge based on their common physical senses and intuitive moral sense.
39. Jon H. Roberts and James Turner, *The Sacred and the Secular University* (Princeton: Princeton University Press, 2000). See also James Tunstead Burtchaell, *The Dying of the Light: The Disengagement of Colleges and Universities from their Christian Churches* (Grand Rapids: Eerdmans, 1998).
40. John F. Wilson, "Introduction" to Roberts and Turner, *The Sacred and the Secular University*, 11. William C. Ringenberg discusses the "old-time college" in chapter 2 of his book *The Christian College: A History of Protestant Higher Education in America* (Grand Rapids: Baker Academic, 2006).
41. On these movements, see William R. Hutchinson, *The Modernist Impulse in American Protestantism* (Durham, NC: Duke University Press, 1992); Garry Dorrien, *The Soul in Society: The Making and Renewal of Social Christianity* (Minneapolis: Fortress, 1995); Shailer Mathews, *The Faith of Modernism* (New York: Macmillan, 1925); and Walter Rauschenbusch, *A Theology for the Social Gospel* (New York: Macmillan, 1919).
42. For an insightful paper on this subject, see Jesse F. Owens, "Free Baptists, the Northern Baptist Convention, and Higher Criticism" (unpublished essay, 2016), 5. Cf. Hutchinson, *Modernist Impulse*.
43. Alfred Williams Anthony, *The Method of Jesus: An Interpretation of Personal Religion* (New York: Silver, Burdett and Company, 1899), 11–12.
44. Anthony, *Method of Jesus*, 243.
45. Anthony, *Method of Jesus*, 248, 250–51. Owens discusses Anthony's rejection of the older doctrine of verbal inspiration of Scripture in the latter's book *An Introduction to the Life of Jesus: An Investigation of the Historical Sources* (Boston: Silver, Burdett and Company, 1896). See Owens, "Free Baptists, the Northern Baptist Convention, and Higher Criticism," 7–9.

46. Edward Cary Hayes, *A Memoir of Prof. Benjamin Francis Hayes, D.D., With Brief Extracts from His Writings* (Boston: Morning Star Publishing House, 1907), 77–80. Elsewhere in the book he talks about his and his wife's embrace of the newer scientific conceptions of human origins and the findings of biblical criticism which taught them not to fear that modern scholarship had cast doubt on older conceptions of the Bible's historical accuracy.
47. Gary Dorrien, *The Making of American Liberal Theology: Idealism, Realism, and Modernity, 1900-1950* (Louisville: Westminster John Knox Press, 2003), 190–99, 216–17, and *The Making of American Liberal Theology: Crisis, Irony, and Postmodernity, 1950-2005* (Louisville: Westminster John Knox Press, 2006), 59–60; 114–15 (the quotation about Case is from p. 191); Owens, "Free Baptists, the Northern Baptist Convention, and Higher Criticism," 9–13; Mathews, *Faith of Modernism*; Shirley Jackson Case, *The Historical Method in the Study of Religion* (Lewiston, ME: Press of the Lewiston Journal, 1907). For Case's mature pronouncements, see, e.g., his *Highways of Christian Doctrine* (Chicago: Willett, Clark and Company, 1936).
48. Minutes of the General Conference (1917), 65.
49. Minutes of the General Conference (1917), 65–67.
50. Baxter, *History of the Freewill Baptists*, 162; Dorrien, *Making of American Liberal Theology* (2003), 107; Owens, "Free Baptists, the Northern Baptist Convention, and Higher Criticism," 17–19.
51. Jack Williams, "The Day We Lost 600 Churches," unpublished essay, https://fwbhistory.com/?page_id=2796; Minutes of the General Conference (1886), 507; Alfred Williams Anthony, "Twenty Years After: The Story of the Union of Baptists and Free Baptists during the Period of Negotiation and Realization, 1904-1924," repr. from *Christian Work* (October 18, 1924), 3.
52. Minutes of the General Conference (1898), 39–40; Robert E. Picirilli, *Little Known Chapters in Free Will Baptist History* (Nashville: Randall House, 2015), 186.
53. Baxter, *History of the Freewill Baptists*, 170–73; Minutes of the General Conference (1904), 128–30; (1907), 104–106.
54. Baxter, *History of the Freewill Baptists*, 171–73. See Baxter for other details on why the General Conference did not go through with a merger with the Disciples of Christ. There was a little talk about uniting with the Congregational Church, but Anthony discouraged it because they were paedobaptist.
55. Baxter, *History of the Freewill Baptists*, 153–62.
56. Minutes of the General Conference (1910), 92.
57. Minutes of the General Conference (1910), 93–98, repr., sans historical information, in Williams, "The Day We Lost 600 Churches." "Baptist state conventions" refers to the ratification of state conventions that were members of the Northern Baptist Convention in regions where there were Free Baptist quarterly and yearly meetings applying for merger.

58. Minutes of the General Conference (1910), 100–102.
59. Minutes of the General Conference (1910), 102–4.
60. Minutes of the General Conference (1910), 40, 119–20; Damon C. Dodd, "The Story of Rev. John H. Wolfe," *Contact* (December 1953) (based on an interview with Wolfe); Damon Dodd, *The Free Will Baptist Story* (Nashville: Executive Department of the National Association of Free Will Baptists, 1956), 107–8; Picirilli, *Little Known Chapters*, 190; Williams, "The Day We Lost 600 Churches"; Baxter, *History of the Freewill Baptists*, 177–78, 181, 191. T. C. Ferguson was originally from Missouri but was serving in Texas at this time.
61. Baxter, *History of the Freewill Baptists*, 178–81; Picirilli, *Little Known Chapters*, 191–99.
62. Some East Tennessee associations were on the roll and had spotty, off-and-on representation (mostly by letter) to the northern General Conference. Despite their opposition to the merger, they did not respond when the vote of constituent bodies was taken, reflecting their aloofness. As mentioned earlier, the northern General Conference was famous for having groups of Arminian Baptists "on the roll" and "in fellowship" that never could really be accounted for. The Committee on Conference acknowledged this when they made their report and admitted how ambiguous the results of the vote of constituent bodies was. See Minutes of the General Conference (1910), 104. Some Oklahoma associations were part of the Southwestern Freewill Baptist General Convention, which was a member of the Free Baptist General Conference, but Oklahoma's origins were almost all from the southern movement.
63. G. W. Million and G. A. Barrett, *A Brief History of the Liberal Baptist People in England and America from 1606 to 1911* (Pocahontas, AR: Liberal Baptist Book and Tract Company, 1911), 235–40, 302–4; William F. Davidson, *The Free Will Baptists in History* (Nashville: Randall House, 1985), 209–10; David A. Joslin, *History of Arkansas Free Will Baptists* (Nashville, n.p., 1998), 8–9; Joshua R. Colson, "Origins of the Southern Illinois Free Will Baptist Movement" (unpublished essay, 2017), 10; T. F. Harrison and J. M. Barfield, *History of the Free Will Baptists of North Carolina*, (Ayden, NC: Free Will Baptist Press, n.d. [1896]), 430. For Poyner, see also chapter 10.
64. Million and Barrett, 235–36, quoting D. B. Montgomery, *General Baptist History* (Evansville, IN: Courier, 1889), 364–67; *A Treatise on the Faith of the Freewill Baptists* (Dover, NH: David Marks, for the Freewill Baptist Connexion, 1834), 112.
65. Million and Barrett, *Brief History of the Liberal Baptist People*, 125–27.
66. Million and Barrett, *Brief History of the Liberal Baptist People*, 125.
67. Million and Barrett, *Brief History of the Liberal Baptist People*, 126.
68. Keith Garrison, *Upon This Rock: Missouri State Association of Free Will Baptists, 100 Years* (Lebanon, MO: Missouri State Association of Free Will Baptists, 2014), 6.

69. Garrison, *Upon This Rock*, 5–11.
70. Colson, "Origins of the Southern Illinois Free Will Baptist Movement," 2–5; George A. Gordon, *The Life and Labors of Rev. Henry S. Gordon: Founder of Free Will Baptist Churches in Southern Illinois* (Campbell Hill, IL: Rev. Geo A. Gordon, 1901), 12–14; Million and Barrett, *Brief History of the Liberal Baptist People*, 218, and "Illinois," in *Free Baptist Cyclopaedia*, 291.
71. Colson, citing Million and Barrett, *Brief History of the Liberal Baptist People*, 219–200. As Robert Picirilli noted in correspondence, the record book of the Charity Church in the Cumberland Association shows that Blankenship preached there several times in the 1850s. See the record book of the Charity Church (1843–1920), held in the Free Will Baptist Historical Collection, Welch College.
72. Colson, "Origins of the Southern Illinois Free Will Baptist Movement," 14–17; Davidson, *Free Will Baptists in History*, 215–16; Minutes of the General Conference (1880), 395; Minutes of the General Conference (1910), 104. The initial name of the Illinois State Association, with the word "original" included, adds another twist to the story. The label "Original Free Will Baptists" is associated with the South and was used by the National Association of Free Will Baptists in the title of its *Treatise* from 1948 until 1981. Up through 1962 the word "original" appeared on the title page as well as the front cover, but from 1962 through 1981 it was dropped from the title page while still appearing on the cover. See *A Treatise of the Faith and Practices of the Original Free Will Baptists* (Nashville: Executive Committee, National Association of Free Will Baptists, 1962 and 1981), see covers and title pages. The 1962 printing was of the 1958 revision.
73. "Virginia," and "West Virginia," in *Free Baptist Cyclopaedia*, 673, 687–89; James H. Cox Jr., *A History of West Virginia Free Will Baptists* (Hurricane, WV, 2013), 19–20.
74. Alton Loveless, James McComas, and Edwin Hayes, *Great Is Thy Faithfulness: Over 200 Years of Ohio Free Will Baptist History, 1805–2009* (Reynoldsburg, OH: Ohio State Association of Free Will Baptists, 2009), 6–8. The Lawrence County Quarterly Meeting was formed after the merger, in 1915, from the Pine Creek Quarterly Meeting (Loveless, McComas, and Hayes, *Great Is Thy Faithfulness*, 20).
75. There were two yearly meetings using the name "Ohio River," one that broke away with Peden but continued using the same name, and the other the earlier-constituted body. One assumes that the former is the one that represented to the triennial General Conference in 1895. Picirilli, *Little Known Chapters*, 161–65, 199.
76. Picirilli, *Little Known Chapters*, 161–65, 199. Alton E. Loveless, "The Ohio State Association," in *History of Free Will Baptist State Associations*, ed. Robert E. Picirilli (Nashville: Randall House, 1976), 78–81. In 1892 the General

Conference became incorporated in the state of Maine as "the General Conference of Free Baptists" and merged all the "societies" of the denomination into one central body. The final minutes of the General Conference in 1917 before it completely dissolved discussed that the "centralization of functions and powers was not acceptable to all of the denomination" and then went on to name Thomas E. Peden and the "Pedenites" who left the General Conference at that time. See the Minutes of the Thirty-Sixth General Conference of Free Baptists (1917), 62.

77. Cox, *History of West Virginia Free Will Baptists*, 11–12; Picirilli, "The West Virginia State Association," in *History of Free Will Baptist State Associations*, 110. Picirilli, *Little Known Chapters*, 175–76; "West Virginia," and "West Virginia College," in *Free Baptist Cyclopaedia*, 687–89.

78. Davidson, *Free Will Baptists in History*, 212–14; *Johnson County, Kentucky: History and Families* (Paducah, KY: Turner, 2001), 35.

79. Minutes of the First Annual Session of the John Thomas Association, 1923. "Free Will" and "Freewill" are used interchangeably for most of its early history, and in 1958 it began to hyphenate its name: "John-Thomas." Minutes of the Eighty-Seventh Session of the John-Thomas Association of Freewill Baptist, 2009; John Sparks, *The Roots of Appalachian Christianity: The Life and Legacy of Elder Shubal Stearns* (Lexington, KY: The University Press of Kentucky, 2001), 277. New Durham is a Virginia conference that joined in 1940, and the Hamilton County Conference from Cincinnati, Ohio, joined in 1958. In the early years of the John-Thomas Association, they referred to the Scripture reading during the worship services as the "lesson." Later it was often said, for example, that the reader "read for a lesson Psalm 23." It was common among the Free Will Baptists of this part of Appalachia to use the traditional term "lesson" or "Scripture lesson" for the public reading of Scripture. One also sees this usage in the Carolinas, Georgia, Alabama, and other states.

80. Davidson, *Free Will Baptists in History*, 262–63.

CHAPTER EIGHT

1. See chapter 5 for more on the Bethlehem tradition associated with Carlisle C. Vandiver. See Bethlehem Association Minutes; Minutes of the Little Brown's Creek Association (1899). The name Little Brown's Creek was changed to Little Brown Creek sometime between 1932 and 1935. See minutes for 1932 and 1935 (those for 1933 and 1934 are not extant).

2. G. W. Million and G. A. Barrett, *A Brief History of the Liberal Baptist People in England and America from 1606 to 1911* (Pocahontas, AR: Liberal Baptist Book and Tract Company, 1911), 201; Rev. John Zedekiah D. "Kai" Lawless, Find-A-Grave #27420901; https://www.ancestry.com/family-tree/person

/tree/33843901/person/18543276174/facts; https://www.ancestry.com/family-tree/person/tree/27443548/person/162102528890/facts; Mississippi, US, Compiled Marriage Index, 1776–1935 (https://www.ancestry.com/search/collections/7842/).
3. The Mount Moriah minutes in 1874 refer to this sister association. See also Million and Barrett, *Brief History of the Liberal Baptist People*, 201.
4. At first glance, one presumes, because Tupelo Association was organized one year after the Mississippi congregations in the Vernon Association were dismissed, that it consisted of those churches. However, the first extant minutes for the Tupelo Association from 1915 show that, like the Jasper Association in Alabama, which was founded three years later, Tupelo used the articles of faith of B. W. Nash's Southern Baptist Association (unlike Vernon). Furthermore, its churches were not the ones that were dismissed from the Vernon Association.
5. Minutes of the Zion Rest Association (1940); Minutes of the Middle Georgia Association of United Baptists (1897); Paul Long, "The Mississippi State Association," in *History of Free Will Baptist State Associations*, ed. Robert E. Picirilli (Nashville: Randall House, 1976), 58.
6. Long, "Mississippi State Association," 61; William F. Davidson, *The Free Will Baptists in History* (Nashville: Randall House, 2001), 286. Also, as will be shown, Elder J. E. McGee, from Vernon, Alabama, later in Oklahoma, sojourned in Mississippi for a time in the 1890s.
7. David A. Joslin, ed., *History of Arkansas Free Will Baptists* (Nashville: n.p., 1998), 28–29, quoting Hudson's 1920 obituary from the Russellville *Daily Democrat*; https://www.ancestry.com/family-tree/person/tree/937514/person/-1741284783/facts?_phsrc=owG1327&_phstart=successSource; Francis Marion Hudson, 1850 US Census, Pope County, Arkansas; roll: 29, p. 262a.
8. Joslin, *History of Arkansas Free Will Baptists*, 11–12; https://www.ancestry.com/family-tree/person/tree/937514/person/-1741284783/facts?_phsrc=owG1327&_phstart=successSource; Francis Marion Hudson Sr., Find-A-Grave #47331937; Million and Barrett, *Brief History of the Liberal Baptist People*, 322–23.
9. Rev. John Zedekiah D. "Kai" Lawless, Find-A-Grave #27420901; https://www.ancestry.com/family-tree/person/tree/33843901/person/18543276174/facts; https://www.ancestry.com/family-tree/person/tree/33843901/person/18543276176/facts; Zedekiah D. Lawless, 1880 U. S. Census, Mountain, Pike County, Arkansas, roll: 53, p. 467B, enumeration district: 126; Z. D. Lawless, 1910 U. S. Census, Wilson, Choctaw County, Oklahoma, roll: T624_1247, p. 3A, enumeration district: 0069, FHL microfilm: 1375260; John H. Lawless, 1880 U. S. Census, Mountain, Pike County, Arkansas, roll: 53, p. 468C, enumeration district: 126; John H. Lawless, 1900 U. S. Census, Mountain, Pike County, Arkansas, roll: 71, p. 1, enumeration district: 0090, FHL microfilm:

1240071; Minutes of the Little Missouri River Association (1891). It is noteworthy that the Lawlesses were living in Lauderdale County, Alabama, the region of the Bethlehem Association, in 1861, when John Henry was born. https://www.ancestry.com/family-tree/person/tree/33843901/person/18543276176/facts.

10. *The Goodspeed Biographical and Historical Memoirs of Northwestern Arkansas* (Chicago: The Goodspeed Publishing Company, 1889), 481; Davidson, *Free Will Baptists in History*, 206–7.

11. Davidson, *Free Will Baptists in History*, 207–8, citing "Church History, To the Union Association of United Baptists to be held at Liberty, Madison County, Arkansas, September 22, 1916," in *Proceedings of the One Hundred Twenty-Ninth Annual Session of the Union Association of United Baptist*, September 21–23, 1979, 36; and "Arkansas," in G. A. Burgess and J. T. Ward, *Free Baptist Cyclopaedia* (Chicago: Free Baptist Cyclopaedia Company, 1889), 22.

12. "Blackburn, Rev. W. J.," in *Free Baptist Cyclopaedia*, 57; https://www.ancestry.com/family-tree/person/tree/172662282/person/242238873589/facts?_phsrc=gfS280&_phstart=successSource; S. W. Blackburn, 1860 U. S. Census, War Eagle and Walnut, Benton County, Arkansas, roll: M653_37, p. 386; Family History Library Film: 803037; Sylvanus Walker Blackburn, Find-A-Grave #9568839. There was another man named Richard Sharp, also from Tennessee, who was visited by the census taker two houses after S. W. Blackburn in 1850. In the 1860 census, Sharp is listed as the next house visited after Blackburn and is also listed as a "Freewill Baptist Clergyman." This places not just one but two men recorded as Free Will Baptist ministers in the same area quite early (https://www.ancestry.com/family-tree/person/tree/153620182/person/322233516799/facts?phsrc=gfS288&_phstart=successSource); Sylvanus W. Blackburn and Richard Sharp, 1850 U. S. Census, Brush Creek, Washington County, Arkansas, roll: 31; p. 347b; S. W. Blackburn and Richard Sharp, 1860 U. S. Census, War Eagle and Walnut, Benton County, Arkansas, roll: M653_37, p. 386; Family History Library Film: 803037). Interestingly, W. J. Blackburn served in the Arkansas state legislature likely at the same time as Francis Hudson from Pope County. This might provide other evidence of cross-pollination between Free Will Baptists in northwest Arkansas and those in other regions of the state. I thank Josh Hunter for putting me onto Blackburn and Sharp.

13. Joslin, *History of Arkansas Free Will Baptists*, 5–8; Minutes of the Old Mount Zion Association (1888); Minutes of the Arkansas Association (1899). These are the first extant minutes of these associations. Old Mount Zion added "Free Will Baptist" to its title in 1889. Some have thought that Charles Rice Kellum in Franklin County, also in northwest Arkansas, was a Freewill Baptist minister from New England but sojourned for a time in North Carolina before going to Arkansas. Yet there is no documentary evidence for this

claim. In 1836, Kellum was ordained by the Baptist (not Freewill Baptist) church in Irasburg, Vermont, as a missionary to the Creek Indians. That was the same year he married the former Elizabeth Pearson in Haverhill, Massachusetts. They went as Baptist missionaries, not to the Creeks, but to the Choctaw Nation in Oklahoma the next year, and by the mid-1840s lived in Franklin County, Arkansas. However, nothing is known about Kellum's ministerial labors or his church affiliation after his move to Arkansas. See Henry Crocker, *History of the Baptists in Vermont* (Bellows Falls, VT: P. H. Gobie, 1913), 322; "Miscellaneous Intelligence," *The Christian Review*, vol. 1, ed. James D. Knowles (Boston: Gould, Kendall, and Lincoln, 1836), 630; https://www.ancestry.com/family-tree/person/tree/167944020/person/102175264289/facts?_phsrc=owG1156&_phstart=successSource; Rev. Charles Rice Kellam, Find-A-Grave #102662318; Charles R. Kellum, New England Historical Genealogical Society, Boston, Massachusetts, Massachusetts Vitals to 1850, Massachusetts, US, Compiled Birth, Marriage, and Death Records, 1700–1850, 186.

14. Davidson, *Free Will Baptists in History*, 209–10; Joslin, *History of Arkansas Free Will Baptists*, 8–9, 29–31; Joshua R. Colson, "Origins of the Southern Illinois Free Will Baptist Movement" (unpublished essay, 2017), 10.
15. T. F. Harrison and J. M. Barfield, *History of the Free Will Baptists of North Carolina*, (Ayden, NC: Free Will Baptist Press, [1896]), 430; https://www.ancestry.com/family-tree/person/tree/156620387/person/432062603638/facts; Rev. David Leroy Poynor, Find-A-Grave #16549397.
16. https://www.ancestry.com/family-tree/person/tree/156620387/person/432062603638/facts; Rev. David Leroy Poynor, Find-A-Grave #16549397; Jesse Diggs Poynor, Find-A-Grave #87233607. Million and Barrett confirm most of these essential facts in their *Brief History of the Liberal Baptist People*, 235–40, 302–4.
17. Million and Barrett, *Brief History of the Liberal Baptist People*, 196.
18. Million and Barrett, *Brief History of the Liberal Baptist People*, 322–23; "James Grant Conner, 1863 – 1897," https://www.therestorationmovement.com/_states/arkansas/conner.htm. Austin also published *The True Blue* in Alabama and the *Gospel Pruning Hook* in Oklahoma.
19. Million and Barrett, *Brief History of the Liberal Baptist People*, 320–22.
20. https://www.ancestry.com/family-tree/person/tree/27443548/person/162102528890/facts; Thos Molloy, 1870 U. S. Census, Betts, Sanford County, Alabama, roll: M593_39, p. 289A; Mississippi, US, Compiled Marriage Index, 1776–1935 (https://www.ancestry.com/search/collections/7842/); Minutes of the Hamburgh Association (1891).
21. Davidson, *Free Will Baptists in History*, 210–11.
22. Davidson, *Free Will Baptists in History*, 284.
23. Robert L. Vaughn, "The Founding of the Free Will Baptist Work in Texas," in Robert E. Picirilli, *Free Will Baptist History: Exploring Our Origins and*

Identity (Nashville: Randall House, 2019), 109–10; Thurmon Murphy, *From Red to the Rio Grande: A History of the Free Will Baptist Work in Texas, 1876–2014* (Columbus, OH: FWB Publications, 2017), 1–43; see also Eugene Richards, "The Texas State Association," in *History of Free Will Baptist State Associations*, 100–103; Davidson, *Free Will Baptists in History*, 284. Regarding Stewart's connection with Tipton and his colleagues, see chapter 4.

24. Vaughn, "The Founding of the Free Will Baptist Work in Texas," 110–12.
25. Vaughn, "The Founding of the Free Will Baptist Work in Texas," 112–13; Minutes of the Chattahoochee Association (1881), "Statistical Table"; Davidson, *Free Will Baptists in History*, 284.
26. Vaughn, "The Founding of the Free Will Baptist Work in Texas," 114–15; See "Texas," in *Free Baptist Cyclopaedia*, 642, which mistakenly refers to Adams as "T. H.," while Vaughn has established that it was "P. H." https://www.ancestry.com/family-tree/person/tree/118991887/person/232027405391/facts?_phsrc=owG1671&_phstart=successSource
27. Bernard Mayfield, "Lone Star," in *Cherokee County History* (Jacksonville, TX: Cherokee County Historical Society, 2001), quoted in Vaughn, "The Founding of the Free Will Baptist Work in Texas," 115–16; see also Vaughn, 116–23; Minutes of the Texas Association (1894), 5–6.
28. Minutes of the Texas Association (1894), 5–6.
29. Harrison and Barfield, *History of the Free Will Baptists*, 429; Million and Barrett, *History of the Liberal Baptist People*, 295; Damon C. Dodd, *The Free Will Baptist Story* (Nashville: Executive Department of the National Association of Free Will Baptists, 1956), 60. More research is needed on Eason and Stetson to corroborate Harrison's and Barfield's account.
30. Murphy, *From the Red to the Rio Grande*, 10; "Ford, Rev. Josephus W.," in *Free Baptist Cyclopaedia*, 198; https://www.ancestry.com/family-tree/person/tree/89749013/person/77001339021/facts?_phsrc=owG1157&_phstart=successSource; Richard G. Ford, 1850 US Census, Brush Creek, Washington County, Arkansas, roll: 31, p. 344b; Missouri State Archives, Jefferson City, MO, Missouri Marriage Records [microfilm], Missouri, US, Marriage Records, 1805–2002, 91; Rev. Josephus Wesley Ford, Find-A-Grave #43727525.
31. See especially Murphy, *From Red to the Rio Grande*, 1–43; see also Richards, "Texas State Association," 100–103.
32. Davidson, *Free Will Baptists in History*, 261–62, 284.
33. Million and Barrett, *Brief History of the Liberal Baptist People*, 295.
34. Delbert Akin, Nancy Draper, and Edwin Wade, *Oklahoma State Association of Free Will Baptists: The First 100 Years, 1908–2008* (Moore, OK: Oklahoma State Association of Free Will Baptists, 2009), 5–6; https://www.ancestry.com/family-tree/person/tree/80742842/person/34425448411/facts?_phsrc=owG1704&_phstart=successSource. Oklahoma achieved statehood in 1907.

35. Akin, Draper, and Wade, *Oklahoma State Association*, 3–4; https://www.ancestry.com/family-tree/person/tree/81190440/person/30446648201/facts; Rev. James M. Roberts, Find-A-Grave #20391103; James M. Roberts, 1900 US Census, Township 13, Cherokee Nation, Indian Territory, roll: 1845, p. 8, enumeration district: 0041, FHL microfilm: 1241845.
36. https://www.ancestry.com/family-tree/person/tree/85978006/person/4253 0084735/facts?_phsrc=gfS360&_phstart=successSource; Rev. Obediah J. "O. J." Taylor, Find-A-Grave #66006433; O. J. Taylor, 1880 US Census, Mountain Township, Logan County, Arkansas, roll: 50, p. 260D, enumeration district: 097. Nothing is known about Taylor's religious background or influences in South Carolina. Regarding Taylor's time in Texas, it is known that Taylor's son William Bayard Taylor was born in Brownwood, Texas, in September 1879. Several archival records bear this out; see, e.g., the latter's death certificate, Arkansas Department of Vital Records, Little Rock, Arkansas, Death Certificates, 1969. The 1900 Census corroborates it and also places the family in Indian Territory by Addie Taylor's birth in December 1892; see Obadiah J. Taylor, 1900 US Census, Township 6, Chickasaw Nation, Indian Territory, roll: 1847, p. 17, enumeration district: 0128; FHL microfilm: 1241847. James Roberts's account also attests to Taylor's sojourn in Texas, but the timeline is sketchy.
37. Rev. James M. Roberts, Find-A-Grave #20391103; Akin, Draper, and Wade, *Oklahoma State Association*, 4.
38. He was still on the roll of ministers in the minutes of 1885. See Minutes of the Mount Moriah Association (1885), "Statistical Table." (There are no extant minutes for 1886–1887.)
39. Rev. Joshua Eiland "J.E." McGee, Find-A-Grave #67059206; https://www.ancestry.com/family-tree/person/tree/78106349/person/48377958238/facts?_phsrc=owG368&_phstart=successSource; https://www.ancestry.com/family-tree/person/tree/78106349/person/290080012652/facts; Peter McGhee, 1850 US Census, Southern District, Pickens County, Alabama, roll: 13, p. 52a; Joshua McGee, 1900 U. S. Census. Township 8, Choctaw Nation, Indian Territory, roll: 1850, p. 10, enumeration district: 0074, FHL microfilm: 1241850; *Lamar* [AL] *News*, April 21, 1887, quoted in Rev. Peter McGee Jr., Find-A-Grave #131137379. McGee's uncle, William Clifton, was still on the roster of ministers in the Mount Moriah Association in its first extant minutes in 1874. See Minutes of the Mount Moriah Association (1874), 8.
40. Akin, Draper, and Wade, *Oklahoma State Association*, 5. The associations adopted these new names about 1903.
41. Davidson, *Free Will Baptists in History*, 185–86; Akin, Draper, and Wade, *Oklahoma State Association*, 6.
42. Minutes of the Cape Fear Free Will Baptist Conference (1866), quoted in Pelt, *Original Free Will Baptists*, 153.

43. Minutes of the Cape Fear Free Will Baptist Conference (1866), quoted in Pelt, *Original Free Will Baptists*, 153–54; Minutes of the Forty-Third Annual Session of the Cape Fear U. A. Free Will Baptist General Conference (1910), 8–9.
44. Harrison and Barfield, *History of the Free Will Baptists of North Carolina*, 265; Pelt, *Original Free Will Baptists*, 155.
45. *An Abstract of the Former Articles of Faith Confessed by the Original Baptist Church Holding the Doctrine of General Provision* (New York: D. Fenshaw, 1855); Davidson, *Free Will Baptists in History*, 242–43.
46. See chapter 3; Robert E. Picirilli, *Little Known Chapters in Free Will Baptist History* (Nashville: Randall House, 2015), 33; Minutes of the Mount Moriah Association (1869), cited in Davidson, *Free Will Baptists in History*, 243–44.
47. Harrison and Barfield, 266–67, 270; "United American Free Will Baptist Church," in *Encyclopedia of African American Religions*, ed. Larry G. Murphy, J. Gordon Melton, and Gary L. Ward (New York: Routledge, 2011), 779; "History of Holly Hill Free Will Baptist Church, Belvoir, North Carolina," http://hollyhillbelvoir.com/media/.
48. *Autobiography of Bishop Isaac Lane, LL.D.* (Nashville: Publishing House of the ME Church, South, 1916), 53–55.
49. *Encyclopedia of African American Religions*, 779; "The UAFWBC Story," United American Freewill Baptist Conference Inc., https://uafwbc.com/the-uafwbc-story/; *Acts and Joint Resolutions of the General Assembly of the State of South Carolina* (Columbia, SC: Gonzales and Bryan, State Printers, 1906), 407.
50. Quoted in K. S. Luckie, "Church History," United American Freewill Baptist Conference Inc., https://uafwbc.com/the-uafwbc-story/.
51. "Our Doctrine," United American Freewill Baptist Conference Inc., https://uafwbc.com/our-doctrine/.
52. Million and Barrett, *Brief History of the Liberal Baptist People*, 192, 201; Minutes of the Chattahoochee Association (1881, 1882); Robert G. Gardner, "African American Free Will Baptists in Georgia," *Viewpoints: Georgia Baptist History* 19 (2004): 5–6.
53. "Our History: The Blessings of Our Past" and Mrs. Jimie Hicks, ed., "Founding Father: Rev. S. H. P. Edmonson," Quad State Annual Conference, Western Division of Free Will Baptists, http://fwbquadstate.org/History.htm.
54. Minutes of the Mount Moriah Association (1869), cited in Davidson, *Free Will Baptists in History*, 243. These minutes do not appear to be extant, but Davidson had access to M. P. Gore's personal collection.
55. Minutes of the Second Annual Session of the Mallet's Creek Association (1891), 4. Held in the Free Will Baptist Historical Collection at Welch College.
56. "Dewey Williams: Shape Note Singer," National Endowment for the Arts, https://www.arts.gov/honors/heritage/dewey-williams#:~:text=Southeast%20Alabama%20is%20the%20only%20area%20in%20the,sung%20by%20African%20Americans%20before%20the%20Civil%20War.

57. Minutes of the Mallet's Creek Association (1891). These connections with the Randall movement lead one to believe that these congregations were influenced by a minister(s) from one of the Louisiana churches founded as a result of the influence of a northern Freewill Baptist minister who was stationed there as a chaplain during the Civil War. See the information on Louisiana below. See also *Treatise* (1954), 41–46.
58. Murphy, *From Red to the Rio Grande*, 2, 4–5; "Church History," St. Paul Free Will Baptist Church, https://revmarcuswhite44.wixsite.com/mysite/church-history.
59. *The Morning Star*, August 13, 1873, cited in Murphy, *From Red to the Rio Grande*, 2–3.
60. *Minutes of General Conference of the Freewill Baptist Connection, Including Ten Sessions—From 1859 to 1889*, compiled by I. D. Stewart (Boston: Free Baptist Printing Establishment, 1887), 2:471, 487.
61. Million and Barrett, *Brief History of the Liberal Baptist People*, 294.
62. Minutes of General Conference (1883), 437. Blackstone is listed as a delegate to the 1883 General Conference.
63. Million and Barrett, *Brief History of the Liberal Baptist People*, 201–2.
64. Million and Barrett, *Brief History of the Liberal Baptist People*, 201–2; Minutes of General Conference (1886), 486–87.
65. Minutes of General Conference (1871), 230–31. How many of these African American churches were absorbed by the Northern Baptist Convention when it merged with the General Conference of Free Baptists in 1911 is unknown.
66. "Shenandoah Mission," in *Free Baptist Cyclopaedia*, 594.
67. "Storer College," in *Free Baptist Cyclopaedia*, 625.
68. "Storer College," 625; Sharon D. Kennedy-Nolle, *Writing Reconstruction: Race, Gender, and Citizenship in the Postwar South* (Chapel Hill: University of North Carolina Press, 2015), 131; the incident with the VMI cadets was reported by Anne S. Dudley, "Address Before the Home Mission Society," *Morning Star*, October 23, 1867.
69. "Storer College," 627. Storer never charged tuition and drew most of its support from Free Baptist congregations. This proved unsustainable after the merger, and the college closed in 1955 owing to financial difficulty.

CHAPTER NINE

1. Ruth B. Bordin, "The Sect to Denomination Process in America: The Freewill Baptist Experience," *Church History* 34 (1965), 77–94. See Ernst Troeltsch, *The Social Teaching of the Christian Churches*, trans. Olive Wyon, 2 vols. (Louisville: Westminster John Knox, 1992 [1912]); William F. Davidson, *The Free Will Baptists in History* (Nashville: Randall House, 2001), 125–26.

"Sect to denomination" is a convenient way of encapsulating the development that occurred. One need not agree with the details of Troeltsch's or Bordin's account or definitions to understand the gist of this phrase.
2. Quoted in Damon C. Dodd, *Marching through Georgia: A History of Free Will Baptists in Georgia* (Colquitt, GA: n.p., 1977), 42. This statement is from the time period before the Chattahoochee United Baptists changed their name to "United Free Will Baptists."
3. Bernard Mayfield, "Lone Star," in *Cherokee County History* (Jacksonville, TX: Cherokee County Historical Society, 2001), quoted in Robert L. Vaughn, "The Founding of the Free Will Baptist Work in Texas," in Robert E. Picirilli, *Free Will Baptist History: Exploring Our Origins and Identity* (Nashville: Randall House, 2019), 115–16. Minutes of the Texas Free Will Baptist Association (1894), 5–6.
4. Minutes of the Toe River Association (1858).
5. Paul Woolsey, *God, A Hundred Years, and a Free Will Baptist Family* (Chuckey, TN: Union Free Will Baptist Association, 1949), 12–13, 43–51; "Woolsey College," in *Free Baptist Cyclopaedia*, 719–20; Robert E. Picirilli, *History of Tennessee Free Will Baptists* (Nashville: Tennessee State Association of Free Will Baptists, rev. 2012), 24.
6. J. M. I. Guyton, "Circular Letter," Minutes of the Mount Moriah Association (1881), 6–9. Guyton was advocating for a school "within the bounds" of the "Southern Baptist Association," which was a group of Arminian and open-communion Baptist associations and churches, mostly Free Will Baptist, across the South.
7. Pelt, *Original Free Will Baptists*, 219–20; Davidson, *Free Will Baptists in History*, 232–34.
8. T. F. Harrison, "Education," *The Free Will Baptist* (May 27, 1896), 2.
9. See Michael R. Pelt, *A History of Ayden Seminary and Eureka College* (Mount Olive, NC: Mount Olive College Press, 1983); Davidson, *Free Will Baptists in History*, 232–34. Some of the material on Ayden/Eureka is adapted from J. Matthew Pinson, *A Free Will Baptist Handbook: Heritage, Beliefs, and Ministries*, 2nd ed. (Nashville: Randall House, 2022), 34–35. For more on the closing of Eureka College, see chapter 13.
10. Minutes of the Toe River Association (1852), handwritten minutes with unnumbered pages held in the Free Will Baptist Historical Collection, Welch College; Minutes of the Cape Fear Conference (1872), 4; Michael R. Pelt, *A History of Original Free Will Baptists* (Mount Olive, NC: Mount Olive College Press, 1996), 175; *An Abstract of the Former Articles of Faith Confessed by the Original Baptist Church, Holding the Doctrine of General Provision, with a Proper Code of Discipline, for the Future Government of the Church* (Newbern, NC: Salmon Hall, 1814).
11. Davidson, *Free Will Baptists in History*, 187–88; William Lumpkin and Enoch

Cobb, eds., *The Free Will Baptist Hymn Book: Containing Hymns and Spiritual Songs, Selected for the Use of the United Churches of Christ, Commonly Called Free Will Baptist and for Saints of all Denominations* (New Bern, NC: John I. Pasteur, 1832); Jesse Heath and Elias Hutchins, eds., *Psalms, Hymns, and Spiritual Songs, Selected for the United Churches of Christ, Commonly Called Free Will Baptists, in North Carolina; and for Saints in All Denominations* (Richmond, VA: Wm. H. Clemmett, 1856); Rufus K. Hearn, Joseph S. Bell, and Jesse Randolph, ed., *Zion's Hymns for the Use of the Original Free Will Baptist Church of North Carolina, and for the Saints of All Denominations* (Pikeville, NC: Elder Daniel Davis, 1854). A copy of the first volume is held in the Free Will Baptist Historical Collection, University of Mount Olive. Copies of the second and third are held there and at the Free Will Baptist Historical Collection, Welch College.

12. *Free Will Baptist Advocate: Published in the Interest of the Original Free Will Baptist Church* 1/7 (April 16, 1874): 2; Pelt, *Original Free Will Baptists*, 172–73.

13. Gary F. Barefoot, "Rufus King Hearn (1819–1894): Free Will Baptist Minister, Historian, and Publisher," *Arminian Baptists: A Biographical History of Free Will Baptists*, ed. David Lytle and Charles Cook (Nashville: Randall House, 2022), 212–15; Michael R. Pelt, "Free Will Baptist," *Encyclopedia of North Carolina*, https://www.ncpedia.org/printpdf/2538. The first extant issue after Hearn became editor is May 23, 1883: *The Free Will Baptist* 3/12. The Convention of Original Free Will Baptists began as the North Carolina State Convention of Original Free Will Baptists after it severed ties with the National Association in 1962. For more information on this body, see chapter 13.

14. Pelt, *Original Free Will Baptists*, 180. Davidson and Pelt rightly discern in Peden's subsequent actions a dissatisfaction with the ecumenism of the northern General Conference. Peden's trajectory is the opposite of that of the northern General Conference, and the theology professor likely did not leave the General Conference and start what Picirilli correctly calls a "rival conference" merely over a name change. However, Picirilli reminds us that it is uncertain precisely what first precipitated Peden's break with the General Conference. Davidson, *Free Will Baptists in History*, 258–59; Pelt, *Original Free Will Baptists*, 182–83; Picirilli, *Little Known Chapters*, 152–53; cf. Norman Allen Baxter, *History of the Freewill Baptists: A Study in New England Separatism* (Rochester: American Baptist Historical Society, 1957), 164n39.

15. Barefoot, "Rufus King Hearn," 207–8.

16. Barefoot, "Rufus King Hearn," 212–14; Hearn, Bell, and Randolph, eds., *Zion's Hymns*; see Davidson, *Free Will Baptists in History*, 84–85, for information on Hearn's interpretation of Free Will Baptist history.

17. Barefoot, "Rufus King Hearn," 213–15.

18. Pelt, *Original Free Will Baptists*, 174–75. See, e.g., Cape Fear, which started recommending it in 1893 (Pelt, *Original Free Will Baptists*, 175); and Chat-

tahoochee, which started recommending it in 1902 (Minutes of the Chattahoochee Association, 1902, 2), after recommending in 1885 the literature from the publishing house in Dover, N.H." (which moved to Boston that year; see "Printing Establishment, The Freewill Baptist," in G. A. Burgess and J. T. Ward, *Free Baptist Cyclopaedia* [Chicago: Free Baptist Cyclopaedia Company, 1889], 543–45) and in 1899 the publisher David C. Cook. See also South Georgia Association, which recommended Ayden literature in 1905 (Minutes of the South Georgia Association, 1905, 4); The Martin Association in Georgia said in 1889: "We will hold a Sabbath school convention at Bellview Church on the Thursday before the first Sabbath in September next and request all Sabbath schools to send representatives to this convention." See the Minutes of the Martin Association (1889), 2.

19. Pelt, *Original Free Will Baptists*, 175, 180–81; Davidson, *Free Will Baptists in History*, 261. The benefit of Free Will Baptist Press, which was eventually located at Ayden, North Carolina, was lost to the National Association in 1962, when the North Carolina State Convention of Original Free Will Baptists separated from the National Association. This separation will be discussed more fully in chapter 13.

20. On the ecumenical thrust in late nineteenth- and early twentieth-century Protestantism, see Eric P. Kaufmann's chapter, "Cosmopolitan Clerics: The Role of Ecumenical Protestantism," in *The Rise and Fall of Anglo-America* (Cambridge: Harvard University Press, 2004), 11–43. See also Davidson, *Free Will Baptists in History*, 255–61.

21. On nineteenth-century Protestant orthodoxy in the South, see E. Brooks Holifield, *The Gentlemen Theologians: American Theology in Southern Culture, 1795–1860* (Durham, NC: Duke University Press, 1978).

22. Robert L. Vaughn and Robert E. Picirilli, "Free Will Baptist Participation in Unity Movements in the South, 1870–1910," in Picirilli, *Free Will Baptist History*, 131.

23. Vaughn and Picirilli, "Free Will Baptist Participation in Unity Movements," 134.

24. Pelt, *Original Free Will Baptists*, 152–53, 157–59. While many used the term "Liberal Baptist" to describe southern Free Will Baptists, northern Freewill Baptists, and midwestern General Baptists, others used it also to include groups such as the Disciples of Christ, Christian Churches, Churches of Christ, and the Churches of God General Conference, which were baptistic and non-Calvinistic in their theology.

25. Pelt, *Original Free Will Baptists*, 159; Vaughn and Picirilli, "Free Will Baptist Participation in Unity Movements," 135–36, 143.

26. See, e.g., the Minutes of the Little Missouri River Association (1891), 3; (1916), 11–13.

27. Minutes of the Little Missouri River Association (1891), 3–5.

28. Vaughn and Picirilli, "Free Will Baptist Participation in Unity Movements," 135, 150. This disaffecting started with the North Carolina General Conference, then Chattahoochee in Georgia, then finally Mount Moriah in Alabama and those in Mississippi and Arkansas who were influenced by it. The Cape Fear Conference in North Carolina was one of the last Free Will Baptist bodies to become disaffected with Nash. He spoke on the subject of union at the annual session of the Cape Fear Conference in 1884, and the delegates voted to send representatives to a union conference the following year. Nash also preached at the meeting, and his Baptist Review Job Office printed the minutes that year. However, the 1885 minutes mention neither Nash nor union, leaving the reader to infer that Cape Fear had lost interest in Nash and the Southern Baptist Association. By 1889, the next extant minutes, Cape Fear voted to support A. D. Williams's Southern Unity movement. See Minutes of the Cape Fear Conference (1884), 3, 5-6; (1885); (1889), 9. Ironically, a small group of Union Baptists from North Carolina migrated to Oklahoma and eventually reunited with the Oklahoma State Free Will Baptist Association a century later in the 1950s (Vaughn and Picirilli, "Free Will Baptist Participation in Unity Movements," 148, 159-60). See also Damon C. Dodd, *The Free Will Baptist Story* (Nashville: Executive Department of the National Association of Free Will Baptists, 1956), 59; Minutes of the Oklahoma State Association (1954), 8, 12; *The Morning Star*, March 7, 1889, 74, 76.
29. Vaughn and Picirilli, "Free Will Baptist Participation in Unity Movements," 161-63; Ollie Latch, *History of the General Baptists* (Poplar Bluff, MO: General Baptist Press, 1954), 390. Williams was one of the visiting brethren at the 1890 Annual Session of the Chattahoochee Association. "The subject of the Southern Unity movement was brought before the body, and Bro. A. D. Williams and others made some remarks, but the question was dropped without definite action." See Minutes of the Chattahoochee Association (1890), 3.
30. Vaughn and Picirilli, "Free Will Baptist Participation in Unity Movements," 164-66. For more on the Unicoi Institute, see Picirilli, *Free Will Baptist History*, 179-232.
31. Vaughn and Picirilli, "Free Will Baptist Participation in Unity Movements," 168-74.
32. Vaughn and Picirilli, "Free Will Baptist Participation in Unity Movements," 176. On Peden and this conference, see especially Robert E. Picirilli, *Little Known Chapters*, 151-80. See also Pelt, *Original Free Will Baptists*, 182-83, and Davidson, *Free Will Baptists in History*, 255-61. Like other historians, I use the adjective "triennial" as a handy way to distinguish the Peden organization from the other General Conferences.
33. Picirilli, *Little Known Chapters* and Pelt, *Original Free Will Baptists*, 182-86. cf. Davidson, *Free Will Baptists in History*, 258-62.
34. This section relies heavily on J. Matthew Pinson, "E. L. St. Claire and the

Free Will Baptist Experience, 1893–1916," *Viewpoints: The Journal of the Georgia Baptist Historical Society* 17 (2000): 19–36.
35. Pinson, "E. L. St. Claire," 22–27, 31–34. The reader will recall that this was the triennial General Conference associated with Thomas Peden.
36. Pinson, "E. L. St. Claire," 27–32; E. L. St. Claire, *The Great Debate at Fanatic's Hall, Prejudiceville: A Witty Book of Rhymes on Church Dissension* (Ayden, NC: Free Will Baptist Print, 1908). Ironically, on the doctrine of original sin and depravity, St. Claire moved away from the more Reformed-oriented total depravity doctrine of most Free Will Baptists in the South and in the North, as illustrated in his pamphlet *The Twin Boys*, about Jacob and Esau. In this work he showed influence of the popular and optimistic Finneyesque teaching of the day. One also sees in St. Claire an optimism that is characteristic of the confidence of late nineteenth- and early twentieth-century Protestantism before World War I brought much of that hopefulness to a crashing end. However, the upshot of St. Claire's preaching and writing was, by and large, to serve as a connection with the older Protestant orthodoxy while safeguarding the confessional uniqueness of the growing Free Will Baptist movement. See E. L. St. Claire, *The Twin Boys* (Raleigh: Edwards and Broughton, 1912). Cf. Charles D. Cook, "E. L. St. Claire (1866–1916): Evangelist, Church Planter, Writer," in *Arminian Baptists*, 241–42.

CHAPTER 10

1. Earlier Calvinist Baptist associations such as the Philadelphia Baptist Association had a polity that was closer to that of the Free Will Baptists.
2. Minutes of the Chattahoochee Association (1879), 12. The Chattahoochee tradition extended from Georgia into Alabama, Florida, and Texas. *Regulas* is the Latin word for "rule."
3. Minutes of the Liberty Association No. 1 (1916), 6–9; Minutes of the Jasper Association (1887), 7. The Liberty tradition extended from Alabama into Florida, Mississippi, and Texas.
4. *An Abstract of the Former Articles of Faith, Confessed by the Original Baptist Church, Holding the Doctrine of General Provision, with a Proper Code of Discipline, for the Future Government of the Church* (New York: D. Fenshaw, 1855); 9; Minutes of the General Conference (1923), 10–11. This use of "ordinance" is the same as that of the Westminster Shorter Catechism in the answer to Question 88 on the outward and ordinary means of grace.
5. *1812 Abstract*, 9. (While the "Rules of Church Discipline" were revised in 1835, for convenience I will hereafter in this chapter refer to this document as the *1812 Abstract*.)
6. See chapter 2 for a fuller discussion of this.

7. Rufus K. Hearn, "Origin of the Free Will Baptist Church of North Carolina," in D. B. Montgomery, ed., *General Baptist History* (Evansville, IN: Courier Company, 1881). Hearn's history was printed earlier in the *Toisnot Transcript* (May 20–June 17, 1875). The reader will recall that Hearn was obviously not denying that Christian believers have experienced saving grace. Rather, he was disagreeing with a technical term used by the New Lights in the Great Awakening to describe a public recitation of the details of this experience. See chapter 2 for more discussion of this phenomenon.
8. E. L. St. Claire, *What Free Will Baptists Believe and Why* (Ayden, NC: Free Will Baptist Press, n.d.), accessed at http://www.onemag.org/stclaire.htm#1.
9. St. Claire, *What Free Will Baptists Believe and Why*. See J. Matthew Pinson, "E. L. St. Claire and the Free Will Baptist Experience, 1893–1916," *Viewpoints: The Journal of the Georgia Baptist Historical Society* 17 (2000): 19–36. This section on the sufficiency of Scripture is adapted from J. Matthew Pinson, *Free Will Baptists and the Sufficiency of Scripture*, a pamphlet (Antioch, TN: Historical Commission, National Association of Free Will Baptists, 2014), 9–12. The Free Will Baptists' *sola scriptura* stance is not to be confused with a "*nuda scriptura*" or "no creed but the Bible" approach. See chapter 3 for a fuller discussion of this distinction.
10. J. Matthew Pinson, "Dissent from Calvinism in the Baptist Tradition," in David L. Allen and Steve W. Lemke, *Calvinism: A Biblical and Theological Critique* (Nashville: B&H Academic, 2022). "Missionary Baptist" was a common designation for non–Free Will Baptists in the South who did not identify with the Primitive Baptists in the anti-mission controversy over local church involvement in missionary societies.
11. For more information on this, see J. Matthew Pinson, *Arminian and Baptist: Explorations in a Theological Tradition* (Nashville: Randall House, 2015). "Imputation" implies that believers stand before God clothed in the righteousness of Christ, whereas "impartation" implies that Christ is making believers more holy, like himself.
12. This is illustrated in Peter Lumpkins's dissertation, which provides numerous examples of the myriad articles of faith used by different groups of Southern Baptists in the nineteenth century. Edgar Peter Frank Lumpkins, "The Decline of Confessional Calvinism among Baptist Associations in the Southern States during the Nineteenth Century" (PhD diss., University of Pretoria, 2018).
13. Hannah Adams, *An Alphabetical Compendium of the Various Sects* (Boston: B. Edes and Sons, 1784), 20. Italics added.
14. John Lawrence Mosheim, *An Ecclesiastical History, Ancient and Modern, from the Birth of Christ, to the Beginning of the Present Century.* . . ., trans. Archibald Maclaine, 4 vols. (New York: Evert Duyckinck, Collins and

Hannay, 1824), 4:131. Maclaine's translation was also widely cited in other reference works, one of which Gore could have owned.

15. That abstract of principles is found in John Asplund, *The Annual Register of the Baptist Denomination in North-America; To the First of November, 1790. . . .* (Southampton County, VA, 1791), 49. See Minutes of the Mount Moriah Association (1874), 7; "The New Hampshire Confession, 1833," in *Baptist Confessions of Faith*, ed. William L. Lumpkin (Valley Forge, PA: Judson, 1969), 362.
16. Asplund, *Annual Register of the Baptist Denomination*, 49.
17. Minutes of the Hamburgh Association (1891), 7.
18. Minutes of the Arkansas Association (1919), 8, 11; Minutes of the Old Mount Zion Association (1889), 5.
19. "Articles of Faith of the Southern Baptist Association," in *The Baptist Review* 38 (1905): p. 3, art. 3 (from the Free Will Baptist Historical Collection, University of Mount Olive), quoted by Robert Vaughn at https://baptistsearch.blogspot.com/2018/01/articles-of-faith-of-southern-baptist.html; Minutes of the Little Brown's Creek Association (1899), 6.
20. *1812 Abstract*, art. 13, repr. in J. Matthew Pinson, *A Free Will Baptist Handbook: Heritage, Beliefs, and Ministries*, 2nd ed. (Nashville: Randall House, 2022), 53; Minutes of the Cumberland Association (1876), 12; Minutes of the Arkansas Association (1919), 8, 11 (italics added). See also the Minutes of the Social Band Association of Arkansas (1913), 7, which said that "infants and idiots" are included in the covenant of grace. ("Idiots" is an archaic term for those mentally disabled persons who were not held accountable for moral choices.) Most Free Will Baptists in the nineteenth century simply asserted the total depravity of humanity and original sin inherited from Adam but did not get into the particulars. These views were universal in southern Free Will Baptist confessional documents in the nineteenth century. In the early twentieth century, E. L. St. Claire made statements that veer from this consensus, reflecting the mentality of many non-Calvinists after the Finneyesque ethos that had exerted great influence on American evangelicalism. See Charles D. Cook, "E. L. St. Claire (1866–1916): Evangelist, Church Planter, Writer," in *Arminian Baptists: A Biographical History of Free Will Baptists*, ed. David Lytle and Charles Cook (Nashville: Randall House, 2022).
21. *1812 Abstract*, arts. 2, 5–6, 8, repr. in Pinson, *Free Will Baptist Handbook*, 150–51.
22. Minutes of the Mount Moriah Association (1874), 7.
23. Minutes of the Chattahoochee Association (1854), 8–9, quoting John 3:19 and Luke 7:30. The reader will recall from chapter 4 that Chattahoochee, while it had rejected strict Calvinism, had not by 1854 made the full transition to confessional Free Will Baptist faith and practice, but D. J. Apperson

would lead the way in this regard in the 1850s or 1860s. However, Apperson, like all Free Will Baptists, would, after his acceptance of the full Free Will Baptist confessional position, agree with the sentiments on conditional election and universal and resistible grace that he had already held before embracing the possibility of apostasy, open communion, and the washing of the saints' feet.

24. *1812 Abstract*, art. 6, repr. in Pinson, *Free Will Baptist Handbook*, 151.
25. Minutes of the Mount Moriah Association (1874), 7; Minutes of the Chattachoochee Association (1854), 5.
26. Minutes of the Mount Moriah Association (1874), 7; Minutes of the Arkansas Association (1919), 11.
27. *1812 Abstract*, art. 9, repr. in Pinson, *Free Will Baptist Handbook*, 152.
28. Minutes of the Mount Moriah Association (1874), 7; Minutes of the Chattahoochee Association (1854), 5.
29. This language, echoing Genesis 6–7, is also seen in the shorter "Articles of Faith" in the *Treatise* of the National Association of Free Will Baptists.
30. "The Life of Rev. John H. Ballard," 4, https://moc.libguides.com/c.php?g=779604&p=5590014.
31. Rufus K. Hearn, Joseph Bell, and Jesse Randolph, eds., *Zion's Hymns, for the Use of the Original Free Will Baptist Church of North Carolina, and for the Saints of all Denominations* (Pikeville, NC: Elder Daniel Davis, 1854), no. 5. This hymn was written by Charles Wesley, whose theology of the nature of atonement in this and other of his hymns does not share the ambiguities of his brother John's views. The former's penal satisfaction understanding of atonement is ironic in view of most Wesleyans' governmental view. For more on this, see J. Matthew Pinson, *40 Questions About Arminianism* (Grand Rapids: Kregel Academic, 2022), 83–96.
32. The northern Freewill Baptists usually affirmed penal substitutionary atonement, but many of them shrank back from the doctrine of the imputation of the righteousness of Christ in justification. See the discussion of these issues in chapter 7.
33. *1812 Abstract*, art. 15, repr. in Pinson, *Free Will Baptist Handbook*, 153.
34. Minutes of the Old Mount Zion Association (1896), 4; Minutes of the Cumberland Association (1876), 12; Minutes of the Chattahoochee Association (1879), 15.
35. *1812 Abstract*, art. 14, repr. in Pinson, *Free Will Baptist Handbook*, 153; Minutes of the Little Brown's Creek Association (1899), art. 11, p. 7.
36. A few United Baptists, especially in Appalachia, still practice the washing of saints' feet in the mid-nineteenth century.
37. Minutes of the Mount Moriah Association (1874), 7. Italics added.
38. Minutes of the Chattahoochee Association (1879), 15; cf. "New Hampshire Confession," art. 11. By 1881, "persevering" was changed to "preserving,"

which remained thereafter, well into the late twentieth century. See Minutes of the Chattahoochee Association (1881), 11–12.
39. J. M. King, "Circular Letter on Apostasy," Minutes of the Chattahoochee Association (1902), 7–8.
40. Minutes of the Cumberland Association (1876), 11–12.
41. Minutes of the Old Mount Zion Association (1889), 6; (1896), 4; Minutes of the Mt. Zion Association (1898). Italics added. No articles of faith were printed in the first extant Old Mount Zion minutes in 1888. In 1925 Old Mount Zion changed its articles of faith to the ones used by the Arkansas Association.
42. Sometimes, the first view above has been referred to as the "backsliding" view, while the second has been referred to as the "apostasy" view. Only one statement has been found in the nineteenth century to the effect that someone can recover from apostasy. A sentence affirming this view is found in Thomas J. Molloy's circular letter in the 1891 Minutes of the Hamburgh Association in Arkansas, 4–6.
43. *An Abstract of the Former Articles of Faith Confessed by the Original Baptist Church, Holding the Doctrine of General Provision, with a Proper Code of Discipline, for the Future Government of the Church* (Newbern, NC: Salmon Hall, 1814), 11. Photocopy of the microfilm of an original copy in the personal library of C. C. Ware, held in the Free Will Baptist Historical Collection, University of Mount Olive.
44. Ellis Gore, "Church Discipline," in the Minutes Mount Moriah Association (1874), 3–6. This was an essay that Gore had already written, which was included in the 1874 Minutes of the Mount Moriah Association because the individual appointed to write the circular letter was unable to do so.
45. Gore, "Church Discipline," 3.
46. Gore, "Church Discipline," 3–4.
47. Gore, "Church Discipline," 3–6.
48. *An Abstract of the Former Articles*, p. 11.
49. Minutes of the North Carolina Original Free Will Baptist General Conference (1853), 4, cited in T. F. Harrison and J. M. Barfield, *A History of the Free Will Baptists of North Carolina* (Ayden, NC: Free Will Baptist Publishing Company, [1897]), 87; William F. Davidson, *The Free Will Baptists in History* (Nashville: Randall House, 2001), 184; Michael R. Pelt, *A History of Original Free Will Baptists* (Mount Olive, NC: Mount Olive College Press, 1996), 146.
50. *An Abstract of the Former Articles*, p. 16.
51. Mt. Moriah tradition. This is representative of similar statements in the Arkansas, Chattahoochee, Tennessee River, and other traditions. Some associations (e.g., Chattahoochee, Tennessee River) used the language of the local church's "independency." Most, however, did not.
52. Minutes of the North Carolina Original Free Will Baptist General Conference

(1853), 4; Minutes of the Flint River Association (1937), 6; see also the Minutes of the Arkansas Association (1921), which said, "In all cases a majority shall rule, except in receiving members which shall be unanimous" (10).
53. Minutes of the Chattahoochee Association (1892), 12. Like the early Randall movement, the Carolina tradition experimented for a time with the concept of "ruling elders"—laymen who would investigate church discipline cases. This usage appeared in the late eighteenth century but began to disappear later in the nineteenth. Still, only ordained ministers were referred to with the title "Elder." Morgan Edwards, "Materials Towards a History of the Baptists in the Provinces of Maryland, Virginia, North Carolina, South Carolina, Georgia" (MS, 1772, held in Furman University Library), https://cdm16821.contentdm.oclc.org/digital/collection/jbt/id/220/rec/1, passim; Davidson, *Free Will Baptists in History*, 178–79.
54. It is hard to tell, for example, whether the Arkansas tradition limited the right to administer baptism to ministers and did not extend it to deacons: "none have a right to administer the same [baptism] only those who are called of God and have come under the hands of the Presbytery of Elders" (Arkansas). The *1812 Abstract* gave deacons the right to baptize if a minister was not present (*An Abstract of the Former Articles*, 15).
55. See, e.g., several issues of the minutes of the Tennessee River and Arkansas Associations. See also the Minutes of the Toe River Association (1855, 1857), handwritten minutes with unnumbered pages held in the Free Will Baptist Historical Collection, Welch College; See, e.g., Mount Moriah: "She may, however, in extreme cases, call aid from sister churches." Minutes of the Mount Moriah Association (1885), Constitution, art. 3, p. 8.
56. The use of "presbytery" is seen in almost all the traditions of church polity in the South (e.g., Carolina, Arkansas, Chattahoochee, Cumberland, Liberty). Some associations had a presbytery of which all ministers were members but which had an examining committee to examine candidates for ordination.
57. Minutes of the Cumberland Association (1876), 14. Often presbyteries and ordaining councils offered care for ministers by offering counsel and admonition, inquiring about their spiritual health and the conduct of their ministries, and recommending reading material.
58. *An Abstract of the Former Articles*, p. 15; Minutes of the Cumberland Association (1876), 14; cf. Arkansas (1919 Minutes): ". . . the Association shall have power, for good cause, to revoke the license or credentials of any minister, licensed or ordained by any church within its jurisdiction."
59. Minutes of the Cumberland Association (1876), 13. The language of "lord it over God's heritage" and "advisory body" or "advisory council" is common. In addition to the Cumberland Association, see, e.g., Minutes of the Mount Moriah Association (1885), 7; Minutes of the 26th Annual Session of the Western Arkansas Association of Freewill Baptists Church of Christ (1894),

2. The one clear historical exception to this view of the self-government of the local congregation among southern Free Will Baptists that I have been able to find is the South Georgia Association in the early twentieth century: "This Association shall be considered an ecclesiastical body and shall control all the various churches composing the same so far as Gospel order extends. Also, no houses or lands shall be sold or disposed of without its consent" (Minutes of South Georgia Association [1909], 14). This statement is not found in the extant minutes before 1909. In 1952, a resolution passed that "we discontinue the printing in our minutes of the part of the church Decorum that conflicts with our National Treatise which we have adopted; and that we substitute that part of our National Treatise which deals with the same" (Minutes of the South Georgia Association [1952], 7).

60. Minutes of the Arkansas Association (1919), 9–10.
61. Westminster Shorter Catechism, Q. 88, http://prts.edu/wp-content/uploads/2013/09/Shorter_Catechism.pdf; David Benedict, *A General History of the Baptist Denominations in America, and Other Parts of the World*, 2 vols. (Boston: Manning and Loring, 1813), 2:107; Edwards, "Materials," 77. Edwards said Lower Fishing Creek Church (General Baptist) in North Carolina practiced the "devoting of children" in the mid-eighteenth century (Edwards, *Materials*, 133).
62. *1812 Abstract*, art. 17; Minutes of the Chattahoochee Association (1892), 14. *A Treatise of the Faith and Practice of the Free Will Baptist[s]* (Purdy, MO: Free Will Baptist Gem, 1936), 38. The *Treatise* wording is the same as the northern *Treatise* after the Usages section of the latter was revised in 1868. The language of "means of grace" remained in the *Treatise* until its 1969 revision. See *A Treatise of the Faith and Practices of the Original Free Will Baptists* (Nashville: Executive Department, National Association of Free Will Baptists, 1969).
63. Minutes of the Arkansas Association (1921), 10, art. 10.
64. *1812 Abstract*, art. 13, repr. Pinson, *Free Will Baptist Handbook*, 153.
65. Harrison and Barfield, *History of the Free Will Baptists of North Carolina*, 148–52.
66. Harrison and Barfield, *History of the Free Will Baptists of North Carolina*, 148–51.
67. Harrison and Barfield, *History of the Free Will Baptists of North Carolina*, 146–47. Ironically, one of the historical authorities Harrison and Barfield quoted on baptism was "Dr. Du Veil on Acts." They likely did not realize that this noted biblical scholar, who was widely quoted from the nineteenth-century reprint of this lengthy commentary on the Acts of the Apostles, was one of their spiritual ancestors. A French convert from Judaism to Catholicism, the distinguished philologist and biblical scholar Carolus M. Du Veil later converted to Anglicanism and subsequently became a General Baptist after discussions with a General Baptist woman who was his housekeeper.

For more on Du Veil, see J. M. Cramp, *Baptist History* (London: Elliot Stock, 1868), 410–11.
68. Minutes of the Chattahoochee Association (1891), 6.
69. *1812 Abstract*, art. 17, repr., in Pinson, *Free Will Baptist Handbook*, 153.
70. Minute of the Toe River Association (1857); Minutes of the Mount Moriah Association (1874), 7.
71. Minutes of the Mount Moriah Association (1885); Grammatical errors in original. See also D. J. Apperson's circular letter on open communion in the Minutes of the Chattahoochee Association (1888), 8–9.
72. Minutes of the Chattahoochee Association (1899), 8.
73. John L. Dagg, "The Duty of Washing the Saints' Feet," *The Virginia Baptist Preacher* 1 (1842): 79–83; John Leadley Dagg, *Manual of Theology. Second Part. A Treatise on Church Order* (Charleston, SC: Southern Baptist Publication Society, 1858), 226–31. See Robert L. Vaughn, *Materials Toward a History of Feet Washing among the Baptists* (Mount Enterprise, TX: Waymark, 2008).
74. Minutes of the Little Missouri River Association (1891), 3, 5–6. These (1891) are the first extant minutes. In the next extant minutes, seventeen years later, they had begun to use the Arkansas Association Articles of Faith (probably because they had been adopted by the Arkansas State Association). Minutes of the Eighth Annual Session of the Little Brown's Creek Association of Free Will Baptists (1899), 7.
75. Minutes of the Social Band Association (September 20–22, 1913), 6.
76. T. F. Harrison and T. H. Harrison, *Feet-Washing* (Ayden, NC: Free Will Baptist Publishing Company, [1896]), 13–15. See my reference to the seventeenth-century Quaker author Robert Barclay, who made the argument that those who disavowed the *pedilavium* should, like the Quakers, disavow baptism and the Lord's Supper on similar grounds. J. Matthew Pinson, *The Washing of the Saints' Feet* (Nashville: Randall House, 2006), 38–39.
77. Harrison and Harrison, *Feet-Washing*, 16–18. The Harrisons thought the quotation from the Roman Catholic scholar came from the president of the University of Notre Dame, but it actually is from the eminent French Roman Catholic liturgiologist Dom Prosper Guéranger's *The Liturgical Year: Passiontide and Holy Week* (Dublin: James Duffy, 1870), 397. See also T. H. Griffin, "Circular Letter," in the Minutes of the Chattahoochee Association (1883), 7–12. For recent defenses of the washing of the saints' feet as an ordinance, see John Christopher Thomas, *Footwashing in John 13 and the Johannine Community* (New York: Bloomsbury, 2004) and Pinson, *The Washing of the Saints' Feet*.
78. D. M. Graham, "Biographical Sketch of Rev. Elias Hutchins," *Freewill Baptist Quarterly* 8 (1860): 96; Elias Hutchins, letter to *The Morning Star* dated June 20, 1830. *Morning Star*, July 28, 1830; Davidson, *Free Will Baptists in History*, 162.

79. Walter B. Shurden, "The Southern Baptist Synthesis: Is it Cracking?" *Baptist History and Heritage* 16 (1981), 2–11.
80. Noah Webster, *American Dictionary of the English Language* (New York: S. Converse, 1830), 770.
81. "How Great, How Solemn is the Work" by Benjamin Beddome, in Hearn, Bell, and Randolph, ed., *Zion's Hymns*, no. 191.
82. Minutes of the Hookerton Free Will Baptist Church (Later Hookerton Disciples Church), 1830–1869 (November 30, 1930), 5.
83. Webster, *American Dictionary* (1830), 461.
84. See the title page as well as the preface of Enoch Cobb, ed., *The Free Will Baptist Hymn Book; Containing Hymns and Spiritual Songs, Selected for the Use of the United Churches of Christ, Commonly Called Free Will Baptists, and for Saints of all Denominations* (New Bern, NC: William G. Hall, 1846).
85. "To Thy Temple We Repair," by James Montgomery, in *Zion's Hymns*, no. 70.
86. Buell E. Cobb, *The Sacred Harp: A Tradition and Its Music* (Athens, GA: University of Georgia Press, 2004).
87. Frank Lawrence Owsley, *Plain Folk of the Old South* (Baton Rouge: Louisiana State University Press, 2008 [1949]), 124–25. The leaders of the shape note singing tradition believed that their methods of teaching people to read music, spurred on by increased literacy, was superior to the older practice of "lining out" hymns, whereby the song leader would read the words of a line of a hymn before the congregation sung that line.
88. Minutes of the Chattahoochee Association (1882), 4.
89. F. L. Smith, "Rise and Progress of Mt. Moriah Church and Mt. Moriah Association with Some of Their Labors," handwritten MS, July 10, 1888, 4. Held in Free Will Baptist Historical Collection, Welch College. For local church benevolence reports and associational benevolence committees, see, e.g., arts. 4 and 6 of the Constitution of the Cape Fear Free-Will Baptist Conference, reprinted in Harrison and Barfield, *History of the Free Will Baptists*, 350.
90. Phillip T. Morgan, "Robert Heaton (1765–1843)," in *Arminian Baptists: A Biographical History of Free Will Baptists*, 150; Minutes of the Toe River Association (1851, 1852). See *Minutes of General Conference of the Freewill Baptist Connection, Including Ten Sessions—From 1859 to 1889*, compiled by I. D. Stewart (Boston: Free Baptist Printing Establishment, 1887), 2:471, 487.
91. Minutes of the Chattahoochee Association (1881), 2; (1882), 3.
92. Minutes of the Free Baptist General Conference (1898), 33.
93. Robert E. Picirilli, *History of Tennessee Free Will Baptists* (Nashville: Tennessee State Association of Free Will Baptists, rev. 2012), 20. See chapter 3 for a discussion of the temperance movement among southern Free Will Baptists.

CHAPTER ELEVEN

1. Minutes of the Co-operative General Association (1916), 1. Damon C. Dodd, "The Story of Rev. John H. Wolfe," *Contact* (December 1953) (based on an interview with Wolfe). The reader will recall that, regardless of the multiplicity of spellings in the northern and southern movements, "Free Will" was more common in the South whereas "Freewill" was more common in the North; thus they are used that way throughout this book. This distinction in nomenclature becomes cumbersome in the following discussion of the movement in the Midwest and Southwest in the early twentieth century, given the fact that Freewill Baptists in this area who stayed out of the merger with the Northern Baptist Convention united with Free Will Baptists in the same area who originated from the southern movement. This phenomenon is exacerbated by the fact that the northern General Conference changed its name to "Free Baptist" in the late nineteenth century.
2. Minutes of the Co-operative General Association (1916), 5–7.
3. Minutes of the Co-operative General Association (1916), 5–7. Robert E. Picirilli, *Little Known Chapters in Free Will Baptist History* (Nashville: Randall House, 2015), 184–99.
4. Minutes of the Co-operative General Association (1917), 9–10.
5. Minutes of the Co-operative General Association (1917), 11–12, 15–16. On Smith, see Picirilli's chapter on the school at Unicoi in *Free Will Baptist History: Exploring Our Origins and Identity* (Nashville: Randall House, 2019), 222. By this time the abbreviation "Rev." for the title "Reverend" for ordained ministers had come into more common use in the Co-operative General Association, as it had in the northern General Conference. The title "Elder" ("Eld.") persisted longer in the South. For example, in the first edition of the new *Treatise* of the National Association of Free Will Baptists in 1935, the Revision Committee's names were printed in the front of the book with "Eld." and a note at the bottom that said, "In the signing of the Treatise, the majority of the committee preferred the title of 'Elder' to that of 'Reverend,' so in love the majority won, with 100 per cent.—Chair." See *Treatise* (1936).
6. Minutes of the Co-operative General Association (1917), 16–17.
7. Minutes of the Co-operative General Association (1917), 17–19.
8. Minutes of the Co-operative General Association (1918), 21; Minutes of the Western General Conference (1937), 9.
9. Minutes of the Co-operative General Association (1918), 10–16.
10. Minutes of the Co-operative General Association (1918), 8. Minutes of the Co-operative General Association (1922), 6–7.
11. Picirilli, *Little Known Chapters*, 240. See this book for the most extensive discussion of this matter, and the entire chapter on John H. Wolfe, for the most in-depth consideration of the Co-operative General Association.

12. Picirilli, *Little Known Chapters*, 239–40.
13. Picirilli, *Little Known Chapters*, 242. The language of "Original Free Will Baptists" dates back to the Carolinas, at least as early as the 1840s. It likely stems from southern Free Will Baptists distinguishing themselves from the Randall movement in the North, which originated about a century later than the Free Will Baptists in the Carolinas. It probably also has some connection to the 1812 *Abstract*'s title, which referred to the "Original Baptist Church, Holding to the Doctrine of General Provision." Outside the Carolinas, the wording was used in both the title of the General Conference in the South in the early twentieth century and the title of the National Association in its early years. While still used in the titles of a few Free Will Baptist churches outside North Carolina, the title is now primarily identified with the Convention of Original Free Will Baptists, which separated from the National Association in 1962 (see chapter 13 for more on this body). See Picirilli, *Little Known Chapters*, 20–25, for more information about the word "Original" when applied to denominational nomenclature.
14. Minutes of the Co-operative General Association (1922); Minutes of the Co-operative General Association (1923), 7, 9, 11; Picirilli, *Little Known Chapters*, 211.
15. Minutes of the Co-operative General Association (1922), 9; Minutes of the Co-operative General Association (1923), 13–14.
16. *Tecumseh College Catalogue and Announcements* (1926–27); Minutes of the Midway Association [Southwest Georgia] ([November] 1926;), 2; ([November] 1927), "Statistical Table"; Minutes of the General Conference ([June] 1927), 1; Picirilli, *Little Known Chapters*, 226–29.
17. Minutes of the General Conference of the Original Free Will Baptists of the United States (1932), 7; Minutes of the Co-operative General Association (1934), 6–7; Picirilli, *Little Known Chapters*, 218. The Co-operative General Association Minutes say "R. V." Shutes, which is almost certainly a misprint of "K. V."
18. Minutes of the General Conference (1933); Minutes of the Co-operative General Association (1934), 3–4, 6–7.
19. Picirilli, *Little Known Chapters*, 242.
20. Minutes of First and Second Annual Sessions of the General Conference of the Original Free Will Baptists of the United States (1921), 3. The group from the Ohio River Yearly Meeting, mentioned later in the Minutes, was probably the delegation that sent the telegram.
21. Minutes of the General Conference (1921), 4, 6.
22. Minutes of the General Conference (1922), 9, 11. Several churches in the Carolinas became Pentecostal in the 1920s, resulting in a group known as the Pentecostal Free Will Baptist Church.
23. Mary Ruth Wisehart, ed., *The Fifty-Year Record of the National Association of*

Free Will Baptists (Nashville: Randall House, 1988), 103–4; Phillip T. Morgan, "The Women of the Cumberland," in Roy W. Harris and Phillip T. Morgan, *The Cumberland Association: Celebrating 175 Years of Leadership, Ministry, and Service* (Lebanon, TN: RHM, 2018), 109–12.

24. Minutes of the General Conference (1923), 5–6, 8, 10.
25. Minutes of the General Conference (1925), 5, 8–9; (1926), 6–8.
26. Minutes of the General Conference (1928), 7–9. "Free Will Baptist League" was the name of the General Conference's youth training organization.
27. Minutes of the General Conference (1931), 16–18; (1935), 16–17.
28. Minutes of the General Conference (1923), 3–4.
29. Minutes of the General Conference (1923), 3–4, 6–9.
30. Minutes of the General Conference (1926), 5–6; "Reverend Henry Oliver, Educator and Minister, Dead at 87," *Contact* (August 1991), 16.
31. Minutes of the General Conference (1928), 15.
32. Minutes of the General Conference (1924), 4, 6–9.
33. Minutes of the General Conference (1924), 4, 6–9; (1928), 14.
34. Minutes of the General Conference (1923), 4–5, 11.
35. Minutes of the General Conference (1923), 10–11.
36. George M. Marsden, *Fundamentalism and American Culture* (New York: Oxford University Press, 1980), 118–23.
37. Minutes of the General Conference (1926), 9.
38. Minutes of the General Conference (1925), 9; (1926), 6. Beginning that year the chief office of the General Conference was no longer referred to as "President."
39. "The Missionary's Farewell" by Samuel Francis Smith, in Rufus K. Hearn, Joseph S. Bell, and Jesse Randolph, ed., *Zion's Hymns for the Use of the Original Free Will Baptist Church of North Carolina, and for the Saints of All Denominations* (Pikeville, NC: Elder Daniel Davis, 1854), no. 258.
40. Minutes of the General Conference (1929), 5. One almost senses impatience from this minister from Georgia, a state that had excelled in home missions (with church planters, e.g., like John T. Knight and his protégé E. L. St. Claire) and from which the first southern Free Will Baptist foreign missionary would emerge.
41. Minutes of the General Conference (1928), 15.
42. Michael R. Pelt, *A History of Original Free Will Baptists* (Mount Olive, NC: Mount Olive College Press, 1996), 236–39.
43. Minutes of the General Conference (1926), 9.
44. Minutes of the General Conference (1929), 6; (1930), 5, 14; (1931), 4, 7. A denominational hymnal would not be published until the Free Will Baptist Press in Ayden, North Carolina, published *The Free Will Baptist Hymnal* in 1958.
45. Minutes of the General Conference (1931), 10.

46. Minutes of the General Conference (1932), 5. Morse, who would also attend the 1933 annual session of the General Conference (see 1933 Minutes), was not active in the Co-operative General Association at this time. The Texas State Convention and Paul Woolsey from the Union Association in East Tennessee were also present and welcomed at the 1932 annual session of the General Conference (16).

47. Minutes of the General Conference (1932), 16.

48. Minutes of the General Conference (1933), 8, 12.

49. Minutes of the Eastern General Association of the General Conference (1934), 19; Minutes of the Co-operative General Association (1934), 7. The 1901 *Treatise* of the Free Baptist General Conference did not include the washing of the saints' feet. Perhaps this matter had already been worked out and assumed, but probably not. The committee called for the meeting to be held with East Nashville Church, but it convened with Cofer's Chapel, the congregation Welch pastored, instead.

50. Minutes of the First Session of the National Association of the Original Free Will Baptists of the United States (1935), 1, 6; Minutes of the Eastern General Association of the Original Free Will Baptists of the United States (1936), title page; Minutes of the Western General Association of Free Will Baptist[s] (1937), 1.

51. Minutes of the National Association (1935), 2.

52. Minutes of the National Association (1935), 3–4.

53. Minutes of the National Association (1935), 5–6.

54. Minutes of the National Association (1935), 5–6, 9, 11.

CHAPTER TWELVE

1. Minutes of the General Conference (1938), 9; Minutes of the National Association (1938), 3. That the constituent bodies of the National Association would be state bodies was intended as a general rule to which certain exceptions would be made. This is evidenced in subsequent practice as well as in the constitution as amended when the General Board was added in 1940 (Minutes of the National Association [1940], 18). However, the "state association" rule became the norm, and when states began to have enough associations to form a state association, this practice, inadvertently or not, resulted in the formation of state associations and representation to the National Association with a delegate to the General Board. This setup has continued to the present. Regional associations exist, such as the Northwest Association or the Northeast Association, which comprise churches in several states where there is a small Free Will Baptist presence. The magnanimity of the Eastern General Association in essentially proposing a 50/50 balance of power between Free Will Baptists east and west of the Mississippi is

noteworthy in view of that Association's overwhelming majority of numbers and resources when compared with the West.
2. Minutes of the National Association (1938), 3-5.
3. Minutes of the National Association (1938), 3, 6, 10-11, 14; Minutes of the National Association (1939), 14.
4. Minutes of the National Association (1940), 18, 21-22; (1942), 7; (1946), 10. Delegates from West Virginia had previously been in attendance as representatives of the Tri-State Association. In 1940 the "West Virginia State Meeting" was admitted for membership in the National Association. Also, in the early sessions of the National Association, the Free Will Baptist orphanages in Middlesex, North Carolina, Greeneville, Tennessee, and Eldridge, Alabama, would be invited to make informal reports.
5. Minutes of the National Association (1941), 21.
6. Minutes of the National Association (1941), 21-23.
7. Minutes of the General Conference (1935), 5, 6, 14; (1936), 14, 16-17; (1937), 15-19; (1938), 4, 11, 13-15; Minutes of the National Association (1935), 9; (1938), 4-5, 9.
8. Minutes of the National Association (1944), 20; (1946), 17; (1947), 20-21, 24; *Into the Darkness: 75 Years of Free Will Baptist International Missions* (Antioch, TN: Free Will Baptist International Missions, 2010), 16-17; Laura Belle Barnard, *Touching the Untouchables*, with Georgia B. Hill (Wheaton: Tyndale House, 1985).
9. Minutes of General Conference (1935), 5-6, 14; Minutes of the Eastern General Association (1936), 14-15.
10. Minutes of General Conference (1935); Minutes of the Eastern General Association (1936), 14-15; Minutes of the National Association (1938), 7, 14; Minutes of the Western General Association (1937), 4, 11.
11. Minutes of the National Association (1939), 8-9; (1940), 16; (1941), 26-27; (1942), 23-24; *Into the Darkness*, 52.
12. Minutes of the National Association (1943), 21-22; (1944), 22; (1946), 16; *Into the Darkness*, 52.
13. *Into the Darkness*, 46-47. See the biography of Thomas Willey, by Jerry Ballard, *Never Say Can't* (Carol Stream, IL: Creation House, 1971), and the autobiography of Mabel Willey, *Beyond the Gate: The Autobiography of Mabel Bailey Willey*, with Mary Ruth Wisehart (Nashville: Randall House, 1998).
14. Minutes of the National Association (1947), 20; *Into the Darkness*, 20-21.
15. Minutes of the National Association (1948), 12, 20, 24; (1950), 23; *Into the Darkness*, 22-25; Mary Ruth Wisehart, ed., *The Fifty-Year Record of the National Association of Free Will Baptists* (Nashville: Randall House, 1988), 59.
16. Mellette would close Zion in 1942 in deference to the new college, donating all its assets to the new institution. Most of Zion's students were from Georgia, Florida, and Alabama, yet other students came from as far away as

Texas and North Carolina. See Benjamin Miller, "The History of Zion Bible School" (unpublished essay, 2006), 6, 11–12, as well as an interview I had with retired minister W. F. McDuffie of Blakely, Georgia, who rode a train from his home in Williamson County, Texas, to attend Zion and never left Early County, Georgia. After Zion closed its doors, Mellette was offered a teaching position at Free Will Baptist Bible College but turned it down owing to family responsibilities (Miller, "History of Zion Bible School," 11–12).

17. Minutes of the General Conference (1933), 15.
18. Minutes of the General Conference (1933), 15.
19. "Story of a College: Free Will Baptist Bible College," in Wisehart, ed., *The Fifty-Year Record*, 34.
20. Agnes Frazier, "Your Opportunity and Mine," *The Free Will Baptist* (January 24, 1940), 3.
21. Minutes of the National Association (1935), 6; (1938), 3, 5.
22. Minutes of the National Association (1939), 3; Phillip T. Morgan and J. Matthew Pinson, *Light and Truth: A Seventy-Fifth-Anniversary Pictorial History of Welch College* (Gallatin, TN: Welch College Press, 2018), 14.
23. Minutes of the National Association (1941), 21, 24; Robert E. Picirilli, *Free Will Baptist History*, 234–35.
24. Minutes of the National Association (1941), 24; Morgan and Pinson, *Light and Truth*, 14.
25. Paul Vernice Harrison, "A Biography of Linton Carroll Johnson," MA thesis, Middle Tennessee State University, 1988, 59–61; Morgan and Pinson, *Light and Truth*, 26–32.
26. Wisehart, ed., *The Fifty-Year Record*, 37.
27. Minutes of the National Association (1935), 7; Free Will Baptist Bible College Bulletin (1943–1944), 8–12; Free Will Baptist Bible College Catalog (1948–1949), 25; (1950–1951), 29–31; Morgan and Pinson, *Light and Truth*, 28.
28. Phillip T. Morgan, "The Promise of a Second Evangelical Mind: Free Will Baptist Bible College and the Hybrid Model of Christian Higher Education," MA thesis, Middle Tennessee State University, 2016, 26–37. I owe the reference to D. L. Moody to my colleague Darrell Holley; see James Findlay, "Moody, 'Gapmen,' and the Gospel: The Early Days of Moody Bible Institute," *Church History* 31 (1962): 322–35; Darrell Hobson, "D. L. Moody's Gap-men: A Vision for Assemblies of God Bible Colleges," *Paraclete* 23 (1989): 1–8.
29. L. C. Johnson, "Over My Shoulder," *Contact* (April 1979), 30; Morgan, "The Promise of a Second Evangelical Mind," 23–26.
30. R. E. Tripp, "The School Problem," *The Free Will Baptist* (January 4, 1939), 3; Morgan, "The Promise of a Second Evangelical Mind," 35–36.
31. Frazier, "Your Opportunity and Mine," 10–11.
32. Frazier, "Your Opportunity and Mine," 10; Morgan, "The Promise of a Second Evangelical Mind," 36–37. Owing to the differences in philosophy of

education vying for prominence in the denomination, Morgan argues, "her approach took time to develop at Free Will Baptist Bible College" (37).
33. Morgan and Pinson, *Light and Truth*, 17–18, 47, 98–99.
34. Minutes of the General Conference (1935), 13; Minutes of the Eastern General Association (1936), 16; (1938), 6; Minutes of the Co-operative General Association (1934), 3; Minutes of the National Association (1935), 10.
35. Minutes of the National Association (1938), 1, 4; (1939), 5, 7, 12.
36. Minutes of the National Association (1941), 9, 21; (1944), 25, 30, 33; (1946), 21–22.
37. Minutes of the National Association (1948), 25–26; "History of the Home Missions Department," in Wisehart, ed., *Fifty-Year Record*, 71.
38. Minutes of the National Association (1949), 26; (1950), 31–32. The minutes list "J. L. Welch," but Robert Picirilli, in email correspondence, said that this was John L. Welch's son Weaver, who was a layman who lived in Kansas City and must have been involved in a church plant there.
39. Minutes of the Western General Association (1937) 9, 11.
40. Minutes of the National Association (1935), 7; (1938), 1, 8; (1939), 12. In 1941 the organization began using the alternate title Woman's National Auxiliary Convention, which by 1950 would be the exclusive title; see Minutes (1941), 2; (1950), 18. In 1993 the name was changed to Women Nationally Active for Christ; see Minutes (1993), A-205–06. In this section "the convention" refers to the WNAC Convention.
41. Minutes of the National Association (1939), 12; (1940), 26–27; Wisehart, ed., *Fifty-Year Record*, 110–12.
42. Wisehart, ed., *Fifty-Year Record*, 110–11; the first edition of Crawford's book was published in 1924: Julius Earl Crawford, *The Call to Christian Stewardship* (Nashville: Publishing House of the Methodist Episcopal Church, South, 1924).
43. Minutes of the National Association (1935), 16–17; (1939), 12, 21; (1940), 26–27; Wisehart, ed., *Fifty-Year Record*, 110–12.
44. Minutes of the National Association (1941), 48.
45. Minutes of the National Association (1941), 48.
46. Minutes of the National Association (1941), 48; (1942), 43.
47. Minutes of the National Association (1942), 43; (1944), 28; (1945), 19–20; (1946), 22.
48. Minutes of the National Association (1941), 48; (1944), 50–55.
49. Minutes of the National Association (1942), 52–53. The Christian Workers Institutes held across the denomination were sponsored by National Executive Secretary L. R. Ennis and the Executive Office of the National Association. For more on these, see Robert E. Picirilli, *Free Will Baptist History: Exploring Our Origins and Identity* (Nashville: Randall House, 2019), chapter 7.
50. Minutes of the National Association (1943), 11–12, 54–55. Opal Bingham's

husband Melvin served on the original Board of Trustees of Free Will Baptist Bible College.
51. Minutes of the National Association (1944), 53; (1945), 14; (1950), 18; Wisehart, ed., *Fifty-Year Record*, 112–13.
52. Minutes of the National Association (1935), 2, 8, 10; (1939), 11. It is impossible to tell who printed the 1946, 1949, and 1951 Minutes.
53. Minutes of the National Association (1935), 2, 8, 10. Minutes of the General Conference (1924), 4–5; Michael R. Pelt, *A History of Original Free Will Baptists* (Mount Olive, NC: Mount Olive College Press, 1996), 203.
54. Minutes of the National Association (1938), 6–7, 12, 14; (1940), 6.
55. Minutes of the National Association (1938), 6–7, 12, 14. This last observation about laymen and women is evidenced by a perusal of annual session Minutes from the 1930s through the 1970s.
56. Minutes of the National Association (1940), 7–11; (1941), 36.
57. Minutes of the National Association (1942), 3, 5, 11, 18, 22–23, 31; (1943), 36.
58. Minutes of the National Association (1943), 12, 27; (1944), 26.
59. Minutes of the National Association (1947), 28, 34.
60. *A Treatise of the Faith and Practices of Free Will Baptists* (rev. 1945), 25, 31; *A Treatise of the Faith and Practices of the Original Free Will Baptists* (rev. 1948), 27, 33, 36–37.
61. Minutes of the National Association (1948), 28.
62. Minutes of the National Association (1944), 28; (1945), 35; (1947), 27. In 1949, the *Gem* did publish a small pamphlet for the board entitled *Personal Soul Winning*. See Minutes of the National Association (1949), 27. The Gem also printed the 1936 and 1940 printings of the *Treatise*. See *Treatise* (1936, 1940).
63. Minutes of the National Association (1949), 27.
64. Minutes of the National Association (1948), 29, 31. Later Charles and Laura Thigpen's son Jonathan would go on to become executive director of ETA, and following his death, his widow Yvonne assumed the post.
65. Minutes of the National Association (1949), 27.
66. Minutes of the National Association (1948), 5–10, 16, 17, 22; (1950), 8. Florida's statistics in this count are from 1950 because statistics in 1947–49 were incomplete. All other statistics are from 1948. These statistics, like all those of the National Association, are "reported" numbers and thus are a less-than-reliable snapshot of the whole, as some churches and associations did not report statistics.
67. Minutes of the National Association (1948), 5–10, 16, 17, 22; (1950), 8.

CHAPTER THIRTEEN

1. Minutes of the National Association (1951), 52.
2. Raymond Riggs, "The Michigan State Association," in *History of Free Will*

Baptist State Associations, ed. Robert E. Picirilli (Nashville: Randall House, 1976), 52; William F. Davidson, *The Free Will Baptists in History* (Nashville: Randall House, 2001), 289–90.

3. For more on these doctrinal positions, see chapter 10.
4. Riggs, "The Michigan State Association," 53; Davidson, *Free Will Baptists in History*, 289–90.
5. W. H. Patterson, "The Indiana State Association," in *History of Free Will Baptist State Associations*, 35–36; Davidson, *Free Will Baptists in History*, 289–90.
6. Patterson, "The Indiana State Association," 37–38. Both the Stone Association and the John-Thomas Association are unaffiliated with the National Association. For more on the Stone Association, see chapter 5. For more on the John-Thomas Association, which comprises churches in Virginia, Kentucky, Indiana, Ohio, and West Virginia, see chapter 7.
7. Jack L. Williams, "The California State Association," in *History of Free Will Baptist State Associations*, 14–16. California Christian College will be discussed in the next chapter.
8. Minutes of the National Association (1981), 104. See also *The 2019 Free Will Baptist Yearbook* (Antioch, TN: Executive Office, National Association of Free Will Baptists, 2019). The Primitive Baptists of New Brunswick came out of the Free Christian Baptists of the Maritime Provinces in Canada in the 1870s. This was an Arminian Baptist denomination of separate origins from the Randall movement, which had correspondence with the latter movement but never united with it. See M. L. Hayward, "George W. Orser and the 'Orserites,'" *Collections of the New Brunswick Historical Society* 11 (1927): 214–37; Joseph McLeod, "A Sketch of the History of the Free Baptists of New Brunswick," in Edward Manning Saunders, *History of the Baptists of the Maritime Provinces* (Halifax, NS: John Burgoyne, 1902), 410–35.
9. See pp. 320–21.
10. "Mount Allen Junior College," and David W. Hansley, "Christian Education," *The Free Will Baptist* (May 28, 1952), 1, 4; see the first issue of *Contact* (November 1953).
11. See chapter 12.
12. Minutes of the National Association (1954), 48; (1957), 52.
13. Minutes of the National Association (1958), 53; (1959), 16–17, 23–24.
14. Michael R. Pelt, *A History of Original Free Will Baptists* (Mount Olive, NC: Mount Olive College Press, 1996), 284–87; "Mount Allen Junior College," *The Free Will Baptist* (March 31, 1954), 1; "Dr. Burkette Raper Dies of Cancer at 83," *Goldsboro News-Argus* (August 1, 2011), http://savannah.newsargus.com/news/archives/2011/0 8/01/dr_burkette_raper_dies_of_cancer_at_83/. See Robert E. Picirilli, "Thunder among the Tar Heels: The 1960s Church Government Controversy" (unpublished essay, 2019).

15. Leroy Forlines-Burkette Raper correspondence, Free Will Baptist Historical Collection, University of Mount Olive.
16. *The Challenger* (February 8, 1960; February 29, 1960); Jerry Ballard, ed., *Perception*, March-April, 1960; W. Burkette Raper, *A Short History of Mount Olive College* (Mount Olive: Mount Olive College Press, 2001), 58.
17. Statement of the Executive Committee of the National Association of Free Will Baptists," *Contact* (September, 1961), 16.
18. "The Western Conference Reports on the Edgemont Church Dispute: Report No. 3," *The Free Will Baptist* (August 16, 1961), 4, 13-14; Pelt, *Original Free Will Baptists*, 308-11.
19. "The Western Conference Reports on the Edgemont Church Dispute: Report No. 3," *The Free Will Baptist* (August 16, 1961), 4, 13-14; ". . . Report No. 4" (August, 23, 1961), 4, 13.
20. Ronald Creech, *The Challenger*, January 2, 1961, quoted in "Western Conference Reports . . . No. 3," 13; "Western Conference Reports . . . No. 4," 16.
21. Billy A. Melvin, "Congregational or Connectional?" *Contact* (February, 1962), 8-9, 11, 16.
22. "If We Had Not," *The Free Will Baptist* (January 10, 1962), 2. For example, the Paul Palmer Conference was formed in January 1964 from several Southwest Georgia churches who sympathized with the North Carolina State Convention. Recently these congregations reunited with the Georgia State Association, an association affiliated with the National Association. See *Minutes of the First Twenty Years of Quarterly Sessions of the Paul Palmer Fellowship Conference of the Original Free Will Baptists*, 2-3, 7.
23. Minutes of the National Association (1961), 13-14, 18; "Statement Adopted on Church Government Issues by the National Association, Norfolk, Virginia, July 1961," *Contact* (August, 1961), 7.
24. "Statement by the Executive Committee of the North Carolina State Convention of Free Will Baptists," *The Free Will Baptist* (January 10, 1962), 4; "Statement by the Executive Committee of the National Association of Free Will Baptists Relative to the Church Government Issue and the North Carolina State Convention of Free Will Baptists," *Contact* (November, 1961), 7, 16. This statement was also carried in *The Free Will Baptist* (January 10, 1962).
25. Minutes of the National Association (1961), 14, 19; Executive Committee of the Western Conference of Original Free Will Baptists of North Carolina, "The National Association and the Ronald Creech and James A. Miles, et al., Lawsuit," *The Free Will Baptist* (January 3, 1962), 4-5.
26. Pelt, *Original Free Will Baptists*, 322-23.
27. Raper, *A Short History*, x, 47, 51-52, 59, 85-86; Gary Fenton Barefoot, "The Free Will Baptist Historical Collection," in Raper, *A Short History*, 90-93; Pelt, *Original Free Will Baptists*, 332.
28. Floyd B. Cherry, *Original Free Will Baptists Believe: A Study of the Articles of*

Faith of Original Free Will Baptists (Pine Level, NC: Carolina Bible Institute, 1996), 31–40, 69–94; "Campbell University Divinity School Signs Agreement with Mount Olive College," *Campbell University—News* (April 15, 2010), https://news.campbell.edu/articles/campbell-university-divinity-school-signs-agreement-with-mount-olive-college/.

29. Opey D. Jeanes, "The Extended Campus," in Raper, *A Short History*, 94–95; "Timeline," University of Mount Olive, https://umo.edu/timeline/#:~:text=Mount%20Olive%20College%20was%20established%20by%20the%20North,now%20known%20as%20the%20University%20of%20Mount%20Olive.

30. Pelt, *Original Free Will Baptists*, 362; "The History of CBIS," http://www.carolinabible.org/history.htm; Cherry, *Original Free Will Baptists Believe*.

31. Pelt, *Original Free Will Baptists*, 335, 345–46.

32. Pelt, *Original Free Will Baptists*, 325–29.

33. Pelt, *Original Free Will Baptists*, 329–31; OFWB International website: https://ofwbi.org/ministries/.

34. Pelt, *Original Free Will Baptists*, 349–50; "Our Ministries," Convention of Original Free Will Baptists, https://ofwb.org/our-ministries/.

35. See Pelt, *Original Free Will Baptists*, 325–50; *Convention of Original Free Will Baptists Directory of Churches* (Mount Olive: Office of Convention Services, 2022); "Our Ministries," https://ofwb.org/our-ministries/.

36. "Our History: The Blessings of Our Past," Quad State Annual Conference, Western Division of Free Will Baptists, http://fwbquadstate.org/History.htm.

37. Richard N. Cote, *Local and Family History in South Carolina: A Bibliography* (Easley, SC: Southern Historical Press, 1981), passim; M. Ruth Little, *Coastal Plain and Fancy: The Historic Architecture of Lenoir County and Kinston, North Carolina* (Kinston, NC: Lenoir County Historical Association, 1998), passim; *Religious Bodies: 1916* (Washington, DC: Government Printing Office, 1919), 119; *Religious Bodies: 1936* (Washington, DC: Government Printing Office, 1940), 179–80; E. O. Watson, ed., *Year Book of the Churches, 1921–22* (New York: Federal Council of the Churches of Christ in America, 1922), 84–85; *Manufacturer's Record* 92 (December 8, 1927): 109.

38. See the Facebook page of the National Convention of Free will Baptists, USA (https://www.facebook.com/NationalConventionofFreeWillBaptistsUSA/); the website of United American Free Will Baptist Bible College in Kinston, NC, the college of the United American Free Will Baptist Denomination Inc. (https://uafwbbiblecollege.com/); the website of the United American Free Will Baptist Conference, headquartered in Lakeland, FL (https://uafwbc.com); the website of the Quad State Annual Conference, a member conference of the Western Division Free Will Baptist Conference, headquartered in St. Louis, Missouri (http://www.fwbquadstate.org/About_Us.htm), which has information about the Western Division; the listing of the incorporation

of the Northeast Original Free Will Baptist Conference in Greenville, NC (https://opencorporates.com/companies/us_nc/0301025); and the Facebook page of the Unified Free Will Baptist Churches Inc. (https://www.facebook.com/UnifiedFreeWillBaptist/).
39. United American Free Will Baptist Bible College website, http://uafwbbiblecollege.com/; *United American Free Will Baptist Bible College Course Catalog*; telephone conversation with Bishop Ronald Mayo, president of United American Free Will Baptist Bible College.
40. Robby Owens, *The Warfield Years: The Story of Edgar Warfield and the Western Division Free-Will Baptist Movement* (El Cajon, CA: Christian Services Network, 2004), 15, 22–23, 31–33, 36, 50, 57, 63–64, 72, 75.
41. Quad State Annual Conference, Free Will Baptist Western Division, "About Us," http://www.fwbquadstate.org/About_Us.htm
42. "Our History: The Blessings of Our Past."
43. "Our History: The Blessings of Our Past."
44. "Our History: The Blessings of Our Past."
45. "Our History: The Blessings of Our Past."
46. "Our History: The Blessings of Our Past."
47. "Our Story," St. Matthews Unison Free Will Baptist Church, https://www.stmatthewsufwbchurch.org/index.php/abut-us2/our-story; https://www.facebook.com/UnifiedFreeWillBaptist/; http://newhopefwbc.org/History; https://www.facebook.com/photo/?fbid=2557090307759363&set=pcb.2557091097759284.
48. Original Free Will Baptist, Middle Eastern District Conference of America Inc. website, https://www.ofwbmed.org/
49. W. Stanley Mooneyham, "Personally...," *Contact* (November 1953), 2.
50. Mark Vandivort, "Black Power," *Contact* (September 1967), 18.
51. Vandivort, "Black Power," 18–19.
52. Vandivort, "Black Power," 19.
53. *2021 Digest of Reports (Includes 2020 Proceedings)* (Antioch, TN: National Association of Free Will Baptists 2021), 240.
54. The Louisiana congregation of which Bishop Raymond Captville, president of the National Convention of Free Will Baptists, is pastor was listed in the 2019 *Yearbook* as being a member of the First Oklahoma Association of Free Will Baptists. *The 2019 Free Will Baptist Yearbook*, B-93.

CHAPTER FOURTEEN

1. *Into the Darkness: 75 Years of Free Will Baptist International Missions* (Antioch, TN: Free Will Baptist International Missions, 2010), 26–29, 58–59, 62–63, 74–77, 100–103, 177–79.
2. *Into the Darkness*, 23–33, 43, 47, 181.

NOTES TO PAGES 350-353   465

3. "In the Vineyard," *Contact* (December, 1960), 2; *Into the Darkness*, 77-81, 124-25, 130, 180, 186. Paul and Amy Robinson were the first lay missionary couple to be sent out by the board. See Minutes of the National Association (1962), 30.
4. William F. Davidson, *The Free Will Baptists in History* (Nashville: Randall House, 2001), 301; *Into the Darkness*, 158, 166, 180-82.
5. *Into the Darkness*, 183; Minutes of the National Association (2011), A-139; (2018), A-21. Recent statistics were provided in an email from the IM Inc. office on August 17, 2022.
6. Phillip T. Morgan and J. Matthew Pinson, *Light and Truth: A Seventy-Fifth Anniversary Pictorial History of Welch College* (Gallatin, Tennessee: Welch College Press, 2017), 17-18, 46-47; Mary Ruth Wisehart, ed., *The Fifty-Year Record of the National Association of Free Will Baptists* (Nashville: Randall House, 1988), 43-45; Free Will Baptist Bible College Catalog (1951-1952), 11.
7. Morgan and Pinson, *Light and Truth*, 28, 52-60, 67-73.
8. Morgan and Pinson, *Light and Truth*, 91-94; *The 1983 Free Will Baptist Yearbook* (Nashville: Executive Office, National Association of Free Will Baptists, 1983), 111; Free Will Baptist Bible College Catalog, (1993-1994), 45; (1996-1997, 1997-1998), 38-39; (1998-1999), 40.
9. *Free Will Baptist Bible College Catalog*, 1996, 7; Morgan and Pinson, *Light and Truth*, 95-97, 119-25.
10. Pat Thomas, "A Brief History of the Home Missions Department," in *Who's Who among Free Will Baptists* (Nashville: Randall House, 1978), 419; Mary Wisehart, ed., *The Fifty-Year Record of the National Association of Free Will Baptists* (Nashville: Randall House, 1988), 55, 71-72; Davidson, *Free Will Baptists in History*, 302-3.
11. Pat Thomas, "A Brief History of the Home Missions Department," 420-21; Wisehart, ed., *Fifty-Year Record*, 72; Davidson, *Free Will Baptists in History*, 302-3.
12. Pat Thomas, "A Brief History of the Home Missions Department," 419-20; Roy Thomas, *Planting and Growing a Fundamental Church* (Nashville: Randall House, 1979); Minutes of the National Association (1979), 55; (1995), A-22; (2001), A-147.
13. Minutes of the National Association (2001), A-147; (2013), A-20; (2014), A-20.
14. Information from the North American Ministries office via email, August 17, 2022.
15. Wisehart, ed., *Fifty-Year Record*, 112-14.
16. Wisehart, ed., *Fifty-Year Record*, 114.
17. Minutes of the National Association (1985), 126; (1986), 117; (1993), A-199, A-229.
18. Minutes of the National Association (1998), A-18, A-195; (2008), A-31; (2010), A-31, A-32; (2014), A-255; (2022), 4.

19. Minutes of the National Association (1961), 57.
20. Minutes of the National Association (1959), 24; (1962), 44–45.
21. Minutes of the National Association (1962), 45; (1963), 48; (1964), 53; (1965), 47; Wisehart, ed., *Fifty-Year Record*, 93–94.
22. Minutes of the National Association (1970), 61; (1971), 19, 69 (compared with 1964 budget in 1963 minutes, 50); (1972), 60; (1973), 73.
23. Minutes of the National Association (1962), 51.
24. Minutes of the National Association (1962), 51; (1963), 51; (1965), 50.
25. Minutes of the National Association (1963), 3; (1964), 16; (1966), 3, 51; (1968), 42; (1969), 2; (1970), 3; Howard F. Vos, *Genesis and Archaeology* (Chicago: Moody, 1963); W. Graham Scroggie, *Is the Bible the Word of God?* (Chicago: Moody, 1950).
26. Minutes of the National Association (1972), 20, 31; (1973), 38.
27. Minutes of the National Association (1993), A-20; (2002), A-22; (2003), 3.
28. Wisehart, ed., *Fifty-Year Record*, 27–28; Minutes of the National Association (1953), 25–26; (1954), 52.
29. Minutes of the National Association (1992), A-28, A-209–12; (2003), A-25; (2005), A-54; (2019), 12.
30. Wisehart, ed., *Fifty-Year Record*, 85–86.
31. Wisehart, ed., *Fifty-Year Record*, 86–88; Minutes of the National Association (2005), A-161–64; (2006), A-136; (2015), A-20; *2022 Digest of Reports (Includes 2021 Proceedings)* (Antioch, TN: National Association of Free Will Baptists 2021), 140.
32. Minutes of the National Association (1980), 92; (1981), 83; (2005), A-164; (2007), A-21, A-222; *2022 Digest of Reports*, 68, 72.
33. Minutes of the National Association (1959), 19; (1960), 9; (1961), 21–22.
34. Minutes of the National Association, (1962), 14; (1963), 22; (1985), 134; (1995), A-230; (1997), A-206; (2000), A-213.
35. Minutes of the National Association (1963), 4, 13, 16.
36. Minutes of the National Association (1964), 4, 22; (1973), 5. Many of these archival materials have been archived at the website of the Historical Commission, www.fwbhistory.com.
37. Minutes of the National Association (1983), 20; (1985), 128; (1986), 126.
38. Minutes of the National Association (1996), A-19; (1997), A-208; (2001), A-218.
39. Minutes of the National Association (1987), 24.
40. Minutes of the National Association, (1988), 19, 23, 138.
41. Jack Williams, "The California State Association," in Picirilli, ed., *History of Free Will Baptist State Associations*, 16; Davidson, *Free Will Baptists in History*, 305–6; "About California Christian College," https://www.calchristian college.edu/about/.
42. "Oklahoma School Has 70 Enrolled," *Contact* (March 1959), 13; "The History of Randall University," Randall University website, https://ru.edu/about

-randall/history/; Davidson, *Free Will Baptists in History*, 306–7; "College Changes Name," *Contact* (May 1971), 13.

43. "Our Story and Purpose"; "Southeastern FWB College Moves to North Carolina," *Contact* (October 1987), 14.

44. J. W. Everton, *Forty Fruitful Years* (Middlesex, NC: Free Will Baptist Children's Home, 1960), 1; Pelt, *Original Free Will Baptists*, 336; Free Will Baptist Children's Home website, https://www.fwbchildrenshome.org/.

45. "Free Will Baptists of Tennessee To Establish Orphanage in Greene, Will Have Formal Opening On May 10th," *The Greeneville Sun* (May 6, 1939); 1; Free Will Baptist Family Ministries website, https://www.fwbfm.com/.

46. Vaudine Lancaster, "Alabama Free Will Baptist Children's Home," in *Alabama State Association of Free Will Baptists: Centential Celebration*, ed. Jimmy Aldridge et al. (n.c.: Alabama State Association of Free Will Baptists, 1997), no page number; Alabama Free Will Baptist Children's Home website, https://fwbhome.org/about/

47. "The Free Will Baptist Home For Children, Turbeville, S.C." (promotional pamphlet, n.d.), 1; "A Look Back: Children's Home Closes," *Manning Times* (January 1, 2015), https://manninglive.com/stories/a-look-back-childrens-home-closes,21827.

48. See the Harvest Free Will Baptist Childcare Ministries website, https://harvestccm.org.

49. Phillip T. Morgan, "The Promise of a Second Evangelical Mind: Free Will Baptist Bible College and the Hybrid Model of Christian Higher Education," MA thesis, Middle Tennessee State University, 2016.

50. F. Leroy Forlines, "A Plea for Unabridged Christianity," *Integrity: A Journal of Christian Thought* 2 (2003), 85–102. These trends mirrored those of the larger evangelical community as chronicled in David F. Wells, *No Place for Truth: Or Whatever Happened to Evangelical Theology?* (Grand Rapids: Eerdmans, 1994).

51. See primarily F. Leroy Forlines, *The Quest for Truth: Theology for the Postmodern Era* (Nashville: Randall House, 2001) and Robert E. Picirilli, *Grace, Faith, Free Will: Contrasting Views of Salvation: Calvinism and Arminianism* (Nashville: Randall House, 2002). Though the southern Free Will Baptists had not produced a systematic theology, some of them had read the northern Freewill Baptist systematic theology by John Butler and Ransom Dunn.

52. Minutes of the National Association (1959), 19; Forlines, *Quest for Truth*; F. Leroy Forlines, *The Bible College Approach to Education* (Nashville, TN: Free Will Baptist Bible College, [1964]); Robert E. Picirilli, "How Broad the Umbrella," paper presented to the Faculty of Free Will Baptist Bible College (n.d.); Morgan, "The Promise of a Second Evangelical Mind," 25–26.

53. Matthew Steven Bracey and W. Jackson Watts, *The Promise of Arminian Theology: Essays in Honor of F. Leroy Forlines* (Nashville: Randall House Academic, 2016). On Reformed Arminianism, see J. Matthew Pinson, *40*

Questions About Arminianism (Grand Rapids: Kregel Academic, 2022). See also Jesse F. Owens, "Scripture and History in the Theology of John Goodwin," paper presented at the Evangelical Theological Society Annual Meeting, November, 2015.

54. F. Leroy Forlines, *The Doctrine of Perseverance* (Ayden, NC: Free Will Baptist Press, 1959); Minutes of the National Association (1968), 17, 19, 21; (1969), 20; *Treatise* of the National Association (2016), 17–18.
55. Minutes of the National Association (1977), 10; (1978), 85–86; (1979), 99; *Treatise* of the National Association (2016), 18–19; Chicago Statement on Biblical Inerrancy (1978), Evangelical Theological Society website, https://www.etsjets.org/files/documents/Chicago_Statement.pdf.
56. Minutes of the National Association (1977), 10; (1978), 85–86; (1979), 99; *Treatise* of the National Association (2016), 18–19. The appendixes on Scripture, perseverance, and the charismatic movement were each written primarily by Forlines or Picirilli.
57. Wisehart, ed., *Fifty-Year Record*, 28; Minutes of the National Association (1971), 21; (1972), 79; (1982), 135. Questions about the NAE had surfaced as early as 1965; see Minutes of the National Association (1965), 20.
58. This synopsis is based largely on an unpublished manuscript from Southeastern Free Will Baptist College entitled, "A Brief Historical Sketch of Southeastern Free Will Baptist College"; *The Record Speaks: Free Will Baptist Bible College* (1982), 1–3.
59. "Our Story and Purpose," Southeastern Free Will Baptist College, https://sfwbc.edu/our-story-and-our-purpose/; *The Record Speaks*, 4–6.
60. Southeastern Free Will Baptist College promotional brochure (1983), held in the Free Will Baptist Historical Collection, Welch College; "Statement of Philosophy and Cooperation for Cooperating Churches," document held in the Free Will Baptist Historical Collection, Welch College; "Our Story and Purpose."
61. Open letter from Randy Cox (January 1983), held in the Free Will Baptist Historical Collection, Welch College; "Our Story and Purpose"; "Southeastern FWB College Moves to North Carolina," *Contact* (October 1987), 14.
62. Dale Burden was senior pastor of Gateway Free Will Baptist Church. "Ange Resigns as Southeastern College President," *Contact* (August 1989), 14; "Billy Bevan Named President at Southeastern College," *Contact* (October 1989), 15; "Our Story and Purpose"; "Gateway Christian College Begins," *Contact* (September 2003), 22; Daniel Edwards, "GCC, My Alma Mater, to Close after 2013 School Year," https://pastordanieledwards.wordpress.com/2013/02/28/gcc-my-alma-mater-to-close-after-2013-school-year-2/.
63. Minutes of the National Association (2008), A-25, A-33; (2016), 19; (2022), 5; *Treatise* of the National Association (2016), 19.
64. Minutes of the National Association, 1935–2022.

65. Minutes of the National Association, 1935–2022. For a definition of "complementarianism," see the Danvers Statement, https://www.reviveourhearts.com/articles/danvers-statement-biblical-manhood-and-womanhood/.
66. The reader will recall that in, in 1947, the Board of Publications and Literature referred to the differences of opinion among premillennialists, amillennialists, and postmillennialists in the National Association. See Minutes of the National Association (1947), 28, 34. Randall House published books from both premillennial and amillennial perspectives. For the premillennial view, see Damon C. Dodd, *The Book of Revelation: A Study Guide* (Nashville: Randall House, 1973) and Douglas J. Simpson, *The Apocalypse* (Nashville: Randall House, 1975). For the amillennial view, see Wade T. Jernigan, *The Unsealed Book: An Amillennial View of Revelation* (Nashville: Randall House, 1975) and Cecil Sanders, *The Future: An Amillennial Understanding* (Nashville: Randall House, 1990). The Convention of Original Free Will Baptists was largely premillennial but allowed for differences. See Chester Pelt, *The Rapture: A Midtribulation Study* (Ayden, NC: Free Will Baptist Press, 1985).
67. This can be seen by perusing the recent minutes of local associations and conferences across the National Association.
68. This is illustrated, for example, by the fact that in the 1990s and 2000s most individuals who attended the annual Symposia and annual session Theological Trends Seminars of the Commission for Theological Integrity were middle-aged and older, whereas in the 2010s those audiences began to skew much younger.
69. Minutes of the National Association (1938), 6. While the National Association did not convene in annual session in 1937, statistics for that year were included in the 1938 minutes. While records are very sparse, the following unaffiliated associations have been documented: French Broad (North Carolina), Jack's Creek (North Carolina), Mount Mitchell (North Carolina), John-Thomas (Virginia, Kentucky, Indiana, Ohio), Boone County (West Virginia), Trinity (West Virginia), Original Stone (Tennessee), Eastern Stone (Tennessee), Stone (Indiana), Muscle Shoals State Line (Alabama, Tennessee), Franklin (Illinois), Freedom (Illinois), Union, (Missouri), and Original Grand River (Oklahoma). Associations I have not been able to document include Western (North Carolina), Ozark (Missouri), Ohiana (Ohio, Indiana), Washita (Oklahoma), and Eastern (Oklahoma). See Albert Wardin, "Independent Free Will Baptist Associations" (unpublished document, 2000), held in the Free Will Baptist Historical Collection, Welch College. Jack's Creek and Muscle Shoals State Line were both in talks with the Tennessee State Association about membership as of 2025.
70. Minutes of the National Association (1948), 5–10, 16, 17, 22; (1950), 8; (1961), 75; (1972), 84; (1982), 137. Florida's statistics in this count are from 1950 because statistics in 1947–49 were incomplete.

71. In 1986 the General Board recommended a feasibility study regarding the formation of an international fellowship, and the delegates to the 1990 annual session approved its establishment. An International Convocation was held in Panama in 1992, and the International Fellowship was founded in Brazil in October 1995. See Minutes of the National Association (1986), 30; (1992), A-29; (1996), A-26. Evidence for greater youth involvement is seen in the larger numbers of attendees at the National Youth Conference. In 1983, the first year National Youth Conference registration was recorded in the Minutes, that number stood at 1,280. It is not known whether this number included adult attendees. In 2019, the year before the onset of the COVID-19 pandemic, 3,299 registered for the conference, 1,444 of which were under age eighteen. See Minutes of the National Association (1983), 104; "Statistical Report: Reporting Period 2019," in Digest of Reports (Antioch, TN: National Association of Free Will Baptists, 2021), 245. The phenomenon is also seen in the age distribution of attendees at events hosted by the Commission for Theological Integrity, which skews young. Furthermore, in 2024, data from sociologist Ryan Burge showed that, out of a study of twenty-three denominations, Free Will Baptists were the second "least gray," i.e., they had the second highest percentage of respondents who listed at least one member of the household who was under the age of 18. Free Will Baptists exceeded larger denominations such as Assemblies of God (ninth), Southern Baptist (fourteenth), and the Episcopal Church (twenty-third). See Ryan Burge, "Which Denominations Are the Grayest? (The Youngest Will Surprise You)," *Church Answers*, https://churchanswers.com/blog/which-denominations-are-the-grayest-the-youngest-will-surprise-you/.

EPILOGUE

1. I say four centuries because, while the American movement dates to the 1680s, its founders in the colony of Carolina were English General Baptists whose religious origins date to 1608.
2. For a treatment of the move away from full-blown Calvinism among Baptists over the course of the nineteenth century, see J. Matthew Pinson, "Dissent from Calvinism in the Baptist Tradition," in *Calvinism: A Biblical and Theological Critique*, ed. David L. Allen and Steve W. Lemke (Nashville: B&H Academic, 2022), 239–82.
3. For more on this democratization, see Nathan O. Hatch, *The Democratization of American Christianity* (New Haven: Yale University Press, 1991). For its effect on Baptist life in the South, see Gregory A. Wills, *Democratic Religion: Freedom, Authority, and Church Discipline in the Baptist South, 1785–1900* (New York: Oxford University Press, 2003).
4. See chapters 7 and 10 for more about these soteriological distinctions.

5. Joseph Wright, *Speculum Haereticis: Or, A Looking-Glass for Hereticks* (London, 1691), 27.
6. James Tunstead Burtchaell, *The Dying of the Light: The Disengagement of Colleges and Universities from their Christian Churches* (Grand Rapids: Eerdmans, 1998), 839–41; D. G. Hart, *The Lost Soul of American Protestantism* (Lanham, MD: Rowman and Littlefield, 2002), xxiii, 20–22.
7. It is important to avoid a blanket condemnation of all movements characterized as "Pietism." Mark Noll argues that pietistic movements in church history have often been good for the church because they emphasize spiritual life and renewal. Yet in their de-emphasis on formal dogma, they "illustrate the perils involved in not treating the mind as a Christian resource" and thus "could be carried to a dangerous extreme." Pietism, Noll says, "played an important role in the revitalization of the church in the seventeenth and eighteenth centuries. Unchecked Pietism, however, played a role in the development of theological liberalism with liberalism's fascination with the forms of religious experience. It played a part in developing the humanistic romanticism of the nineteenth and twentieth centuries, where a vague nature mysticism replaced a more orthodox understanding of God and the world." See Mark A. Noll, *The Scandal of the Evangelical Mind* (Grand Rapids: Eerdmans, 1994), 49. One sees echoes of this interpretation of pietism in the popular evangelical writer Francis Schaeffer, who argued that while early pietism was a "healthy protest against formalism and a too-abstract Christianity," it had a "deficient, 'platonic' spirituality." See Francis A. Schaeffer, *A Christian Manifesto* (Westchester, IL: Crossway, 1981), 18–19.
8. Free Will Baptist Church Covenant, repr. in J. Matthew Pinson, *A Free Will Baptist Handbook: Heritage, Beliefs, and Ministries*, 2nd ed. (Nashville: Randall House, 2022), 157–58.

BIBLIOGRAPHY

PRIMARY SOURCES

Books

A Treatise of the Faith and Practice of the Free Will Baptist[s]. Purdy, MO: Free Will Baptist Gem, 1936.
A Treatise of the Faith and Practices of Free Will Baptists. Nashville: Board of Publications and Literature of the National Association of Free Will Baptists, 1945.
A Treatise of the Faith and Practices of the National Association of Free Will Baptists. Antioch, TN: Executive Office, National Association of Free Will Baptists, 2016.
A Treatise of the Faith and Practices of the Original Free Will Baptists. Nashville, TN: Board of Publications and Literature of the National Association of Free Will Baptists, 1948, 1951.
A Treatise on the Faith and Practice of the Freewill Baptists. Dover, NH: Freewill Baptist Printing Establishment, 1871.
A Treatise on the Faith of the Free-will Baptists. Dover, NH: Free-will Baptist Printing Establishment, 1854.
A Treatise on the Faith of the Freewill Baptists. Dover, NH: David Marks, for the Freewill Baptist Connexion, 1834.
Adams, Hannah. *An Alphabetical Compendium of the Various Sects*. Boston: B. Edes and Sons, 1784.
An Abstract of the Former Articles of Faith Confessed by the Original Baptist Church, Holding the Doctrine of General Provision, with a Proper Code of Discipline, for the Future Government of the Church. Newbern, NC: Salmon Hall, 1814.
An Abstract of the Former Articles of Faith Confessed by the Original Baptist Church Holding the Doctrine of General Provision, with a Proper Code of Discipline, for the Future Government of the Church. New York: D. Fenshaw, 1855.
An Orthodox Creed: Or, a Protestant Confession of Faith. Being an Essay to Unite and Confirm All True Protestants in the Fundamental Articles of the Christian Religion, against the Errors and Heresies of the Church of Rome, http://baptiststudiesonline.com/wp-content/uploads/2007/02/orthodox-creed.pdf.

Anthony, Alfred Williams. *An Introduction to the Life of Jesus: An Investigation of the Historical Sources*. Boston: Silver, Burdett and Company, 1896.

———. *The Method of Jesus: An Interpretation of Personal Religion*. New York: Silver, Burdett and Company, 1899.

Arminius, Jacobus. *The Works of James Arminius*, 3 vols. Translated by James Nichols and William Nichols. Nashville: Randall House, 2007.

Asplund, John. *Annual Register of the Baptist Denomination, in North-America; To the First of November, 1790*. Southampton County, VA, 1791.

Barnard, Laura Belle. *Touching the Untouchables*. With Georgia B. Hill. Wheaton: Tyndale House, 1985.

Burkitt, Lemuel, and Jesse Read. *A Concise History of the Kehukee Baptist Association, from its Original Rise Down to 1803*. Revised by Henry L. Burkitt. Philadelphia: Lippincott, Grambo and Company, 1850.

Burlingame-Cheney, Emeline. *The Story of the Life and Work of Oren B. Cheney, Founder and First President of Bates College*. Boston: Morning Star Publishing House, 1907.

Butler, J. J., and Ransom Dunn. *Lectures on Systematic Theology*. Boston: Morning Star, 1892.

Butler, John J. *Commentary on the New Testament: Critical and Practical: Acts, Romans, Corinthians*. Biddeford, ME: J. E. Butler, 1871.

———. *Commentary on the New Testament: Critical and Practical: The Gospels*. Dover, NH: G. T. Day and Company, 1870.

———. *Natural and Revealed Theology*. Dover, NH: Freewill Baptist Printing Establishment, 1861.

———. *Thoughts on the Benevolent Enterprises, Embracing the Subjects of Missions, Sabbath Schools, Temperance, Abolition of Slavery, and Peace*. Dover, NH: Trustees of the Freewill Baptist Connection, 1840.

Buzzell, John. *A Religious Magazine, containing a short history of the Church of Christ, gathered at New-Durham, N.H., in the year 1780 . . . also a particular account of the late Reformations and revivals of religion*. Portland, ME: J. M'Kown, 1822.

———. *Life of Elder Benjamin Randall*. Limerick, Maine: Hobbs, Woodman, and Co., 1827.

"Carlisle G. Vandivere" in *A Memorial and Biographical History of McLennan, Falls, Bell and Coryell Counties, Texas*. Chicago: Lewis Pub. Co., 1893.

Case, Shirley Jackson. *Highways of Christian Doctrine*. Chicago: Willett, Clark and Company, 1936.

———. *The Historical Method in the Study of Religion*. Lewiston, ME: Press of the Lewiston Journal, 1907.

Catalogue of the Officers and Students of Bates College. Lewiston, ME: Daily Journal Office, 1863.

Chicago Statement on Biblical Inerrancy (1978). *Evangelical Theological Society*. https://www.etsjets.org/files/documents/Chicago_Statement.pdf.

Cobb, Enoch, ed. *The Free Will Baptist Hymn Book: Containing Hymns and Spiritual Songs, Selected for the Use of the United Churches of Christ, Commonly Called Free Will Baptist, and for Saints of all Denominations*. New Bern, NC: William G. Hall, 1846.

Comer, John. *The Diary of John Comer*. Edited by C. Edwin Barrows. In *Collections of the Rhode Island Historical Society* 8 (1893).

Convention of Original Free Will Baptists Directory of Churches. Mount Olive, NC: Office of Convention Services, 2022.

Cooper, Christopher. *The Vail Turn'd Aside: Or, Heresie Unmask'd, Being a Reply to a Book Entituled The Moderate Trinitarian*. London, 1701.

Crawford, Julius Earl. *The Call to Christian Stewardship*. Nashville: Publishing House of the Methodist Episcopal Church, South, 1924.

Dagg, John Leadley. *Manual of Theology. Second Part. A Treatise on Church Order*. Charleston, SC: Southern Baptist Publication Society, 1858.

Davis, Almond H. *The Female Preacher, Or, Memoir of Salome Lincoln, Afterwards the Wife of Elder Junia S. Mowry*. Providence, RI: Elder J. S. Mowry, 1843.

Dodd, Damon C. *The Book of Revelation: A Study Guide*. Nashville: Randall House, 1973.

Early, Joe, Jr. *The Life and Writings of Thomas Helwys*. Early English Baptist Texts. Macon, GA: Mercer University Press, 2009.

Fifth Annual Report of the Freewill Baptist Anti-Slavery Society. Dover, New Hampshire: Wm. Burr, Printer, 1851.

Forlines, F. Leroy. *Classical Arminianism: A Theology of Salvation*. Nashville: Randall House, 2011.

———. *Romans*, Randall House Bible Commentary. Edited by Robert E. Picirilli. Nashville: Randall House, 1987.

———. *The Quest for Truth: Theology for the Postmodern Era*. Nashville: Randall House, 2001.

Free Will Baptist Bible College Bulletin. 1943–1944.

Free Will Baptist Bible College Catalog. 1948–1952, 1996.

"Freewill Baptist Church Covenant." *Allardt Freewill Baptist Church*. https://allardt fwbc.wordpress.com/fwb-covenant/.

Grantham, Thomas. *Christianismus Primitivus, Or the Ancient Christian Religion*. London, 1678.

Guéranger, Dom Prosper. *The Liturgical Year: Passiontide and Holy Week*. Dublin: James Duffy, 1870.

Harrison, T. F., and J. M. Barfield. *History of the Free Will Baptists of North Carolina*. Ayden, NC: Free Will Baptist Publishing Company, [1896].

Harrison, T. F., and T. H. Harrison. *Feet-Washing*. Ayden, NC: Free Will Baptist Publishing Company, 1894.

Hayes, Edward Cary. *A Memoir of Prof. Benjamin Francis Hayes, D.D., With Brief Extracts from His Writings*. Boston: Morning Star Publishing House, 1907.

Hearn, R. K. "Origin of the Free Will Baptist Church of North Carolina." *Toisnot*

Transcript (May 20–June 17, 1875). Reprinted in *General Baptist History*. Edited by D. B. Montgomery. Evansville, IN: Courier, 1889.

Hearn, Rufus K., Joseph Bell, and Jesse Randolph, eds. *Zion's Hymns, for the Use of the Original Free Will Baptist Church of North Carolina, and for the Saints of all Denominations*. Pikeville, NC: Elder Daniel Davis, 1854.

Heath, Jesse, and Elias Hutchins, eds., *Psalms, Hymns, and Spiritual Songs, Selected for the United Churches of Christ, Commonly Called Free Will Baptists, in North Carolina; and for Saints in All Denominations*. Richmond, VA: Wm. H. Clemmett, 1856.

Jernigan, Wade T. *The Unsealed Book: An Amillennial View of Revelation*. Nashville: Randall House, 1975.

Lane, Isaac. *Autobiography of Bishop Isaac Lane, LL.D.* Nashville: Publishing House of the M.E. Church, South, 1916.

Lewis, John W. *The Life, Labors, and Travels of Elder Charles Bowles, of the Free Will Baptist Denomination, Together With an Essay on the Character and Condition of the African Race*. Watertown, ME: Ingalls and Stowell's Steam Press, 1852.

Lumpkin, William L., ed. *Baptist Confessions of Faith*. Valley Forge, PA: Judson, 1959.

Lumpkin, William and Enoch Cobb, eds. *The Free Will Baptist Hymn Book: Containing Hymns and Spiritual Songs, Selected for the Use of the United Churches of Christ, Commonly Called Free Will Baptist and for Saints of all Denominations*. New Bern, NC: John I. Pasteur, 1832.

Marks, Marilla, ed. *Memoirs of the Life of David Marks*. Dover, N.H.: The Free-will Baptist Printing Establishment, 1847.

Mathews, Shailer. *The Faith of Modernism*. New York: Macmillan, 1925.

McGlothlin, W. J., ed. *Baptist Confessions of Faith*. Philadelphia: American Baptist Publication Society, 1911.

Pelt, Chester H. *The Rapture: A Midtribulation Study*. Ayden, NC: Free Will Baptist Press, 1985.

Picirilli, Robert E. *I, II Corinthians*, Randall House Bible Commentary. Edited by Robert E. Picirilli. Nashville: Randall House, 1987.

———. *Grace, Faith, Free Will: Contrasting Views of Salvation; Calvinism and Arminianism*. Nashville: Randall House, 2002.

Rauschenbusch, Walter. *A Theology for the Social Gospel*. New York: Macmillan, 1919.

Sacred Melodies. Dover, N.H.: The Free-will Baptist Printing Establishment, 1851.

Sanders, Cecil. *The Future: An Amillennial Understanding*. Nashville: Randall House, 1990.

Scroggie, W. Graham. *Is the Bible the Word of God?* Chicago: Moody, 1950.

Simpson, Douglas J. *The Apocalypse*. Nashville: Randall House, 1975.

Smart, Moses M. *A Brief View of Christian Doctrine*. Lowell, MA: N. L. Daton, 1843.

Stanley, Francis. *Christianity indeed, OR, The well-disciplin'd Christian the Delight of Christ*. London, 1667.

St. Claire, E. L. *The Great Debate at Fanatic's Hall, Prejudiceville: A Witty Book of Rhymes on Church Dissension*. Ayden, NC: Free Will Baptist Print, 1908.
———. *The Twin Boys*. Raleigh: Edwards and Broughton, 1912.
———. *What Free Will Baptists Believe and Why*. Ayden, NC: Free Will Baptist Press, n.d.
Tecumseh College Catalogue and Announcements. 1926–27.
The Book of Catechisms. Louisville: Presbyterian Church, U.S.A., 2001.
The Church Member's Book: Or Admonitions and Instructions for All Classes of Christians. Dover, N.H.: The Free-will Baptist Printing Establishment, 1847.
The Free Will Baptist Hymnal. Ayden, N.C.: Free Will Baptist Press, 1958.
The Freewill Baptist Selection of Spiritual Songs with Music for the Church and the Choir. Dover, NH: Freewill Baptist Printing Establishment, 1881.
The Humble Advice of the Assembly of Divines, Now by Authority of Parliament, sitting at Westminster, Concerning a Shorter Catechisme. . . . London, 1647.
Thomas, Roy. *Planting and Growing a Fundamental Church*. Nashville: Randall House, 1979.
United American Free Will Baptist Bible College Course Catalog, 2023.
Usages of the Free-will Baptist Connexion. Revised by Order of the Thirteenth Annual General Conference, Assembled in October 1847.
Vos, Howard F. *Genesis and Archaeology*. Chicago: Moody, 1963.
Willey, Mabel. *Beyond the Gate: The Autobiography of Mabel Bailey Willey*, with Mary Ruth Wisehart. Nashville: Randall House, 1998.
Wilson, Samuel. *An Account of the Province of Carolina in America*. London, 1682.
Wright, Joseph. *Speculum Haereticis: Or, A Looking-Glass for Hereticks*. London, 1691.

Minutes

Unless otherwise indicated, the following church records are housed at the Free Will Baptist Historical Collection at Welch College.

English General Baptists
Whitley, W. T. *Minutes of the General Assembly of the General Baptist Churches in England: with Kindred Records*. London: Kingsgate, 1909.

Alabama
Minutes of the Annual Sessions of the Liberty Association of The United Freewill Baptist Church of Christ. 1906, 1916.
Minutes of the Annual Sessions of the Mount Moriah Free-Will Baptist Association. 1874, 1885.
Minutes of the Fifth Annual Session of the Southern Union Association United Freewill Baptist Church of Christ. 1931.
Minutes of the Fifty-Sixth Annual Session of the Flint River Freewill Baptist Association. 1937.

Minutes of the First Annual Session of the East Alabama Free Will Baptist Association. 1958.
Minutes of the First Annual Session of the Jasper Free-Will Baptist Association. 1887.
Minutes of the First Session of the Birmingham District Association of the United Free-Will Baptist Church of Christ. 1939.
Minutes of the Fourth Annual Session of the Vernon Free-Will Baptist Association. 1883.
Minutes of the Second Annual Session of the Mallet's Creek Association. 1891.
Minutes of the Seventh Annual Session of the Muscle Shoals State Line Association of the Freewill Baptist. 1927.
Minutes of the Sixteenth Session of Liberty Association No. 2 of the United Freewill Baptist Church of Christ. 1925.
Minutes of the Sixty-Eighth Annual Session of the Southeastern Free Will Baptist Association. 1946.
Minutes of the Third Annual Session of the Liberty Free Will Baptist Association. 1936.

Arkansas
Hamburgh Association, Freewill Baptists. Fourth Annual Session. 1891.
Minutes of the 26th Annual Session of the Western Arkansas Association of Freewill Baptists Church of Christ. 1894.
Minutes of the Annual Sessions of the Arkansas Association of Freewill Baptists. 1899, 1919, 1921.
Minutes of the Annual Sessions of the Little Missouri River Free Will Baptist Association. 1891, 1916.
Minutes of the Old Mount Zion Association. 1888.
Minutes of the Old Mount Zion Association of Free Will Baptists. 1889, 1896, 1898.
Minutes of the Thirty-Ninth Session of the Social Band Baptist Association. 1913.
Proceedings of the One Hundred Twenty-Ninth Annual Session of the Union Association of United Baptist. 1979.

Florida
Minutes of the Twenty-Third Annual Session of the West-Florida and South-East Alabama Liberty Free Will Baptist Association. 1911.

Georgia
Minutes of the Annual Sessions of the Chattahoochee United Baptist Association. 1847–1848, 1850–1851, 1854.
Minutes of the Annual Sessions of the Chattahoochee United Free-Will Baptist Association. 1879, 1881–1883, 1885.

BIBLIOGRAPHY   479

Minutes of the Annual Sessions of the Chattahoochee United Freewill Baptist Association. 1888, 1899, 1902.
Minutes of the Annual Sessions of the Chattahoochee Free Will Baptist Association. 1890–1891.
Minutes of the Annual Sessions of the Midway Free Will Baptist Association. 1926–1927.
Minutes of the Fifty-Seventh Annual Session of the Chattahoochee United Free Will Baptist Association, September 30, October 1-2, 1892.
Minutes of the First Annual Session of the Martin Freewill Baptist Association. 1887.
Minutes of the First Annual Session of the Union Association of the United Free Will Baptists. 1926.
Minutes of the First Twenty Years of Quarterly Sessions of the Paul Palmer Fellowship Conference of the Original Free Will Baptist. 1963–1983.
Minutes of the Seventy-Fifth Annual Session of the South Georgia Association of Original Free Will Baptists. 1952.
Minutes of the Sixth Annual Session of the Ga. Union Association. 1900.
Minutes of the Third Annual Session of the Martin Free-Will Baptist Association. 1889.
Minutes of the Thirtieth Annual Session of the Little River Association of the United Free Will Baptists. 1936.
Minutes of the Thirty-Fourth Annual Session of the Middle Georgia Association of United Baptists. 1897.
Minutes of the Thirty-Second Annual Session of the Ogeechee Association of the Original Free Will Baptists. 1940.
Minutes of the Annual Sessions of the South Georgia Free Will Baptist Association. 1903, 1909.
Proceedings of the First Session of the Marietta Union Conference of Free Will Baptist. 1912.

Kentucky
Minutes of the Annual Sessions of the John Thomas Association. 1923, 2009.

Mississippi
Minutes of the Annual Sessions of the Tupelo Free Will Baptist Association. 1915–1916.
Minutes of the Annual Sessions of the Little Brown's Creek Association of Free Will Baptists. 1899, 1932.
Minutes of the Forty-Fifth Annual Session of the Little Brown Creek Association of the Freewill Baptists. 1935.
Minutes of the Thirty-Third Annual Session of the Zion Rest United Free Will Baptist Association. 1940.

North Carolina
Minutes of the North Carolina Original Free Will Baptist General Conference. 1853.
Minutes of the Free-Will Baptist Association. Salisbury, NC: Philo White, 1830.
Minutes of the Hookerton Free Will Baptist Church (Later Hookerton Disciples Church), 1830–1869. November 30, 1930.
Minutes of the General Court of North Carolina, including Chancery Court minutes. September 24–29, 1694. In Parker, Mattie Erma Edwards, ed. *Colonial Records of North Carolina* (Second Series). Raleigh: Department of Archives and History, 1963.
Minutes of the Perquimans Precinct Court, North Carolina. January 10, 1698. In Parker, Mattie Erma Edwards, ed. *Colonial Records of North Carolina* (Second Series). Raleigh: Department of Archives and History, 1963.
Minutes of the Perquimans Precinct Court, North Carolina. July 7–9, 1701. In Parker, Mattie Erma Edwards, ed. *Colonial Records of North Carolina* (Second Series). Raleigh: Department of Archives and History, 1963.
Minutes of the General Court of North Carolina (1720–1722). In William Laurence Saunders, ed., *Colonial Records of North Carolina*, 2:409–11, 415–16, 442, 444, 471, https://docsouth.unc.edu/csr/.
Minutes of the Annual North Carolina (Bethel) Conference. Transcribed by Robert E. Picirilli. 1829–1832, 1834–1842.
Minutes of the Fifty-Sixth Annual Session of the Cape Fear U. A. Free Will Baptist General Conference. 1910.
Minutes of the North Carolina Free Will Baptist General Conference. 1845.
Minutes of the Second Biennial Conference of the Cape Fear Freewill Baptist Convention. 1872.

Oklahoma
Minutes of the Forty-Sixth Annual Session of the Oklahoma State Association of Free Will Baptists. 1954.

South Carolina
Minutes of the First Annual Session of the South Carolina State Association. 1943.

Tennessee
Minutes of the Thirty-Third Annual Convention of Free Will Baptists, Cumberland Free Will Baptist Association. 1876.
Minutes of the Annual Sessions of the Tennessee River Association of Freewill Baptists. 1891, 1924.
Minutes of the Cumberland Association of Separate Baptists. 1843.
Minutes of the Forty-Ninth Annual Session of the Tennessee River Association of Free Will Baptists. 1927.

Minutes of the Nolynn Association of Separate Baptists. 1819–1884. http://www
.separatebaptist.org/downloads/nolynn/NolynnMinutes1819-1884.pdf.
Minutes of the Toe River Association.
Minutes of the Twenty-Eighth Annual Meeting of the Bethlehem Association of
Free Will Baptists. 1871.

Texas
Minutes of the Texas Free Will Baptist Association. 1894.

General Conference (Randall)
Minutes of the General Conference of Free Baptists. 1898, 1907, 1910.
Minutes of the General Conference of the Freewill Baptist Connection (1827–1859).
Dover, NH: Freewill Baptist Printing Establishment, 1859.
Minutes of General Conference of the Freewill Baptist Connection, Including Ten Sessions—From 1859 to 1889. Compiled by I. D. Stewart. Boston: Free Baptist Printing Establishment, 1887.

Co-Operative General Association
Minutes of the First Adjourned Session of the Co-operative General Association
of Freewill Baptists. 1917.
Minutes of the First Triennial Session of the Co-operative General Association of
Freewill Baptists. 1916.
Minutes of the Fourth Adjourned Session of the Co-operative General Association
of Free Will Baptist. 1922.
Minutes of the Second Regular Session of the Western General Association of Free
Will Baptist. 1937.
Minutes of the Seventh Tri-ennial Session of the Co-operative Association of Freewill Baptists. 1934.
Minutes of the Triennial Sessions of the Co-operative General Association of
Freewill Baptists. 1918. 1923.

General Conference [Southeast]
Minutes of Annual Sessions of the General Conference of the Original Free Will
Baptists of the United States. 1921–1935.
Minutes of the Annual Sessions of the Eastern General Association of the Original
Free Will Baptists of the United States. 1936–1938.

National Association
Digest of Reports (Includes 2021 Proceedings). Antioch, TN: National Association of
Free Will Baptists, 2021.
Minutes of the Annual Sessions of the National Association of the Original Free
Will Baptists of the United States. 1939–1941.

Minutes of the Annual Sessions of the National Association of the Free Will Baptists of the United States. 1942–1953.
Minutes of the Annual Sessions of the National Association of Free Will Baptists. 1954–2022.
Minutes of the National Association of the Original Free Will Baptists of the United States. 1935, 1938.
The Free Will Baptist Yearbook. Antioch, TN: Executive Office, National Association of Free Will Baptists, 2018, 2019.
The Free Will Baptist Yearbook. Nashville: Executive Office, National Association of Free Will Baptists, 1983.

PAMPHLETS, ARTICLES, CHAPTERS, AND PERIODICALS

"A Discovery." *The Baptist* (November 21, 1846): 194–95.
"Ange Resigns as Southeastern College President." *Contact* (August 1989): 14.
Anthony, Alfred Williams. "Twenty Years After: The Story of the Union of Baptists and Free Baptists during the Period of Negotiation and Realization, 1904–1924." Repr. from *Christian Work* (October 18, 1924). Held in the Free Will Baptist Historical Collection, Welch College.
Ball, Fleetwood. "Cleveland Calls Christly Clans—Tennessee Baptists Meet, Undaunted by Rain." *Baptist and Reflector* (November 20, 1919): 5–6.
Ballard, Jerry, ed. *Perception.* March-April, 1960.
"Billy Bevan Named President at Southeastern College." *Contact* (October 1989): 15.
Boyd, Ernest Hurston. "Boyd on the Christian Baptists." *Putnam County Herald.* November 19, 1953. http://osafreewillbaptist.org/blog1/history/.
"Carlisle G. Vandivere." *A Memorial and Biographical History of McLennan, Falls, Bell and Coryell Counties, Texas.* Chicago: Lewis Pub. Co., 1893.
"College Changes Name." *Contact* (May 1971): 13.
"Congregational or Connectional?" *Contact* (February, 1962): 8–9, 11, 16.
Dagg, John L. "The Duty of Washing the Saints' Feet." *The Virginia Baptist Preacher* 1 (1842): 79–82.
"Dr. Burkette Raper Dies of Cancer at 83." *Goldsboro News-Argus.* August 1, 2011. http://savannah.newsargus.com/news/archives/2011/08/01/dr_burkette_raper_dies_of_cancer_at_83/.
"Elias Hutchins in North Carolina." *Freewill Baptist Quarterly* 10 (1862): 285–308.
Everton, J. W. *Forty Fruitful Years.* Middlesex, NC: Free Will Baptist Children's Home, 1960.
Executive Committee of the Western Conference of Original Free Will Baptists of North Carolina. "The National Association and the Ronald Creech and James A. Miles, et al., Lawsuit." *The Free Will Baptist* (January 3, 1962): 4–5, 16.

Forlines, F. Leroy. "A Plea for Unabridged Christianity." *Integrity: A Journal of Christian Thought* 2 (2003): 85–102.
———. *The Bible College Approach to Education*. Nashville, TN: Free Will Baptist Bible College, 1964.
———. *The Doctrine of Perseverance*. Ayden, NC: Free Will Baptist Press, 1959.
"Former Missionary Accepts Post as President of Hillsdale College." *Contact* (August 1971): 15.
Frazier, Agnes. "Your Opportunity and Mine." *The Free Will Baptist* (January 24, 1940): 3, 10–11.
Free Will Baptist Advocate. Published in the Interest of the Original Free Will Baptist Church. April 16, 1874.
"Free Will Baptists of Tennessee to Establish Orphanage in Greene, Will Have Formal Opening On May 10th." *The Greeneville Sun* (May 6, 1939): 4.
"Gateway Christian College Begins." *Contact* (September 2003): 22.
Hansley, David W. "Christian Education," *The Free Will Baptist* (May 28, 1952): 4.
Harrison, T. F. "Education." *The Free Will Baptist* (May 27, 1896): 2.
"Harvest Day Set." *Contact* (October 1966): 12–13.
"Hillsdale Names New President, Dean." *Contact* (November 1982): 19.
"Hillsdale Names Tim Eaton President." *Contact* (October 2004): 19.
"Hillsdale's First Debt Free Building Housing Men Students." *Contact* (November 1975): 11.
Howe, J. A. "The Relation of the Doctrine of Total Depravity to Other Christian Doctrines." *Freewill Baptist Quarterly* 13 (1865): 311–21.
"If We Had Not." *The Free Will Baptist* (January 10, 1962): 2.
"In the Vineyard." *Contact* (December 1960): 2.
Johnson, L. C. "Over My Shoulder." *Contact* (April 1979): 30–31.
"Miscellaneous Intelligence." *The Christian Review*, vol. 1. Edited by James D. Knowles. Boston: Gould, Kendall, and Lincoln, 1836.
"Mount Allen Junior College." *The Free Will Baptist* (May 28, 1952): 1.
"Mount Allen Junior College." *The Free Will Baptist* (March 31, 1954): 1.
"Oklahoma Bible College Becomes Trinity College." *Contact* (November 1970): 13.
"Oklahoma School Has 70 Enrolled." *Contact* (March 1959): 13.
"Oklahoma State Meeting." *Contact* (November 1964): 12.
"President Named." *Contact* (August 1961): 12.
Root, S. E. "The Philosophy of Divine Worship." *Freewill Baptist Quarterly* 16 (1868): 221–31.
"Southeastern College Names Stox President." *Contact* (April 2003): 18.
Southeastern Free Will Baptist College promotional brochure (1983). Held in the Free Will Baptist Historical Collection, Welch College.
"Southeastern FWB College Moves to North Carolina." *Contact* (October 1987): 14.

"Statement Adopted on Church Government Issues by the National Association, Norfolk, Virginia, July 1961." *Contact* (August 1961): 7.
"Statement by the Executive Committee of the National Association of Free Will Baptists Relative to the Church Government Issue and the North Carolina State Convention of Free Will Baptists." *Contact* (November 1961): 7, 16.
"Statement by the Executive Committee of the North Carolina State Convention of Free Will Baptists." *The Free Will Baptist* (January 10, 1962): 4–5.
"Statement of the Executive Committee of the National Association of Free Will Baptists." *Contact* (September 1961): 16.
"The Baptismal Question in the Light of the Scriptures and Church History." *The Freewill Baptist Quarterly* 7 (1859): 121–60.
The Challenger. February 8, 1960; February 29, 1960.
The Free Will Baptist. May 23, 1883.
"The Free Will Baptist Home for Children, Turbeville, S.C." Promotional pamphlet, n.d. Held in Free Will Baptist Historical Collection, Welch College.
The [Milledgeville, GA] Reflector. Nov. 17, 1818.
The Morning Star. 1820, 1827–1834, 1867, 1873, 1889.
"The Presidential Election in 1864." *Freewill Baptist Quarterly* 13 (1865): 70–90.
The Record Speaks: Free Will Baptist Bible College. Nashville: Free Will Baptist Bible College, 1982.
"The Western Conference Reports on the Edgemont Church Dispute" [Report No. 3, Report No. 4] *The Free Will Baptist* (August 16, 1961): 4–5.
Tripp, R. E. "The School Problem." *The Free Will Baptist* (January 4, 1939): 3.
Vandivort, Mark. "Black Power." *Contact* (September 1967): 18–19.

Unpublished Sources

Ballard, John H. "The Life of Rev. John H. Ballard." *University of Mt. Olive, Moye Library.* https://moc.libguides.com/c.php?g=779604&p=5590014.
"Campbell University Divinity School Signs Agreement with Mount Olive College." Campbell University—News (April 15, 2010), https://news.campbell.edu/articles/campbell-university-divinity-school-signs-agreement-with-mount-olive-college/.
Comer, John. *Diary of John Comer* (1704–1731, 2 volumes in one). Original manuscripts at the Rhode Island Historical Society.
Edwards, Morgan. "Materials Towards a History of the Baptists in the Provinces of Maryland, Virginia, North Carolina, South Carolina, Georgia." MS, 1772, held in Furman University Library. https://cdm16821.contentdm.oclc.org/digital/collection/jbt/id/220/rec/1.
———. "Tour of Rev. Morgan Edwards of Pennsylvania, To the American Baptists in North Carolina in 1772–73." MS, University Library, University of North Carolina at Chapel Hill. https://archive.org/details/tourofrevmorgane1893edwa/page/n5/mode/2up.

Letter from Henry Boyett to Jeremiah Heath. Held in the Jeremiah Heath papers, Free Will Baptist Historical Collection, University of Mount Olive, reprinted in Pelt, Chester H. *A History of the Salem Association of Free Will Baptists of West Florida*. Marianna, FL: Salem Free Will Baptist Association, 1987.
Open letter from Randy Cox. January 1983. Document held in the Free Will Baptist Historical Collection, Welch College.
"Our Doctrine." *United American Freewill Baptist Conference, Inc.* https://uafwbc.com/our-doctrine/. Accessed August 9, 2022.
"Statement of Philosophy and Cooperation for Cooperating Churches." Southeastern Free Will Baptist College. Document held in the Free Will Baptist Historical Collection, Welch College.
"The Danvers Statement on Biblical Manhood and Womanhood." *Revive Our Hearts*. https://www.reviveourhearts.com/articles/danvers-statement-biblical-manhood-and-womanhood/.
Welch, John L. Interview with Robert E. Picirilli, Free Will Baptist Bible College, April 25, 1971. Document held in the Free Will Baptist Historical Collection, Welch College.

Genealogical and Archival Sources

1809–1885, Alabama, US, County Marriage Records, 1805-1967, Marriage Records. Alabama Marriages, County courthouses, Alabama.
Alabama Department of Archives and History, Montgomery, Alabama, *Confederate Pension Applications, 1880–1940*, collection #: Microfilm in the Research Room, roll description: Boyd, Jasper—Bradford, Wm. N.
Bureau of Land Management. *U.S., General Land Office Records, 1776–2015*. Washington DC, Federal Land Patents, State Volumes.
"Carlisle G. Vandivere." *A Memorial and Biographical History of McLennan, Falls, Bell and Coryell Counties, Texas*. Chicago: Lewis Pub. Co., 1893.
County Court Records at Kenansville, NC and FHL # 0422156 item 2. North Carolina, US, Marriage Index, 1741–2004.
Griffen, Levi. County Court Records - FHL # 0296803-0296808. North Carolina, US, Marriage Index, 1741–2004. North Carolina State Archives, Raleigh, North Carolina.
Griffin, John. North Carolina, US, Compiled Census and Census Substitutes Index. 1790-1890.
Index to Marriage Bonds—Abstracts (1780–1865). North Carolina County Registers of Deeds, Microfilm, Record Group 048. North Carolina State Archives, Raleigh, NC.
"Kellum, Charles R." New England Historical Genealogical Society, Boston, Massachusetts, Massachusetts Vitals to 1850. Massachusetts, US, Compiled Birth, Marriage, and Death Records, 1700–1850.

Letter from Richard Everard to Edmund Gibson (October 12, 1729) in Saunders, *Colonial Records of North Carolina*, 3:48.
Loose Wills and Estate Papers, 1746–1890. North Carolina, County Court of Pleas and Quarter Sessions (Craven County, NC).
Marriages, Book AA, 1824-1841, Georgia, U.S., Marriage Records From Select Counties, 1828-1978. County Marriage Records, 1828–1978. The Georgia Archives, Morrow, Georgia.
Marriages, Vol 1A, 1809-1816, Georgia, U.S., Marriage Records From Select Counties, 1828-1978. County Marriage Records, 1828–1978. The Georgia Archives, Morrow, Georgia.
McKenzie, Wm. Schedules of the Florida State Census of 1885. National Archives Microfilm Publication M845, 13 Rolls. Records of the Bureau of the Census, Record Group 29. National Archives, Washington DC.
Mississippi, U.S., Compiled Marriage Index, 1776-1935, https://www.ancestry.com/search/collections/7842/
Missouri State Archives, Jefferson City, MO, Missouri Marriage Records [microfilm]. Missouri, Marriage Records, 1805-2002.
"Moore, Reddin." South Carolina Department of Archives and History, Columbia, South Carolina. US Census Mortality Schedules, South Carolina, 1850–1880, roll: 3. Marion, South Carolina, 1849.
Murrie, Pauline Shirley, ed. "Marriage Records of Nacogdoches County, Texas, 1824–1881." Houston: n.p., 1968. https://www.seekingmyroots.com/members/files/H011199.pdf.
Somerset County Judicial Records [Maryland]. 1735–1737. Vol. 851.
Texas, U.S., Marriage Index, 1824-2017, Texas Department of State Health Services, Austin, Texas.
The North Carolina Historical and Genealogical Register. 1900–1903.
U. S. Censuses, 1810–1880, 1900–1920.

SECONDARY SOURCES

Books

Adams, George F. *History of the Baptists in Maryland*. Baltimore: Weishampel, 1885.
Akin, Delbert, Nancy Draper, and Edwin Wade. *Oklahoma State Association of Free Will Baptists: The First 100 Years, 1908-2008*. Moore, OK: Oklahoma State Association of Free Will Baptists, 2009.
Ballard, Jerry. *Never Say Can't*. Carol Stream, IL: Creation House, 1971.
Bangs, Carl. *Arminius: A Study in the Dutch Reformation*. Nashville: Abingdon, 1971.
Barefoot, Gary F., Alan K. Lamm, Michael R. Pelt, and Ricky J. Warren. *A History of the Cape Fear Conference of Original Free Will Baptists, 1855–2010*. [no city], NC: Cape Fear Conference Historical Committee, 2011.

BIBLIOGRAPHY   487

Baxter, Norman Allen. *History of the Freewill Baptists: A Study in New England Separatism*. Rochester, NY: American Baptist Publication Society, 1957.
Benedict, David. *A General History of the Baptist Denomination, and Other Parts of the World*, vol. 1. Boston: Lincoln and Edmands, 1813.
———. *General History of the Baptist Denomination in America, and Other Parts of the World*, vol. 2. Boston: Manning and Loring, 1813.
———. *A General History of the Baptist Denomination in America and Other Parts of the World*. New York: Lewis Colby and Company, 1848.
———. *A General History of the Baptist Denomination in America and Other Parts of the World*. New York: Lewis Colby and Company, 1850.
Bodie, William Willis. *History of Williamsburg: Something About the People of Williamsburg County, South Carolina, From the First Settlement by Europeans about 1705 until 1923*. Columbia, SC: State Company, 1923.
Bolton, Charles C. *Poor Whites of the Antebellum South: Tenants and Laborers in Central North Carolina and Northeast Mississippi*. Durham, NC: Duke University Press, 1994.
Bozeman, Theodore Dwight. *Protestants in an Age of Science: The Baconian Ideal and Antebellum American Religious Thought*. Chapel Hill: University of North Carolina Press, 1977.
Bracey, Matthew Steven, and W. Jackson Watts, eds. *The Promise of Arminian Theology: Essays in Honor of F. Leroy Forlines*. Nashville: Randall House Academic, 2016.
Brackney, William H. *Historical Dictionary of the Baptists*. Lanham, MD: Scarecrow, 2009.
Brewster, J. M. *Fidelity and Usefulness: Life of William Burr*. Dover, NH: Freewill Baptist Printing Establishment, 1871.
Bryant, Scott. *The Awakening of the Freewill Baptists: Benjamin Randall and the Founding of an American Religious Tradition*. Macon, GA: Mercer University Press, 2011.
Burgess, G. A., and J. T. Ward. *Free Baptist Cyclopaedia*. Chicago: Free Baptist Cyclopaedia Company, 1889.
Burtchaell, James Tunstead. *The Dying of the Light: The Disengagement of Colleges and Universities from their Christian Churches*. Grand Rapids: Eerdmans, 1998.
Chute, Anthony L. *A Piety Above the Common Standard: Jesse Mercer and the Defense of Evangelistic Calvinism*. Macon, GA: Mercer University Press, 2004.
Cobb, Buell E.. *The Sacred Harp: A Tradition and Its Music*. Athens, GA: University of Georgia Press, 2004.
Cole, Charles G. *The Social Ideas of the Northern Evangelists, 1826–1850*. New York: Columbia University Press, 1954.
Cox, James H., Jr. *A History of West Virginia Free Will Baptists*. Hurricane, WV: 2013.

Crocker, Henry. *History of the Baptists in Vermont*. Bellows Falls, VT: P. H. Gobie, 1913.

Crowley, John G. *Primitive Baptists of the Wiregrass South, 1815 to the Present*. Gainesville, FL: University Press of Florida, 1998.

Davidson, William. *The Free Will Baptists in America, 1727-1984*. Nashville: Randall House, 1985.

———. *The Free Will Baptists in History*. Nashville: Randall House, 2001.

Dodd, Damon C. *Marching through Georgia: A History of Free Will Baptists in Georgia*. Colquitt, Georgia: n.p., 1977.

———. *The Free Will Baptist Story*. Nashville: Executive Department of the National Association of Free Will Baptists, 1956.

Dorrien, Gary. *The Making of American Liberal Theology: Crisis, Irony, and Postmodernity, 1950-2005*. Louisville: Westminster John Knox Press, 2006.

———. *The Making of American Liberal Theology: Idealism, Realism, and Modernity, 1900-1950*. Louisville: Westminster John Knox Press, 2003.

———. *The Soul in Society: The Making and Renewal of Social Christianity*. Minneapolis: Fortress, 1995.

Gardner, Robert. *Baptists of Early America: A Statistical History, 1639-1790*. Atlanta: Georgia Baptist Historical Society, 1983.

Garrison, Keith. *Upon This Rock: Missouri State Association of Free Will Baptists, 100 Years*. Lebanon, MO: Missouri State Association of Free Will Baptists, 2014.

George, Timothy. *Theology of the Reformers*. Nashville: Broadman, 1988.

———, ed. *Evangelicals and the Nicene Faith: Reclaiming the Apostolic Witness*. Grand Rapids: Baker, 2011.

Goadby, J. Jackson. *Bye-Paths in Baptist History: A Collection of Interesting, Instructive, and Curious Information not Generally Known Concerning the Baptist Denomination*. London: Elliot Stock, 1871.

Gordon, George A. *The Life and Labors of Rev. Henry S. Gordon: Founder of Free Will Baptist Churches in Southern Illinois*. Campbell Hill, IL: Rev. Geo A. Gordon, 1901.

Harper, Keith. *A Mere Kentucky of a Place: The Elkhorn Association and the Commonwealth's First Baptist*. America's Baptists. Knoxville: University of Tennessee Press, 2021.

Harris, Roy W., and Phillip T. Morgan. *The Cumberland Association: Celebrating 175 Years of Leadership, Ministry, and Service*. Lebanon, TN: RHM, 2018.

Harrison, Harrold, ed. *Who's Who Among Free Will Baptists*. Nashville: Randall House, 1978.

Harrison, T. F., and J. M. Barfield. *History of the Free Will Baptists of North Carolina*. Ayden, NC: Free Will Baptist Publishing House, [1896].

Hart, D. G. *The Lost Soul of American Protestantism*. Lanham, MD: Rowman and Littlefield, 2002.

Hatch, Nathan O. *The Democratization of American Christianity*. New Haven: Yale University Press, 1989.
Hatton, T. J., Kevin H. O'Rourke, and Alan M. Taylor, eds. *The New Comparative Economic History: Essays in Honor of Jeffrey G. Williamson*. Cambridge: MIT Press, 2007.
Holder, Naomi Dail. *History of Wheat Swamp Christian Church*. LaGrange, NC, 1977.
Holifield, E. Brooks. *The Gentlemen Theologians: American Theology in Southern Culture, 1795–1860*. Durham, NC: Duke University Press, 1978.
Hooker, Richard J., ed. *The Carolina Backcountry on the Eve of the Revolution: The Journal and Other Writings of Charles Woodmason, Anglican Itinerant*. Chapel Hill: University of North Carolina Press, 1953.
Hutchinson, William R. *The Modernist Impulse in American Protestantism*. Durham, NC: Duke University Press, 1992.
Into the Darkness: 75 Years of Free Will Baptist International Missions. Antioch, TN: Free Will Baptist International Missions, 2010.
Johnson, Oliver. *W. L. Garrison and His Times*. Miami: Mnemosyne Publishing Company, 1969 [1881].
Johnson, Paul E. *A Shopkeeper's Millennium: Society and Revival in Rochester, New York, 1815–1837*. New York: Hill and Wang, 2004.
Johnson County, Kentucky: History and Families. Paducah, KY: Turner, 2001.
Jonas, W. Glenn, Jr., ed. *The Baptist River: Essays on Many Tributaries of a Diverse Tradition*. Macon, GA: Mercer University Press, 2006.
Jones, Marvin. *The Beginning of Baptist Ecclesiology: The Foundational Contributions of Thomas Helwys*. Eugene, OR: Pickwick Publishers, 2017.
Joslin, David A., ed. *History of Arkansas Free Will Baptists*. Nashville: n.p., printed by Randall House, 1998.
Kennedy-Nolle, Sharon D. *Writing Reconstruction: Race, Gender, and Citizenship in the Postwar South*. Chapel Hill: University of North Carolina Press, 2015.
Kidd, Thomas S. *George Whitefield: America's Spiritual Founding Father*. New Haven: Yale University Press, 2014.
Kim, Do Hoon. *John Eliot's Puritan Ministry to New England "Indians."* Eugene, OR: Pickwick Publishers, 2021.
Latch, Ollie. *History of the General Baptists*. Poplar Bluff, MO: General Baptist Press, 1954.
Little, John Buckner. *The History of Butler County, Alabama, from 1815 to 1885*. Cincinnati: Elm Street Printing Company, 1885, https://www.ancestry.com/search/collections/22980/.
Loveless, Alton, James McComas, and Edwin Hayes. *Great Is Thy Faithfulness: Over 200 Years of Ohio Free Will Baptist History, 1805–2009*. Reynoldsburg, OH: Ohio State Association of Free Will Baptists, 2009.

Lytle, David and Charles Cook. *Arminian Baptists: A Biographical History of Free Will Baptists*. Nashville: Randall House, 2022.
Maclay, Isaac W. *The Descendants of Henry Sater of Maryland*. New York: Barnes, 1895.
Marini, Stephen A. *Radical Sects in Revolutionary New England*. Cambridge: Harvard University Press, 1982.
Marsden, George M. *Fundamentalism and American Culture*. New York: Oxford University Press, 1980.
McBeth, H. Leon. *The Baptist Heritage: Four Centuries of Baptist Witness*. Nashville: Broadman Publishers, 1987.
McKivigan, John R. *The War Against Proslavery Religion: Abolitionism and the Northern Churches, 1830–1865*. Ithaca: Cornell University Press, 1984.
Million, G. W. *A History of Free Will Baptists*. Nashville: Board of Publications and Literature, National Association of Free Will Baptists, 1958.
Million, G. W., and G. A. Barrett. *A Brief History of the Liberal Baptists in England and America from 1606 to 1911*. Pocahontas, AR: Liberal Baptist Book and Tract Company, 1911.
Montgomery, D. B., ed. *General Baptist History*. Evansville, IN: Courier Company, 1882.
Morgan, Phillip T., and J. Matthew Pinson. *Light and Truth: A Seventy-Fifth-Anniversary Pictorial History of Welch College*. Gallatin, TN: Welch College Press, 2018.
Mosheim, John Lawrence. *An Ecclesiastical History, Ancient and Modern, from the Birth of Christ, to the Beginning of the Present Century. . . .* Translated by Archibald Maclaine, 4 vols. New York: Evert Duyckinck, Collins and Hannay, 1824.
Mulder, Philip N. *A Controversial Spirit: Evangelical Awakenings in the South*. New York: Oxford University Press, 2002.
Murphy, Thurmon. *From the Red to the Rio Grande: A History of the Free Will Baptist Work in Texas, 1876–2014*. Columbus, OH: FWB Publications, 2017.
Newman, Albert Henry. *A History of Anti-Pedobaptism: From the Rise of Pedobaptism to A.D. 1609*. Philadelphia: American Baptist Publication Society, 1896.
———. *A History of the Baptist Churches of the United States*. New York: Charles Scribner's Sons, 1902.
Noll, Mark A. *America's God: From Jonathan Edwards to Abraham Lincoln*. New York: Oxford University Press, 2005.
———. *The Scandal of the Evangelical Mind*. Grand Rapids: Eerdmans Publishers, 1994.
Owens, Robby. *The Warfield Years: The Story of Edgar Warfield and the Western Division Free-Will Baptist Movement*. El Cajon, CA: Christian Services Network, 2004.

Owsley, Frank Lawrence. *Plain Folk of the Old South.* Baton Rouge: Louisiana State University Press, 2008 [1949].
Paschal, George Washington. *History of North Carolina Baptists,* 2 vols. Raleigh: The General Board, North Carolina Baptist State Convention, 1930.
Patterson, James A. *James Robinson Graves: Staking the Boundaries of Baptist Identity.* Studies in Baptist Life and Thought. Edited by Michael A. G. Haykin. Nashville: B&H Academic, 2012.
Pelt, Chester H. *A History of the Salem Association of Free Will Baptists of West Florida.* Marianna, FL: Salem Free Will Baptist Association, 1987.
Pelt, Michael R. *A History of Original Free Will Baptists.* Mount Olive, NC: Mount Olive College Press, 1996.
Picirilli, Robert E., ed. *History of Free Will Baptist State Associations.* Nashville: Randall House, 1976.
———. *Free Will Baptist History: Exploring Our Origins and Identity.* Nashville: Randall House, 2019.
———. *Grace, Faith, Free Will: Contrasting Views of Salvation: Calvinism and Arminianism.* Nashville: Randall House, 2002.
———. *Little Known Chapters in Free Will Baptist History.* Nashville: Randall House, 2015.
Pinson, J. Matthew. *40 Questions About Arminianism.* Grand Rapids: Kregel Academic, 2022.
———. *A Free Will Baptist Handbook: Heritage, Beliefs, and Ministries,* 2nd ed. Nashville: Randall House, 2022. First edition published in 1998.
———. *Arminian and Baptist: Explorations in a Theological Tradition.* Nashville: Randall House, 2016.
———. *The Washing of the Saints' Feet.* Nashville: Randall House, 2006.
Raper, W. Burkette. *A Short History of Mount Olive College.* Mount Olive: Mount Olive College Press, 2001.
Raven, James. *London Booksellers and American Customers: Transatlantic Community and the Charleston Library Society, 1478–1811.* Columbia, SC: University of South Carolina Press, 2002.
Ready, Milton. *The Tar Heel State: A New History of North Carolina.* Columbia, SC: University of South Carolina Press, 2020.
Riley, B. F. *A History of the Baptists in the Southern States East of the Mississippi.* Philadelphia: American Baptist Publication Society, 1898.
Ringenberg William C. *The Christian College: A History of Protestant Higher Education in America.* Grand Rapids: Baker Academic, 2006.
Roberts, Jon H., and James Turner. *The Sacred and the Secular University.* Princeton: Princeton University Press, 2000.
Schweiger, Beth Barton. *A Literate South: Reading before Emancipation.* New Haven: Yale University Press, 2019.

Sernett, Milton C. *Abolition's Axe: Beriah Green, Oneida Institute, and the Black Freedom Struggle*. Syracuse, NY: Syracuse University Press, 1986.
Shurden, Walter B. *Not a Silent People: Controversies That Have Shaped Southern Baptists*. Macon, GA: Smyth and Helwys Publishers, 1995.
Smith, Timothy L. *Revivalism and Social Reform in Mid-Nineteenth-Century America*. Nashville: Abingdon Press, 1957.
Sparks, John. *The Roots of Appalachian Christianity: The Life and Legacy of Elder Shubal Stearns*. Lexington, KY: The University Press of Kentucky, 2001.
Spencer, J. H. *A History of Kentucky Baptists from 1769 to 1885*. Revised by Mrs. Burilla B. Spencer, 2 vols. Cincinnati: J. R. Baumes, 1885.
Stanglin, Keith. *The Letter and Spirit of Biblical Interpretation: From the Early Church to Modern Practice*. Grand Rapids: Baker Academic, 2018.
Stewart, I. D. *The History of the Freewill Baptists for Half a Century*. Dover, NH: Freewill Baptist Printing Establishment, 1862.
Sweeney, Douglas A. *The American Evangelical Story: A History of the Movement*. Grand Rapids: Baker, 2005.
Taylor, Adam. *The History of the English General Baptists*, 2 vols. London: T. Bore, 1818.
The Free Baptist Woman's Missionary Society: Faith and Works Win, 1873–1921. Providence, RI: The Free Baptist Woman's Missionary Society, 1922.
Thomas, John Christopher. *Footwashing in John 13 and the Johannine Community*. New York: Bloomsbury, 2004.
Thomas, John L. *The Liberator: A Biography of William Lloyd Garrison*. Boston: Little, Brown and Company, 1963.
Torbet, Robert G. *A History of the Baptists*. Valley Forge, PA: Judson Press, 1963.
Troeltsch, Ernst. *The Social Teaching of the Christian Churches*. Translated by Olive Wyon, 2 vols. Louisville: Westminster John Knox Publishers, 1992 [1912].
Vaughn, Robert L. *Materials Toward a History of Feet Washing among the Baptists*. Mount Enterprise, TX: Waymark, 2008.
Ware, Charles Crossfield. *Albemarle Annals*. Wilson: NC, 1961.
———. *North Carolina Disciples of Christ: A History of Their Rise and Progress, and of Their Contribution to Their General Brotherhood*. St. Louis: Christian Board of Publication, 1927.
———. *Pamlico Profile*. New Bern, NC: Owen G. Dunn, 1961.
———. *Tar Heel Disciples*. New Bern, NC: Owen G. Dunn, 1942.
Watts, Joseph T. *The Rise and Progress of Maryland Baptists*. Baltimore: Maryland Baptist Union, 1953.
Webb, Jo Smith. *Linkage: The Study of a Family*, vol. 2. Self-Published, 1984.
Webster, Noah. *American Dictionary of the English Language*. New York: S. Converse, 1830.
Wells, David F. *No Place for Truth: Or Whatever Happened to Evangelical Theology?* Grand Rapids: Eerdmans Publishers, 1994.

Wills, Gregory A. *Democratic Religion: Freedom, Authority, and Church Discipline in the Baptist South, 1785–1900.* Religion in America. Edited by Harry S. Stout. New York: Oxford University Press, 1997.
Winiarski, Douglas L. *Darkness Falls on the Land of Light: Experiencing Religious Awakenings in Eighteenth-Century New England.* Chapel Hill: University of North Carolina Press, for the Omohundro Institute of Early American History and Culture, Williamsburg, Virginia, 2017.
Wisehart, Mary Ruth, ed. *The Fifty-Year Record of the National Association of Free Will Baptists.* Nashville: Randall House, 1988.
Wolever, Terry. *The Life of John Gano, 1727–1804.* Springfield, MO: Particular Baptist Press, 2012.
Woolsey, Paul. *God, A Hundred Years, and a Free Will Baptist Family.* Chuckey, TN: Union Free Will Baptist Association, 1949.

Theses and Dissertations

Crist, Timothy. "Francis Smith and the Opposition Press in England, 1660–1688." PhD thesis, Cambridge University, 1977.
Harrison, Paul Vernice. "A Biography of Linton Carroll Johnson." MA thesis, Middle Tennessee State University, 1988.
Larson, Timothy. "Faith by Their Works: Our Progressive Tradition." BA thesis, Bates College, 2005. https://www.bates.edu/150-years/history/progressive-tradition/chapter-2/.
Lumpkins, E. Peter Frank. "The Decline of Confessional Calvinism among Baptist Associations in the Southern States during the Nineteenth Century." PhD diss., University of Pretoria, 2018.
Morgan, Phillip T. "The Promise of a Second Evangelical Mind: Free Will Baptist Bible College and the Hybrid Model of Christian Higher Education." MA thesis, Middle Tennessee State University, 2016.
Pinson, J. Matthew. "Religious Social Reform in the Antebellum North: Anti-Slavery and Temperance Reform among the Northern Freewill Baptists, 1800–1860." MA thesis, University of West Florida, 1993.
Reeves, Russ Patrick. "Countering Revivalism and Revitalizing Protestantism: High Church, Confessional, and Romantic Critiques of Second Great Awakening Revivalism, 1835 to 1852." PhD diss., University of Iowa, 2005.

Encyclopedia Entries

Fick, Virginia Gunn. "Hatting." In *Encyclopedia of North Carolina.* Ed. William S. Powell. Chapel Hill: University of North Carolina Press, 2006. https://www.ncpedia.org/hatting.
Fitzmier, J. R. "Second Great Awakening." In *Dictionary of Religion in America.* Edited by Daniel G. Reid. Downers Grove, IL: InterVarsity Press, 1990.

Hester, Kevin L. "Free Will Baptists." In *Encyclopedia of Religious Revivals in America*. Edited by Michael J. McClymond and Lisa Smith. Westport, CT: Greenwood Press, 2007.

Pelt, Michael R. "Free Will Baptist." In *Encyclopedia of North Carolina*. https://www.ncpedia.org/printpdf/2538.

Pinson, J. Matthew. "Free Will Baptists." In *Encyclopedia of Religious Controversies in the United States*, vol. 1. Edited by Bill J. Leonard and Jill Y. Crainshaw. Santa Barbara, CA: ABC-CLIO, 2013.

Stevenson, George. "Laker, Benjamin." In *Dictionary of North Carolina Biography*, vol. 4. Edited by William S. Powell. Chapel Hill: University of North Carolina Press, 1991.

———. "Palmer, Paul," "Parker, Joseph," and "Surginer, William." In *Dictionary of North Carolina Biography*, vol. 5. Edited by William S. Powell. Chapel Hill: University of North Carolina Press, 1991.

"United American Free Will Baptist Church." In *Encyclopedia of African American Religions*. Edited by Larry G. Murphy, J. Gordon Melton, and Gary L. Ward. New York: Routledge, 2011.

Pamphlets, Articles, and Book Chapters

Aldridge, Jimmy, et al., eds. *Alabama State Association of Free Will Baptists: Centennial Celebration*. n.p.: Alabama State Association of Free Will Baptists, 1997.

"Baptists in the Colonies till 1750." *Transactions of the Baptist Historical Society* 7 (1920): 31–48.

Betteridge, Alan. "Early Staffordshire Baptists: A Further Note." *Baptist Quarterly* 38 (1999): 200–01.

Bordin, Ruth B. "The Sect to Denomination Process in America: The Freewill Baptist Experience." *Church History* 34 (1965): 77–94.

Davidson, William F. "The National Association of Free Will Baptists." *The Baptist River: Essays on Many Tributaries of a Diverse Tradition*. Edited by W. Glenn Jonas, Jr. Macon, GA: Mercer University Press, 2006, Chapter 6.

Davis, B. P. "Notes from Records of Reedy Creek Church, Tar River Association." *North Carolina Baptist Historical Papers* 3 (1899–1900): 8–23.

Dodd, Damon C. "The Story of Rev. John H. Wolfe." *Contact* (December 1953): 4, 6 (based on an interview with Wolfe).

Durso, Pamela R. "She-Preachers, Bossy Women, and Children of the Devil: Women Ministers in the Baptist Tradition, 1609-2012." *Review & Expositor* 110 (2013): 33–47.

Findlay, James. "Moody, 'Gapmen,' and the Gospel: The Early Days of Moody Bible Institute." *Church History* 31 (1962): 322–35.

Fisher, Abial. "History of the First Baptist Church, Swansea, Massachusetts." *The Baptist Memorial and Monthly Record* 4 (1845): 225–35.

Gardner, Robert G. "African American Free Will Baptists in Georgia." *Viewpoints: The Journal of the Georgia Baptist Historical Society* 19 (2004).
Goodfriend, Joyce D. "The Baptist Church in Prerevolutionary New York City." *American Baptist Quarterly* 16 (1997): 219–40.
Graham, D. M. "Biographical Sketch of Rev. Elias Hutchins." *Freewill Baptist Quarterly* 8 (1860): 84–108.
Hasty, Steven. "Did They Survive?" *Contact* (July 1988): 12–13.
Hathaway, J. R. B., ed., "Births, Deaths and Marriages in Berkeley, Later Perquimans Precinct, N.C.," *The North Carolina Historical and Genealogical Register* 3 (1903): 204.
Hester, Kevin L. *Free Will Baptists and the Priesthood of All Believers*. Antioch, TN: Historical Commission, National Association of Free Will Baptists, 2010.
Hobson, Darrell. "D. L. Moody's Gap-men: A Vision for Assemblies of God Bible Colleges." *Paraclete* 23 (1989): 1–8.
Holley, E. Darrell. *Without a Monument: The Life of Elder Paul Palmer*. Nashville: Free Will Baptist Bible College, 2000.
Hufham, J. D. "Notes, Queries and Criticisms." *North Carolina Baptist Historical Papers* 3 (1899–1900): 224–28.
———. "The Baptists in North Carolina." *North Carolina Baptist Historical Papers* 1 (1896–1897): 143–78.
———. "The Baptists of North Carolina. Part II—Third Paper." *North Carolina Baptist Historical Papers* 3.1 [1899]: 1–23.
Hume, Robert D. "The Value of Money in Eighteenth-Century England: Income, Prices, Buying Power—and Some Problems in Cultural Economics." *Huntington Library Quarterly* 77 (2014): 373–416.
Kaufmann, Eric P. "Cosmopolitan Clerics: The Role of Ecumenical Protestantism." In *The Rise and Fall of Anglo-America*. Cambridge: Harvard University Press, 2004.
Kidd, Thomas S. "Calvinism Is Not New to Baptists: Grace Unleashed in the American Colonies." *Desiring God* (June 13, 2015), https://www.desiringgod.org/articles/calvinism-is-not-new-to-baptists.
Le Beau, Bryan F. "'The Acrimonious, Controversial Spirit' Among Baptists and Presbyterians in the Middle Colonies During the Great Awakening." *American Baptist Quarterly* 9 (1990): 167–83.
Lennon, Donald R., and Fred D. Ragan. "Searching for Greener Pastures: Out-Migration in the 1800s and 1900s." *Tar Heel Junior Historian* 34 (1995), https://www.ncpedia.org/anchor/searching-greener-pastures.
Lynch, James R. "Baptist Women in Ministry Through 1920." *American Baptist Quarterly* 13 (1994): 304–18.
Mayfield, Bernard. "Lone Star." In *Cherokee County History*. Jacksonville, TX: Cherokee County Historical Society, 2001.
Mooneyham, W. Stanley. "Personally . . ." *Contact* (November 1953): 2.

"Notes and Comments." *North Carolina Baptist Historical Papers* 1 (1896–1897): 132–136.

Owen, Ernest, and Darrell Holley. "A Brief History of the Florida State Association." *The Historical Review: A Journal of Church History Published by the Florida State Association of Free Will Baptists* 2 (1994): 49–56.

Pelt, Michael R. *A History of Ayden Seminary and Eureka College*. Mount Olive, NC: Mount Olive College Press, 1983.

Picirilli, Robert E. "A Study of Separate, Free Will Baptist Origins in Middle Tennessee." *The Quarterly Review* 37 (1977): 44–52.

———. *History of Tennessee Free Will Baptists*. Nashville: Historical Commission, Tennessee State Association of Free Will Baptists, 2012.

Pinson, J. Matthew. "E. L. St. Claire and the Free Will Baptist Experience, 1893–1916." *Viewpoints: The Journal of the Georgia Baptist Historical Society* 17 (2000): 19–35.

———. "Dissent from Calvinism in the Baptist Tradition." In *Calvinism: A Biblical and Theological Critique*. Edited by David L. Allen and Steve W. Lemke. Nashville: B&H Academic, 2022.

———. *Free Will Baptists and Church Government*. Antioch, TN: Historical Commission, National Association of Free Will Baptists, 2008.

———. *Free Will Baptists and the Sufficiency of Scripture*. Antioch, TN: Historical Commission, National Association of Free Will Baptists, 2014.

"Progress of Universalism in North and South Carolina." *The Universalist Magazine* (August 11, 1827). https://universalistchristian.net/universalist-history/progress-of-universalism-in-north-and-south-carolina-1827/.

"Reunion of the Synods of New York and Philadelphia." *Presbyterian Quarterly Review* 28 (1859): 529–63.

Ruark, Elmer F. "Our Baptist Heritage." *The Quarterly Review* 27 (1967): 53–58.

Salley, Alexander S., ed. "Reverend John Blair's Mission to North Carolina, 1704." In *Narratives of Early Carolina, 1650–1708*. Original Narratives of Early American History. Edited by J. Franklin Jameson. New York: Charles Scribner's Sons, 1911.

Shurden, Walter B. "The Southern Baptist Synthesis: Is it Cracking?" *Baptist History and Heritage* 16 (1981): 2–11.

Sketch of Rev. John Averett Fonville. Montgomery Alabama, Alabama Department of Archives and History.

Smith, Elizabeth. "The Former Articles of Faith of the North Carolina Free Will Baptists." *The Free Will Baptist* (July 27, 1960): 9–11.

"The Early General Baptist Churches in the United States." *Freewill Baptist Quarterly* 3 (1855): 422–34.

"The North Carolina Freewill Baptists." *Freewill Baptist Quarterly* 4 (1856): 221–28, 328–37.

Thomsen, Eric. "In the North." *FWBHistory.com*. https://fwbhistory.com/?page_id=88.

Urner, Clarence H. "Early Baptist Records in Prince George County, Virginia." *The Virginia Magazine of History and Biography* 41 (1933): 97–101.
Wheeler, S. J. "History of the Meherrin Church." *North Carolina Baptist Historical Papers* 1 (1896): 41–76.
Whitley, W. T. "General Baptists in Carolina and Virginia." *Crozer Quarterly* 13 (1936): 21–27.
———. "General Baptists in Carolina and Virginia." *The Free Will Baptist* 75 (1960): 12–14.
———. "Thomas Hammersley." *Baptist Quarterly* 8 (1937): 316.
Williams, Daniel. "Origins of the Free Will Baptists in Georgia." *The Journal of Baptist Studies* 6 (2014): 31–59.

UNPUBLISHED SOURCES

"A Brief Historical Sketch of Southeastern Free Will Baptist College." unpublished manuscript, Southeastern Free Will Baptist College.
"A Brief History." https://www.bates.edu/150-years/history/.
"About California Christian College." *California Christian College.* https://www.calchristiancollege.edu/about/.
"Church History." *St. Paul Freewill Baptist Church.* https://revmarcuswhite44.wixsite.com/mysite/church-history.
"Churches." *Original Stone Association of the Free Will Christian Baptist Church of Christ.* http://osafreewillbaptist.org/blog1/churches/.
Colson, Joshua R. "Origins of the Southern Illinois Free Will Baptist Movement." unpublished essay, 2017.
"Dewey Williams: Shape Note Singer." *National Endowment for the Arts.* https://www.arts.gov/honors/heritage/dewey-williams#:~:text=Southeast%20Alabama%20is%20the%20only%20area%20in%20the,sung%20by%20African%20Americans%20before%20the%20Civil%20War.
Edwards, Daniel. "GCC, My Alma Mater, to Close after 2013 School Year." https://pastordanieledwards.wordpress.com/2013/02/28/gcc-my-alma-mater-to-close-after-2013-school-year-2/.
"Gum Swamp OFWB History." https://gumswampchurch.org/gum-swamp-ofwb-church-history/. Accessed August 2, 2021.
Hillsdale College. Sketch of Its History—Recent Loss of Its Buildings—Change of Plans and Description of the New. Booklet printed in September 1874.
"History." *New Hope Free Will Baptist Church.* http://newhopefwbc.org/History.
"History of Holly Hill Free Will Baptist Church, Belvoir, North Carolina." http://hollyhillbelvoir.com/media/.
"James Grant Conner, 1863–1897." https://www.therestorationmovement.com/_states/arkansas/conner.htm.

Leroy Forlines-Burkette Raper correspondence. Free Will Baptist Historical Collection, Mount Olive College.

Luckie, K. S. "Church History." *United American Freewill Baptist Conference, Inc.* https://uafwbc.com/the-uafwbc-story/. Accessed August 9, 2022.

Miller, Benjamin. "The History of Zion Bible School." Unpublished essay, 2006.

Notes of M. P. Gore, grandson of Ellis Gore. McShan, Pickens County, Alabama, November 12, 1971. Held in Free Will Baptist Historical Collection, Welch College.

"Our History: The Blessings of Our Past." *Quad State Annual Conference, Western Division of Free Will Baptists.* http://fwbquadstate.org/History.htm.

"Our Ministries." *The Convention of Original Free Will Baptist Churches.* https://ofwb.org/our-ministries/.

"Our Story." *St. Matthews Unison Free Will Baptist Church.* https://www.stmatthewsufwbchurch.org/index.php/abut-us2/our-story.

"Our Story and Purpose." *Southeastern Free Will Baptist College.* https://sfwbc.edu/our-story-and-our-purpose/.

Owens, Jesse F. "Free Baptists, the Northern Baptist Convention, and Higher Criticism." Unpublished essay, 2016.

———. "Scripture and History in the Theology of John Goodwin." Unpublished essay, 2015.

———. "When General Baptists Became Particular Baptists." Unpublished essay, 2014.

Picirilli, Robert E. "How Broad the Umbrella." Paper presented to the Faculty of Free Will Baptist Bible College (n.d.).

———. "Thunder among the Tar Heels: The 1960s Church Government Controversy." Unpublished essay, 2019.

Pinson, J. Matthew. "Baconianism and Scottish Common Sense Philosophy among the Northern Freewill Baptists." Unpublished essay presented at Yale University American Religious History doctoral study group, 1993.

Smith, F. L. "Rise and Progress of Mt. Moriah Church and Mt. Moriah Association with Some of Their Labors." Handwritten MS, July 10, 1888. Held in Free Will Baptist Historical Collection, Welch College.

"The History of CBIS." *Carolina Bible Institute & Seminary.* http://www.carolinabible.org/history.htm.

"The History of Randall University." *Randall University.* https://ru.edu/about-randall/history/.

"The UAFWBC Story." *United American Freewill Baptist Conference, Inc.* https://uafwbc.com/the-uafwbc-story/. Accessed August 9, 2022.

"Timeline." *University of Mount Olive.* https://umo.edu/timeline/#:~:text=Mount%20Olive%20College%20was%20established%20by%20the%20North,now%20known%20as%20the%20University%20of%20Mount%20Olive.

Whitworth, Jerry. *The History of Nettle Ridge Church, 1856–1994.* 1994.

Williams, Jack. "The Day We Lost 600 Churches." Unpublished essay. https://fwbhistory.com/?page_id=2796.

INDEX

1660 Confession. *See Standard Confession*
1812 Abstract, 60, 62–66, 92, 105, 108, 110, 112, 116–17, 188, 210, 224, 226, 238–39, 245–48, 250–51, 256, 259–60, 262, 288, 341, 396n45, 399nn6–7, 399nn9–12, 407n10, 444n5, 446nn20–21, 447n24, 447n27, 447n33, 447n35, 449n54, 450n62, 450n64, 451n69, 454n13. *See Discipline*
1911 merger, 3, 124, 140, 146, 155, 173, 185–86, 188, 199, 215, 217, 275–76, 295, 323–24, 372, 422n23, 426n5, 439n65

abolition, 134, 150, 152–54, 156, 372, 420n6, 421n9, 424n48, 424nn53–54, 425n68, 427n36
Abstract of Principles, 103, 243–45, 446n15
Account of the Province of Carolina in America, An, 18, 384n4
African American Free Will Baptists, 3, 8–9, 11, 13, 68, 71, 92, 111, 124, 134, 145, 149–57, 169, 199, 204–17, 269, 271–72, 336–45, 366–67, 400n21, 421n10, 439n65
Alfin, Jesse, 67, 72
Alford, J. W., 283, 286, 288, 294
amillennialism, 318, 324, 366, 469n66, 357
Anabaptist, 4–7, 26, 33, 44, 264, 325, 371, 405n59

Anglican(ism), 4, 6, 18, 20–21, 25, 28, 31–32, 35, 47, 50, 52–53, 371, 385n10, 395n30, 450n67
anointing the sick, 2, 65, 229, 239, 259–60
Anthony, Alfred Williams, 173–77, 180–81, 186, 422n25, 428nn43–45
antislavery, 134, 139, 141, 144–45, 149–54, 156, 424n48
apostasy, 1, 89, 93, 99, 102–4, 107, 109, 113, 118–20, 136, 178, 187, 195–96, 238, 251–54, 262, 288, 324, 357, 361–62, 375–76, 407n3, 412n38, 412n40, 447n23, 448n39, 448n42
Apperson, D. J., 199–200, 247–48, 446n23
Apperson, Joseph L., 199–200
Arminian(ism), 1, 3, 5–8, 10, 25, 34–35, 37–38, 47–48, 52, 59–60, 63, 65, 74, 83, 90–91, 93, 102–4, 109, 111–14, 118–19, 121–22, 126, 135–36, 138, 150, 161–63, 171, 176–78, 184, 193, 195–96, 198, 227–29, 238, 241–44, 246, 248–49, 251–53, 264, 277, 326, 361, 371, 373–74, 376, 381, 394n15, 401n25, 405n50, 417nn19–20, 419n41, 430n62, 440n6, 441n13, 444n36, 445n11, 446n20, 447n31, 452n90, 461n8, 467n51, 467n53; Reformed, 6, 361–62; Wesleyan, 242, 376
Arminius, Jacobus, 6–7, 246, 250, 360
atonement, 1, 6, 162–63, 242, 247–49, 251, 262, 376, 447n31;

499

atonement (*cont.*)
  general/universal, 1, 6–7, 31, 33, 63, 102–3, 135–36, 162, 242–43, 246, 248, 417n19; particular/limited, 1, 6, 63, 89, 102, 119, 251; penal substitutionary, 162–63, 242, 249–50, 361, 376, 447n31–32
Austin, W. C., 194, 197, 277, 435n18
Ayden Seminary, 222–24, 233, 236, 287, 440n9. *See* Eureka College

backsliding, 324, 357, 448n42
Bacon, Francis, 171, 428nn37–38
Ball, George, 177, 279
Ballard, John H., 125–26, 249, 272, 419nn41–42, 447n30, 462n16
baptism, 20, 22–23, 26, 31–33, 35–36, 38, 43–44, 48, 66, 69, 71–73, 76, 86, 103, 116, 119, 137, 159, 165, 184, 215, 226, 229, 240–41, 257, 259–63, 265–66, 270, 375, 412n40, 425n2, 449n54, 450n67, 451n76; believer's, 5, 26, 33, 36, 43–45, 50, 65, 116–17, 126, 163–64, 230, 239, 254, 259–61, 371, 375, 387n28, 395n31; immersion, 45, 50, 126, 164–65, 230, 240, 254, 260–62, 401n25; infant, 135, 160, 166, 260, 262–63, 375; requisite for church membership, 240, 260; succession of, 5
baptismal regeneration, 116, 177, 261
baptistic non-Calvinists, 114, 200, 229–30, 245, 411n30, 442n24
Baptist Review, The, 231, 443n28, 446n19
Baptists
  – American, 9, 12, 23, 140–42, 179, 384n1, 385n12, 387n20, 388n30, 393n6, 394n21, 397n45, 424n47
  – Arminian, 3, 10, 34–35, 47, 52, 74, 83, 93, 114, 177, 228, 277, 326, 381, 430n62, 461n8
  – Arminianizing, 10, 91, 102, 113, 119, 121, 193, 198, 228, 251, 419n41
  – Calvinist, 3, 28–29, 34, 41, 45, 49, 52, 56–58, 63, 102–4, 119, 122–23, 133, 137, 226, 229, 239, 242, 244–45, 268, 371, 383n1, 388n30, 444n1
  – Free Communion, 154, 184, 428n37
  – General, 1–7, 10, 13, 17–18, 20–39, 41–53, 55–57, 59–63, 73–74, 82, 89, 136–40, 160, 162–63, 166–67, 177, 182, 184–85, 196, 226, 231–32, 238–41, 246, 250, 257, 260, 264, 277, 279, 335–36, 361, 366, 373–74, 377, 379, 383n1, 384nn2–3, 385n5, 386nn13–14, 387n20, 387n28, 388n29, 388nn36–37, 389n40, 390n45, 390n51, 391n52, 391n54, 392n61, 393n4, 393nn7–8, 394n11, 394nn17–18, 395n23, 395n25, 396n45, 397n45; 398n1, 411n30, 430n64, 442n24, 443n29, 445n7, 450n61, 450n67, 470n1; General Assembly, 17, 21, 384n3, 394n11; General Association (England), 21–22, 25, 377, 386n14, 387n15; General Association (American Midwest), 21, 74, 184, 264, 335–36, 403n36; Six Principle, 29, 43–44, 52, 379, 389n37, 419n20
  – Liberal, 229–33, 415n9, 442n24
  – Missionary, 95, 98, 104, 125, 182, 184, 212, 215, 237, 263, 402n34, 409n18, 445n10
  – Northern, 3, 124–25, 140–42, 144, 146, 148, 155, 173, 177–78, 180–81, 183–85, 188, 199, 215, 217, 275, 281, 288, 323–25, 372, 376–77, 379, 383n1, 396n45, 406n1, 422n23, 428n42, 428n45, 429n47, 429n50, 429n57, 439n65, 453n1
  – Particular, 1–2, 6, 30, 36, 39, 42, 46, 55, 63, 237, 388n30, 393n4, 393n7, 394nn17–18, 395n25, 398n58
  – Primitive, 2, 195, 212, 237, 241, 244, 263, 326, 374, 395n30, 421n18, 445n10, 461n8

INDEX 501

- Regular, 9, 47, 50, 58, 61, 63, 66, 81, 90, 103, 111, 113, 117, 119, 128, 136–37, 195, 243–45, 266, 395n21, 407n2
- Separate, 10, 50, 89–91, 102, 104, 115, 117–20, 122–23, 128, 137, 237, 251, 259, 266, 373–74, 395n21, 395n31, 406n2, 407n3, 416n18, 417nn19–20, 418n25, 418n29
- Seventh-Day, 28
- Southern, 12, 34, 41, 53, 61, 102, 107, 117, 125, 127, 229–31, 234, 237, 239, 243, 245, 251, 259, 263–64, 266–67, 334, 371, 380, 383n1, 390n44, 393n4, 396n45, 410n18, 412n40, 433n4, 440n6, 443n28, 445n12, 446n19, 452n79, 470n71
- Union, 83, 105, 229–31, 413n43, 443n28
- United, 84, 90, 93, 95, 98–100, 102–6, 108–10, 114, 119–20, 128, 179, 181, 187, 191, 193, 195–96, 198, 232, 251, 253, 402n33, 410n23, 411n25, 413n43, 414n52, 419n41, 433n5, 434n11, 440n2, 447n36

Barefoot, Gary, 11–12, 334, 406n62, 411n28, 441n13, 441nn15–17, 462n27
Barfield, J. M., 77, 81, 196, 200, 223, 227–28, 260–61, 335, 383n1, 396n45, 399n12, 401nn29–32, 402nn34–35, 403nn36–37, 404n43, 405nn51–52, 405n57, 405n60, 406n61, 406nn63–68, 406n70, 407n5, 407nn7–8, 408n14, 413nn43–44, 413n47, 430n63, 435n15, 436n29, 438n44, 438n47, 448n49, 450nn65–67, 452n89
Barnard, Laura Belle, 290, 299–301, 306, 457n8
Barrett, G. A., 89, 182–83, 197, 201–2, 384n1, 390n45, 397n45, 406n2, 411n28, 416n17, 419n39, 430nn63–67, 431nn70–71, 433nn2–3, 433n8, 435nn16–19, 436n33, 438n52m 439n61, 439nn63–64

Bates College, 12, 143, 145–46, 173–75, 216, 423nn38–39, 424n50
Belgic Confession, 6
Bell, Joseph, 85, 225, 268, 441n16, 447n31, 452n81, 455n39
Benedict, David, 27, 103, 121, 383n1, 387n22, 390n45, 391n52, 398n58, 412n39, 418n30, 419n41, 450n61
Bentley, Richard, 19
Bethel Conference, 59, 72–76, 79–81, 92, 94, 105–8, 399n6, 399n12, 401nn29–32, 402nn34–35, 403n37, 405nn51–52, 407n5, 408n14, 413n43, 413n50
Bethlehem Association, 112, 114–17, 191–92, 194, 197–98, 257, 415n11, 416nn13–14, 432n1, 434n9
Biblical School, the, 142–43, 146
Billings, William, 269
bi-vocational, 211, 224, 349
Black Free Will Baptists. *See* African American Free Will Baptists
Blackwelder, I. J., 281, 294–95, 299–301
Blair, John, 20, 385n11
Blanton, John Abraham, 92, 108, 414n51
Blighton, George, 20–21
Bloss, J. B., 310, 416n17
Bond, Robert, 67, 75, 105
Bordin, Ruth, 219, 439n1
Bowles, Charles, 134, 421n10
Boyett, Henry, 91–92, 94–100, 107, 109, 114, 199, 409nn15–16, 410n20
Bracey, Matthew Steven, 467n53
Brackney, William, 389n44, 390n45
Braxton, Levi, 67, 72
Brown, B. F., 280, 294, 310
Brown, David, 355
Brummitt, John, 354
Bryant, Scott, 135–38, 421nn15–17, 422n20, 425n1, 426n7
Burden, Keith, 354
Burges, William, 27–28

Burgess, G. A., 216–17, 383n1, 396n45, 416n11, 416n16, 421n10, 434n11, 442n18
Burkitt, Lemuel, 36–37, 44, 47–48, 52, 58–60, 63, 383n1, 392n61, 392n64, 394n11, 394n21, 396n45, 397n47, 398n57, 398n59, 399n8
Burtchaell, James, 53–54, 378–79, 396nn40–42, 428n39, 471n6
Butler, John J., 142–43, 156, 160, 163, 166–67, 169–70, 279, 386n14, 409n16, 425n68, 426n5, 426n15, 427n22, 427nn24–26, 427n31, 427n33, 467n51
Buzzell, John, 66–67, 91, 93–94, 139–40, 142, 166, 421n13

California Christian College, 325, 357, 461n7, 466n41
Callaway, Elijah, 67, 91, 93–95, 408n13
Calvin, John, 5–7
Calvinism, 1–3, 6–8, 25, 28–30, 34, 36–39, 41–49, 51–52, 55–59, 63, 74, 81, 89, 102–4, 106, 113–14, 117–19, 121–23, 126, 131–38, 154, 161–63, 177–78, 200, 226, 228–30, 238–46, 251, 263, 266, 268, 326, 371, 373–74, 377–78, 383n1, 386n14, 388n30, 393n3, 395n21, 395n25, 397n47, 402n33, 403n36, 411n30, 412n35, 417nn18–20, 419n41, 426nn7–8, 442n24, 444n1, 445n10, 445n12, 446n20, 446n23, 467n51, 470n2; New Light, 42, 44–45, 48–52, 55, 59, 82, 117, 134, 136–38, 240, 371, 379, 395n21, 395n31, 445n7; Old Light, 44–45, 48–49, 82, 132, 136, 395n31
Campbell, Alexander, 78, 127
Campbell, Thomas, 78, 127
Cape Fear Conference, 83–86, 100, 205–6, 230, 232, 294, 333, 338, 406n62, 411n28, 437n42, 438nn43–44, 440n10, 441n18, 443n28, 452n89

Cape Fear United American Free Will Baptist Conference, 205–6
Case, Shirley Jackson, 175, 429n47
Charles II, 18, 60, 64
Charleston Tradition, 267
Chattahoochee Association, 93, 98–109, 114, 199–200, 210, 220, 235, 238, 247, 252, 257, 259, 261, 263, 265, 270, 410n23, 411nn25–27, 412n36, 412n38, 413nn41–42, 413n46, 413nn48–49, 436n25, 438n52, 440n2, 443nn28–29, 444n1, 446n23, 447n34, 447n38, 448n39, 448n51, 449n53, 449n56, 450n62, 451n68, 451nn71–72, 451n77, 452n88, 452n91
Cheney, Oren B., 142, 145–46, 186, 216, 424n50, 425n69
Cherry, Floyd, 335, 462n28, 463n30
Chestnut Ridge Church, 31–32, 44–45, 389n44, 390n45, 391n52
Christian Workers Institutes, 305, 315, 459n49
Christianismus Primitivus, 18, 20, 22
Christology, 21
church discipline, 33, 44–45, 85, 166–67, 206, 241, 254–56, 258, 270, 330, 332, 402n35, 418n34, 444n5, 448nn44–47, 449n53, 470n3
Churches of God, General Conference, 177, 264, 442n24
Church Member's Book, 154, 160, 168–71, 425n64, 425n3, 427nn28–30, 427n32, 427n34–36
church membership, 43–45, 47, 49–51, 85, 137, 144, 164–65, 168, 177–78, 180, 205–6, 240, 254–55, 260, 321, 355
Church of Christ, 80, 120, 126–27, 197, 414n53, 421n16; Free Will Baptist, 109, 123, 419n46, 449n59
Church of England. See Anglican(ism)
Church Training Service (CTS), 313, 353
Chute, Anthony, 412n35

INDEX 503

circumstances (of worship), 239–40
Civil War, 77, 85–86, 90, 123–24, 126,
   131, 144, 191, 204, 206–8, 214, 217,
   219–20, 230, 271–72, 371, 400n21,
   439n57
classical education, 223, 276, 307
Cobb Divinity School, 143, 145–46, 173,
   175
Cobb, Enoch, 224, 268, 441n11, 452n84,
   452n86
Coffey, Rufus, 354
Colson, Joshua, 184, 430nn63–64,
   431nn70–72, 435n14
Comer, John, 24–29, 35, 37–38, 43,
   383n1, 387n25, 388n31, 389nn38–40,
   391n58, 392n65, 393n10
communion, 8, 51, 66, 105, 150, 154,
   164–65, 168, 184, 231–32, 254, 259–65,
   373, 375, 383n1, 422n25, 428n37,
   451n76; close(d), 2, 90, 104, 106, 109,
   117–18, 122, 165, 178, 182, 213, 262–63,
   374, 383n1, 402n33, 417n20, 419n41;
   open, 2, 66, 83, 93, 99, 102–4, 109,
   111, 114, 118, 122, 126–27, 165, 176,
   178, 187, 195, 200, 227–30, 235, 238,
   245, 251, 253–54, 260–63, 374–75,
   383n1, 401n25, 407n3, 417n20, 440n6,
   447n23, 451n71
Community, 335
Confederacy, 85, 126, 271–72, 410n20
confessional(ism), 2, 3, 8, 10, 22, 53,
   55, 78–81, 84, 90–91, 109, 118, 120,
   128, 161, 178, 195, 210, 226, 228–29,
   233–36, 241, 243–44, 251–52, 260, 275,
   284, 288, 303, 318, 332, 361, 367–68,
   372, 374–75, 377–81, 405n50, 405n59,
   407n3, 417n20, 420n3, 444n36,
   445n12, 446n20, 446n23
confirmation (rite), 2, 26, 32, 38, 229,
   387n28. *See* Laying on of hands
Congregationalist, 2, 41, 44–45, 50, 82,
   117, 131, 165, 395n31

Contact, 326, 331, 333, 342–43, 354, 356,
   423n40, 430n60, 453n1, 455n30,
   458n29, 461n10, 462n17, 462n21,
   462nn23–24, 464nn49–50, 465n3,
   466n42, 467n43, 468nn61–62
Convention of Original Free Will
   Baptists, 3, 8, 13, 225, 326, 336,
   344, 366–67, 380, 442n19, 454n13,
   463nn34–35, 469n66
Cooper, Anthony Ashley, 18
Cooper, Christopher, 22
Co-operative General Association, 13,
   181–82, 184, 188, 201, 275–83, 288,
   292–96, 299, 301, 303–4, 309–11, 316,
   323, 373, 453nn1–11, 454nn14–15,
   454nn17–18, 456n46, 456n49, 459n34
Coville, W. E., 297–98, 317–18
Crawford, Robert, 299, 305, 310, 315
Creech, Ronald, 329–31, 333, 355,
   462n20, 462n25
creed(s), 22, 33, 53–54, 78–79, 82,
   118–19, 123, 173, 178, 241, 377, 391n52,
   401n25, 445n9
Cronk, Dan, 302–3, 306
Cronk, Trula, 302, 306
Crowe, David, 350
Crowley, John, 50, 137, 395n30, 421n18
Cumberland Association, 115, 117–21,
   127, 182, 185, 196, 245, 253, 258, 264,
   278–79, 287, 294, 304, 417n19, 418n25,
   418n27, 418n29, 431n71, 446n20,
   448n40, 449nn57–9, 455n23

D6 Family Ministry, 351, 353–54
Dagg, John Leadley, 241, 263, 451n73
Danforth, Clarissa, 147
Davidson, J. R., 304–6
Davidson, William F., 7, 10, 12, 17, 21, 23,
   34, 57, 62, 71, 117, 135, 148, 156, 184–85,
   195–96, 266, 356, 383n1, 384n1,
   385nn6–7, 386n14, 387n19, 387nn21–
   22, 388nn31–33, 388n37, 389nn42–43,

Davidson, William F. (*cont.*)
39n0n44–45, 390n48, 391n56, 392n67, 393n4, 393n9, 394n15, 394nn17–18, 396n45, 397n45, 397nn49–50, 398nn56–57, 398n1, 398n3, 399nn5–9, 400nn12–13, 401n26, 402nn34–35, 403n38, 404nn45–46, 406n61, 406n65, 415n1, 415n3, 415n8, 418n25, 418n29, 419n41, 420n8, 421n13, 422n21, 423n33, 424nn48–49, 425n67, 430n63, 431n72, 432n78, 432n80, 433n6, 434nn10–11, 435n14, 435nn21–22, 436n23, 436n25, 436n32, 437n41, 438nn45–46, 438n54, 439n1, 440n7, 440n9, 440n11, 441n14, 441n16, 442nn19–20, 443nn32–33, 448n49, 449n53, 451n78, 461n2, 461nn4–5, 465n4, 465nn10–11, 466n41, 467n42
Davis, Winford, 293–95, 301, 305, 316–17, 337
deacon, 2, 35, 60, 62–63, 80, 101, 166, 194, 202, 216, 255, 257–59, 374–75, 377, 384n3, 425n3, 449n54
Dearmore, W. E., 202, 276, 292
Democratic Party, 149, 154, 156
depravity, 132–33, 161, 241–49, 376, 444n36; total 1, 6, 118, 162, 241–49, 361, 426n10, 444n36, 446n20
Devotion, Constant, 29, 35–36, 38
Disciples of Christ, 59, 71, 78–81, 123, 126, 177, 230–31, 261, 371, 375, 377–79, 397n45, 397n48, 398n57, 398n4, 402n35, 404n47, 405n52, 405n57, 411n30, 442n24
Discipline, 62–64, 69, 78–79, 84–85, 96, 110, 112, 206, 210, 224, 375. *See* 1812 Abstract
dispensational premillennial, 335, 366
Dodd, Damon C., 8, 299, 302, 305–6, 323, 349, 356, 384n1, 397n45, 421n9, 421n12, 430n60, 436n29, 440n2, 443n28, 453n1, 469n66

Dorrien, Gary, 175–76, 428n41, 429n47, 429n50
Drake, John, 29
Dunbar, George, 306, 310
Dunn, Ransom, 143–44, 163, 279, 423n36, 426n5, 426n15, 467n51
Durso, Pamela, 423n47
Dutch Waterlander Mennonites, 4, 6

Eason, J. T., 91, 200, 436n29
Eastern Orthodox, 265
ecclesiology, 2, 4, 7, 54, 64, 366, 376
ecumenism, 3, 126, 155, 173, 176, 228, 232–36, 263, 288, 372, 377–80, 441n14, 442n20
Edwards, Eunice, 351
Edwards, Jonathan, 42, 51, 420n1
Edwards, Morgan, 23, 28, 31, 33–37, 42, 47–48, 59, 383n1, 385n12, 388n30, 388n34, 389n40, 389n44, 390n45, 390nn51–52, 391nn53–54, 391nn56–57, 392n61, 392n63, 392n69, 393nn6–7, 394n13, 394n16, 396n45, 398n58, 449n53, 450n61
election, 50, 113, 136; conditional, 102, 243, 447n23; unconditional, 102, 119, 251
elements (of worship), 167, 239–40
Enlightenment, 53
Ennis, L. R., 291, 299, 304–5, 307, 459n49
episcopal, 8, 57, 82, 159, 207, 340, 376, 459n42, 470n71
eschatology, 64, 171, 173, 228, 366, 420n8
eternal security, 90, 106, 109, 371, 374
Eureka College, 222–24, 286–87, 291–92, 299, 303–4, 312, 336, 440n9. *See* Ayden Seminary
Evangelical Training Association, 320, 352
Evans, William, 354–55

INDEX

executive secretary, 299, 305–6, 310, 312–13, 315–16, 323, 327, 331, 340, 342, 350–52, 354, 363
experience of grace, 43, 45–52, 58, 137, 240–41

family worship, 49, 226
feet washing. *See* washing of the saints' feet
fellowship, 44, 74, 76, 93, 102, 115, 123, 125, 154–55, 164–65, 167, 176, 180, 205, 212, 231, 234, 255–59, 263, 288, 332, 334, 339, 341–43, 367, 369, 430n62, 470n71
Ferguson, T. C., 180, 201, 275, 277, 430n60
Finney, Charles, 8, 55, 132–35, 174, 228, 243, 250, 379, 444n36, 446n20
Fonville, Frederick, 66, 174, 402n34
Footwashing. *See* washing of the saints' feet
Ford, H. M., 121, 177, 272
Ford brothers (TX), 201, 436n30
Forlines, Fay Gilbert, 416n17
Forlines, F. Leroy, 307, 328–29, 348–49, 355–56, 360–62, 364, 416n17, 462n15, 467nn50–53, 468n54, 468n56
Forlines, James, 348
Frazier, Agnes, 304, 307–8, 310–16, 327, 350, 458n20, 458nn31–458n32
Free Baptist Woman's Missionary Society, 146, 423n42
Freemasonry, 82–85, 134, 230, 256–57, 405n60
Free Soil Party, 149
Free Will Baptist, The, 225–27, 233, 235, 276, 284, 286, 291, 304, 308, 318, 331, 333, 399n7, 399n9, 440n8, 441nn12–13, 458n20, 458n30, 461n10, 461n14, 462nn18–19, 462n22, 462nn24–25, 462n27
Free Will Baptist Advocate, The, 225, 338, 441n12

Free Will Baptist Banner, 197, 201
Free Will Baptist Bible College. *See* Welch College
Freewill Baptist Education Society, 142
Freewill Baptist Foreign Mission Society, 139–40
Free Will Baptist Gem, 313, 316–8, 325, 450n62
Freewill Baptist Home Mission Society, 139, 141, 147, 152
Free Will Baptist Hymnal, The, 335, 455n44
Free Will Baptist Hymn Book, The, 224, 268, 356, 441n11, 452n84
Free Will Baptist League, 294–95, 297, 301, 316, 318, 320, 351–53, 455n26. *See* Church Training Service
Freewill Baptist Printing Establishment, 139–41, 144, 152
Free Will Baptist Publishing Company/Press, 116, 225–27, 233, 236, 276, 286, 313–14, 316–19, 327, 331, 335–36, 340, 351–52
Freewill Baptist Quarterly, 133, 159–60, 171, 281, 395n22, 396n37, 396n45, 401nn26–27, 420n7, 422n19, 424n60, 425n2, 426n4, 426n10
Freewill Baptist Repository, The, 154
Free Will Baptist Theological Seminary, 219, 222
French, Richard, 19–20
Fry, Mae, 351
Fry, Malcolm, 353
Fulsher, William, 32, 39, 55, 58–61
fundamentalism, 8, 288–89, 329, 335, 349, 358, 363–64, 368, 371, 378–81

Gano, John, 37, 41–43, 45–47, 393n8, 395n21
Gardner, Robert, 41, 210, 384n1, 388n37, 393n1, 393n9, 397n45, 438n52
Garrison, Keith, 183, 430n68, 431n69

Gateway Christian College, 365, 468n62
General Association of General Baptists, 21, 264, 336
General Conference: in North Carolina, 11, 56, 62, 64, 67, 72, 80–86, 91, 93, 105–7, 205–7, 209–10, 222, 225–27, 230–31, 256–57, 379, 397n48, 399n6, 405nn55–56, 407n8, 413n49, 443n28; in the North (Randall), 11, 121, 124–25, 134, 139, 142, 146, 149, 151–52, 154–56, 163, 165, 170–71, 173, 175–86, 188, 214–15, 225, 271–72, 275, 289, 372, 377, 420n8, 421n9, 422nn21–23, 422n25, 422n27, 422n30, 423n32, 423n41, 424n56, 424n59, 425n63, 425n66, 426n12, 426n15, 427n35, 429nn48–49, 429nn51–54, 429nn56–57, 430nn58–60, 430n62, 431n72, 439n60, 439n62, 439nn64–65, 441n14, 452n90, 452n92, 453n1, 453n5; Southeast, 11, 13, 280–96, 298–301, 303–4, 309–11, 316, 373, 376, 444n4, 454n13, 454nn16–18, 454nn20–22, 455nn24–35, 455nn37–38, 455nn40–41, 455nn43–45, 456nn46–49, 456n1, 457n7, 457nn9–10, 458nn17–18, 459n34, 460n53; triennial/Thomas Peden's, 11, 233–35, 239, 276, 278, 431nn75–76, 443n32, 444n35; United American Free Will Baptist, 337–41, 438n43
George, Timothy, 7, 404n48, 405n50
Goen, G. C., 294, 301
Gore, Ellis, 9, 91–92, 111–14, 128, 192, 198, 204, 222, 230, 243–45, 254–56, 406n2, 415nn3–4, 415n9, 438n54, 445n14, 448nn44–47
Gower, Wilson, 118–20, 315
grace, 1, 5–7, 33, 42–43, 45–52, 54, 58, 63, 65, 112–13, 120–21, 127, 132, 135–37, 139, 160, 162–63, 170, 178, 208, 237–38, 240–43, 246–53, 259, 265, 268–69, 284, 319, 362, 373, 376, 393n3, 418n20, 422n25, 425n3, 428n37, 444n4, 445n7, 446n20, 450n62, 467n51; irresistible, 7, 89, 102, 104, 119, 242, 246, 251, 413n49; prevenient, 162, 242, 248–49; resistible, 102, 242, 252, 447n23. See experience of grace; means of grace
Grantham, Thomas, 4, 7, 18, 20, 22, 167, 246, 361, 385n5
Great Awakening, 25, 42–43, 45, 48–49, 51–53, 55, 82, 131, 133, 135–36, 240, 379, 394n15, 394n21, 405n59, 416n18, 445n7; Second, 53, 55, 82, 131–34, 136, 160, 238, 379, 420nn2–4
Great Depression, 224, 291
Griffin, J. C., 298, 304–5, 312, 314, 318–20, 327, 335, 410n21
Griffin, Levi, 91, 97–100, 107, 410n21
Griffin, Mrs. J. C., 312, 314, 327
Griffin, T. H., 105, 265, 451n77
Guyton, J. M. I., 221–22, 440n6

Hammersley, John, 21, 384n2
Hammersley, Thomas, 17, 19, 377, 386nn13–14, 387n29
Hampton, Ralph, 349, 357
Hanna, Carlisle, 348
Hanna, Marie, 309, 348
Hansley, David W., 461n10
Harper, Keith, 12, 416n18
Harris, Roy, 417n19, 454n23
Harrison, Harrold, 352
Harrison, Paul, 458n25
Harrison, T. F., 77, 81, 196, 199–200, 223, 227–28, 260–61, 265, 335, 352, 383n1, 396n45, 399n12, 401nn29–32, 402nn34–35, 403nn36–37, 404n43, 405nn51–52, 405n57, 405n60, 406n61, 406nn63–68, 406n70, 407n5, 407nn7–8, 408n14, 413nn43–44, 413n47, 430n63, 435n15, 436n29,

438n44, 438n47, 440n8, 448n49,
   450nn65–67, 451nn76–77, 452n89
Hart, D. G., 53–54, 378–79, 396n43,
   405n59, 418n34, 470n3
Hart, Josiah, 32, 34–38, 42, 59, 391n57,
   392n61
Hartsfield, David, 78–79, 106, 402n35
Hartsfield, James, 91–92, 106–7, 413n46
Hartsfield, Lewis, 73–74, 92, 402n35
Harvey, Thomas, 18–19
Hatch, Nathan, 2, 54, 82, 123, 396n39,
   396n43, 471n6
Hearn, Howell, 62, 72, 226
Hearn, Rufus K., 45, 52, 57, 62, 70,
   72–73, 83–85, 106, 138, 206–27,
   225–28, 235, 240, 268, 383n1, 392n61,
   394nn15–16, 395n22, 396nn36–37,
   396n45, 397n51, 398n1, 399n5, 401n23,
   421n18, 422n19, 441n11, 441n13,
   441nn15–17, 445n7, 447n31, 452n81,
   455n39
Heath, Jeremiah, 67, 79, 94–97, 107,
   408n15, 409n16
Heath, Jesse, 61–62, 64–72, 74–75,
   82, 91, 93–94, 224, 398n1, 399n12,
   400n14, 400n19, 441n11
Heaton, Robert, 117–20, 128, 184, 206,
   271, 417n19, 452n90
Heidelberg Catechism, 6
Helwys, Thomas, 3–6, 246, 361, 412n40
Hersey, Herman, 354
Hester, Kevin, 12, 396n44
High, Danita, 351
Hillsdale College (Michigan), 143–46,
   276, 423nn35–37
Hillsdale Free Will Baptist College. See
   Randall University
Hinnant, R. N., 287
*History of the Free Will Baptists of
   North Carolina*, 196, 227, 260, 335.
   See T. F. Harrison; J. M. Barfield

Holder, B. B., 86, 91, 200
Holiness movement, 1, 8, 132, 229,
   242–43, 264, 284
Holley, Darrell, 12, 384n1, 387n19,
   397n45, 412n33, 458n28
Hollis, Brinson, 67, 91, 94–100, 107, 109,
   114, 199, 408n14, 409n16, 410n19
Hollis, M. L., 193, 292, 309–10
Hood, Thomas, Jr., 93, 401n27,
   408nn11–12
Hood, Thomas, Sr., 72, 92, 401n27,
   408nn11–12
Hooke, Joseph, 22
Hubmaier, Balthasar, 4
Hufham, J. D., 34, 383n1, 391n55, 418n20
Hunter, Ronald, 353
Hutchins, Elias, 48, 65, 67, 70–72, 74–
   76, 92, 138, 155, 224, 265–66, 400n13,
   401n24, 401nn26–28, 441n11, 451n78
Hyatt, Marie, 306
hymn(s), hymnal(s), 48, 69, 96, 138, 150,
   167, 211, 224–27, 231, 249, 267–69, 288,
   290, 292, 335, 356–57, 416n14, 441n11,
   441n16, 447n31, 452n81, 452nn84–85,
   452n87, 455n39, 455n44

IM, Inc., 294–95, 297, 299–303, 310–11,
   324, 336, 347–48, 355, 369, 457n8,
   464n1, 465n5
imputed righteousness, 1, 6, 65, 163,
   242, 245, 250–51, 254, 361, 376
Ingram, Robert, 30

Jackson, Bobby, 355
Jernigan, Wade, 357–58, 469n66
Johnson, L. C., 306–7, 309, 318, 348–49,
   360, 458n25, 458n29
Johnson, Ruth, 306, 309
Johnson, Samuel, 353
Jones, D. W. (Selph), 282, 304–5
Jones, Richard, 24, 27, 35, 59

Joslin, David, 430n63, 433nn7–8, 434n13, 435n14
justification, 1, 5–6, 65, 120, 163, 220, 242, 245, 249–51, 253, 261, 361, 376, 447n32

Kehukee Baptist Association, 36, 44, 47, 52, 63, 383n1, 392n61, 392n64, 394n11, 394n21, 396n45, 398n57, 398n59, 399n8
Ketteman, Paul J., 306, 320, 355
Kidd, Thomas, 41, 393n3, 393n5
Knight, John Thomas, 101, 235, 455n40

Ladies Aid Society, 284–86, 289, 291, 311, 313–14, 358–59
Laker, Benjamin, 17–24, 28–29, 206, 377, 384nn2–3, 385nn7–8, 385n10, 385n12, 386nn13–14
Latham, Thomas J., 68–70, 72, 78–79, 400n20
Lawless, Zedekiah, 192, 194–95, 202
laying on of hands, 2, 26, 31–32, 38, 44, 65, 118, 229, 239, 259–60, 387n28
Ledbetter, Henry, 38, 42, 46
Lewis, Ray, 354
Liberal(ism), 3, 8, 83, 175, 228, 230, 235, 287, 289, 329, 355–56, 363, 379, 381, 471n7
Locke, John, 18
Lord's Supper. *See* communion
Loveall, Henry, 29, 389n40, 390n44
Loveless, Alton, 353, 431n74, 431n76
Lucas, J. W., 91, 100, 232, 411n28
Ludwell, Philip, 19
Lumpkin, William, 224, 416n18, 440n11, 445n12, 446n15
Lupton, Alice, 284–85
Luther, Martin, 5, 164

Malone, Thomas, 349
Marks, David, 134, 139–41, 144, 325, 421n11, 422n22, 422n25, 422nn27–28

marriage, 19–20, 169–71, 365, 402n35
Marsden, George, 455n63
Masonic controversy. *See* Freemasonry
Massey, Kimbrel, 92, 105, 413n45
Master's Men, 350, 353, 355
McAdams, Hiram, 201, 277–78, 310
McAdams, Lizzie, 201, 278, 309–10, 315
McBeth, Leon, 384n1, 368n36, 389n44, 390n45, 395n1, 397n45
McDonald, Ruth, 351
McGee, J. E., 203–4, 437nn35–37
McNab, Robert, 73–74, 401n32
means of grace, 45, 48–49, 51, 65, 160, 238, 251, 259, 265, 425n3, 444n4, 450n62
meditation, 49
Mellette, T. B., 281, 283–84, 288, 292, 297, 303–04, 457n16
Melvin, Billy, 331, 354, 363, 462n21
Melvin, D. H., 285–86
Melvin, Henry, 294–95, 304–6, 316–18, 353
Mercer University, 12
messenger, 20, 23–24, 28, 30–31, 36, 72–73, 75, 388n36, 391n52, 427n23
Messer, Trymon, 350
Methodist, 1, 7, 95, 104, 116, 125–26, 131, 165, 182, 197–98, 207–8, 229, 309, 372, 375–76, 401n25, 459n42
Miley, LaVerne, 348
Miller, Benjamin (Georgia), 458n16
Miller, Benjamin (North Carolina), 46
Miller, J. F., 310, 319
Million, G. W., 89, 182–83, 197, 201–2, 384n1, 390n45, 397n45, 406n2, 411n28, 416n17, 419n39, 421n14, 430nn64–67, 431nn70–71, 432n2, 433n3, 433n8, 435nn16–19, 436n29, 436n33, 438n52, 439n61, 438nn63–64
missions, 101, 134, 141, 179, 236, 284–86, 289, 299–301, 303, 306, 312–16, 335–36, 343, 369, 409n18, 425n68; foreign,

145–46, 285, 289–90, 294–95, 297, 299–303, 310, 312, 324, 336, 347–48, 355, 457n8, 464n1; home, 146, 285, 289, 297, 306, 309–11, 323, 336, 349–50, 355, 459n37, 465nn10–12
Modernism, 8, 173–6, 228, 236, 288–89, 355, 379–81, 428nn41–42, 429n47
Molloy, Thomas, 113, 192, 198, 245, 435n20, 448n42
Montgomery, D. B., 383n1, 391n52, 392n61, 398n1, 421n18, 430n64, 445n7
Montgomery, James, 268, 452n85
Moody, Edward, 354
Mooneyham, Stanley, 340, 342, 352, 354, 363, 464n49
Moore, Alfred, 83
Moore, James, 67, 82–83, 105–7, 398n1
Moore, Redding (Reading), 71–72, 75–77, 267, 403nn38–39
Morgan, Clint, 348
Morgan, Phillip, 11, 271, 307, 417n19, 452n90, 455n23, 458n22, 458n28, 465n6, 467n49
Morning Star, The, 66–70, 73, 76, 78, 91, 93, 122, 134, 139–40, 142, 144, 151–54, 201, 213, 231–32, 398n1, 399n12, 400nn13–20, 401n24, 401n26, 401n32, 404n39, 407n5, 408n13, 422n24, 439n59, 439n68, 443n28, 451n78; *New*, 275–78, 280–82
Morning Star Publishing House, 212
Morris, E. C., 281, 283, 292
Morris, S. L., 180, 201, 275–77, 281
Morse, M. L., 279–82, 292, 456n46
Mosheim, John, 244, 445n14
Mount Moriah Association, 9, 112–14, 128, 192, 198, 204, 206, 211, 221–22, 231–32, 243–45, 247–48, 252, 262, 270, 406n2, 413n49, 415n3, 415nn8–9, 433n3, 437nn38–39, 438n46, 438n54, 440n6, 443n28, 446n15,

446n22, 447nn25–26, 447n28, 447n37, 448n44, 449n55, 449n59, 451nn70–71
Mount Olive College. *See* University of Mount Olive
Moye, J. C., 283, 334

Nash, B. W., 101, 229–32, 234–35, 239, 264, 398n1, 411nn30–31, 415n9, 443n28
National Association of Evangelicals, 354, 363
National Association of Free Will Baptists, 3, 11–12, 13, 89, 101, 116–17, 127, 161, 181, 187–88, 232, 259–60, 275, 280, 282–83, 285–86, 293–94, 296–303, 306, 308–21, 323–29, 331–33, 340, 342–44, 347, 350–58, 361–63, 365–69, 372–73, 376, 380–81, 406n1, 426n3, 441n13, 442n19, 453n5, 454n13, 456n1, 462n22; Board of Education, 292, 305, 315; Board of Publications and Literature, 314, 318–20 (*see* D6 Family Ministry); Board of Retirement and Insurance, 354–55; Board of Superannuation, 354; Commission for Theological Integrity, 355–56; Executive Office, 299, 315, 354, 356, 459n49; Foreign Missions Department/International Missions (*see* IM Inc.); Free Will Baptist Foundation, 355; Historical Commission, 12, 356; Home Missions (*see* North American Ministries); Media Commission, 356; Music Commission, 357; Sunday School Board, 317, 327–28, 351–52; Woman's National Auxiliary Convention, 295, 309, 311–12, 316, 335, 350, 358, 459n40
National Convention of Free Will Baptists, USA, 3, 339–40, 463n38, 464n54

National Sunday School Convention, 320
New Hampshire Confession of Faith, 103, 161, 243–45, 251–52, 446n15, 447n38
Newman, Albert Henry, 383n1, 386n14, 396n45
new measures, 132, 160
Noll Mark, 131, 420nn1–2, 426n8, 471n7
Norden, Robert, 20–21, 23–24, 59
North American Ministries, 297, 303, 306, 309–11, 336, 349–50, 355, 459n37, 465nn10–12, 465n14
North Carolina State Convention of Original Free Will Baptists, 326, 380, 441n13, 442n19, 462n24
Northern Baptist Convention, 3, 124–25, 141–42, 144, 173, 177–78, 184, 188, 201, 217, 275, 323, 325, 372, 376–77, 422n23, 428n42, 428n45, 429n47, 429n50, 429n57, 439n65, 453n1
nuda scriptura, 78, 404n48, 405n59, 445n9

O'Donnell, J. D., 358, 415n3, 415n8
Oliver, William Henry, 287, 291, 455n30
ONE Magazine, 354
ordinance(s), 2, 38, 43, 65–66, 68, 71, 76, 79, 101–2, 105, 107, 118, 127, 137, 159–60, 165, 182–83, 238–39, 253, 255, 259–63, 265–66, 279–80, 282, 284, 288, 373, 444n4
ordination, 2, 29, 38, 42, 75, 79, 91, 94, 98, 101, 112, 114, 123, 134, 138, 148, 151, 167, 185, 195, 205, 211, 221, 245, 257–58, 286–87, 314, 317, 330–31, 365, 377, 397n47, 449n56
ordination council. *See* presbytery
original sin, 5–6, 444n36, 446n20
Origin of the Free Will Baptist Church of North Carolina, 45, 70, 226,

240, 392n61, 394nn15–16, 395n22, 396nn36–37, 397n51, 398n1, 401n23, 421n18, 422n19, 445n7
orphanage, 144, 146, 270, 276, 286, 302, 312, 315, 334, 358–59, 467n45
Orthodox Creed, 33, 241
Owen, Ernest, 101, 412n33
Owens, Jesse, 12, 175, 384n2, 393n4, 393nn7–8, 394nn17–18
Owsley, Frank Lawrence, 452n87

paedobaptist, 28, 48, 104, 165, 177, 260, 375, 429n54
Palmer, Joanna, 9, 22–23, 25–26, 30, 33, 206
Palmer, Paul, 3, 10, 17, 19, 22–39, 41, 43–44, 48, 52–53, 55, 59, 377, 383n1, 384n2, 387nn18–19, 387n22, 387n24, 387nn26–27, 388nn29–30, 388n36, 389nn40–42, 389n44, 390nn45–46, 390n48, 390n50, 391nn52–53, 394n15, 396n45, 406n1, 411n25, 462n22
Palmer movement, 10–11, 13, 28, 41, 44, 55, 89–92, 166, 181–83, 188, 201, 215, 275, 282, 356, 372–73, 377, 379, 398n1, 406n1
Parker, Joseph, 27, 34, 36–39, 55–57, 59–61, 383n1, 388n31, 388n36, 391n54, 392nn65–68, 393n8, 396n45, 397n47, 397nn49–50
Parker, William, 57–61
Parrish, Neal, 239, 283, 286–87
Parsonfield Academy, 142–43
Parsonfield Seminary, 156, 161, 422n30
Paschal, George Washington, 23, 27, 34–38, 46, 48, 55, 57–58, 60, 384n1, 387n21, 387n27, 388nn31–32, 389n40, 390n45, 390n57, 392n60, 392n68, 393n2, 393n6, 394n19, 395n24, 396n38, 396n45, 397n46, 397nn50–51, 397n55, 398n59

Peden, Thomas E., 11, 186–87, 225, 233–34, 288, 431n75, 432n76, 441n14, 443n32, 444n35
pedilavium, 2, 104, 165, 229, 252, 263, 265, 374, 390n52, 451n76. *See* washing of the saints' feet
Pedobaptism. *See* baptism: infant
Pelagianism, 6, 8, 161, 238, 243
Pelt, Chester, 98, 100, 109, 409nn15–18, 410nn21–23, 411n26, 411n28–29, 411n31, 412n32, 469n66
Pelt, Michael R., 7, 11–12, 17, 28, 34, 46–47, 205, 333–34, 384n1, 385n6, 386n14, 388n30, 388n32, 388n34, 388n36, 389n38, 389n42, 390n45, 391nn56–57, 392n60, 392n63, 392n66, 392n70, 393n4, 393n7, 394n18, 394n20, 395n32, 397n45, 397n47, 397n49, 398n2, 399nn5–6, 401nn25–26, 401n29, 404n48, 405nn49–50, 405nn52–53, 405nn57–58, 406nn61–62, 406n70, 407n4, 437n42, 438nn43–44, 440n7, 440nn9–10, 441nn12–14, 441n18, 442nn24–25, 443nn32–33, 448n49, 455n42, 460n53, 461n14, 462n18, 462nn26–27, 463nn30–35, 467n44
Pentecostal(ism), 264, 371, 378–79
Perquimans Precinct, 17, 19–27, 30–31, 385n7, 385n9, 386nn13–14
perseverance of the saints, 1, 65, 117–18, 163, 177, 251, 357, 361, 413n41, 417nn19–20, 419n41, 468n54, 468n56
Peterson, Moses, 121–22
Philadelphia Baptist Association, 29, 41, 240, 373, 444n1
Phillips, E. T., 227–28, 284
Picirilli, Robert E., 7, 10–12, 86, 102–3, 118, 127, 229, 231, 233, 279–80, 305, 307, 349, 356–57, 360–62, 399n12, 400nn13–14, 401n24, 401n27, 401n29, 401n32, 403nn38–39, 404n40, 404n42, 404n44, 404n46, 406n62, 406nn69–70, 407n3, 407n5, 411nn27–28, 411n31, 412nn34–39, 413nn49–50, 414nn51–52, 415n3, 415n9, 417n19, 418nn21–24, 418n26, 418nn28–29, 418n36, 419n43, 419n45, 422n25, 429n52, 430n60, 430n61, 431n71, 431nn75–76, 432n77, 433n5, 435n23, 438n46, 440n3, 440n5, 441n14, 442nn22–23, 442n25, 443nn28–33, 452n93, 453n3, 453n5, 453n11, 454nn12–14, 454nn16–17, 454n19, 458n23, 459n38, 459n49, 461n2, 461n14, 466n41, 467nn51–52, 468n56
pietism, 2, 8, 53–55, 81–82, 137, 173–74, 178, 307, 372, 377–81, 471n7
Pinson, L. V., 12, 416n17
Pittman, R. F., 276–78, 292
polity, 2–4, 123, 166, 177, 214, 229, 238, 254, 256, 329–33, 340, 373–75, 405n54, 405n59, 444n1, 449n56; congregationalism, 331, 374, 462n21; connectionalism, 3, 8, 331–33, 366, 375–76, 462n21; intercongregational, 4, 374
Polston, Fannie Mae, 284–86, 294, 304, 311–33, 315
postmillennialism, 133, 171, 173, 228, 318, 366, 420n8, 469n66
Powell, Larry, 350
Poyner, David L., 91, 115, 181–82, 185, 196–97, 202, 264, 430n63
prayer, 44, 49, 72, 81, 85, 95, 132, 160, 168, 208, 210, 212, 239, 255, 257, 259, 268–69, 281, 301, 312–13, 316, 342, 385n10
predestination, 25, 29, 89, 113, 135–36, 373. *See* election
Premillennialism, 318, 324, 357, 366, 469n66

Presbyterian(ism), 2, 8, 20, 41, 44–45, 82, 126, 131, 162, 165, 208, 305, 359, 374, 394n21
presbytery, 2, 80, 117, 257–58, 329–30, 449n54, 449n56
Psalms, Hymns, and Spiritual Songs, 224, 441n11
Puritan(ism), 4–6, 49–52, 163, 239, 267, 361
Pursell, Cleo, 351

Quaker, 20, 22, 24, 28, 47, 52–53, 150, 265, 451n76

Randall, Benjamin, 3, 10, 66, 135–39, 142, 147, 159, 161, 165–66, 176, 183, 420n8, 421nn13–15, 422n20, 424n49, 425n1, 426n7
Randall House. *See* D6 Family Ministry
Randall movement, 3, 9, 11, 13, 55, 89, 121, 124–25, 131, 135, 139, 159–61, 163, 166–67, 169, 181–87, 198–99, 201, 212–15, 231–32, 250, 271, 275, 282, 293, 323–25, 361, 365, 372–73, 376–77, 381, 406n1, 411n31, 425n3, 427n23, 439n57, 449n53, 454n13, 461n8
Randall University, 340, 344, 357–58, 366, 466n42
Randolph, Jesse, 225, 268, 441n11, 441n16, 447n31, 452n81, 455n39
Raper, W. Burkette, 328–29, 334–35, 461n14, 462nn15–16, 462n27, 463n29
Read, Jesse, 36–37, 44, 47–48, 52, 58–60, 63, 383n1, 392n61, 392n64, 394n11, 394n21, 396n45, 397n47, 398n57, 398n59, 399n8
Record Speaks, The, 364, 468nn58–59
redemption; general. *See* atonement: general; particular
Reeds, Roger, 328, 352, 357
Reformation, Protestant, 4–7, 53–54, 237, 243, 421n16

Reformed movement, 1, 4–8, 33, 161, 238, 249, 360–62, 371, 376, 391n52, 444n36, 467n53
Reformers, 135; Magisterial, 5; Radical, 4, 424n48
Remonstrants, 6, 243–44, 246, 248
Republican Party, 145, 149, 230, 385n5, 401n25
Restoration movement, 1, 64, 104. *See* Stone-Campbell movement
revivalism, 2, 8, 41, 48, 53–55, 82, 123, 132–33, 136, 138, 379, 401n25, 420n3, 420nn6–7
Revolutionary War. *See* War for Independence
Riggs, Raymond, 311, 319, 324, 347, 460n2, 461n4
Roach, James, 56, 61–62, 64, 398n2, 399n5
Rogers, B. F., 282, 292, 294, 301
Rogers, Peleg, 36, 392n59
Roman Catholicism, 6, 159, 175, 241, 255, 263, 265, 451n77
Rowe, Jermiah, 67, 81

Sabbath school, 134, 156, 167, 212, 214, 224–25, 227, 425n68, 442n18
sacrament(s), 51, 65, 76, 239, 259, 262–63, 265, 267, 373
Sacred Harp, The, 211, 269, 452n86; Colored, 269
Sacred Melodies, 150, 424n52, 425n70
sanctification, 163, 242, 284, 319, 361, 364, 376, 420n8
Sater, Henry, 29, 31, 389n44, 390n45, 398n58
second work of grace, 1, 137, 376
segregation, 205, 210, 232, 271, 345, 367
self-governance (of the church), 56, 115, 167, 256–57, 331–32, 450n2
sexuality, 169–70, 270, 365
Shiloh Conference, 72, 79, 399n6

INDEX 513

Shockey, Robert, 350
Shurden, Walter, 266–67, 412n40, 452n79
Shute, K. V., 281, 309, 318–19, 354, 454n17
Shute, Lora, 354
Simpson, Douglas, 469n66
Simpson, Mrs. J. E., 298, 354
singing schools, 269
Six Principles, 43–44, 52, 379, 418n20
Sloan, Gladys, 351
Smart, Moses, 161, 163–65, 426nn9–10, 427nn19–20
Smith, Elizabeth, 64, 399n9
Smith, F. L., 111, 414n1, 452n89
Smith, Francis, 18, 384n5, 391n52
Smith, Henry, 59, 62, 67, 72, 79, 398n57
Smith, Rolla, 347–48
Smyth, John, 4–6, 412n40
social gospel, 8, 173, 176, 428n41
social reform, 8, 133–34, 142, 144–45, 148–49, 156, 173, 372, 378–79, 420n2, 420nn6–7, 424n48, 427n36
soteriology, 1, 6–7, 161, 366, 374, 403n36
South Carolina Conference, 75–78, 402n34
Southeastern Free Will Baptist Bible College, 344, 358, 363–66, 467n43, 468nn58–60, 468n62
Southern Harmony, 269
Southern Unity Movement, 231–32, 443nn28–29
Southwestern General Convention, 201, 275
Spivey, Caleb, 92, 108
Spivey, Matthew, 92–93, 108, 413n50
Standard Confession of 1660, 17, 21–22, 44, 52, 60–65, 245–46, 248, 250, 385n5, 394n12, 395n35, 399n7
Stanglin, Keith, 404n48
Stanley, Francis, 33, 44, 391n52
Staten, Ralph, 318, 328

St. Claire, E. L., 101, 227, 235–36, 241, 412n32, 426n9, 443n34, 444nn35–36, 445nn8–9, 446n20, 455n40
Stearns, Shubal, 117, 394n15, 432n79
Stetson, Charles, 91, 201, 418n21, 436n29
Stevenson, George, 17–18, 21–25, 30, 34, 38, 43, 57, 384nn1–3, 385n7, 385n10, 385n12, 386nn13–14, 387nn18–19, 387n22, 387n24, 387nn26–27, 388n30, 388n36, 389n38, 389nn41–42, 390nn45–46, 390n48, 390n50, 391n53, 391n56, 391n58, 392n59, 392n62, 392nn66–68, 393n8, 397n45, 397n47, 397nn49–50
Stewart, A. M., 91, 100, 199–200, 220–21, 411n27
Stewart, I. D., 147, 155, 383n1, 396n45, 421n12, 423n45, 439n60, 452n90
Stinson, Benoni, 74, 184, 403n36
Stone, Corder, 126
Stone Association, 115, 121, 126–27, 325, 419n46, 461n6
Stone-Campbell movement, 1, 8, 78, 82, 104, 229, 261, 401n25, 404n48, 405n59
Storer College, 141, 146, 186, 216–17, 439nn67–69
sufficiency of Scripture, 5, 45, 159–61, 238, 241, 265–66, 425n1, 445n9
suffrage, 153, 169, 257
Sunday School Convention, 317–18, 320
Superannuation Board, 298
Surginer, William, 34–38, 42, 389n38, 390n51, 391n56, 391n58, 392nn58–59, 392n62
Synod of Dort, 6

Taylor, O. J., 203–4, 437n36
Tecumseh College, 276–78, 280–82, 303, 454n16

Thigpen, Charles 309, 324, 327, 348–49, 353, 460n64
Thigpen, Laura, 309, 324, 348–49, 353, 460n64
Thomas, Roy, 350
Thomsen, Eric, 12, 421n10
Tipton, Benjamin, 91, 97–100, 107, 109, 199, 410n24, 436n23
Toe River Association, 86, 115, 121–25, 221, 224, 258, 262, 271–72, 418nn32–35, 418n37, 419n41, 440n4, 440n10, 449n55, 451n70, 452n90
Toisnot Transcript, The, 225, 392n61, 398n1, 421n18, 445nn6–7
Toleration Act, 24, 27
tongues (gift of), 362
Townsend, T. J., 202, 204
Treatise, 117, 124–25, 159, 161–66, 182, 213, 259, 280, 292–93, 295, 298, 316, 318, 331, 361–62, 365, 376, 420n8, 425n1, 425n3, 426n6, 426nn11–12, 426nn14–16, 427nn17–18, 427n21, 427nn23–24, 430n64, 431n72, 439n57, 447n29, 449n59, 450n62, 451n73, 453n5, 456n49, 460n60, 460n62, 468nn54–56, 468n63
Trinity Online Bible College, 340

Unified Free Will Baptists, 339, 341–42, 464n38
Union (army), 214, 272
Union Association, 125, 184, 195, 232, 408n10, 414n51, 414n53, 419n40, 434n11, 456n46
United American Free Will Baptist Bible College, 338–39, 463n38, 464n39
United American Free Will Baptist Church, 3, 199, 209–11, 217, 337–39, 341, 344, 438n47, 438n49
United American Free Will Baptist Denomination Inc., 339, 463n38

United Baptist Association, 93, 98–99, 102–3, 108, 119, 253, 410n23
University of Mount Olive, 11–12, 222, 326, 328–29, 334–36, 344, 380, 384n2
Urmston, John, 20

Vandiver, C. C., 92, 114–16, 128, 191–92, 194, 196–97, 415n11, 416n12, 432n1
Vanhoose family, 187, 278, 295, 305, 319
Vanhorn, Peter, 46
Vaughn, Robert, 199, 229, 231, 233, 411n27, 411n31, 415n9, 435n23, 436nn24–27, 440n3, 442nn22–24, 443nn28–32, 446n19, 451n73
Vause, Jesse, 75, 82, 105

Waddell, Eugene, 348, 355
Walker, William, 36, 42, 392n61, 394n19
War for Independence, 33, 131, 134–35, 390n51
War of 1812, 97
Ward, J. T., 216–17, 383n1, 396n45, 416n11, 416n16, 421n10, 434n11, 442n18
Ware, C. C., 397n45, 398n57, 398n4, 399n5, 402n35, 404n47, 405nn49–50, 405n53, 405n57, 414n50, 448n43
washing of the saints' feet, 2, 4, 66, 68, 90, 99, 101–2, 104–5, 107, 109, 118, 121–22, 127, 164–65, 177–78, 182–83, 187, 195, 227, 229–31, 235, 238, 241, 251–54, 260, 263–65, 272, 279–80, 282, 288, 292–93, 371, 373–75, 391n52, 402n33, 407n3, 415n9, 419n41, 427n21, 447n23, 447n36, 451n73, 451nn76–77, 456n49
Watts, Isaac, 211, 226, 268
Watts, W. Jackson, 467n53
Welch, John L.: Jr., 276, 278–80, 283, 286, 289, 291–94, 297, 303–6, 309, 311, 316, 319; Sr., 37, 127, 232, 456n49

Welch, Mary Ann, 286, 311, 313
Welch College, 7, 11–2, 222, 232, 287, 299–300, 302–3, 306, 310, 312, 315, 320, 324, 326–29, 338–40, 344, 348–49, 351, 353–61, 362–66, 400n13, 414n1, 458n16, 458n19, 458nn27–28, 459n32, 465n6, 465nn8–9, 467n49, 467n52, 468n58
Welch Divinity School, 7, 349
Wells, David F., 467n50
Wesley, Charles, 226, 268, 436n30, 447n31
Wesley, John, 226
Wesleyan, 1, 8, 132, 136, 161, 163, 229, 242, 264, 371, 376, 447n31
Westminster Confession of Faith, 240
Westminster Shorter Catechism, 48, 259, 444n4, 450n61
Wheeler, John, 121, 124–25
Wheeler, S. J., 38, 57–59, 396n45
White, Cyrus, 102
Whitefield, George, 42–43, 49, 51, 135–36, 393n5, 395n25
White Free Will Baptists, 11, 92, 121, 169, 199, 201, 205–8, 210, 213, 217, 219–20, 236, 269, 271–72, 324, 340, 342–45, 400n21, 407n10
Whitley, W. T., 23, 384n1, 384n3, 386nn13–14, 387n15, 387n20, 387n23, 394n11, 395n25
Whitsitt, William, 34, 41, 53, 61, 383n1, 395n25
Willey, Mabel, 300–302, 347, 457n13
Willey, Thomas H., 300–302, 347, 457n13
Williams, Daniel, 421n35
Williams, Jack, 176, 325, 356, 429n51, 466n41
Willis, Homer, 350
Wills, Gregory, 123, 418n34, 470n3
Wilson, Reford, 348

Wilson, Samuel, 18, 384n4
Winfield, John, 55, 57–62, 399n5
Winiarski, Douglas, 48–49, 51, 395n26–34
Wisehart, Mary Ruth, 312, 349, 351, 454n23, 457n13, 457n15, 458n19, 458n26, 459n37, 459nn41–43, 465n6, 465nn10–11, 465nn15–16, 466n21, 466n28, 466nn30–31, 468n57
Wolfe, John H., 180, 182, 275–77, 279–82, 430n60, 453n1, 453n11
Woman's Home Mission societies, 284–85, 289
Woman's National Auxiliary Convention, 295, 309, 311–12, 316, 335, 350, 358, 459n40
Women's Auxiliary. *See* Woman's National Auxiliary Convention
Women's National Convention. *See* Woman's National Auxiliary Convention
Woolsey, Paul, 302, 328, 418nn31–32, 419n41, 440n5, 456n46
Woolsey, William Bonaparte, 100, 121–22, 126, 221, 302
Woolsey College, 100, 122, 221, 302, 440n5
Workman, Marjorie, 351
World War II, 185, 315, 323, 360
worship, 5, 21, 27, 49, 58, 71, 123, 145, 147, 160–61, 164, 167–68, 226, 240, 265–69, 292, 317, 324, 340, 363, 385n10, 425n3, 426n4, 432n79. *See* circumstances (of worship); elements (of worship)
Worthington, Melvin, 354, 357
Wright, Joseph, 471n5

Yandell, I. W., 203–4
Yeley, Bessie, 300–301, 350

Zion Bible School, 222, 281, 292, 297, 303–4, 312
Zion's Hymns, 225–26, 249, 267–68, 441n11, 441n16, 447n31, 452n81, 452n85, 455n39
Zwingli, Huldrych, 5

www.ingramcontent.com/pod-product-compliance
Lightning Source LLC
Chambersburg PA
CBHW020246010526
44107CB00002B/116